Virginia Women

Virginia Women
THEIR LIVES AND TIMES

Volume 1

EDITED BY

*Cynthia A. Kierner and
Sandra Gioia Treadway*

The University of Georgia Press *Athens and London*

© 2015 by the University of Georgia Press
Athens, Georgia 30602
www.ugapress.org
All rights reserved
Set in Minion Pro by Graphic Composition, Inc.

Most University of Georgia Press titles are
available from popular e-book vendors.

Printed digitally

Library of Congress Cataloging-in-Publication Data

Virginia women : their lives and times / edited by Cynthia A. Kierner
and Sandra Gioia Treadway.
volumes cm
Includes bibliographical references and index.
ISBN 978-0-8203-4741-7 (ebook) —
ISBN 978-0-8203-4262-7 (volume 1 : hardcover : alk. paper) —
ISBN 978-0-8203-4263-4 (volume 1 : pbk. : alk. paper)
1. Women—Virginia—History. 2. Women—Virginia—Social conditions.
3. Women—Virginia—Biography. I. Kierner, Cynthia A., 1958–
II. Treadway, Sandra Gioia.
HQ1438.V5V57 2014
305.409755—dc23
2014023190

British Library Cataloging-in-Publication Data available

Contents

Introduction
CYNTHIA A. KIERNER AND SANDRA GIOIA TREADWAY   1

Grace Sherwood
The Virginia Witch
CYNTHIA A. KIERNER   11

Cockacoeske and Sarah Harris Stegge Grendon
Bacon's Rebellion and the Roles of Women
KRISTALYN M. SHEFVELAND   33

Jane Webb and Her Family
Life Stories and the Law in Early Virginia
TERRI L. SNYDER   55

Clementina Rind
Widowed Printer of Williamsburg
MARTHA J. KING   74

Sarah Jerdone
Negotiating Revolution
LINDA L. STURTZ   95

Anne Henry Christian
Chronicling Family and Business on the Revolutionary Frontier
GAIL S. TERRY   116

Mary Draper Ingles
A Survivor in Her Time and a Legend Ever Since
MARY C. FERRARI   138

Elizabeth Henry Campbell Russell
Champion of Faith in the Early Republic
JON KUKLA 160

Elizabeth Jacquelin Ambler Brent Carrington
*A Founder of the Female Humane Association
for Orphan Girls in Richmond*
SARAH HAND MEACHAM 180

Dolley Madison
A Case Study in Southern Style
CATHERINE ALLGOR 201

Harriet Hemings
Daughter of the President's Slave
CATHERINE KERRISON 222

Edy Turner
The Nottoway Indians' "Female Chief"
HELEN C. ROUNTREE 244

Ann R. Page and Mary L. Custis
From Annfield and Arlington to Africa, with Love
DEBORAH A. LEE 260

Ellen Wayles Randolph Coolidge
Thomas Jefferson's Granddaughter in New England and Beyond
LISA A. FRANCAVILLA 283

Elizabeth Van Lew
Southern Lady, Union Spy
ELIZABETH R. VARON 305

Antonia Ford Willard
Southern Belle, Yankee Wife
MICHELLE A. KROWL 323

Sally Louisa Tompkins
Confederate Healer
E. SUSAN BARBER   344

Contributors   363

Index   367

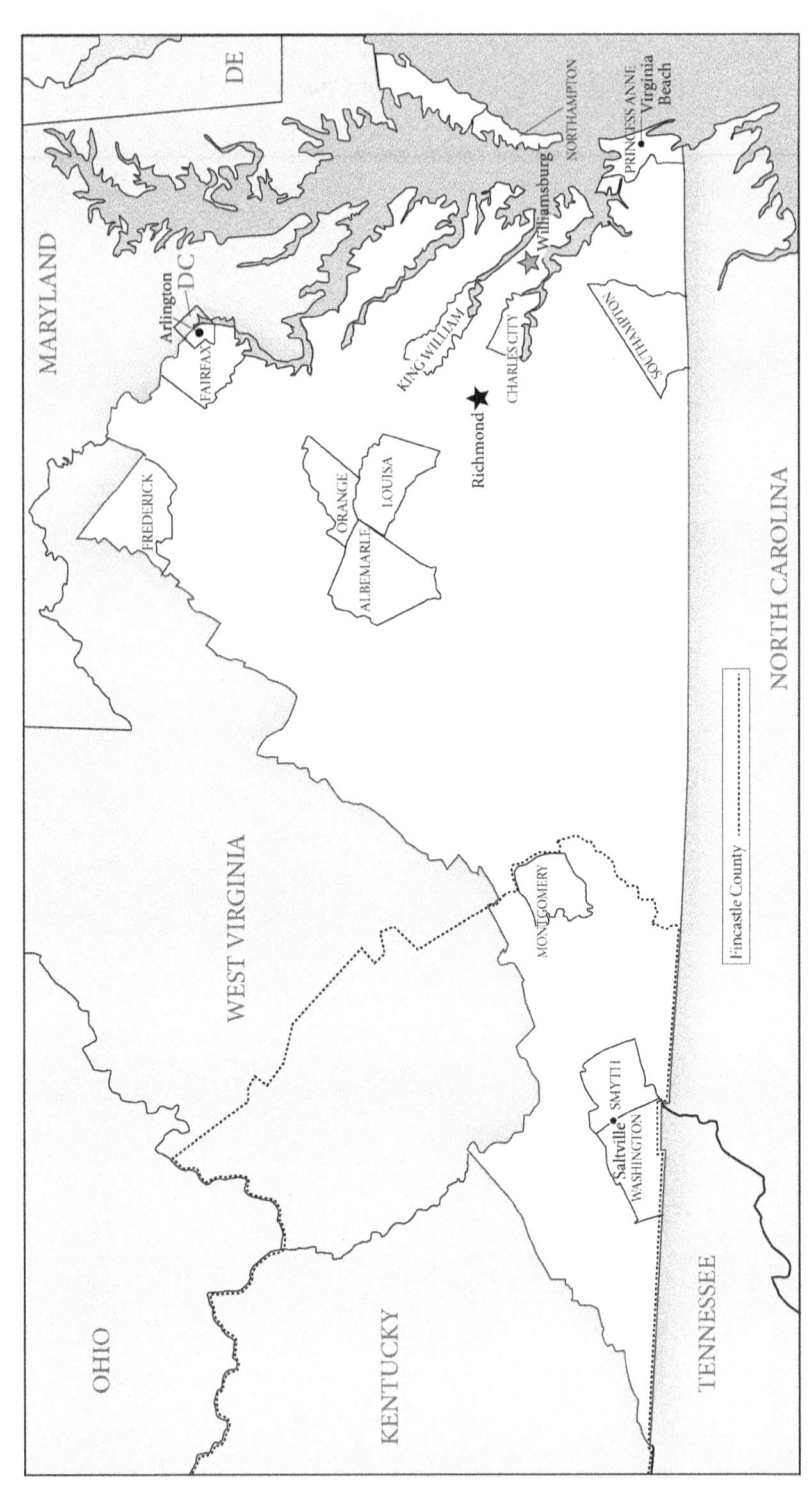

Virginia Women

Introduction

CYNTHIA A. KIERNER AND SANDRA GIOIA TREADWAY

The essays in *Virginia Women: Their Lives and Times* recount the history of women in the Old Dominion through the lives of individuals who were both unique and representative of their times. Virginia's history spans more than four centuries, and women were significant actors in every historical era, from before the first English settlement at Jamestown in 1607 to our own new millennium. In both economic and cultural terms, women's work has been valuable. Their involvement in public life, though sometimes barely visible, has been both ongoing and productive, and at times its effects have been transformative. The authors of these essays seek to engage general readers, teachers, and students—as well as historians—in both the personal stories of their subjects and their larger historical contexts.

A whirlwind survey of four centuries of Virginia women's history suggests the rich diversity of our subject. At the first colonial outpost, Jamestown, Pocahontas forged relationships between English settlers and Powhatan Natives. Decades later, Lady Frances Berkeley was a political force in transatlantic imperial politics, traveling to London to secure the king's assistance in suppressing Bacon's Rebellion. In the eighteenth century, Virginia women such as the Williamsburg milliner Catherine Rathell brought London fashions to eager colonial consumers, while the patriotic Anne Dabney Terrell of Bedford County later used her pen to rally female Virginians to America's Revolutionary cause. Nineteenth-century Virginia women included Mary Randolph, who authored America's first regional cookbook; Jane Minor of Petersburg, a former slave who used her earnings to purchase the freedom of sixteen enslaved women and children; and Elizabeth Keckley, who escaped slavery to become Mary Todd Lincoln's dressmaker and to found an organization that aided newly emancipated African Americans during and after the Civil War. In the twentieth century, Lila Meade Valentine and Zelda Kingoff Nordlinger fought for women's political and civil rights—via suffrage and the Equal Rights Amendment—and Lorena Bobbitt, an abused wife who became famous for slicing her husband's penis in 1993, established a nonprofit organization to stop domestic violence.[1]

With the exception of the much-mythologized Pocahontas, none of these women are widely known today, at least among people who are not specifically interested in women's history. The continued obscurity of such consequential historical figures—none of whom is the subject of a chapter here—shows that there is still much work to be done. At the same time, their obscurity also underscores the fact that, despite decades of groundbreaking research by historians of women and gender, women's individual and collective activities and achievements still tend to be unrecorded or underrepresented in general surveys of both American and Virginia history, as well as in the public's historical consciousness.

Indeed, the massive tome that for decades was the premier single-volume history of the Old Dominion barely mentioned women. That book's index had more than fifteen hundred entries, only forty-four of which referenced Virginia women. (An additional twelve entries referenced women who were not Virginians, including two English queens and two wives of U.S. presidents.) The four-hundredth anniversary of the founding of Jamestown brought the publication in 2007 of two new Virginia history surveys, which, to varying degrees, included women in their stories, but mainly as supporting actors in a familiar historical narrative. These accounts showed how women contributed to historical events and trends, but they ignored the more challenging question of how gender shaped history and whether women's historical experiences expose errors or deficiencies in the existing historical narrative.[2]

Nor have women's distinctive stories and experiences been adequately reflected in movies, monuments, and other artifacts of public memory and popular historical consciousness. Ironically, the welcome twenty-first-century addition of a monument on Richmond's Capitol Square "to commemorate the contributions of the women of Virginia" is compelling evidence of their overall absence from the state's otherwise prolific culture of commemoration. A comparably generic monument to Virginia men is unnecessary—and, indeed, would be redundant—because there are countless monuments and memorials to generals on horseback, soldiers, statesmen, businessmen, and other male notables dispersed throughout the commonwealth. How Virginia women have been remembered—or, more commonly, how they have been misremembered or forgotten—is an important theme in many of the essays in these volumes.[3]

Taken collectively, the contents of these books represent a major step in the direction of redressing this frustratingly persistent historiographical imbalance.

A few of the women featured here and in our second volume are famous and have even been the subject of book-length biographies: First Lady Dolley Madison, the Pulitzer Prize–winning novelist Ellen Glasgow; the iconic singer Patsy Cline.[4] Others, such as the Civil War spy Elizabeth Van Lew and the civil rights activist Sarah Patton Boyle, are well known among historians and, indeed, have been the subjects of fine scholarly work,[5] but we aim to introduce these Virginia women to a wider audience. Most of the women whose stories are included in this collection, however, are comparatively unknown, even among historians. In some cases, the information an author presents here may be all we will ever know about her subject.

In choosing the subjects for this two-volume collection, one of our main objectives was to show how the experiences of Virginia women varied by race, class, age, marital status, and sexual orientation, and across both space and time. We were most successful in achieving fairly balanced geographic coverage and a roughly equitable chronological distribution. Volume 1 begins with chapters on four very different sorts of seventeenth-century women: a white woman of marginal means who was rumored to be a witch; a white trader and a Pamunkey Indian leader, both of whom played important roles in Bacon's Rebellion; and a mixed-race woman who was remarkably adept at using Virginia's courts and laws to defend her own (and her children's) freedom. Essays that focus on the Civil War and Reconstruction eras are respectively situated at the end of the first volume and the beginning of the second, which closes with two chapters that provide dramatically different windows onto the late twentieth century. One of these concluding essays focuses on two northern Virginia women who secured election to the state legislature in the 1960s and rose to leadership positions by the 1980s. The other compares the experiences of two lesbian mothers who were involved in highly publicized child custody cases—with vastly different outcomes—in the 1990s.

Beyond the issues of chronology and geography, however, observant readers will notice that certain categories of women seem under- or overrepresented. For the most part, these imbalances result from a lack of sources, especially for the earlier periods when the vast majority of Virginia women were illiterate and relatively few surviving public or private documents provide information about their lives. On the one hand, only two essays in our first volume deal with women of African American descent, both of whom were in fact atypical because they were mixed-race and free. Historians know about Jane Webb and Harriet Hemings only because Webb was a frequent litigant and Hemings was the daughter of Thomas Jefferson: these extraordinary women left their marks in court records and family papers, respectively. On the other hand, widows are seemingly overrepresented in volume 1 both because most early American women—who were typically younger than their husbands—eventually became widows and because widows had both family responsibilities and legal rights that made them far more likely than other women to leave an evidentiary trail in the form of either private letters or public documents. (Despite significant changes in state law as a result of the Revolution, Virginians did not abandon the English common-law doctrine of coverture—which prevented wives from owning and controlling property—until after the Civil War.) An important turning point, widowhood often led women to become more heavily involved in religious or civic activities or in managing family businesses or properties. Happily for historians, all of these undertakings produced letters, ledgers, and public documents that we can use to reconstruct their lives.

Recognizing the significant variations among women's lived experiences, we nonetheless embrace the findings of a generation of historians who have shown that gender matters profoundly in shaping women's lives.[6] As readers make their way through these volumes, they will encounter events and topics that punctuate conventional surveys of Virginia history and American history generally. The American Revolution, westward migration, industrialization, the Civil War, Progressive reform, and the long struggle for African American freedom and equality are all here, but these familiar historical mileposts often look different from the perspective of the essays' female subjects. In early Virginia, for instance, most free women—along with children, slaves, and the mentally ill—were subservient dependents under a legal system that white men cherished as a bulwark of their rights and liberties. A century later, when men sought prosperity and independence on the western frontier, women found jobs, female companionship, and opportunities for philanthropy and other forms of meaningful public activism in the growing cities of the commonwealth. In the antebellum era, motherhood discouraged most African American women from joining men's efforts to flee slavery, and the same concern for children led their female descendants to devise innovative strategies to educate black youth when public schools closed in the 1960s in an attempt to stop court-ordered desegregation.

Paying attention to women's experiences sometimes destabilizes widely accepted historical metanarratives, the big stories that we construct to discern meaning in the past. For example, the prevailing interpretation of the history of the Virginia colony has been a story of progress: in the eighteenth century, according to this argument, stability, prosperity, and harmony supplanted disease, death, and social conflict. Our contributors, however, tell a different story, one in which perceived stability and harmony rested on patriarchy and white supremacy, as law, demography, and custom combined to suppress the autonomy of women, blacks, and Indians, thereby improving the status of white men and easing tensions among them. To counter the overly simplistic narratives that emphasize Virginia's leadership in the Civil War era—when Richmond was the capital of the Confederacy and Arlington's Robert E. Lee was the revered commander of the rebel forces—historians have shown that Virginia women's attitudes toward the war (and toward the issue of slavery, which caused it) often were moderate, ambiguous, or even radically heterodox. The most pervasive American narrative of all, which sees history as a progressive triumph of democracy, also looks different from the perspective of Virginia feminists, whose state waited until 1952 to accept the Nineteenth Amendment (which, in 1920, gave adult women the right to vote) and never ratified the ERA, despite the fact that polls showed that most Virginians supported it.[7]

Taken together, these essays form a cautiously optimistic narrative of Virginia women's history. Women's rights have expanded over time: enslaved women became free; wives became property holders; women of all races attained greater access to education, employment, suffrage, and other basic civil rights. Despite this overarching theme of improvement and progress, however, some gains have been slow in coming, and improvements in education, income, working conditions, and other areas have varied by class, race, and region.

Above all, the chapters in these volumes represent a small but compelling sample of the diversity and complexity of Virginia women's experiences over four centuries. In the colonial period, Virginia women were slaves and servants, but they were also ladies who owned (and sometimes mistreated) their servants and slaves. In the nineteenth century, Virginia women worked in factories, wrote novels, did religious and benevolence work, honored Confederate defenders of slavery and white supremacy, and strove to improve the circumstances of freed African Americans and poor whites. Generations later, some Virginia women fought hard to preserve time-honored gender and racial hierarchies, opposing woman suffrage and defending Jim Crow, while others devoted themselves to progressive causes, such as labor unions, the ERA, and civil rights. But as many of these essays show, women's choices were not always quite so stark. Some slaveholding women who claimed to hate slavery acted on those principles, though many others did not. Strong, independent women paid lip service to conventional gender ideals that relegated white southern women to passive dependence. Improvements in education could lead women into professional careers, or schooling could be preparation for domestic life as, indeed, it has been since the post-Revolutionary era.

All of the essays in *Virginia Women: Their Lives and Times* speak to one or more of our three overarching themes for this collection: making women visible, recovering women's voices, and chronicling both the better- and less-known ways in which Virginia women strove—often on the public stage—to improve society and to obtain and protect their rights. Rather than the conventional editors' summary of each chapter and its author's contributions, what follows is an elaboration on each of these three themes, with specific references to the women who are the subjects of the essays in this volume.

For starters, it is surely worth emphasizing that without historians' research, most of the women discussed in these essays would be invisible to posterity—and their invisibility would be quite literally true for those who lived before the advent of photography. Of the nineteen women who are the subjects of the seventeen essays in the first volume of *Virginia Women*, only three had their portraits painted. Not surprisingly, they came from the highest echelons of Virginia society. Dolley Madison was the wife of a president. Ellen Wayles Randolph Coolidge was Thomas Jefferson's favorite granddaughter. Elizabeth Campbell Russell was Patrick Henry's sister. For historians, the vast majority of Virginia women (and men) who lived in the era before the Civil War are faceless and anonymous.

Many are also voiceless because so many Virginia women were illiterate in the seventeenth and eighteenth centuries, and even later, especially in rural areas. Historians can glimpse such women through material artifacts and, more commonly, by searching for them in official records, travelers' accounts, and other third-person documents. Official government records are among the best sources of information on Native Americans, such as the Pamunkey Cockacoeske, and Edy Turner, the nineteenth-century Nottoway chief, though historians must read these documents carefully, in light of the assumptions and biases of the white men who produced them. Like Sarah Harris Stegge Grendon, who was accused of treason in the wake of Bacon's Rebellion, women were most likely to appear in the historical record when they caused trouble. The otherwise obscure Grace Sherwood can be traced in the records of her local county court, where she frequently tangled with her neighbors who, in turn, accused her of witchcraft. Jane Webb's litigiousness also generated records that make it possible to reconstruct her challenging life as a mixed-race woman in Northampton County on Virginia's eastern shore, where she tenaciously fought to retain her freedom, while she lived on the margins of a society that increasingly equated blackness with slavery.

Even some relatively well-known Virginia women lived remarkably shadowy lives. Mary Draper Ingles has long been a celebrated frontier heroine in western Virginia. Taken prisoner by the Shawnees in 1755, she escaped her captors and returned home to resume her place as a member of a prominent frontier family. But since Ingles herself left no documents—she was probably illiterate—

historians must parse various accounts of her captivity to distinguish myth from reality. Harriet Hemings, the light-skinned daughter of Sally Hemings and Thomas Jefferson, may have learned to read and write, but she purposefully left no clues about her life after she left Virginia in 1822, having decided to change her name and pass as white. Hemings's carefully reconstructed—but still vexingly incomplete—story is important because it shows not only the malleability of racial identities but also how gender shaped and constrained her options in both slavery and freedom. Harriet Hemings's brothers began their lives in freedom as skilled workers, but for her—as for most women—the surest road to respectability and safety was to find herself a husband.

Although Virginia had few public schools until after the Civil War, literacy rates improved with the expansion of private academies, Sunday schools, and a burgeoning print culture that included newspapers, advice books, devotional tracts, and novels. While access to what women read yields insights into their world views and values, their letters, diaries, and other writings help us to hear their voices. By the middle decades of the eighteenth century and especially after the Revolution, Virginia women were increasingly likely to commit their thoughts and experiences to paper, and some even became published authors. While Ellen Glasgow is probably the best known of Virginia's female writers, the work of Virginia women appeared in print as early as the eighteenth century.

Two contributors to this first volume draw on women's literary work to illuminate their lives and times. Although Virginia women may have contributed anonymous essays and poems to the *Virginia Gazette* from its inception in the 1730s, Clementina Rind arguably became the colony's first woman of letters when she assumed the job of printing and editing one of Williamsburg's two newspapers following the death of her husband in 1773. In her published writings and by the choices she made for what to publish in her newspaper, Rind defined herself as a hard-working printer, a female patriot, and a widow whose family depended on the continuing patronage of her community. Decades later, Elizabeth Jacquelin Ambler Brent Carrington tried her hand at writing a novel based on the tragic wartime experiences of a girlhood acquaintance, who was seduced and became pregnant by a French soldier during the American Revolution. Carrington hoped that her story would be a cautionary tale for females, who needed to protect themselves from predatory men in perilous and uncertain times. Although she never finished her novel, the same impulse that motivated her to write it led her to assume a leading role in the civic life of Richmond, where her benevolence work focused mostly on efforts that she believed would prevent poor orphan girls from succumbing to vice and prostitution.

Women's voices emerge most clearly from their surviving letters and other private writings. For Virginia women, these sources are relatively scarce for the colonial period, though during the Revolution the separation of wives from husbands (who fought and, in some cases, died in the war) made letter writers of literate women from many propertied families. One such woman was Anne Henry Christian, sister of the famed Revolutionary orator Patrick Henry, whose letters chronicle her transformation from a young wife and mother wholly absorbed in domestic concerns to a woman of business representing her family's economic interests in the wider world. Letters and business records also attest to the business acumen of Sarah Jerdone, a Louisa County widow who approached the American Revolution with a combination of gender-inflected political flexibility and single-minded determination to preserve her family's property.

Generations later, women reflected in writing on how sectional tensions and the eventual Civil War challenged them to sort out their loyalties and priorities. A careful reading of the letters and diary of Ellen Wayles Randolph Coolidge, who left Virginia to settle in her husband's native Massachusetts in 1825, reveals not only the importance of letters in maintaining family ties and female friendships but also her self-conscious construction of herself as a Virginian and a southerner during the antebellum decades. In the 1860s, young Antonia Ford of Fairfax expressed her allegiance to her family, her Virginia community, and the Confederate cause in her letters, which also reveal her boundless devotion to the Union officer whom she married after a wartime courtship in March 1864.

Family life was central to these women—nearly all of whom were wives and mothers—but the essays in this collection also highlight the ways in which Virginia women acted, often on a public stage, to benefit society or to secure or defend their rights. Because southern women remained largely aloof from antebellum feminism—a movement whose signal achievements included the first women's rights convention in Seneca Falls, New York, in 1848—and later were less assertive than their northern counterparts in demanding suffrage and other changes, it is easy to underestimate the extent to which Virginia women pursued reform and feminist agendas. It is also easy to assume, mistakenly, that Virginia women's political activism occurred only after the Civil War, or even only in the twentieth century. Indeed, Dolley Madison, who was born in 1768, may have been the most politically significant woman in Virginia history, at least in terms of her long-term legacy. Between 1809 and 1817, when her husband was president, Madison used her social skills and political savvy to invent the job that would become known as the "First Lady," setting important precedents and becoming an enviable political asset to her brilliant but bookish husband, whom she deeply loved.

Notwithstanding Madison's remarkable career and the occasional Virginia woman who invoked the ideals of the American Revolution to criticize her lack of political rights, most of the public initiatives that Virginia women pursued before the Civil War were religious or philanthropic. Elizabeth Henry Campbell Russell, another of Patrick Henry's sisters, became a committed evangelical and a leading benefactor of the Methodist Church in western Virginia. Her efforts helped spark a larger transformation of Virginia's religious landscape in the post-Revolutionary era, which afforded women more authority and influence than they had known in the more hierarchical Church of England (later Episcopal) parishes. As a founding member of Richmond's Female Humane Association, Elizabeth Jacquelin Ambler Brent Carrington was at the forefront of the women's benevolence movement, which emerged in cities in Virginia and throughout the United States beginning in the 1790s. During the Civil War, Sally Louisa Tompkins ran an unusually successful and widely known Confederate hospital. Despite her lack of formal training, Tompkins's facility treated more than thirteen hundred sick and wounded soldiers with only seventy-three fatalities.

Some Virginia women also acted, individually or collectively, to undermine slavery. In the colonial period, Jane Webb went to court repeatedly to protect her own status as a free woman and to ensure that her children—who were born free but nonetheless were bound into service until they were adults—would be free as well. Subsequent generations of African Americans continued this practice of turning to white authorities to obtain their liberty or to verify their status as free people, petitioning either the courts or the legislature. Meanwhile, some white evangelical women, such as Elizabeth Henry Campbell Russell, freed their slaves as a matter of principle, while others were active in Virginia's version of the antislavery movement, which operated chiefly under the auspices of the American Colonization Society. Although African Americans often resented the ACS efforts to deport them to the west African colony of Liberia, pious white women like Ann Randolph Meade Page and Molly Lee Fitzhugh Custis truly believed that they and their associates were striking a blow against the vile institution of slavery when they sent freed African Americans to Liberia. Some black Virginians agreed, starting new lives as free people in Africa and maintaining affectionate relationships with the white women who sponsored their emigration. Elizabeth Van Lew also supported colonization, hoping for a gradual end to slavery, until secession made her an abolitionist, a Union spy, and ultimately a staunch friend to Richmond's newly emancipated African American community.

All of these women have terrific stories with important implications for how we think about the history of Virginia, of the South, and of the United States generally. We hope that scholars and teachers will use these essays to enrich their own work and that general readers will appreciate the opportunity to move beyond the curiously resilient stereotypes of southern women's history. These examples demonstrate some of the myriad ways in which women have influenced and even changed the history of the Old Dominion—both on their own and alongside men—and also the complex and varying ways in which gender shaped their lives.

NOTES

1. Information about the women mentioned in this paragraph can be found in Cynthia A. Kierner, Jennifer R. Loux, and Megan Taylor Shockley, *Changing History: Virginia Women through Four Centuries* (Richmond: Library of Virginia, 2013), on the following pages: Pocahontas, 6–7; Berkeley, 19, 20, 21; Rathell, 31, 39, 40, 41, 56–57; Terrell, 57, 60; Randolph, 104, 126; Minor, 97–98; Keckley, 110, 111, 112; Valentine, 223, 229, 233, 234; Nordlinger, 333, 334, 335–36; Bobbitt, 348.

2. The classic twentieth-century survey of Virginia history, which went through multiple editions, is Virginius Dabney, *Virginia, the New Dominion: A History from 1607 to the Present* (Charlottesville: University of Virginia Press, 1971). Of the women who are the subjects of essays in our two volumes, only Mary Draper Ingles and Ellen Glasgow appear in Dabney's book. The quadricentennial surveys are Ronald L. Heinemann, James G. Kolp, Anthony S. Parent Jr., and William G. Shade, *Old Dominion, New Commonwealth: A History of Virginia, 1607–2007* (Charlottesville: University of Virginia Press, 2007), and Peter Wallenstein, *Cradle of America: Four Centuries of Virginia History* (Lawrence: University Press of Kansas, 2007). Wallenstein is by far the more inclusive of the two newer surveys, including more material on women and on social and cultural history generally. For the difference between "contribution" history and using the history of women and gender to interrogate the existing historical narrative, see Gerda Lerner, "Placing Women in History: Definitions and Challenges," *Feminist Studies* 3 (1975): 5–14.

3. On the monument, see the press release dated March 28, 2013, at http://womensmonument com.virginia.gov/PDFs/WomenMonumentRelease.pdf, and more generally the Women's Monument Commission website at http://womensmonumentcom.virginia.gov (accessed May 21, 2013).

4. Full-length biographies of the better-known women who are the topics of essays in this collection include Catherine Allgor, *A Perfect Union: Dolley Madison and the Creation of an American Nation* (New York: Henry Holt, 2006); Susan Goodman, *Ellen Glasgow: A Biography* (Baltimore, Md.: Johns Hopkins University Press, 2003); and Margaret Jones, *Patsy: The Life and Times of Patsy Cline* (New York: HarperCollins, 1994).

5. See Elizabeth R. Varon, *Southern Lady, Yankee Spy: The True Story of Elizabeth Van Lew, a Union Agent in the Heart of the Confederacy* (New York: Oxford University Press, 2003); and Jennifer Ritterhouse, "Introduction," in Sarah Patton Boyle, *The Desegregated Heart: A Virginian's Stand in the Time of Transition* (Charlottesville: University of Virginia Press, 2001).

6. See especially Joan Wallach Scott, "Gender: A Useful Category of Historical Analysis," *American Historical Review* 91 (1986): 1053–75.

7. A 1979 poll found that 59 percent of Virginians favored passage of the Equal Rights Amendment, which failed by one vote in the state senate in 1982. See Kierner, Loux, and Shockley, *Changing History*, 327–29.

Grace Sherwood

The Virginia Witch

CYNTHIA A. KIERNER

In July 2006 Governor Timothy M. Kaine restored the "good name" of a supposed witch named Grace Sherwood who had lived and died in the now-defunct county of Princess Anne, in Virginia's southeastern corner. In 1706 Sherwood had been "ducked" in the Lynnhaven River to determine her guilt or innocence and, having failed that test, seemed headed for trial in Virginia's highest court. Three centuries later, after repeated requests from a Virginia Beach resident who had spent years researching Sherwood's case and lobbying on her behalf, the governor condemned her "trial by water" and celebrated the fact that modern women "have the freedom to pursue their hopes and dreams." In April 2007 a statue of Sherwood was erected in Virginia Beach, inscribed with both a brief biographical sketch and Kaine's exculpatory declaration.[1]

In some ways, Grace Sherwood's story is comparable to that of Pocahontas, arguably the most intriguing woman in Virginia's early history. In both cases, the historical record is frustratingly incomplete. No one truly knows how Pocahontas understood her relationship with John Smith, why she married the Englishman John Rolfe, or how she saw her role in the often tense relations between her people and the English colonizers. Similarly, we can never know for sure if Grace Sherwood considered herself a witch and, if so, how she defined witchcraft and sought to use it in her daily life. Like Pocahontas, Sherwood became a legendary figure (albeit a less famous one). Oral tradition held that she sailed to England and back in an eggshell in a single day, and that she magically made the herb rosemary grow in thickets on the banks of the Lynnhaven River. Some believed that Sherwood had the power to make bad soil fertile. Others thought her spirit haunted the river, frightening men who dared to fish where she was ducked.[2]

THE SWIMMING OF MARY SUTTON

This illustration from an English witch-hunting manual recommended ducking as "a strange and most true trial how to know whether a woman be a witch or not." Although Grace Sherwood failed this test, she escaped the sad fate of Mary Sutton and her daughter, both of whom were executed as witches in England in 1613. Reproduced by permission of The Huntington Library, San Marino, California.

GRACE SHERWOOD

Erected in 2007, this life-size bronze statue by Robert G. Cunningham stands on Witchduck Road in Virginia Beach, not far from the site where Sherwood was ducked. Private donations funded this commemoration of Sherwood, who was increasingly viewed as benign and wrongly persecuted. Photograph by Cynthia A. Kierner.

Unlike the celebrated and much-mythologized Pocahontas, Grace Sherwood is a relatively obscure figure, in part because she was not connected to a powerful man who left a cache of revealing personal papers or made an otherwise lasting impression on the history of the colony. The three best-known women from Virginia's early decades are Pocahontas (daughter of the mighty chief Powhatan), Lady Frances Berkeley (the wife of Governor William Berkeley and a political force in her own right), and Lucy Parke Byrd (the wife of the great planter and diarist William Byrd II, who famously "rogered" her on the billiard table and complained when she plucked her eyebrows). Historians encounter less well-connected women mostly in county court records and other public documents. Party to a total of five court cases, Grace Sherwood is the best known of Virginia's alleged witches precisely because her involvement with the courts is relatively well documented.[3]

Sherwood is the subject of a children's book, several modern local history plays, and popular histories of varying accuracy and quality. Early accounts portrayed her variously as a pitiable victim, a whimsical folkloric figure, and a symbol of local, state, or even southern sectional identity. More recently, she has been celebrated as an independent woman who suffered persecution at the hands of superstitious and sexist neighbors. In her own time, however, Sherwood was someone who made the most of the limited autonomy that law and custom afforded to women. An assertive and relatively autonomous person in a society in which women were supposed to be subordinate and dependent, she became known as a troublesome neighbor or, worse, as a woman who might use magical powers to wreak havoc in her community.

Grace Sherwood and her neighbors likely believed in witchcraft and in the responsibility of the state to punish those who practiced it. Following English law, Virginia's earliest white settlers made minor witchcraft offenses punishable by imprisonment for one year; death by hanging was the prescribed penalty for a major infraction or for a second offense. Michael Dalton's *Countrey Justice*, an important guide that went through many seventeenth-century editions and was used and cited by magistrates in Virginia and other English colonies, included detailed instructions for the effective detection of witches and *maleficium* (harmful magic or sorcery). Dalton emphasized the need for physical evidence to convict an accused witch. He urged magistrates to search for "some big or little Teat" on the body of the accused or some other "Devils marks." He also advocated searching the house of an alleged witch for "Pictures of Clay or Wax" or "Hair cut, Bones, Powders, Books of Witchcraft, Charms, and Pots or Places where their Spirits may be kept" or other incriminating artifacts.[4]

Although no law defined practitioners of maleficium as exclusively female, women predominated in both the court proceedings and the popular culture of witchcraft. The predisposition to see witches as women—and women as witches—was rooted in theology and folklore, as well as in the gender conventions of the early modern era. Authors of early Christian treatises explicitly argued that women were far more likely than men to consort with Satan. As daughters of Eve, they asserted, women were inherently more evil and corruptible; having comparatively little temporal authority, they were also more apt to covet supernatural powers. The image of woman as the devil's handmaiden persisted even as English Protestants increasingly lauded feminine virtue. Once they idealized women as submissive wives, nurturing mothers, and benevolent neighbors, they stigmatized and shunned assertive, independent, or cantankerous women who did not fit this ideal. Those accused of witchcraft included many such women.[5]

In 1626 the first recorded witch trial in any English colony took place in Kecoughtan, a Virginia community located about twenty miles upriver from Jamestown. The proceedings against Joan Wright foreshadowed key aspects of subsequent Virginia witchcraft cases, including those involving Grace Sherwood decades later. First, Wright was a woman, as were all but two of the sixteen colonists who are known to have appeared in Virginia courts as a result of witchcraft accusations. Second, the defendant appeared in court at the behest of her neighbors, who claimed that Wright, a midwife, caused the death of a neighbor's infant, predicted the deaths of three men in her neighborhood, "bewitched" Sargeant Booth so that despite "having very fayre game to shute . . . he could never kill any thinge," and threatened to make Elizabeth Gates "dance naked and stand before the Tree." Third, though clergy were often involved in New England witch trials, secular authorities handled Wright's case, as they did all later Virginia cases. Finally, Wright was also typical in that she was not convicted. In fact, her case never even came to trial, perhaps because her husband, Robert, testified on her behalf.[6]

Joan Wright was the first woman in any English colony to defend herself against a criminal charge of witchcraft, and Grace Sherwood was the last. Both were Virginians. A total of eight witchcraft cases are known to have come before the Virginia General Court, the body charged with adjudicating serious criminal cases in the colony, but only one of the eight is known to have resulted in a conviction. The court delivered a guilty verdict in the case of William Harding, the sole male criminal defendant, and sentenced him to ten lashes and banishment in 1655. The Virginia General Court heard its last witchcraft case, with the exception of Sherwood's, in 1679. Although nearly half of all Virginia witchcraft incidents occurred after that date, they were instead adjudicated as civil cases in the colony's county courts.⁷

While criminal cases resulted in part from the willingness of the magistrates—first at the county level and then in the General Court—to take witchcraft charges seriously, civil cases arose from the accused witch's determination to protect her reputation. In civil cases related to witchcraft, the accused witch confronted her accuser head-on by suing for defamation. Because wrongful gossip and slander could lead to a "tyranny of neighbors," defamation suits were common, especially in the seventeenth century, when colonial communities were new and their members' reputations and social standing were still fluid. Under such circumstances, colonists often enlisted the authority of the courts to protect their reputations from irreparable damage and potentially ruinous consequences.⁸

Women were often plaintiffs and defendants in defamation cases, in part because they lacked the legal or cultural authority to pursue their enemies by other means. Unlike men, who typically filed defamation suits to defuse gossip about failed or shady business dealings, most female plaintiffs sued to defend their sexual reputations. For both sexes, however, the underlying issue was economic. Men had a vested interest in having their neighbors believe that they were honest and financially competent; chastity and sexual trustworthiness enhanced a woman's ability to attract a suitable husband and, later, to ensure the legitimacy of her offspring, who stood to inherit the property of her spouse. Nevertheless, one study of defamation suits in seventeenth-century Maryland found that after sexual impropriety, witchcraft was the second most common charge leveled against—and contested by—that colony's women.⁹

Although court-ordered settlements of cases involving unruly speech could resolve potentially violent quarrels, some Virginia authorities sought to stem the seemingly endless tide of private defamation suits, especially those involving women. In 1662, reacting to the high volume of lawsuits and perhaps acting on complaints from "poore husbands" who were liable for the fines and court costs their litigious wives incurred, colonial legislators enacted a law that gave men the choice of either paying their wives' fines or having their "brabling" women publicly ducked. A few years earlier, in 1655, magistrates in Lower Norfolk County adopted a parallel—though less explicitly misogynistic—strategy in hopes of specifically limiting witchcraft accusations. "Whereas divers dangerous & scandalous speeches have been raised by some p[er]sons concerning sevrall women in this Countie, termeing them to be Witches, whereby theire reputacons have been much impaired," the court imposed the sizable fine of 1,000 pounds of tobacco on anyone who voiced "any such like scandall" that could not be proven in court.¹⁰

Lower Norfolk (part of which became Princess Anne County in 1691) was the site of most of Virginia's known witchcraft-related court proceedings, including those involving Grace Sherwood. Of eighteen documented Virginia witchcraft cases, eight involved residents of Lower Norfolk/Princess Anne. Three were criminal cases that local magistrates remanded to the General Court for trial; the others were civil suits for slander or defamation. Some historians suggest that hostility between orthodox Anglicans and dissenting Protestants (first Puritans and later Quakers) made this county uniquely contentious and that these religious conflicts occasionally led to witchcraft accusations. In the late 1670s, criminal proceedings against the accused witches Joan Jenking and Alice Cartwright also may have resulted at least in part from social tensions and personal conflicts related to Bacon's Rebellion. In the 1690s, the decline of tobacco prices may have caused hardships and animosities that inspired the county's last significant spate of witchcraft accusations.[11]

Yet there was something special about Grace Sherwood. Neither a Quaker nor an activist on either side during Bacon's Rebellion and its aftermath, she nonetheless accounted for three of the eight witchcraft cases reported in the county's court records and two of four such cases that the court heard in the 1690s. In September 1698, Grace was a co-plaintiff (with her husband, James) in two civil suits arising from witchcraft accusations, which resurfaced in another case eight years later. Although two Princess Anne men accused Anne and John Byrd of witchcraft in 1698, and the Byrds initiated two suits for defamation that July, there is no discernible connection (besides the timing) between the Byrds' cases and the Sherwoods'. The court dismissed the Byrds' suits, thereby implying either that their accusers' allegations were truthful—and therefore not actionable under civil law—or more likely (since no criminal charges ensued) that the gossip was so preposterous that it posed no real threat to the Byrds' reputations. Either way, the Byrds' careers as accused witches ended in 1698 with the court's ruling, while Grace Sherwood's continued and intensified during the next decade.[12]

By 1698, Grace Sherwood was a middle-aged wife and mother to at least three living children, but her fortunes had declined in ways that may have compromised her claim to respectability. Grace was the daughter of John White, a literate man who, as a carpenter, possessed skills that were valued in the colony. In 1674, White received a patent for 195 acres in Lower Norfolk County's Lynnhaven Parish, in "the northern branch of Curratuck." Although White was no great planter, he was a substantial middling landowner. By 1680 Grace White, his only surviving child, had married James Sherwood, who was neither skilled nor landed. James, like Grace, was also illiterate, lacking even the ability to sign his name to legal documents. In October 1680, John White transferred

50 acres to James Sherwood, who received the rest of his acreage when the older man died a few months later. Relations between father- and son-in-law were cordial. White, who piously consigned his "Soule to Almighty god and to Jesus Christ by whose death and passion I hoope to have Remission of all my sines," made his "Loving Sone In Law James Sherwood" the sole executor of his estate.[13]

Despite inheriting all of White's property, except some livestock and his "great gun," the Sherwoods did not prosper. They did not acquire more land. Instead, they lost some, selling a fifteen-acre portion of White's former holdings to Captain Plomer Bray in 1690. James owed money to the estate of Thomas Jackson, whose widow successfully sued him, and he may have had other debts. Like most small planters, James had no slaves, though he did own some livestock: five head of cattle, seven pigs, seven sheep, and "one old poor mangy scabby horse." A 1701 inventory of his estate described nearly all the contents of the Sherwoods' house as "old," which suggests that they had acquired their furniture and other implements years earlier from Grace's father. Also included among their possessions were milk pails, cider casks, and a wheel for spinning wool, all of which was essential gear for doing women's domestic work in colonial Virginia.[14]

Neither debts nor old furniture was a cause for shame, but evidence from public records confirms the impression that the Sherwoods, though still landowners, were at best marginal members of the county's yeomanry. James Sherwood never held a position of public trust, though men whose property holdings were comparable to his routinely served as jurors, appraisers, and other minor functionaries, if the local gentry who ran the county court and the parish vestry deemed them prudent and trustworthy. In one colonial Virginia county, roughly one-third of all male heads of household held some county or parish post at any given time; officeholders changed from year to year to spread the jobs—and whatever hardships or benefits they brought—among those considered suitable for service. Unlike the men who filled these positions, James Sherwood appeared in the county court records only as a litigant. Significantly, the Sherwoods accounted for three of the sixteen defamation suits that the court heard during the 1690s.[15]

In 1698, James and Grace Sherwood filed three lawsuits, all of which pertained to Grace, who would not have been party to a suit that only involved her husband. Under the common-law doctrine of coverture, when a woman married her entire legal identity was subsumed in that of her spouse, who was legally responsible for her actions. That meant that, in theory at least, husbands always represented their wives at law and in all property-related matters. In practice, however, colonial women often appeared as plaintiffs in defamation cases that pertained specifically to them, doing so most commonly as co-plaintiffs with their husbands.[16]

So, in February 1698, when "James Sherwood and Grace his wife" sued Richard Capps for defamation, seeking a whopping £50 sterling in damages, they were contending that Capps had defamed Grace (and perhaps James as well). Like the Sherwoods, the Cappses were middling landowners in Lynnhaven Parish. Richard was either the brother or cousin of William Capps Jr., whom Margery Mulligan had identified as the father of her child when she was presented in court for bastardy in 1697. Perhaps some altercation between the Sherwoods and Richard Capps—which may or may not have involved the temporarily disgraced William—provoked Richard's alleged defamation of Grace. Court records do not indicate what Capps said, but since most women sued to defend themselves against either sexual innuendo or witchcraft accusations, it seems likely that one of these was at issue in *Sherwood v. Capps*. Court records indicate that this suit was "Ended by the parties" without a verdict, but whatever Capps said had been sufficiently damaging to motivate the Sherwoods to initiate their first suit as plaintiffs in the county court, where they sought damages roughly equivalent to $4,255 in 2000 U.S. dollars.[17]

The next time the Sherwoods headed to court, on September 10, 1698, they filed two slander suits against respectable people from their neighborhood who had accused Grace of witchcraft, citing specific acts of maleficium that she supposedly committed against them. The defendants in the first of these cases, John and Jane Gisbourne, had known Grace Sherwood for many years. John Gisbourne's farm was adjacent to the Sherwoods', and he had witnessed John White's initial deed of land to James Sherwood in 1680. The defendants in the second case were Anthony and Elizabeth Barnes, who were also landowners in Lynnhaven Parish. The fact that Elizabeth Barnes formally witnessed the will of a local planter, William Brocke, and later served as forewoman of a court-appointed jury of women charged with searching for evidence of witchcraft indicates that she was a highly regarded member of the community.[18]

In these lawsuits, the Sherwoods claimed that the Gisbournes and the Barneses had "wronged and abused" Grace by spreading malicious and untrue stories about her supposed supernatural powers. John and Jane Gisbourne had claimed that Sherwood "bewitched their pigs to Death and bewitched their Cotton" crop, causing them financial loss. Elizabeth Barnes had declared that Grace came to her one night and rode her (like a horse or a broomstick) before escaping through "the Key hole or crack of the door like a black Catt." The assembled jurors would have recognized all of these actions—killing animals and crops, shape-shifting, the ability to fly through the air by riding a normally earthbound being or object—as behaviors commonly attributed to witches in both folklore and learned treatises.[19]

The Sherwoods took these charges seriously and fought them strenuously. The fact that they sought £100 in damages in each of these suits—twice what they had demanded from Richard Capps—suggests that these new allegations were more damaging and also that the Sherwoods feared the cumulative effects of the continuing gossip among their neighbors. In 1698, the Sherwoods brought nine witnesses to court to testify on Grace's behalf, all of whom were to receive compensation from the suits' losing parties. Of the sixteen defamation cases heard in Princess Anne County during the 1690s, only the two that the Sherwoods initiated against the Gisbournes and the Barneses were specifically classified as "slander" suits in the court's records. This unusual designation may have indicated that the plaintiffs (and the authorities) deemed the gossip about Grace Sherwood more serious than the recent allegations against Anne and John Byrd, who had also been accused of witchcraft but whose lawsuits the court placed in the more ordinary category of "defamation."[20]

The Sherwoods lost both of their cases, despite the fact that every other known Virginia civil case concerning witchcraft resulted in either dismissal—as in the case of the Byrds—or judgment in favor of the plaintiff (the accused witch). In the Sherwoods' cases, by contrast, a jury of twelve local men ruled against them and in favor of the defendants. Court records yield no clues as to the jurors' logic. The Sherwoods presented witnesses, who presumably either attested to Grace's good character or recounted earlier altercations between her and her accusers to establish the defendants' motives for spreading damaging gossip about her. The Gisbournes and the Barneses produced no witnesses in their own defense. Nevertheless, the jurors found in the defendants' favor, leaving the Sherwoods to pay the court costs. One can only conclude that Grace's reputation led the jurors to believe that she had behaved maliciously, regardless of whether she actually employed maleficium against her neighbors.

While large-scale witch hunts occurred in times of social stress, isolated accusations, such as those that plagued Grace Sherwood, arose from the small politics of everyday life. The Salem witch hunts of 1692—which involved at least 144 defendants and resulted in the execution of 20 convicted witches—were unique in scale even for New England, where criminal trials for witchcraft were comparatively common in part because of the unusual intimacy among villagers in Puritan communities. Scholars attribute the Salem debacle variously to popular anxiety over the decline of religious orthodoxy, the trauma of recurrent Indian wars, and uncertainty about the political future of the Massachusetts colony. In Salem, each round of accusations produced revelations about other supposed witches, eventually including some defendants who were not local people and who were known to their accusers mainly by reputation. In Princess Anne County, by contrast, whatever circumstances led the Gisbournes and the Barneses to accuse Grace Sherwood of witchcraft were personal. Perhaps John Gisbourne, who died deeply indebted, was already financially vulnerable in 1698. Sherwood, who lived nearby, was a convenient scapegoat for the death of his pigs and the failure of his crops.[21]

What was it about Grace Sherwood that made her such a plausible target, both for her accusers and for the jurors who concluded that the defendants were not slandering her when they accused her of witchcraft? A middle-aged woman of marginal or declining economic status, Sherwood fit the description of most accused witches in colonial America, though obviously many more colonists who met these general criteria were never accused of witchcraft. In Grace Sherwood's case, whatever gossip Richard Capps spread previously may have heightened her neighbors' suspicions, whereas some of the witnesses who testified in her favor may not have been especially credible. Elizabeth and Thomas Williams were notably problematic. Elizabeth ran off to live with a man whom her husband, Thomas, then sued "for Carrying away and entertening" his spouse; Elizabeth soon took up with another man, and a second lawsuit ensued. Another member of the Williams family had been sued for defamation by John Gisbourne, who then became the defendant in the Sherwoods' slander case.[22]

Oral tradition, which persisted for centuries in Princess Anne County, described Grace Sherwood as independent, assertive, and often unwilling to conform to the gender conventions of her community. Stories about her dancing naked in the moonlight and flirting with other women's husbands were common, as were assertions that she was a midwife or a "healer," occupations that made women particularly vulnerable to suspicion because of the unusual powers they seemed to confer on them. Some accounts describe Sherwood as having worn men's trousers, which implied a dangerous and objectionable appropriation of male authority and autonomy. Although no contemporary sources document these stories, given Sherwood's continuing problems with her neighbors, it makes sense to take them seriously.[23]

Grace Sherwood revealed her desire for independence after her husband died in 1701. James's death deprived her of the status and protection that marriage afforded and left her alone to fight her battles. Yet, unlike many Virginia widows of her era, Grace did not remarry, and she took an unusually keen interest in her husband's property. James died without leaving a will, and Grace was there to witness the proceedings when the court conducted an inventory of his estate. Though she had three sons, the eldest of whom was twenty years old at the time of his father's death, it appears that Grace alone was involved in the estate inventory, and she apparently expected to retain control over the family plantation and its house. At a time when wives could not own property and when a widow with mature sons typically received only a life interest in one-third of her husband's estate, being the sole owner of a farm would have made Sherwood an unusual figure in Princess Anne, and perhaps also a threatening one.[24]

For reasons that are unclear, however, neither Grace nor her sons obtained a clear title to James's property. According to the law of escheat, the property of people who died without a will reverted to the Crown if they had no heirs to inherit it, but James Sherwood had left behind a wife and three sons. Nevertheless, in 1704, colonial authorities inexplicably ruled that his property—145 acres in all—was to be escheated to the queen and issued a warrant to that effect. (Since James had 180 acres after the sale to Plomer Bray in 1690, it seems likely that he had already conveyed 35 acres to James Jr., his eldest son.) Although there is no evidence that Grace was forced to leave her farm at that point, there was a very real possibility that the government would sell the escheated land to someone else. Any efforts Grace might have made to contest this official ruling or otherwise protect the property she saw as her own probably figured into the drama that soon engulfed her.[25]

In December 1705, Grace Sherwood sued Luke Hill and his wife, Elizabeth, for assault and battery, asserting that Elizabeth "had Assaulted Brused Maimed & Barbarously Beaten" her and seeking £50 sterling in damages. No witnesses appeared for either side, but Sherwood must have been injured sufficiently to convince the jury that Hill had assaulted her. The jurors found in Sherwood's favor, but two factors suggest that they sympathized with the Hills nonetheless. For one thing, the jury ordered the Hills to pay only twenty shillings (the equivalent of £1) in damages. More remarkably, Sherwood was unable to collect even that small sum because the foreman of the jury "Omitted to Signe" the verdict, thereby rendering it invalid. Although the justices ordered the foreman, Mark Powell, to return to court in January to validate the court's verdict against the Hills, that never happened.[26]

Instead, when the court reconvened in January, Luke Hill took the offensive, asking the justices to initiate criminal proceedings against Sherwood on the grounds that she had "been for a long time Suspected of witchcraft." Specifically, Hill claimed that Grace had "bewitched" his wife, Elizabeth, and that Sherwood's maleficium was therefore a mitigating factor in the recent assault and battery suit against her. The magistrates responded by ordering the sheriff to bring Sherwood to the court in February, when they "Long debated" these new allegations with mixed results. On the one hand, the justices' order for

Luke Hill to pay court costs suggests that the court elected not to pursue the criminal case against Sherwood, at least for the time being. On the other hand, the magistrates also commanded Sherwood to return to court in March "to be Searched . . . by a Jury of women" for some bodily marking that might constitute physical evidence to corroborate Hill's accusation. In so doing, the justices followed the instructions set out in Dalton's *Countrey Justice* and other legal treatises, which enabled them to satisfy both Sherwood's accusers (who may or may not have actually believed she was a witch) and also the growing skepticism of better-educated colonists about witchcraft beliefs generally.[27]

In March, the justices impaneled a jury of twelve women to examine Grace Sherwood. Colonial courts typically employed female jurors to conduct physical examinations of women defendants to search for signs of pregnancy in fornication, adultery, and bastardy cases, and also to look for witches' marks. Although the court records indicate that Sherwood agreed to the full-body search, she really had no other option because the magistrates could have forced her to submit to it. If Sherwood believed that enduring such humiliation would prove her innocence, the choice of her former accuser Elizabeth Barnes as the jury's forewoman must have given her pause. Barnes and her fellow jurors soon reported that they had "Sercht Grace Sherwood & have found Two things like titts with Severall other Spotts."[28]

Although the magistrates in Princess Anne were still reluctant to initiate criminal proceedings against Sherwood, Luke Hill insisted that she stand trial and he took the unusual step of petitioning the governor's council in Williamsburg to request that she be prosecuted as a witch in the General Court. Whatever its source—perhaps they coveted her land—the Hills' hostility toward Sherwood ran deep. The governor's council forwarded Hill's petition to the attorney general, who rejected it for two reasons. First, he maintained, the charge against Sherwood was "too general." Second, only an action of the county court could cause the higher court to initiate criminal proceedings against a defendant. Accordingly, the attorney general ordered the justices of Princess Anne County to "make a further Examination of the matters of fact . . . & if they thought there was sufficient cause" to send Sherwood to the "Genll prison of this Colony" in Williamsburg to await appearance before a grand jury in the General Court.[29]

Hill and his supporters must have pressed the magistrates to continue their investigation because on May 2, 1706, the county court ordered the sheriff to take Sherwood into custody while the authorities gathered additional evidence, dispatching the constable to her farm to search for potentially incriminating "Images & Such like things." The court also tried to convene a second "Able Jury of Women" to reexamine Sherwood, but this time the local women—who either sympathized with Sherwood or feared her vengeance—refused to serve and were held in contempt of court. By July, convinced that no local women would obey their summons, the justices took a daring step. They decided to tie Sherwood hand-to-foot and submerge her in water. If she floated, that meant she was a witch; sinking would prove her innocence.[30]

Although a 1662 Virginia law prescribed "ducking" as an appropriate punishment for women's "brabling" or scandalous speech, there is no evidence that witch ducking had been practiced previously in the colony. Trial by water had been used in witch trials in England, however, and the famed English "witchfinder" Matthew Hopkins recommended ducking in his influential pamphlet, *The Discovery of Witches*, in 1647. Citing King James I, who had published a major treatise on demonology decades earlier, Hopkins asserted that because "Witches deny their baptisme when they Covenant with the Devill ... when they be heaved into the water, the water refuseth to receive them into her bosome ... and suffers them to float, as the Froath on the Sea." In fact, few people in early modern England knew how to swim, so binding the limbs of the accused (whose body was also sometimes tied to a special ducking stool or chair) made it virtually certain that the accused would sink—and likely perish in the ordeal—even if they somehow managed to escape whatever ropes or chains the authorities used to bind them.[31]

Why did the county magistrates mandate such an unusual procedure, given their initial reluctance even to remand Sherwood's case to the General Court? The court records mention no stunning new evidence that warranted a more aggressive prosecution of Sherwood's case, only that she supposedly consented to "have all means possible tryed either to acquit her or to Give more Strength to the Suspicion that she might be Dealt with as Deserved" and thereby put the matter to rest. Popular pressure likely caused the magistrates to step up their efforts to prosecute Sherwood. In Virginia and elsewhere, county courts were supposed to foster order, stability, and social cohesion. Under other circumstances, colonial justices' desire to maintain order likely discouraged witchcraft prosecutions and promoted leniency toward both accusers and accused. In this instance, however, the justices may have vigorously pursued Sherwood's case to placate her enemies, who by then included, at a minimum, the Cappses, the Gisbournes, the Barneses, the Hills, and the twelve female jurors who had found the "titts" and "Spotts."[32]

In implementing the trial by water, the magistrates strove to be compassionate and impartial. When the weather was "very Rainy and Bad" on July 5, 1706, they postponed the procedure, fearing that it "might endanger [Sherwood's] health." Five days later, when Sherwood was delivered to John Harper's riverfront plantation to undergo the test, the justices stipulated that she would be submerged only "into [water] above man's depth ... always having care of her life to preserve her from drowning." As it turned out, however, when Sherwood was bound and dunked, she inexplicably freed herself, and spectators saw her "swimming ... contrary to custom." The court then prevailed on five "antient women" to examine her body, and they declared under oath that Sherwood was "not like them nor noe other woman" because she had "two things like titts on her private parts of a Black coller being blacker than the rest of her body." This new empirical evidence, along with the results of the ducking and the fact that Sherwood said "little or nothing in her own behalf," led the justices to put her in the county jail to await transportation to Williamsburg for criminal trial in the General Court.[33]

Sherwood must have gone to Williamsburg, but the papers of the General Court have not survived, so there is no record of her having stood trial there. If convicted, she might have received as light a sentence as one-year imprisonment, though the justices could have ordered her hanged if they considered her maleficium especially serious or if they interpreted the bewitching of Elizabeth Hill as not being her first offense. It seems unlikely that the court would have imposed the maximum sentence. No Virginia witchcraft case had ever resulted in an execution, England's last witch hanging had occurred in 1685, and the notoriously high death toll at Salem made colonial judges even more cautious when adjudicating witchcraft cases and sentencing defendants. Indeed, the last English colonists executed for witchcraft died at Salem in 1692.[34]

The historical record indicates only that Grace Sherwood survived and that— if she was, in fact, imprisoned—she was back in Princess Anne County by 1708, when she was one of many debtors sued by Christopher Cocke, to whom she was ordered to pay 600 pounds of tobacco plus court costs. Six years later, in 1714, George Hancock, a member of the gentry and a frequent plaintiff in local debt cases, successfully sued Sherwood to recover the 357 pounds of tobacco she owed him. Sherwood's appearance as a litigant in such mundane cases suggests that she had assimilated herself into the routine life of her community. Moreover, she managed to get along with her neighbors—and they with her—until she died in 1740. There are no more documented encounters between Sherwood and the Hills. The Capps family and the Gisbournes still lived nearby, but if their relations with Sherwood remained tense, they never again led to lawsuits. When the aged Richard Capps found himself in poverty in 1728, he petitioned the county for poor relief instead of blaming Sherwood or anyone else for his predicament. In sum, in the thirty-four years following her ducking, Sherwood made only two unremarkable appearances in the county court.[35]

During these years, the widowed Sherwood also maintained her independence and became an acknowledged landowner in her own right. In 1714, she sought and received official legal title to the 145 acres that had been escheated to the Crown a decade earlier. In response to her petition—and in exchange for two pounds of tobacco per acre—Governor Alexander Spotswood issued royal letters patent that granted the land to Sherwood "and to her heirs & assigns forever." The governor's patent recognized her position as a property-owning member of the community. In 1731, when court-appointed "processioners" produced a complete list of the county's landowners, Grace Sherwood was one of only five women listed in her precinct. Of the five, she was the only one not designated as a "widow" in the official record because she was not merely a caretaker for her late husband's estate but rather, by virtue of the governor's patent, the actual owner of acreage in Princess Anne County.[36]

Sherwood showed how highly she valued her property when, rejecting her husband's example, she prepared her last will and testament in 1733. Otherwise a shadowy figure, her son John emerges in that document as her most likely source of labor and companionship. Grace bequeathed to him "my plantacon whereon I now live" as well as her entire personal estate, which included ten head of cattle, one "Inglish" blanket, and a pewter dish and basin. A step up from the "old" things that had been listed on her husband's estate inventory, these items signified Grace's modest success as a planter, something her unfortunate husband never attained. Her son James, who lived on a farm adjacent to his mother's, probably already had received some land from his father's estate; Grace left him five shillings, clearly a token bequest. The third son, Richard, who did not reside in Princess Anne, also received a token five shillings from his mother.[37]

For nearly a century after Grace Sherwood's death in 1740, her story was fodder for local lore and oral tradition, though it never appeared in early written histories of the Virginia colony. The educated Virginians who typically authored these early histories and memoirs found the witchcraft beliefs of their ancestors profoundly embarrassing. In 1736 Parliament's repeal of the anti-witchcraft statute was tantamount to an official rejection of traditional beliefs in maleficium, though two years later Virginia's first newspaper, the self-consciously urbane *Virginia Gazette*, printed a letter whose author lamented that "the Law for Abolishing the Act against Witches has not abolish'd the Credulity of the Country People." As late as 1770, a Virginia almanac poked fun at those who believed in witchcraft and praised the rational clergy of the Old Dominion for resisting these popular prejudices. Belief in witchcraft, magic, and the occult persisted, however, as did the story of Grace Sherwood, who was increasingly viewed as a curious but benign figure from Virginia's colonial era.[38]

Early nineteenth-century retellings of Sherwood's story almost inevitably featured comparisons to New England witchcraft, since Virginia and Massachusetts, the oldest and most influential of the colonies, competed for primacy in the nation's historical consciousness. In 1833, when Jonathan P. Cushing—the president of Hampden-Sydney College, cofounder of the Virginia Historical Society, and a New Hampshire native who craved acceptance in his beloved adopted state—included the records of the court proceedings against Sherwood in the inaugural volume of the society's published collections, he implied that colonial Virginians were not all that different from their New England contemporaries. At least one Massachusetts newspaper, the *Salem Gazette*, reprinted the substance of Cushing's piece, agreeing that Sherwood's case deserved "a conspicuous place among the annals of Salem Witchcraft." In 1844, however, a New Englander used Sherwood's story to tweak Virginians' outsized pride in their history, reminding them that their ancestors shared the dubious "honor of persecuting poor old women for dealing with the devil."[39]

In the aftermath of the Civil War, some Virginia writers used the Grace Sherwood story to reimagine their state's place in the larger history and culture of a forcibly reunited and reconstructed republic. In 1869, four years after the defeat of the Confederacy, an anonymous Virginian, writing for a national magazine, struck a conciliatory note, observing that his own state and Massachusetts shared an equally embarrassing colonial history, which included religious intolerance, the mistreatment of Indians, and the foolish and inhumane persecution of women like "poor Grace Sherwood" as supposed witches. In 1904, however, another anonymous Virginian, addressing a local audience, compared the record of the Old Dominion favorably with that of New England's inhumane "fanaticism" on the witchcraft issue. Conceding that his own colonial forebears shared the superstitions of their times, this proud Virginian nevertheless oversimplified the problem of Virginia witchcraft, attributing the rarity of prosecutions solely to the "common sense, conservatism, and staunch stability of character" of these early "Southerners."[40]

These accounts portrayed Sherwood as a sympathetic victim of superstition and ignorance, but others viewed her (and accused witches generally) in a more unambiguously positive light. The transformation of popular conceptions of witches from evil crones to hapless victims and then to benevolent enchantresses attuned to the natural world originated as a corollary to the Romantic critique of scientific rationalism and industrialization and emerged most forcefully in tandem with the fight for women's rights. Thus the suffragist Matilda Joslyn Gage included witches in her feminist history of women's spirituality; Gage's radical son-in-law, the writer L. Frank Baum, created a world in *The Wonderful Wizard of Oz* where—with the notable exception of the Wicked

Witch of the West—witches were good characters. (Baum's male characters were decidedly less attractive, both physically and morally.) Modern accounts, some of which approach Sherwood's story from a feminist perspective, describe her as beautiful, noble, and independent. According to one local historian, she was simply "born before her time." Another claimed that Sherwood "might have become a great actress, a social lioness, or a leader of womens [sic] causes" had she lived in another era.[41]

The transformation of Grace Sherwood from feared practitioner of maleficium to valiant free spirit or feminist role model derived from a sea change in attitudes toward magic, witches, and women. Not surprisingly, the statue of Sherwood in Virginia Beach reflects these new sensibilities. Because no one knows what Sherwood looked like, the sculptor's main task was to capture her personality and her spirit, which he depicted not as cantankerous or aggressive, but rather as kindly and modest. While Sherwood's contemporaries would have regarded her animals (known as "familiars") and herbs as accoutrements of maleficium, the sculptor's inclusion of the raccoon at her feet and the rosemary and garlic in her hands signify an admirable affinity with nature. The historical record suggests that the real Grace Sherwood was less tranquil—and certainly more formidable. Still, the sculptor's imagined heroine stands erect and alone, just as Grace Sherwood confronted her accusers at the spot known even today as Witchduck Point on the banks of the Lynnhaven River.

NOTES

1. *Washington Post*, July 12, 2006; *Richmond Times-Dispatch*, July 11, 2006; *Wall Street Journal*, eastern ed., August 4, 2006; *Norfolk Virginian-Pilot*, July 10, 2006; Timothy M. Kaine to Belinda Nash, July 10, 2006, Grace Sherwood Vertical File, Virginia Historical Society.

2. The literature on Pocahontas is vast; for a suggestive overview, see Sarah J. Stebbins, "Pocahontas: Her Life and Legend," at http://www.nps.gov/jame/historyculture/pocahontas-her-life-and-legend.htm (accessed January 9, 2012). For the Sherwood legends, see William Whitehurst Old, *The Story of Grace Sherwood* (n.p., n.d.), 3; John Cooke Esten, "Grace Sherwood: The One Virginia Witch," *Harper's New Monthly Magazine* 69 (June 1884): 99–102; Elizabeth Dabney Coleman, "The Witchcraft Delusion Rejected," *Virginia Cavalcade* 9 (Summer 1956): 28; Floyd Painter, "An Early 18th Century Witch Bottle: A Legacy of the Witch of Pungo," *Chesopiean* 18 (1980): 62–65, 67; Florence Kimberly Turner, *Gateway to the New World: A History of Princess Anne County, Virginia, 1607–1824* (Easley, S.C.: Southern Historical Press, 1984), 79–80.

3. Notable uses of Virginia colonial court records to do women's history include Kathleen M. Brown, *Good Wives, Nasty Wenches, and Anxious Patriarchs: Gender, Race, and Power in Colonial Virginia* (Chapel Hill: University of North Carolina Press, 1996); Terri L. Snyder, *Brabbling Women: Disorderly Speech and the Law in Early Virginia* (Ithaca, N.Y.: Cornell University Press, 2003); and John Ruston Pagan, *Anne Orthwood's Bastard: Sex and Law in Early Virginia* (New

York: Oxford University Press, 2003). On Berkeley, see Snyder, *Brabbling Women*, 19–32. On Byrd, see Paula A. Treckel, "'The Empire of My Heart': The Marriage of William Byrd II and Lucy Parke Byrd," *Virginia Magazine of History and Biography* 105 (1997): 125–56. A list of known Chesapeake court proceedings involving witchcraft appears in Maureen Rush Burgess, "The Cup of Desolation and Ruin: Seventeenth-Century Witchcraft in the Chesapeake" (PhD diss., University of Hawaii, 2004), 217–19.

4. Michael Dalton, *The Countrey Justice* (1611; London: G. Sawbridge, 1677), 383–85. See also Edward L. Bond, "Source of Knowledge, Source of Power: The Supernatural World of English Virginia, 1607–1624," *Virginia Magazine of History and Biography* 108 (2000): 105–8, 116–20; Ivor Noel Hume, "Witchcraft and Evil Spirits: Weird Sisters, Hand in Hand," *Colonial Williamsburg* 21 (Autumn 1999): 17–18; Philip Alexander Bruce, *Institutional History of Virginia in the Seventeenth Century*, 2 vols. (New York: G. P. Putnam's Sons, 1910), 1:283; Keith Thomas, *Religion and the Decline of Magic* (New York: Scribner's, 1971), 442–43, 460, 553–54, 557, 561; Jon Butler, "Magic, Astrology, and the Early American Religious Heritage, 1600–1700," *American Historical Review* 84 (1979): 322, 325–34; David D. Hall, *Worlds of Wonder, Days of Judgment: Popular Religious Belief in Early New England* (Cambridge, Mass.: Harvard University Press, 1989), chap. 2.

5. See especially Carol F. Karlsen, *The Devil in the Shape of a Woman: Witchcraft in Colonial New England* (New York: Norton, 1987), chap. 5.

6. Richard Beale Davis, "The Devil in Virginia in the Seventeenth Century," *Virginia Magazine of History and Biography* 65 (1957): 138–41; Brown, *Good Wives*, 102–4. There may have been additional criminal trials for witchcraft, but many of the records of the General Court are not extant. See H. R. McIlwaine, ed., *Minutes of the Council and General Court of Colonial Virginia* . . . (Richmond: Virginia State Library, 1924), v.

7. Bruce, *Institutional History*, 1:288; Burgess, "Cup of Desolation and Ruin," 217–19.

8. Helena M. Wall, *Fierce Communion: Family and Community in Early America* (Cambridge, Mass.: Harvard University Press, 1990), chap. 2.

9. Snyder, *Brabbling Women*, esp. 2–8; Brown, *Good Wives*, 94–98, 145–49; Mary Beth Norton, "Gender and Defamation in Seventeenth-Century Maryland," *William and Mary Quarterly*, 3rd ser., 44 (1987): 3–9, 16; Norton, *Founding Mothers and Fathers: Gendered Power and the Forming of American Society* (New York: Knopf, 1996), 211–17, 232–76.

10. Clara Ann Bowler, "Carted Whores and White Shrouded Apologies," *Virginia Magazine of History and Biography* 85 (1977): 412–13; Snyder, *Brabbling Women*, 2, 21, 37–38; Brown, *Good Wives*, 147–48; Edward W. James, comp., "Witchcraft in Virginia," *William and Mary Quarterly*, 1st ser., 2 (1893–94): 58; Lindsey M. Newman, "'Under an Ill Tongue': Witchcraft and Religion in Seventeenth-Century Virginia" (MA thesis, Virginia Tech, 2009), 36, 43, 58, 78.

11. James Horn, *Adapting to a New World: English Society in the Seventeenth-Century Chesapeake* (Chapel Hill: University of North Carolina Press, 1994), 382, 388–89; Edward L. Bond, *Damned Souls in a Tobacco Colony: Religion in Seventeenth-Century Virginia* (Macon, Ga.: Mercer University Press, 2000), 156–57n; James, "Witchcraft," 59; Lorena S. Walsh, *Motives of Honor, Pleasure, and Profit: Plantation Management in the Colonial Chesapeake* (Chapel Hill: University of North Carolina Press, 2010), 210–17.

12. Princess Anne County (hereafter PA) Order Book 1, 1691–1709, 168, 178–79, Library of Virginia. Unless otherwise noted, all public records cited are located in the Library of Virginia in Richmond. Many court documents pertaining to Sherwood's trials have been previously published. See, especially, Edward W. James, comp., "Grace Sherwood, the Virginia Witch," *William and Mary Quarterly*, 1st ser., 3 (1894–95): 96–101, 190–92, 240–42, and 4 (1895–96): 18–22.

13. Land grant to John White, October 26, 1674, Land Office Patents no. 6, 1666–79, 528; White's

deed to James Sherwood, October 15, 1680, Norfolk County Deed Book 4, 85; Will of John White, February 9, 1680, ibid., 98. Most sources give 1660 as Grace White's date of birth. Though undocumented, this date is a reasonable estimate, given the average marrying age for Virginia women in this period. See Darrett B. Rutman and Anita H. Rutman, "'Now Wives and Sons-in-Law': Parental Death in a Seventeenth-Century Virginia County," in *The Chesapeake in the Seventeenth Century: Essays on Anglo-American Society and Politics*, ed. Thad W. Tate and David L. Ammerman (Chapel Hill: University of North Carolina Press, 1979), 157–60; Daniel Blake Smith, *Inside the Great House: Planter Family Life in Eighteenth-Century Chesapeake Society* (Ithaca, N.Y.: Cornell University Press, 1980), 117–18.

14. James Sherwood's deed to Plomer Bray, September 15, 1690, Norfolk County Deed Book 5, 137; PA Order Book 1, 1691–1709, 68; Appraismt of James Sherwood Estate, September 8, 1701, PA Deed Book 1, 301.

15. Darrett B. Rutman and Anita H. Rutman, *A Place in Time: Middlesex County, Virginia, 1650–1750* (New York: Norton, 1984), 142–52.

16. Norton, "Gender and Defamation," 31–32.

17. PA Order Book 1, 1691–1709, 111, 122, 150. On the Capps family, see PA Deed Book 1, 138, 280. Fathers of illegitimate offspring paid court-ordered child support but generally suffered no long-term damage to their reputations. See Pagan, *Anne Orthwood's Bastard*, 125–34; Cornelia Hughes Dayton, "Taking the Trade: Abortion and Gender Relations in an Eighteenth-Century New England Village," *William and Mary Quarterly*, 3rd ser., 48 (1991): 21–22, 32. Currency conversion is based on John J. McCusker, *How Much Is That in Real Money?* (Worcester, Mass.: American Antiquarian Society, 1992), 333, and Scott Derks, *The Value of a Dollar: Prices and Incomes in the United States, 1860-2004* (Millerton, N.Y.: Grey House, 2004), xvii.

18. John White's deed to James Sherwood, October 15, 1680, Norfolk County Deed Book 4, 85; Processioners' Report on Lands, October 19–November 4, 1731, PA Minute Book 2, 1709–17, 269–71; PA Order Book 1, 1691–1709, 435; Will of Joseph Lake, 1687, in Charles Fleming McIntosh, ed., *Brief Abstract of Lower Norfolk County Wills* (Richmond, Va.: Colonial Dames of America, 1914), 115; Will of William Brocke, February 1686, ibid., 111.

19. PA Order Book 1, 1691–1709, 178–79.

20. Ibid., 168, 178–79. Defamation can be slander (oral communication) or libel (print). Because libel was a criminal offense, all civil cases concerning actionable speech were, strictly speaking, slander suits, so it is unclear what the court meant by applying that label to the Sherwoods' suits only. This unique designation may have been used, at least on this occasion, to identify an extreme instance of "defamation per se"—that is, words that defamed by their very nature or substance. My thanks to Lee Shepard of the Virginia Historical Society for help puzzling out the probable meaning of this distinction. See also Wall, *Fierce Communion*, 31–33.

21. See PA Minute Book 5, 1737–44, for the court order to sell "all the perishable Estate" of John Gisbourne "at public outcry" to pay his debts. Important studies of Salem witchcraft include Paul S. Boyer and Stephen Nissembaum, *Salem Possessed: The Social Origins of Witchcraft* (Cambridge, Mass.: Harvard University Press, 1974); John P. Demos, "Underlying Themes in the Witchcraft of Seventeenth-Century New England," *American Historical Review* 75 (1970): 1311–26; and Mary Beth Norton, *The Devil's Snare: The Salem Witchcraft Crisis of 1692* (New York: Knopf, 2002).

22. PA Order Book 1, 1691–1709, 66, 207, 216.

23. Karlsen, *Devil in the Shape of a Woman*, 118–19, 142–43; John Demos, *The Enemy Within: A Short History of Witch-Hunting* (New York: Viking, 2008), 39–43, 117–20; Lyndal Roper, *The Witch in the Western Imagination* (Charlottesville: University of Virginia Press, 2012), 84, 99–100, 107–8;

123–24. More accounts that cite oral tradition have appeared in the *Washington Post*, July 12, 2006; and *Richmond Times-Dispatch*, July 11, 2006. See also Nona Stuck, "Saving Grace," *Ladies Home Journal* (October 2006): 118, in Grace Sherwood Vertical File, Virginia Historical Society.

24. Appraismt of James Sherwood Estate, September 8, 1701, PA Deed Book 1, 301. On Virginia widows and property, see Marylynn Salmon, *Women and the Law of Property in Early America* (Chapel Hill: University of North Carolina Press, 1986), 151–56.

25. Alexander Spotswood's patent to Grace Sherwood, June 16, 1714, Land Office Patents no. 10, 1710–19, 179.

26. PA Order Book 1, 1691–1709, 426.

27. Ibid., 429, 431, 433, 435; Journal of the Governor and Council, March 28, 1706. On the increasing skepticism toward witchcraft accusations in eighteenth-century America, especially among colonial officials and educated elites, see Butler, "Magic, Astrology," 335, 343.

28. PA Order Book 1, 1691–1709, 435; Julia Cherry Spruill, *Women's Life and Work in the Southern Colonies* (Chapel Hill: University of North Carolina Press, 1932), 326–27; George Lincoln Burr, ed., *Narratives of the Witchcraft Cases, 1648–1706* (New York: Charles Scribner's Sons, 1914), 436.

29. Journal of the Governor and Council, March 28, 1706.

30. PA Order Book 1, 1691–1709, 441–42, 444–45. In 1979, archaeologists in the area found "a small glass phial containing a mass of brass pins," which may have been used to ward off witches' curses (Painter, "An Early 18th Century Witch Bottle," 62).

31. Matthew Hopkins, *The Discovery of Witches* (London: Matthew Hopkins, 1647), 6. On swimming, see Kevin Dawson, "Enslaved Swimmers and Divers in the Atlantic World," *Journal of American History* 92 (2006): 1329–33.

32. PA Order Book 1, 1691–1709, 444–45. On the stabilizing and integrative functions of colonial county courts, see Warren M. Billings, "Law and Culture in the Colonial Chesapeake Area," *Southern Studies* 17 (1978): 336–37, 343–44, 346–47; David Thomas Konig, *Law and Society in Puritan Massachusetts: Essex County, 1629–1692* (Chapel Hill: University of North Carolina Press, 1979), xii–xv; A. G. Roeber, *Faithful Magistrates and Republican Lawyers: Creators of Virginia Legal Culture, 1680–1810* (Chapel Hill: University of North Carolina Press, 1981), 74–75; Rhys Isaac, *The Transformation of Virginia, 1740–1790* (Chapel Hill: University of North Carolina Press, 1982), 88–94; Rutman and Rutman, *A Place in Time*, 86–93, 125–27, 246–47.

33. PA Order Book 1, 1691–1709, 445; Jonathan P. Cushing, comp., "Record of Grace Sherwood's Trial for Witchcraft," in *Collections of the Virginia Historical and Philosophical Society* 1 (1833): 77–78. This description of Sherwood's body led one author to infer incorrectly that she was a "mulatto of the despised 'free nigger' order, if not a negress." Court records generally identified African Americans and mulattoes as such, and after 1692 slave defendants were tried (without juries) in a special Court of Oyer and Terminer, not in the General Court. See [W. C. Elam], "Old Times in Virginia and a Few Parallels," *Putnam's Monthly Magazine of American Literature* 20 (August 1869): 208; Philip J. Schwarz, *Twice Condemned: Slaves and the Criminal Laws of Virginia, 1705–1865* (Baton Rouge: Louisiana State University Press, 1988), 16–18.

34. Thomas, *Religion and the Decline of Magic*, 452; Butler, "Magic, Astrology," 335; Archibald Taylor to Jonathan P. Cushing, October 1, 1832, in Cushing, "Record of Grace Sherwood's Trial," 71.

35. PA Minute Book 2, 1709–17, 207, 269–71, 477; PA Minute Book 3, 1717–28, 318; PA Deeds and Wills no. 5, 1735–40, 501; Processioners' Report on Lands, October 19–November 4, 1731.

36. Alexander Spotswood's patent to Grace Sherwood, June 16, 1714, Land Office Patents no. 10, 1710–19, 179; Processioners' Report on Lands, October 19–November 4, 1731, PA Minute Book 2, 1709–17, 269–71.

37. Will of Grace Sherwood, August 20, 1733, in PA Deeds and Wills no. 5, 1735–40, 501; PA Minute Book 5, 1737–44, 120.

38. *Virginia Gazette*, January 20, 1738; *The Virginia Almanack for the Year of Our Lord God 1770* (Williamsburg, Va.: Purdie and Dixon, 1769). See also Mechal Sobel, *The World They Made Together: Black and White Values in Eighteenth-Century Virginia* (Princeton, N.J.: Princeton University Press, 1987), 82.

39. Cushing, "Record of Grace Sherwood's Trial"; *Salem Gazette*, August 13, 1833; *Barre Gazette*, April 26, 1844; David James Kiracofe, "The Jamestown Jubilees: 'State Patriotism' and Virginia Identity in the Early Nineteenth Century," *Virginia Magazine of History and Biography* 110 (2002): 35–68. On Cushing, see "Biographical Sketch," *Southern Literary Messenger* 2 (February 1836): 163; George M. Dame, "Sketch of the Life and Character of Jonathan M. [sic] Cushing," *American Quarterly Register* 11 (November 1838): 119, 129.

40. [Elam], "Old Times in Virginia," 207–8; "Witchcraft in Virginia," *Jamestown Bulletin* (July 16, 1904): 1, 5.

41. Marion Gibson, "Retelling Salem Stories: Gender Politics and Witches in American Culture," *European Journal of American Culture* 25 (2006): 88–89; Silvia Bovenschen et al., "The Contemporary Witch, the Historical Witch and the Witch Myth: The Witch, Subject of the Appropriation of Nature and Object of the Domination of Nature," *New German Critique* 15 (Fall 1978): 110–13, 116; Demos, *Enemy Within*, 246–49; Turner, *Gateway to the New World*, 79–82; Painter, "An Early 18th Century Witch Bottle," 65.

Cockacoeske and Sarah Harris Stegge Grendon

Bacon's Rebellion and the Roles of Women

KRISTALYN M. SHEFVELAND

In 1676 a massive force of colonists led by Nathaniel Bacon unleashed its wrath against Virginia's indigenous people and the colony's royal governor, Sir William Berkeley. While early histories of this episode focused on the political ramifications of Bacon's Rebellion, social historians have seen it as a central factor in the emergence of a plantation economy in which the predominant labor system was race-based chattel slavery. Other scholarship, however, emphasizes the significance of gender in Bacon's Rebellion, noting the high level of women's involvement on both sides. This chapter focuses on two of those women: Cockacoeske, who was the leader of the Pamunkeys between 1656 and 1686, and Sarah Harris Stegge Grendon, the wife of the trader Thomas Stegge and aunt of William Byrd I. Both of these women were prominent participants in the rebellion.[1]

Although it is unclear whether Sarah and Cockacoeske ever met, their life stories became intertwined with the introduction of the skins trade and the Indian slave trade, and they played major roles on the opposing sides of Bacon's Rebellion. For each woman, moreover, the rebellion constituted a turning point. Sarah's influence reached its height in the chaos of the rebellion, and her power declined quickly in its aftermath. Cockacoeske, who experienced much hardship during the rebellion itself, ultimately suffered little as a result of it, and she maintained her high position as the leader of the Pamunkey community. In short, while the status and influence of the English regime increased after the rebellion, the status of English women decreased; Native peoples' situation overall declined, but the case of Cockacoeske suggests that their matrilineal

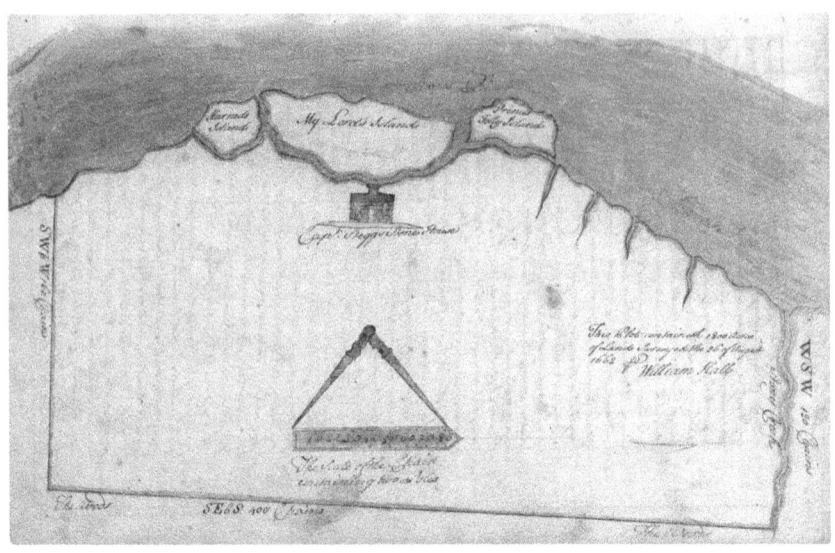

FALLS PLANTATION

Contained in William Byrd's "Title Book" of patents, deeds, and leases related to his landholdings in Charles City County, this map shows the stone house of his aunt Sarah Harris Stegge, located at the falls of the James River. The Battle of Bloody Run took place downriver from the plantation. Virginia Historical Society.

COCKACOESKE, QUEEN OF PAMUNKEY

In this composite illustration by Rose Powhatan (Pamunkey/Tauxenent/Dogue), the artist utilized a descendant of the Pamunkeys, Georgia Mills Jessup, to bring to life the detailed description of Cockacoeske in the English record. Rose Powhatan, Powhatan Museum of Indigenous Art and Culture, 2008.

customs remained intact, and the women leaders adapted to the changed circumstances of the post-rebellion era.

Women's voices are frequently omitted from the historical record, yet the stories of Sarah and Cockacoeske can be gleaned from the surviving official and personal records pertaining to Bacon's Rebellion. Those sources, written by men, portray both women as rather outspoken and strong, though the records also suggest that men responded to their assertiveness in different ways. As one prominent historian has argued, "language tells us what people thought, not what they did; that language is contested and contextual; and that language reflects the viewpoint of speakers."[2] Because English men increasingly expected their own women to be weak or passive, they described Sarah and other English women who were involved in the rebellion as sources of disorder, chaos, and upheaval of the natural order. By contrast, English men expected Native American females to be powerful, hardworking, and in many other respects unlike European women. Over the course of the rebellion, Sarah Harris Stegge Grendon gradually conformed to white men's expectations—at least according to men's rendering of her in the historical record—while Cockacoeske's voice as a political sovereign, speaking out against the problems affecting her people and demanding recognition, seemed to become more powerful.

A colonial housewife, particularly one living on the periphery of the English settlements, had a difficult and demanding life. While Sarah likely played helpmeet to both her husband Thomas Stegge and her next husband, the planter Thomas Grendon, in Charles City County, she was also the mistress of a trade post and a tobacco plantation. To survive and succeed in these circumstances required a degree of fluidity in gender roles since women often needed to do work that did not conform to the increasingly domestic ideal of the English social order. A plantation wife would have been responsible for cooking, cleaning, childcare, and other domestic work, but she would also have tended to the gardens, prepared meats, milked cows, and cared for other livestock. In addition, a trader's wife would have dealt with many visitors and traders moving through her household, and she would sometimes be involved in trade negotiations. Records show that Sarah was knowledgeable and savvy about her husband's business—so much so that Thomas felt comfortable leaving her in charge of his trade after he died in 1670.

English women like Sarah, living in the new settlements along the falls of the James River in close proximity to both trading paths and sometimes violent Native peoples and colonial traders, had to be resilient, industrious, and willing to manipulate life's circumstances to meet their own needs and advance their interests. In 1676, Sarah clearly had good reasons to support Bacon's Rebellion, as did some other women colonists. After the rebellion waned, the commissioners sent by King Charles II to investigate the upheaval wrote that Bacon had utilized these women to "preach Rebellion." It is clear in most narratives of the events of 1676 why women played such a role: the wife of Anthony Haviland, for example, supported her husband, who went off with Bacon to fight the Occoneechee and other Indians. Sarah's motivations are less clear, but she was deeply committed to the rebellion, and it seems likely she acted on her own initiative in part to protect the trading interests in which she had become invested during her marriage to Thomas Stegge.[3]

Little is known of the life of Sarah apart from her marriages. Her first husband, George Harris, a merchant in Charles City County, died in 1663, and she married Thomas Stegge, a merchant, county official, and trader in the same county, in 1664. Stegge's family had a history of opposing Governor Berkeley: his father had supported Parliament against the royalist governor during the English Civil War in the 1640s and 1650s. After Stegge died in 1670, Sarah married Colonel Thomas Grendon, who was also a local officeholder in Charles City County. When the rebellion started in 1676, however, Sarah's husband was in England. So, unlike most other female participants, she did not act simply to support her husband during the rebellion, but instead chose to support Bacon to further the interests of the Indian trade, in which she had become active during her marriage to Stegge. That trade included Indian enslavement, a practice deeply tied to the roots of the rebellion itself. Like others who were involved in the Indian trade in slaves and other commodities, Sarah and her nephew William Byrd resented Governor Berkeley's trade regulations, which aimed to protect the Native people and thereby limited white traders' ability to make profits.[4]

In the mid-seventeenth century, a number of social pressures and expectations caused a host of anxieties for women like Sarah. In early colonial Virginia, women of rank, particularly widows, exercised some degree of authority outside the household, especially early in the century when mortality rates were high, leaving relatively few adult men to manage families' public interests and finances. By the time of the rebellion, however, men sought increasingly to tighten gender roles, although some women opposed this trend. For example, Lady Frances Berkeley, the politically aware and outspoken wife of the governor, boldly defended her husband's policies. Conversely, the rebellion's male adherents disparaged Bacon's female supporters, and popular literature of the era painted widows, such as Sarah, as especially unsavory and manipulative. For instance, as one scholar observes, in her 1690 play, *The Widdow Ranter; or, The History of Bacon in Virginia*, Aphra Behn "represented Virginia widows and fictive widows in various ways that emphasized their autonomy, sexuality, and violence," thereby suggesting that widowhood "sanctions a questionable agency that allows [women] not only to objectify and command men but also to pursue them for sexual pleasure."[5]

Gender categories well established in English literature and society—namely, that a woman's role was defined by her husband, whose authority over his dependents was supreme—were rarely attainable in seventeenth-century Virginia, though male legislators increasingly passed laws meant to curtail women's autonomy. Indeed, on three separate occasions—in 1662, 1677, and 1699—Virginia's colonial legislature, the House of Burgesses, responded directly to the threat of women's unruly speech by giving husbands stronger authority over their wives and specifically encouraging them to confine women's speech to the "domestic realm." Women like Sarah Harris Stegge Grendon were particularly disturbing because, as one historian has noted, "these women, who in theory ought to be under the control of their husbands, often acted with the most freedom." Virginia men feared their inability to control both their households and the larger society.[6]

While English men's concerns about widows and other assertive women reflected their fear of women in positions of power, the expectations of the Powhatan and Pamunkey peoples were different, which accounts in part for the dissimilarity in the descriptions of Sarah and Cockacoeske in English historical documents. Gender roles in the eastern woodlands of North America allowed Native men and women to play complementary but distinctly different roles, but women's roles within the community were highly valued, and women from important Native families involved themselves in matters of diplomacy and trade. Native peoples of the eastern woodlands used a matrilineal line of descent, passing property and positions of authority down through the family's female line. They believed that women, in their roles as mothers and wives, had a right to be involved in social, economic, and political activities related to the community.[7]

The traditional structure of Powhatan society was a paramount chiefdom, a political organization with three tiers of authority: paramount *weroance* (or chief), district weroance, and town weroance. Weroances (or, in the case of female chiefs, *weronsquas*) were typically related to one another because Native leaders found that giving one's sibling control of a subsidiary territory provided good training and promoted orderly relations between the territories. Most weroances and weronsquas got their positions through matrilineal inheritance. Cockacoeske's lineage and ties to power went from Wahunsonacock (known to the English as the chief Powhatan) to Opitchapam, who was soon replaced by Opechancanough, the paramount chief who oversaw the last of two Anglo-Powhatan wars. Cockacoeske was related to Opechancanough. Upon Opechancanough's death at the hands of his English guards, a Pamunkey warrior named Necotowance took over, but the old paramount chiefdom disintegrated with the utter defeat of the Powhatans in 1646, when Native leaders signed a treaty in which they acknowledged their defeat and agreed to pay tribute to the English victors. For that reason, the Powhatan people, including the Pamunkeys, were known as Native tributaries.[8]

The historical record reveals little about the Pamunkeys and other Virginia Natives during this early period, except for their involvement in trade and diplomacy. Much of what we know about Powhatan and Pamunkey women is confined to generalizations based on scarce ethnographic evidence. In daily life, work was largely gendered, but equally important was the fact that women's work and men's work were reciprocal and intertwined. Women gathered wood for the domestic and communal hearths. They made pottery, mats, baskets, and tools related to the preparation and storage of food. In addition, women were responsible for the cultivation of crops, primarily the three sisters: corn, beans, and squash. Women built and owned the houses in which they and their kin lived. The work of women and men overlapped in some areas, including the clearing of land and, notably, in the ruling positions of their chiefdoms, where women were clearly present.[9]

In seventeenth-century Virginia, Native women of rank had much more power than English women had. There is strong evidence in the archaeological and ethnographic data that Native women not only held the sorts of power that English observers expected to be held by men, but that formal power in the chiefdoms was not solely vested in males. Additionally, the record indicates that Native women contributed significantly to the incomes of their families well into the late seventeenth century. Although scholars believe that female authority in Powhatan societies declined as a result of contact with the English, Native women were still more influential in their communities than were their English counterparts. They also had far more sexual freedom, and their involvement in trade and diplomacy throughout the eastern woodlands has been well documented.[10]

Native women played vital roles in this early period through their relationships with colonists, relationships that the women could at times manipulate to further their interests. The relationships resulting from Anglo-Indian encounters were bred in war, trade, and sexual intimacies, and caused a reordering of the known world for both parties. Cockacoeske's and Sarah Harris Stegge's lives would begin to intertwine following the end of the last Anglo-Powhatan war in 1646, when the resulting treaty set the stage for a number of disagreements between the defeated former Powhatan chiefdom and the English settlers, and opened the door to the Native slave trade, which became a precondition for Bacon's Rebellion.

As part of their tributary agreement in the 1646 treaty, the former Powhatan towns, including the Pamunkeys', had to provide military assistance to the colonists when they needed it. English expectations of Pamunkey military assistance came with the arrival of the Westo people at the falls of the James River. In 1656, the Battle of Bloody Run took place near what is now Richmond, close to the growing settlements of Indian traders and hopeful planters in Henrico and Charles City counties. Colonel Thomas Stegge, Sarah's second husband, had developed the Falls Plantation with his entry into the Indian trade after the 1646 peace. His property included three small islands and a stone house with a chimney in the middle, marked as "Col. Stegge's Stone house" in William Byrd's "Title Book."[11]

After the Battle of Bloody Run, the Stegges entered the Indian slave trade and Cockacoeske rose to power in the Pamunkey community. By 1649, Totopotomoy, Cockacoeske's husband, had replaced Necotowance as leader of the Pamunkeys. When the House of Burgesses heard of the arrival of the Westos, it ordered Colonel Edward Hill to muster his militia along with friendly Pamunkey and Chickahominy people to remove the foreign Indians from the region—if possible without war. Hill ignored the assembly's orders and with his Native allies attacked the Westos almost immediately. Although five of the Westo leaders died at the hands of the Pamunkeys, the Westos remained in their new Virginia homelands. Totopotomoy died during the battle, and Cockacoeske, a descendant of Opechancanough and a relative of Powhatan, then assumed his leadership position. The colonists came to call her "Queen of the Pamunkey."[12]

The Falls Plantation's location as a trading venue near the site of the Battle of Bloody Run played a major role in the lives of both Sarah and Cockacoeske. Because of its proximity to the battlefield, the Falls Plantation gave Stegge an advantage in capitalizing on the peace made with the Westos. In 1656, the council of Virginia lifted certain trade restrictions to allow individual colonists to trade directly with the Natives. After defeating the Pamunkeys and Hill's militia, the Westos secured agreements with Virginia traders to procure Native slaves from the interior in exchange for guns. Once in Virginia, the Westos acted as one of the dominant Indian trading groups on the frontier, and they took advantage of the colonists' inexperience and ignorance about the interior geography of Virginia and about Native peoples. In this era before the large-scale importation of enslaved Africans to the colony, Indian slavery emerged as a quick, easy, and highly profitable enterprise for traders such as Thomas and Sarah Harris Stegge.[13]

The Stegges' involvement in the slave trade, in turn, was part of the backdrop for Bacon's Rebellion, as the English and their Indian allies used slave raids to create fear and to achieve military superiority over their Native enemies, who in 1676 bore the brunt of the rebels' violence. The Indian slave trade created the circumstances that allowed Cockacoeske's and Sarah's lives to intersect. While the slave traders largely targeted Indian groups on the periphery of English settlement, tributary Natives—such as the Pamunkeys—became targets as well, which worried Cockacoeske and the other leaders of the former Powhatan chiefdom. The English obtained slaves from Indian raiders such as the Westos, but they also gained them through extralegal means, including coercing tributaries into handing over their children, ostensibly for education and apprenticeships. This ruse did not fool the tributaries for long, however. By the late seventeenth century they refused to provide children to the English, remarking on "the breach of a former contract made long ago," where their children were sent to "other Countrys" as slaves.[14]

Thomas Stegge died in 1670, passing his trade enterprise to his nephew William Byrd and to his widow, Sarah. In Thomas's will, dated March 31, 1670, and proved on May 15, 1671, he provided well for Sarah. He left her "ornaments for her person" and a young Indian slave girl as a "loving remembrance." He provided instructions for his wife's accommodations in case she desired to travel to England. Additionally, he instructed Thomas Grendon of London to pay his wife the remainder of her inheritance after all his accounts were settled. As was the custom among the English, Stegge left all of his landed property to Byrd, his closest male relative. In his will, however, Stegge revealed something about Sarah's role in his life and just how important she was to his enterprises when he instructed her to "continue the managing of the estate" for the eighteen-year-old Byrd until he acquired more experience "governed by the prudent and provident advice of his aunt." By 1673, Byrd's Falls Plantation, with the help of his aunt Sarah, was an "active trading post," where Native people were likely held captive and sold. Byrd sent parties of traders of up to fifteen men and one hundred packhorses into the interior, and such caravans became common sights at the Falls Plantation. Byrd quickly expanded his uncle's trade into Carolina and, playing both merchant and planter, he developed the trade in skins and slaves.[15]

To prevent disorder and war in the colony, Virginia's House of Burgesses had sought to regulate this trade and to protect the colony's tributary allies. Between 1646 and 1660, colonists engaged in the Indian trade therefore were required to have a commission from the governor. Despite strict regulation, however, illicit trade with foreign Indians, the enslavement of Indians, and unpaid debts to Virginia's Native allies quickly began to grow, and Native people began to lash out at interior English settlements in Charles City and Henrico counties. Governor William Berkeley sought to prevent hostilities along the fall line of the James River by arming garrisons in the frontier counties. Not surprisingly, the individual men and the families who were involved in the Indian slave trade—and the most likely causes of the problems with the Native people—were members of the new local militia companies. These people included Sarah, now married to Thomas Grendon, and William Byrd. In 1674, Byrd became the captain of the Henrico County militia and headed a garrison of fifty-five men near the falls of the James River.[16]

That same year, Nathaniel Bacon, Governor Berkeley's cousin by marriage, immigrated to the colony, and he quickly associated himself with Byrd and the interior trade. The House of Burgesses sought to prevent war by banning the sale of arms or ammunition to Indians, making it a capital crime. The burgesses also sought to stop previously licensed traders from doing business as they began to reorganize the Indian trade. Nathaniel Bacon and William Byrd were among those banned by the new regulations. Bacon angrily accused the governor of monopolizing the trade and ignoring the interests of white traders in the interior counties. He soon attracted a following among colonists who shared his resentment toward the governor and his policies.[17]

The outbreak of hostilities that led to what became called Bacon's Rebellion directly resulted from the Indian trade and therefore involved Sarah Harris Stegge Grendon and William Byrd. It is likely that the Susquehannock attacks that set off the rebellion targeted both Byrd and Bacon because of their activities as Indian slave traders. In response to the retributive raids on both sides, in March 1676 at a special meeting of the assembly, Governor Berkeley decided to rebuild and fortify the garrisons around the perimeter to protect the colonists. The militia of Charles City and Henrico counties began to organize companies into "trainbands," small groups that could root out Indian raiding parties with greater ease and efficiency. Corruption and inefficient management led the residents of the area to remark that the arms "lye in sand and rust," while Anglo-Indian relations deteriorated into abuse and outright war.[18]

Colonists living in those regions, including Sarah, thought the plan for defensive forts was too expensive and inadequate, and instead they supported Bacon's plan to attack the Indians, which Berkeley, who had labeled Bacon a rebel, refused to allow. Bacon favored an Indian genocide to eradicate the problems of the interior. Berkeley complained of Sarah's support of Bacon and his plans, stating that she was an agitator alongside other women whose inflammatory claims that Berkeley was "a greater friend to the Indians than to the English" had "presently spread through the whole country and in every part the Rabble so threatened the better sort of people that they durst not sterr out of their houses." While conflicts arising from the Indian trade precipitated the rebellion, it was women who spread the word, and they played important roles in the ensuing upheaval. Women were present on both sides, with Lady Frances Berkeley among the most outspoken of Bacon's opponents. Indeed, the rebels blamed her for the governor's hated policies. "Under the influence of Lady Berkeley's misrule," one averred, the governor "became covetous, relishing Indians presents . . . so wel, that many Christians Blood is pukkuted up, with other mischievs."[19]

Sarah Harris Stegge Grendon became especially notorious for her public actions supporting Bacon and his followers. Governor Berkeley later remembered her as "a great encourager and assister in the late horrid Rebellion." In particular, Berkeley argued, Sarah "helped the rebels by her lyeing and scandalous reports." Indeed, she and other rebel women were active in spreading the news of Bacon's efforts and at times acted as propagandists on the rebels' behalf. For example, the rebel woman known only as Mrs. Haviland, whom Berkeley referred to as an "Excelent divulger of news," traveled throughout the countryside to spread the word of Bacon's cause. Sarah played a similar role, and she also, according to Berkeley, offered material aid, including guns, to some of Bacon's men and was one of the "first great incourager[s] and Setter[s] on of the Ignorant Vulgar."[20]

Desperate to pacify the rebellious settlers and to stop Bacon's raids, Governor Berkeley tried to regain control of the situation when the burgesses convened that spring. He invited Cockacoeske, the weronsqua of the tributary Pamunkeys, to meet with Virginia authorities, who asked for her military assistance as part of the tributary agreement. Cockacoeske initially refused to help the governor. Instead, the tributaries sought to navigate the English colonial system through interpreters and by acting as traders and guides for English colonists while attempting to maintain control over their own towns and to protect their own interests.[21]

A subsequent exchange between Cockacoeske and English authorities provides an interesting perspective on how colonial leaders viewed her. One contemporary English observer, John Clayton, noted that in general Virginia Natives were seldom seen to be "affected w[i]th pleasure, or transported with passion [anger], and even among themselves they discourse . . . little[,] sit[t]ing several hours & perhaps not one word." Cockacoeske's appearance at the meeting of the Virginia council directly contradicts Clayton's portrayal of the Pamunkeys as somber, quiet people. By the time she met with Berkeley and his councilors in 1676, Cockacoeske had been leading the Pamunkeys for twenty years. When she appeared before the English leaders, she was a "commanding personage," entering the chamber "with a comportment gracefull to admiration, bringing on her right hand an Englishm[a]n interpreter, and on her left, her son, a stripling twenty years of age," believed to be the son of the English captain John West. Cockacoeske wore a black-and-white wampum headdress and a deerskin mantle with "deep, twisted fringe." The English man who recorded what transpired at the meeting described her as "majestic."[22]

One historian has concluded that Native women were involved in "virtually every major encounter between Europeans and Indians in the New World" as counselors, translators, wives, or mistresses. In short, they acted as guides and cultural mediators. Native women who established intimate personal relationships with European men were especially influential, because of both the power they wielded in their communities and their even more powerful impact on their husbands or consorts and their children. Cockacoeske's sexual liaison with Captain John West caused quite a stir in the English community: his English wife, Unity, left him because of it. The English viewed Cockacoeske as important, in part because she was weronsqua but also because of her relationship with West and the child they had together, who the English thought might inherit her position as Pamunkey leader.[23]

In 1676, Cockacoeske maintained her role as a political sovereign and chose to address the governor's council on her terms. The council alleged that she spoke English well, but she nonetheless insisted on communicating through an interpreter. When the councilors pressed Cockacoeske to provide men to serve as guides for expeditions against the Susquehannocks, she did not respond. After further demands from the English, she broke her silence; according to the English, she appeared close to tears and quite agitated. Cockacoeske then launched into a fifteen-minute tirade, "often interlacing with a high shrill voice and vehement passion," stating repeatedly, "Tatapatomoi chepiack," or "Totopotomoy is dead." This statement was an accusation, an indication that she held the council responsible for the death of her husband and one hundred of her bowmen at the Battle of Bloody Run in 1656. Her people had not yet been compensated for these losses, and the colonists' involvement in the Indian slave trade, which thrived after the Westos' victory, had led to the enslavement of tributary peoples and the loss of their land to encroaching English settlers. For its part, the council was not moved by her remarks: "Her discourse ending and our morose chairman not advancing one cold word toward asswaging the anger and grief her speech and demeanor manifested under her oppression, nor taking any notice of all she had said." Cockacoeske eventually agreed to provide 12 bowmen to the English, though the council believed she had at least 150 under her command.[24]

On June 22, 1676, Bacon arrived at the statehouse in Jamestown and, backed by at least five hundred men, he demanded a commission to attack the Indians. The governor capitulated and issued Bacon the commission. Berkeley soon recanted, however, claiming the commission was void because Bacon had obtained it by force. But recent elections had brought a pro-Bacon majority to the House of Burgesses, which acted decisively against the governor's comparatively humane Indian policies. Reflecting the land-hungry white colonists' growing resentment of Native peoples—a sentiment that, for many, was the core of Bacon's appeal—the burgesses decided that any Indians, tributary or not, who left their towns without English permission were enemies. As such, all of their lands were subject to confiscation. At this juncture, the assembly abandoned plans for the frontier forts and instead voted to raise more troops—a total of a thousand men drawn from several counties. These troops were authorized to confiscate Indian guns, furs, and corn. In addition, the assembly provided that "Indians taken in warr be held and accounted slaves dureing life." The chaotic violence that erupted throughout the colony lasted through the fall of 1676, during which time, among other things, Bacon offered freedom to white servants and black slaves who joined his uprising. Rebels plundered their enemies' estates and attacked Indians throughout the colony, killing and enslaving many.[25]

Of particular interest is Bacon's attack on the Pamunkeys and Cockacoeske. For her part, Cockacoeske had instructed her people that "if they found the English coming upon them that they should neither ffire a gun nor draw an arrow upon them." Bacon located the Pamunkey people in the Great Dragon Swamp between the Mattaponi and Piankatank riversheds in New Kent County. He and his men seized furs, trading cloth, and wampum that belonged to the Pamunkey people. They also captured forty-five Indians and killed at least eight. According to contemporary accounts, the captured Indians "were some of them sold by Bacon & the rest disposed of by Sr. Wm. Berkeley, all but five w'ch were restored to the Queen by Ingram who was Bacon's Gen'll." Cockacoeske later reported that she herself was chased by the rebels off into the "wild woodes where shee was lost and missing from her owne people fourteen days." She, along with a ten-year-old boy, stayed alive by "gnawing sometimes upon the legg of a terrapin" that the boy found. While in the woods she saw a Pamunkey woman lying dead in the road, which "struck such terror in the Queen that fearing by that gastly example" she plunged farther and farther into the woods.[26]

The rebels clearly had targeted Cockacoeske who, as the leader of her people, they regarded as a great prize. Bacon and his men captured an older Pamunkey woman, likely related to Cockacoeske, in the hopes that she would lead them to the weronsqua. Instead of doing so, the colonists alleged, she "led them quite contrary." Realizing that the woman would not cooperate, Bacon ordered his soldiers to kill her by a blow to the skull. The rebels continued to wander through the swamps until they found the main trading path and the Nanzaticos, another Native community. There they took hostage a young woman, "half starved, and so not able to escape." Many of the Nanzaticos attempted to flee, but they were soon discovered, and the English "killed two or three Indian men and as many women." The rebellion ended that fall with the October death of Bacon from typhus and bloody flux, but the repercussions of the Indian slave war, the activities of Sarah Grendon and William Byrd, and the rebel attacks on Cockacoeske were far from over.[27]

The loyalist retaliation proved quick and violent, with Berkeley confiscating estates and ordering prosecutions that resulted in the execution of twenty-three English men for their involvement in the rebellion. The new pro-Berkeley assembly that met in February 1677 also targeted rebel women like Sarah Grendon and Mrs. Haviland, whom they called "the fore runners of tumult and rebellion." Under the common-law doctrine of coverture, a wife had no legal identity apart from that of her husband, so when a married woman committed a crime, she usually was not held accountable for it because—at least in theory—the law assumed that her husband controlled her actions. Although the crime of treason was a significant exception to this rule, the House of Burgesses was reluctant to charge rebel women with that capital crime. Perhaps believing that the courts would be unlikely to convict supposedly apolitical women of such an obviously political crime, Virginia's leaders instead accused most rebel women of seditious libel. In keeping with the gender conventions of the era, they charged women with uttering unruly words, rather than with the more serious crime of purposefully disloyal political action.[28]

Penalties for wives convicted of seditious libel were uniquely harsh. A man convicted of seditious libel paid a heavy price: one thousand pounds of tobacco for the first offense, double that amount for the second, plus standing in the pillory for two hours. Married women, however, unless they could pay the fine, were subject to twenty lashes for a first offense and thirty lashes for the second. One scholar has argued that the law thus "invited husbands to maintain social order by not paying their wives' fines and therefore subjecting them to flogging." The assembly also might have sought to "intimidate married women with the possibility of humiliating punishment for future misbehavior."[29]

Sarah's actions and the governor's particular antipathy toward her, however, had uniquely dire consequences. She was the only woman involved in the rebellion whom Berkeley charged with treason and whom the assembly refused a general pardon and "indemnity" for her actions, instead issuing a warrant for the seizure of the Grendon estate. Defendants convicted of treason lost both their property and their lives. Likely realizing the gravity of her situation, Sarah retreated from her earlier rebellious statements and allowed her recently returned husband, Thomas Grendon, to speak for her. Thomas lobbied the royal commissioners—sent by the king to reestablish order in the colony—in hopes of saving both his wife and his estate. The commissioners eventually agreed that Sarah, like the other women involved in the rebellion, was simply foolish and misguided, and therefore incapable of committing treason. The commissioners criticized Berkeley, arguing that "Some mens Estate [were] being taken away for the indiscreet tattle of their Wives here, and while they were absent about their lawfull affaires in England." Sarah assumed the role of the foolish and apolitical wife in order to save her husband's property and her own life. When questioned by the commissioners, she readily admitted providing gunpowder to Bacon's men, but she now claimed that she thought the powder would be used only against enemy Indians. To receive a pardon, Sarah declared that her words and deeds were those of "an ignorant woman."[30]

The commissioners ruled against the governor and in favor of the notion of women as foolish and apolitical. The warrant against Sarah, they argued, was not properly executed, and the estate seized was that of her husband and not her own. Most important, the commissioners concluded that "the speaking of some foolish words by a simple woman (thought tending to disturbance in those ill times) was no pretence sufficient to seize the estate of a husband so far absent, especially without due proof and conviction." On May 10, 1677, the commissioners dismissed the charge of treason against Sarah Harris Stegge Grendon. That very same day, in a separate hearing, colonial authorities deemed that there was insufficient cause to try Sarah for her life because she had done nothing more than many other colonists had during the rebellion.[31]

While sorting out the divisions among English colonists in the aftermath of the rebellion, the royal commissioners also sought to rectify the situation with the Native tributaries, and these negotiations and the resulting Treaty of Middle Plantation reveal the extent to which Cockacoeske attempted to turn the tragic events of the rebellion to her favor. It is here that one can surmise that Native women in positions of power understood the rules of cultural mediation and took advantage of them when opportunities arose. The arena in which Cockacoeske was most successful was her dealings with the royal commissioners. The king's representatives considered Cockacoeske to be a victim of the rebellion, called her the "faithfull friend to and lover of the English," and recommended that she be compensated for her suffering and losses with gifts from the English government. Cockacoeske's considerable influence in the negotiation of the Treaty of Middle Plantation has been well documented. She clearly attempted to recreate the former Powhatan chiefdom, with herself as its paramount weronsqua. On June 11, 1677, commissioner Herbert Jeffreys reported on the treaty and the signing process, including the fact that the "queen" of the Pamunkeys signed "on behalf of herself and Severall Nations now reunited under her Subjection and Government as anciently." One historian has argued persuasively that "this latter sentence is especially significant, for it refers to article 12 of the treaty, which committed several smaller, unspecified Indian nations to Cockacoeske's rule, tangible evidence of her success in manipulating the treaty agreement to her own people's advantage."[32]

By October 1677, the London-based Lords of Trade and Plantation recommended an expansion of the Virginia treaty to include Maryland, and King Charles II commissioned gifts for the Indian leaders who signed the original treaty: the weronsqua of the Weyanock, the weroance of the Nottoways, the weroance of the Nansemonds, and Cockacoeske. As a sign of the English Crown's goodwill toward its Native tributaries, London authorities commissioned crowns and royal robes for the Indian leaders. Fashioned for each of the four were crimson velvet hats trimmed with ermine fur and "small crowns or coronets of thinne silver plate, gilt and adorned with false stones of various colours" with a Latin inscription that signified the recipients' connection to the English king: "A Carolo Secondo Magna Brittaniae Rege." Cockacoeske and her son, John West, received additional recognition as well. Cockacoeske, the king's commissioners reported, "was robbed of her rich matchcoat by the rebels," and therefore they asked for a "crown and robe, together with a stript [striped] Indian gown of gay colours and a Bracelet of falce stones" in addition to a silver pendant to be made for her. John West was to receive "a scarlett coate belayered with gold and silver lace, with breeches, shoes and stockings, hatt, sword and belt suitable, and a pair of good pistols."[33]

When the gifts arrived with the new governor, Thomas Culpeper, in June 1680, the Virginia council objected to their distribution because by then the treaty's signatories had grown to include some twelve Native leaders, who represented seven Indian groups. The council asked that the presentation of Cockacoeske's gifts be delayed, "fearing those people may be heightened thereby especially by such Marks of Dignity as Coronets, wch as they conceive ought not to be prostituted to such mean persons." The councilors further explained their reasoning on behalf of the colonists, who suffered "fatal returnes for considerable presents given unto" Native peoples, and the council argued that presents of this nature were "a wrong way of manageing of those people[,] they esteeming presents to be the effects of fear, and not kindness." Importantly, the council also took issue with the preferential treatment of Cockacoeske, alleging that there were several other neighboring and foreign Indian groups that "deserved of the English at least as well as the called Queen of Pomunkey" and that those groups "will shew their Resentment at least against them which is almost as bad."[34]

It was not only the councilors who took exception to the adornment of Cockacoeske and the power granted to her and the Pamunkeys in articles 12 and 18 of the treaty. Article 12 gave Cockacoeske dominion over "several scattered Indian nations," and article 18 placed several of the tributaries under Pamunkey rule. Cockacoeske seemingly had attempted to return the Pamunkey leadership to the "chiefly dominance" of the era before Opechancanough's death. The Chickahominy and Rappahannock people greatly resented this intrusion, and the colonial secretary, Thomas Ludwell, indicated in his letters regarding the second version of the treaty that the several nations under Cockacoeske were "dissatisfied" and "contemptible at their new subjection" to her. Indeed, in a list of grievances compiled by Cockacoeske and her son on June 5, 1678, they alleged that the Chickahominys were refusing to pay tribute and obey her commands. In the list of nine grievances, they accused the Chickahominy people of poisoning one of Cockacoeske's great men while the Chickahominys complained that the Pamunkey leader "cutt off soe many Chickahominy heads." In another letter later that month, Cockacoeske noted that the Rappahannocks and the Chickahominys were both "very disobedient to my commands." These groups retained their independence while they upheld their commitment to the terms of the Anglo-Indian treaty. Despite her efforts, Cockacoeske did not successfully re-create the Powhatan chiefdom's paramountcy.[35]

Both Sarah and Cockacoeske began to fade from the public record in the aftermath of Bacon's Rebellion. Thomas Grendon remained an important person in William Byrd's life, and therefore so did Sarah in the immediate years after the rebellion. In the county court of Henrico, on April 1, 1678, Byrd gave to Thomas Grendon and Abel Gower, his "trusty and well-beloved friends," full power of attorney. In 1684, Thomas Grendon died, and Sarah remarried quickly. William Byrd wrote derisively of this marriage in his correspondence, including letters to his suppliers, Perry and Lane of London, a further indication that his aunt had some connection and dealings with his merchant endeavors. On March 29, 1685, he complained that "Mr. Brain (who hath marryed Mrs. Grendon) pretends great matters though I cannot conceive what encouragement they found this year." Byrd wrote of the marriage again to Warham Horsmanden, his father-in-law, explaining that "my Aunt was marryed again in about the latter end of Jan'ry to one Mr. Edward Brain a stranger to all here, but pretends to bee worth money, if not the Old Woman may thanke herself."[36]

Byrd clearly resented Sarah's decision to marry Edward Braine. He alleged that his aunt remarried because she could not stand to "lie alone," indeed that she was not able to "be alone," but it is just as likely that, as one historian has noted, "the real source of his anger . . . originated in a woman's control over him." Byrd likely objected to Sarah's ongoing role in Thomas Stegge's trade. At a time when women were less and less likely to wield economic power, her control over financial and household decisions seemingly subverted the natural order of things. Indeed, in 1685, shortly after Sarah married Braine, Byrd worried that—perhaps because of her new husband's dubious financial situation—Sarah Harris Stegge Grendon Braine had the power to "sweep away all the Virginia estate."[37]

As for Cockacoeske, George Smith, the Pamunkey interpreter, informed the governor on July 1, 1686, that she was "lately dead" and that her heir was her niece, not her son, thus confirming that a matrilineal inheritance line was still in place in the Pamunkey community. A reference from 1702 names the niece as "Ms. Betty Queen ye Queen," and in 1708 there was a Pamunkey leader named "Queen Ann."[38]

Women, both English and Native, were significant actors in Virginia politics and society in the era of Bacon's Rebellion. English women were propagandists and purveyors of secret intelligence for the public relations campaign needed by Bacon to whip the countryside into a frenzy of support for his genocidal Indian campaign. The reshaping of Native tributary relationships in the Treaty of Middle Plantation in 1677 was due in large part to the plans of Cockacoeske. She likely knew that the English believed she would pass her power to her son, John West, and she attempted to use the unfortunate circumstances to maintain her authority and to promote the interests of her people. The royal commissioners chose to ignore women's agency and instead classified all women who were involved in the rebellion as victims—including Cockacoeske, the "good Queen of the Pamunkey."[39]

Sarah Harris Stegge Grendon managed to secure her pardon by embracing coverture and the gender conventions of foolish, passive English womanhood; she allowed her husband to speak for her and thereby tacitly admitted that she was incapable of acting for herself. One analysis of Aphra Behn's play *The Widow Ranter* contends that Behn depicted the Native woman as "a victim of the sociopolitical conflicts within the Virginia colony and of the mercantilist economy of English colonial expansionism."[40] While this analysis refers to the largely farcical fictional representation of Native women in a play meant for entertainment, the statement has hints of truth. As Behn's Indian queen Semernia opines, "The more I gaze upon this English Stranger, the more Confusion struggles in my Soul. . . . And ever when he spoke, my panting heart, with a Prophetick fear in sighs reply'd, I shall fall such a Victim to his Eyes."[41] Although Cockacoeske differed from the fictional Semernia in significant ways, it is worthwhile to analyze the changes wrought by the effects of the Indian slave trade and consider why Native and English women would be appealing subjects for contemporary playwrights and their patrons.

Each woman, thrust into the rebellion by her position in the slave trade, experienced it as a turning point in her life. Sarah Harris Stegge Grendon and her family rose to power in the colony through the frontier exchange economy, but her personal autonomy and influence declined in the aftermath of the rebellion. Cockacoeske, in an attempt to reclaim the power of the Powhatan chiefdom over the Native tributaries, played the political game aptly but gained little for the Pamunkey community, whose power in the colony decreased with the exponential growth of the white population and the rising entrenchment of a plantation economy.

NOTES

1. An important social history account of the rebellion is Edmund S. Morgan, *American Slavery, American Freedom: The Ordeal of Colonial Virginia* (New York: Norton, 1974). On women specifically, see Susan Westbury, "Women in Bacon's Rebellion," in *Southern Women: Histories and Identities*, ed. Virginia Bernhard, Betty Brandon, Elizabeth Fox-Genovese, and Theda Perdue (Columbia: University of Missouri Press, 1992); Terri L. Snyder, *Brabbling Women: Disorderly Speech and the Law in Early Virginia* (Ithaca, N.Y.: Cornell University Press, 2003), esp. 32–36; Kathleen M. Brown, *Good Wives, Nasty Wenches, and Anxious Patriarchs: Gender, Race, and Power in Colonial Virginia* (Chapel Hill: University of North Carolina Press, 1996), esp. 162–67.

2. Nancy Shoemaker, "An Alliance between Men: Gender Metaphors in Eighteenth-Century American Indian Diplomacy East of the Mississippi," *Ethnohistory* 46 (1999): 240.

3. Julia Cherry Spruill, *Women's Life and Work in the Southern Colonies* (Chapel Hill: University of North Carolina Press, 1937), 83; Westbury, "Women in Bacon's Rebellion," 33; Lois Green Carr and Lorena S. Walsh, "The Planter's Wife: The Experience of White Women in Seventeenth-Century Maryland," *William and Mary Quarterly*, 3rd ser., 34 (1977): 550; Charles M. Andrews, ed., *Narratives of the Insurrections, 1675–1690* (New York: Charles Scribner's Sons, 1915), 111.

4. Westbury, "Women in Bacon's Rebellion," 39; Andrews, *Narratives of the Insurrections*, 111; Sarah Grendon to Herbert Jeffries, n.d., Coventry Papers, 78, Bath 65, ff. 5, 6, Longleat House, Warminster, Wiltshire, England.

5. Mary Beth Norton, *Separated by Their Sex: Women in Public and Private in the Colonial Atlantic World* (Ithaca, N.Y.: Cornell University Press, 2011), 2, 34; Brown, *Good Wives*, 163–64; Snyder, *Brabbling Women*, 123–24.

6. Kathleen M. Brown, "The Dilemma of Colonial Masculinity," in *Gender and the Southern Body Politic*, ed. Nancy Bercaw (Jackson: University of Mississippi Press, 2000), 37–43; Brown, *Good Wives*, 73; Snyder, *Brabbling Women*, 21, 127. See also Carr and Walsh, "Planter's Wife."

7. On Native women in the eastern woodlands generally, see Theda Perdue, *Cherokee Women: Gender and Culture Change, 1700–1835* (Lincoln: University of Nebraska Press, 1998); Theda Perdue, ed., *Sifters: Native American Women's Lives* (New York: Oxford University Press, 2001); Steven C. Hahn, *The Life and Times of Mary Musgrove* (Gainesville: University Press of Florida, 2012); Kathryn E. Holland Braund, *Deerskins and Duffels: The Creek Trade with Anglo-America, 1685–1815* (Lincoln: University of Nebraska Press, 1993).

8. Helen C. Rountree, *The Powhatan Indians of Virginia: Their Traditional Culture* (Norman: University of Oklahoma Press, 1989), 93, 117; Martha W. McCartney, "Cockacoeske, Queen of Pamunkey: Diplomat and Suzeraine," in *Powhatan's Mantle: Indians of the Colonial Southeast*, ed. Gregory A. Waselkov, Peter H. Wood, and Tom Hatley (Lincoln: University of Nebraska Press, 1989), 243–45.

9. Helen C. Rountree, "Powhatan Indian Women: The People Captain John Smith Barely Saw," *Ethnohistory* 45 (1998): 1–29.

10. Charles R. Cobb, "Mississippian Chiefdoms: How Complex?," *Annual Review of Anthropology* 32 (2003): 75; Helen C. Rountree, *Pocahontas's People: The Powhatan Indians of Virginia through Four Centuries* (Norman: University of Oklahoma Press, 1990), 150; Brown, *Good Wives*, 50; Heidi Hutner, *Colonial Women: Race and Culture in Stuart Drama* (New York: Oxford University Press, 2001), 12. See also Hahn, *Life and Times of Mary Musgrove*; Braund, *Deerskins and Duffels*; Perdue, *Cherokee Women*.

11. William Waller Hening, comp., *The Statutes at Large: Being a Collection of All the Laws of Virginia*, 13 vols. (Richmond, Va.: Samuel Pleasants Jr., 1810–23), 1:322–26; Alan Vance Briceland, *Westward from Virginia: The Exploration of the Virginia-Carolina Frontier, 1650–1710* (Charlottesville: University of Virginia Press, 1987), 24; W. Stitt Robinson, ed., *Virginia Treaties, 1607–1722* (Frederick, Md.: University Publications of America, 1983), 67–69; "Letters of the Byrd Family," *Virginia Magazine of History and Biography* 35 (1927): 221–45, 226.

12. Martha McCartney, "Cockacoeske," in *Dictionary of Virginia Biography* (Richmond: Library of Virginia, 1998–), 3:321–22; Hening, *Statutes at Large*, 1:415, 422; Jon Kukla, *Speakers and Clerks of the Virginia House of Burgesses 1643–1776* (Richmond: Library of Virginia, 1981), 39; Rountree, *Pocahontas's People*; McCartney, "Cockacoeske, Queen of Pamunkey," 172–95.

13. Edward Ragan, "A Brief Survey of Anglo-Indian Interactions in Virginia during the Seventeenth Century," in *A Study of Virginia Indians and Jamestown: The First Century*, ed. Danielle Moretti-Langholtz (Williamsburg, Va.: National Parks Service, 2005), 23; Robbie Ethridge, "Introduction," in *Mapping the Mississippian Shatter Zone: The Colonial Indian Slave Trade and Regional Instability in the American South*, ed. Robbie Ethridge and Sheri M. Shuck-Hall (Lincoln: University of Nebraska Press, 2009), 25; William G. Stanard, ed., "Thomas Stegg," *Virginia Magazine of History and Biography* 24 (1916): 357; Stanard, ed., "Auditor Stegge's Accounts," *Virginia Magazine of History and Biography* 51 (1943): 176. See also Kristalyn M. Shefveland, "'Wholly Subjected'?: Anglo-Indian Interaction in Colonial Virginia, 1646–1718," (PhD diss., University of Mississippi, 2010).

14. R. A. Brock, ed., *The Official Letters of Alexander Spotswood, Lieutenant-Governor of the Colony of Virginia 1710–1722*, 2 vols. (Richmond: Virginia Historical Society, 1882), 1:125.

15. "Letters of the Byrd Family," 227–28; William G. Stanard, ed., "Thomas Stegg [sic] Will," *Virginia Magazine of History and Biography* 35 (1927): 227, 233; Maureen Meyers, "From Refugees to Slave Traders: The Transformation of the Westo," in *Mapping the Mississippian Shatter Zone*, 92;

Louis B. Wright, "William Byrd and the Slave Trade," *Huntington Quarterly* 8 (1945): 379–87; Benjamin Weisiger, ed., *Henrico County, Virginia, Deeds, 1677–1705* (Richmond: Weisiger, 1986), 134.

16. Hening, *Statutes at Large*, 2:20–21; Meyers, "From Refugees to Slave Traders," 93; Philip A. Bruce, ed., "Westover," *Virginia Magazine of History and Biography* 3 (July 1895): 290.

17. Louis B. Wright and Marion Tinling, eds., *The Secret Diary of William Byrd of Westover, 1709–1712* (Richmond, Va.: Dietz, 1941), 3; Hening, *Statutes at Large*, 2:336; Wilcomb E. Washburn, *The Governor and the Rebel: A History of Bacon's Rebellion in Virginia* (Chapel Hill: University of North Carolina Press, 1957), 20–21.

18. Meyers, "From Refugees to Slave Traders," 92; C. S. Everett, "'They shalbe slaves for their lives,'" in *Indian Slavery in Colonial America*, ed. Alan Gallay (Lincoln: University of Nebraska Press, 2009), 67–108; James P. Whittenburg and John M. Coski, eds., *Charles City County, Virginia: An Official History* (Salem, Va.: Don Mills , 1989), 32.

19. Pierre Marambaud, "William Byrd I: A Young Virginia Planter in the 1670s," *Virginia Magazine of History and Biography* 81 (1973): 140; William Berkeley to Thomas Ludwell, July 1, 1676, in Warren M. Billings, ed., *The Papers of Sir William Berkeley 1605–1677* (Richmond: Library of Virginia, 2007), 537; Snyder, *Brabbling Women*, 27.

20. "Heroines of Virginia," *William and Mary Quarterly*, 1st ser., 15 (1906): 41; Public Records Office (hereafter PRO) C.O. 1/39, ff. 64–65; Brown, *Good Wives*, 162; William Berkeley to Thomas Ludwell, July 1, 1676, in Billings, *Papers of Sir William Berkeley*, 537.

21. Andrews, *Narratives of the Insurrections*, 25–27; Hening, *Statutes at Large*, 2:346.

22. Rountree, *Powhatan Indians of Virginia*, 96; John Clayton, "Another Account of Virginia," ed. Edmund Berkeley and Dorothy S. Berkeley, *Virginia Magazine of History and Biography* 76 (1968): 434; McCartney, "Cockacoeske, Queen of Pamunkey," 263.

23. Clara Sue Kidwell, "Indian Women as Cultural Mediators," *Ethnohistory* 39 (1992): 97–98, n14.

24. McCartney, "Cockacoeske, Queen of Pamunkey," 246–47; *The Beginning, Progress, and Conclusion of Bacon's Rebellion in Virginia, in the Years 1675 and 1676* (Washington, D.C.: Peter Force, 1835), http://memory.loc.gov/ammem/collections/jefferson_papers/tm.html (accessed March 21, 2013).

25. Morgan, *American Slavery*, 261–66; Andrews, *Narratives of the Insurrections*, 25–27; Hening, *Statutes at Large*, 2:346.

26. Philip Alexander Bruce and William Glover Stanard, eds., "Narrative of Bacon's Rebellion," *Virginia Magazine of History and Biography* 2 (1896): 138, 140 (marginal note in original); Andrews, *Narratives of the Insurrections*, 66–71, 129–36; Andrew Marvell to Henry Thompson, November 14, 1676, HM 21813, Huntington Library; CO 1/42, f. 178; John Berry, Francis Moryson, and Herbert Jeffreys, "A True Narrative of the Rise, Progress, and Cessation of the Late Rebellion," in *Samuel Wiseman's Book of Record: The Official Account of Bacon's Rebellion in Virginia, 1676–1677*, ed. Michael Leroy Oberg (Lanham, Md.: Lexington, 2005), 142–86.

27. Bruce and Stanard, "Narrative of Bacon's Rebellion," 138.

28. Westbury, "Women in Bacon's Rebellion," 40; Snyder, *Brabbling Women*, chap. 1; Hening, *Statutes at Large*, 2:385; Sir William Blackstone, *Commentaries on the Laws of England in Four Books* (Chicago: Callaghan, 1899), 4:28–29.

29. Spruill, *Women's Life and Work*, 320, 339.

30. "Heroines of Virginia," 41; Brown, *Good Wives*, 176; Oberg, *Samuel Wiseman's Book*, 261; Andrews, *Narratives of the Insurrections*, 111; Sarah Grendon to Herbert Jeffries, n.d., Coventry Papers, Bath 65, 78, ff. 5, 6, Longleat House, Warminster, Wiltshire, England.

31. Oberg, *Samuel Wiseman's Book*, 261; "Personal Grievances," *Virginia Magazine of History and Biography* 24 (1916): 370.

32. McCartney, "Cockacoeske, Queen of Pamunkey," 250; Herbert Jeffreys to Right Honorable, June 11, 1677, Coventry Papers, 77, Bath 65, ff. 64–65, Longleat House, Warminster, Wiltshire, England.

33. A frontlet still survives but is no longer with the Pamunkeys; it is in the collections of the Virginia Historical Society in Richmond. In May 2010, at Williamsburg, the Pamunkeys received an exact replica commissioned by the Colonial Williamsburg Foundation. See McCartney, "Cockacoeske, Queen of Pamunkey," 251–52.

34. Ibid., 253–54; H. R. McIlwaine et al., comps., *Executive Journals of the Council of Colonial Virginia*, 6 vols. (Richmond: Virginia State Library, 1925–66), 1:4; Hening, *Statutes at Large*, 2:275–77.

35. McCartney, "Cockacoeske, Queen of Pamunkey," 255–56; "Queen of Pamunkey (Cockacoeske), the Agrievances of the Queen of Poemunkey and Her Sonn Captain John West," June 5, 1678, in PRO, CO 1/42, f. 177; Cockacoeske to Colonel Francis Moryson, June 29, 1678, PRO, CO 1/42, f. 276; Hening, *Statutes at Large*, 2:275–77; Thomas Ludwell to Right Honorable, January 30, 1678, Coventry Papers, 77, Bath 65, ff. 202–3, Longleat House, Warminster, Wiltshire, England.

36. Marambaud, "William Byrd I," 141; William Byrd to Perry and Lane, March 29, 1685, in Marion Tinling, ed., *The Correspondence of the Three William Byrds of Westover, Virginia, 1684–1776*, 2 vols. (Charlottesville: University of Virginia Press, 1977), 1:31; Byrd to Warham Horsmanden, March 1685, ibid., 1:32; "Personal Grievances," 370.

37. Byrd to Warham Horsmanden, March 1685, in Tinling, *Correspondence of the Three William Byrds*, 1:32; Byrd to Nordest Rand, March 31, 1685, ibid., 1:35–36; Byrd to Robert Coe, April 1, 1685, ibid., 1:39; Byrd to Thomas Gower, June 8, 1685, ibid., 1:42–43; Snyder, *Brabbling Women*, 126.

38. McCartney, "Cockacoeske, Queen of Pamunkey," 259–60; Francis Nicholson to the Council, October 22, 1702, PRO, CO 5/1312, pt. 1, f. 318.

39. Brown, *Good Wives*, 176.

40. Hutner, *Colonial Women*, 90.

41. Aphra Behn, *The Widdow Ranter; or, The History of Bacon in Virginia*, in *The Works of Aphra Behn*, ed. Montague Summers (1690; New York: B. Blom, 1967), 246. In this fictional take on Bacon's Rebellion, Behn alleges that Bacon's great motivation was to be a hero and to steal the Indian queen for himself to make her his princess. Semernia, the Indian queen, spoke in an aside here about Nathaniel Bacon. There is evidence that Behn was familiar with the commissioner's report on the rebellion. See Jenny Hale Pulsipher, "*The Widow Ranter* and Royalist Culture in Colonial Virginia," *Early American Literature* 39 (2004): 43, 45; Hutner, *Colonial Women*.

Jane Webb and Her Family

Life Stories and the Law in Early Virginia

TERRI L. SNYDER

In July 1726 Jane Webb stood at the common whipping post in Northampton County, on the eastern shore of Virginia. Webb, a free, mixed-race woman of about forty-three years of age, had run afoul of the local magistrates after a setback in a bitter and protracted lawsuit against Thomas Savage, a middling white planter. According to witnesses, Webb had openly declared that "if all Virginia negros had as good a heart as she had, they would all be free." The justices found these to be "dangerous words, tending to the breach of the peace," and they punished Webb with ten lashes "well laid on." Yet behind her seditious words lay a tangled skein of family history spanning over two decades that stemmed from the fact that Thomas Savage owned Jane Webb's husband, an enslaved man known only in the records as Left. Although Left was a slave, the Webb marriage was legally recognized, and the seven children born to the couple, following the legal principle of *partus sequitur ventrem*, took their free status as well as their surname from their mother. Legal doctrine did not translate seamlessly into local practice, however, and as a result of her effort to protect the precarious freedom of her family, Webb wound up at the whipping post on that July day.[1]

At first glance, Jane Webb may not appear to be a good subject for biographical study: she was ordinary, obscure, and utterly unconnected to anyone famous. She left no private letters or journals; it is not clear if she could write. Only traces of Webb can be found in early Virginia court records, filtered through the pens of court clerks, formal legal mechanisms, and standard procedures for pleas. Some documents reflect her own legal subjectivity—her consciousness under the law—but her private persona is mostly lost to us. Except for her disorderly words, the records offer few clues to the interior Webb, a view that biographers

"THE HUMBLE PETITION OF JANE WEBB"

In this 1722 petition, Jane Webb affirmed her own free status, asserted the legality of her marriage, and defended the free status of her children. In doing so, she directly challenged the power of the local court over her family.
Library of Virginia.

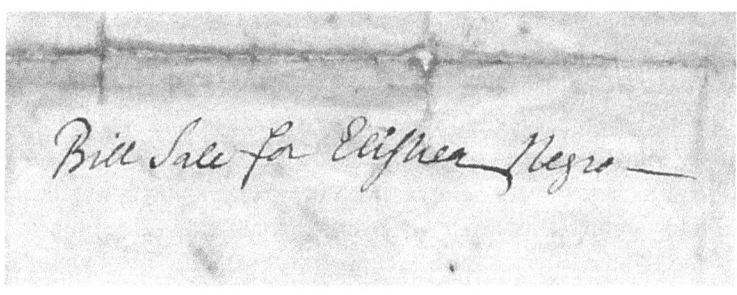

"BILL OF SALE FOR ELISHEA A NEGRO"
This document from Portsmouth, New Hampshire, illustrates the erasure of Elisha Webb's last name, a key marker of her free status, and reveals the terms of her illegal enslavement. The bill of sale stipulated that she was sold "for ever" to Daniel Wentworth, a merchant, for the sum of £120 sterling. New Hampshire State Archives, Concord.

often seek. In many ways, she is the antithesis of the typical subject and the rich subjectivity that often attract scholars to life stories.

Biographies of women in early America are often focused on famous individuals about whom much is known and can be discovered, and for good reasons. Studies of Sally Hemings and Martha Jefferson Randolph, for instance, are possible because these women—one enslaved, one free, both occupying the same household—were well known by their contemporaries by virtue of their connection to Thomas Jefferson. Since his importance in the history of Virginia and the United States is unquestioned, his papers have been deemed exceptionally worthy of preservation. It is because of this, in part, that the stories of Hemings and Randolph can be told. Even in famous families, however, the history of women can be overshadowed, if not overlooked and misunderstood, when biographers rely on traditional definitions of historical and political worthiness. The biographies of Hemings and Randolph, in contrast, approach these women as central subjects in their own right, not simply as appendages to Jefferson. Their stories are rendered not to augment or deepen our understanding of Jefferson (although some of that is inevitable) but rather to illuminate the complexities of women's roles, family matters, and the history of slavery and race in early America. Getting at the stories of early American women also requires innovative methods. Sally Hemings left no written evidence for her biographer, but her life is rendered concretely through the stories of her parents, siblings, children, and descendants as well as through Jefferson's records. Along with her own letters, accounts of Martha Randolph are set in the context of the public and private lives of her contemporaries, enabling readers to understand what was both ordinary and extraordinary about her.[2]

These approaches for studying early Virginia women also can be brought to bear on the unknown and ordinary but exceptional Jane Webb. As one of the more legally active women in early eighteenth-century Virginia, her life exemplifies a finely tuned legal consciousness honed by multiple experiences as a woman before the bar during that time. Webb's story is worth telling because it reflects the distinct experiences of some of the most marginalized of women in the early southern colonies. Unlike the daughters and wives of middling and small planters, who were Webb's contemporaries, for instance, free women of color who married across status lines did not enjoy the advantages of a liberal marriage market born of early Virginia's uneven sex ratio; if indentured, they could not count on their husbands to purchase their contracts; and when widowed, they would not gain substantial control over property. From her status under the law and her experience at the bar to her position in the household polity, a free woman of color in an across-status marriage, like Jane Webb, was not, in nearly all respects, a planter's wife.[3]

As a mixed-race, free woman who married a slave rather than a planter, Jane Webb's story exemplifies the social and political realities of relations of gender and race as they existed in the households, neighborhoods, and courts of early eighteenth-century Virginia. The lives of women like Webb—the laboring and often peripatetic poor—are difficult to get at because the sources that document their lives are sporadic, incomplete, and intensely local.[4] What we know of Webb's life has been pieced together through the documents of her court appearances, petitions, and suits in the surviving court records of Northampton County. Aside from local sources, such as the county court, parish, and land records, little other surviving evidence allows us to explore the experiences of free black women like Webb, despite the fact that everywhere in Virginia and in much of what became the South up to the Civil War, they outnumbered their male counterparts by as much as two to one. A conservative estimate suggests that about 10 percent of them, also like Webb, found mates from the ranks of the enslaved and became married women who headed households.[5] In order to best present Webb's story, this chapter examines her life from three distinct but related vantage points: the role of geography and local culture in shaping her legal consciousness, her strategies for protecting her marriage and children, and the ways in which her consciousness and strategies translated into legal legacies, particularly for her daughters.

Jane Webb spent her entire life on the eastern shore of Virginia, and geography played a meaningful role in shaping her legal consciousness. The eastern shore is composed of two counties, Accomack and Northampton, which occupy the entire peninsula that separates the Chesapeake Bay from the Atlantic Ocean. From the middle of the seventeenth century until the eve of the Civil War, the eastern shore, which held about 8 percent of Virginia's colonial population, was home to one of its largest concentrations of free blacks, who filled out the ranks of the colony's servant class. Nor was this a region of intense slavery: even after transatlantic slave shipments began to arrive in the colony with greater frequency, only about 20 percent of the households on the eastern shore claimed ownership of slaves.[6]

In this geographically remote and racially mixed region, free, indentured, and enslaved people—English, Native, Caribbean, African—labored and lived together. In 1682 Jane Webb was born of this intermingling: her mother, Ann Williams, was an English indentured servant, and her father, Daniel Webb, was a slave whose origins are uncertain. Because of her mixed-race parentage and out-of-wedlock birth, Webb was bound out for service more or less in accordance with English law on orphans. *More* because she was indentured only until she was eighteen years of age; she was lucky to have been born ahead of the

1691 statute that specified a term of thirty years of service for individuals born in similar circumstances. *Less* because on her master's death, she was explicitly named as part of his widow's inheritance, to be "att her disposal during her life, and at her decease to be divided amongst [her] children," a statement that sounds ominously permanent, although Webb was in fact freed around 1700. During her youth, Jane Webb would have seen that manumission by will, deed, or self-purchase was possible—two enslaved men were freed in the household in which she labored—but also that the temporary bondage of servitude could easily shade into the permanent state of slavery. She would have learned that the law on slavery and freedom was ever changing in Virginia, and that recourse to the local court was a necessity in safeguarding the fragile liberties of free blacks.[7]

While the legal culture on the eastern shore of Virginia was accessible to free blacks through the early eighteenth century, statutes regulated free black women with regard to marriage and taxation. Colonial Virginia law neither proscribed nor endorsed marriage between free and enslaved blacks. Statutes in the Old Dominion prevented interracial marriage and sex, regulated consanguinity, and stipulated the proper form for the solemnization of vows, but no law expressly prevented free people of color from marrying enslaved people. Yet, while free women of color were allowed to marry from the ranks of the enslaved, they were also burdened with taxation, unlike their white counterparts.[8] A 1643 law decreed that adult black women were to be taxed in the same manner as adult men, regardless of race; white women, however, remained untaxed. A couple of decades later, confusion apparently arose as to whether free women of color were exempt from taxation. In 1668 a new law clarified the matter, stipulating that while free black women ought to "enjoy their freedome," they should not "be admitted to a full fruition of the exemptions and impunities" of English women. The regulations about interracial marriage and taxation, as one historian has argued, made race rather than class a "cornerstone" of womanhood.[9]

Growing up as a mixed-race orphan on Virginia's eastern shore, then, Jane Webb would have learned lessons that animated her legal consciousness for the rest of her life. She would have understood that nominally free people like her shared in some possibilities of liberty; that the court allowed for legal improvisations but these were subject to the consent of masters; and that indeterminacy under the law was dangerous. Surely, by the time she was freed from servitude in 1700, Webb was likely aware of several mixed-status marriages on the eastern shore. These marriages were often formalized through the efforts of wives, who insisted that their unions be given express mention in legal documents in order to protect their own freedom and that of any children born to the marriage. There would be no need for this in the reverse case. Since the status of the child followed the mother, free black men who married enslaved women had no reason to formalize their unions because their offspring would be enslaved, like their mothers. Given these legal lessons, Webb devised legal strategies to reinforce her claims to liberty.[10]

In 1703, a few years after Jane Webb was freed from her indenture, she had, as she expressed it, "a strong desire to intermarry with a certain . . . slave commonly called Left." Left's owner, Thomas Savage, consented to the match in a legal contract, and from that point forward, Jane and Left Webb were understood to be husband and wife. Who solemnized this marriage is unclear, although some of the Savages were Quakers, and they might have helped to arrange the marriage.[11] Getting married at all required sacrifice on Jane Webb's part, as her contract with Savage makes apparent.[12] In order to marry Left, Webb reentered servitude for seven years and agreed that any children born to the marriage through 1711 would serve Savage for eighteen years. After 1711 Left would be freed, and any children born to the couple after that would bear no obligation to Savage. Jane Webb's motives seem clear: she traded servitude in order to marry, to ensure the legal legitimacy of her progeny, and to keep the family free and together.[13]

Jane Webb went to considerable pains to mention the legal status of her marriage whenever she appeared in court. That it was never assumed or taken for granted points to the legal fragility of the union and the vulnerability of the Webb children, at least five of whom survived to adulthood. Failing to obtain legal recognition of the union—if only a simple mention in a court order book—risked the freedom of any children born to the marriage. Since much was at stake, clearly legal attestation to these marriages functioned as formal records of free black status throughout the entire colonial period, decades before free blacks were legally required to register their status. In Virginia, for instance, registration would not be required until 1793, during the great wave of manumissions that occurred in the wake of the Revolution.[14] Nearly a century earlier, Jane Webb recognized the importance of generating a legal record of her status. For a free woman like Jane Webb, who was the legal face of her family, registration was a crucial protective device.

As a free woman married to a slave, Jane Webb held an anomalous position in household governance. It likely was not immediately clear to anyone how the English common law of domestic relations, or coverture, encompassed the free wives of enslaved husbands. Under the doctrine of coverture, the legal identity of a husband subsumed that of his wife; husband and wife were assumed to be one in the eyes of the law. Wives, for instance, could not sue or be sued independently nor enter into contracts; they were not entitled to their wages. Yet the practice in early Virginia defied a strict interpretation of coverture, a fact that worked in favor of Jane Webb. In the early Old Dominion, free women, even married women, were in and out of the courts, enjoying relatively more freedom, legally speaking, than they would after the Revolution.[15]

A free black woman who married an enslaved man was both a *feme sole* (unmarried woman) and a *feme covert* (married woman), simultaneously the head of the household and married to a man who had no personhood under the law. Moreover, unlike the white planter's white wife, who had little direct relationship to the polity during her marriage, a free black woman who married an enslaved man was the legal face of her household. It was up to her to pursue legal strategies that would protect and sustain her progeny in Virginia's increasingly racialized environment. While local courts and masters initially tolerated and may have even encouraged across-status marriages, because they resulted in female-headed households and lineages these marriages existed in tension with patriarchal models in a slave society.[16]

For all of these reasons, Jane Webb's marriage challenged early American understandings of household status in ways that the reverse situation (that is, when free men of color married enslaved women) simply did not. In a society in which patriarchal authority was enshrined in the law, free women of color who married enslaved men initially must have posed challenges to the logic of coverture. Under the law of domestic relations, any woman's "only freely chosen legal obligation was to her husband," and he was vested in rights to her property and her body. Treatises on domestic relations referred to coverture as the law of "baron and feme," meaning "not husband and wife, but lord and woman." This challenge was easily resolved, however: lawmakers in Virginia and elsewhere eventually extended coverture to mixed-status marriages and, when necessary, vested wives' legal identities in the masters of their enslaved husbands. The same treatises on *baron et feme* encompassed all household relations, including not just those between husbands and wives but also those between masters and servants.[17]

In theory, the logic was all of a piece: all of these relations were subject to the same structural hierarchies. And, in practice, legal authorities on the eastern shore had confronted this very issue in the latter part of the seventeenth century. When the free Sarah King married the enslaved Thomas Driggus, she initially lived with him in his master's household. But, by the mid-1670s, the Northampton County court ordered that she should not "depart the house of [her husband's master] without *the leave and order of both* her said husband and [his master]."[18] Local custom made the rights of the enslaved husband and his master strikingly equal: in this instance patriarchy trumped the law of slavery and, at the very least, operated contrary to our assumptions. Sarah King did, as Jane Webb would do nearly fifty years later, eventually choose to live separately from her husband so that she could live in a household apart from his master's control.

Tracing Jane Webb's life in the aftermath of the 1703 marriage contract allows us to understand the logic of legal paternalism and comprehend why customary law in local circumstances accommodated these nontraditional unions. Jane and Left had three children before 1711 and four children thereafter.[19] Yet, as 1711 came and went, Jane Webb remained in the Savage household, Left remained a slave, and Thomas Savage successively bound to his service every single one of the Webb children. Masters like Savage, along with local legal and religious authorities, agreed to recognize marriages between free women and enslaved men for both ideological and material reasons. Because the children of these unions were free, the sole responsibility for providing their material support rested with their mothers, who typically possessed few resources beyond their own labor. Masters also assumed that families would seek to stay together, which, in Jane Webb's case, meant that they stayed in the Savage household with Left. Occasionally enslaved husbands and their free wives ran away, but masters most likely supported these irregular marriages because they believed the unions would discourage that: local masters and justices counted on marriage to root families to the slave owners' households.

Justices and masters also condoned improvisations in local practice because they understood that ultimately the law was on their side. Because their families were typically poor, free black children, like the Webb offspring, were likely to be bound over as servants for the first two or three decades of their lives.[20] Moreover, it did not matter whether Jane Webb chose to indenture her children because Virginia's justices, following English practice, had discretionary powers to indenture children whose parents' "poverty" prevented them from giving their children "breeding," a loosely defined quality indeed. From the viewpoint of the law, it was, as it had been in England since the sixteenth-century Statute of Artificers, perfectly acceptable to compel free individuals, if they were poor, to labor. The integrity of poorer families (that is, keeping them together) was relatively less important to the law than forcing the poor to work.[21]

All of this is evident in the case of Jane Webb. When she refused to bind over her younger children (those born after 1711, who were to be free from service, according to the terms of the original contract), Thomas Savage petitioned the court, stating that he had the "best right" to the Webb children since their mother had "no visible means to support the said children . . . and they may be induced to take ill courses."[22] The justices agreed, and the children were bound over to Savage. Judicial paternalism may have allowed Jane Webb's irregular marriage, but the master of her husband was a primary beneficiary of this practice under the law, since his rights to the children superseded those of their mother. Ultimately, then, local custom accommodated Jane Webb's union and other similar marriages across status because they strengthened the power of masters, undermined the rights of free blacks, particularly free black women, and helped stabilize slavery.

Despite these disabilities, Jane Webb had some powerful legal weapons in her arsenal, and she drew on them to protect her family. In August 1722, for instance, nearly two decades after drawing up the contract with Savage, Webb questioned the court about the terms of her children's service.[23] When her oldest children, Dinah and Daniel, had each reached the age of eighteen and were not freed from Savage, Webb appealed to the court. Her petition was carefully composed to stress her family's freedom: "The humble petition of Jane Webb a free malatto . . . baptized by the name Jane the said petitioners mother being a white woman and whereas . . . the petitioner having served seven years for the Liberty of Intermarying with one negroman named Left, manslave . . . [*the petitioner*] *prays that* [*the*] *children being born in Lawfull Wedlock may not be adjudged to servitude* [*and that the*] *Court* [*is*] *not Intending to Enslave* [*the*] *petitioner's children.*" The petition featured several legal markers of freedom. It described Webb as a "free malatto," who was "baptized" and whose mother was a "white woman." It indirectly referred to her contract with Savage ("the petitioner having served several years") and established her "Lawfull Wedlock" with Left and, therefore, the free status of her children.[24]

The meaning of the last line of this 1722 petition—Jane Webb's concern that the court was intending to "Enslave" her children—is not immediately apparent. A consideration of pending colonial legislation, however, makes her intentions clear. In 1722 Virginia's governor complained of a "conspiracy [of slaves] . . . wherein the Free-Negros . . . were much Suspected to have been Concerned." And also in 1722 Virginia's legislators responded by enacting new statutes that were intended to fix a "perpetual Brand upon Free-Negros & Mulattos" by excluding them from the "great privileges of a freeman," which included voting and officeholding and, eventually, would encompass their exclusion from juries except in cases in which slaves were being tried. These exclusions were necessary because, as the governor put it, free blacks "always did, and ever [would], adhere to and favour slaves." Moreover, as soon as slaves were manumitted, he argued, they viewed themselves as "good [people] as the Best of [their] Neighbours."[25]

In light of these concerns, three new laws went into effect in 1723. The first declared that any child born to a free woman of color during her term of servitude was to serve her master for a term of thirty or thirty-one years, while the second made manumission impossible except by the governor's approval. These two laws virtually enslaved free black children and effectively closed down all but one avenue by which slaves might gain their freedom.[26] The third statute, initiated by the Northampton County representative George Harmanson, focused specifically on the threat posed by free black women.[27] According to Harmanson, his constituents had complained about the "great numbers of free negros of which the women pay no taxes."[28] The grievance resulted in a new statute that stipulated that free black women, married or not, were to be taxed like any other male or enslaved female resident of the colony above the age of sixteen, signaling an intensification of legal efforts to legislate difference based on race and sex.[29] As will become clear, Harmanson's experience with the Webb family likely propelled his support of these new laws. Perhaps he believed that an additional financial burden on free families of color would be a means of quelling dissent by free women of color like Jane Webb.

Jane Webb's petition, then, made in August 1722, strongly suggests that she anticipated this legislation. When she used the word "Enslave," she directly challenged the power of the law to constrain the freedom of her children. Under the new statutes, she believed, the court would adjust her children's terms of service to fit the new thirty-year requirement, and she also probably assumed that Left would never gain his freedom. The critical aspects of Jane Webb's 1703 contract now must have appeared to her to be nearly unattainable.

In 1725, in an effort to forestall the enslavement of her children, Jane Webb brought a suit in chancery against Thomas Savage. Her complaint in *Webb v. Savage* recounted the original terms of the contract and argued that Savage had failed to live up to the conditions. Although Savage claimed that he had lost the document, he disputed Webb's version of its stipulations, arguing that he was entitled to the service of all of the Webb children and that he had never agreed to free Left. Moreover, he also produced two witnesses—including George Harmanson, the burgess for Northampton County—who claimed to have seen the contract and swore to Savage's version of it. Webb, in turn, produced a free black witness; the existing law rejected the testimony of slaves and non-Christians, but it did not yet explicitly prevent free blacks from being witnesses. The justices, uncertain of how to proceed, deliberated but ultimately denied her request.[30]

When legal strategies failed, Jane Webb resorted to resistance through intimidation. Immediately after the entry in the court order book that outlined the testimony of the witnesses who swore to Thomas Savage's version of the contract, it was noted that George Harmanson had "heard that Jane Webb has uttered dangerous words tending to the breach of the peace."[31] Disorderly speech such as this was an effective avenue of resistance for women in small, volatile, and insular societies like the early eastern shore of Virginia. But this was no idle gossip. Webb's words were politically charged, a calculated demonstration of her own racial consciousness and a deliberate threat of collective resistance.

The hazard of Jane Webb's words was not lost on the court. On the very next day, at the very next court session, punishing Webb was the first order of business. She was brought to the bar, witnesses swore to her disorderly words, and she was ordered to receive "ten lashes well laid on at the common whipping post on her bare back and that the sheriff perform the same *immediately*." Given that telling detail and the subsequent entry, it appears that court adjourned for several minutes; most of those in attendance likely listened or watched as Jane Webb was stripped to the waist, tied to the post, and whipped. When the sheriff finished, she was brought back to the bar, and court resumed. The second order of business: "Jane Webb (having received her punishment) is discharged ... upon payment of fees." Court fees were a corollary to corporal punishment.[32]

Although Webb ultimately failed to hold Thomas Savage to the terms of their original contract, as she understood it, and although she ran afoul of the Northampton justices and burgesses, she did succeed in providing meaningful legal lessons to her children. Her instrumental use of the courts, her knowledge of law, and her legal resourcefulness were skills that all free black women needed if they wanted their families to remain free and enjoy some economic mobility. The eldest and youngest Webb daughters, Dinah and Elisha, respectively, became adept litigators.

Dinah was born in 1704 and indentured to Thomas Savage three years later, in 1707. When she was eighteen, her mother complained to the court that Savage had held Dinah beyond the terms of the indenture, but this petition failed. However, two years later, Dinah sued for her freedom, bringing to court evidence of her birth record from the parish register. This time the justices ruled in her favor. In 1727, after she had married a free black man, Gabriel Manley, Dinah again appeared in court. Her petition complained that Thomas Savage had failed to provide her freedom dues, and had neglected to teach her to read as was originally promised. Again, the court agreed. By 1735 Dinah and Gabriel left the eastern shore for North Carolina, a more hospitable environment for free blacks in the early eighteenth century. In her persistence in securing her freedom dues and compensation for the literacy that Savage did not provide, Dinah Webb exhibited some of the same persistence at the bar as did her mother.[33]

The same is true of Elisha Webb, whose legal skills and tenacity were very much evident in her efforts to maintain her freedom. Elisha was the youngest of the Webb daughters; she was born in 1716 and indentured to Thomas Savage in 1726.³⁴ In May 1737 she boarded a ship in Virginia and sailed up the eastern seaboard to Portsmouth, New Hampshire. For some reason—perhaps at her own request—her labor contract had been sold to the ship's captain. Despite her race, in the eyes of the law, Elisha Webb was understood to be a free, if indentured, woman. Yet, by the time she reached Portsmouth, someone had altered her status, erased her surname, and sold her into slavery. Elisha Webb had become, as the bill of sale put it, "Elishea a negro," and for £120 sterling, she had been sold into slavery "for ever."³⁵

It would take several years, several letters, and the intercession of her mother, but eventually Elisha would use the courts in New Hampshire and Virginia to reestablish her status as a free woman. In order to bring about this feat of justice, Elisha Webb drew on the same kind of legal skills as her mother and set into motion local, neighborhood, and intercolonial networks. Yet she had bided her time: her bill of "sale" was dated May 3, 1737, but she did not legally complain of her enslavement for another two years, which was about the same amount of time she had left to serve on her indenture. What is clear is that someone sympathetic to Elisha was coasting up and down the eastern seaboard in 1739 because someone carried a letter from her to a court clerk, Thomas Cable, on the eastern shore of Virginia.³⁶

Elisha's letter, most likely carried by mariners, set into motion the eastern shore neighborhood—Webbs, Savages, and local legal officials—and mobilized them to take measures that would help her secure freedom. The clerk's reply to Elisha's letter reiterated her assertion that she had been sold into slavery for "one hundred and one years." This, he claimed, was "very unjust" and bluntly added, "the party who keeps you after knowing you to be a free person will be liable to be damaged." In other words, he threatened a lawsuit.³⁷ Cable then sent Elisha's letter to Esther Savage, the widow of the now-deceased son and heir of Thomas Savage. She replied to Elisha, asserting that "my husband sold thee . . . for eleven months and some few days" plus a year for each of the out-of-wedlock children that Elisha had while in Virginia. Savage added, "If there is any thing more against thee with his name to it I verily believe it is forged." In other words, Esther Savage declared the Savages innocent of wrongdoing and laid the blame on parties up in Portsmouth.³⁸

Elisha's strategy was to involve the eastern shore neighborhood in the injustice that had been done to her and put the local court and her former master in a defensive position. Eventually, this strategy worked. When the clerk replied to Elisha, he included Savage's letter and urged Elisha to show it to her owner, who would be "satisfied that you are a free person, and no doubt will set you free without putting your poor father and mother to the expense of the seal of the Governor."³⁹ In the end, it would require three additional letters from the

Savage heirs, a lawsuit, and legal counsel provided by one of the most influential lawyers in New Hampshire, but Elisha gained her freedom and collected damages from the man who claimed to own her.[40]

In addition to mariners, legal officials, and her former masters, the networks that secured Elisha Webb's freedom also encompassed family. Jane Webb, now nearly sixty years of age, once again maneuvered her way through Virginia legalities. Once Elisha's letter reached Virginia, a justice summoned Jane Webb. In an act that at once bespeaks the power of her oppression and the meaning of her freedom, Jane Webb ferried Elisha's first letter from the justice to Esther Savage: "this day," Savage wrote, "thy mother brought me a letter signed by thee and directed to Coll. Cable." Jane Webb then ferried Savage's response back to the justice and asked him to convey to Elisha, as he did in a postscript, that her "mother and father" sent their "blessing." And Jane Webb, once again, appeared in the Northampton court to make sure that the depositions and affirmations from the Savages that supported Elisha's freedom were made a matter of legal record, given the justice's seal, remunerated, and sent up to Portsmouth—all costly matters.[41]

After Elisha Webb won her freedom in 1742, she remained in Portsmouth. For Elisha, as for Dinah, the eastern shore of Virginia no longer seemed to be a hospitable environment for free blacks. Elisha and her enslaved husband, Cesar, had six children. Once again reflecting legal lessons learned from her mother, Elisha requested that the town clerk record the names and birthdates of the couple's children and asked him to note that they were "born free."[42] The last of Elisha and Cesar's children was a daughter, born in 1762; they named her Jane.

As a case study, Jane Webb offers an opportunity to study the intersections between women's life stories and the law of race and slavery in early Virginia. Her multiple appearances at the bar of the local court display a sharp legal consciousness and an array of legal strategies. In part, her life offers a potent challenge to assumptions about women's legal incapacity in early Virginia precisely because she used the remedies of petition, contract, and chancery to keep her children free and to negotiate local legal paternalism on the eastern shore of Virginia. And she passed those legal lessons on to her daughters.

At the same time, however, her story illustrates the overreaching power of statute law and of local legal officials to reach into the lives of free women of color. Legal patriarchy, locally and at the colony level, was inextricably linked to the interests of masters and sharply responsive to white anxieties over free black women, their children, and their alliances, marital and otherwise, with slaves. All around her, as Jane Webb well knew, Virginia's legislators, sometimes taking their cues from the specific locale of the eastern shore, codified the law of slavery and shaped the legal system to erode the numbers, rights, and independence of free blacks like herself. Webb's appearances at the bar, seen in light of the actions of local legal officials and the evolution of the colony's race-based law, suggest a bleaker legal reality for free women of color in early Virginia.

If the intersection of her life story and the law reflects Jane Webb's equivocal legal capacities, it also allows us to glimpse her political subjectivity. In addition to the episode of subversive speech discussed above, the changing designations of Jane Webb's surname offer insight into the gender and racial politics of early Virginia. Initially, she was referred to as Jane Williams, the surname of her British mother, which was most likely bestowed at her out-of-wedlock birth.[43] At some point, at least by 1703, she was called or began calling herself Jane Webb, using her enslaved father's surname. Perhaps this was to emphasize that her paternity was, in fact, known and to legitimize her parents' union, if only informally, in defiance of the law. Webb was the surname that descended to her children, and through the mid-1720s, Jane Webb was the name she used for her court appearances. In the years of the rancorous court battles with Thomas Savage, however, her husband's first name began appearing as her surname; in tax lists she was referred to as "Jane Left" in 1724 and as "Jane Webb, alias Left" in 1727. And when she died in November 1764, at the age of eighty-two, she was buried as "Jane Left."[44]

We might be tempted to write off these variations in naming—Jane Williams, Jane Webb, Jane Left—as simply erratic record keeping. Yet they might also be read as expressions of Webb's objections to the ways that the law defined her. As Jane Williams, she was, in the legal parlance of the day, a bastard. As Jane Webb, she connected herself to a paternal, if enslaved, lineage, conferring the name of her father on her children and using it as the legal face of her household. And when she called herself Jane Left, she similarly asserted a patriarchal, male-headed model for her family. These name changes carried a politically significant valence. By taking her enslaved father's surname as her own and, later, her enslaved husband's first name as her surname, she challenged prevailing ideas about slavery, manhood, and race. These assertions of paternal and traditional family models were deeply political designations. Through them, Webb claimed a patriarchal dependency that was, ironically, quite radical in the racially charged environment of early Virginia.

Finally, if the stories of Sally Hemings and Martha Jefferson Randolph capture women who lived at the center of power in early America, the story of Jane Webb, in contrast, is a study of life on the margins of early Virginia. Her biography challenges us to rethink the familiar categories of women's history. Situated somewhere between the good wife and the nasty wench, *feme covert* and *feme sole*, free and unfree, black and white, her story uniquely captures the ways in which the intersections of race, status, and legalities shaped the experiences of women in early Virginia. For free black women like Jane, Dinah, and Elisha Webb, the law conferred but mostly constrained their freedom. Ironically, it is the records of the harsh reality of those legalities that allow us to recover their life stories and to write a new history of women in early Virginia.

NOTES

1. Northampton County Orders (hereafter NCO), 1722–29, July 1726, ff. 247–48, and *Webb v. Savage*, Chancery Court Records, Northampton County Judgments, 1727-001 (hereafter NCJ). Unless otherwise indicated, all Northampton County, Virginia, documents cited in this chapter are in the Library of Virginia, Richmond.

2. See Annette Gordon-Reed, *The Hemingses of Monticello: An American Family* (New York: Norton, 2008); and Cynthia A. Kierner, *Martha Jefferson Randolph, Daughter of Monticello: Her Life and Times* (Chapel Hill: University of North Carolina Press, 2012).

3. Lois Green Carr and Lorena S. Walsh, "The Planter's Wife: The Experience of White Women in Seventeenth-Century Maryland," *William and Mary Quarterly*, 3rd ser., 34 (1977): 549, 550, 556, 569.

4. Exceptions include J. Douglas Deal, "A Constricted World: Free Blacks on Virginia's Eastern Shore," in *Colonial Chesapeake Society*, ed. Lois Green Carr, Philip D. Morgan, and Jean B. Russo (Chapel Hill: University of North Carolina Press, 1998), 275–305; Deal, *Race and Class in Colonial Virginia: Indians, Englishmen, and Africans on the Eastern Shore during the Seventeenth Century* (New York: Garland, 1993); Kathleen M. Brown, *Good Wives, Nasty Wenches, and Anxious Patriarchs: Gender, Race, and Power in Colonial Virginia* (Chapel Hill: University of North Carolina Press, 1996); Jane G. Landers, *Against the Odds: Free Blacks in the Slave Societies of the Americas* (London: Routledge, 1996); and Terri L. Snyder, "Marriage on the Margins: Free Wives, Enslaved Husbands, and the Law in Early Virginia," *Law and History Review* 30 (2012): 141–71.

5. For statistics, see Tommy L. Bogger, *Free Blacks in Norfolk Virginia, 1790–1860: The Darker Side of Freedom* (Charlottesville: University of Virginia Press, 1997), 109; Suzanne Lebsock, *The Free Women of Petersburg: Status and Culture in a Southern Town, 1784–1860* (New York: Norton, 1984), 87–111; Leonard P. Curry, *The Free Black in Urban America, 1800–1850* (Chicago: University of Chicago Press, 1981), 8–9, 11–14; Carl N. Degler, *Neither Black nor White: Slavery and Race Relations in Brazil and the United States* (New York: Prentice Hall, 1971), 83–84; Eva Sheppard Wolf, *Race and Liberty in the New Nation: Emancipation in Virginia from the Revolution to Nat Turner's Rebellion* (Baton Rouge: Louisiana State University Press, 2006); Ira Berlin, *Slaves without Masters: The Free Negro in the Antebellum South* (New York: Random House, 1974); John H. Russell, *The Free Negro in Virginia, 1619–1865* (Baltimore, Md.: Johns Hopkins University Press, 1913); John Hope Franklin, *The Free Negro in North Carolina, 1790–1860* (Chapel Hill: University of North Carolina Press, 1943); Herbert Klein, *African Slavery in Latin America and the Caribbean* (New York: Oxford University Press, 1988), 227.

6. One tithable list created in the mid-seventeenth century listed 29 percent of Northampton's black population as free. See John Ruston Pagan, "Law and Society in Restoration Virginia" (PhD diss., Oxford University, 1996), 416–34; Edmund S. Morgan, *American Slavery, American Freedom: The Ordeal of Colonial Virginia* (New York: Norton, 1974), 414–15, table 4; and T. H. Breen and

Stephen Innes, *"Myne Owne Ground": Race and Freedom on Virginia's Eastern Shore 1640–1676* (New York: Oxford University Press, 1980), 68–69. In the post-Revolutionary era, the free black population on the eastern shore outstripped other Virginia counties by as much as 2–6 percent (Wolf, *Race and Liberty in the New Nation*, 43, table 1). On the labor composition of early Chesapeake households, see Carole Shammas, "Black Women's Work and the Evolution of Plantation Society in Virginia," *Labor History* 26 (1985): 5–28; Russell Menard, "From Servants to Slaves: The Transformation of the Chesapeake Labor System," *Southern Studies* 16 (1977): 355–90; and John C. Coombs, "Beyond the Origins Debate: Rethinking the Rise of Virginia Slavery," in *Early Modern Virginia: Reconsidering the Old Dominion*, ed. Douglas Bradburn and John C. Coombs (Charlottesville: University of Virginia Press, 2011), 239–78.

7. On Jane Webb's origins, see the Will of Henry Warren, December 16, 1693, NCO, no. 13, ff. 261–62; Deal, "Constricted World," 299–300; Terri L. Snyder, "Webb, Jane," in *African American National Biography*, ed. Henry Louis Gates and Evelyn Brooks Higgenbotham (New York: Oxford University Press, 2008), 8:186–87; and "Webb Family," in *Free African Americans of Virginia, North Carolina, and South Carolina*, ed. Paul Heinegg, http://www.freeafricanamericans.com (accessed September 5, 2012). For the 1691 statute, see W. W. Hening, comp., *The Statutes at Large: Being a Collection of All the Laws of Virginia*, 13 vols. (Richmond, Va.: Samuel Pleasants Jr., 1810–23), 3:86–88.

8. Virginia statutes in 1691 and 1705 criminalized interracial marriage and sex and levied heavy penalties on white women who violated these laws; the laws, however, did not proscribe marriage between enslaved and free people (Hening, *Statutes at Large*, 3:86–87, 452–54). John Hope Franklin notes that North Carolinians did not restrict marriage across free-slave status until 1787, and then to note only that the master must be paid a fee. After the rise of the antislavery movement, in 1830 marriage between free and enslaved blacks was prohibited altogether (Franklin, *Free Negro in North Carolina*, 184–85). More recently, Richard C. Rohrs argued that the restrictions against marriage or cohabitation between slaves and free blacks came in the wake of the publication of David Walker's incendiary *Appeal*. See Rohrs, "The Free Black Experience in Antebellum Wilmington, North Carolina: Refining Generalizations about Race Relations," *Journal of Southern History* 78 (2012): 619.

9. Brown, *Good Wives*, 116–28. For the 1643 law, see Hening, *Statutes at Large*, 1:242; for the 1645 law, ibid., 1:292. For a 1658 law that taxed imported African or Native American servants—exempting Christians, those born in Virginia, or those who were free when their parents imported them in the colony—see ibid., 1:454. In 1662, a new statute taxed all women—regardless of race—who worked "in the ground" (ibid., 2:170). In 1668 the law specified that all free black women were to be taxed (ibid., 2:267). A further revision in 1705 once again exempted free black women, but a 1723 revision not only reiterated their taxable status, it also made taxable all women who were married to free men of color (ibid., 3:258, 4:133).

10. See Snyder, "Marriage on the Margins," 155–58.

11. Her language and affirmation suggest that Esther Savage was a Quaker; see *Elisha Webb v. Daniel Wentworth*, Provincial Court Records, no. 26121 (1739), New Hampshire State Archives, Concord (hereafter NHSA).

12. *Webb v. Savage* (1725–27), NCJ.

13. By the terms of a 1691 law, enacted a decade before Webb and Savage made their bargain, no slave was to be set free unless payment was provided for transportation out of the country within six months (Hening, *Statutes at Large*, 3:87–88). I am puzzled about Jane and Left Webb's plans in this regard.

14. Ibid., 14:440, 448.

15. Holly Brewer, "The Transformation of Domestic Law," in *The Cambridge History of Law in America*, vol. 1: *Early America, 1580–1815*, ed. Christopher Tomlins and Michael Grossberg (Cam-

bridge: Cambridge University Press, 2008), 298–99; Terri L. Snyder, *Brabbling Women: Disorderly Speech and the Law in Early Virginia* (Ithaca, N.Y.: Cornell University Press, 2003); Linda L. Sturtz, *Within Her Power: Propertied Women in Colonial Virginia* (New York: Routledge, 2002); and Joan R. Gundersen and Gwen Victor Gampel, "Married Women's Legal Status in Eighteenth-Century New York and Virginia," *William and Mary Quarterly*, 3rd ser., 39 (1982): 116–33.

16. On the clash between English and nonconjugal-centered households in early America, see Carole Shammas, *A History of Household Government in America* (Charlottesville: University of Virginia Press, 2002), 20–21, 43–44. On coverture and the law of domestic relations, see Linda K. Kerber, *No Constitutional Right to Be Ladies: Women and the Obligations of Citizenship* (New York: Hill and Wang, 1998), 12, 15; Linda K. Kerber, "A Constitutional Right to Be Treated like American Ladies: Women and the Obligations of Citizenship," in *U.S. History as Women's History*, ed. Linda K. Kerber, Alice Kessler Harris, and Katherine Kish Sklar (Chapel Hill: University of North Carolina Press, 1995), 21; and Brewer, "Transformation of Domestic Law," 288–323. On the evolution of the law of slavery and race in early Virginia, see generally Anthony S. Parent, *Foul Means: The Formation of a Slave Society in Virginia, 1660–1740* (Chapel Hill: University of North Carolina Press, 2006); Brown, *Good Wives*; and Morgan, *American Slavery*.

17. Kerber, *No Constitutional Right to Be Ladies*, 12, 15. See also Kerber, "A Constitutional Right," 21; Brewer, "Transformation of Domestic Law," 297–311.

18. Emphasis mine. NCO, 1664–74, f. 122.

19. Dinah (1704), Daniel (1706), Frances (1708), Ann (1711), Elizabeth (1713), Elisha (1716), and Abimelech (1720). See Heinegg, *Free African Americans*, for the genealogy.

20. Holly Brewer, *By Birth or Consent: Children, Law, and the Anglo-American Revolution in Authority* (Chapel Hill: University of North Carolina Press, 2005), 273. The terms of service for mixed-race children depended on the marital status of their parents. Because the Webb children were born to married parents, their terms of service could be negotiated; mixed-race children born out of wedlock, however, faced statutory indentures that lasted until they were thirty or thirty-one years of age; see Hening, *Statutes at Large*, 3:87, 452–53; 4:133.

21. Brewer, *By Birth or Consent*, 12, 255–58, 271–75; Kerber, *No Constitutional Right to Be Ladies*, 52–53; and Christopher Tomlins, "Law, Population, Labor," in *The Cambridge History of American Law*, ed. Michael Grossberg and Christopher Tomlins (New York: Cambridge University Press, 2008), 232–39.

22. Petition of Thomas Savage, February 10, 1725, Northampton County Free Negro and Slave Records.

23. The court order notes the indenture of Dinah, Daniel, and Frances Webb but does not specify a term other than "according to law," March 21, 1710/11, NCO, no. 15, f. 10; see also *Webb v. Savage* (1723), and Indenture dated April 17, 1711, Northampton County Free Negro and Slave Records.

24. Petition of Jane Webb, August 22, 1722, Northampton County Free Negro and Slave Records.

25. William Gooch to Alured Popple, May 18, 1736, in Emory G. Evans, "A Question of Complexion: Documents concerning the Negro and the Franchise in Eighteenth-Century Virginia," *Virginia Magazine of History and Biography* 71 (1963): 414. Despite the 1736 date, Gooch was writing about legislation enacted in 1723.

26. Hening, *Statutes at Large*, 4:132 (manumission) and 133 (terms of service for children of mixed-race women servants).

27. George Harmanson was both a justice and a burgess who represented Northampton County in 1720–22 and 1723–26; see H. R. McIlwaine, ed., *Journals of the House of Burgesses of Virginia, 1712–14, 1715, 1718, 1720–22, 1723–26* (Richmond: Virginia State Library, 1912), x–xi.

28. McIlwaine, *Journals of the House of Burgesses, 1723–26*, 369.

29. Hening, *Statutes at Large*, 4:133.

30. *Webb v. Savage*, NCJ, 1727-001. The suit was subsequently dismissed; see NCO, no. 18, 1722–29, f. 287. By 1705, slaves could not be witnesses in trials against whites; in 1723, the law prevented free black men from voting; and in 1732 the law prevented free blacks from serving as witnesses in trials against whites (Hening, *Statutes at Large*, 3:298, 4:133, 327).

31. NCO, 1722–29, no. 18, July 12, 1726, f. 247.

32. Ibid., July 13, 1726, f. 248, emphasis mine.

33. NCO, March 21, 1710/11, f. 10; NCO, 1722–29, March 11, 1725 (Dinah's petition), April 14, 1725 (discharge judgment), ff. 17, 179; ibid., November 15, 1727, f. 304. Petition of Dinah Manley, February 12, 1727, Northampton County Free Negro and Slave Records; Bill of Sale, *Elisha Webb v. Daniel Wentworth*, Provincial Court Records, no. 26121 (1739), NHSA.

34. The indenture was demanded by Savage. See Petition of Thomas Savage, February 10, 1725, Northampton County Free Negro and Slave Records.

35. Bill of Sale, *Elisha Webb v. Daniel Wentworth*, Provincial Court Records, no. 26121 (1739), NHSA. See also Robert Dishman, "Breaking the Bonds: The Role of New Hampshire's Courts in Freeing Those Wrongly Enslaved, 1640–1740s," *Historical New Hampshire* 59 (2005): 86–91; and Catherine Adams and Elizabeth H. Pleck, *Love of Freedom: Black Women in Colonial and Revolutionary New England* (New York: Oxford University Press, 2010), 136. Both incorrectly identify Elisha's mother as a white woman. On black Portsmouth, see also Mark J. Sammons and Valerie Cunningham, *Black Portsmouth: Three Centuries of African-American Heritage* (Durham: University of New Hampshire Press, 2004).

36. Elisha eventually married the enslaved Cesar, who was owned by a Portsmouth shipping merchant, so perhaps it was through such connections that she got her letter to Virginia. Slaves regularly managed coastal vessels in the West Indies, the Chesapeake, and the lower South; see W. Jeffrey Bolster, *Black Jacks: African American Seamen in the Age of Sail* (Cambridge, Mass.: Harvard University Press, 1997), 129–570.

37. Col. Thomas Cable to Elisha Webb, July 28, 1740, *Webb v. Wentworth*, NHSA.

38. Esther Savage to Elisha Webb, March 23, 1739/40, ibid. Thomas Savage III was the son of Thomas Savage II, who made the original contract with Webb. The younger Savage, who died in 1739, sold Elisha to the ship captain. Esther was his widow.

39. Thomas Cable to Elisha Webb, July 28, 1740, ibid. See also the affirmation of Esther Savage and the Depositions of John Savage and Margaret Ellegood, ibid.

40. Affirmation of Esther Savage and Depositions of John Savage and Margaret Ellegood, ibid.

41. Esther Savage to Elisha Webb, March 23, 1739/40; Thomas Cable to Elisha Webb, July 28, 1740, ibid.

42. Dishman, "Breaking the Bonds," 89.

43. For the reference to the "free malatto formerly Jane Williams," see Petition of Jane Webb, August 22, 1722, Northampton County Free Negro and Slave Records.

44. In 1725 "Jane Lef malatto" was listed under "Masters of Families" on the Northampton County Tithable list; see John B. Bell, *Northampton County, Virginia, Tithables, 1720–1769* (Bowie, Md.: Heritage, 1993), 94, 102. See also "Webb Family" at www.freeafricanamericans.com (accessed January 24, 2012). For Jane Left's burial record, see Howard Mackey, *Vestry Book of Hungar's Parish, Northampton County, Virginia, 1757–1785* (Camden, Maine: Picton, 1997), 19.

Clementina Rind

Widowed Printer of Williamsburg

MARTHA J. KING

It was not a typical sweltering summer day in Williamsburg on August 21, 1773. The newly widowed Clementina Rind, the mother of a brood of small children, had just bid farewell to her late husband, William Rind, a public printer for the Virginia colony and the editor of the *Virginia Gazette*. William had died two days earlier. On the day of the funeral, the Williamsburg fraternity of the Free and Accepted Masons met at midafternoon in their lodge in the colonial capital and then gathered at the Rind house on Duke of Gloucester Street; "after staying there as long as the necessary preparations required," they processed "before the Corpse" in the order of their rank. The widow Rind, her fatherless children, and other inhabitants followed behind the casket to the service and burial at Bruton Parish Church. The Reverend John Dixon, a professor of divinity at the College of William and Mary, delivered the sermon, and Peter Pelham played an organ dirge.[1] When the service was over, the late printer's fellow Masons paid their respects and then solemnly escorted the family back to the door of their home before retiring to the lodge. A bereft and "most grateful" Clementina paused in the doorway to her rented two-story Georgian tenement after an exhausting and emotionally draining day.[2]

At that moment of departure, Clementina Rind stood at a threshold—both literally and symbolically—as she looked back on her past and faced an uncertain future. Unusually literate for her time and place, the Williamsburg woman, born about 1740, had married around the age of twenty-five to William Rind, the apprentice printer and eventual partner of Jonas Green in Annapolis, Maryland.[3] The Rinds moved to Williamsburg in late 1765, in the midst of the Stamp Act crisis, when William accepted an invitation to establish a free and open press at the urging of several patriot-minded Virginia politicians, including Thomas Jefferson.[4]

William Rind's *Virginia Gazette* premiered on May 16, 1766, publishing under the lofty motto "Open to All Parties, but Influenced by None." The Rind *Virginia Gazette* was neither the first nor last newspaper by this name in the history of the Old Dominion. In 1736, William Parks established the first *Virginia Gazette* in Williamsburg and was succeeded as printer on his death by his journeyman, William Hunter. When Hunter died in 1761, the printing office had a succession of owners, including Joseph Royle and the Scotsman Alexander Purdie. In 1765, before William Rind's arrival in Williamsburg, Purdie, in partnership with John Dixon, published a newspaper whose masthead promised to deliver "the freshest advices, both foreign and domestick." In late 1774, however, Purdie dissolved the partnership to start another rival *Virginia Gazette*.[5]

In addition to producing regular issues of the weekly *Gazette* from his Williamsburg printing office, the young William Rind issued almanacs, sold stationery items, bound books, did government job work, and printed blank forms, while Clementina dutifully cared for their five children (William, John, Charles, James, and Maria) in a household that also included a kinsman, John Pinkney, who may have been William's brother-in-law, and Dick, a black slave who probably worked as a semiskilled artisan. Isaac Collins, who had worked for the Wilmington printer James Adams, served the final year of his apprenticeship in the Rind household until he turned twenty-one and headed to Philadelphia in 1767 to become a journeyman printer.[6]

William's death in August 1773 left the Rind household without its master printer, husband, and father. As Clementina traversed the liminal space that Saturday morning after the funeral, she was not simply retreating to a private domestic life but also entering a public arena as a printer's widow. Home and work were integrally tied. With living quarters and printing office under the same roof, it is likely that Clementina and her older children had worked alongside William Rind. In many ways the colonial printing office was a family enterprise with wife and children receiving an informal apprenticeship in the trade. Spouses shared economic goals, and both work and family prosperity relied on the cooperation of and negotiation with the members of the entire family unit, though the extent of a woman's direct participation in the artisanal trade of her husband varied and often depended on her place in the life cycle and the needs of her family. But printers' wives often acted as almost silent partners, working in the printing office without advertising their activities or seeking public sanction for their contributions.[7]

BEING now unhappily forced to enter upon Business on my own Account, I flatter myself those Gentlemen who shall continue to oblige me with their Custom will not be offended at my requesting them, in future, to be punctual in sending Cash with Advertisements, &c. The ardent Desire I have of rendering this Paper as useful and entertaining as possible urges the Necessity of attending to this Request, as it must be obvious to every one that Business of so extensive a Nature cannot be carried on with that Spirit which is necessary, without a sufficient Fund to support it: Mine, in great Measure, depends on the Punctuality of those who favour me with their Commands. May that All Ruling Power, whose chastening Hand has snatched from my dear Infants and myself our whole Dependence, make me equal to the Task! An unaffected Desire to please, an indefatigable Attention to my Business, and the Assistance of Persons whose Abilities and Attachment I can rely on, will, I hope, make me not entirely unworthy of Encouragement from the Public in general, and from the Honourable House of Burgesses in particular; whose Favour I once more take the Liberty to solicit, and in whose generous Breasts it lies to bestow Happiness and Plenty on my orphan Family, if they find me capable of being their Servant. Cheared by that pleasing Hope, I will try to support, with Fortitude, the painful Sensation of Incertainty, by a firm Reliance on that Candour and Generosity, which have ever been the Characteristic of that honourable Body.

I am, with great Respect,
The Public's most faithful,
And most obedient,
CLEMENTINA RIND.

WILLIAMSBURG, September 2, 1773.

C. RIND, *VIRGINIA GAZETTE*, SEPTEMBER 2, 1773

In this first issue printed after her husband's death, Clementina Rind announced her plan to continue his printing business. She also pledged to make her newspaper "useful and entertaining" and exhorted her customers to continue their subscriptions and her advertisers to be punctual in their payments.

Special Collections, John D. Rockefeller Jr. Library,
The Colonial Williamsburg Foundation.

A SUMMARY VIEW OF THE RIGHTS OF BRITISH AMERICA
The author of this work was not identified on its title page but was known to be the Virginia patriot Thomas Jefferson. The full name of its printer, Clementina Rind, however, boldly appeared on this important Revolutionary-era pamphlet, printed in Williamsburg in 1774. Library of Congress, Rare Book and Special Collections Division.

Clementina's perceived security had dimmed as her husband's health waned. After "sustaining a tedious and painful illness with the most Christian fortitude,"[8] William eventually died on August 19, 1773, at the age of thirty-nine. Rival printer Alexander Purdie, a recently remarried widower, and his business partner, John Dixon, noted William's death that day in their own *Gazette*: "He was a Gentleman of a very amiable Character, being a tender Husband, a kind parent, an indulgent Master, and a faithful Servant of the Publick."[9] The following week they added, "His Impartiality in the Conduct of his Gazette . . . cannot fail of securing to his Memory the Esteem of all who are sensible how much the Freedom of the Press contributes to maintain and extend the most sacred Rights of Humanity."[10] With his brief life over and few printed words to mark his passing, William might have soon faded from memory.

As the caretaker of her husband's legacy, Clementina played an important role in safeguarding William's reputation, and in doing so, helped to secure her own place in the political, economic, and religious life of her community. The funeral and highly ritualized burial customs commonplace in eighteenth-century Anglican Virginia restored order to the public sphere and maintained patriarchal structures. While a grieving widow might be stoic in her participation in the typical observances of Virginia deathways, including mourning clothes, postmortem meals, and a formalized order for the location and burial of the deceased, her individual response to widowhood was unique.[11] Widowhood was a life-changing event, and what ensued for Clementina was constant adaptation. William's death created the potential and opportunity—and, indeed, the need—for her to negotiate and to some extent transform her position in her community's gendered social hierarchy. During her thirteen-month tenure as Virginia's public printer and the editor of Rind's *Virginia Gazette*, Clementina would carefully navigate the boundaries that both informed and constrained women's status in pre-Revolutionary Virginia. She would also play a significant, if short-lived, role in the public life of the colony.

Like other eighteenth-century widows, Clementina Rind's legal status changed on the death of her spouse. While a married woman's legal identity was subsumed under that of her husband according to the English common-law doctrine of coverture, widowed women had more legal rights. As a *feme sole* (single woman), a widow could buy and sell property, sue and be sued in court, execute a power of attorney, act as the executor or administrator of an estate, sign and receive documents, and initiate legal and commercial transactions in her own name. When a man died without making a will, the law also guaranteed his widow her dower right to a life interest in one-third of his land and slaves.

Virginia widows were entitled to their dower bequests—the so-called widow's third—in real property and in a comparable amount of personal property forever. Some widows fared even better and were allowed more than their third. Yet though these colonial laws may have helped a widow to survive economically, they rarely fostered her autonomy or independence.[12]

A widow could wallow in her grief and depend on friends and kin, remarry if the opportunity presented itself, or muster the strength to do the best she could for a family suddenly deprived of the economic support of its head of household. Scholars have acknowledged women's participation in the southern colonial economy, but they disagree about how to interpret the significance of women's involvement in business and other public matters. Some historians argue that women typically acted conservatively in order to protect the interests of their male kin, rather than seeking autonomy and promoting their own interests. Others see widowhood mainly as a source of women's temporary independence. Still others contend that widows who did not remarry were constantly negotiating the space between home and community and that they were not marginal—but rather central—to both, neither overturning nor supporting the male-dominated gender hierarchy.[13]

Clementina's response to her altered life situation was rooted in immediacy. On September 2, 1773, only two weeks after her husband's demise, she lamented publicly in the *Gazette* what weighed heavily in her heart:

> Being now unhappily forced to enter upon Business on my own Account, I flatter myself those Gentlemen who shall continue to oblige me with their Custom will not be offended at my requesting them, in future, to be punctual in sending Cash with Advertisements.... May that All Ruling Power, whose chastening Hand has snatched from my dear Infants and myself our whole Dependence, make me equal to the Task! An unaffected Desire to please, an indefatigable Attention to my Business, and the Assistance of Persons whose Abilities and Attachment I can rely on, will, I hope, make me not entirely unworthy of Encouragement from the Public in general, and from the Honourable House of Burgesses in particular; whose Favour I once more take the Liberty to solicit, and in whose generous Breast it lies to bestow Happiness and Plenty on my orphan Family, if they find me capable of being their Servant.[14]

This public statement of her plight revealed dependency, self-doubt, and anxious uncertainty. Like many young widows, she used a language of deference and expressed a lack of confidence in her own abilities, along with an almost victimized sense of God's fate at work in her life.

At the same time, Clementina's lament reflected her conscientiousness and also her implicit role in the family business prior to her newly assumed *feme sole* status. Like other widows of working men, Clementina had to balance the need to mourn with the need to take action. These women did not have the luxury to linger nostalgically over memories of a bygone married life. There were mouths to be fed, bodies to be clothed and cared for, bills to be paid, and accounts to be reconciled. While death and short life expectancies were ever-present realities in colonial societies riddled with fevers, fires, wars, and natural disasters, life for the survivors—with all its demands—had to go on. Widowhood was so common that many people fully expected widows to express emotional distress while simultaneously shouldering many of their late husbands' responsibilities, including supervising the family finances and dealing with merchants, apprentices, and subscribers.[15]

William Rind may even have unknowingly helped prepare his wife for this solo state when he published "The Widower's Soliloquy" in his *Gazette* on New Year's Eve 1772. The author of this advice column cautioned against immoderate grief for the dead. A proper tribute of tears and sorrow was acceptable, but not to the neglect of duty and the business of life.[16] Clementina probably had seen and read this piece and recalled its wisdom as she confronted her own changed life in the wake of the loss of her spouse.

Widowhood not only marked a profound shift in a woman's legal status but also presented her with the opportunity to reevaluate her dependence on others and find new reserves of strength within herself. New rights to manage land, control property, enter into contracts, and execute a will or deed came with additional responsibilities. Moreover, a widow typically lost both the prestige and income she had enjoyed previously because of her husband's standing in the community. After William's death, Clementina faced the probable loss of most of her family's material possessions. In less than a month, the deputy sheriff of Williamsburg announced a sale to be held on October 2 at the family's home of "all the estate of the said Rind, consisting of household and kitchen furniture." The estate needed to be settled to pay off William's creditors.[17]

Clementina had much to lose. An inventory of William's estate taken on September 27, 1773, by the rival printers Purdie and Dixon with John Pinkney and Robert Prentis appraised his property at just over £272. William's estate included sheets, pillowcases, silver teaspoons, a tea table, mahogany chairs, a fish kettle, coal, two cows, and a slave named Dick, who was valued at £30. William's printing equipment, which consisted of two presses, four typefaces, and many assorted printing tools, was worth more than anything else in the house. Clementina could potentially lose many of these possessions and also the family residence. On September 30, the owner of the house that William had leased placed an advertisement in the widow's *Virginia Gazette*, announcing the sale of three Williamsburg tenements, including "the brick house on the Main Street where Mrs. Rind lives."[18]

While Clementina had to move from her lodgings and part with some of the family's accumulated household goods, she managed to keep her husband's printing equipment, clearly her most valuable possession. Continued use of the printing press gave her a chance for survival and respectability. Because William had been the public printer when he died, Clementina as his widow could justify her need to continue his work to make good on his contract with Virginia's colonial government. Although William's outstanding debts had to be paid on his death, and the contents of his household were offered for sale to pay his creditors and settle his estate, his widow was able to purchase on six months' credit some of these family goods, including the printing equipment. When full payment came due in April 1774, Clementina executed a deed of trust with Williamsburg mayor John Blair and three other gentlemen. She listed as security for this timely loan the printing press and the very household goods she had purchased earlier.[19]

Despite her diminished means as a new widow, Clementina had at least one significant model for approaching this new phase of her life. Prior to moving to Williamsburg, her husband had apprenticed and then partnered with the Annapolis printer Jonas Green, who may have been a member of William's extended family. Sometime during the men's seven-year business partnership, which lasted from 1758 to 1765, Clementina married William and came to know the master printer's wife, Anne Catharine Hoof Green. The Greens and the Rinds worked together; they also may have lived near each other and worshiped at the same church. William was a godparent for more than one of the Greens' children when they were presented for baptism at St. Anne's Parish Church in Annapolis.[20] It is likely that the printers' wives maintained a cordial association, if not a more personal friendship, since their husbands' work and lives were so closely joined. After the dissolution of the Green-Rind printing partnership and the Rinds' departure from Maryland, the opportunity for regular interaction undoubtedly grew less frequent, but Anne Catharine's experience as a printer's widow in Annapolis would presage Clementina's.

A year after the Rinds moved to Virginia, an April 1767 issue of the *Maryland Gazette* announced the death of Jonas Green, who had been the printer to the province for twenty-eight years and the editor of the *Maryland Gazette* for twenty-one. Anne Catharine mourned his death by printing on the second page of the *Gazette* in a box bordered with bold double black lines a brief obituary in which she expressed her grief over "the Loss of him, in the various Stations of

Husband, Parent, Master and Companion."[21] In the same issue of the newspaper, she solicited the support of her subscribers. The mother of fourteen children, eight of whom had died in infancy, she appealed to her readers in a deferential style but fully noted the faithful service of her late husband and the hope that her right to follow in his steps had been clearly established. Although Jonas had died intestate, Anne Catharine managed to circumvent any debate about the legitimacy of her newly assumed role as a printer. As the widow of Jonas Green, she relied on an almost unspoken claim to succeed her husband. Anne Catharine cast her managerial efforts and her work as a printer as part of her wifely duties in compliance with her late husband's wishes. She requested the favor of her subscribers, described her "numerous Family" as being "almost destitute of Support," and stated her desire to supply her customers on the same terms and conditions that her late spouse had. Acknowledging the interdependence of their enterprise, she and her son pledged to continue as public printers with the kind indulgence and encouragement of their readers.[22]

For almost nine months after Jonas Green's death, his widow continued to operate the *Maryland Gazette* under her own name and to act as the public printer for the colony. In the latter capacity, she published the *Laws of Maryland* and *Votes and Proceedings of the Lower House of Assembly of the Province of Maryland*; her shop also produced *The Maryland Almanack for the Year 1768*. The widowed mother printed alone and in partnership with her three sons, William, Frederick, and Samuel, for nearly eight years until her own death in March 1775. The Maryland widow undoubtedly learned of Clementina's widowhood since the Greens' newspaper ran a reprint of William Rind's obituary in mid-September 1773.[23]

Whether Clementina considered a similar partnership with her own young sons, her relative John Pinkney, or other male printers is not known, but she proceeded "on her own account" as a printer in Williamsburg for thirteen months after the death of her spouse. Both Anne Catharine Green and Clementina Rind addressed their respective plights in print, alerting their communities to their husbands' deaths and their own new status as widows, and articulating the need for their neighbors' ongoing support as they carried on their husbands' trade and made a living for themselves and their dependents. Neither widow remarried.

By the middle of the eighteenth century, the dominant trend was for widows to avoid remarrying. One reason for this change was that women had fewer opportunities to remarry because of increasingly even sex ratios and the demographic reality that women usually married men older than themselves, thus decreasing the pool of marriageable men for widowed women. While Virginia widows often had remarried in the seventeenth and early eighteenth centuries, by 1750 they were less likely to do so. Only one-fourth of the colony's widows remarried in the decades before 1776, and this figure dropped to one-fifth in the post-Revolutionary era.[24]

Cultural and economic concerns reinforced the tendency of widows not to marry again. Some eighteenth-century moralists cautioned that by remarrying a woman would dishonor her deceased husband. Others urged widows to cultivate thrift, piety, and benevolence toward their dependents rather than pursuing a new spouse. Affluent and middling widows stood to lose wealth or property on remarriage, and any widow lost her *feme sole* status when she took a new husband. Whereas men were socialized to pursue self-interest, a widow who suddenly found herself responsible for her family's financial situation had to learn this trait by necessity, even though in so doing she challenged common notions about women's supposedly domestic nature and the prevailing sexual division of labor.[25]

In Clementina's case, religion offered additional material and spiritual support in widowhood. Indeed, Clementina's involvement in Williamsburg's Anglican community may have ameliorated her difficult situation as a single female head of household. Membership in a faith community such as the Bruton Parish Church provided a ready-made safety net for families in need. The tenets of Christian charity toward widows and orphans helped to keep food on one's table, at least temporarily. Additionally, the religiously themed publications that Clementina offered for sale—pocket Bibles, Common Prayer books, and hymnals—found a ready market among her fellow believers and added a revenue stream to the Rind household. These religious publications were part of Clementina's larger commercial business of selling legal blanks, handbills, broadsides, pamphlets, stationery, and paper, which supplemented her income from the *Virginia Gazette* and her public printing contract, just as it had done when William ran the family business.[26]

Widows' use of material and social resources to support their children revealed not only their new status as heads of households in the absence of fathers but also a broader pattern of reciprocal assistance among kin and within associational and occupational communities. In addition to appealing to gendered tropes of feminine weakness, widows could rely on aid from family and other personal connections. Such mutual exchanges within Williamsburg's small community of printers help explain why widows remained involved in managing businesses and households even after their sons reached manhood. Clementina's kinsman John Pinkney assisted her in the printing office, and after her death he continued the *Virginia Gazette* briefly for the benefit of her estate and later to help her children before he moved to North Carolina. Another Williamsburg printer, John Dixon, became guardian of the Rind children in February 1776, and the local Masonic lodge apportioned money for the children's maintenance, clothing, and education (at least for William and John) as late as 1779.[27]

Maternal obligation often gave widows such as Clementina a legitimate justification for taking on unconventional public roles. They acted not solely for themselves or even as extensions of their deceased husbands but rather out of a single parent's devotion to their dependents' best interests. Clementina expressed to readers of her *Virginia Gazette* in April 1774 her "grateful thanks" and a desire to continue with the "public business . . . whereby I may make a tolerable provision for myself and children."[28] She thus presented herself as a wise negotiator and especially as a self-sacrificing parent. Some widowed printers also used the tropes of maternal devotion and female vulnerability in their encounters with the patriarchal structures of their respective colonial legislatures. Rather than being saddled by unpaid debts due to them or denied opportunities for government printing contracts, some widows confronted the authorities with moderate success—all the while maintaining their gendered language of deference.[29]

When Virginia's House of Burgesses convened in May 1774, an important order of business was to elect a printer for the colony. Three printers submitted separate petitions to be considered for the government job: Clementina Rind (continuing in the place of her late husband), Alexander Purdie, and John Dixon. When the votes were tallied, the burgesses recorded sixty votes for the widow to act alone, twenty-five votes for her to act in conjunction with rival printer Purdie, and two votes for her to act jointly with rival Dixon. The burgesses all agreed that Clementina should have some share of the government printing, and no one had considered hiring her merely to assist one of her male competitors. The crux of the ballot decision rested on whether she would act in a solo or joint capacity. The assembly overwhelmingly gave its support to Clementina Rind acting alone, because she had demonstrated over the previous nine months since the death of her husband and in the completion of his contract not only that she needed the work to provide for her family but, equally important, that she was capable of maintaining the printing operation "on her own account."[30]

As the burgesses doubtless knew, Clementina Rind's *Virginia Gazette*, a four-page weekly issued on Thursdays, retained much of the character and content of her husband's newspaper, though she also took some subtle steps to make the newspaper her own. Despite employing the language of polite deference, she continued the paper under her own name.[31] Her paper had the usual news from Europe as well as intelligence from colonial ports and cities. It also included poems and acrostics, lighthearted bantering between the sexes, and more descriptive death notices than were printed in some of her contemporaries' papers.[32] In April 1774, moreover, a month before the burgesses met, Clementina announced plans to enlarge her paper and to acquire an "elegant set of types from London" in an effort to support the "dignity of her gazette." A shrewd but possibly risky move, acquiring expensive new type would make her paper distinctive and stylish, while the smaller typeface would allow her to publish more news at a time when deteriorating relations with Great Britain made politics routinely newsworthy. By the end of June 1774 the new type had arrived, and Clementina's *Virginia Gazette* appeared in the much smaller font. While she had difficulty collecting what she was owed from some subscribers and advertisers, she noted her gratitude toward those who were "punctual in their payments," including Thomas Jefferson and George Washington, and thanked those who continued to do business with her. She also reminded delinquent customers to send prompt cash payments or settle with her at the meeting of the next General Court.[33]

In printing the newspaper, Clementina admittedly depended on the aid of a wide network of friends, subscribers, and neighbors, and she certainly benefited from living in a colonial capital with its constellations of kin, friends, colleagues, and strangers visiting from the Tidewater to the Piedmont and beyond. Besides family connections, Clementina relied on other women in the community to help support her family, and she constructed social and business networks, extending friendship ties to widen her subscription and customer bases.

Print culture helped some women to extend their geographic and social reach and allowed Clementina in particular to participate in the day-to-day commercial life of the colony. Through the advertisements in her *Gazette*, she fostered (and profited from) the burgeoning commercial growth of the British Atlantic world and supported the efforts of merchants and artisans in Williamsburg and beyond. She was also part of a large informal economy of women. In addition to posting notices of ship arrivals in the James, York, or Rappahannock rivers and alerts about runaway slaves and servants, her newspaper included advertisements from women shopkeepers who operated in ways not unlike she did. The pages of the *Virginia Gazette* were full of notices for and by milliners, cooks, tavern keepers, school mistresses, maids, midwives, and other traditionally female occupations—all local women whose skills and services were offered for a price by themselves or others acting as their agents.[34] Jane Vobe ran several taverns, the last being the King's Arms Tavern, which she operated from 1772 to

1789. Margaret Hunter ran a successful millinery business in a brick shop in the 1770s and 1780s. Elizabeth Dickinson's store advertised jewelry and millinery in 1773. Jane Charlton and Catherine Rathell ran competing millinery and jewelry shops, and Clementina included advertisements from them both, sometimes in adjacent columns of her *Gazette*.[35] From 1767 to 1789, Hannah Ludwell Lee was the owner of Ludwell Paradise House, which for a time Clementina and her family leased as their office and residence.[36]

Notices placed by these women reveal the real connection between women's work and Atlantic commerce as vital conduits in the supply of imported goods to local consumers. Williamsburg's wealth and continued commercial ties to England made shopkeeping a viable female livelihood and allowed Virginia women to emerge as debtors and creditors in their own right. Most women, like Clementina, did not have extensive international credit, but they often had credit locally, especially in their immediate neighborhoods. Whether she sought to buy, rent, or sell goods for herself in the marketplace or whether she simply facilitated the ability of others to do so, as a printer Clementina suddenly had increased status and key community connections. The simple words often placed at the end of an advertisement, "enquire of the printer hereof," subtly attest to the true power of printers in these neighborhood transactions.[37]

Clementina also asserted herself as a responsible gatekeeper of information in her neighborhood by setting editorial standards and refusing to publish unsigned letters in her newspaper. In late December 1773, she defended herself against attacks by rival printers Purdie and Dixon, who accused her of partiality in refusing to publish an exposé of a recent scandal, which, in their view, was the "only Method by which the guilty Great might be punished." Clementina disagreed, declaring that her newspaper would not be a vehicle for spreading gossip about matters that related to "individuals only." As the editor and publisher, she would not "indiscriminately" print everything she was offered, and she especially recoiled at the prospect of publishing anonymous allegations. Clementina argued that the allegations of the anonymous author, known only as "An Attentive Observer," would be better reviewed in a court of law than in the columns of her paper. In response to her critics' strident complaints that her refusal to publish the item amounted to a restriction on the freedom of the press, she asserted that she was "not conscious of having deviated from that Spirit of freedom which I shall always think it my duty to maintain."[38]

In August 1774, on the one-year anniversary of her assuming the editorship of the *Virginia Gazette*, Clementina printed a lengthy reminder to her customers and an eloquent accounting of her own understanding of her role as a printer. Hopeful for restored health after an undisclosed illness, she announced "her particular endeavor to amuse and instruct and, at the same time, her firm determination, ever to preserve the *dignity* of her paper."[39] In the pages of her *Gazette*, Clementina carefully balanced her public editorial independence and her personal economic dependence on her subscribers and fellow Virginians.

Clementina also expressed interest in the "other," or those whose race and class made them different from herself. The arrival of Lady Dunmore (Charlotte Stewart Murray), the aristocratic wife of the royal governor, and her six children in Virginia's colonial capital in March 1774 brought "great joy to the inhabitants" and the newsworthy spectacle of British high society. Clementina covered the ensuing cannon salutes in Yorktown, the illuminated houses and fireworks in Williamsburg, and the throngs of people who gathered to watch the entourage pass in their fancy carriages. She included a poem to mark the occasion, "Hail, Noble Charlotte," in her *Gazette* as well. Seeking to appeal to genteel readers and perhaps most especially to women, Clementina included more detailed coverage of Lady Dunmore's arrival and her reception by the townspeople of Williamsburg than any of her contemporaries did in their newspapers.[40]

While both Clementina Rind and her rivals often ran advertisements from the same customers or items on similar topics, Clementina's unusual concern with the less fortunate members of her community is evident. News of the opening in 1773 of the new Public Hospital for Persons of Insane and Disordered Minds, the first hospital in the colonies for the mentally ill, appeared in both her paper and Purdie and Dixon's. But in January 1774, she alone included "A letter on the Improvement of the Mind. Addressed to a Young Lady," in which the author urged benevolence and charitable giving to the downtrodden no matter what the stage of one's life. In April 1774 she and her competitors printed an announcement for a meeting for a fund for the relief of widows and orphans. The next month, however, only her printing office produced for sale a sermon preached in Bruton Parish Church for the relief of poor widows and orphans of clergymen in Virginia. Perhaps Clementina's own fate as a widow increased her sensitivity to the need for charity on behalf of others who had suffered losses. Yet her charity did not extend to everyone. Reacting to news from the West, she asserted in September 1774, "The Indians are daily committing some murder or other. Their cruel and inhuman treatment towards the people on the frontiers loudly calls for vengeance."[41]

Nor did Clementina's words or actions indicate any discomfort with the institution of slavery. As a printer, Clementina served as a channel of information about slaves for sale and hire, slave ship arrivals, slave auctions and uprisings, and slave runaways, all with their richly descriptive summaries of tribal origins, physical characteristics, clothing, and their relative value as set by the return reward. As a slave owner herself, Clementina benefited from the work done by her enslaved man Dick, and by the extra money he could earn for her, if she chose to hire him out. We do not know whether Clementina was a stern or benevolent slave mistress, but we do know that she relied heavily on Dick, who most likely had at least some basic literacy from his employment in the printing office.

While Clementina took seriously the motto of her *Gazette* to be open to all parties, the newspaper became increasingly more partisan in the course of the thirteen months in which she printed it on her own in part because her tenure as printer coincided with heightened colonial resistance to British imperial policies. If news of the destruction of the tea in Boston harbor in December 1773 sparked the further boycotting of British goods, the passage of the Coercive Acts, with their "intolerable" closure of the port of Boston, was met with an explosion of patriotic animosity against the British in the columns and pages of the *Virginia Gazette*. Clementina felt obligated, as a patriotic publisher of intelligence "at a time when the liberties of the colonies are daringly infringed," to expose any illegal or arbitrary measures by Britain toward the colonies.[42]

The Rind *Gazette* under William's control had carried articles on the major political and constitutional issues of the time, including the nonimportation agreements, the repeal of the Townshend duties on imports in 1770, and warnings of Parliament's encroachments on colonists' liberties and rights. As a shaper of political consciousness and with an awareness of British injustices moving closer to home, Clementina followed suit and included news of the Virginia legislature's resolution, in May 1774, to have a day of public fasting and prayer in solidarity with the New England patriots. When Governor Dunmore dissolved the House of Burgesses in outrage over this resolution, the legislators reconvened just down the street at Williamsburg's Raleigh Tavern. In June 1774 Clementina reported the arrival of "fresh advices" from a vessel from Philadelphia and concluded they contained "material pieces relative to the unhappy disputes now subsisting in America." She promised her readers a supplement especially "when we consider that the proceedings of the firm, animated, and patriotic conduct, of all the colonies, must be agreeable to every native of this country, and all others who wish well to the rights and liberties of AMERICA." The pages of Clementina's *Gazette* throughout the summer of 1774 were replete with patriotic expressions of support for the plight of Boston. Her editorial coverage reflected the important role Virginia played in unifying sentiment against British imperial authority as extralegal colonial conventions gained legitimacy and popularity.[43]

In August 1774 Clementina printed *A Summary View of the Rights of British America*, a pamphlet written by Thomas Jefferson, which was crucial in the development of the Revolutionary ideology that ultimately justified independence.[44] According to its preface, *A Summary View* was intended to convey the sentiments of a delegate who was prevented by illness from attending the Virginia Convention in Williamsburg, and "without the knowledge of the author, we have ventured to communicate his sentiments to the public."[45] Although the pamphlet was an attack on King George III, it affirmed the colonists' recognition of the authority of the British monarch while denying the powers of Parliament. The delegates to the Virginia Convention in Williamsburg that August selected Peyton Randolph, Richard Henry Lee, George Washington, Patrick Henry, Richard Bland, Benjamin Harrison, and Edmund Pendleton to represent them in the Continental Congress that would assemble in Philadelphia that fall.

Accounts of contemporary events in pre-Revolutionary Virginia filled the columns of the papers, and the dissemination of such news became a printer's bread and butter. Likewise, information about tobacco cultivation or educational reform at the College of William and Mary became not just nuggets of local news but keys to a printer's vitality in the colonial capital.[46] Just as the colonists struggled and many Virginians came to see autonomy from Great Britain as essential to their survival, Clementina Rind sought every avenue to be sure the news got out and thus provided for the security, safety, and well-being of her family. While the sources for weaving the life of an eighteenth-century woman are often frustratingly scarce and incomplete, the pages of Clementina Rind's *Virginia Gazette* and the output of her printing office provide a colorful tapestry of a year of her life as a widow at a time equally crucial in Virginia's allegiances and future.

Many colonial newspapers consisted of reprinted news and letters from other papers, and Clementina's was no exception. But the *Virginia Gazette* under her editorship was not merely a cut-and-paste operation but rather revealed her own unique interests and editorial proclivities as she exercised control over what to print and when to print it. Sometimes she offered her readers apologies for the delayed publication of a piece of news because of lack of space.[47] The two *Virginia Gazette*s in Williamsburg operated on similar publication schedules, but the issues of September 15, 1774, offer striking examples of how Clementina's paper could appeal to a different target audience. Whereas Purdie and Dixon chose to extract a 1678 sermon by Archbishop Tillotson on their front page and to highlight European news, especially from Paris and London, on their first two pages, Clementina's front page for the same date included not one but two letters focused on women's colonial response to the dreaded tea tax. She reprinted a letter from the *South Carolina Gazette* by "A Planter's Wife," who called on her sisters and countrywomen to promise "to forego use of all foreign tea." Under an August 7, 1774, Williamsburg dateline, Clementina also included a letter from the countrywomen of Virginia to the "Ladies of Pennsylvania," exhorting them "to be firm in withstanding luxuries of every kind; but above all, as the most pernicious of all, that you will (as we have universally done) banish India tea from your tables" and substitute aromatic herbals instead.

Clementina's status as a literate woman and her occupation as a printer gave her real influence over the economic fortunes of others and a central political role in her specific locale in a specific, albeit brief, time.[48] Women printers helped shape what the public read in their role as booksellers and publishers and became conduits of political news in their role as editors. As a gatekeeper and a source of information, a woman printer exercised a type of power and authority that women in other occupations simply did not have. She was at once a consumer and creator of information and a provider of access to it. Print culture uniquely positioned Rind by engaging her intellect in the diffusion of knowledge and information, establishing her in a large network of social, economic, and political connections in her Virginia community.

After only thirteen months as a widowed Virginia printer, Clementina Rind succumbed to a brief illness and died on September 25, 1774, without a will but not without public notice of her contributions to both her family and her community.[49] In a rhyming eulogy contributed by a "Constant Reader" and printed in tribute to her in the *Virginia Gazette*—now overseen by John Pinkney—the author mentioned the many roles Clementina assumed and the vital connection she provided not just to her family but to the Williamsburg community: "She answer'd well creation's utmost end; / The mistress, mother, wife, and bosom friend . . . / How sad the parting, when one fatal stroke / Those rich connections prematurely broke! / This happy neighbourhood so well approv'd / Are scatter'd up and down, one link remov'd."[50]

Just as printers were enmeshed in their neighborhood networks, widows were important figures who bound their families together. While widowhood cut the marital ties to their husbands, widowhood actually strengthened the kinship webs of friends and family in ways born of necessity and maintained through dedication, loyalty, and the desire to preserve a printing enterprise. Within the parameters of her family and community networks, and in a complex interplay of gendered notions of both dependence and independence, this widowed printer forged her own distinctive identity. A closer examination of the life and publications of Clementina Rind increases our understanding of both the limits and possibilities of women's lives in pre-Revolutionary Virginia.

NOTES

1. Purdie and Dixon, *Virginia Gazette*, August 26, 1773.

2. C. Rind, *Virginia Gazette*, August 26, 1773, 2; C. Rind, *Virginia Gazette* supplement, September 30, 1773, 2.

3. Edward Papenfuse, Archivist for the state of Maryland, suggested that Clementina Rind may have been the English immigrant Clementina Van Grierson. See letter from Clementina Van Grierson to unnamed woman, October 31, 1756, Annapolis, PRO/HCA/30/258-4932, Maryland State Archives, Annapolis.

4. Roger P. Mellen, "Thomas Jefferson and the Origins of Newspaper Competition in Pre-Revolutionary Virginia," *Journalism History* 35 (Fall 2009): 151–61. Mellen contends that it was highly unlikely that the young, inexperienced Jefferson recruited Rind to establish the rival *Virginia Gazette*. He claims that Jefferson's recollections years later that "we procured Rind" have been misinterpreted, and the "we" simply meant either the collective people of Virginia or its more radical politicians. See also William Waller Hening to Thomas Jefferson, July 8, 1809, and Jefferson to Hening, July 25, 1809, Jefferson Papers, Library of Congress, Manuscript Division.

5. See John Clyde Oswald, *Printing in the Americas* (New York: Gregg, 1937), 94, 135, 139; and Clarence S. Brigham, *History and Bibliography of American Newspapers, 1690–1820*, 2 vols. (Worcester, Mass.: American Antiquarian Society, 1947), 2:1161–63.

6. Of the Rind children, William Jr., was probably born in Maryland. In 1767 at Bruton Parish Church, John Grierson Rind was baptized with a middle name that may have been his mother's maiden name, as was customary for the time. Another son, Charles, was also baptized in this Williamsburg church the following year. See William Archer Rutherford Goodwin, *The Record of Bruton Parish Church*, ed. and rev. Mary Frances Goodwin (Richmond, Va.: Dietz, 1941), 145, 152. For Pinkney and Collins, see Rosamond Randall Beirne and Edith Rossiter Bevan, *The Hammond-Harwood House and Its Owners* (Annapolis, Md.: n.p., 1941), 39, 41; Richard F. Hixson, *Isaac Collins: A Quaker Printer in 18th Century America* (New Brunswick, N.J.: Rutgers University Press, 1968), 11–14.

7. On women as economic partners, see Susan Branson, "Women and the Family Economy in the Early Republic: The Case of Elizabeth Meredith," *Journal of the Early Republic* 16 (1996): 47–71; Julie Matthaei, *An Economic History of Women in America: Women's Work, the Sexual Division of Labor, and the Development of Capitalism* (New York: Schocken, 1982), 71; Jeanne Boydston, *Home and Work: Housework, Wages, and the Ideology of Labor in the Early Republic* (New York: Oxford University Press, 1990), 1–29; Cynthia A. Kierner, *Beyond the Household: Women's Place in the Early South, 1700–1835* (Ithaca, N.Y.: Cornell University Press, 1998), 20; Linda L. Sturtz, *Within Her Power: Propertied Women in Colonial Virginia* (New York: Routledge, 2002), esp. chap. 6.

8. C. Rind, *Virginia Gazette*, August 26, 1773, 2.

9. Purdie and Dixon, *Virginia Gazette*, August 19, 1773, 2. On March 28, 1772, Alexander Purdie had mourned the passing of his wife, Mary Purdie, the twenty-seven-year-old mother of four sons and a daughter who had died as a toddler. But the widower remarried within the year to Peachy Davenport. See *Bruton Parish Churchyard and Church: A Guide to the Tombstones, Monuments, and Mural Tablets with a Foldout Map* (Williamsburg, Va.: Bruton Parish Church, 1976), 35; W. Rind, *Virginia Gazette*, December 31, 1772.

10. Purdie and Dixon, *Virginia Gazette*, August 26, 1773, 2.

11. For death and burial customs in colonial Virginia, see John K. Nelson, *A Blessed Company: Parishes, Parsons, and Parishioners in Anglican Virginia, 1690–1776* (Chapel Hill: University of North

Carolina Press, 2001), 225–32; Lauren F. Winner, *A Cheerful and Comfortable Faith: Anglican Religious Practice in the Elite Households of Eighteenth-Century Virginia* (New Haven, Conn.: Yale University Press, 2010), esp. 151–59; Thad W. Tate, "Funerals in Eighteenth Century Virginia," *Colonial Williamsburg Research Report* 85 (1956).

12. Marylynn Salmon, *Women and the Law of Property* (Chapel Hill: University of North Carolina Press, 1986), 14; Linda E. Speth, "More than Her 'Thirds': Wives and Widows in Colonial Virginia," in Linda E. Speth and Alison Duncan Hirsch, *Women, Family, and Community in Colonial America: Two Perspectives* (New York: Routledge, 1983), 7–10.

13. Inge Dornan, "The Rise and Fall of Womanhood: Ideal and Reality in Women's Status and Experience in the Carolina Low Country," *RSA Journal* 15-16 (2004–5): 149–67; Dornan, "Masterful Women: Colonial Women Slaveholders in the Urban Low Country," *Journal of American Studies* 39 (2005): 387–88; Vivian Bruce Conger, *The Widow's Might: Widowhood and Gender in Early British America* (New York: New York University Press, 2009), 6–7, 91, 109, 113–17.

14. C. Rind, *Virginia Gazette*, September 2, 1773, 3.

15. Kirsten E. Wood, "Broken Reeds and Competent Farmers: Slaveholding Widows in the Southeastern United States, 1783–1861," *Journal of Women's History* 13 (2001): 34–57; Jan Lewis, *The Pursuit of Happiness: Family and Values in Jefferson's Virginia* (Cambridge: Cambridge University Press, 1983), 69–70, and chap. 3.

16. W. Rind, *Virginia Gazette*, December 31, 1772, 2.

17. Terri L. Premo, *Winter Friends: Women Growing Old in the New Republic, 1785–1835* (Chicago: University of Chicago Press, 1990), 29–38; Alexander Keyssar, "Widowhood in Eighteenth-Century Massachusetts: A Problem in the History of the Family," *Perspectives in American History* 8 (1974): 83; C. Rind, *Virginia Gazette*, September 23, 1773, 3.

18. "Inventory of the Estate of William Rind," *William and Mary Quarterly*, 2nd ser., 17 (1937): 53–55; C. Rind, *Virginia Gazette* supplement, September 30, 1773, 2.

19. Deed of mortgage, Clementina Rind to John Blair, Robert Miller, James Southall, John Tazewell, April 13, 1774, Virginia Historical Society, MS 2 R4715 a 1.

20. While the precise marriage date of the Rinds is not known, William was still a bachelor as late as July 1762, when he appeared in the St. Anne's Parish Vestry under a "List of Batchelors in this Parish viz . . . of the Value of £100 and under £300." See "Vestry Proceedings, St. Ann's [sic] Parish, Annapolis, Md.," *Maryland Historical Magazine* 10 (1915): 38; Lawrence C. Wroth, *A History of Printing in Colonial Maryland* (Baltimore, Md.: Typothetae of Baltimore, 1922), 85. William Rind's father, Alexander, was first married to Abigail Green, who may have been of the same family as Jonas Green; see William C. Kiessel, "The Green Family: A Dynasty of Printers," *New England Historical and Genealogical Register* 104 (April 1950): 81–93.

21. *Maryland Gazette*, April 16, 1767.

22. Ibid.

23. Ibid., September 16, 1773.

24. Speth, "More than Her 'Thirds,'" 27; Joan R. Gundersen, *To Be Useful to the World: Women in Revolutionary America, 1740–1790* (New York: Twayne, 1996), 46.

25. Martha Saxton, *Being Good: Women's Moral Values in Early America* (New York: Hill and Wang, 2003), 165–170; Vivian Conger, "'Being Weak of Body but Firm of Mind and Memory': Widowhood in Colonial America, 1630–1750" (PhD diss., Cornell University, 1994), chaps. 2–3; Allison Levy, "Widow's Peek: Looking at Ritual and Representation," in *Widowhood and Visual Culture in Early Modern Europe*, ed. Allison Levy (Burlington, Vt.: Ashgate, 2003), 2–5.

26. See, for example, C. Rind, *Virginia Gazette*, April 7 and May 26, 1774.

27. Cara Anzilotti, *In the Affairs of the World: Women, Patriarchy, and Power in Colonial South Carolina* (Westport, Conn.: Praeger, 2002), 166; Wood, "Broken Reeds and Competent Farmers," 38–39; Martha J. King, "Making an Impression: Women Printers in the Southern Colonies in the Revolutionary Era" (PhD diss., College of William and Mary, 1992); Pinkney, *Virginia Gazette*, October 16 and December 8, 1774; Dixon and Hunter, *Virginia Gazette*, June 27, 1777. For details on the Rind children, see Jane D. Carson, "Clementina Rind: A Research Report," *Colonial Williamsburg Foundation Research Report* 47 (n.d.): 4–5; and Lyon G. Tyler, ed., "Williamsburg Lodge of Masons," *William and Mary Quarterly*, 1st ser., 1 (1892): 10–11, 13–14.

28. C. Rind, *Virginia Gazette*, April 14, 1774, 3.

29. For other examples of the language of constructed helplessness more generally, see an analysis of women's petitions in Cynthia A. Kierner, *Southern Women in Revolution, 1776–1800: Personal and Political Narratives* (Columbia: University of South Carolina Press, 1998).

30. John Pendleton Kennedy, ed., *Journals of the House of Burgesses of Virginia 1773–1776 Including the Records of the Committee of Correspondence* (Richmond: Virginia State Library, 1905), 13:77, 124–25.

31. The new colophon read "Printed by Clementina Rind, at the New Printing Office, on the Main Street" (C. Rind, *Virginia Gazette*, August 26, 1773).

32. For an example of an acrostic, see *Virginia Gazette*, March 17, 1774.

33. Ibid., April 14, 1774, 3; James A. Bear and Lucia C. Stanton, eds., *Jefferson's Memorandum Books: Accounts, with Legal Records and Miscellany, 1767–1826*, 2 vols. (Princeton, N.J.: Princeton University Press, 1997), 1:14, 16, 19, 21, 31, 79, 325, 350; W. W. Abbot and Dorothy Twohig, eds., *Papers of George Washington, Colonial Series* (Charlottesville: University of Virginia Press, 1994), 9:363.

34. See, for example, C. Rind, *Virginia Gazette*, September 30, October 21 and 28, 1773.

35. Ibid., October 21, 1773, 2. Purdie and Dixon also ran ads from Charlton and Rathell in the May 12, 1774, postscript issue of the *Virginia Gazette*.

36. For details about the residents of Williamsburg in the eighteenth century, I am indebted to the resources of the Colonial Williamsburg Foundation, many of which are now available online at http://research.history.org/JDRLibrary/Online_Resources.cfm (accessed April 2, 2013).

37. Ellen Hartigan-O'Connor, *The Ties That Buy: Women and Commerce in Revolutionary America* (Philadelphia: University of Pennsylvania Press, 2009), 129–60; Hartigan-O'Connor, "'She Said She Did Not Know Money': Urban Women and Atlantic Markets in the Revolutionary Era," *Early American Studies* 4 (2006): 343. For specific examples, see C. Rind, *Virginia Gazette*, June 2 and 23, 1774.

38. See "An Attentive Observer," Purdie and Dixon, *Virginia Gazette*, December 23, 1773, 1; C. Rind, *Virginia Gazette*, December 30, 1773.

39. C. Rind, *Virginia Gazette*, August 25, 1774.

40. Ibid., March 3, 1774, 3.

41. Ibid., January 13, April 7, May 26, and September 8, 1774.

42. Ibid., May 19, 1774.

43. Ibid., June 9, July 21, and July 28, 1774. For the imperial crisis brewing in Virginia over the reach of parliamentary authority, especially its power to tax without representation, see John E. Selby, *The Revolution in Virginia, 1775–1783* (Williamsburg, Va.: Colonial Williamsburg, 1988), 7–40.

44. Andrew Jackson O'Shaughnessy, "'If others will not be active, I must drive': George III and the American Revolution," *Early American Studies* 2 (2004): 1–47, esp. 17; William L. Hedges, "Telling Off the King: Jefferson's *Summary View* as American Fantasy," *Early American Literature* 22 (1987): 166–74.

45. [Thomas Jefferson], *A Summary View of the Rights of British America* (Williamsburg, Va.: printed by Clementina Rind, 1774). Peyton Randolph and not Jefferson may have submitted the piece to Clementina for publication. For background, see Julian P. Boyd, ed., *Papers of Thomas Jefferson*, 39 vols. to date (Princeton, N.J.: Princeton University Press, 1950–), 1:672.

46. For educational reforms, see the letters of "Academicus" and "A Country Justice," in C. Rind, *Virginia Gazette*, December 30, 1773, and May 19, 1774, respectively.

47. For examples of her justification for delayed printing, see C. Rind, *Virginia Gazette*, December 23, 1773, 3.

48. Terri L. Snyder, "Refiguring Women in Early American History," *William and Mary Quarterly*, 3rd ser., 69 (2012): 421–50.

49. "John Pinkney for the Benefit of Clementina Rind's Estate," *Virginia Gazette*, September 29, 1774, 3. Pinkney continued publication for the benefit of the Rind children until April 1775 and then as owner of the *Virginia Gazette* until February 1776.

50. Pinkney, *Virginia Gazette*, October 16, 1774, 1.

Sarah Jerdone

Negotiating Revolution

LINDA L. STURTZ

Of her house, Jerdone Castle, Sarah Jerdone could properly boast "George Washington slept here," and that the president also stayed for breakfast in June 1791. Yet years earlier, Sarah Jerdone had been forced to submit a petition to Virginia's Revolutionary legislature to protect her family's land from state confiscation acts that seized the property of loyalists (also known as Tories) who opposed the Revolution and remained loyal to King George III after the colonists declared their independence. Allegiance was complicated during the American Revolution. Accusations of loyalism plagued the Jerdone family during the war and after it was over.

Back in 1771, Francis Jerdone, a Scots merchant who had settled in Virginia, died, leaving his widow, Sarah, to raise their eight surviving children, who were all still minors. Then as now, ambitious families often sustained transoceanic ties, and while the circulation of individuals across the Atlantic over several generations expanded the opportunities the Jerdones enjoyed, the rising tensions of the 1770s placed Sarah in an awkward position: how would her allegiance be defined? With disputes raging between Britain and its North American colonies, it was an inauspicious time to be widowed. Once the war began, Sarah Jerdone was conspicuously silent about her family's political loyalties, walking a tightrope between rival camps. Her transatlantic personal and trading networks suggest that transnational, rather than national, allegiances shaped her outlook. Her wartime actions reveal how she carefully negotiated her place in the complicated legal and cultural landscape of Revolutionary Virginia.

In retrospect, American independence seems inevitable, but Virginia's House of Burgesses still drank toasts to the king into the early 1770s. Like all their

JERDONE CASTLE, LOUISA COUNTY

The older, one-and-a-half-story portion of Jerdone Castle (*left*) was built in the mid-eighteenth century but was later overshadowed by the 1858 addition. Neither spartan nor ostentatious, the house was built of wood on a foundation of Flemish-bond brick with glazed headers while the interior included paneling and built-in cupboards around the fireplaces of several rooms, no doubt necessary for storing the Jerdones' extensive library.

Virginia Department of Historic Resources.

FRAME FOR MOURNING LOCKET IN MEMORY OF SARAH JERDONE AND HER DAUGHTER-IN-LAW

Initially, the copper frame encircled a miniature portrait, now lost. The frame is inscribed with the names and death dates of the two women and a line from Alexander Pope's poem "Elegy to the Memory of an Unfortunate Lady": "How Lovd. How Valued once avails thee not." Jerdone Family Papers, Special Collections Research Center, Swem Library, College of William and Mary.

contemporaries in Virginia and the other colonies, the Jerdones saw themselves as part of the British Empire. How did Anglo-Americans with strong ties to Britain determine their allegiance during the war years? How did they negotiate the consequences of their choices? Historians have shown that individuals' allegiances shifted over time, with people sometimes switching sides in order to remain on friendly terms with whichever army was marching through their region. Communities often forgave or overlooked disaffection among their otherwise highly regarded neighbors.[1]

Although Sarah Jerdone lived through a period of political upheaval, her life bore no resemblance to those of more politically motivated loyalist women, such as the outspoken Charlotte Thornton, who "disapprov[ed] of the illegal proceedings of the people of Virginia." As the widow of a member of the royal governor's council, Thornton proudly proclaimed that she acted "from a dislike of the Conduct of the Americans proceeding to open War with England and their insisting she should join them or quit the Colony." Given this ultimatum, she "determined on the latter & left her House, Estate, and every Comfort she enjoyed rather than Act against her King and Conscience." She declared herself "the only Widow in the Colony of Virginia, whose Loyalty emboldened her to quit her Possession there, & fly to Great Britain."[2]

Because not everyone was as outspoken as Thornton, leaders on both sides were often perplexed (and sometimes paranoid) when it came to distinguishing enemies from friends. One historian refers to the "threshing operation" performed by Whig and Tory leaders during the early months of the war as the precursor to the winnowing process by which they attempted to sort out potential enemies from supporters, though hostilities or neighborly pressure often forced fence sitters to make some kind of public statement of political allegiance. Even so, women and children proved particularly difficult to categorize, especially given expectations on both sides that civility should be accorded to elite white women, while the women themselves manipulated tropes of helplessness to their own advantage. Furthermore, state laws that sought to minimize the disruptive impact of loyalism by regulating movements of men (through imprisonment or exile) or by sequestering their property still included clauses exempting married women and children from these penalties. They were exempt because the common law considered wives and minors to be incapable of managing property in their own right.[3]

The status of widows, who had both more legal rights and more practical autonomy than wives, was more ambiguous. Those who were not clearly Whigs often faced suspicion from their independence-minded neighbors. Sarah Jerdone occupied a point on a spectrum of women of fluctuating or non-Whig allegiances on which Charlotte Thornton—the councilor's widow who proudly proclaimed her allegiance to George III and then went into exile—was poised on one extreme. Closer to the center of the spectrum was Mary Willing Byrd, the wealthy, well-connected, and highly visible widow of another member of the governor's council, who counted both Whigs and Tories among her family and friends and defended her family's property from predators on both sides. The more equivocal Byrd remained in Virginia and negotiated with two successive governors to retain her family's extensive property, despite recurring suspicions that she opposed the Revolution. Byrd eventually contributed to the Virginia war effort, noting tartly that "I have paid my taxes, and have not been Personally or Virtually represented" in the legislature because of her sex. By contrast, Jerdone tried to remain neutral—even silent—on political matters, at least until her family's property was threatened, when she endeavored cautiously to defend it.[4]

The Jerdones were probably neither avid patriots nor committed loyalists but instead fit into the broad category of disaffected people who were bewildered by the collapse of a familiar world that had provided them with opportunities for upward mobility in the transatlantic economy. Sarah Macon Jerdone was descended from prominent seventeenth-century Virginia settlers, and her father and grandfather had served in the House of Burgesses, but she chose as her husband Francis Jerdone, a tough, six-foot-tall Scotsman from outside that Virginia-centered circle. In 1752 Francis had left his native Scotland to serve as an apprentice to a London merchant before becoming the representative of a British trading firm in Virginia. He soon set up his own store in Yorktown, where in competition with the town's established merchants he sold British manufactured goods and newly imported slaves. His risks paid off, and profits allowed him to diversify his investments.[5]

By the 1770s the Scots, who had gained legal access to restricted British imperial markets after the Act of Union in 1707, controlled about half of the Tidewater tobacco market, but they remained suspicious outsiders to many Virginians. Planter antipathy toward these merchants was evident in denunciations of them as "Caledonian Jews." Virginians patronized stores owned by Scots because they provided the best terms and the highest quality merchandise, but customers resented the debts they amassed as a result of these exchanges. Scots merchants were also suspect because they often supported London's imperial policies during the unrest of the 1760s and early 1770s, in part because they wished to collect the debts owed by their Virginia customers. Moreover, Scots firms perpetuated the outsider status of their employees by contractually prohibiting them from marrying local women, though some, like Francis Jerdone, took Virginia wives after they had served out the terms of their contracts.[6]

Francis and Sarah, who may have met through his commercial transactions with her family, married in 1753, after he had established himself in his own business. As newlyweds, the couple seemed blissfully happy. Francis wrote to Sarah during a brief separation that "in the morning that I parted with you My ever beloved I found my self dull and heavy." Francis considered his wife an "agreeable companion." They often took trips together, and when he was forced to journey alone, Francis described his misery by comparing their marital partnership to the rapport between their horses: "my little bay horse would hardly go along as he had not his fellow traveler to lead the way." Shortly after the birth of their first son Francis declared, "I think I am as happy as my fellow creatures are in common in this world: being bless'd & with a sufficiency to make life comfortable with an agreeable bosom companion, a fine prattling girl & a boy but a few weeks old." Sarah spent almost half of the eighteen years of their marriage pregnant. The Jerdones had nine children in all, two of whom died in childhood.[7]

Although his marriage to Sarah connected Francis to an impressive network of established Virginia planters, he remained a proactive merchant who studied emerging opportunities keenly. He examined local agricultural production methods, determined that tools being sent from Britain could be improved, and sent back new designs for tools he wanted to sell to his customers. Rather than simply provide off-the-shelf goods, he developed his own distinctive line of merchandise appropriate to his Virginia customers' needs. Planning for the longer term, he also acquired labor—both white indentured servants and black slaves—and land in the province's interior Piedmont region.[8]

Eventually the Jerdone family businesses included Providence Forge in New Kent County, a grist mill, a saw mill, and thousands of acres of land on plantations geographically dispersed across Virginia. Enslaved people provided the primary labor force for these operations. The Jerdones moved into a new house, which they called Jerdone Castle, in rural Louisa County. After the French and Indian War began in 1754, however, the family retreated to New Kent County to live with Sarah's parents until hostilities ceased.[9]

Marriage to a merchant had its material advantages. The family accumulated an extensive library of imported books, a collection that survives intact today at the College of William and Mary. The selections they made for their library reveal the importance of literature to the family, as does a locket inscribed with a passage from a poem by Alexander Pope that commemorated the deaths of Sarah and her daughter-in-law. Sarah also had access to the best goods because her husband bought them for the family when he ordered merchandise for his customers. On one occasion, Francis ordered blue stockings and a leghorn hat for Sarah, along with eighteen yards of what must have been a splendid striped fabric "of gay colours" for his daughter. One can imagine the twelve-year-old girl rolling her eyes at her papa's mistake as he quickly revised the request because "she now informs me that 20 yds is the patern." Despite her ready access to fine imports, Sarah shunned extravagance and once, when supplied with an elaborate carriage, she exchanged it for a simpler one that was both better suited for local roads and less likely to arouse envy among her neighbors.[10]

Sarah was not a passive partner, and her working relationship with her husband during his lifetime became an apprenticeship for her autonomous direction of their businesses after he died in 1771. Francis filled her in on the details of their far-flung enterprises when she was at one place and he at another, relying on her—and on her father and sister—to manage their various business interests. Francis's will, written in 1770, made Sarah coexecutor, and in doing so, he followed the tradition in Sarah's family: her grandmother had been the executor of her own husband's will. Francis wanted Sarah to continue to manage the family's affairs with the assistance of her coexecutors while the children were minors. He also granted Sarah the use of their home plantation and its slaves during her widowhood, as well as the right to dispose of the plantation. If she chose to marry again, he instructed her to dispose of the property according to her own wishes before the wedding—an unusual provision that reflected Francis's trust in his wife's judgment and his belief that she had a near-equal stake in the property they had acquired during their marriage. If Sarah did not remarry, the property would be divided among the children after her death.[11]

In his will, Francis also provided for the children's education, a matter that Sarah took to heart. In addition to raising her own children, Sarah took in other young relatives after their parents died, including a grandson who eventually became a South American revolutionary.[12] Although her own sons ultimately remained in Virginia—one became a Virginia planter after returning from school in England and the other trained as a physician—two of her daughters married immigrant merchants and eventually moved to Britain, and a third actively directed the business of her family. Sarah Macon Jerdone's grandchildren grew up in Virginia, Scotland, and England, sustaining their family's transatlantic ties in the post-Revolutionary period.

As a widow after August 1771, Sarah had extensive responsibilities. To protect the significant family investment in Providence Forge, she had to learn the iron business quickly, especially because Francis's partner, William Holt, eventually defaulted on his loans, leaving Sarah as the forge's sole owner. The relationship with Holt precipitated a long-running lawsuit between the Holts and the Jerdones that lasted into the next generation. Although Sarah was less involved in the mercantile branch of the family business after Francis's death, her expertise in trade was sufficiently noteworthy that her son-in-law Alexander Macaulay respectfully asked her opinions concerning shipping as he planned his own business.[13]

In taking a more central role in the family business, Sarah followed the pattern established by many merchants' widows in eighteenth-century Virginia. But the Revolution changed everything, both by creating an unstable and highly politicized business environment and by making the widowed Sarah a potential political actor. Because Francis died in 1771, "which side he would have supported is a tantalizing, if moot, question," as his biographer points out.[14] His death left that choice to Sarah, who followed a complicated path that allowed her family to flourish both during and after the Revolution, despite their being politically suspect.

Sarah Jerdone could negotiate and conceal her allegiance during the war because she was a woman living in a society that had difficulty imagining women as purposeful political actors. Jerdone probably adopted a flexible approach in part because she did not feel strongly committed to one side or the other. Rather, she was one of the cautiously disaffected who simply hoped that the war would end soon, before she was forced to take a strong stand either for or against it. How did people in this muddled middle manage? Jerdone pursued her business interests quietly as best she could, effectively classifying herself by her decisions about where she resided (remaining in Virginia), which government she petitioned, and how she negotiated her children's status.

Jerdone's clearest support for the Revolution came when she supplied the Continental and French armies that traversed the state in 1781. After Lafayette's troops made firewood from hundreds of yards of fences on Jerdone land, the Virginia government paid for the wood (and other items) that Sarah provided to the army, including goods and services "requisitioned" by state and Continental forces. The fact that she submitted claims for payment for grain and beef, as well as for services such as carting, cooperage, and blacksmith work, suggests that her property served as an all-purpose rest stop for the army on its way to Yorktown. Supplying troops was not always voluntary, but submitting claims for compensation to the Virginia government suggested her recognition of its authority, if not her outright support. Even if Sarah's support for independence and the resulting war was lukewarm, her choice of where to submit her claims demonstrated a tacit acceptance of the new Revolutionary regime.[15]

Sarah was trusting in business, but she was not naïve. The most persistent worry that emerged from her wartime business resulted from the protracted lawsuit against William Holt, Francis's Providence Forge business partner. The Jerdones continued to operate the forge in partnership with him, and they renewed their arrangement in 1777. During the war, however, cash lost value rapidly, and in 1783 the Jerdones became suspicious of Holt's accounting. Only after auditors were brought in did it become clear that Holt had credited the Jerdones' forge accounts with depreciated paper currency while paying himself in the more valuable and stable specie. By his accounting, Holt claimed the Jerdones owed him money rather than vice versa. The Jerdones sued in 1783, beginning what became a decades-long battle.[16]

Sarah Jerdone also faced ongoing resistance from her slaves before, during, and after the war, as they exploited unsettled circumstances in the Jerdone family and in the larger society. Enslaved people were well-enough informed to take advantage of auspicious moments to improve their condition. For example, two months after Francis died, an enslaved man named Cooper attempted to join his wife in Fredericksburg, where he had once lived with her. Two other enslaved workers from the Jerdone property ran away and were assumed to be "lurking" near the homes of their former masters, presumably so that they, too, could reunite with their families. On another occasion, a slave woman named Hannah decided that she wanted to live at Jerdone Castle, not at Providence Forge. The woman went on her own to Jerdone Castle because, as the forge manager wrote in exasperation, "Hannah has made Her choice" of where to live. The manager suggested that Sarah grant Hannah's wish, noting that "she is but of little service here."[17]

Running away in wartime could be more dramatic and its consequences more enduring. In 1775 Virginia's last royal governor, John Murray, Earl of Dunmore, issued a proclamation declaring all indentured servants or "Negroes or others (appertaining to the Rebels)" free if they took up arms and joined the king's troops. Several hundred joined Dunmore's Ethiopian Regiment. Dunmore's initiative was confirmed and expanded in 1779 when Sir Henry Clinton issued the Philipsburg Proclamation, which allowed any slave, male or female, adult or child, to use the proximity of British troops to seek their own liberation. In 1780 a slave named Kent, who lived on the Jerdone property, sought his freedom. Although he had been only thirteen when Dunmore issued his proclamation—old enough to understand the excitement surrounding it but too young to act on his own or join the troops—by 1780 the eighteen-year-old Kent was strong enough to venture out on his own, and he exploited the disruption of wartime to seek his own independence. Kent left for good, unlike Cooper and others who had run away to reunite with families who resided elsewhere, only to return or be forced back to their masters' plantations.[18]

Unlike Kent's mother, who presumably never saw her son again, Sarah could hope to reunite with her own absent sons. In 1776 Francis Jerdone Jr. was twenty years old and his brother John was twelve. Sarah's decision to send her two surviving sons abroad during the war and her subsequent use of a petition to reclaim property seized by the state in their absence exemplifies her cautious approach to the war and its potential economic impact. Historians may quibble about what constituted allegiance, but Virginia law was clear: to "prevent doubts who shall be deemed British subjects," it declared that anyone who was absent from the state after April 19, 1775 (the date of the Battle of Lexington) would be considered "subjects of his Britannick majesty." Material penalties came with that distinction. Although the law protected the property of minors, wives, and those of "insane mind" who were suspected of loyalism—on the grounds that they lacked the capacity to make political choices—the widowed Sarah and Francis Jr., who had reached legal adulthood in 1777 while abroad, were liable to these penalties. This left the Jerdones in a quandary and the family's property at least theoretically subject to seizure.[19]

By 1777 fragmentary evidence suggests that family conversations were at least somewhat accepting of the political changes in Virginia. When young John Jerdone wrote home that year, he mused "how happy would it be for us all, if this unnatural dispute between the Mother and the Daughter could be effectually made up." One historian plausibly suggests that this comment refers to a personal disagreement between Sarah Jerdone and her daughter, who was on the verge of marrying. However, John's wording—his use of "the" mother and "the" daughter—suggests that he was discussing the more public dispute between the mother country and the colonies. Although that comment alone suggests merely that the Jerdones wanted peace—and perhaps a reinstatement of British rule—John also informed his mother that his schoolmaster "often calls me his Little American Rifleman," which may indicate that his teacher believed the Jerdones to be sympathetic to independence.[20]

Still, the family's ambivalence left them vulnerable and, with her sons in Britain, Sarah took it upon herself to deal with the Revolutionary state legislature on their behalf. As the war progressed and the state's financial situation grew more desperate, laws concerning loyalist property became more draconian. At the beginning of the war, Virginia only sequestered lands owned by loyalists, theoretically leaving open the possibility of returnees reclaiming the property. Within a few years, however, the cash-strapped state began selling seized loyalist land. Virginia property owners who were absent from the state and who were declared loyalists under the law would find recovering their property difficult, if not impossible, once the land was sold.[21]

The Albemarle County property of Sarah's absent son Francis was seemingly lost when, in October 1779, at an inquisition before the public escheator, a jury condemned his holdings in the county, which included three thousand acres and fifty-two enslaved people. At this point Sarah swung into action, petitioning the state legislature to protect the property from confiscation. To preserve her family's property Sarah now had to interact with the political authorities of her state. Wording her petition carefully, she claimed that in sending her sons abroad she had taken no political stance but merely acted "agreeable to the desire of her deceased husband." In fact, her husband's will had stipulated how she would pay for the children's education but left unspecified where they would be schooled. Nevertheless, in her petition Sarah claimed that her husband had sent their eldest son to school in Britain and "desired that his younger sons might also be sent there as soon as they were old enough to . . . bear the voyage." (The youngest of the Jerdones' three boys died at age three, in 1772, the year after his father's death.) Sarah's argument was disingenuous. Even if the couple had discussed sending the boys abroad prior to 1771, war certainly afforded Sarah an acceptable excuse to change these plans in favor of keeping her sons, like her daughters, at home in Virginia.[22]

Sarah Jerdone was one of growing numbers of women who petitioned their state legislatures during the Revolution. Her request, like those of most female petitioners, was reactive, personal, and deferential. In approaching the state's lawmakers, she sought redress for her particular grievance. The right to petition was long established for women and others who could not vote and had no other formal political voice. By petitioning, Jerdone was not claiming any new rights for women generally or even for herself, but she was claiming membership in Virginia's political society, and she expected her application to receive a fair hearing from the legislators.[23]

In framing her petition, Jerdone went to great lengths to portray herself as a dutiful wife and mother, selectively citing documents that showed her fulfilling her husband's wishes and showed her sons deferring to parental dictates. Though she sought to show the legislators that all the Jerdones were behaving in a dutiful and unobjectionable fashion consistent with gendered social norms, her story was not entirely persuasive. Assuming the role of the weak and foolish woman, Sarah asserted that she was the source of her family's troubles, having created a situation that was "exceedingly hard" for her son and "greatly distressing to her who is the innocent cause of her son's misfortune."[24] In this formulation, she portrayed herself as innocent—unaware of the laws and the consequences of breaking them—but also as sufficiently authoritative and calculating to protect her near-adult son by sending him off to England. Sarah wanted her son's land back; she hedged her bets by claiming both that she forced Francis Jr. to leave and that she weakly submitted to the will of her dead husband. Perhaps she hoped that the legislators were too busy to examine the details of the will too closely—and she seemingly got lucky. The legislative committee never reported any final disposition of her case. As a result of benign neglect, the issue was allowed to languish and the Jerdones retained their property.

What actually happened concerning the boys' education is more complicated than Sarah indicated in her petition. By 1774 Francis Jr. had completed his studies in Britain and returned to Virginia. By then, ten-year-old John was ready to start school, but Sarah believed that John was too young to travel alone, so she "with some difficulty prevailed" on Francis to accompany his brother. In August 1775 the nineteen-year-old Francis took his brother to England, where they remained until Francis's twenty-first birthday, following the wishes of their mother. Then, although Francis was "very impatient to return to his own Country" and endangered his property by remaining abroad, he dutifully waited to return until he had permission from his mother.[25] By contrast, Sarah claimed in her petition that she had instructed Francis to come home and had been expecting him "for some time past." Yet Sarah also claimed that she had hoped that "the unhappy difference between G.B. & this state would have been soon accommodated," making his immediate return unnecessary. If we take the petition at face value—and we might well not—Sarah believed that the disputes that caused her neighbors to go to war could have been resolved quickly. She was pragmatic, optimistic, and opportunistic. She strategically referred to Virginia as a "state," not a colony, in her petition. In 1775 she might well have been content to have the "unhappy difference" concluded without independence but in any case, she ultimately chose loyalty to Virginia over adherence to any larger power.

Jerdone's request—and how she pursued it—paralleled those of other Virginia families with transatlantic interests. Once the fighting ended, elite refugees flocked back to the state and sought to resume life as they had known it before the war. However, British subjects who had abandoned Virginia during the war, remained abroad until 1782, and then returned to the state without becoming citizens were to be held as prisoners unless they secured special leave from the governor. A new law was deemed necessary because of the growth in the number of refugees seeking readmission, but even then, local authorities often permitted their former neighbors to return to their communities.[26]

With the official end of the war in 1783, even more exiled Virginians sought to return home. Some found tolerance. Ralph Wormeley petitioned the assembly to admit his son John to citizenship and, like Sarah Jerdone, stated that the young man had left before the war for Scotland to pursue his education. John Wormeley had served in the British forces but claimed he merely did so because he had been unable to support himself financially during the war years when remittances from home could not reach him. Wormeley was readmitted to the state after taking an oath of allegiance but prohibited from holding office for four years. Presley Thornton claimed that he, too, had absented himself from Virginia because he had been sent to England for his education. A parent's decision to send a child to Britain, it appears, provided a viable excuse for that child's residence abroad during the war years. By 1783 exiles found it easier to come home, though they generally did not recover estates that had been forfeited to the state. Sarah's 1779 petition therefore had been crucial in saving the family's property for her sons.[27]

Choosing a place of residence in wartime could be a strategic decision for disaffected people who could afford to send family members abroad and who sometimes benefited from the assumptions about gender that pervaded Anglo-American law and society. Women who remained behind while their husbands or children went to England or elsewhere could protect at least a portion of their husbands' estates. While women could be charged with treason, authorities typically assumed that a wife who simply followed the wishes of her loyalist husband was under his control. Wives of loyalists were rarely held accountable for their politically objectionable actions because a higher priority in this society was to uphold the authority of husbands. Although a widow's position could be more ambiguous, Sarah Jerdone was able to invoke the authority of her dead husband to good effect, sending her sons abroad while she remained at home in Virginia.[28]

Although Jerdone never described her decision to stay in Virginia during the war as a deliberate strategy to preserve her sons' property, other families used this ploy. The loyalist Humphrey Roberts left his wife in charge of their children, land, and slaves when he escaped Norfolk, hoping that her continuing presence there would safeguard his property. Margaret Goodrich had a husband and sons in active service on behalf of the British, though she herself, as part of a long-tailed Virginia family, was able to cite her father's patriotism when she sought to return to her family's estates. Virginia-born Margaret Parker, her sister Rebecca Aicheson, and their sister-in-law Mary Ellegood also stayed in Virginia, despite the pro-British stances of their husbands. After the war, the newly widowed Rebecca remained in the state, while Margaret very reluctantly left to join her husband in England. Margaret's son, like the Jerdone sons, was educated in England during the war. His absence made him suspicious, but his mother's conduct protected him, and he went into business in Virginia after the war was over.[29]

By working strategically to keep property in the hands of wives who remained in Virginia, even the families of active loyalists could shelter property from seizure during the war and provide the means for children to return later. Courts in Virginia permitted widows or wives whose loyalist husbands went into exile to claim their dower rights, so long as the women remained in the state. Dower was the portion (usually a one-third share) that the common law gave a woman from her husband's property for her own use while she was a widow. During the war, the state set aside an equivalent share of land for the wives of loyalists who, by virtue of their husbands' political transgressions, were now de facto widows. That decision afforded the wives of such absent husbands opportunities to protect their estates. Because their chances to preserve at least a portion of the family property improved significantly if they resided in the state, many wives of loyalists stayed in Virginia while their husbands were at war, in prison, or in exile. Because the law also deemed children incapable of making independent decisions, loyalist parents who wished to preserve their children's property could cite their status as minors to argue that their estates should be returned to them when they reached adulthood. As we have seen, Sarah Jerdone used this strategy.[30]

Sarah Jerdone's carefully deferential and legalistic strategy contrasts markedly with that of her contemporary Mary Willing Byrd. Another widow—albeit more prosperous and well connected than Jerdone—who also faced the suspicions of neighbors about her loyalty, Byrd was the second wife of William Byrd III of Westover. A native Virginian, William Byrd inherited vast wealth in land, slaves, and speculative investments but squandered much of it gambling before dying by his own hand less than six months after the declaration of independence. William had supported Lord Dunmore until he issued his proclamation providing freedom to the slaves of rebels, at which point Byrd, an experienced military commander, volunteered his services to Virginia's patriot leaders, who declined his offer. Demonstrating how this war divided families, Thomas, one of Byrd's sons from his first marriage, joined the British forces and commanded Dunmore's Ethiopian Regiment at the Battle of Great Bridge. Mary Willing Byrd had strong family ties to other loyalists, including her father, sister, and brother-in-law, and she was related by marriage to Benedict Arnold, who actively helped her during the war, making her particularly suspect. Some people believed that she maintained a treasonous correspondence with high-ranking British officers who were also her kinsmen, and even assisted the British military effort.[31]

Unlike Sarah Macon Jerdone, Mary Willing Byrd openly interacted with the British, with whom she was often on friendly terms. When some of her slaves ran off to fight for the king, Byrd negotiated to reclaim them, and the British commanders offered goods to help compensate for her losses. Perhaps in part to protect her property from British depredations, she lavishly entertained enemy officers, including the reviled Benedict Arnold. Then, Byrd had the audacity to seek sympathy from Governor Thomas Jefferson, whom she addressed in a letter, not a formal petition, to make the case that she had, in fact, been loyal to her "country." But even Byrd used her status as a widow (one with many children) as a cover for her suspicious activities. Women and minors, she suggested, had to do what was necessary to protect their interests and their safety in such dangerous times.[32]

Nevertheless, like Byrd's neighbors, Jefferson concluded that her consorting with the enemy exceeded the bounds of legally accepted acts. Mary Willing Byrd was subsequently scheduled for trial for her offenses, but the trial was postponed and then canceled due to a lack of witnesses for the prosecution. Byrd's solidarity with the Virginia gentry families, who were extensively intermarried by 1776, was decisive, but general discomfort at charging a woman with treason likely played a role as well. Either way, the patriot Arthur Lee predicted that Byrd would escape trial because "means were taken to keep witnesses out of the way."[33]

In some respects, Byrd's and Jerdone's situations seem similar. Both knew prominent Virginia officials who were willing to work on their behalf. After Byrd's gentry friends stepped in, witnesses against her conveniently disappeared. Jerdone's troubles ended, at least according to tradition, when she appealed to George Washington, through her friendship with Martha Washington, to advance her cause. But Byrd's statements in her own defense were far more strident—and also far more political. In her letters to Jefferson and his successor, Thomas Nelson, she carefully constructed herself both as an aggrieved and helpless widow and as a stalwart citizen possessed of rights and honor. She demanded a reconsideration of the gendered norms of citizenship on the basis of her position both as a mother who sent a son to fight as a Revolutionary soldier and as a property-owning taxpayer. Both a distinctly feminine justification (motherhood) and what would later be labeled a liberal feminist stance (equality) factored into her argument. Ironically, when she demanded her "property," Byrd was referring to enslaved people. Perhaps not surprisingly, gendered difference—not equality—was the winning argument. When General F. W. von Steuben, speaking for the revolutionaries, permitted Byrd to receive her property, or goods in replacement, it was *because* she was a woman. "Was the same case to happen in Europe," he claimed, "the Suffering person; especially as she is a female and a widow, would be allowed to receive them."[34]

While Byrd's loyalties may have shifted according to her situation, Sarah Jerdone seems to have tried to remain neutral for the duration of the war. She never made a statement in which she explicitly professed allegiance to either side. Other Virginia women were more forthright, politically speaking. Charlotte Thornton proudly and publicly proclaimed her loyalty to Britain, abandoning her position and estates in order to retain her Britishness. There were others like her. Countless others, by contrast, committed themselves wholeheartedly to the Revolutionary cause.

Sarah Macon Jerdone valued her property highly. She did her best to preserve it during the war, and later, when she wrote her will, she distributed it in such a way as to ensure equity among her children and to secure her daughters' independence. The only son to survive Jerdone had been extremely well provided for in his father's will, so she favored her daughters in her bequests in order to "do Justice to all your descendants," in the words of her attorney. She made an exception to the equal division of her property, granting extra cash to Isabella, "whom I mean so far to prefer," with instructions that her daughter would have power over the property "notwithstanding her Coverture . . . at no time subject to the Controul of her husband." Sarah's reasons for favoring Isabella are not clear, but this daughter lived nearby and her husband frequently assisted Sarah in business and in personal matters; the family understood that Isabella played a signal role in her mother's life. Sarah's decision to grant her daughter independent funds reflected her desire to provide some autonomy to Isabella, rather than distrust of a man on whom she herself relied. Sarah also protected her other daughters' property in this fashion. Her bequests suggest that she believed, based on her own experience, that a wife's separate estate shielded her family from creditors and economic crises.[35]

In keeping with her concern for equity, Sarah also deducted from her daughter Elizabeth Jerdone Macaulay's share a sum comparable to a loan made to her previously. Elizabeth's husband had taken grand financial risks in his lifetime—including running goods into British-occupied New York and speculating in the Dismal Swamp Company—leaving his destitute widow to watch the family's goods sold at auction shortly after he died. Widowed at age thirty-nine, Elizabeth had four surviving children, and Sarah clearly understood her daughter's situation. Sarah had generously advanced funds to Elizabeth, but she now deducted the sum from her legacy, albeit without interest.[36] In dividing her property into relatively equal holdings for her daughters, Sarah split up the community of enslaved people on her estate. Providing for her daughters equally was her primary concern, and she divided enslaved peoples' families to achieve that goal.

Although biographies alone cannot begin to exhibit the widely differing experiences of Virginia women during the Revolution, the repercussions of Sarah Jerdone's choices suggest ways that citizenship and allegiance came to be defined for those who were neither staunch loyalists nor active revolutionaries. If well-behaved women rarely make history, sneaky ones, or those who strategically keep a low profile, sometimes succeed.[37] In contrast to committed and overt loyalists, Sarah Jerdone negotiated the complex wartime world while avoiding taking strong public stands that would jeopardize the interests and safety of her family. By the end of the war, Sarah's choices concerning securing her property, supplying the army (however reluctantly), selecting a residence, and appealing to government officials made both her and her children Virginians and Americans. Jerdone's life—like those of her contemporaries Mary Willing Byrd and Charlotte Thornton—shows the limited ways that most women participated in the affairs of the public sphere, as well as the ways in which their doing so contributed to the construction of new post-Revolutionary identities.

The story about Sarah Jerdone hosting George Washington with which this chapter opened is famous and has often been repeated. Its various versions typically focus on the Jerdone family's crypto-loyalism and the friendship between Sarah and Martha that subverted the logical male political order, making it plausible for the patriots' commander in chief to lodge at a Tory's home. According to the Library of Virginia catalog, for instance, "Francis Jerdone, Jr. (1756–1841), inherited 'Jerdone Castle,' as well as lands and businesses in Louisa and New Kent Counties upon his father's death, but may have almost lost them during the American Revolution. Jerdone reputedly was a Tory, but his mother was a friend of Martha Washington and his property was not confiscated."[38]

Is the story of the Jerdones' connection to the Washingtons and their reliance on this friendship to save them true? Certainly, the families were acquainted. Before the war, Sarah Jerdone's sons and son-in-law had cooperated with Washington in their attempts to speculate in western lands. Much later, in 1791, George Washington found himself stranded en route to another destination and was forced to make an unexpected stop at Jerdone Castle after traversing bad roads and missing a turn to the route he wanted. (Apparently, even the former commander in chief was man enough to eschew asking directions.) He stayed overnight at Mrs. Jerdone's and referred to being "kindly entertained" there. But Washington described the encounter in an impersonal tone, suggesting that Jerdone was more an acquaintance at best, not a close friend. Not an official stay, the visit was merely an accidental necessity. Another version of the story suggests that the visit was casual and that Sarah Jerdone was remarkably down-to-earth, even when unexpectedly hosting the greatest hero of the American Revolution, who was also the sitting president. According to this account, "When the General came to Jerdone Castle, he was duly announced, and a servant ran to tell his mistress that the distinguished man was arrived. Mrs. Jerdone without ado ordered the servant go and tell the President that she would be in as soon as she finished setting her hen." This story, along with a 1930s history celebrating the "more ancient and less pretentious dwelling of the early Jerdones," rather than the grand later addition to the house, is in keeping with a narrative that showcased the homespun values celebrated by Depression-era historians.[39]

The story about how Sarah Jerdone's friendship with the Washingtons saved the Jerdone land when her family was suspected of allegiance to the Crown has enjoyed a long shelf life, but it vastly oversimplifies the politics of the period and the role of gender in shaping women's (and men's) strategies and choices in perilous times. In Revolutionary Virginia, Sarah Jerdone's cautious behavior and her carefully worded petition probably had more to do with her ultimate success. Negotiating a revolution was tricky business.

NOTES

I would like to thank Linda Baumgarten, Matthew Dziennik, Cathy Hellier, Lindsay Keiter, Cynthia Kierner, Joan Lovelace, Debra Majeed, Beatrice McKenzie, Ami Pflugrad-Jackisch, Julie Richter, James C. Robertson, Linda Rowe, Taylor Stroemer, Fredrika Teute, Samuel Whittaker, and the seminar of the Colonial Williamsburg Foundation Library, August 7, 2012. I received research support from a Colonial Williamsburg Foundation Gilder Lehrman Fellowship and Beloit College's Keefer Fund.

1. Isaac Samuel Harrell, *Loyalism in Virginia* (Durham, N.C.: Duke University Press, 1926), 30; Adele Hast, "Loyalism and Community: The Lower Chesapeake Pocket of Virginia," in *Virginia in the American Revolution*, 3 vols., ed. Richard Rutyna and Peter Steward (Norfolk, Va.: Old Dominion University, 1977–83), 2:42–59.

2. *Virginia Gazette* (Purdie and Dixon), March 15, 1776; National Archives of Great Britain (hereafter NAGB) AO 12/54/331, 99/258, 13/31/14–18, 264–74, as cited by Peter Wilson Coldham, *American Migrations* (Baltimore, Md.: Genealogical Publishing, 2000), 571; NAGB AO 13/32, f. T II; ibid., f. T II[2]; Colonial Williamsburg, reel 490. See, more generally, Carol Berkin, *Revolutionary Mothers: Women in the Struggle for America's Independence* (New York: Knopf, 2005), 24, 92–106, 100–101, 141–42.

3. Judith Van Buskirk, *Generous Enemies: Patriots and Loyalists in Revolutionary New York* (Philadelphia: University of Pennsylvania Press, 2002), 5; Mary Beth Norton, "Eighteenth-Century American Women in Peace and War," *William and Mary Quarterly*, 3rd ser., 33 (1976): 386–409; Linda Sturtz, *Within Her Power: Propertied Women in Colonial Virginia* (New York: Routledge, 2002), 20. Works that raise key issues about both the loyalist diaspora and loyalists who remained in America include Robert M. Calhoon, "The Reintegration of the Loyalists and the Disaffected," in *The American Revolution: Its Character and Limits*, ed. Jack P. Greene (New York: New York University Press, 1987), 51–74; Jack P. Greene, "Colonial History and National History," *William and Mary Quarterly*, 3rd ser., 64 (2007): 243; Maya Jasanoff, *Liberty's Exiles: American Loyalists in the Revolutionary World* (New York: Knopf, 2011).

4. Sara B. Bearss, "Mary Willing Byrd," in *Dictionary of Virginia Biography* (Richmond: Library of Virginia, 1998), 2:457–59. See also Mary Willing Byrd to Thomas Jefferson, February 23, 1781, in Julian P. Boyd et al., eds., *The Papers of Thomas Jefferson* (Princeton, N.J.: Princeton University Press, 1950–), 5:691; Byrd to [Thomas Nelson], August 10, 1781, ibid., 703–4.

5. Malcolm Harris, *Old New Kent County*, 2 vols. (West Point, Va.: Harris, 1977), 1:133–37; Edward Riley, "Development of Yorktown, Virginia," *Virginia Magazine of History and Biography* 60 (1952): 522–36; "Francis Jerdone to William Buchanan, May 26, 1750," *William and Mary Quarterly*, 1st ser., 11 (1903): 157; J. H. Soltow, "Scottish Traders in Virginia," *Economic History Review*, 2nd ser., 12 (1959): 84–85.

6. Albert H. Tillson, *Accommodating Revolutions: Virginia's Northern Neck in an Era of Transformations, 1760–1810* (Charlottesville: University of Virginia Press, 2010), 153–67; John Selby, *The Revolution in Virginia* (Williamsburg, Va.: Colonial Williamsburg, 1988), 27.

7. William Cuninghame and Company Letter Books, 1767–73, as cited by Soltow, "Scottish Traders," 86; Francis Jerdone Sr. (hereafter FJ) to Sarah Macon Jerdone (hereafter SMJ), July 12, 1753, February 12, 1756, July 10, 1759, Jerdone Family Papers, Manuscripts and Rare Books Department, Swem Library, College of William and Mary (hereafter Swem), box 1, f. 1. All additional Jerdone correspondence is from this collection unless otherwise noted.

8. FJ to Messrs Tappenden and Hanboy June 25, 1756; FJ to Capt. Archbd. Crawfurd, June 26, 1756; FJ to Messrs Morgan Thomas and Co., June 16, 1757, all in FJ Letter Book. On FJ's cross-county travels, see James Soltow, "Role of Williamsburg," *William and Mary Quarterly*, 3rd ser., 15 (1958): 470.

9. "Will of Francis Jerdone," *William and Mary Quarterly*, 2nd ser., 11 (1931): 7–10; FJ to Capt. Hugh Crawfurd, May 15, 1756, FJ Letter Book.

10. David Null, "The Library of Francis Jerdone" (MA thesis, College of William and Mary, 1978); FJ to Jacob Hewitt, January 17, 1763, FJ Letter Book; Donald to FJ Jr., December 6, 1784, box 1, f. 3; Ann Smart Martin, *Buying into the World of Goods: Early Consumers in Backcountry Virginia* (Baltimore, Md.: Johns Hopkins University Press, 2006), 17. For the locket, see Swem, ser. 7, box 18; inscription on the copper frame: "How Lovd. How Valued once avails thee not / Mary Jerdone died March 12th 1821 / Sarah Jerdone died October 23rd 1818." The line is a passage from Alexander Pope's "Elegy to the Memory of an Unfortunate Lady."

11. "Will of Francis Jerdone"; FJ to SMJ, July 12, 1753, and July 10, 1759, box 1, f. 1. Sarah's grandmother Martha Macon was the executor for Gideon Macon, a burgess and vestryman (Harris, *Old New Kent County*, 1:132–37). For a more general account of Virginia women in merchant family enterprises, see Sturtz, *Within Her Power*, 141–76.

12. Sarah Jerdone's grandson Alexander Macaulay was the son of Elizabeth Jerdone Macaulay and her husband, also named Alexander Macaulay. Enrique Martinez, "Alexander Macaulay . . . Liberation of Colombia," *William and Mary Quarterly*, 3rd ser., 23 (1943): 235–48; "Alexander Macaulay, Unknown Hero," *Hispanic American Historical Review* 25 (1945): 528–35. The Jerdone records for the Belsches orphan are discussed in Sturtz, *Within Her Power*, 135–37.

13. "Providence Forge," *William and Mary Quarterly*, 1st ser., 5 (1896): 20–22; "Journal of Alexander Macaulay," ibid., 1st. ser., 11 (1903): 190.

14. Null, "Library of Francis Jerdone."

15. Janice Abercrombie and Richard Slatten, eds., *Virginia Revolutionary "Publick" Claims*, 3 vols. (Athens, Ga.: Iberian, 1992), 1:185, 636, 638, 641, 643, 644, 706, 710, 712–13, 720; 2:18, 30; Anne Reddy, "Lafayette at Providence Forge," *William and Mary Quarterly*, 1st ser., 11 (1931): 241.

16. The case from the Jerdones' perspective appears in the following, all in Swem, box 1, unless otherwise noted. [William Douglass] to FJ, May 19, 1787, f. 6; William Browne to FJ, September 10,

1812, box 5, f. 5; Wm Douglass to FJ, October 12, 1783, f. 2; Wm Douglass to FJ, December 11, 1783, f. 2; John Jerdone to FJ, November 20, 1784, f. 3; Wm. DuVal to FJ, July 14, 1785, f. 4; Donald and Burton to FJ, July 24, 1785, f. 4; Wm DuVal to FJ, March 19, 1786, May 5, 1786, October 7, 1786, f. 5.

17. Wm Douglass to FJ Jr., January 16, 1788, box 2, f. 1; Francis Jerdone Slave Book 1749–1873, ff. 18–20.

18. Selby, *Revolution in Virginia*, 66–67; Andrew O'Shaughnessy and Philip Morgan, "Arming Slaves in the American Revolution," in *Arming Slaves: From Classical Times to the Modern Age*, ed. Christopher Brown and Philip Morgan (New Haven, Conn.: Yale University Press, 2006), 209.

19. W. W. Hening, comp., *The Statutes at Large: Being a Collection of All the Laws of Virginia*, 13 vols. (Richmond, Va.: Samuel Pleasants Jr., 1810–23), 10:66–71.

20. M. H. Beals, "The Sojourning Settler: Transatlantic Networks and Identities in the British-American Tobacco Trade, 1740–1841," *Journal of Irish and Scottish Studies* 3 (2009): 157–73; John Jerdone to SMJ, March 21, 1777, box 1, f. 1.

21. Peter Mitchell, "Loyalist Property and the Revolution in Virginia" (PhD diss., University of Colorado, 1965); "Petitions and Letters," *Richmond College Historical Papers* 1 (1915): 336–55. Key cases of British sympathizers, legally defined as "aliens," recovering land included *Hunter v. Fairfax* (1794) and *Reed v. Reed* (1804) in Charles Hobson and Joan Lovelace, eds., *St. George Tucker's Law Reports and Selected Papers* (Chapel Hill: University of North Carolina Press, 2013), 298–306, 631–48, 830–35, 1793–98. I am grateful to Ms. Lovelace for prepublication access to these materials.

22. *Journal of the House of Delegates of . . . Virginia, Begun . . . 4 Oct[ober] 1779* (Richmond, Va.: Thomas W. White, 1827), 12.

23. Cynthia A. Kierner, *Southern Women in Revolution, 1776–1800: Personal and Political Narratives* (Columbia: University of South Carolina Press, 1998), xxiv–xxv, 153.

24. *Journal of the House of Delegates*, 12.

25. Edgar Woods, *Albemarle County in Virginia* (Charlottesville: Michie, 1901), 48; Petition of SMJ, Swem Special Collections, add. 17; Norton Family Papers, Colonial Williamsburg, MS no. 36.3, f. 140; "Petition of Sarah," enclosing a 1779 bill of exchange for funds to pay for British schooling; John Jerdone to SMJ, June 27, 1783, box 1, f. 2; Beals, "Sojourning Settler," 157. Men of Francis Jerdone's status were underrepresented in the military forces during the war. See Allan Kulikoff, *The Agrarian Origins of American Capitalism* (Charlottesville: University of Virginia Press, 1982), 152–80.

26. Hening, *Statutes at Large*, 13:136; H. J. Eckenrode, *Revolution in Virginia* (Boston: Houghton Mifflin, 1916), 287.

27. Eckenrode suggests that the language of kindness toward prisoners was "usual" and therefore perhaps a bit formulaic (*Revolution in Virginia*, 289, 291). See Petition of Ralph Wormeley, November 18, 1783, Westmoreland County, Legislative Petitions, Library of Virginia; Petition of Presley Thornton, November 18, 1783, Northumberland County, ibid. See also Joseph S. Ewing, ed., "The Correspondence of Archibald Mccall and George Mccall, 1777–1783," *Virginia Magazine of History and Biography* 73 (1965): 312–53, 425–54.

28. Linda K. Kerber, *Women of the Republic: Intellect and Ideology in Revolutionary America* (Chapel Hill: University of North Carolina Press, 1980), 53n31, 122–26, 130–36; Norton, "Eighteenth-Century American Women," 386–409; Calhoon, "Reintegration of the Loyalists." See also Wallace Brown, *The King's Friends* (Providence, R.I.: Brown University Press, 1966): 245, 189; Joan R. Gundersen, "'We Bear the Yoke with a Reluctant Impatience': The War for Independence and Virginia's Displaced Women," in *War and Society in the American Revolution: Mobilization and Home Fronts*, ed. John Phillips Resch and Walter L. Sargent (DeKalb: Northern Illinois University Press, 2007), 264–65. For an attempt to shield property that backfired, see the case of Walter Dulany of

Maryland in Bryan Rindfleisch, "'The World Turned Upside Down': The Impact of the American Revolution on the Patterns of Inheritance, Marriage, and Kinship among Southern Planter Loyalist Families," *Southern Historian* 31 (2010): 55.

29. Christopher Doyle, "Judge St. George Tucker and the Case of *Tom v. Roberts*," *Virginia Magazine of History and Biography* 106 (1998): 425–26, 441. See also Gregory Palmer and Lorenzo Sabine, *Biographical Sketches of Loyalists of the American Revolution* (Westport, Conn.: Meckler, 1984), 10, 253, 324, 670.

30. Linda K. Kerber, *No Constitutional Right to Be Ladies: Women and the Obligations of Citizenship* (New York: Hill and Wang, 1988), 15, 18, 317n45; Kerber, *Women of the Republic*, 9; Hast, "Loyalism and Community," 58; Ewing, "Correspondence of Archibald Mccall and George Mccall."

31. Selby, *Revolution in Virginia*, 66. Although a "tantalizing undocumented statement" suggested that Byrd submitted claims for £6,600 worth of supplies used by the British and was supported in her efforts by no less than General Cornwallis, no records survive in the British Treasury to document her efforts to claim restitution. The initial claim by B. F. Stevens and subsequent efforts to track down affidavits or a petition are reported in "The Affair of Westover: An Editorial Note," in Boyd et al., *Papers of Thomas Jefferson*, 5:671–705.

32. "The Affair of Westover," n. 14; events from the perspective of "Mr. Walter Harris," one of the escaped Westover slaves, in NAGB AO 12/99, 334–35.

33. "The Affair of Westover," n. 55, citing letter of Lee to Bland, March 21, 1781, 5:685.

34. Mary Byrd to [Thomas Nelson?], [August 10, 1781], in Boyd et al., *Papers of Thomas Jefferson*, 5:703–4; Steuben to Thomas Jefferson, February 21, 1781, ibid., 4:680; Mary Byrd to Thomas Jefferson, February 23, 1781, ibid., 4:690–92.

35. John Warden to SMJ, August 16, 1811; John Jerdone to SMJ, June 27, 1783, box 1, f. 2.

36. Will of Sarah Jerdone, written March 20, 1813, codicil May 29, proved November 9, 1818, official copy in Helen M. Anderson Papers, MS 89.13, Colonial Williamsburg; Charles Royster, *The Fabulous History of the Dismal Swamp Company* (New York: Borzoi, 1999), 395.

37. Laurel Thatcher Ulrich discusses the interpretation and proliferation of this phrase in her *Well-Behaved Women Seldom Make History* (New York: Knopf, 2007), esp. xiii.

38. See, generally, Elizabeth Stone, *Black Sheep and Kissing Cousins: How Our Family Stories Shape Us* (New York: Crown, 1989). For the overlap between public and Revolutionary era family mythology, see Gail S. Terry, "Defining Family, Defining Nation: A Nineteenth-Century Family and Its Eighteenth-Century Past," unpublished manuscript from DePaul Early American Writing Group, Chicago, Ill., November 2007; "Guide to the Jerdone Family Papers: A Collection in the Library of Virginia," acc. no. 21607, http://ead.lib.virginia.edu/vivaxtf/view?docId=lva/vi00560 .xml;query (accessed August 7, 2012).

39. "Petition of Joseph Harper, Francis Jerdone . . . Forty Thousand Acres," in *The Papers of George Washington: Colonial Series*, 10 vols., ed. W. W. Abbot et al. (Charlottesville: University of Virginia Press, 1983–85), 8:31; entry for June 9, 1791, in *The Diaries of George Washington*, vol. 6: *January 1790–December 1799*, ed. Donald Jackson and Dorothy Twohig (Charlottesville: University of Virginia Press, 1979), 162–63; Malcolm H. Harris, *History of Louisa County, Virginia* (Richmond: Dietz Press, 1936), 123–26; *Journal of the House of Delegates*, 12; Petition of Sarah Jerdone, October 4, 1779, Swem, add. 17.

Anne Henry Christian

Chronicling Family and Business on the Revolutionary Frontier

GAIL S. TERRY

Anne Henry Christian was one of the seven sisters of Patrick Henry, a leading American revolutionary and governor of Virginia. Today she is much less well known than her famous elder brother or her younger sister, Elizabeth Henry Campbell Russell, an important Methodist lay leader whom a nineteenth-century descendant recalled as sharing their brother's extraordinary oratorical skill.[1] When Anne Christian is remembered at all, it is mostly for a series of letters documenting her reluctant move to the Kentucky frontier in 1785 with her husband, William, a land speculator, soldier, and member of Virginia's western elite.

Christian excelled as a chronicler of her own life. Even before narrating her family's trans-Appalachian migration, she had produced a remarkable record of her life on southwestern Virginia's Revolutionary frontier in dozens of letters written to family members during the 1770s and 1780s. Her clear and legible script resembles that of an eighteenth-century clerk or merchant, and her letters have an easy narrative flow, suggesting someone comfortable with the written word. The style is straightforward, displaying neither self-conscious erudition nor the literary wordplay found in letters written by some of her contemporaries.

As Christian's letters show, both before and after her migration across the Appalachians, she was first and foremost committed to her family. Early letters reveal a dutiful young wife and mother fully engaged in the domesticity of what she once described as "the blessed retreat of a Country Life." When the Revolution impinged on that life, she complained. In 1777 she wrote to her brother

Patrick, then governor of Virginia, urging him to persuade her husband to quit "the publick employments that he is engaged in" and return home. Although some women responded to the challenges of war by becoming ardent patriots or by assuming responsibility for family businesses during their husband's absences, Christian did not; instead, she struggled to preserve her collapsing domestic world.[2] The war's outcome, however, facilitated the westward movement of Virginians, including the Christians, and Anne's letters chronicle her experiences as a new settler in Kentucky and also her response to William's death while he was leading an attack against the Wabash Indians in 1786. As it turned out, widowhood expanded her horizons in ways that the Revolution had not, transforming her into an assertive and successful woman of business who stabilized her family's enterprises and secured the prosperity of the next generation.

Despite her remarkable abilities as a letter writer, little is known about Anne Henry's early life and education. The fifth child of Sarah Winston Syme and her second husband, John Henry, Anne was probably born in 1738 or 1739. Known as "Annie" throughout her life, she met her future husband, William Christian, while he was reading law with her brother Patrick. They married in early 1768, and shortly after William's father provided him with a substantial marriage portion in the form of land. Anne may have brought little property to the marriage. At the time her father noted that he could not provide a marriage portion but promised her a significant legacy after her parents' death. Whether or not the legacy materialized remains unclear.[3]

After they married, twenty-nine-year-old Anne and twenty-six-year-old William set up housekeeping near his parents on the Stone House lands (present-day Cloverdale, near Roanoke). William's younger sister, also named Anne, and her husband, William Fleming, lived about five miles away. The sisters-in-law developed a close and enduring friendship. Anne Fleming spent the rest of her life at Belmont, her home in western Virginia, and eventually became the keeper of the family archives, which included approximately fifty of Anne Christian's letters. Nineteenth-century manuscript collectors and chroniclers of the history of Virginia and the early American West later siphoned off the papers from Fleming's collection that they deemed most significant for documenting the political and military history of the state and the nation, including a few letters by Anne Christian. The remaining papers stayed in the family until the early twentieth century, when they found their way into a public repository.[4]

In the first decade and a half of their marriages, the two Annes exchanged visits, family news, seeds and produce, dress patterns, books, and, of course, letters. Only Anne Christian's side of the correspondence survives. She wrote

My dear Sister   Bear Grass August 17th 1786

The day your Mother left us was a terrible days — journey we had worse roads than ever I saw before in my life, we came 24 miles, & had a very wet night. We got to Inglishes in 6 days from Maitins on August the Second, & got to Mr Wallaces the fourth day, safe & well, which mercies I hope we shall never forget, the goodness of God to us was very great, we had our health & strength, continued to us all the way & no accident at all. We got here the 11th day. We now want much to hear from your dear Mother & hope she got in safe & well, we wait with impatience to hear, & hope will write us as soon as possible, I must give you a short account of what part of this Country I have seen, as we came through Lincoln we found a very rich Country of Land but broken in many places, & exceeding bad water & a great scarcity of it, — Nelson County is better watered & I think more level — We came through Beards Town & saw Mr Gibbon there very well he writes in the Clerks office, We came by Salisburg that place looks high & pleasant but no water there fit to drink at all We had a very fine level road from there here through a beech Country, & this place all round us in sight of the Houses is covered with beech, we have a very good Spring, there are six families living here the people are a good deal afraid of the Indians, they have stolen horses near here, & they attackd a house at Clashers Mills a few days ago but were beat off — there was a man wounded in Brackenrige's lane this Summer, however I ventured to go to see the falls last wendsday there were fire arms men, it is a place capable of being made very pretty the river there is quite beautifull, but sickly, Mr Daniel & your sister were here, the Children there are all well we wish ————— here to go to the falls

ANNE HENRY CHRISTIAN LETTER

Anne Christian wrote this letter to her sister-in-law Anne Fleming shortly after the Christians arrived at Beargrass Creek in August 1787. In it she described the last stages of her journey along Wilderness Road before being reunited with family and friends who had relocated earlier. She also noted her neighbors' fear of Indians.

Virginia Historical Society.

ANNE HENRY CHRISTIAN LETTER

The clear, regular script is typical of Christian's handwriting, as is the signature. Folding and sealing a letter to make a kind of envelope was common during this period.

Virginia Historical Society.

mostly about the births of children and domestic life, only rarely discussing what she termed "publick business." Her letters also documented the movements of her family. William Christian moved or contemplated moving his household often enough for a niece to describe him as a "rolling stone." The first of these moves, completed by December 1770, took the couple (and William's parents and youngest sister) some fifty miles southwest to Mahanaim at Dunkard's Bottom in the New River valley.[5]

After the Christians moved, the two Annes continued their friendship by letter, exchanging information about their families and domestic work and—in Christian's case at least—lamenting the loss of face-to-face companionship. "We are now settled in our new Habitation," she wrote soon after her arrival at Mahanaim, "& I can't say but it is full as agreeable as I expected, but when I reflect on the great distance which is now between us it makes me a little melancholy, but I comfort myself with the thought of seeing you this Christmas with Mr. Fleming." In another letter written the next day, she added, "I send the chintz pattern, & I hope to see you flaunting in it at Mr. Madison's Ball, where we intend going." The following autumn Christian explained, "I flattered myself that I shou'd have been down to see you all this Court, but in the first place I have no horse & in the next I have the worst Cold ever I had in my life, & for the third the weather has got almost too cold . . . to Venture so far." From time to time the women exchanged gifts. Fleming sent Christian a cheese; Christian sent "1 & 1/2 bushels [of] dried apples for Mamma & you to divide between you," commenting that "I am really sorry they are such bad ones, but they were dried in wet weather which makes them black." When Christian gratefully accepted some books from her sister-in-law, she noted, "I have been so busy making Our Negroes Clothes I have not had time to give them a reading yet." By January 1772 Christian's first child, Prissey, was beginning to talk; Fleming's son Lenny was learning to read; and Fleming's youngest sister, who was still unmarried, was living with Anne and William Christian.[6]

Anne Christian noted the days when the county court sat, more because they offered potential chances for the two women to visit than because of any interest in court business. Until 1772, when the Christians' home became part of the new county of Fincastle, both William Christian and William Fleming served as justices on the Botetourt County court. After Fincastle was separated from Botetourt, the men were justices on separate courts, so Anne Christian had fewer opportunities to see Anne Fleming. The growing size of the women's young families might also have made travel more difficult. In April 1772 Christian wrote to Fleming about the birth of her second child. "I was safely delivered of a fine daughter on Friday the 27th of March," and "my little daughter takes up chief of my Time nursing her, & now & then Prissey [her two-year-old], who I cannot cast off yet. All here say the young one will be the Beauty, but be that as it will I hope to have the pleasure of presenting you with your new Niece this summer." The newborn, named Sarah Henry Christian for her maternal grandmother and called Sally, resembled her father. Anne Christian would give birth to four more children in the next decade, but she still traveled across Virginia in the 1770s and early 1780s to visit her Henry and Christian relatives. After the birth of Lenny in the 1760s, Fleming suffered several miscarriages or stillbirths, although she successfully gave birth to seven more children after 1775.[7]

Just as Anne Christian's letters offered no details about the business of the county courts, they contained few references to public business during the political controversies with Britain and the Virginians' war against the Shawnees, which preceded the declaring of American independence. These events proved vitally important to the men in her family, but Anne's interest in war and politics was confined to their immediate impact on those closest to her. Three examples illustrate this point.

The Proclamation Line of 1763, established by the king at the end of the French and Indian War, imperiled the fortunes of William Christian, Patrick Henry, William Fleming, and other elite Virginians who were large-scale speculators in western lands. Intended to promote peace by separating the Native peoples and the settlers, the principal effect of the line on the Virginia elite was to jeopardize their western land claims. Speculators tried to circumvent the new policy, first by attempting to purchase the land from the Iroquois and then by negotiating a new western boundary with the Cherokees. But the Shawnees defended their hunting rights by building a Native American coalition and threatening white settlers on the frontier.[8] In the autumn of 1774 Virginia's royal governor, Lord Dunmore, retaliated by leading an expedition against them that became known as Dunmore's War.

The governor led one army down the Ohio River from Fort Pitt (present-day Pittsburgh), while Anne's husband and William Fleming were part of a second force moving from western Virginia northward through the Kanawha River valley to join the governor. In October, Virginia forces fought the Shawnees at Point Pleasant (in present-day West Virginia). William Christian's company of soldiers arrived too late to fight, but Fleming was seriously injured in the battle. Outnumbered and short of powder, the Shawnees surrendered and were forced to give up their lands south of the Ohio River.[9]

Fearing a possible Indian attack, Anne Christian and her in-laws had retreated east from the New River valley before the war began. Anne stayed first with a sister in Hanover County and then at Patrick Henry's residence at Scotchtown. William Christian's parents moved to Belmont to stay with Anne Fleming, who received letters from both her husband and her brother before the battle and relayed their news to her anxious sister-in-law. In early October Christian wrote from Hanover County to Fleming in Botetourt, "I . . . am extremely glad to hear you are all well & in no fear of the Indians, . . . the uneasiness I have suffered in the Absence of your Dear Brother [William] has had such an effect on my health that you wou'd scarce know me, but I trust he will yet be preserved safe till his return in, & then I hope to lie at ease in my mind. I am in great hopes of seeing him this week, for this day the Assembly meets & the Governor was to be in by that time." Christian concluded, "I have no news to write, only what regards to the publick & that is too tedious to mention." By mid-October she had finally heard from William, although his letters appear to have been written before the battle.[10]

In October 1774 Anne Christian's brother Patrick was at the center of another drama that was unfolding in Philadelphia, one that—if her letters reflect her consciousness—she ignored almost completely. Perhaps because she was staying at her brother's house, Christian reported that "Pat is not returned from Philadelphia," where he was representing Virginia in the First Continental Congress. Anne never mentioned any of the events or controversies that occasioned the calling of that meeting: the Boston Tea Party in December 1773, Parliament's retaliatory passage of the Coercive Acts in May 1774, and the Quebec Act, which annexed the area west of the Appalachians and north of the Ohio River to the formerly French but now British colony of Quebec.[11]

In 1774 Anne's only interest in imperial politics was its potential impact on those closest to her. The land issue was paramount. From 1772 through July 1774, in violation of his instructions from London, Dunmore was still issuing land grants to Virginians who had fought in the French and Indian War, including Anne's relatives. Her "Brother Billy" had gone to Williamsburg in an attempt to secure some "plotts of Ohio Land." Christian conveyed the bad news to her sister-in-law that "all were received but Mr. Flemings." Christian had intended "to send Mr. Flemings [surveys] to Col. Byrd to get altered, as he had not inserted the service he served in." Despite her attempts, and although some Virginia speculators gained confirmation of their pre-Revolutionary land grants after independence, Fleming never received a clear title to these Ohio lands.[12]

The winter of 1774–75 and the following spring found Anne back at Mahanaim and fully engaged in domestic matters, while her husband and brother were in eastern Virginia where events were slowly moving the colony toward independence. First elected to the House of Burgesses in 1773, William Christian served in that body and in the extralegal conventions that gradually supplanted it. In

1775 he attended the convention in Richmond that selected Virginia's delegates to the Second Continental Congress, and witnessed his brother-in-law Patrick Henry's famous "Give me liberty, or give me death" speech. After Dunmore orchestrated the seizure of gunpowder from the magazine at Williamsburg in April—two days after the Battles of Lexington and Concord—Patrick led a group of volunteers to Williamsburg to confront the governor. Anne's husband came home temporarily, only to return to Williamsburg when the House of Burgesses reconvened in June. When the increasingly embattled royal governor, Dunmore, fled to a ship in the York River, William was one of four burgesses appointed to formally protest his flight and his seizure of the gunpowder.[13]

As these events unfolded in eastern Virginia, Anne Christian's correspondence remained firmly focused on family and household matters. She wrote to her sister-in-law from Mahanaim to congratulate her "on the birth of your Dear Little girl & hope it will please God to Continue her Life & health & make her a Blessing to you, & the Comfort you will then have in her, may in some measure make up for the many losses you have sustain'd in that way." She asked Fleming to send "some Turnip seed [I left] behind a glass in your Hall . . . [and] some Colewort seed or Cabbage seed from you, as all that Mr. Christian brought me up, seems good for nothing." Anne also worried that William was contemplating a move to the Holston River valley that would take her still farther from her sister-in-law and the other kin whose companionship she valued.[14]

When the third Virginia Convention met to organize for war in July 1775, once again William Christian was there. Volunteers flocked to Williamsburg to oppose the governor, and Patrick Henry, in Philadelphia at the meeting of the Second Continental Congress, was chosen to serve as colonel of what would eventually become the First Virginia Regiment; William Christian would briefly serve as lieutenant colonel and then colonel of the same regiment. After carrying news of the convention's proceedings to his backcountry constituents, Christian returned east for the early fighting. In September open warfare broke out between the governor's forces and the Virginia militia near Hampton Roads. In November Dunmore issued a proclamation offering freedom to slaves and servants who would join him in the fight. In December Virginia troops won an important victory at Great Bridge, but in the aftermath of the battle, Dunmore's forces burned several buildings in nearby Norfolk, though it was a loyalist stronghold. The Virginia militia then went on a three-day rampage, looting and burning much of the town.[15]

Anne Christian's movements and activities in the last months of 1775 are not clear, but by January 1776 she was in Williamsburg with her husband. Perhaps the enormity of events and her proximity to the action led her to break her habit of not discussing public business. "I hate much to enlarge on the publick news for none of it is good," she began, before informing her sister-in-law about the burning of Norfolk. She added that most of the Virginia troops were there, leaving only three hundred soldiers to protect Williamsburg. She claimed that the common view was that the governor would attack Yorktown soon, and fearing he would obtain reinforcements she awaited "an alarm which may drive us up to Hanover." Still, Christian's primary concerns were her immediate circumstances. "Nothing here is to be expected but wars & fighting in the Spring, I wish to God we were out of the reach of them, living peaceably at home again, which is one of the greatest blessings this life can afford.... God only can see the event of all this Confusion which at present our lower Country is in—but I heartily wish I may see an end to it soon & once more enjoy the blessed retreat of a Country Life." William, however, she observed, seemed "very well & what Surprizes me much, seems more contented than I can possibly be, at this great distance from home." He appeared to thrive on being near the center of the action.[16]

Anne's movements during the remainder of 1776 are less certain than those of her brother and husband. When the Continental Congress took the Virginia regiments into the Continental army, Patrick Henry resigned his commission in the First Virginia Regiment, and William, always popular among the men, replaced him. When Richard Henry Lee introduced the motion calling for independence in Congress, William was returning from the backcountry to Williamsburg to confirm rumors that the Cherokees were preparing for war on the western frontier. In the summer of 1776, Congress declared independence, and the Virginia Convention chose Patrick Henry as the first governor of the commonwealth. Meanwhile, William Christian resigned his commission in the Continental army to lead a war against the Cherokees.[17]

The Revolutionary War on Virginia's western frontier was primarily an Indian war, and William's most notable service came during the expedition against the Cherokees. In 1776 young Cherokee warriors had broken with their more cautious elders and attempted to take back lands claimed by white settlers along the southern frontier. In the summer and fall of 1776, North and South Carolina forces destroyed many southern Cherokee towns, and the surviving inhabitants fled northward to Cherokee towns located on land now claimed by Virginians. By late October William Christian and his men had arrived there, but the warriors had departed, leaving behind women and children. Some Cherokee leaders sought peace, but either would not or could not meet Christian's demands to hand over the British representative to the tribe and the young Cherokee leader Dragging Canoe. In retribution, Christian's troops burned the towns at Big

Island, Tellico, Chilhowee, and Settico. The older chiefs sued for peace, while the younger ones headed southwest to build new towns along the Chickamauga River. By November 1776 Christian was headed home, but in the winter and spring of 1777 he returned to the Long Island (present-day Kingsport, Tennessee) to act as a commissioner for Virginia in the treaty negotiations with the Cherokees, which continued into the summer. By then, Patrick Henry had appointed his brother-in-law to oversee the running of a boundary line between Virginia and the Cherokee country.[18]

William's involvement in the Cherokee war and its aftermath led Anne to pen the letter in which she complained to the governor (her brother Patrick) about her husband's Revolutionary activities. Claiming that family came first, she asked Patrick to "by any means be instrumental towards his [William's] quitting the publick employments that he is engaged in, [even] if it were only for [a] while, until he could get his affairs brought into some better way than at present." Anne argued that "someone certainly may be had that would answer as well to act in his place for the future, & at the same time save a whole Family from ruin, as his stay[ing] at home might yet do." She added, "I am sorry to see that he is entering from one thing to another without considering his private affairs which even are almost desperate." Anne probably feared for her husband's life and would not have expressed her concerns so bluntly had the governor not been her brother. But her focus on her family's immediate needs and her attempt to have her husband removed from active service clearly show that politics—even when they involved securing potentially lucrative western land claims—were not a high priority.[19]

Many men and women in the southern backcountry preferred to remain neutral in the conflict with Britain, and Anne Christian certainly was not the only woman who proved reluctant to part with her husband in wartime. However, her lack of enthusiasm for the Revolutionary cause is all the more striking because of the fervor with which both her husband and brother embraced it. The Christians' neighbors typically included loyalists and others who were "disaffected"—that is, they did not support the Revolution and mostly wanted to be left alone. William and his fellow revolutionaries in western Virginia actively pressured members of these groups to support the Revolutionary regime. That Anne should refuse to support William's political activities is remarkable, especially given the extent to which she generally acquiesced in his decisions in other areas.[20]

Anne's appeal to her brother was not successful, perhaps because both he and William perceived more clearly than she did the extent to which the so-called public business and their own private economic affairs were intertwined. Britain's refusal to suspend the Proclamation Line of 1763 and the passage of the Quebec Act in 1774 propelled them to support independence because the economic interests of the western elite rested on land speculation. In 1781 William was again appointed as a commissioner to represent Virginia at treaty negotiations. He was also elected to a four-year term in the Virginia Senate, representing the West: Botetourt, Greenbrier, Montgomery, and the Kentucky counties. While men of William's generation may have valued public service as a source of fame, he and his wife clearly had different views about how best to preserve their family's private fortune.[21]

Even before the war ended, William, ever the "rolling stone," began looking ahead to his next move. His fascination with the West and its potential for development led him in 1779 to consider a future move to Kentucky, where he intended to develop a town at a salt springs (known as Saltsburg) that he had patented in 1774. One brother-in-law had already preceded him westward; however, the British surrender at Yorktown in 1781 had not ended the fighting in the West, and Christian's brother-in-law was killed at the Battle of Blue Licks in 1782. Anne commented sadly on the loss and the war in a letter to her sister-in-law, "Oh how many parts of America has been fields of blood, and how oft of late have the savages triumphed victors. . . . When will the happy time of peace arrive when the sound of war shall be no more heard in our land."[22]

After the official winning of American independence in 1783, William continued to watch as the confusion over Kentucky land claims unfolded, before finally deciding to make his move in 1785. It was a calculated risk. He had traveled to Kentucky at least once by then, and brother-in-law William Fleming had sat on two commissions created by Virginia to oversee the settlement of conflicting land claims there. Two of William's sisters and their husbands had already moved across the Appalachians, and while one of the men had died fighting Indians, the other was well established near Danville. Family connections and potential prosperity pulled William toward Kentucky, while Virginia's deteriorating economic situation pushed him westward. In February 1785 he sold Mahanaim and prepared to move.[23]

Anne and William Christian were on the leading edge of American imperialism when they joined what would become a flood of migrants across the Appalachians and into the interior of the continent. Historians disagree about the extent to which women's opinions influenced the decision to move—or not—but agree that men often were more enthusiastic than their wives about starting anew. William apparently did not solicit Anne's opinion about the move to Kentucky, but he must have known that she preferred not to go. When he explained the reasons behind the timing of the move, however, she acquiesced.

As she explained to Anne Fleming, "we are amazeingly in debt at the Saltworks, which seems to be a bad prospect before us, as we were in hopes by selling here to get clear of debt & be on a good footing when we got to Kentucky." William had toured his Kentucky saltworks in 1783 with an eye toward expanding it, but left it under the control of an agent instead. By 1785 the agent had abandoned his post to live in Louisville and rented out the saltworks to people in its immediate vicinity. According to Anne, the man left in charge was rumored to draw a salary of £600 per year, "So upon the whole we must go there or be ruined, Since we have sold here."[24]

In early May William, Anne, their six children, his widowed mother, at least fourteen slaves, and an unknown quantity of livestock set out for Kentucky. After some indecision, the group took the Wilderness Road route, and Anne chronicled their progress for her sister-in-law. By mid-May they were at the Long Island on the Holston, and William's mother, Elizabeth, was feeling the ill effects of travel. From there the slaves were sent ahead, and the white people settled in to spend the summer in present-day Tennessee. In August William, Anne, and the children made the trek through the Cumberland Gap into Kentucky, but the journey proved too demanding for William's aging mother, who joined an eastward-bound party and returned safely to Virginia. After the Christians arrived in Danville, they rested with William's sister and her husband before proceeding north to the saltworks. The journey from east Tennessee had taken eleven days.[25]

William and Anne established a homestead on Beargrass Creek, about six miles from Louisville, and their enslaved laborers immediately began erecting cabins on the site, two for the family and one for "Company." Husband and wife both noted Indian activity in the neighborhood, but offered contradictory views about it. William claimed that they were "not afraid of the Indians hurting us . . . only of their taking our Horses," while Anne maintained that "the people are a good deal afraid of the Indians; they have stolen horses near here, & they attacked a house at Clarkes Ville a few days ago but were beat off." Although both initially wrote otherwise favorable reports, William quickly came around to Anne's way of thinking about the Indians. He advised William Fleming to remain in Virginia for at least two or three more years and secretly confessed to his mother some regrets about the move. He followed news of treaty negotiations with the Shawnees, and both he and Anne anticipated the coming of a general Indian war. When winter came in early December, the Indian raids temporarily ceased, but William began talking about moving the family south to safety in Danville the following spring. Anne was eager to go, but she also thought that William might opt to abandon Kentucky altogether. As she confessed to Anne Fleming, "Your Brother seems to be much displeas'd with Kentucky generally & I fear to have to move again."[26]

The late winter and early spring of 1786 brought two important transitions in Anne Christian's life. In February her eldest child, fifteen-year-old Prissey, married a fellow Virginian, Alexander Scott Bullitt, and set up housekeeping about a half mile from the Beargrass farm. William described Bullitt as "an accomplished young gentleman & Possessed of good Fortune." He owned some land and about fifty slaves, which William supplemented with a gift of a thousand acres and ten more slaves. The other development proved life altering: after an Indian raid in their neighborhood in April, William led a party of men north across the Ohio River in pursuit of some Wabash Indians and was killed.[27]

William's death sent shockwaves through the family and left Anne stunned with grief. His men carried William's body back to Beargrass Creek, and his family buried him on his land there. A nineteenth-century oral tradition maintained that Anne's grief was so great that she would not allow the horse that he had ridden to be returned because she could not bear to look at it. In May she went with her children to Danville, where they spent the summer in a cabin on the property of William's youngest sister, Rosanna, and her husband, Caleb Wallace. In a short note to her sister-in-law Anne Fleming, Anne wrote, "what I have so long dreaded [William's death] is at length come to pass"; she hoped God would give her the strength to bear it, adding, "I beg you dear Sister to excuse me from breaking off, I cannot yet write." Rosanna explained to Anne Fleming that Christian "took on after this misfortune happened amaseingly, it had like to hurt her health, but one thing that I think is very happy—She is not with Child as was thought at first." Anne asked her brother Patrick to publish news of William's death in the *Virginia Gazette* and to provide mourning rings for her daughters.[28]

With William's death, Anne entered a new stage in her life. Under English common law, at marriage women lost their legal right to control property, although some wives circumvented these limitations—generally with their husband's support—and participated in family business enterprises, often acting as temporary heads of their families during their husband's absence. Anne seems to have done this in a limited and informal way in 1774, when she recognized the deficiency in William Fleming's land survey and tried to rectify it. But widowhood changed everything. With widowhood, Anne regained the formal legal rights she had lost when she married and became the head of her family, representing their interests in the wider economic and legal realms.[29]

The post-Revolutionary economy of the 1780s offered tremendous possibilities for prosperity but at great risk. William's economic enterprises were substantial, including the developing plantation on Beargrass Creek and the expanding saltworks, whose workforce included a significant number of enslaved laborers. His death in 1786 thrust Anne into a leading role in these sophisticated and complex business ventures. She faced a steep learning curve, but the future of her children depended on her transformation into a successful woman of business. Although William had maintained an account book, it has been lost, and no systematic archive of the family's eighteenth-century business ventures survives today. Instead, documentation of their economic affairs and Anne's transformation is preserved in fragments—loose receipts and orders, a few loose individual accounts, letters concerning her mother-in-law's annuity and property, and an account book kept by her son-in-law Alexander Scott Bullitt.[30]

William's assets at the time of his death included somewhere between six thousand and ten thousand acres of Kentucky land, forty-six slaves, and the saltworks. No list of his debts survives, but they were substantial as well. Anne later confessed to a brother-in-law that William owed "considerably more than £2000" when he died, including part of a £1,700 debt for sixteen slaves contracted in 1785 and payable "in one, two, three, and four years credit." In his will, William left five hundred acres (including the farm on Beargrass Creek where the couple lived) to Anne, along with ten slaves, all the household furniture and plantation tools, a wagon and four workhorses, two riding horses, and all the cattle and hogs. Each of his four minor daughters was to receive land and slaves when she married, and William also left three slaves to his mother. The saltworks and two slaves were to go to the only son, John, when he came of age. Two tracts of land were to be sold to help pay off debts, and the profits of the saltworks were to be used to cover any remaining ones. To support and educate the children, Anne was to receive all the profits of the saltworks for seven years (provided she remained a widow) "without . . . being called to any Account [then or] . . . at any future period." However, William chose not Anne, but their son-in-law Alexander Scott Bullitt and two other men, as his executors.[31]

In addition to confusion over Kentucky land claims, the general economic uncertainty of the 1780s in the West and the nation at large, and the overlapping responsibilities for administering William's estate (especially the saltworks), Anne's situation was further complicated by the fact that William had been his father's executor. William's father, Israel Christian, died in 1784, leaving a personal estate valued at £440 and approximately nine thousand acres of land beyond the Appalachians, some surveyed and patented and some not. Israel left his livestock, five slaves, and an annuity of £100 to his wife, Elizabeth. He stipulated that some of his land should be sold, both to pay his debts and to fund his widow's annuity, and he bequeathed additional lands to his youngest daughter and to several grandchildren. William and his sister Anne Fleming were to share any land remaining after debts. When Elizabeth set out for Kentucky with William and Anne Christian in 1785, she took her livestock and slaves with her. When she turned back, her assets continued on to Kentucky. By 1786 the estates of father and son were inseparably intertwined.[32]

Even as Anne grieved during the weeks immediately following William's death, correspondence from creditors and agents began to arrive. By May 1786 she was signing receipts, issuing orders payable, and writing notes of instruction to her agents. She issued demands in a clear, confident voice, and her subordinates invariably addressed her as "Madam." Her fragmentary business papers illuminate the operation of a credit-based economy with minimal usage of coins or other cash. Anne used credit in salt to pay her debts and to purchase items, but she also instructed her agent at the saltworks to sell salt to specific individuals, preferred customers for a rare commodity.[33]

After she had been a widow for about six months, Anne wrote to both her brother and mother-in-law expressing her desire to live independently. At about the same time, she and her five youngest children left the Wallaces' place in Danville. Because she feared Indian attacks in the area around her Beargrass farm, Christian rented farms in what she called the "safe parts" of Kentucky for 1786–87 and then again for 1787–88.[34]

Anne Christian's relatively rapid progress from grieving widow to woman of business was not necessarily atypical among widows of means. Many moved quickly to master their new duties as heads of households and representatives of their families' wider economic interests. Wealthier widows generally had more clout than less well-to-do ones, even if much of their wealth was encumbered by debt. Widows of means often relied on agents, became involved in the courts, and drew on or manipulated kin to assist them. It was apparently not unusual for sons-in-law to perceive their widowed mothers-in-law and the women's new authority as threatening, however, and Alexander Scott Bullitt probably did.[35]

One particularly vexing problem with Bullitt involved bonds (promises to pay) that circulated like currency and complicated the management of William's and his father's intertwined estates. The example of Matthew Flournoy's bond best illustrates this problem. Flournoy had owed Israel Christian £150, and his bond came to William, as his father's executor. Sometime between the summer of 1786 and 1787, on Bullitt's instructions as William's executor, Anne apparently used Flournoy's bond to pay a debt to a Louisville merchant. Bullitt then complained that Anne had no right to pass the bond because it belonged to the estate of William's father. In distress, Anne wrote to her sister-in-law Fleming, "I must enjoin secrecy from you on this distressing subject, the Man [Bullitt] whose connection ought to have promised protection to my family has turned our enemy. . . . what I beg of you is to tell your dear Mother about the bond & write me if She is Satisfied with it, I hope to raise a great deal of money this winter from Salt, & will send it to her as I can get it." Anne's daughter Sally, now about fifteen years old, also wrote to her grandmother Elizabeth, asking her to "send me Power Letters [i.e., power of attorney]," presumably so that she could help with financial matters. Shortly after, Elizabeth wrote to Bullitt, asking him to collect Flournoy's bonds and place the one for £150 in Anne's hands "till it is convenient for [William's] Estate to pay it." Bullitt appears to have dragged his feet, and by the fall of 1787 a frustrated Anne was attempting to collect some of Israel's debts to help pay her mother-in-law's annuity. In 1788 Elizabeth stepped in, demanding that Bullitt deliver Flournoy's three remaining bonds, each for £100, to her agents in Kentucky. Anne received the bonds, and her daughter Sally witnessed the transaction.[36]

A twentieth-century historian described Bullitt in 1788 as "sober but immature and inconsiderate"; however, he was drinking heavily by the early 1790s. Anne's suspicion of him continued as she became more knowledgeable about her family's business interests. She began to follow the proceedings of the General Court, especially lawsuits brought by William's estate for the collection of debts. She routinely updated her mother-in-law about attempts to track down and secure payment of Israel's debts and also about the state of her slaves who remained in Kentucky. A vigilant proprietor of the family saltworks, she admonished her agent there to be "very particular in keeping an order book—to prevent mistakes." She also informed her son-in-law Bullitt that she had been "advised to apply to the Genl. Court to get appointed guardian to Johnny [her son], which I accordingly did." As Anne explained, because "Saltsburg is Johnny's whole dependance [inheritance] I wish to carry the works in a manner most conducive to his interest." She was appalled to learn that Bullitt had leased out the entire works for seven years, "a term I cannot agree to," and insisted instead that they were to be rented out annually and worked with their own slaves until all the debts of the estate were discharged. Her plan would help to preserve timber, which she thought was being cut at much too rapid a rate.[37]

As a widow, Anne became more aware of wider political developments and their impact on her economic interests. In the fall of 1786, the Spanish closed the Mississippi River—the route Kentuckians used to ship produce to distant markets—to American trade. Patrick Henry wrote to his sister that Congress intended to acquiesce and surrender navigation rights on the Mississippi, and he asked her to contact several men in Kentucky and urge them to petition against this action.[38] Whether Anne was also aware of ongoing political developments intended to separate Kentucky from Virginia (and in some cases from the United States) remains uncertain, but she addressed neither these topics nor the 1788 debate over ratification of the new U.S. Constitution in her correspondence.

In the spring of 1788, Anne began to think seriously about returning to Virginia for an extended stay. She carefully assessed her financial situation, and by July she had made up her mind. As she explained to Elizabeth, "I think I can leave my affairs in such a way as may prevent their suffering in my absence." Anne hired someone to dispose of the salt, and she planned to hire out the slaves currently at the rental plantation for next year, except about a half dozen whom she would send to Beargrass under an overseer to make a crop on the farm there. She expected the corn crop at Beargrass to generate enough income to support the slaves working there. The wheat crop currently in the field at the rental farm she proposed to have ground into flour and sold at Louisville, where "it bears a good market." The livestock would be left in the care of the enslaved drover Edinburgh, who could see to them over the winter and then drive them down to the farm in the spring. Finally, Anne noted, "I am happy to inform you that we are almost out of debt," and she detailed a plan for paying off those debts that remained.[39]

Anne's plan for the management of her economic affairs during her absence shows that she had become both knowledgeable and authoritative in a relatively short time. She had a keen grasp of her own assets and of local market conditions. Like most other slave owners, male or female, she was remarkably insensitive to the plight of her human workforce. Neither she nor William hesitated to send slaves to the saltworks—which were particularly vulnerable to Indian raids in the 1780s—or to keep them at Beargrass (which she now called "Fort William" in honor of her late husband). Slaves not employed at the saltworks or on the farm during Anne's absence were to be rented out, a process that typically separated enslaved people from their families.[40]

Her affairs in order, Anne Christian recrossed the Appalachians and headed east with her five youngest children in August 1788. She spent the next year visiting family and friends in the Piedmont and southwestern Virginia. Her mother-in-law, Elizabeth, died in the late summer of 1789, and sometime during that year Anne developed a persistent cough. Doctor's orders sent her to Yorktown for her health, but when recovery proved elusive, she was advised to spend the winter of 1789–90 in the West Indies. In October Anne made her will, left her four youngest children with her brother Patrick, and prepared to set sail for Antigua. In December she wrote to her children that she had arrived safely and promised to bring presents when she returned—fashionable things for the older daughters, a doll for the youngest, and "some rareties suitable for" her son, Johnny. She never saw any of them again. Christian set sail for Norfolk in April 1790 and died there on May 4, a day or two after her arrival. Her burial place remains unknown.[41]

Anne Christian's death in 1790 at the age of fifty-one cuts off the possibility of definitively answering the question of whether she—like so many other women—would have become caught up in the partisan political fervor of the 1790s, but that seems unlikely. As a widow and a businesswoman, Christian saw herself primarily as a steward safeguarding her children's inheritances. As a member of the white propertied elite, she operated from a position of privilege. Both she and her husband saw Native Americans primarily as obstacles to their own family's prosperity, and they displayed little sensitivity to the human suffering that their decisions created for their enslaved workforce. As a woman, even a widow, however, Christian faced social, economic, and legal challenges, as her struggles with Bullitt illustrate.[42]

By the terms she set for herself, Christian ultimately succeeded as a woman of business. Her daughters became women of property, married well, and returned to Kentucky, although her only son died unmarried at the age of nineteen. But perhaps Alexander Scott Bullitt, the son-in-law who so frustrated Anne, did best of all. After her death one of the executors of Anne's will refused to serve, explaining that the business of William's estate was "in such a channel, that it cannot be diverted, without creating ... displeasure." He noted that Bullitt, as William's executor, would certainly "have a right to possess himself of the Salt Works," and added (appearing to confirm Anne's earlier view of Bullitt), he "is greatly reformed [and] I have now hopes of his being an useful member of Society." Bullitt did take control of the saltworks—although after their brother's death the Christians' daughters held shares in it—and the Bullitt family became a Kentucky dynasty. Their estate, Oxmoor, was eventually built on William and Anne's Beargrass Creek farm, and in perhaps a final twist of irony, Bullitt's descendants were responsible for preserving much of the written documentation of Anne Christian's business activities.[43]

The remarkable written record that she left behind distinguishes Anne Henry Christian from most of her eighteenth-century Virginian contemporaries. It enables us to trace her transformation from a young wife and mother focused on domestic concerns within her household to a widowed woman of business representing her family's interests in the wider economic and legal world. Although this transition may have been typical for many eighteenth-century women, Christian's account of it was anything but. Her letters provide an intimate glimpse of one woman's perceptions of life on Virginia's Revolutionary frontier. They deepen our understanding not only of her life but also of the multifaceted experience of the American Revolution. For Anne Christian, the Revolutionary era represented a watershed, but she resisted the changes it brought. The roots of her transformation lay in a more personal and traditional cause: the loss of her husband.

NOTES

Research for this chapter was supported by fellowships at the Virginia Historical Society and the Filson Historical Society. I am grateful to the staffs of both for their assistance.

1. On Elizabeth Henry Campbell Russell, see the chapter by Jon Kukla in this volume.

2. Anne Christian (hereafter AC) to Anne Fleming (hereafter AF), January 14, 1776, Hugh Blair Grigsby Papers (hereafter Grigsby), Virginia Historical Society (hereafter VHS); AC to Patrick Henry (hereafter PH), May 22, 1777, transcript, Bullitt Family Papers, Filson Historical Society (hereafter FHS). On the impact of the Revolution, see Mary Beth Norton, *Liberty's Daughters: The Revolutionary Experience of American Women* (Boston: Little, Brown, 1980); Laurel Thatcher Ulrich, "Introduction," to her *A Midwife's Tale: The Life of Martha Ballard, Based on Her Diary, 1785–1812* (New York: Knopf, 1990); and Carol Berkin, *Revolutionary Mothers: Women in the Struggle for America's Independence* (New York: Knopf, 2005), chap. 3.

3. "Christian, Annie," *Dictionary of Virginia Biography* (Richmond: Library of Virginia, 2006), 3:223–24 (hereafter *DVB*). Christian signed her letters "Annie Christian" or "A. Christian." For birth date, see Edith Poindexter to Brent Tarter, April 3, 2003, private communication from Tarter to the author. John Henry to Israel Christian, January 12, 1768, in William Wirt Henry, ed., *Patrick Henry: Life, Correspondence, and Speeches*, 2 vols. (New York: Charles Scribner's Sons, 1891), 1:122–23.

4. "Christian, William," *DVB*, 3:234. See also Gail S. Terry, "Family Empires: A Frontier Elite in Virginia and Kentucky, 1740–1815" (PhD diss., College of William and Mary, 1992), 39–40, 191, 264–65; Anna C. Baxter to Lyman C. Draper, January 3, 1845, Draper Collection, 8 CC 38, Wisconsin State Historical Society, Madison; Louisa P. Baxter to Hugh Blair Grigsby, February 20, August 2, August 6, 1858, and August 25, 1873; Elizabeth H. Baxter to Hugh Blair Grigsby, July 10, 1867, all in Grigsby. The bulk of AC's letters are in the William Fleming Papers (hereafter Fleming), Washington and Lee University Library, Lexington, Va.

5. Eliza Ramsey to Lyman C. Draper, February 22, 1842, Draper Collection, 8 ZZ 4; AC to AF, December 3, 1770, Fleming.

6. AC to AF, December 3 and 4, 1770; November 11, 1771; n.d.; and January 16, 1772, all in Fleming. I have standardized Christian's spelling and modernized the punctuation.

7. AC to AF, January 29, 1770; November 11, 1771; April 11, 1772, Fleming. On AF's miscarriages or stillbirths, see AC to AF, April 29, 1775, ibid. For a list of AF's children who survived to adulthood, including Lenny and six children born in 1775 and after, see the Collection Control Folder for Fleming.

8. Woody Holton, *Forced Founders: Indians, Debtors, Slaves, and the Making of the American Revolution in Virginia* (Chapel Hill: University of North Carolina Press, 1999), chap. 2; Colin G. Calloway, *The Shawnees and the War for America* (New York: Viking, 2007), chap. 3.

9. Calloway, *The Shawnees and the War for America*; John E. Selby and Edward M. Riley, *Dun-*

more (Williamsburg: Virginia Bicentennial Commission, 1977), chap 2; "Introduction," in Reuben G. Thwaites and Louise P. Kellogg, eds., *Documentary History of Dunmore's War, 1774* (Madison: State Historical Society of Wisconsin, 1905), ix–xxviii.

10. William Fleming (hereafter WF) to AF, September 4, 7, 9, and 27, 1774; and William Christian (hereafter WC) to AF, September 18, 1774, all in Draper Collection, 2 ZZ 1–5 and 10; AC to AF, October 3 and 15, 1774, Fleming.

11. AC to AF, October 15, 1774, Fleming.

12. Ibid.; John M. Hemphill II, "Introduction," in *Cavaliers and Pioneers: Abstracts of Virginia Land Patents and Grants*, vol. 7, ed. Dennis Ray Hudgins (Richmond: Library of Virginia, 1999), vii–xvi.

13. AC to AF, January 30, 1775, Fleming; "Christian, William," 234. See also John E. Selby, *The Revolution in Virginia, 1773–1783* (Williamsburg, Va.: Colonial Williamsburg, 1988), prologue and chap. 3; Michael A. McDonnell, *The Politics of War: Race, Class, and Conflict in Revolutionary Virginia* (Chapel Hill: University of North Carolina Press, 2007), chaps. 1–2.

14. AC to AF, April 29, 1775, Fleming.

15. WC to William Preston, August 17, 1775, Preston Family Papers, Perkins Library, Duke University, Durham, N.C.; McDonnell, *Politics of War*, chaps. 3–5; Selby, *Revolution in Virginia*, 41–88.

16. AC to AF, January 14, 1776, Grigsby.

17. "Christian, William," 234; Arthur Campbell to William Campbell, June 12, 1776, Campbell-Preston-Floyd Papers, vol. 1, Manuscripts Division, Library of Congress; William Campbell to Elizabeth Henry Campbell, August 18, 1776, ibid.; Selby, *Revolution in Virginia*, chaps. 5–6; McDonnell, *Politics of War*, chaps. 7–8.

18. Colin G. Calloway, *The American Revolution in Indian Country* (Cambridge: Cambridge University Press, 1995), 26, 43–44, 49, 182–202; Selby, *Revolution in Virginia*, 184–88; WC to PH, October 6, 14, 15, and 23, 1776, *Virginia Magazine of History and Biography* 17 (1909): 52–64; WC to William Russell, November 12, 1776, transcript, Bullitt Family Papers; WC et al., "Record of Negotiations with Cherokee, January 22–April 21, 1777," Draper Collection 4 QQ 76–153; WC to Evan Shelby, [c. July 1777], Shelby Papers, vol. 1, Library of Congress.

19. AC to PH, May 22, 1777, transcript, Bullitt Family Papers.

20. Albert H. Tillson Jr., *Gentry and Common Folk: Political Culture on the Virginia Frontier, 1740–1789* (Lexington: University of Kentucky Press, 1991), 101–16; Emory G. Evans, "Trouble in the Backcountry: Disaffection in Southwest Virginia during the American Revolution," in *An Uncivil War*, ed. Ronald Hoffman et al. (Charlottesville: University of Virginia Press, 1985), 179–212; Proceedings of Montgomery and Botetourt Counties, August 1780, Draper Collection, 5 QQ 3–79; Berkin, *Revolutionary Mothers*, chap. 3; Terry, "Family Empires," 191–204.

21. Nathanael Greene, Commission Appointing WC et al., February 26, 1781, and WC's speeches at treaty negotiations, July 1781, Draper Collection, 1 XX 30, 45, 49; Thomas Jefferson to William Preston, WC, and Joseph Martin, March 24, 1781, transcript, Preston Family Papers, VHS; Calloway, *American Revolution in Indian Country*, 49–51, 58, 202–8; "Christian, William," 234–35. See also Douglass Adair, "Fame and the Founding Fathers," in *Fame and the Founding Fathers: Essays by Douglass Adair*, ed. Trevor Colborn (New York: Norton, 1974), 3–36.

22. WC to William Campbell, July 11, 1779, Campbell-Preston-Floyd Papers; WC to WF, December 21, 1779, Grigsby; Calloway, *American Revolution in Indian Country*, 272, 280–84; AC to AF, October 7, 1782, Fleming; WC to Benjamin Harrison, September 28, 1782, Governor's Letters Received, July 1776–November 1784, Library of Virginia.

23. WC to William Preston, February 7, 1782, Preston Family Papers, VHS; AC to AF, October 7,

1782, and January 17, 1785, Fleming; WC to Elizabeth Christian (hereafter EC), February 19, 1785, Grigsby. On land claims, see Patricia Watlington, *The Partisan Spirit* (Chapel Hill: University of North Carolina Press, 1972), chap 1.

24. For women vetoing or delaying moves, see George Thompson to John Breckinridge, December 15, 1792, and Mary Howard to John Breckinridge, July 22, 1792, Breckinridge Family Papers, Library of Congress; John Mack Faragher, *Daniel Boone: The Life and Legend of an American Pioneer* (New York: Henry Holt, 1992), 63–65. On the debate, see Joan E. Cashin, *A Family Venture: Men and Women on the Southern Frontier* (New York: Oxford University Press, 1991), chap. 2; Jane Turner Censer, "Southwestern Migration among North Carolina Planters: 'The Disposition to Emigrate,'" *Journal of Southern History* 57 (1991): 407–26; and Gail S. Terry, "Writing Migration: White Women's Letters and Emigration from the Valley of Virginia," paper delivered at the Annual Meeting of the American Historical Association, New York, January 3, 1997. See also AC to AF, March 15, 1785, Fleming; Robert E. McDowell, "Bullitt's Lick: The Related Saltworks and Settlements," *Filson Club Historical Quarterly* 30 (1956): 241–69. See also WC Power of Attorney to Robert Daniel (hereafter RD), August 23, 1783; WC and RD, Partnership Agreement, August 31, 1783; and RD, Relinquishment of Rights in Saltworks, November 15, 1785, Bullitt Family Papers; Mary Trigg Daniel to WC, November 21 and December 25, 1783, transcripts, Robert Emmett McDowell Collection, vol. 1, Bullitt's Lick Papers, FHS.

25. EC to AF, January 25, 1785, Fleming; AC to AF, March 15 and May 18, 1785, ibid.; AC to AF, June 9 and August 17, 1785, Grigsby.

26. WC to EC, August 17, November 4, and December 12, 1785, Grigsby; AC to AF, August 17, September 13, November 3, and December 15, 1785, ibid.; WC to WF, September 25, 1785, ibid.

27. WC to EC, March 30, 1786, Grigsby; AC to WC, March 22, 1786, Draper Collection, 2 U 140; AC to AF, March 26, 1786, Grigsby; "Christian, William," 235.

28. Lucien Beckner, ed., "Rev. John Dabney Shane's Interview with Mrs. Sarah Graham," *Filson Historical Quarterly* 9 (1930): 9. I am grateful to Ellen Eslinger for this reference. AC to AF, June 25, 1786, Fleming; Rosanna Wallace to AF, June 26, [1786], ibid.; AC to PH, n.d., Bullitt Family Papers.

29. Laurel Thatcher Ulrich, *Good Wives: Image and Reality in the Lives of Women in Northern New England 1650–1750* (New York: Oxford University Press, 1983), 35–50; and Linda L. Sturtz, *Within Her Power: Propertied Women in Colonial Virginia* (New York: Routledge, 2002), esp. chap. 3.

30. On the lost account book, see AC to EC, October 30, 1787, Fleming. Except for letters regarding EC's property, Anne's business papers and the records of William's estate are in the Bullitt Family Papers. For the evolution of this collection, see Honor Sachs, "Reconstructing a Life: The Archival Challenges of Women's History," *Library Trends* 56 (2008): 656–58.

31. AC to WF, April 12, 1787, Grigsby; WC to EC, December 12, 1785, ibid.; Will of WC, March 13, 1786, certified copy, Misc. Papers, FHS.

32. Will of Israel Christian, July 12, 1784, and Appraisement of Israel Christian's Personal Estate, January 14, 1785, Montgomery County Deeds and Wills, book B, 1773–97, 66–68, microfilm, Library of Virginia.

33. J. Donne to AC, May 1, May 10, and June 14, 1786, and Orders of AC, May 18, 1786–May 7, 1787, all in Bullitt Family Papers. On women and personalism, see Suzanne Lebsock, *The Free Women of Petersburg: Status and Culture in a Southern Town, 1784–1860* (New York: Norton, 1984).

34. AC to EC, September 18, 1786, and May 11, 1788, Grigsby; AC to PH, September 1786, transcript, and AC's lease with Jacob Myers, August 20, 1787, both in Bullitt Family Papers.

35. Kirsten E. Wood, *Masterful Women: Slaveholding Widows from the American Revolution*

through the Civil War (Chapel Hill: University of North Carolina Press, 2006), 5, 7, 62–65, 82, 87–90, 101–2.

36. AC to AF, [1786–87]; Sarah Winston Christian to EC, n.d.; EC to [ASB], n.d., and to Caleb Wallace, n.d.; AC to EC, [no month], October 30, 1787, and January 2, 1788, all in Fleming; EC to ASB, July 11, 1788, receipt on verso, Bullitt Family Papers. See also Caleb Wallace to WF, August 13, 1788; WF to ASB, October 27, 1788; and AC to AF November 13, 1788, all in Fleming.

37. On Bullitt, see Watlington, *Partisan Spirit*, 142. On AC's increasing business acumen, see James McCorkle to AC, January 7 and 25, 1788; AC to James Asturgus, January 28, March 1 and 11, 1788; Daniel Brodhead Jr. to Richard Woolfolk, March 21, 1788; AC to ASB, April 24, 1788, all in Bullitt Family Papers; AC to EC, March 22 and May 11, 1788, Grigsby; AC to EC, March 28, 1788, Fleming.

38. Watlington, *Partisan Spirit*, 105; PH to AC, October 20, 1786, transcript, Bullitt Family Papers.

39. AC to EC, May 11 and July 18, 1788, Grigsby.

40. Ibid. See also AC to [?], 1787, Bullitt Family Papers; WC to EC, November 4, 1787, Grigsby; *Kentucky Gazette*, December 13 and 20, 1788, and November 21, 1789, cited in Penn Bogart, "Citations to African Americans in Kentucky Newspapers before 1815," FHS. More generally, see Ellen Eslinger, "The Shape of Slavery on the Kentucky Frontier," *Register of the Kentucky Historical Society* (1994): 1–23; Wood, *Masterful Women*, 6–7.

41. Caleb Wallace to WF, August 13, 1788, Fleming; AC to EC, September 20, 1788, ibid.; AC to AF, [1788], ibid.; AC to AF, November 13, 1788, and September 11, 1789, Grigsby; AC to AF and WF, September 28, 1789, ibid.; Will of AC, October 10, 1789, certified copy, Bullitt Family Papers; AC to her children, December 11, 1789, transcript, ibid.; AC to John Breckinridge, February and June 15, 1789, Breckinridge Family Papers; PH to John Breckinridge, July 3, 1789, ibid.; *Norfolk and Portsmouth Chronicle*, May 8, 1790; [Richmond] *Virginia Independent Chronicle and General Advertiser*, May 12, 1790; "Christian, Annie," 224.

42. On women and political parties in the 1790s, see Rosemarie Zagarri, *Revolutionary Backlash: Women and Politics in the Early American Republic* (Philadelphia: University of Pennsylvania Press, 2007), esp. chap. 2.

43. Harry Innes to WF, July 31, 1790, Fleming, but cf. Watlington, *Partisan Spirit*, 142; ASB, Account Book, Bullitt Family Papers; Thomas W. Bullitt, *My Life at Oxmoor* (1911; updated and privately reprinted, 1995), 11–15. ASB later purchased the Beargrass farm from a third party (Shirley Harmon, FHS, conversation with the author, August 10, 1999).

Mary Draper Ingles

A Survivor in Her Time and a Legend Ever Since

MARY C. FERRARI

In the summer of 1755 Mary Draper Ingles, her husband, William, and their two sons were living at the Draper's Meadow settlement on the edge of the Virginia frontier. At the end of July Shawnee Indians attacked the settlement, capturing Mary, her sons, and her sister-in-law, and killing several people, including Mary's mother. The Natives and their captives traveled for one month into the Ohio Territory. Mary, separated from her sons and sister-in-law, lived among the Indians for several weeks, until she and another woman (whose name is unknown) escaped and began the long journey back to the Virginia settlements. The journey of more than four hundred miles, undertaken without many provisions, involved following the Ohio River to the Kanawha and then to the New River, where both women were rescued. The dramatic story of her escape and eventual return home turned Mary Draper Ingles into a legend that has been embraced by a region, a town, and a university.

Born in the 1730s and dying in 1815, Mary Draper Ingles led a long and eventful life. Her story is important for the insights it provides into women's lives and work on the Virginia frontier, especially in the New River valley, where she and her family were among the earliest and most prosperous white settlers. A hardworking mother and wife who played integral roles in the family's enterprises—which included a ferry and a tavern—Mary was in some ways a representative woman of the backcountry planter elite. At the same time, the narrative of her escape from captivity has lived on in both oral tradition and written accounts, the first of which was penned by one of her sons in the 1820s. The popularity of Mary's story, which secured her unlikely fame after her death, reflected the white population's continuing fascination with Native Americans and especially with episodes that pitted white women against the so-called savages. The public telling—and retelling—of Mary's story made her a key figure in the historical memory of western Virginia. From her son's dramatic portrait of a daring and determined woman who bore the emotional scars of her ordeal, to twentieth-century celebrations of the frontierswoman as American patriot, the successive iterations of her saga have reflected Virginians' evolving ideas about gender, race, and the frontier in the history of the Old Dominion.

Mary Draper Ingles rarely appears in the historical record, where her husband, William Ingles, is amply represented. Mary's testimony was recorded in deed books when William's estate was settled after his death. Her name is listed in two surviving daybooks from stores at which she purchased goods. The story of her escape appeared in several colonial newspapers. And sometime before his death in 1836, as a result of pressure from relations and friends, her son John wrote a short history of "the defficulties and sufferings my fathers own family had to undergo at that early day," including the scenes "through which they had to pass in their first settling on the Western Watters of Virginia." His work, published under the title *Escape from Indian Captivity*, was the first of three nineteenth-century renditions of the Mary Draper Ingles story. It was also probably the most accurate.[1]

John Ingles's account was based on the stories his parents told, which "made such deep and lasting impressions on my youthfull mind that they will never be forgotten by me as long as I live." He admitted that his narrative might seem "fabulous or romantick" but insisted that it was based on facts "that could have been abundantly established by many witnesses." Still, captive stories typically blended fact with fiction. The brief newspaper accounts that appeared after Mary's return corroborate some of John's details, such as his claim that she was exempt from running the gauntlet and from other forms of ritual humiliation typically imposed on captives. Other parts of John's story, if not totally fictional, reflected the biases of his time. For example, he went to great lengths to explain why his father did not rescue the captives, thus justifying William's failure to play his socially prescribed protective role. Nineteenth-century ideas about gender and motherhood likewise shaped John's account. In his version of her story, Mary escaped because she was "so distressed in being separated from her children & her situation such a disagreeable one that she came to the determined resolution that she wood leave them & try to get Home or dy in the woods."[2]

The real-life Mary Draper was born to George and Eleanor Draper sometime

MONUMENT IN HONOR OF MARY DRAPER INGLES
Located in the West View Cemetery in Radford, the monument was erected in 1909 and is partially built of bricks from her house's chimney.
Photo by Lora Gordon.

RECONSTRUCTED INGLES CABIN

A historical interpreter, John Jefferies, a direct descendant of
Mary Draper Ingles, stands in front of the reconstructed cabin
located on the family's property in Radford, Virginia.
Photo by Lora Gordon.

around 1732. The family may have been in Augusta County, then the westernmost county of Virginia, as early as 1742, when a George Draper was listed among the members of George Robinson's militia company. In 1747 Mary's father became the constable in Augusta County. Two years later he was dead, and when his wife, the administrator of his estate, called for an inventory, it was performed by William Ingles and his father. Around this time, William Ingles and Mary Draper married. In 1745 the council of Virginia granted James Patton and his Wood's River Company a hundred thousand acres of land on the New and Holston rivers. The next year, families began to move into the area. Within a decade Patton had settled more than a hundred families on his land, including the Ingleses. By that time Mary and William had two sons, Thomas and George.[3]

Mary and William lived in Draper's Meadow, which was part of the Tom's Creek settlement. Virginia's frontier people formed clusters of farmsteads with miles between them and other groups of settlers. Speculators tended to survey only the good land, skipping over other areas and consequently leaving white settlements dispersed. Settlers were committed to their local neighborhoods—so much so that when the Indians threatened, families often fled or stayed in neighborhood groups. Settlements consisted of "ethnically diverse, white Protestant, freehold-farm families" who lived and traded together. The largest ethnic group in the New River valley was the Scots Irish, who comprised 40 percent of the population; another 28 percent were English, 22 percent were German, and 10 percent were Welsh. Most inhabitants of the Tom's Creek settlement were German. Indeed, the German-born Adam Harmon was the first person Mary encountered on her return from captivity in 1755. The fact that Harmon recognized her voice without seeing her suggests that he knew her well.[4]

Men in places as far off as London, Quebec, Ohio, Williamsburg, and Philadelphia made decisions that resulted in the violence that Mary, her family, and so many others experienced or witnessed in the 1750s. The horrific Indian raid of July 1755 had its roots in centuries-old hatreds that originated in Europe and flourished in America. As Mary and William built their lives in western Virginia, tensions were increasing on two continents as the French, the English, and their respective Native American allies battled over who would control the Ohio Territory. The Virginia frontier became embroiled in that contest. With the territory between the Blue Ridge and the Ohio River theoretically under British influence, Virginia governor Robert Dinwiddie and his friends sought to profit by land speculation in that area, which was inhabited mainly by Delaware and Shawnee Indians. The Ohio Natives were increasingly cautious in their dealings with both the French and the British, but after 1752, because of their concerns about British land speculation, they allied themselves decisively with the French.[5]

By 1754 the French and Indian War had begun in the colonies, and within two years it became a world war. French Canada was much smaller than British North America, so the French used their own military forces to defend the St. Lawrence and Hudson rivers and tried to entice their Native allies to attack the frontiers of the more central British colonies, including Virginia. But the Shawnees and Delawares were not just pawns of the French. They were also eager to stop the movement of British colonists toward their territory, and they avidly pursued honor, prisoners, and plunder by attacking white colonial settlements. Between 1754 and 1758 small war parties of Shawnees terrorized the Virginia backcountry. The Shawnees adopted a purposeful war strategy to maximize destruction and, they hoped, discourage further white settlement in their territory. Larger war parties attacked forts and supply depots—though they usually waited until the target was weakened by disease or undermanned—while smaller parties raided settlements where women and children predominated.[6]

White families in western Virginia and Pennsylvania suffered tremendously as a consequence of Indian raids. Between 1755 and 1758 Ohio Natives took as many as a thousand captives and killed two thousand people. In Virginia, the western counties of Augusta, Frederick, and Hampshire were the main targets of these attacks, but raids also occurred farther east in Bedford, Halifax, and Albemarle. Fear of attack caused the frontier to empty of settlers. In fact, residents abandoned their homes in such large numbers that Indians complained that they had to travel too far to reach white settlements to raid. Augusta County's population dropped by half between 1754 and 1758; it did not return to prewar levels until 1764. War also hurt the Ohio Indians, who suffered crop shortages, a smallpox epidemic, and battle losses.[7]

Mary Draper Ingles and her family were the victims of an Indian raid in late July 1755, when the Shawnees attacked the settlement at Draper's Meadow. Colonel James Patton, Mary's mother, and others were killed in the raid, while Mary, her four- and two-year-old sons, and her sister-in-law, Betty Draper, were captured. The men at Draper's Meadow were working in the fields, far enough away that they did not realize that the attack had happened until it was too late to save anyone. In John Ingles's version of the story, his father returned while the Indians were still there, but the attackers chased the unarmed Ingles into the woods, where he fell and hid in the underbrush while his pursuers continued running. The Shawnee raiders may have known that Patton, a leading land speculator, was in the settlement when they attacked. Several years earlier, Patton had attended a conference at Logg Town at which two Shawnee headmen were present. The Natives who heard Patton's speech at the conference interpreted his words as a threat and were angered by his actions.[8]

The Shawnees struck fast, seized people and goods, set fire to buildings, and then retreated quickly before they could be followed. At Draper's Meadow, they took "their prisoners and plunder and started and steared their course down the New River." Though prisoners generally were "roughly treated," Mary later claimed that she was treated with respect and that she and her two children were often allowed to ride a horse. Mary attended to Betty Draper's injured arm, and her captors permitted her to go into the woods to get supplies to dress the wound. Although Mary's escape would have been easier if she had run off before reaching the Ohio country, she "could not think of leaving her children," according to her son. Ingles, Draper, and the two boys were brought to the Ohio Valley, traveling for a month until they reached an Indian village at the mouth of the Scioto River. As they approached the village, the Shawees forced most of the captives to run the gauntlet, which in this case consisted of "forming . . . two lines of all the Indians in the nation men women and children and the prisoners to start at the Head of the two rows formed & run down between the lines & every Indian giving them a cut or a pelt with switch sticks or such things." For some reason, Mary was not required to perform this ritual, though when the Natives gathered to divide and adopt the prisoners, Mary was separated from her young sons.[9]

The Shawnee world that Mary then entered might not have been completely foreign to her. Native towns had longhouses, used for ritual dances and gatherings, but most families lived in small cabins, some of which had chimneys and cellars. Decades of trade with the Europeans had filled Indian settlements with familiar items, such as kettles, European hardware, cloth, ceramics, and jewelry. Mary's boys could have played with the same imported toys they enjoyed at Draper's Meadow. Cloth was already more widely used for clothing than buckskin among the Indians, and the Native diet had expanded from the local staples of corn, beans, and squash to include cabbage, turnips, cucumbers, chocolate, and tea. The large number of white captives who came to the Ohio Territory accelerated these changes. By the 1760s travelers noted that Native Americans enjoyed cardplaying and European dances and games.[10]

Mary stayed in the Shawnee village for two or three weeks and then accompanied a group of Indians to Big Bone Lick, in present-day Kentucky, to make salt. There, she decided to attempt an escape, encouraging an "old Dutch woman" (who was probably a German woman from her neighborhood) to join her. Under the guise of gathering grapes, the two women wandered off with a blanket, a tomahawk, and perhaps a knife. They did not take any other supplies or clothing to avoid arousing the suspicions of their captors.[11]

Big Bone Lick was a hundred miles from the Ohio River, which Ingles and her companion needed to follow to find their way home. The women followed the Ohio to the Kanawha and ultimately to the white settlements on the New River. They likely traveled even farther because the streams and creeks connected to the rivers sometimes forced them to go offtrack in search of shallow areas where they could cross before returning to the main river. Early in the endeavor, they found an abandoned cabin with corn and a horse, but they later lost the horse trying to cross a stream; mostly, they lived on whatever food they could find in the woods, such as nuts and grapes. Often they were "so pushed with hunger that they would dig up roots & eate that they knew nothing of." At one point, the "Dutch Woman" inexplicably attempted to kill her companion, but Mary avoided injury and traveled on alone. John Ingles also reported that "the little clothing which she had started with was nearly or entirely worn out or dragged off of her by the Brush on her long Journey & her mocosans intierly worn out." Traveling in the fall, Mary found the nights quite cold, and she found shelter in hollow logs or under leaves. After six weeks she reached Adam Harmon's home on the New River. He brought her to the fort at Dunkard's Bottom, where she was reunited with her brother and husband. The "Dutch Woman" was also rescued. Oddly, the reunion between the two women was said to be joyful.[12]

In 1756 Shingas, a Delaware war captain, claimed to not be afraid of the English, whom he viewed generally as "old women" who could not travel "without loaded Horses and Waggons full of Provisions and a great deal of Baggage." But Mary Ingles, a woman in her twenties, accompanied by an older woman, traveled more than four hundred miles and forty-two days without any baggage and with very few provisions. The younger of Mary's two sons at the time, George, never returned from captivity. The older boy, Thomas, spent thirteen years among the Indians; his family eventually paid for his return, with William making two trips to the Ohio country before he retrieved his son. According to his brother John, the seventeen-year-old Thomas was "an entier Indian in his manner & appearance & could not speake one word of English." Family members worked hard to reintroduce Thomas to their world, but the transition was not easy, and he never completely reacclimated. Eventually, he was sent to school in Albemarle County under the watchful eye of Thomas Walker, a leading explorer and land speculator. After three or four years, he had become more acculturated, though he retained some of his "Indian actions."[13]

The extent to which Mary's successful journey was remarkable is well illuminated by comparing it to an ill-fated expedition to the Ohio River by the Augusta County militia. In 1755 Governor Dinwiddie ordered 350 men to be drafted from the Augusta County militia to attack the same Indian town where Mary was held captive. The group, led by Colonel Andrew Lewis, assembled in February 1756 and attempted to go down the Big Sandy River to the Ohio, a 350-mile trip. The men brought enough food for only fifteen days, which was still much more than Mary had to begin her journey. A shortage of horses and heavy rains hindered the troops' progress, forcing Lewis to cut the troops' rations in half. After a month of travel that saw desertions and mutinous attitudes among the men, the food ran out, and the troops refused to continue. Unlike Mary, they never reached their destination.[14]

After Mary's return home, the war raged on and she and William, like many white people in their area, took shelter in the local Fort Vause. Most frontier forts, like Vause, were simple and even improvised structures. Fort Vause was the home of Ephraim Vause, who had fortified his house and built a stockade around it. The Ingleses moved there in the spring of 1756, but they did not stay long, supposedly because Mary was restless and uneasy. They then went to Bedford County, on the other side of the Blue Ridge Mountains. Their move was fortuitous because the Shawnees attacked Fort Vause on July 16, 1756, and "there being only 4 or 5 men in the fort they could not go out to give the enemy battle."[15]

The Ingleses remained in Bedford County for several years. In 1757 William Ingles bought a town lot in Bedford and some larger lots just outside the town center. By 1762, however, he and his family returned to the New River valley and settled near what is now Radford, where they operated a ferry across the river. Because this part of the frontier was still vulnerable to Indian attacks, William, like Ephraim Vause, built a fort at his house, and every season local families gathered at what Ingles called Fort Hope. In 1763, when a group of Indians returning from attacking some families on the Smith River passed near the Ingleses' house, William led a force of between fifteen and eighteen men against them. Ingles reported with satisfaction that his men "all behaved like good soldiers," forcing the Natives to run off, abandoning thirty horses, their plunder, and their prisoners.[16] As the frontier moved west, Indian raids on the New River became less frequent, but Mary's family still experienced tragedy, as some family and friends moved west with the frontier and became victims of violence.

For the next decade and a half, Mary and William expanded their fortunes and family with the addition of four children—Susanna, Rhoda, Mary, and John, who was born in 1766. One traveler described the scenery around the Ingles home on the New River as "romantic to a degree the river very beautifull, the hills well wooded, the low grounds well improved & well stocked." Mary played many roles in her long life: daughter, wife, keeper of a household, director of slaves, mother, and grandmother. William Ingles, too, wore many hats: farmer, government official, tax collector, tavern owner, merchant, ferryman, and militia officer. Much of the historiography of the New River valley has focused on how much and how quickly the social stratification of the Tidewater moved westward.[17] Surviving sources for the frontier area—most of which are public records—make political and military studies more feasible than a detailed reconstruction of the essential work that women performed in frontier households and communities. While it is relatively easy to document William's move up the economic and political ladder in the county, it is harder to show how Mary's roles and circumstances adapted to her new status as a female member of the local elite.

William Ingles profited from his various business and agricultural ventures. In 1766 he took out an ordinary (tavern) license with a partner, David Robinson. Two years later he received another ordinary license in his name only. Then, when Fincastle County was created in 1773, Ingles was one of the first to get an ordinary license from the new county. In addition to providing places for locals to drink and travelers to stay, taverns served many public and private functions. Taverns fostered the development of community connections and served as sites of political discussion and business transactions, as post offices, and as newsrooms. The taverns, like the ferry he operated, would have been reliable sources of both information and income for William and his family.[18]

Like most people in the area, William was also a farmer. Farmers in the New River valley grew corn, wheat, and rye, but their biggest cash crops were hemp and flax. In 1774 William registered a certificate for 1,750 pounds of hemp, and he probably also grew flax. Like most Virginia farmers, William also raised livestock. The 1782 tax lists show that he owned fifty-one horses and sixty-seven cattle, a far higher number than the average of eight horses owned by each New River valley head of household. Since William sold bacon to the military, he must have had pigs as well.[19]

All of these enterprises required more labor than William could have performed alone. He paid taxes on three slaves in 1770, and in the ensuing years, as his wealth increased, his slaveholdings more than tripled. In 1782 only 11.65 percent of the county's households included slaves. William paid taxes on ten enslaved people, far exceeding the county average of 3.62 slaves per slaveholding household. William may have generated additional income by hiring out some of his enslaved workers. In 1774 he sued Joseph Hicks, who allegedly had "beat, wound[ed] and ill treat[ed]" one of William's hands to the point that he "lost the service and labor of his said slave." In his will, William left Mary a life interest in two enslaved people, James and Ester.[20]

Both before and after the Indian attack and her famous escape, Mary Ingles was the wife of a frontier farmer. Acquiring land required either hiring a licensed surveyor to perform a survey and then registering the claim or petitioning the governor and council for a grant, after which a survey was ordered. Both approaches left a relatively small number of local and colonial officials as the gatekeepers to landownership. As a result, during the quarter-century after the creation of Augusta County in 1738, two-thirds of its adult white male inhabitants did not own land. From the start, therefore, William Ingles was part of a privileged minority, owning 255 acres in the Tom's Creek area, where he lived with his family, and an additional 440 acres he held jointly with Mary's brother John. William continued to acquire land, hiring William Preston to perform four surveys of 4,200 acres in 1774. His will gave Mary 100 acres of the "upper end of the tract of land I now live on" for her maintenance and support during her widowhood. His younger son, John, received Mary's land after her death along with all the land that his father owned on both sides of the New River. William gave his older son, Thomas, and two sons-in-law acreage that he owned elsewhere. The Ingleses' unmarried daughter, Mary, inherited the profits from the family ferry for five years, along with three enslaved people, which became her marriage portion when she wed a few years later. Overall, William's will shows that, in terms of landownership and other indicators of wealth, the Ingleses were members of the backcountry elite.[21]

Nevertheless, William's wealth did not afford Mary a life of leisure. She was responsible for many tasks, including cooking, gardening, preserving food, cloth production, sewing, and laundering. Housework also included building fires, hauling and chopping wood, and carrying water. William's prolific economic endeavors also must have added to her responsibilities. Virginia women often ran taverns, either with or without their husband's help. In his will, William left Mary all the "Plantation Utinsials and loot of husbandry also six milk cows and four good horses or mares together with all my sheep and hogs to her and her heirs forever." The large amount of livestock she received suggests that she was the one who oversaw them, which would have included making butter and cheese, curing bacon, and processing wool. Much of the harvesting and processing of flax—a twenty-two-step process—was also women's work, which Mary would have performed or overseen. Mary's workload would have varied with her age, wealth, skills, and access to help. She gave birth to three daughters after her return from captivity, and as they grew older, they would have assisted her with various tasks, in the process learning the skills they would need when they married and took over their own households. Neighbors and sometimes very young or old female slaves also might have helped.[22]

Like many Virginia women, for whom sewing was a near-universal occupation, Mary was an adept seamstress. During her captivity, she made shirts using linen that her captors purchased from French traders. According to her son, Mary's work "pleased [the Shawnees] so that they wood do any thing for her to get a shirt made and the Frenchmen finding it a considerable advantage to them in selling their check & linen to the Indians incouraged her very much." Account books from local stores show that a combination of Mary's handiwork and imported goods clothed the Ingles family. A 1774 account book from New Dublin (modern-day Newbern, in Pulaski County) lists a tailor making purchases for William Ingles that included silk, shallron (a wool product used to line clothing), and colored thread. At that time, men's coats and breeches were made by tailors, but other items, including shirts, were hand sewn at home. William also bought Irish linen, which would have been less coarse than American homespun. Mary or one of her daughters most likely turned the Irish linen into clothes.[23]

Another surviving daybook, which covers the years 1798–1802, shows that Mary remained an active producer of food and clothing even as a widow with grown children. During that period, her food purchases consisted solely of sugar and coffee; while her farm could furnish her with meat, vegetables, eggs, and dairy products, sugar and coffee were two items that she could not produce herself. Overall, most of her store purchases were related to sewing and included calico and muslin, both of which were imported. She also purchased tea wares, including an entire set of cups and saucers.[24]

While store records and social contexts can help us envision key aspects of Mary's life and work, her personality is more elusive in part because she left behind no letters, diaries, or other personal papers. Indeed, although William Ingles was literate, his wife may not have been. Like her mother, Eleanor Draper—who affirmed her appointment as the executor of her husband's will by making her mark—perhaps Mary Draper Ingles could not write (or read). A ferry customer who met Mary in middle age left the only surviving firsthand account of her. In 1779, while a prisoner of war, the lieutenant governor of Detroit, Henry Hamilton, crossed the New River via Ingles Ferry and spent a day at the Ingles house. The family apparently shared the story of Mary's captivity and escape, which Hamilton recorded in his journal, adding that "terror and distress had left so deep an impression on her mind that she appeared absorbed in a deep melancholy, and left the management of household concerns, & the reception of Strangers to her lovely daughter." One isolated journal entry is not conclusive as to whether melancholy was Mary's permanent mental state—and, if so, whether her sadness was a long-term result of the horrors of 1755—or whether she was just inhospitable to her British guest, who by his own admission was seen by the people in the area as "being of kindred manners with the Savages."[25]

Hamilton's visit occurred during the American War for Independence, which was another challenging time for Mary and her family. Before the war, William had military and political responsibilities consistent with his wealth and status in the community. He served as justice of the peace, sheriff, and tax collector, and also as a colonel in the militia. William's leadership continued into the pre-Revolutionary era. As a member of the Fincastle County Committee of Safety, he supported the patriot cause. William was present at a meeting on January 20, 1775, at which local freeholders unanimously resolved to risk their lives, if need be, to defend colonial rights against the evil designs of a corrupt Parliament. Significantly, even on the brink of revolution, the perils of frontier living were never far from the minds of the backcountry people. This meeting produced a document—the "Fincastle Resolves"—in which freeholders duly noted that they were mostly immigrants who had crossed the Atlantic "and explored this then uncultivated wilderness, bordering on many nations of savages, and surrounded by mountains almost inaccessible to any but those very savages, who have incessantly been committing barbarities and depredations on us since our first seating the country."[26]

Yet, perhaps because William sought to profit from the war and because neither he nor his sons ever left home to fight, he found himself charged with treason in 1780. There was little evidence of support for the British in the New River valley until after the successful beginning of Britain's Southern Campaign in 1779–80. Then, loyalism on the Virginia frontier typically manifested as passive support for the British and short-term acts of defiance against the local patriot elite. In 1780 local authorities charged William Ingles with loyalism, but the court ruled that the charge was not proven and deferred final judgment pending the presentation of additional evidence. William was ordered to post a bond guaranteeing his future appearance if called. Was William a loyalist? He did not fight on the British side, and there is no evidence that he was involved in any local loyalist disturbances. Moreover, both he and his sons participated in the local militia throughout the war. In 1779 William Preston, the county commander, ordered Ingles to draft "several Companies of Militia, which with those already on foot he is to take the Command of, as a Touchstone of his Sincerity in the American Cause, and March immediately against the Insurgents." Preston noted that Ingles "seemed willing to undertake the Business and promises the utmost Exertion in Quelling the Insurrection." Doubts about William's views seem to have been prompted by the same economic ambitions he had demonstrated all his life. The loyalist James Duggless mentioned that Ingles had recently driven beef cattle north and sold them to the British because "he received hard money for them."[27]

Perhaps because the war had brought hardship for many in their backcountry community, this incident apparently did not stigmatize the Ingleses. By 1780 residents of Montgomery County (formed in 1776 and named in honor of the recently slain patriot general) informed the state legislature that Indian attacks and bad weather had prevented them from harvesting their crops for several years. That same year William Preston protested that food shortages made the area incapable of absorbing the British prisoners of war whom Congress hoped to relocate there. The state government increased taxes to pay for the war, including a tax on cattle, which would have particularly hurt the Ingleses. At the same time, state and continental currency rapidly lost value, and the ferry rates and tavern prices that were part of the family's income were regulated in wartime. County-mandated prices never kept pace with inflation (though the war presumably would have increased demand and prices for William's hemp and livestock). Whatever the toll on William's reputation and finances, he remained both wealthy and influential.[28]

In 1782, with American independence virtually secured by the decisive victory at Yorktown, Mary experienced two separate family tragedies: the death of her husband and another Indian attack on members of her family. William Ingles had resigned his militia commission as a result of "his infirmities" and died soon thereafter. Mary's son Thomas was living with his family on the frontier at a settlement known as Burks Gardens when—in an echo of the events at Draper's Meadow twenty-seven years earlier—Indians attacked the settlement while Thomas was out in his fields. His family was captured and their house burned, but Thomas was able to raise a force of between fifteen and twenty men to pursue the raiders, catching up to them within a few days. The Indians had inflicted violence on their prisoners: Thomas's wife was struck several times in the head but survived her injuries, while their daughter died of her wounds a few days later. Mary Ingles thus lost members of three generations of her family to Native American violence: her mother and her son George in 1755, and now her granddaughter. From the Ingleses' perspective, the Indians were entirely to blame for frontier violence. Years later, Mary's son John condemned the Shawnees and referred to their "Hethan thirst for bloodshed and plunder" as the cause of the attack at Draper's Meadow.[29]

According to John Ingles, Mary "still continued to live in New River & Injoyed an extraordinary portion of good health" until her death in 1815 at the age of eighty-three or eighty-four.[30] Curiosity about her captivity and escape continued after her death, which inspired John to write his account. In her lifetime, Mary does not seem to have been a legend or a local celebrity: she was instead the wife of a successful man who witnessed more than her share of violence. Betty Draper, Mary's sister-in-law, who lived among the Shawnees for six years before her release, never had her story told. Nor was the unnamed "Dutch Woman" who shared Mary's painful walk home the subject of a captivity narrative.

From the late seventeenth through the early twentieth century, captivity narratives were a popular literary genre. Scholarly studies of such narratives have found, however, that the genre changed somewhat over time. Those written in the colonial era typically described white captives as beleaguered victims (who ultimately survived their ordeals), while those written in the first part of the nineteenth century emphasized the white settlers' physical strength, cunning, and stamina.[31] The three nineteenth-century narratives written about Mary Draper Ingles reflect this trend. By contrast, authors of twentieth-century renditions of Mary's story admit they are writing fiction—a novel, a play—though those who read or watch their narratives tend to see the fictions as truth.

In the nineteenth century, three versions of the Mary Draper Ingles story were produced. John Ingles's *Escape from Indian Captivity* was the first. Letitia Preston Floyd, the daughter of William Preston whose uncle James Patton was killed in the 1755 raid, produced the second account based on local oral tradition, which was probably less reliable than the family stories on which John Ingles had drawn. Letitia Preston Floyd first told the Ingles story in an 1843 letter to historian Lyman C. Draper; her account was republished in the form of a letter to her son Benjamin Rush Floyd in a series of articles in the *Richmond Standard* newspaper in 1880.

Letitia Floyd's account, written eighty-eight years after the attack, follows the pattern of many captive narratives of the era. The stereotypical captivity account included a frightful scene of capture, murder, fire, and a violent interruption of the ensuing forced migration. John Ingles's account simply stated there was killing and the taking of prisoners, going on to focus instead on what his father was doing, perhaps to defend his reputation. Floyd's more melodramatically graphic version described the killing of "old Mrs. Draper and two children of Colonel Ingles, by knocking their brains out on the ends of the cabin logs." Floyd invented and killed off two Ingles children who never existed. She also incorrectly described Thomas as being ten years old, and she credited her kinsman James Patton with killing two Indians with his sword. The most controversial new information Floyd presented, however, was the assertion that Mary was pregnant and gave birth to a baby three days out on the trail, after which she and the infant remained with the Indians for three months until Mary "left her child in a bark cradle asleep, knowing that as soon as she was missed the Indians would kill the infant."[32]

While Letitia Preston Floyd portrayed Mary Draper Ingles as a seemingly emotionless woman who abandoned her child in order to return home, in John Ingles's version of the story Mary escaped only after her captors had forcibly separated her from her children. Floyd's story has some internal inconsistencies: Mary could not have stayed three months with the Indians because doing so would have had her returning home in February, though it is known that she arrived in the fall. Floyd's description of Mary's interaction with the "Dutch woman" is also bizarre: she told readers that the two women cast lots to see who would be eaten by the other. She wrote, "the lot fell on Mrs. Ingles, who, understanding her traveling companions temper, promised her a sum of money if she would refrain from killing her. Colonel Ingles was a rich man, and this had the desired effect."[33] By portraying Mary Draper Ingles as a heartless mother turned potential cannibal, Floyd told a titillating story while implying that Mary had been corrupted by the putative barbarism of her captors. In addition, William was neither rich nor a colonel in 1755.

In 1886 John P. Hale published *Trans-Allegheny Pioneers: Historical Sketches of the First White Settlements West of the Alleghenies 1748 and After*. Hale described himself as "one of the oldest surviving descendants of those early pioneers" and as someone who had "taken some pains to collect the family records." Although John Ingles had said nothing of his parents' backgrounds in his book, Hale included information about the European origins of the Draper and Ingles families. Hale's version, even more than Floyd's, however, emphasized the almost Amazonian strength of the captive Mary, a common theme in nineteenth-century narratives. Hale claimed that Mary could jump as well as her brother and that "she could stand and jump straight up nearly as high as her head; could stand on the ground, beside her horse, and leap into the saddle unaided; could stand on the floor and jump over a chair-back." He also described Mary as "an extraordinary woman and equal to any emergency," repeating Floyd's story about her pregnancy and subsequent abandonment of the baby.[34] Because Hale's book was published in three separate editions, it was by far the most accessible of the Ingles narratives. As a result, the information (and misinformation) it included became part of the myth of Mary Draper Ingles, which many people accepted as fact.

Sometime around the turn of the twentieth century, Ingles became a local and regional heroine whose image and reputation transcended the captivity narrative as a new generation—which included many educated and civic-minded women—looked for women from history to commemorate and honor. Mary's name and story were widely celebrated throughout the Appalachian region. West Virginia has a Mary Draper Ingles Trail in Kanawha State Forest and a

Mary Draper Ingles Bridge in Summers County. Kentucky's Boone County erected a statue of her in front of a public library. But nowhere is the Ingles story more celebrated than in the Virginia localities that today surround the New River: the city of Radford and Pulaski County. In 1909 Mary's descendants erected a monument to her—built of the bricks from her house's chimney—in the West View Cemetery in Radford. The following year the Virginia General Assembly chartered the State Normal School for Women (modern-day Radford University), which also embraced the Mary Draper Ingles story. Before the school opened its doors to students, its faculty created two literary societies. The faculty wanted to name the societies for outstanding women. The meeting to name the societies was held at the Radford home of H. P. Anderson. When the committee asked Anderson to name the most "outstanding woman in the history of Southwestern Virginia," citing Hale's book he nominated Mary Draper Ingles. The committee named one society "Pocahontas" and the other "Ingles."[35]

At the dedication of a tablet donated to the Ingles Literary Society of Radford Normal School by the Ingles descendants, Beverly Taylor, member of the class of 1916, praised Mary in terms that obscured the roughness, rigor, and violence of eighteenth-century frontier life. Mary Draper Ingles, Taylor mused, like all the women of colonial America, "was known far for her grace, sweetness, modesty, loyalty, and Christian womanhood." She went on to describe Mary's "charming manner, cordiality radiating from every feature, inconspicuous in her dress, and busy with a thousand duties." Taylor and the other members of the Ingles Literary Society turned Mary Draper Ingles into a model of true womanhood that early twentieth-century girls from respectable families could emulate: domestic, pious, modest, and well mannered. It was a portrait that was at odds with reality and that also conflicted with the image of Mary presented in the captivity narratives written by her son and others in the preceding century. By 1915 more Virginia women were becoming educated and entering professions, and some even demanded the right to vote. Yet Taylor invoked Ingles in order to maintain the status quo. "There is no new woman," she declared. "The Virginia woman of today is the same as in 1800." It was the love of home that drove Mary those many miles, and "today's woman is the same great homemaker as she was in the days of Mary Draper Ingles."[36]

In 1971 a new wave of interest in Mary Draper Ingles came to Radford when the Drama Committee of the New River Historical Society commissioned the outdoor drama *The Long Way Home*, written by Earl Hobson Smith. The play was a community effort. To build the stage on which it premiered in June 1971, hundreds of people from the area, including members of several civic groups, "met on the grounds and worked far into the night." The play's script contains imagined dialogue that reflects both the influence of Hale's book and the values and preoccupations of the time in which Smith wrote. Nevertheless, the local newspaper described the play's story as "true and ... one of the most dramatic ones ever told." The *News Journal* praised *The Long Way Home* as "the pride of Southwest Virginia, and the drama backers are thrilled to present the beautiful and colorful story to the nation and the world."[37]

Written while the country was divided by the Vietnam War, civil rights, feminism, and other sources of real and imagined social upheaval, in this version of her story Mary Draper Ingles and her family became symbols of conservative patriotic American values. In the play Mary's mother says, "We all got married young, raised our families by the good book, and kept busy livin each day as it comes without complainin." To which Colonel Patton replies, "it's families like you Drapers and Ingles who are willing to stay and work the land and build your homes and help each other that will make this new country of ours strong." Despite the fact that in 1755 Virginians did not see themselves as making a "new country," the play's last line suggests otherwise: "And thus a nation was raised upon the strong backs of these early pioneers. Their legacy to us is the United States of America still as free today as the people who love her." The playwright portrayed Mary as a loving mother beset by tragedy: instead of leaving her baby, the infant seemingly dies shortly after its birth.[38]

In the play Mary is strong, resourceful, a healer, and intuitive—neither an Amazon nor the dependent, modest, and wholly domestic lady that Beverly Taylor imagined. Early in the play, Mary announces, without consulting William, that if the baby she is carrying is a girl she will name the child Martha. Her brother John comments, "You know when Mary makes up her mind to do something there's no changing it." To which an appeasing William answers, "HaHa, don't I know it! But I wouldn't want her any other way." Thousands watched or performed in the outdoor drama *The Long Way Home*, which played every summer from 1971 to 2000 in a thousand-seat amphitheater built on the Ingleses' property. A similar version of the story was told in the novel *Follow the River* (1981) by James Alexander Thom.[39]

Local people have found new ways to commemorate Mary Draper Ingles and the frontier farming experience in the twenty-first century. The land on which *The Long Way Home* was staged has been converted into a living history museum that features a reconstructed Ingles cabin based on archaeological research done on the site. The descendants of Mary Draper Ingles occasionally allow visitors to tour the cabin and its farm, which features livestock from the Colonial Williamsburg and Mount Vernon breeding programs.[40]

To John Ingles, Mary Draper Ingles was a "very good sewer," daring and determined when she escaped, and restless and uneasy when she returned home.[41] Floyd and Hale presented a Mary with extraordinary Amazon-like strength and resolve, but they embellished her story with melodramatic incidents and imagined details. For the students at the early Radford Normal, Ingles was repackaged to represent their era's version of domesticated true womanhood. To the thousands who watched *The Long Way Home*, Mary embodied a conservative resilience, the spirit it took to settle the frontier and create the United States. The real Mary Draper Ingles was a survivor whose true and mostly imagined life became for many both an inspiration for and a validation of the prevailing cultural values of their times.

NOTES

I would like to thank Ann Smart Martin, Lora Gordon, Gene Hyde, Anna Chrysostomides, and John Jefferies for their assistance with this project.

1. John Ingles Sr., *Escape from Indian Captivity: The Story of Mary Draper Ingles and Son Thomas Ingles*, 2nd ed., ed. Roberta Ingles Steele and Andrew Lewis Ingles (Radford, Va.: privately printed, 1982), 5; *Maryland Gazette*, March 18, 1756; Montgomery County Deed Book B, 54, Montgomery County Courthouse, Christiansburg, Va.; Day Book, New Dublin, 1774, 5, 13, 18, 21, 32, scanned image, private collection of John Jefferies; Ferry Hill Le[d]ger, 8, 29, 54. 84, 92, 144, Ingles Family Collection, box 1, Virginia Tech Special Collections, Blacksburg.

2. Ingles, *Escape from Indian Captivity*, 5, 11; June Namias, *White Captives* (Chapel Hill: University of North Carolina Press, 1993), 23; *Maryland Gazette*, March 18, 1756; John Demos, *The Unredeemed Captive: A Family Story from Early America* (New York: Knopf, 1994), 81.

3. Ingles, *Escape from Indian Captivity*, 4; "Militia Companies in Augusta County, in 1742," *Virginia Magazine of History and Biography* 8 (1901): 281; Turk McCleskey, "The Price of Conformity, Class, Ethnicity, and Local Authority on the Colonial Virginia Frontier," in *Diversity and Accommodation: Essays on the Cultural Composition of the Virginia Frontier*, ed. Michael J. Puglisi (Knoxville: University of Tennessee Press, 1997), 218; Augusta County Will Book 1, 127, 247, Augusta County Courthouse, Staunton, Va.; Augusta County Order Book 2, 104, Augusta County Courthouse; Chester Raymond Young, "The Effects of the French and Indian War on Civilian Life in the Frontier Counties of Virginia, 1754–1763," (PhD diss., Vanderbilt University, 1969), 17–18.

4. Robert D. Mitchell, "The Southern Backcountry: A Geographical House Divided," in *The Southern Colonial Backcountry: Interdisciplinary Perspectives on Frontier Communities*, ed. David Colin Crass et al. (Knoxville: University of Tennessee Press, 1998), 22–23; Turk McCleskey, "Shadow Land: Provisional Real Estate Claims and Anglo-American Settlement in Southwestern Virginia," ibid., 64; Albert Tillson Jr., *Gentry and Common Folk: Political Culture on a Virginia Frontier, 1740–1789* (Lexington: University of Kentucky Press, 1991), 55–56; Warren R. Hofstra, *The Planting of*

New Virginia: Settlement and Landscape in the Shenandoah Valley (Baltimore, Md.: Johns Hopkins University Press, 2004), 84; Albert H. Tillson, "The Localist Roots of Backcountry Loyalism: An Examination of Popular Culture in Virginia's New River Valley," *Journal of Southern History* 54 (1988): 392; Kenneth W. Keller, "The Outlook of Rhinelanders on the Virginia Frontier," in Puglisi, *Diversity and Accommodation*, 117; McCleskey, "Price of Conformity," 220; Ingles, *Escape from Indian Captivity*, 16.

5. Hofstra, *Planting of New Virginia*, 103; Michael N. McConnell, *A Country Between: The Upper Ohio Valley and Its Peoples, 1724-1774* (Lincoln: University of Nebraska Press, 1992), 20, 89, 93, 103, 112-14.

6. Matthew C. Ward, "Fighting the 'Old Women': Indian Strategy on the Virginia and Pennsylvania Frontier, 1754-1758," *Virginia Magazine of History and Biography* 103 (1995): 298, 300, 309; Ward, *Breaking the Backcountry: The Seven Years' War in Virginia and Pennsylvania, 1754-1765* (Pittsburgh, Pa.: University of Pittsburgh Press, 2004), 31, 35.

7. Ward, "Fighting the 'Old Women,'" 301, 310, 312, 315, 316, 317; Ward, *Breaking the Backcountry*, 61, 70; McConnell, *A Country Between*, 128.

8. Ingles, *Escape from Indian Captivity*, 7-9; Preston, "A Register of the Persons who have been either killed, wounded or taken Prisoners by the Enemy in Augusta county, as also of such have made their Escape," State Historical Society of Wisconsin, Draper Manuscript Collection, microfilm, 1 QQ 83; *Pennsylvania Gazette*, August 21, 1755; McConnell, *A Country Between*, 95.

9. Ward, "Fighting the 'Old Women,'" 310; Ward, *Breaking the Backcountry*, 53; Ingles, *Escape from Indian Captivity*, 9-11.

10. McConnell, *A Country Between*, 211-13, 219.

11. The Dutch woman was most likely the same woman Preston listed as captured from the New River in a raid on July 3, 1755. The victims of this raid were described as "Dutch Jacob and his wife." He was listed as wounded; she was listed as captured and escaped. Preston, "Register of Persons," 1 QQ 83; Ingles, *Escape from Indian Captivity*, 12.

12. *Maryland Gazette*, March 18, 1756; Ingles, *Escape from Indian Captivity*, 13-15, 17-18.

13. John Craig, Deposition, March 30, 1756, Penn MSS, Indian Affairs, 2:78, Historical Society of Pennsylvania, qtd. in Ward, "Fighting the 'Old Women,'" 297. In the 1982 reprint of John Ingles's book, the editors quote Cecil C. Lawson, a certified land surveyor, who determined the distance of her route (Ingles, *Escape from Indian Captivity*, 16, 37-38); see ibid., 27.

14. Ward, *Breaking the Backcountry*, 104; Nathaniel Turk McCleskey, "Across the First Divide: Frontiers of Settlement and Culture in Augusta County, Virginia, 1738-1770" (PhD diss., College of William and Mary, 1990), 311.

15. Young, "Effects of the French and Indian War," 82, 85; Ingles, *Escape from Indian Captivity*, 18-19; letter describing the attack on Fort Vause, Draper Manuscripts, 1 QQ 134.

16. "New London, Bedford County, Va.," *Virginia Magazine of History and Biography* 19 (1912): 431-32; William Waller Hening, comp., *The Statutes at Large: Being a Collection of All the Laws of Virginia*, 13 vols. (Richmond, Va.: Samuel Pleasants Jr., 1810-23), 7:588; Ingles, *Escape from Indian Captivity*, 20, 21; William Ingles to William Preston, Fort Hope, September 13, 1763, Draper Manuscripts, 2 QQ 43.

17. John D. Barnhart and R. E. Banta, eds., *Henry Hamilton and George Rogers Clark in the American Revolution with the Unpublished Journal of Lieut. Gov. Henry Hamilton* (Crawfordsville, Ind.: R. E. Banta, 1951), 200. Turk McCleskey argues that eastern hierarchies, though imperfectly replicated on the frontier, nonetheless influenced land distribution. Albert Tillson sees frontier people as less inclined to accept elite political authority and more attached to their local neighbor-

hoods. See McCleskey, "Rich Land, Poor Prospects: Real Estate and the Formation of a Social Elite in Augusta County, Virginia, 1738–1770," *Virginia Magazine of History and Biography* 98 (1990): 486; Tillson, "Localist Roots," 387, 392.

18. Augusta County Ordinary Bonds, 1745–75, 135, 168, Augusta County Courthouse; Montgomery County Order Books 1, 3, Montgomery County Courthouse, Christiansburg, Va.; Daniel B. Thorp, "Doing Business in the Backcountry: Retail Trade in Colonial Rowan County, North Carolina," *William and Mary Quarterly*, 3rd ser., 48 (1991): 391–92; Thorp, "Taverns and Tavern Culture on the Southern Colonial Frontier: Rowan County, North Carolina, 1753–1776," *Journal of Southern History* 62 (1996): 661–62, 674; Ward, *Breaking the Backcountry*, 15.

19. B. Scott Crawford, "Economic Interdependence along a Colonial Frontier: Capitalism and the New River Valley, 1745–1789" (MA thesis, Old Dominion University, 1996), 29; Montgomery County Order Book 1, 7, and 2, 8; Mary Kegley, ed., *Tax Lists of Montgomery County, Virginia, 1782* (Radford, Va.: printed privately, 1974), 17; "Virginia Militia in the Revolution," *Virginia Magazine of History and Biography* 10 (1902): 83.

20. *Ingles, William v. Joseph Hicks*, Warrant Envelope 106, Montgomery County Courthouse; Mary Kegley, ed., *New River Tithables 1770–1773* (Radford, Va.: privately printed, 1972), 3, 4, 6, 19, 22, 23; Crawford, "Economic Interdependence," 31; Kegley, *Tax Lists of Montgomery County*, 17; Montgomery County Deed Book B, 54, Montgomery County Courthouse.

21. McCleskey, "Rich Land, Poor Prospects," 451–52, 461; McCleskey, "Price of Conformity," 216; William Preston, "Surveyors' Fees, Botetourt County, Va. and Fincastle, Va. from about May 4, 1770, to about December 5, 1787," 6:32, Campbell-Preston-Floyd Papers, microfilm, Virginia Tech; Montgomery County Deed Book B, 54.

22. Laurel Thatcher Ulrich, *Good Wives: Image and Reality in the Lives of Women in Northern New England, 1650–1750* (New York: Knopf, 1982), 13–33; Laurel Thatcher Ulrich, "Martha Ballard and Her Girls: Women's Work in Eighteenth-Century Maine," in *Work and Labor in Early America*, ed. Stephen Innes (Chapel Hill: University of North Carolina Press, 1988), 75, 77, 104; Linda L. Sturtz, *Within Her Power: Propertied Women in Colonial Virginia* (New York: Routledge, 2002), chap. 4; Carole Shammas, "Black Women's Work and the Evolution of Plantation Society in Virginia," *Labor History* 26 (1985): 23–24; Joan R. Gundersen, *To Be Useful in the World*, rev. ed. (Chapel Hill: University of North Carolina Press, 2006), 74; Montgomery County Deed Book B, 54; Kenneth W. Keller, "From the Rhineland to the Virginia Frontier: Flax Production as a Commercial Enterprise," *Virginia Magazine of History and Biography* 98 (1990): 499.

23. Ingles, *Escape from Indian Captivity*, 11; Day Book, New Dublin, 1774, 5, 13, 18, 21, 32, scanned image, private collection of John Jefferies; Florence M. Montgomery, *Textiles in America, 1650–1870* (New York: Norton, 1984), 346–47; Ulrich, "Martha Ballard and Her Girls," 75; Keller, "From the Rhineland to the Virginia Frontier," 497; Cynthia A. Kierner, *Beyond the Household: Women's Place in the Early South, 1700–1835* (Ithaca, N.Y.: Cornell University Press, 1998), 14–15.

24. Ferry Hill Le[d]ger, 8, 29, 54. 84, 92, 144, Ingles Family Collection, box 1, Virginia Tech Special Collections; Montgomery, *Textiles in America*, 184–85, 304.

25. Augusta County Will Book 1, 128; Barnhart and Banta, *Henry Hamilton and George Rogers Clark*, 200.

26. Montgomery County Order Book 2, 141, 152–53; Kegley, *New River Tithables*, 3, 4, 6, 19, 23–24; William Van Schreeven and Robert Scribner, comps., *Revolutionary Virginia: The Road to Independence*, 7 vols. (Charlottesville: University of Virginia Press, 1975), 2:254–56.

27. Tillson, "Localist Roots," 388, 394, 396, 402; "At a meeting of the Justices of Montgomery County and Botetourt for the Examination of Colonel William Ingles," August 1780, Draper Manu-

scripts, 5 QQ 73; William Preston letter, July 1779, ibid., 3 zz 19; "James Duggless confession," August 18, 1780, ibid., 5 QQ 59.

28. Tillson, *Gentry and Commonfolk*, 2, 89–90, 119; Richard K. Macmaster, "The Cattle Trade in Western Virginia, 1760–1830," in *Appalachian Frontiers: Settlement, Society, and Development in the Pre-Industrial Era*, ed. Robert D. Mitchell (Lexington: University of Kentucky Press, 1991), 135–36; Robert D. Mitchell, *Commercialism and Frontier Perspectives on the Early Shenandoah Valley* (Charlottesville: University of Virginia Press, 1977), 170, 183.

29. Colonel William Preston to Governor Harrison, March 15, 1782, in *Calendar of Virginia State Papers and Other Manuscripts*, ed. William P. Palmer (1883; rpt., New York: Kraus Reprint, 1968), 3:100; Ingles, *Escape from Indian Captivity*, 7, 22, 32–33; Montgomery County Order Book 2, 322; William Preston to the Governor of Virginia, Botetourt, April 26, 1782, Draper Manuscripts, 5 QQ 108; Ward, *Breaking the Backcountry*, 4.

30. Ingles, *Escape from Indian Captivity*, 22.

31. Demos, *Unredeemed Captive*, 76; Namias, *White Captives*, 33–34.

32. Ellen Apperson Brown, "What Really Happened at Drapers Meadow? The Evolution of a Frontier Legend," *Smithfield Review* 7 (2003): 10, 15; Peter Wallenstein, *Cradle of America: Four Centuries of Virginia History* (Lawrence: University Press of Kansas, 2007), 5–59; "Incidents of Border Life in Virginia, Related by Mrs. Letitia Floyd in a letter to her son, Colonel Benjamin Rush Floyd," transcribed from *Richmond Standard*, June 5, 1880, in Montgomery County Muster Roll, 1772–1900, 253–57, Montgomery County Courthouse; Namias, *White Captives*, 22–23.

33. Brown, "What Really Happened at Drapers Meadow?" 15; "Incidents of Border Life in Virginia," 256.

34. John P. Hale, *Trans-Allegheny Pioneers: Historical Sketches of the First White Settlements West of the Alleghenies 1748 and After* (1886; rpt., Raleigh, N.C.: Derreth Printing Company, 1971), 10–14, 27, 35–36.

35. Scott L. Gardner, *Radford, Then and Now* (Charleston, S.C.: Arcadia, 2010), ix; M'Ledge Moffett, "A History of the State Teachers College at Radford Virginia 1910–1930," 280, http://Library.radford.edu/archives/RUHistory/Moffett%20all%20with%20search.pdf (accessed March 12, 2013).

36. Beverly Taylor, "Virginia Womanhood Ever the Same," *Radford Norman Bulletin* 3 (1915): 5–6.

37. *News Journal*, February 25, 1990, and June 22, 1971.

38. Earl Hobson Smith, *The Long Way Home* (1976), Special Collections, Radford Public Library, 7, 10, 101.

39. Ibid., 4; James Alexander Thom, *Follow the River* (New York: Ballantine, 1981).

40. "Ingles Ferry," http://www.inglesferry.com (accessed September 2, 2012).

41. Ingles, *Escape from Indian Captivity*, 10, 11, 18.

Elizabeth Henry Campbell Russell

Champion of Faith in the Early Republic

JON KUKLA

Elizabeth Henry Campbell Russell was the daughter of a planter, the sister of a famous patriot, and the wife of two Revolutionary generals. Her lifetime spanned a pivotal period when Virginia was transformed from a colonial society dominated by the gentry to a somewhat more egalitarian republic confronting the challenges of the post-Revolutionary era. Often overshadowed by her connections to Patrick Henry, William Campbell, and William Russell, her life of devotion, prayer, and patronage contributed to Virginia's religious transformation from Anglicanism to Protestant pluralism. Indeed, the dynamic cultural impact of the religious revivals of the eighteenth century known as the Great Awakening shaped the life of Elizabeth Henry Campbell Russell from the moment of her birth on July 10, 1749, at Studley, her mother's six-hundred-acre tobacco plantation on Totopotomoy Creek in Hanover County, to the hour of her death on March 18, 1825. That religious orientation, in turn, led her to play a significant but largely overlooked role in the development of the evangelicalism that came to dominate Virginia's religious landscape in the post-Revolutionary era.

Elizabeth Henry was the eighth of nine children born to Sarah Winston Syme and John Henry. Soon thereafter, when her half brother John Syme Jr. came of age and took possession of Studley, Elizabeth's family moved to Mount Brilliant, a 630-acre plantation in western Hanover County.¹ Hanover was a booming county during Elizabeth's youth, sending tobacco from warehouses on the meandering Pamunkey River through the Chesapeake Bay to world markets. The annual value of the colony's overall exports—tobacco, grain, lumber, and pig iron—was about £160,000, or roughly one-quarter of all exports from British North America.[2]

Elizabeth Henry's heritage was shaped by the Scottish immigrants who swarmed into Virginia and the middle Atlantic colonies after the 1707 union of Scotland and England. Elizabeth's father came to Virginia about 1727, worked at Studley for John Syme Sr., and married his widow. Trained as a surveyor at the University of Aberdeen, John Henry laid out the streets of Newcastle in 1729 and published "A New and Accurate Map of Virginia" in 1770.[3] His brother, the Reverend Patrick Henry, followed him to Hanover County in the early 1730s. Ordained in the Scottish Episcopal Church after taking a master's degree at Marischal College, Elizabeth's uncle was the rector of St. Paul's Parish in Hanover County from 1737 to his death.[4]

Every autumn Elizabeth and her siblings might have enjoyed Hanover's annual St. Andrew's Day festival, with its prizes for dancing, singing, jumping, wrestling, and "Foot-ball-play" (a game closer to rugby than soccer). Elizabeth and her sisters doubtless hoped to win the "fine Pair of Silk Stockings" given each year "to the *handsomest Maid* upon the Green." As young women, however, they were denied admission to the Society of St. Andrew's banquet.[5] The popularity of St. Andrew's Day reflected social changes in Great Britain's oldest, largest, and wealthiest colony. Virginia's population grew from 114,000 to 231,000 between 1730 and 1750, with Scottish immigrants especially prevalent in the Piedmont. Scottish merchants quadrupled their share of the Chesapeake tobacco trade from 10 percent in 1730 to 40 percent in 1765. During that same period, the colony's slave population doubled to 60,000, more than a quarter of the overall population.[6]

The religious revival known as the Great Awakening came to Hanover County four years before Elizabeth Henry's birth. Her uncle first sounded an alarm about what he regarded as an invasion of evangelical preachers in a February 1745 letter to Commissary William Dawson, the head of the established Church of England in Virginia. Although Pastor Henry's tone was hostile, his observations were accurate. "The New Preachers," Elizabeth's uncle complained, were maligning Virginia's established clergy as unconverted imposters who had "no authority to meddle with Holy things" and disparaging the Anglican liturgy and prayer book as an "abundance of lies."[7]

By law Virginians paid tithes to support their local Anglican parishes, attended church at least monthly, and honored the Sabbath. Church wardens and grand juries suppressed drunkenness, swearing, cursing, blasphemy, adultery, and fornication. Only Anglican ministers could perform marriages, and

ELIZABETH HENRY CAMPBELL RUSSELL

An oil portrait of Russell by the Charleston artist James De Veaux was exhibited at the Virginia Historical Society in 1929. This print based on the De Veaux portrait, which is now in private hands, hangs at Patrick Henry's Scotchtown in Hanover County. Courtesy of Preservation Virginia.

colonial courts were required to report "all Public or Private Meetings of any other Religion than the Church of England." Anglican parishes also cared for orphans and the disabled, kept up roads and bridges, and oversaw the annual "processioning" of land boundaries.[8]

Like her father, uncle, and many of her siblings, Elizabeth Henry found meaning in the worship and sacraments of the Church of England and its elegant Georgian churches. Records suggest that Anglican clergymen baptized as many as 85 percent of white Virginians as infants, and many slaves as well. Gentry and yeoman planters, tenant farmers, their families, and many of their slaves found weekly solace and joy in the cadences of the Book of Common Prayer, the sacraments of baptism and communion, and well-written sermons delivered with more dignity than drama. Ministers aimed not to summon the elect into an exclusive church nor call worshipers to sudden conversion, but rather to encourage all the residents of their parishes to accept God's offer of redemption and live good and moral lives.[9]

Denominational tensions spurred by the Great Awakening quickly penetrated the Henry family. In 1745 Virginia's highest court fined Elizabeth's grandfather Isaac Winston for allowing John Roan (one of the dissenting ministers denounced by her uncle) to preach in his home, despite a jury ruling that none of the people gathered at his house had acted "in a riotous manner" or "against the canons of the Church of England." That October Elizabeth's uncle reluctantly allowed the Anglican evangelist George Whitefield, widely regarded as an ally of the Methodist leaders John and Samuel Wesley, to preach from the pulpit at St. Paul's Church rather than flaunt his popularity by addressing thousands out of doors.[10]

Elizabeth's father served on the vestry, or church council, of St. Paul's, where Elizabeth was baptized as an infant and later attended services. On many Sundays, however, Elizabeth's mother skipped Pastor Henry's Anglican services and took her children by carriage to Polegreen Church or Ground Squirrel Chapel and the Presbyterian services of Samuel Davies, who moved to Hanover County in 1748.[11] In his decade of ministry in Virginia, Davies led a Presbyterian revival that attracted Elizabeth's mother and her elder sisters Jane and Lucy. Their response to Davies acquainted Elizabeth with the opportunity for escape from the highly structured and patriarchal limits of Virginia's established church that evangelical faith offered, even as Davies's eloquent sermons influenced the oratorical style for which her brother Patrick became famous.[12]

The course of Elizabeth's life shifted early in 1775 with the death of her brother Patrick's first wife, Sarah Shelton Henry. She and their widowed mother moved to Scotchtown, the orator's residence in western Hanover County, to manage the household and help care for his five children. When Patrick was elected colonel of the First Virginia Regiment in August, twenty-six-year-old Elizabeth and her married sister Anne Henry Christian moved with him to a house in Williamsburg, where they acted as his hostesses and housekeepers. Anne's husband, William Christian, had studied law with Patrick and served as the lieutenant colonel of his mentor's regiment.[13]

Elizabeth Henry charmed the young officers stationed in Williamsburg on the eve of independence. She stood "above medium height," according to a grandnephew's admiring biography, "with a most attractive face and imposing presence." Foremost among Elizabeth's suitors was a young militia captain from Fincastle County, who joined her father's regiment in September 1775. Four years her senior, William Campbell was raised a Presbyterian and studied at Augusta Academy, a forerunner of Washington and Lee University, before inheriting a large estate in southwestern Virginia in 1767. The next year he established his own plantation, Aspenvale, along the Great Wagon Road twenty miles north of modern Abingdon. Renowned both for his fiery temper and his great courtesy, Campbell stood six foot two and had sandy red hair, blue eyes, and the capacity for frontier leadership.[14]

Elizabeth Henry and William Campbell were married at Scotchtown on April 2, 1776.[15] After her brother Patrick Henry became the first elected governor of the newly independent commonwealth of Virginia on June 29, Elizabeth returned with him to Scotchtown and nursed him through a life-threatening illness that lingered into the autumn. Assigned to the regiment guarding the capital that August, William Campbell sent his wife the only letter of his to her that survives. Writing from the house on England Street "where I was first blessed with the sight of my dear Betsy," Campbell declared that "from that happy moment I date the hour of all my bliss."[16] The couple reunited at Aspenvale in November after Campbell left Williamsburg to defend his western neighborhood against hostile Cherokees.

Elizabeth's new home was a story-and-a-half log house, bisected by a breezeway, which the couple shared with William's widowed mother and his unmarried sister until Margaret Buchanan Campbell died and her daughter Anne married in 1777. The house was surrounded by Campbell's inheritance of a thousand fertile acres on the middle fork of the Holston River.[17] The couple named their first child, born April 21, 1778, Sarah Buchanan Campbell in honor of their mothers. The couple's second child, Charles Henry Campbell, was born February 20, 1780, but lived only five years. As was common for American women during the War for Independence, the responsibilities for childrearing fell to

Elizabeth, especially when public service took her husband away from home. She also helped the sick and needy of the settlements near Seven Mile Ford.[18]

Throughout the war, Elizabeth's husband strove to protect Virginia's frontier settlements, ruthlessly suppressing loyalists, destroying their property, and executing as many as twelve Tories without trial—"necessary measures," according to the general assembly, "justifiable from the immediate urgency and imminence of the danger" even if not "strictly warranted by law."[19] In one incident that summer, William and Elizabeth Campbell were riding home from church when a man approaching on horseback bolted into the woods, but not before he was recognized as the notorious loyalist Francis Hopkins. William Campbell and several companions chased Hopkins to the Holston River. After a search confirmed the spy's identity and revealed messages intended for dangerous Cherokee leaders, his captors hanged Hopkins from a sycamore and rejoined their families. "What did you do with him, Mr. Campbell?" Elizabeth asked. "Oh, we hung him, Betty," the colonel replied, "that's all."[20]

The following autumn, Elizabeth Campbell shared once again the common wartime experience of frontier women when her husband led his county militia to a rendezvous of nine hundred frontiersmen in the Carolina backcountry. Campbell planned and led the assault against a key loyalist stronghold at Kings Mountain, South Carolina—west of Charlotte—in a battle celebrated as one of the most dramatic and important American victories in the war's southern theater. While Elizabeth took charge of their family and plantation, Congress celebrated William as the hero of Kings Mountain in 1780. The next year Virginia's legislature gave him a sword and a horse and named Campbell County in his honor.[21] William Campbell remained with General Nathanael Greene's forces until he was dispatched as a brigadier general in June 1781 to assist the Marquis de Lafayette in eastern Virginia. Struck down by fever and chest pains in August, William retired to Rocky Mills in Hanover County, the residence of Elizabeth's half brother John Syme, where he died at thirty-six of an apparent heart attack on August 22, 1781. Buried initially near Elizabeth's father and her brother's late wife at Mount Brilliant, Campbell's body was re-interred in the family graveyard at Aspenvale in 1832 on the fifty-first anniversary of his death.[22]

After her husband's death and the surrender of the British army at Yorktown in October 1781, Elizabeth Campbell, now thirty-two, remained at Aspenvale to raise three-and-a-half-year-old Sarah and twenty-month-old Charles and manage their inheritance. The end of hostilities also brought Colonel William Russell back to a property he owned at Seven Mile Ford, a few miles from Aspenvale. A forty-eight-year-old widower whose son had served at Kings Mountain, Russell had served throughout the War for Independence and was present at

Yorktown when Cornwallis surrendered. Made a brigadier general as he retired from the Virginia militia, Russell used that honorary title until his death. Elizabeth Campbell and William Russell were married on May 29, 1783. Two of their four children survived infancy. General Russell represented Washington County from 1784 through 1786 in Virginia's House of Delegates, where he engineered the creation of a new county named in his honor, and then represented a district composed of more than a dozen western counties in the Virginia Senate until 1791.[23]

When she remarried, Elizabeth ceded control of her property to her new husband. The general embraced his rights under the common-law doctrine of coverture, which stipulated, as the English jurist William Blackstone wrote, that "husband and wife are one person in law" and "the very being or legal existence of the woman is suspended during the marriage." When her five-year-old brother died in 1785, Elizabeth's daughter Sarah Campbell inherited the sole ownership of an undeveloped tract known as the Salt Lick (later known as the Salt Works and now the village of Saltville). Acting for his stepdaughter, General Russell built a furnace for distilling salt from the area's briny water, dug the first brine well in 1788, and soon was producing more than ninety thousand bushels of salt a year. He also built a log residence at the Salt Works that in time became known as the Madam Russell House.[24]

Elizabeth seems to have stood aside as her husband took these steps, perhaps because the general was creating an economic foundation that would amass a fortune for his stepdaughter. His austere discipline pressed harshly on Sarah, however, and she appealed to her uncle Arthur Campbell for help. Elizabeth apparently did not intervene when the general fought with his former compatriot for legal control of Sarah's inheritance, a dispute exacerbated by their political clash over Arthur's flirtation with a separatist movement aimed at creating a new state of Franklin in western North Carolina. Finally, in May 1790 Virginia's High Court of Chancery ruled that this claim against Sarah's inheritance "ceased by [Elizabeth's] second marriage," after which Arthur Campbell became his niece's guardian.[25]

Another change in Elizabeth's life indirectly related to her decision to remarry and return to the backcountry was her religious conversion in the late 1780s. Little is known about Elizabeth's religious life during the Revolution, when she resided in an area with few churches and fewer clergy. After the Revolution, however, evangelical churches grew rapidly on the Virginia frontier. Itinerant preachers appealed to residents of newly settled and thinly populated agricultural communities who yearned for direct supernatural interventions in everyday life and the freedom to seek their own salvation. Three months after the Russells moved into the log house, itinerant Methodist preachers in the Holston River valley gathered about three miles away at Keywood, midway between Glade Spring and the Salt Works, for their first governing conference, or annual meeting, west of the Blue Ridge. While they awaited the arrival of Bishop Francis Asbury, the principal Methodist leader in the southern states, the itinerants held a series of worship services. As the Reverend Thomas Ware later wrote, on Sunday, May 11, 1788, William and Elizabeth Russell were among the crowd who heard the cadaverous John Tunnell preach an excellent sermon "followed by a number of powerful exhortations."[26]

After the conference ended, Elizabeth Russell privately approached Ware. She had thought she was a Christian, she confided, but now she felt herself "the veriest sinner upon earth." She asked Ware and Tunnell to come to the log house, "pray for us, and tell us what we must do to be saved." On Monday the preachers spent the afternoon in prayer with Elizabeth until they were exhausted. While they recuperated nearby, General Russell tried to assuage his wife by reading to her from *An Appeal to Matter of Fact and Common Sense; or, A Rational Demonstration of Man's Corrupt and Lost Estate* by John William Fletcher, a close associate of the Wesley brothers whose theological sophistication stood out in a movement reliant upon self-taught itinerant preachers.[27]

Hearing the clapping of hands and the repeated shouts of "Glory!" the preachers hurried to the house. They "found Mrs. Russell praising the Lord" while the general paced the floor, weeping bitterly and praying "O Lord, thou didst bless my dear wife while thy poor servant was reading to her—hast thou not a blessing also for me?" Both the initial conversion of Elizabeth Russell, Ware recalled, and the "penitential grief so conspicuous in the General" prior to his conversion "made a deep impression on the minds of many, and numbers [of additional converts] were brought in before the Conference closed."[28]

As this scene suggests, evangelical revivals had a self-validating quality in which religious ecstasy seemed a visible token of divine favor. "The usual manner of [Methodist] conversion looked like this," an itinerant preacher reported from Petersburg: "People fell to the earth and lay in agonies . . . till they beat the earth with their hands, head and feet." Converts felt the presence of God through dreams, visions, miraculous healings, speaking in tongues. At camp meetings they swooned, fell into trances, and experienced "the jerks," spasmodic twitchings of the head, upper torso, or entire body.[29]

Although Methodist leaders believed, as Bishop Asbury remarked, that the Presbyterians and Baptists took "the rich and . . . the slaves" and left them "the simple-hearted poor people," evangelical leaders of all persuasions competed for opportunities to publicize the attendance of wealthy, well-educated, or prominent people at their services and camp meetings.[30] In this respect the Russells' conversion anticipated the transformation of Methodism in the nineteenth century as its adherents climbed the social ladder and shifted away from overt enthusiasm toward Victorian ideals of gentility. "God Almighty bless them and reward them," exclaimed Asbury, who became a frequent visitor at the Salt Works.[31]

During their remaining years together, Elizabeth and William Russell were "lavish in attention and kindness" toward Asbury and the itinerant Methodist preachers of southwest Virginia. Late in 1792, however, the fifty-eight-year-old general caught a cold as he traveled toward Richmond and died of influenza in Shenandoah County on January 14, 1793. Visiting "Sister Russell" that spring, Bishop Asbury presided over a five-hour memorial service at the log house, with weeping, shouting, several exhortations, and a sermon based on Hebrews 7:4: "Now consider how great this man was." Remembering the general as "a living flame and a blessing to his neighbourhood," Asbury prayed that "the Gospel may continue in this house!" Buried initially near Front Royal, Russell's remains were re-interred at Arlington National Cemetery in 1943.[32]

During the remaining thirty-two years of her life, Elizabeth Russell joined the legion of widows, particularly those of independent means, who "formed the backbone of the early Methodist movement." For women of prominent families, Methodism offered direct opportunities to shape the religious and moral character of their communities.[33] Widows like Russell made important contributions to the Wesleyan movement by supporting the itinerant ministers whose travels were a hallmark of frontier Methodism in the early republic. A typical itinerant preacher was a young single man who lodged and ate with members of perhaps two dozen local congregations along a four-hundred-mile circuit that required four weeks of travel and almost daily preaching. Entering the itinerant ministry was tantamount to taking vows of poverty, chastity, and obedience. Traveling Methodist preachers were fortunate if they could collect their stipulated allowance of $80 per year plus expenses. Marriage was discouraged by rule and practice (as well as by Bishop Asbury's bachelor example).[34]

The Wesleyan movement appealed to a broad spectrum of Americans in the early republic who were, as one itinerant preacher noted in 1803, "looking for miracles and things out of the common order" by which "they expected God to tell them every thing they ought to do." Between 1770 and 1820 Methodists grew from about a thousand to more than a quarter million adherents, and from about 2 percent to more than 34 percent of the nation's total church membership by 1850. About 87 percent lived below the Mason-Dixon line in 1790. At the same time, the Episcopalian (formerly Anglican) share of church membership in the southeastern states fell from 27 percent in 1776 to 4 percent in 1850.[35]

Worshipers who gathered at Elizabeth Russell's house experienced the full repertoire of frontier revivalism. When John Kobler "preached at the Saltworks" on Christmas Day 1794, he and his hostess witnessed "the loudest shout that I have heard for six months past." Kobler's account reflects the intensity of Elizabeth Russell's religious environment, in which an individual's daily relationship with God eclipsed abstract concepts about salvation. Although sympathetic to the Calvinist belief in innate human depravity, frontier Methodists seeking personal redemption rejected the passivity that predestination seemed to encourage.[36]

The essentials of Elizabeth Russell's faith are evident in a letter she wrote on the first anniversary of William Russell's death to "Brother" Stith Mead, then an itinerant preacher on the Holston circuit. Like the other correspondence Mead copied into his letter book (mostly from preachers rather than laity), Russell's letter reflected both her anguished conviction of personal wickedness and her joyful assurance of personal redemption by the grace of her "Dear Redeemer," all in terms that her coreligionists recognized as "the language of Canaan":

> Eternal Glory to the King of Heaven, My Brother, for his great Mercy in sparing me and my lovely Daughters. I take pleasure in thanking you for your welcome favour [i.e., receipt of Mead's recent letter delivered] by my much Esteemed Brother [John] Kobler.
>
> Blessed be our great Creator, for his great refreshment to Your precious Soul. Indeed nothing but pure Religion can afford real Comfort to an Immortal Soul. Oh! my Brother I trust I am bound for Heaven with grace to enable me. I can never love, nor praise, my Dear Redeemer enough for his wonderful love to unworthy me.
>
> My great God has been very Merciful to me of late. Supported me under great trials—Glory, Glory for ever and for ever more to my God, for my dear Saviour's Sake. My dear Brother help me praise Jesus the friend of Sinners. Oh! that I may feel more and more of the Religion of Jesus in my heart and my little all to be devoted to my Heavenly Father.
>
> My dear Brother Mead go on in the strength of Christ to Preach his holy word, and may you still continue to be a pattern [i.e., an example] to all around you, of true piety. I should be Extreamly glad to see you where ever you are. My very dear Brother pray for me and all my dear Children and Family to be enabled to serve God all our days. And Now my Brother I bid you fare-well. May the Grace of our Lord Jesus Christ be with you and all of us Now and forever more. Amen
>
> Eliza. Russell

Only the postscript alluded to the parental responsibilities for her surviving daughters—"now nine and five years old"—that fell to the widow and her slaves. "My sweet little Betty Henry and Jane Robertson's best love to you," she wrote, "desiring you would accept of some Plumbs."[37]

Elizabeth Russell and Stith Mead had much in common. Both came to Methodism from politically active gentry families. Both had parents and siblings who enjoyed what many Virginians regarded as "innocent recreations" and "civil mirth," such as whist, dancing, fencing, fox hunting, cock fighting, and other games. Mead was bitterly estranged from his parents and siblings, and he eschewed politics. Likewise, Russell's faith had no political implications; her distance from politics (and the reform movements increasingly associated with northern Protestantism) stemmed from the intensity of her concern for individual conversions and personal faith. She quietly chose to free her slaves, but in other respects she and southern evangelicals in general agreed with Bishop Asbury's comment during a visit to Washington, D.C.: "Congress does not interest me: I am a man of another world: I am Christ's."[38]

Madam Russell, as Elizabeth came to be called, seems to have supplemented her immersion in a life of prayer and charity (and the care of her daughters) by adopting the Methodist itinerant preachers in lieu of her geographically dispersed extended family. At the time she wrote to Stith, her parents and four siblings were deceased, her brother Patrick was ailing and retired in distant Charlotte County, two older sisters were also living east of the Blue Ridge, and her youngest sister was in Kentucky. Nevertheless, the evidence suggests that Russell preferred a pious and retiring life even when she was among kin. An acquaintance who visited her late in life remembered that when she had briefly resided near her daughter Sarah in Abingdon "the gay society of that place, particularly among her own relatives, was uncongenial to her."[39]

Religion led Elizabeth Russell to eschew fashion and other hallmarks of earthly indulgence. Visitors and descendants remembered her daily attire as having been "in the style of '76." She wore unfashionable dresses—dark calico in summer, gray flannel in winter—which reached the tops of her shoes and had sleeves that reached below the elbows. Long half-handed gloves covered her forearms. Russell sometimes wore a white linen apron and almost always a linen kerchief around her neck and a simple fluted cap. On Sundays and ceremonial occasions she donned black silk and an old-fashioned bonnet, but when she worked in her garden she often wore an old beaver hat discarded by Asbury when she gave him a new one.[40]

In her later years, Elizabeth Russell increasingly devoted herself to the Methodist movement, giving up superfluous earthly possessions, resigning in 1795 as the administrator of William Russell's estate, and relinquishing to her daughter Sarah Campbell Preston her dower rights in her first husband, William Campbell's, estate. Although by 1808 American Methodists had eased their initial opposition to slavery, in 1795 Elizabeth chose to manumit the slaves she owned. When she did so, she prepared a formal manumission document in which she stated her principled opposition to slavery:

> Whereas by the wrongdoing of men it hath been the unfortunate lot of the following negroes to be slaves for life, to wit, Vina, Adam, Nancy senior, Nancy, Kitty and Selah. And whereas believing the same have come into my possession by the direction of providence, and conceiving from the clearest conviction of my conscience . . . that it is both sinful and unjust, as they are by nature equally free with myself, to continue them in slavery, I do therefore . . . make free the said Negroes, hoping while they are free of man they will faithfully serve their Maker through the merits of Christ.

For several other slaves who had belonged to her first husband and in whom she held a life interest by virtue of her dower right in his estate, Russell arranged freedom during her lifetime and provided them with lodgings and gardens at the Salt Works. These slaves remained legally bound to her daughter's estate, however, and after Russell's death most of these people were "incorporated among the slaves of [her son-in-law] General Francis Preston, and some of them were made house and body servants and distributed among his children."[41]

Elizabeth Russell declined to accompany Sarah and Francis Preston when they moved in 1812 from the Salt Works to Abingdon, where they built an imposing mansion that is now the main building of the Martha Washington Inn. Instead she retired to a new house at Chilhowie, about eight miles from Saltville, near her daughter Jane Russell Thompson. A large room on the ground floor served as a place of worship, and she reserved another room, sometimes called the prophet's chamber, as lodging for impoverished preachers riding the circuit. No visitor left her house empty-handed, as she generously provided clothing, horses, and money for clergymen in need—and plums for Stith Mead.[42]

Converted in the heyday of Methodism's young circuit-riding itinerant preachers, Elizabeth Russell contributed to its transition from a frontier sect to a mainstream denomination. George Whitefield and the Wesley brothers had often preached to large outdoor audiences in both Britain and America, but in the 1790s southern preachers began to organize religious meetings that extended over several days. Campgrounds became institutionalized, with tents arranged in horseshoe, rectangular, or circular patterns under the shade of large trees. Preachers occupied a raised platform toward one end of the camp, with rough-hewn benches arranged on either side of an aisle that separated men and women. Near the front, a special "mourner's bench" welcomed those who felt the call to conversion. Fires built on tall pylons illuminated the camp at night. Straw and sawdust covered the ground where ecstatic converts fell, shouted, shook, and trembled during the course of three- or four-day meetings. Francis Asbury recognized the camp meeting as a powerful proselytizing tool, Methodism's "battle ax and weapon of war."[43]

At a typical Virginia camp meeting in 1803, twenty-seven Methodist preachers delivered thirty-four sermons and exhortations between noon on Friday, September 30, and noon on Monday, October 3. Forty-five white people and "a number of black people" experienced conversion at the meeting, and "the prayers, cries and shouts of the people in the dead hours of the night might be heard at the distance of 2 or 3 miles." Three years later Elizabeth Russell's friend Stith Mead organized twenty-two camp meetings attended by 64,500 people in central Virginia during the seven-month "season." By 1810 camp meetings had become signature events for Methodist circuits throughout the country, increasing annually from about four hundred in 1811 to six hundred in 1816 and a thousand by 1820.[44]

Elizabeth Russell was known for her eloquent prayers in small groups, but she rarely spoke in camp meetings or other public assemblies, shrank from all notoriety, and carefully supported the male leaders she admired in the Methodist organization. During the colonial Great Awakening and the Virginia revivals of the 1780s, as worshipers literally abandoned their assigned seating in pews arranged by social rank for open fields and rough-hewn benches, evangelicals had occasionally challenged hierarchies of race, wealth, ethnicity, and education with ideals of Christian fellowship and spiritual equality. After 1800, however, personal salvation trumped all other concerns in the Wesleyan movement in the southern states. Although women were a numerical majority of early Methodist adherents, power in the family of God was organized "along distinctly hierarchical and patriarchal lines." A perceptive young clergyman's wife who visited Russell in 1824 wrote that Elizabeth "insisted that [the woman's husband] might have served God better in single blessedness"—and then clapped her hands and exclaimed that her own favorite pastor "loved the Church better than he did his wife." Preaching was the province of white men, and for all the appearances of lay influence, the bishop and preachers exercised autocratic control of Methodism for many years after Elizabeth Russell's death.[45]

Yet the fact that prominent Virginia leaders figured in two widely circulated stories about Russell's prayers suggests that many believed she wielded a subtle influence in matters of religion. James Madison was said to have visited Elizabeth and her son-in-law Francis Preston at the Salt Works while campaigning for the presidency. According to this story, Madison got a hearty welcome and had scarcely stepped inside her house before "she placed her hands on his shoulders, gently pressed him to his knees, and prayed for him as the prospective head of the nation." Madison was then reported to have said: "I have heard all the first orators of America, but I have never heard any eloquence as great as that prayer of Mrs. Russell." On another occasion, the jurist Spencer Roane paid her a short visit. "It has been long since we met, and [we] may not meet again," said Russell as he prepared to depart, "will you please to pray with us before leaving?" Judge Roane, a steadfast Episcopalian, immediately reached for his pocket but found it empty. "I would do so with great pleasure," he said, "but I have forgotten my prayer book." "Well," Russell replied, "if you will join I will try to pray without a book," and "so they all kneeled and solemn fervent prayer was offered."[46]

In the 1820s Elizabeth Russell donated land at the Salt Works for a church and cemetery. Elizabeth Chapel was dedicated in 1824, the forerunner of the Madam Russell Memorial United Methodist Church built at Saltville in 1900 with large stained-glass windows honoring Elizabeth Russell and Bishop Francis Asbury. Russell's grandson Thomas L. Preston invented the myth that Emory and Henry College was named in her honor. Twenty-first-century scholarship has proven that the college was named for her brother Patrick Henry and Methodist bishop John Emory (also the namesake of Emory University in Atlanta).[47]

At the age of seventy-six, Elizabeth Henry Campbell Russell suffered a fall at her home. She died several weeks later on March 18, 1825, and was buried at Chilhowie according to her expressed wish. Decades later her daughter Sarah moved Elizabeth's body to the Aspenvale graveyard at Saltville, where the inscription on her gravestone describes her remarkable life:

ELIZABETH RUSSELL
Born Henry
By a first marriage Wife of Gen. Wm. Campbell
By a second Wife of Gen. Wm. Russell
A devoted and devout member of the Methodist Church
Her life was passed in the love and practice of its doctrines.[48]

Although Elizabeth Henry Campbell Russell's life of devotion and prayer was often overshadowed by her close ties to three Revolutionary heroes, she played a significant and underappreciated role in Virginia's post-Revolutionary religious and cultural development. "Methodists were few and scattered," Elizabeth Russell reminded a visitor shortly before her death, "but now they have become a great people, and just as far as the human foot has trod the soil there is a Methodist."[49] She may have recognized that the astonishing success of the Wesleyan movement in America was reaching far beyond camp meetings and chapels. Once a marginal sect with little influence, her church became a major religious denomination and a bastion of Victorian respectability as the nineteenth century progressed.

With the collapse of the colonial state-sponsored churches, Methodists led the way toward the modern American model of voluntary churches that compete for souls in a pluralistic religious environment. Methodist experiments with communication in meetings and in print also molded the political culture of the era, injecting vernacular Christianity and revivalism into the political bloodstream of nineteenth-century America. Russell's famous brother Patrick Henry had spoken the language of civic republicanism when he expressed the hope that his fellow citizens would sustain the new republic by embracing righteousness, practicing virtue, and encouraging it in others.[50] Setting her eyes on the world to come and expressing her hopes in the language of Canaan, Elizabeth Henry Campbell Russell earned a distinctive place in the history of the republic as a champion of the Methodist Church and the evangelical tradition that shaped American culture in the post-Revolutionary era.

NOTES

I am grateful to Edith C. Poindexter for information about the Henry family, Sarah-Jane Poindexter for documents from the Filson Historical Society, Lisa S. McCown for advice about collections at the Leyburn Library of Washington and Lee University, and Kathy Juliano of Drew University Library and David Grabarek of the Library of Virginia for arranging access to Stith Mead's rare memoir.

1. Mark Couvillon, *Patrick Henry's Virginia: A Guide to the Homes and Sites in the Life of an American Patriot* (Brookneal, Va.: Patrick Henry Memorial Foundation, 2001), 9–19; Robert Douthat Meade, *Patrick Henry: Patriot in the Making* (Philadelphia: Lippincott, 1957), 44–45.

2. Martha W. McCartney, *Nature's Bounty, Nature's Glory: The Heritage and History of Hanover County, Virginia* (Hanover, Va.: Heritage and History of Hanover County, 2009).

3. Meade, *Patrick Henry*, 3–34; Roger L. Emerson, *Professors, Patronage and Politics: The Aberdeen Universities in the Eighteenth Century* (Aberdeen, Scotland: Aberdeen University Press, 1992); Paul B. Wood, *The Aberdeen Enlightenment: The Arts Curriculum in the Eighteenth Century* (Aberdeen, Scotland: Aberdeen University Press, 1993).

4. Leon M. Bazile, ed., "Wills of the Reverend Patrick Henry and Walter Coles of Hanover County, Virginia," *Virginia Magazine of History and Biography* 58 (1950): 122.

5. *Virginia Gazette*, November 26, 1736; October 7 and December 9, 1737; December 15, 1738; December 14, 1739; Francis P. Magoun Jr., "Scottish Popular Football, 1424–1815," *American Historical Review* 37 (1931): 11.

6. Lorena S. Walsh, *Motives of Honor, Pleasure, and Profit: Plantation Management in the Colonial Chesapeake, 1607-1763* (Chapel Hill: University of North Carolina Press, 2010), 147-50.

7. Patrick Henry Sr. to William Dawson, February 13, 1745, Dawson Manuscripts, Library of Congress. An imperfect transcription is printed in "Letters of Patrick Henry, Sr., Samuel Davies, James Maury, Edwin Conway, and George Trask," *William and Mary Quarterly*, 2nd ser., 1 (1921): 261.

8. George Webb, *Office and Authority of a Justice of the Peace* (Williamsburg, Va.: William Parks, 1736), 78; Edward L. Bond, *Spreading the Gospel in Colonial Virginia: Preaching, Religion, and Community* (Lanham, Md.: Lexington Books, 2005), 3-71; William Waller Hening, comp., *The Statutes at Large: Being a Collection of All the Laws of Virginia*, 13 vols. (Richmond, Va.: Samuel Pleasants Jr., 1810-23), 3:170-71; William H. Seiler, "The Anglican Parish in Virginia," in *Seventeenth-Century America: Essays in Colonial History*, ed. James Morton Smith (Chapel Hill: University of North Carolina Press, 1959), 119-42; Seiler, "Land Processioning in Colonial Virginia," *William and Mary Quarterly*, 3rd ser., 6 (1949): 416-36.

9. On colonial Virginia Anglicans, see generally, Lauren F. Winner, *A Cheerful and Comfortable Faith: Anglican Religious Practice in the Elite Households of Eighteenth-Century Virginia* (New Haven, Conn.: Yale University Press, 2010); Jewel L. Spangler, *Virginians Reborn: Anglican Monopoly, Evangelical Dissent, and the Rise of the Baptists in the Late Eighteenth Century* (Charlottesville: University of Virginia Press, 2008), 9-42; Edward L. Bond, *Damned Souls in a Tobacco Colony: Religion in Seventeenth-Century Virginia* (Macon, Ga.: Mercer University Press, 2000), 238-303; John K. Nelson, *A Blessed Company: Parishes, Parsons and Parishioners in Anglican Virginia, 1690-776* (Chapel Hill: University of North Carolina Press, 2001), 357n28, 359n60, 387n24.

10. William Henry Foote, *Sketches of Virginia: Historical and Biographical* (Philadelphia: William S. Martien, 1850), 161; Rodger M. Payne, "New Light in Hanover County: Evangelical Dissent in Piedmont Virginia, 1740-755," *Journal of Southern History* 61 (1995): 672-76.

11. George William Pilcher, *Samuel Davies: Apostle of Dissent in Colonial Virginia* (Knoxville: University of Tennessee Press, 1971), 4, 186. Davies visited Hanover County in 1747 but moved there in 1748.

12. Joan R. Gundersen, *To Be Useful to the World: Women in Revolutionary America, 1740-1790* (New York: Twayne, 1996), 98-99; Monica Najar, *Evangelizing the South: A Social History of Church and State in Early America* (New York: Oxford University Press, 2008), 37, 45-59; Meade, *Patrick Henry*, 71-74.

13. William J. Van Schreeven, Robert L. Scribner, and Brent Tarter, eds., *Revolutionary Virginia: The Road to Independence*, 7 vols. (Charlottesville: University of Virginia Press, 1973-83), 2:257, 5:25, 7:654. See also Gail S. Terry's chapter in this volume.

14. Paul David Nelson, "Campbell, William," in *Dictionary of Virginia Biography* (Richmond: Library of Virginia, 1998-), 2:582-84; William Wirt Henry, ed., *Patrick Henry: Life, Correspondence, and Speeches*, 3 vols. (New York: Charles Scribner's Sons, 1891), 1:329-30.

15. Although most accounts of Russell's life place her marriage at Scotchtown, David Rice McAnally, an acquaintance late in her life, wrote that "the marriage was celebrated at the house of Col. [Samuel] Meredith, of Hanover county, who had married her oldest sister," Jane Henry Meredith (1737-1819). See McAnally, *Life and Times of Rev. William Patton* (St. Louis, Mo.: Methodist Book Depository, 1858), 60.

16. William Campbell to Elizabeth Henry Campbell, August 18, 1776, in Thomas L. Preston, *A Sketch of Mrs. Elizabeth Russell, Wife of General William Campbell, and Sister of Patrick Henry* (Nashville, Tenn.: Publishing House of the Methodist Episcopal Church, South, 1888), 11-3; the location of the original manuscript is unknown. Rumors of Governor Henry's death circulated

early in July 1776. See Jack P. Greene, ed., *Diary of Colonel Landon Carter of Sabine Hall, 1752–778* (Richmond: Virginia Historical Society, 1965), 1057.

17. Douglas Summers Brown, "Elizabeth Henry Campbell Russell: Patroness of Early Methodism in the Highlands of Virginia," *Virginia Cavalcade* 30 (1981): 110–17.

18. Elva Runyon, "Madam Russell, Methodist Saint" (MA thesis, University of Virginia, 1941), 16, 25; Preston, *Sketch of Mrs. Elizabeth Russell*, 7, 43; Laura Copenhaver, "Madame Russell," *Scribner's Magazine* 83, no. 6 (June 1928): 728; Margaret C. Pilcher, "Mrs. Elizabeth Henry Campbell Russell," *American Monthly Magazine [of the Daughters of the American Revolution]* 8 (1896): 885.

19. John Redd, "Reminiscences of Western Virginia, 1770–790," *Virginia Magazine of History and Biography* 7 (1899): 119–22; "An Act to indemnify William Campbell, Walter Crockett, and others," October 1779, in Hening, *Statutes at Large*, 10:195.

20. Lyman C. Draper, *King's Mountain and Its Heroes: History of the Battle of King's Mountain, October 7th, 1780* (Cincinnati, Ohio: Peter G. Thompson, 1881), 384–87.

21. Emory G. Evans, "Trouble in the Backcountry: Disaffection in Southwest Virginia during the American Revolution," in *An Uncivil War: The Southern Backcountry during the American Revolution*, ed. Ronald Hoffman, Thad W. Tate, and Peter J. Albert (Charlottesville: University of Virginia Press, 1985), 179–212; E. T. Crowson, "Colonel William Campbell and the Battle of Kings Mountain," *Virginia Cavalcade* 30 (1980): 22–29.

22. Nelson, "Campbell, William," 2:584; Jim Glanville and John M. Preston, "Aspenvale Cemetery and Its Place in the History of Southwest Virginia," *Smithfield Review* 13 (2009): 22, 135n134.

23. Hening, *Statutes at Large*, 12:110; Cynthia Miller Leonard, comp., *The General Assembly of Virginia, July 30, 1619–January 11, 1978: A Bicentennial Register of Members* (Richmond: Library of Virginia, 1978), 153–86; Preston, *Sketch of Mrs. Elizabeth Russell*, 7–8.

24. Gladys Stallard, "Madam Russell: Elizabeth Henry Campbell Russell," *Appalachian Quarterly* 1 (1996): 12–15; Robert C. Whisonant, "Geology and the Civil War in Southwestern Virginia: The Smyth County Salt Works," *Virginia Minerals* 42 (1996): 24–26; William Blackstone, *Commentaries on the Law of England*, 4 vols. (Oxford: Clarendon, 1765–69), 1:430. On coverture, see also Linda L. Sturtz, *Within Her Power: Propertied Women in Colonial Virginia* (New York: Routledge, 2002), 19–21; Carole Pateman, "Women and Consent," *Political Theory* 8 (1980): 149–68; and Hendrick Hartog, "Wives as Favorites," in *Law as Culture and Culture as Law: Essays in Honor of John Phillip Reid*, ed. Hendrick Hartog, William E. Nelson, and Barbara Wilcie Kern (Madison, Wis.: Madison House, 2000), 292–321.

25. Preston, *Sketch of Mrs. Elizabeth Russell*, 21–22; Emilee Hines, *More than Petticoats: Remarkable Virginia Women* (Guilford, Conn.: Globe Pequot, 2003), 29–30; Stallard, "Madam Russell," 12–15. Arthur Campbell's proposed terms of guardianship for Sarah Buchanan Campbell, dated July 1787, bear the notation "refused by Wm Russell." Arthur Campbell's 1786 petition and the chancery court's May 27, 1790, ruling are in sections 6 and 7 of the Preston Family Papers, Virginia Historical Society. See also Peter J. Kastor, "Campbell, Arthur," in *Dictionary of Virginia Biography*, 2:554–56; and Kastor, "'Equitable Rights and Privileges': The Divided Loyalties in Washington County, Virginia, during the Franklin Separatist Crisis," *Virginia Magazine of History and Biography* 105 (1997): 193–226.

26. Thomas Ware, *Sketches of the Life and Travels of Rev. Thomas Ware* (New York: T. Mason and G. Lane, 1839), 152; Greg McMillan, "A Brief Historical Sketch of the Events at Keywood, May 1788," *Bulletin of the Historical Society of Washington County, Virginia*, ser. 2, no. 43 (2006): 55–61. William W. Bennett's *Memorials of Methodism in Virginia* (Richmond, Va.: Published by the Author, 1871), 267–70, introduced many transcription errors into his often-reprinted text of Ware's narrative.

For John Tunnell, see William B. Sprague, *Annals of the American Pulpit; or, Commemorative Notices of Distinguished American Clergymen of Various Denominations* (New York: Robert Carter and Brothers, 1859), 7:48; and R. N. Price, *Holston Methodism: From Its Origin to the Present Time*, 5 vols. (Nashville, Tenn.: Publishing House of the Methodist Episcopal Church, South, 1903–14), 1:129–30. Methodist publicists portrayed this "First Conference West of the Alleghenies" as a harbinger of the denomination's "onward march into the Mississippi Valley and the great West"; ibid., 125.

27. Ware, *Sketches*, 152–53. Fletcher's *Appeal* was first published in London in 1772; a Philadelphia edition was published in 1783. See Patrick P. Streiff, "Fletcher, John William, 1729–85," in *Oxford Dictionary of National Biography* (Oxford: Oxford University Press, 2004).

28. Ware, *Sketches*, 152–53.

29. "An Account of the Revival of the Work of God at Petersburg in Virginia," *Arminian Magazine* (June 1790): 300; John H. Wigger, "Taking Heaven by Storm: Enthusiasm and Early American Methodism, 1770–820," *Journal of the Early Republic* 14 (1994): 173; Roger Robins, "Vernacular American Landscape: Methodists, Camp Meetings, and Social Respectability," *Religion and American Culture: A Journal of Interpretation* 4 (1994): 171; Christine Leigh Heyrman, *Southern Cross: The Beginnings of the Bible Belt* (New York: Knopf, 1997), 74, 77; William Brent Jones, "Moving Mountains: Southern Appalachia and the Faith of the Nation, 1730–1835" (PhD diss., University of Virginia, 2011), 122–30.

30. Elmer T. Clark, J. Manning Potts, and Jacob S. Payton, eds., *Journal and Letters of Francis Asbury*, 3 vols. (Nashville, Tenn.: Abingdon, 1958), 2:423–24; John B. Boles, *The Great Revival, 1787–1805: The Origins of the Southern Evangelical Mind* (Lexington: University of Kentucky Press, 1972), 169–70.

31. Robins, "Vernacular American Landscape," 183, 171; Wigger, "Taking Heaven by Storm," 193; Richard L. Bushman, *The Refinement of America: Persons, Houses, Cities* (New York: Knopf, 1992), 319–26, 346–48; Clark, Potts, and Payton, *Journal and Letters of Francis Asbury*, 1:633.

32. Clark, Potts, and Payton, *Journal and Letters of Francis Asbury*, 1:570, 758; Elizabeth Yarrington Russell, "Brigadier General William Russell of Virginia," *Virginia Magazine of History and Biography* 52 (1944): 267–72.

33. Heyrman, *Southern Cross*, 10–18, 269–70n13; Wigger, "Taking Heaven by Storm," 184; Catherine A. Brekus, *Strangers and Pilgrims: Female Preaching in America, 1740–845* (Chapel Hill: University of North Carolina Press, 1998), 133. Joan Gundersen found differences in attitude between older Virginians who remembered the effective colonial establishment and younger citizens familiar only with the desiccated postwar church ("Drawing the Line: Disestablishment in Powhatan County, Virginia," paper presented at the American Society of Church History Conference, Chicago, Ill., December 28, 1991; cited by permission of the author).

34. Wesley Marsh Gewehr, "Some Factors in the Expansion of Frontier Methodism, 1800–1811," *Journal of Religion* 8 (1929): 100–106.

35. Wigger, "Taking Heaven by Storm," 167–75, 192 (quotation at 173); Jacob Young, *Autobiography of a Pioneer; or, The Nativity, Experience, Travels, and Ministerial Labors of Rev. Jacob Young* (Cincinnati, Ohio: L. Swornstedt and A. Poe, 1857), 126; Roger Finke and Rodney Stark, *The Churching of America, 1776–2005: Winners and Losers in Our Religious Economy*, 2nd. ed. (New Brunswick, N.J.: Rutgers University Press, 2005), 55–56; Nathan O. Hatch, "The Puzzle of American Methodism," *Church History* 63 (1994): 178–80.

36. John Kobler to Stith Mead, December 30, 1794, in Stith Mead Letter Book, 1792–95, 140–41; *Works of the Rev. John Fletcher with a Life by the Rev. Abraham Scott*, 2 vols. (London: Thomas Allman, 1836), 1:4–5; Wigger, "Taking Heaven by Storm," 178–80; Robins, "Vernacular American

Landscape," 171; Cynthia Lynn Lyerly, "Enthusiasm, Possession, and Madness: Gender and the Opposition to Methodism in the South, 1770–1810," in *Beyond Image and Convention: Explorations in Southern Women's History*, ed. Janet L. Coryell et al. (Columbia: University of Missouri Press, 1998), 61–63.

37. Russell to Stith Mead, January 14, 1794, in Stith Mead Letter Book, 53–54; Heyrman, *Southern Cross*, 4–5; Mead, *A Short Account of the Experience and Labors of the Rev. Stith Mead, Preacher of the Gospel, and an Elder of the Methodist Episcopal Church* (Lynchburg, Va.: For the Author, 1829).

38. Mead, *Short Account*, 30–33; Heyrman, *Southern Cross*, 51–260; Clark, Potts, and Payton, *Journal and Letters of Francis Asbury*, 2:497; Boles, *The Great Revival*, 171–82; Lyerly, "Enthusiasm, Possession, and Madness," 71. Ann Smart Martin treats Mead's gentry family in *Buying into a World of Goods: Early Consumers in Backcountry Virginia* (Baltimore, Md.: Johns Hopkins University Press, 2008), 36–41, 200.

39. Edith C. Poindexter, "Patrick Henry's Siblings" (June 2009), unpublished paper in possession of author; Julia A. Tevis, *Sixty Years in a School-Room: An Autobiography* (Cincinnati, Ohio: Western Methodist Book Concern, 1878), 200.

40. Preston, *Sketch of Mrs. Elizabeth Russell*, 33–34; Tevis, *Sixty Years in a School-Room*, 199–202, 269–71.

41. Francis Preston's son Thomas wrote proudly that "not one of the dower negroes attempted to escape during the period of their temporary freedom" (Preston, *Sketch of Mrs. Elizabeth Russell*, 25–29). The manumission document is reprinted in William Warren Sweet, *Virginia Methodism: A History* (Richmond, Va.: Whittet and Shepperson, 1955), 195. Slaves whom Russell and her siblings inherited from their mother are listed in Senner Higginbotham MacFarlane, ed., "Will of Patrick Henry's Mother," *William and Mary Quarterly*, 2nd ser., 8 (1928): 117–19. Sylvia Frey tracks the evangelical retreat from antislavery in "Inequality in the Here and Hereafter: Religion and the Construction of Race and Gender in the Post-Revolutionary South," in *Inequality in Early America*, ed. Carla Gardina Pestana and Sharon V. Salinger (Hanover: University of New Hampshire Press, 1999), 87–108.

42. Preston, *Sketch of Mrs. Elizabeth Russell*, 31–32.

43. Kenneth O. Brown, *Holy Ground: A Study of the American Camp Meeting* (New York: Garland, 1992); Russell E. Richey, *Early American Methodism* (Bloomington: Indiana University Press, 1991); Robins, "Vernacular American Landscape," 168–73; Karen B. Westerfield Tucker, *American Methodist Worship* (New York: Oxford University Press, 2001), 75; Francis Asbury to Jacob Gruber, September 1, 1811, in Clark, Potts, and Payton, *Journal and Letters of Francis Asbury*, 3:453.

44. "Camp-Meeting," *Independent Chronicle* (Boston, Mass.), November 21, 1803; "Camp Meetings," *American Citizen* (New York City), December 25, 1806; "Camp Meetings," *Poulson's American Daily Advertiser* (Philadelphia), January 2, 1807; Stith Mead, "Camp Meeting," *William and Mary Quarterly*, 2nd ser., 4 (1924): 210.

45. Tevis, *Sixty Years in a School-Room*, 265; Frey, "Inequality in the Here and Hereafter," 87–108; Brekus, *Strangers and Pilgrims*, 133; Wigger, "Taking Heaven by Storm," 184; Runyon, "Madam Russell," 58.

46. Price, *Holston Methodism*, 1:132; McAnally, *Life and Times of Rev. William Patton*, 64–65. Roane was married to Elizabeth Russell's sister Anne from 1786 to her death in 1799. See Timothy S. Huebner, "Spencer Roane, Virginia Legal Culture, and the Rise of a Southern Judiciary," in his *The Southern Judicial Tradition: State Judges and Sectional Distinctiveness, 1790–890* (Athens: University of Georgia Press, 1999), 10–39.

47. Preston, *Sketch of Mrs. Elizabeth Russell*, 38–39; Robert J. Vejnar II, "From a Bishop and a

Patriot to a Bishop and a Saint: Rival Understandings of the Naming of Emory and Henry College," *Smithfield Review* 12 (2008): 35–61.

48. Glanville and Preston, "Aspenvale Cemetery," 122–23, 135n135.

49. Tevis, *Sixty Years in a School-Room*, 271; Jane C. French, "Madam Russell," *Addresses Delivered Before the Washington County Historical Society* 6 (1941): n.p.

50. Hatch, "Puzzle of American Methodism," 186–89; Henry, *Patrick Henry: Life, Correspondence, and Speeches*, 1:81–82. For a different view of the political impact of evangelicalism, see Amanda Porterfield, *Conceived in Doubt: Religion and Politics in the New American Nation* (Chicago: University of Chicago Press, 2012).

Elizabeth Jacquelin Ambler Brent Carrington

A Founder of the Female Humane Association for Orphan Girls in Richmond

SARAH HAND MEACHAM

❊ ❊ ❊

Elizabeth Jacquelin Ambler Brent Carrington was born in 1765 and died in 1842. She was the eldest of four girls born to a well-to-do Yorktown merchant, Jacquelin Ambler, and his wife, Rebecca Burwell Ambler. Jacquelin Ambler was active in Virginia's state government. He joined the fight for independence from Great Britain, serving first on the Council of State and then as treasurer of the commonwealth. Although Elizabeth—or Betsey, as she was called in childhood—was only eleven when Virginia and the other colonies declared their independence, the ensuing Revolution had a profound and lasting impact on her life.

In 1781, when Betsey Ambler was fifteen years old, her family fled as British troops advanced toward Yorktown. She chronicled her family's odyssey—first to Richmond, then to Charlottesville, and then back to Richmond—in lively letters to her friend Mildred Smith. Mostly, the Ambler sisters found fleeing in carriages and staying in new places to be great fun.[1] While the patriotic Betsey was proud of her father's role in the Revolution, she was too young to contribute to the war effort, aside from making homespun and stockings to replace necessities that Virginians used to import from Britain. Still, the wartime tragedy of a childhood acquaintance named Rachel Warrenton, who was seduced by a French soldier and became pregnant at a time when unwed mothers were shunned, preyed on her mind all of her life. The plight of Rachel Warrenton, along with the formative experience of female friendship, convinced Elizabeth Jacquelin Ambler Brent Carrington that girls needed strong female assistance, supervision, and protection. That conviction eventually led to decades of public activism on behalf of girls in the largest city in the commonwealth.

In 1785 Betsey Ambler married William Brent of Stafford County. She was devastated when he died of unknown causes less than three months later. Seven years later, in 1792, she married Edward Carrington of Richmond. Their marriage lasted eighteen years until he died in October 1810. Elizabeth Carrington spent the next thirty-two years as a widow in Richmond. Without children of her own to raise, she had time for civic projects. Among Virginia women of her era, Carrington was unusual in not having any children—surely the result of infertility—but middling and well-off women increasingly used birth control and abortificants to limit the size of their families, using their greater freedom to establish and work for benevolent associations.[2]

Even before she was widowed, Carrington engaged in benevolence work in her Richmond community. Perhaps recalling the sad case of Rachel Warrenton, in 1805 she joined with other elite women in Richmond to form the Female Humane Association, an organization that sought to protect and provide for orphaned and needy girls in Virginia. This group's signature accomplishment was to build an asylum, or home, for white female orphans in 1811.

Many historians explain the origins of women's organized benevolence in the 1790s as a logical extension of their public activism during the American Revolution. In Revolutionary Boston, the Daughters of Liberty had marched with the Sons of Liberty and burned tax collectors in effigy. Women throughout America participated in the anti-imperial movement by making the homespun that replaced imported English cloth and by substituting infusions of sassafras and other local plants for imported British East India Company tea. During the war, some women collected money and supplies for the troops. Poorer women traveled with the army as nurses, cooks, and laundresses. Winning the war did not bring women new rights, but some scholars believe that the Revolutionary rhetoric of liberty and women's Revolutionary activism led them to see themselves as members of a larger political community. As women, many believed, they could promote the American experiment in liberty and republicanism by being competent and civic minded. As republican wives and republican mothers, they could keep frugal households and raise industrious and self-reliant children, who would be the future citizens of the republic.[3]

Other scholars have argued that religious fervor—either on its own or coupled with republican civic values—catalyzed women's benevolence. Beginning in the 1790s a series of religious revivals known collectively as the Second Great Awakening swept through the United States, leading evangelical converts

MEMORIAL HOME FOR GIRLS, RICHMOND

The Female Humane Association orphanage (later renamed the Memorial Home for Girls) is shown in a postcard image from 1921. There are no images for the original building, which burned in 1892 and which was likely half the size of the orphanage pictured here. The original building was also probably more homelike, a visual symbol of public mothering, while the new building looked more institutional. Virginia Commonwealth University Libraries.

GRAVE OF EDWARD CARRINGTON, RICHMOND

It is unknown where Elizabeth Carrington is buried. Like many early American women, no one made a gravestone for her. It is likely, however, that she is buried next to her second husband, Edward Carrington, whose tombstone is pictured here, with the inscription that Elizabeth Carrington wrote. Photo by Sarah Hand Meacham.

to undertake a wide range of charitable and reform activities. Following the revivals, evangelical women raised funds to support missionaries, established associations to raise money and support their churches, and took food and religious pamphlets to poor people in their communities. Starting in the 1820s women inspired by religion also founded the first Sunday schools, where thousands of children learned to read and write.[4]

Significantly, Elizabeth Carrington's letters suggest that women's reasons for pursuing benevolence work varied widely and that her own motivation was neither republican nor evangelical. On the one hand, as an adolescent during the Revolution, she was more interested in beaus, novels, and local gossip than in the ideals of civic virtue and republican citizenship. On the other hand, she was a staunch Episcopalian who never embraced either the proselytizing spirit or the denominational fervor of committed evangelicals. Carrington helped to build a women's association and an orphanage for girls because of her personal knowledge of, and identification with, women's vulnerability and sufferings. The plight of Rachel Warrenton taught her that even white women's fortunes were precarious and that girls needed women's protection. Similar convictions inspired other efforts to ameliorate the distress of vulnerable women and children, which were increasingly undertaken by middle-aged upper- and middle-class women in cities in post-Revolutionary America.[5]

While Carrington's benevolence was born of her experiences during the American Revolution, it was prompted by her personal encounters during the war, not by her political convictions concerning independence or republicanism. At least in her case, the war created an environment in which a foreign soldier could seduce, impregnate, and abandon one of her acquaintances, a respectable young woman who lived with her elderly and unwatchful aunt in Yorktown. Carrington could imagine all too easily a similar calamity befalling herself, her mother, or her nieces, had they been just slightly less fortunate. For Carrington, it was not political or religious concerns that led to her public activities, but rather personal experience led her to an emotional conviction that girls needed women's protection and guidance.

Some historians have portrayed the half-century following the American Revolution as a sort of golden age of women's benevolence: Carrington's letters and the few remaining records of Richmond's Female Humane Association support that view. Before the Revolution, charity was assumed to be the responsibility of each locality. In Virginia, men who sat on county courts and parish vestries dispensed relief to the deserving poor in their communities. After the Revolution, however, urban areas especially became overwhelmed with those seeking support, and by 1800 Americans of both sexes were establishing charitable organizations to address the need, with women's groups focused mainly on aiding widows and children. Men's charities tended to be more limited than women's, seeking to place boys as apprentices with families or craftsmen, rather than building orphanages for them. Women like Carrington feared that such a system would leave girls unprotected and unskilled, so they were more likely to build orphanages to teach girls sewing and housekeeping, as well as to keep them safe. After 1840, however, a combination of the increasing financial needs of such organizations and men's fear of women's growing public prominence led men to assume leadership positions in many charities, relegating women to auxiliary roles.[6]

Most of what can be learned about Elizabeth Carrington and her ideas about helping orphan girls comes from fifteen surviving letters she wrote between 1780 and 1823, mostly to her friend Mildred Smith Dudley. It is unclear how these two friends met. They may have been part of a set of girls and young women that had tea and socialized together in Yorktown, which likely included Rachel Warrenton. The fact that the two friends did not exchange letters until Carrington's family fled Yorktown during the war suggests that they did not need to write earlier because they saw each other frequently.

These letters reveal above all the importance of female friendship and the persistent longing to associate with other women. The word "friend" and the concept of friendship have a somewhat complex history. In the seventeenth and early eighteenth centuries, because a "friend" was what would now be called a "patron"—in other words, a superior who provided goods or services for one less powerful than himself—that term was reserved for men alone. A young man called an older man who helped him make connections to find work, buy land, or start a business a "friend." It was only in the mid-eighteenth century that friendship became a relationship between equals and thus a relationship open to women. "Friends" were different from family relations and neighbors. When marriage or some other change in circumstances put great distances between female friends, letters helped them to maintain their connection over space and time, often resulting in a lifelong correspondence.[7]

Carrington wrote of female friendship without feeling the need to defend it, indicating that female friendships had become more acceptable than they had been only a generation earlier. Esther Burr was a girl in New Jersey in the 1750s when a family tutor said that he "did not think women knew what friendship was, they were hardly capable of anything so cool and rational as friendship." Eliza Lucas Pinckney of South Carolina had also heard insinuations that women were not capable of friendship, but she disagreed. As she intimated to a female correspondent in England, the letters they exchanged "show how capable women are of both business and friendship."[8]

Like hundreds of other female friends, Elizabeth Carrington and Mildred

Dudley exchanged letters that included memories of time spent together, which furnished them with decades of succor and sustenance. Women often confided in female friends, rather than in husbands or brothers. "When you left our dear little town, I felt as if every ray of [sunshine] had fled," Mildred began her first letter in 1780. "Oh my dear loved Betsey . . . how shall I exist without you?" she asked, adding, "Life seems a dreary waste since deprived of your loved society." Even girls or women who met only once or twice might develop and maintain a friendship for decades through letters. For instance, when Elizabeth was mourning the death of her first husband, her father asked her to visit a young English woman named Frances Caines, who had come to Virginia to enjoy the mild climate to improve her health. Although the two visited only briefly, Elizabeth later wrote to Caines that their meeting was "one of the greatest blessings of my life." Eight years later, Carrington was still writing to Caines that "my affection for you is unabated," and calling her "dear loved friend." In 1802, when Carrington was temporarily depressed, she worried that Caines might think she had stopped writing because of "want of affection." Carrington insisted that this was not the case and asked Caines to "continue to love me and make allowance for my weaknesses." As in the case of Carrington's short-term depression in 1802, women turned to their female friends in times of trial. When Elizabeth's first husband died after they had been married for only three months, she was heartbroken. "Oh my friend," she wrote to Dudley, "[I am] widowed, wretched and forlorn."[9] When faced with hardship, women believed that those who would listen best and help them most were other women.

Nineteenth-century women's letters so frequently mention love and physical ways of showing love that modern readers may wonder if the correspondents were lovers. For instance, during the war Mildred reveled in how "delightful the thought of being again in the arms of my first best of friends, how do I look forward with delight to the period our infant attachment shall be ripened into maturer friendship that the usual advantages we shall derive from shall be lasting as our lives." In all likelihood, however, the girls were not lovers. Rather, they were comfortable using a language of love with people of the same sex perhaps because the idea of same-sex sexual relationships was so foreign to them that it did not cross their minds. As one historian of southern women has argued, "because women had few alternatives to marriage and motherhood, their affection for each other posed no serious threat to heterosexual relationships; indeed, many women combined traditional married life with intense female friendship." Men and women believed that they were so different from each other that they would find understanding and comfort only with members of their own sex. So, it is not surprising that as adults they built separate organizations to address the needs of members of their own sex.[10]

Girls also used friendship to practice being mothers, instructing each other on how they should conduct themselves and practicing their maternal nurturing on each other. In the 1780s Mildred Smith told Betsey Ambler that while she preferred to live in her native Yorktown, she would gladly move to Richmond because "then I should be always near you always ready with my watchful tenderness to guard you against those juvenile extravagancies that you must allow me to say need some restraint." In this exchange, Mildred looked on Betsey as a child, chiding her for her "giddiness." Playing the role of the concerned maternal figure, she also worried that Betsey, like Rachel Warrenton, might fall under the influence of a French officer. "It is well for my loved Betsy," she concluded, "that she [was] removed from these scenes of amusement and dissipation, her giddy brain would also be turned were she here." For her part, Betsey invoked an imaginary Mildred to reprimand herself when she thought she might have been too coquettish. In Williamsburg a man invited her to a ball that he said was in her honor. "I delighted with an opportunity of shewing my consequence by accep[ting] his invitation and playing off a thousand airs," Betsey reported, "that would have provoked a le[cture] from you, an hour long."[11]

Other than separating the young friends, the American Revolution affected them very little initially. It is true that the Amblers fled Yorktown several times, and that Jacquelin decided that Betsey and one of her sisters would spend the duration of the war near Winchester with their elderly aunt and uncle, for safety, without their parents. Jacquelin wanted his wife, Rebecca, to stay with the girls, but she decided that the air in Winchester was bad for her health and insisted on leaving. Early Americans believed that miasmas—pockets of poor-quality air—caused illness, but it seems equally likely that Rebecca Burwell Ambler did not want to give up being mistress of her own household in order to live in small rented quarters or with elderly relatives.[12]

Although the topic of the Revolution must have filled her family's discussions, Betsey rarely wrote about it. She wrote one letter to her friend in which she briefly asserted that Americans must fight or face "British tyranny," and she wrote as well that she respected her beau for joining the Continental army. Mostly, her letters conveyed her excitement about the more personal impact of war. In 1781 she wrote of her family's "too certain confirmation of the British having landed and being actually on their way to town not a moment was to be lost and we were off in a twinkling." Amid confusion and impending danger, she confided, "I would have almost risked a view of them to have peeked in on you ... but my Father seemed to think that we had not a moment to lose. Such terror and confusion you have no idea of. Governor, counsel, everybody scampering. What an alarming crisis is this." She begged to know where her friend "hid when the enemy passed your door."[13]

Completing the same letter a few days later, the young refugee was decidedly less thrilled with the situation, but only because she was now forced to live in what she considered a dull place. In Newcastle, unlike in Yorktown, she complained, there were no dances and no friends. "What a gloomy time do I look forward to," she sighed, "oh that you were with us to beguile the tediousness of these immeasurable days, now at there [sic] longest."[14]

In a grander sense, however, the war shaped Elizabeth Carrington's life permanently as a result of her knowledge of the seduction and disgrace of her Yorktown acquaintance Rachel Warrenton. Even before the battle that made Yorktown famous by resulting in a British surrender, large numbers of soldiers had arrived in that coastal community. One of these soldiers was Viscount Rochambeau, the son of the commander of the French military forces in America and the man who seduced, impregnated, and abandoned the unfortunate Warrenton. Not only did Rochambeau leave instead of marrying Warrenton, he also refused to acknowledge her son or provide for his support. Instead, Rochambeau returned to France alone after the war was over. Legally, there was nothing that Warrenton could do to make him support the child whom she named Louis (later anglicized to Lewis). Indeed, only the fact that Warrenton's aunt reluctantly agreed to house and support both mother and child prevented the county from hauling the unwed mother into court and charging her with the humiliating crime of bastardy.

But the consequences of Warrenton's error were still damning. Her family was mortified, and her aunt—who left Lewis £1,000 when she died—disowned Rachel. Her sister, Camille, also suffered as a result of Rachel's tarnished social status. As Betsey reminded both herself and Mildred, "a departure from female rectitude . . . involves a family so irremediably." Thirteen years after her affair with Viscount Rochambeau, Warrenton married "an obscure man in her neighborhood," with whom she had two more children. That family of four lived in poverty, while Warrenton's son, who inherited money from his mother's aunt, left for school and grew up to become an admiral.[15]

While it sounds extraordinarily unfair to twenty-first-century ears to blame Warrenton for her own sad fate, elite women of her era considered it women's responsibility to stop men's sexual overtures. When the friends discussed Warrenton's situation in their letters, they were reminding themselves to mind their own conduct. Smith denounced Warrenton because she had "lost . . . every thing that is dear to woman," and condemned her for forgetting "the dignity of her sex." She believed that the consequences of Rachel's misconduct were, indeed, far reaching: Warrenton's "sisters mortification is beyond description," and her aunt tried to ignore the new baby, who was "so painful a disgrace."

Perhaps because she was so "mortified & chagrined . . . at the conduct of her eldest ward Rachel," the aunt embraced Mildred after a visit, pressing her "to her bosom, and weeping would exclaim Oh that these girls that I have reared with so much care would have spared me the torture I now endure Rachel *lost & undone forever*."[16]

Poor Rachel Warrenton probably could not resist the viscount's attentions and promises of marriage. A woman who married had the chance to become mistress of her own household and enjoy some authority. While some single women in urban areas such as Philadelphia were able to support themselves, and a few even thrived, most women who did not marry could look forward only to a lifetime of serving in other people's households and taking care of other people's children. Not just any man would do, though. In an age when married women could not legally own property, testify in court, sue, or keep money they earned, and when divorce was virtually unattainable, the choice of a spouse was crucial. Men decided where women lived, where their children went to school or apprenticed, whether their wives could spend money, and whether they could visit their families. At the same time, in an era when people increasingly valued companionship in marriage and when men and women alike idealized physical attraction and romantic love, the dashing viscount must have seemed like a most promising husband. A father's or mother's careful inquiries might have revealed otherwise, but orphan girls such as Warrenton, who lived with less vigilant—and perhaps less authoritative—relatives, lacked such assistance and had to make these crucial determinations on their own.[17]

No one, including Rachel Warrenton's female friends, blamed the viscount for the unfortunate fate that befell her. In fact, in 1782, Mildred Smith declared roundly, "why blame the Viscount. Had she but kept in view the dignity of her sex. . . . Poor deluded girl." Smith's statement reflected the prevailing wisdom that it was a woman's fault if she involved herself with a man who was not worthy of her trust. At the same time, however, Betsey and Mildred did not shun Rachel because, as an orphan, she lacked the close attention and guidance only a mother could provide. Though she was at fault, she had been forced to operate without the usual safeguards that a fully functioning family ideally offered to dependent females. Mildred concluded, "had she poor soul been blest with a mothers care in early life and been taught the heinousness of such a departure from female rectitude all might yet have been well." Betsey agreed that if she had had a "mother's care" Rachel Warrenton would not have found herself pregnant and abandoned.[18]

As Elizabeth Carrington aged and reflected on Warrenton's experiences, she concluded that she was lucky not to have ended up orphaned or pregnant and unwed herself, and she advised other women about how to protect vulnerable girls. In 1809 the forty-four-year-old Carrington advised her younger sister Nancy Ambler Fisher "never to leave your daughters a hundred and fifty miles from you with any but a Mother or a Sister. . . . [Other] relations however amiable and respectable generally are either too much engaged or too negligent to have charge of thoughtless girls all I will add at present is to warn you that girls at the age of 12 & 13 require a mothers care." She continued to concentrate on the topic, writing in another letter, "Our female relation was truly amiable, but young and inexperienced and almost as childish as ourselves. . . . a girl of 13 left without one adviser; of a gay and frivolous temper, fancying herself a woman, stands on a precipice that trembles beneath her. . . . It is not a pleasant thing to retrace the follies of youth but I have determined by a candid representation of different periods of my life to guard our dear little girls against errors that I have fallen into."[19]

Carrington had faith in the power of education, and she believed that stories of good and ill behavior could lead young people to emulate virtue and avoid vice. To that end, like many elite and middling women who had the time and the ability to read, Carrington and her friends read novels. Novels were a new literary genre that became extremely popular, especially after 1760. The histories and other literature of the sixteenth, seventeenth, and early eighteenth centuries taught moral lessons and featured men as the main characters. Novels told stories that often had female characters at their center; the main plot often revolved around women without mothers or guides to help them navigate the tricky waters to attain financially stable and fulfilling marriages. The plots of the most popular novels turned on whether a girl would make a bad marriage, or find herself seduced, pregnant, and abandoned. In the novels read by post-Revolutionary American women, men were rakes who were not to be trusted.[20]

Carrington even tried to write her own novel to warn girls and their mothers of the threat faced by girls, especially orphans, and the causes and consequences of seduction. She titled her unfinished novel "Variety; or, The Vicissitudes of Long Life," and she began it with a woman named Rebecca, who did not want to give up drinking tea during the American Revolution. In the novel, two distant relatives take in two orphaned girls. The main male character, Abram, tells his wife that "there is nothing earthly that interests me so much as helpless little female orphans and when our three little girls . . . are playing around us, it often occurs to me how helpless their situation would be if deprived of our care." Carrington never finished her novel, perhaps thinking herself untalented, or perhaps deciding to focus instead on protecting vulnerable girls in more concrete ways.[21]

In her novel and letters, Carrington emphasized—almost obsessively—the risk of girls becoming motherless, what could befall them, and how to educate them. She wondered what would have become of her own orphan mother had she not been taken in by family friends. She worried about what might have happened to her if she had been only a touch more risqué when she lived with her aging aunt. She wrote to her sister that "after asking ourselves who we are; and what we are, it naturally arises from whom we are. . . . particularly, when years increase, we love to trace our genealogy. . . . we hear with tenfold delight, of a noble act or pious deed done by those from whom we have descended; while a departure from rectitude in those whom the ties of nature bind us too [sic] would fill the virtuous mind with horror and lead to that sort of conduct, which gains respect and love, thereby shewing that vice and folly are by no means hereditary." In another letter, Carrington reflected on which textbooks she considered best, and how her father had educated her and her eldest sister by having them write letters to the children of his friends, noting approvingly that "a boarding school was no where in Virginia to be found" when she was a youngster.[22]

Although Carrington never said so explicitly, it is reasonable to infer that her reflections on Warrenton's situation, her own mother's inattention, and her hopes for the power of education led her to join with several other elite Richmond women to found the Female Humane Association in 1805. Such associations were still new at that time, but they were becoming more common. Anne Parrish had led a group of young white Quaker women in founding the nation's first female charity, the Female Society for the Relief of the Distressed, in Philadelphia in 1795, and women founded the Society for the Relief of Poor Widows in New York in 1797. Similar organizations followed in Baltimore in 1798, Boston in 1799, Savannah in 1800, and Norfolk in 1804. Southern and northern women's benevolent associations were very similar until after 1830, when some more radical northern women's groups became involved with temperance, abolitionism, and women's rights. Until 1840 benevolent societies also were homosocial worlds, meaning that men and women generally founded separate organizations that operated independently of each other.[23]

The founders of Richmond's Female Humane Association nonetheless benefited from men's charitable activities, which also expanded in the post-Revolutionary decades. The men's Amicable Society was founded in December 1788 for the "relief of strangers" then arriving in Richmond. The Amicable Society and the Female Humane Association were on good terms. In 1841, when the Amicable Society disbanded, its officers gave their group's fifty shares of bank stock to the Female Humane Association. This bequest and the donation of an empty lot enabled the Female Humane Association to erect a new orphanage on the corner of Seventh and Leigh Streets in Richmond in 1843. This building was used for nearly seventy years until the orphanage moved to Highland Park. In 1921, it became known as the Memorial Home for Girls.[24]

From the start, members of the Richmond Female Humane Association aimed to raise money specifically to help poor women and girls. Each member of the association was required to pay dues of one dollar annually, plus fines ranging from twelve to twenty-five cents for missing meetings. In the 1820s, like many women's benevolent societies, the Richmond group began holding an annual fair at which they sold "things to please the palate, the mind and the eye." Announcements told potential buyers that they were contributing "to this good work and [should] feel the sunshine of an approving conscience."[25]

Carrington and her associates sought to educate the girls who came under their care, but when they prepared their charges for the future they presumed that they would continue to occupy an inferior social rank. To be sure, during this period, schools instructed both rich and poor girls in the basic ideals of white womanhood in order to make them virtuous, useful, and pliable members of society. Yet girls from affluent families were encouraged to become sensitive, sympathetic, and civic leaders of other women, while poor girls were taught to be obedient, deferential, and industrious, so that they could earn a living in domestic service as adults.

Elite Virginia girls studied with private tutors at home or they attended the increasingly popular ladies academies. These schools for girls became widespread throughout the United States after the Revolution, educating the daughters of both middle-class and wealthy families. Students read literature, learned about ancient Greece and Rome, and practiced music, painting, and letter writing. At school, they gave speeches on stage—which were open to the public—and they put on tableaus. They were also taught that women were morally superior to men because of women's greater sensibility or sensitivity. Because women were more sensitive, so the argument went, they both needed protection and were at the same time uniquely suited to inculcating morality in others.[26]

The education offered by the Female Humane Association, in contrast, was more narrowly religious and practical. In 1827 members reported having "fourteen indigent and helpless children" who were "fed and clothed, and (what is more important) instructed by a respectable Matron in the rudiments of education and in their moral and religious duties." The board was proud to have "maintained and instructed, and put into a respectable way of living, who would else have been wretched themselves, and nuisances to the town," and complimented themselves for the "rescue [of] female orphans from misery and shame."

In addition to attending what were surely stern lectures on prayer, humility, deference, and purity, the girls spent most of their days spinning and weaving. The matron of the school took the children to "Christian worship" on Sundays and saw to it that they learned "those fundamental truths, wherein all Christians are agreed." An 1833 request for donations highlighted the larger purpose of making these poor girls useful to—rather than a problem for—society. Lamenting that "great numbers of poor female children are annually lost to society from the inability of this Institution to provide for them," the association argued that "many who might have been rescued from guilt and misery . . . into the paths of virtue and peace, will now exert only an evil and injurious influence upon society," adding, "Who can calculate the advantages to society of saving one poor child from guilt and infamy, and sending her forth to the world in purity and innocence, strong in virtuous principles, and rich in useful knowledge?" The desire to send girls "forth to the world . . . strong in virtuous principles" suggests that an additional goal was to reduce prostitution and thereby shield men such as their own husbands and sons from corruption.[27]

The supply of orphans (and potential prostitutes and beggars) was enormous partly as a result of high mortality rates. While the demographics of orphans in Richmond have yet to be analyzed, research on other regions is suggestive. One historian found that in Charleston, South Carolina, "among white men born there between 1761 and 1800, approximately 33 percent of those who reached the age of twenty died before their fortieth birthday." So many women died during childbirth that they called labor "going down to death's door." Many early nineteenth-century Americans also died of waterborne diseases, such as typhoid and cholera, which have since been reduced by access to cleaner drinking water. Others died because clothes, sheets, flatware, and medical instruments were washed infrequently. Germ theory would not spread to the United States until after the Civil War. Until then, few people washed utensils and cups that a sick person had used, or boiled forceps between births.[28]

One did not have to be an "orphan" in today's sense of the word in order to qualify as such in the early nineteenth century. In the early 1800s at least 10–20 percent of children in orphanages still had a living parent, usually a mother, but the parent was too poor or incapacitated to care for the child. As part of the effort to make domestic servants who would be pliable and not sexually appealing to men, the Female Humane Association separated "orphan" girls from any relatives—if they had them—because they feared that poor relatives would be negative influences on their charges. As one association pamphlet proudly proclaimed, "upon entrance in the home [a girl] was entirely separated from her family."[29]

Once a girl reached thirteen or fourteen years old, she was "bound out," meaning that she was rented to a family who wanted a servant. It is possible that Female Humane Association girls were bound out to the kitchens and sculleries of the same women who gave money to the orphanage, though the association's records are not clear on this point. These fledgling domestic servants might live in the houses of their new mistresses; if the mistresses lived close enough to the orphanage, the girls could return there to sleep. The girls were not paid for their work. Any payments went to the orphanage to fund its operating costs and projects.[30]

If Carrington had her way, then, the Female Humane Association home was a strict and restrictive place. The only records that exist from the early days of the association and its orphanage are some bylaws approved in 1827 and an earlier act of incorporation passed by the general assembly in January 1811, which gave the Female Humane Association the power to acquire and hold property, the right to sue and be sued, and the right to bind out orphan girls. No records survive that indicate what the girls ate or wore, what rules they followed, or what they thought of the orphanage. Carrington herself approved of corporal punishment. In a letter to her sister, she recalled that their own "dear" father had used "the rod" (for whipping) frequently and "most conscientiously," and though "he was considered a most rigid disciplinarian but I have since discovered that his superior knowledge of human nature led him to pursue the right course, and in my own subsequent experience in the education of children, I have found that the present prevailing opinion that youth may be reared and matured by indulgence is altogether erroneous." Carrington concluded that "with a very few exceptions it will be always proper to observe a well regulated discipline." She further advised her sister that "restraint is certainly never pleasant, and to children is insupportable, but it is prod[uc]tive of every good, in every situation; and gives a zest to . . . life that, nothing else can supply; that it forms the mind to bear its ills has never been denied,—the advantages I have experienced through life from my fathers supposed inflexibility are incalculable."[31]

While elite women like Carrington really did want to protect girls and truly did care about their moral and spiritual development, they also wanted to prevent poor girls from becoming threats to respectable middling and elite families. It was women's job to raise virtuous boys and girls: boys who would go on to run the republic's political and commercial endeavors and girls who would be mothers to another generation of republican sons. Rootless girls, who might be prostitutes or otherwise turn young men astray, jeopardized both national survival and family tranquility, besides producing illegitimate children who would have to be supported with local taxes. For the good of the community and the nation, then, it was important that orphan girls learn to serve families, be modest and self-supporting, and accept their place in the social hierarchy.

The fact that benevolent women's subtly expressed fears that girls without strict oversight would degenerate into unwed mothers or prostitutes who would debauch their own sons makes assessing the Female Humane Association's work tricky. Carrington can be viewed as both progressive for her time when it came to protecting white girls, and conservative for perpetuating the idea that stopping sexual advances was the sole responsibility of girls. Worse, her tainted compassion for white girls did not extend to black girls in any way. In 1784 she inherited a "negro girl, Judith," from her aunt Martha Jacquelin, but Carrington never mentioned Judith in her letters. In addition, she mocked an enslaved woman in her unfinished novel: when her black character is asked about the location of a letter, Carrington had her respond, "pray God Miss if me knows one word bout em—Dey come heap pon heap, so fast, dat me never know which place I put em me taut when massa tell missa to read um wid de bit tear runnin down he old eyes some mischief was hatching. . . . my heart beat pit a pat so hard, dat me no member where me put de let[t]er."[32] Carrington's legacy, and that of her associates, is thus complex. They were progressive in their efforts to help some girls, and at the same time they were retrograde in their assumptions about sexual responsibility and in their willful ignorance concerning the circumstances of both enslaved and free African Americans.

Recovering the stories of women like Carrington can be challenging. The work of the women who founded Richmond's Female Humane Association and hundreds of similar benevolent associations is hidden in the historical record, in part because women themselves masked their own activities. A striking example is the tablet placed at the entrance of the Memorial Home for Girls in 1933:

This tablet is placed in grateful memory of

Mrs. James Wood

Mrs. Edward Carrington

Mrs. Philip Nicholas

who began the work of this institution in 1805, and of the successive officers and members of the governing board who helped to make possible its unbroken tradition of loving service.[33]

This plaque, like hundreds of similar ones, clouds women's endeavors and accomplishments by defining women solely as extensions of their husbands. Indeed, the only indication on the plaque that the home was founded, funded, and maintained by women is the "Mrs." in front of three men's names. Elizabeth

Jacquelin Ambler Brent Carrington thus disappears from history, her identity subsumed in that of a man who died many years before she completed her accomplished and eventful life.

Disturbingly, it was women themselves who began to hide their public roles, starting in the 1840s. Just as the 1840s witnessed men first intervening in and then taking control of women's benevolent associations, that decade also saw other transitions in relationships between men and women. It was then that it became commonplace for women to identify themselves by their husbands' names. It was also in the 1840s and 1850s that men and women began to conclude that women should not speak to public audiences. And, for the most part, after 1840 women's work and achievements in the area of benevolence were often credited to men.[34]

As a result of these nineteenth-century conventions, historical sources such as plaques and institutional histories can mislead, so we must read them carefully and critically. For instance, a book published by the Memorial Home for Girls in 1938 to celebrate its history at no point listed either the first names or maiden names of the three women who founded the institution. And the book's author spent far more time on "Mr. Edmund Walls," who bequeathed an empty lot to the association in his will, than to the women who founded, donated to, worked for, or lived in the home.[35] In 1965 the renamed Memorial Foundation for Children published a new pamphlet that gave some credit to the women who founded the home, opening with "it is the story of how the ideal of a determined, dauntless woman resulted in the formation of Virginia's oldest charitable institution." The authors lauded "Mrs. James E. Wood," the "wife of General Wood, an ex-governor of Virginia." The other founding members were listed only as "a sister-in-law of John Marshall, Mrs. Philip Norborne Nicholas, wife of the Attorney General of Virginia, and Mrs. Edward J. Carrington, wife of Colonel Carrington of Revolutionary War fame, Commissioner of the United States for Virginia, and a friend of George Wythe and George Washington," and "pretty Mrs. John Bell."[36] This pamphlet, likely well intentioned, still obscured women's initiative and work by describing them only as the "pretty" wives of famous men.

Elizabeth Jacquelin Ambler Brent Carrington died on February 15, 1842, and was buried in St. John's churchyard in Richmond.[37] Like most early American women, she was interred in an unmarked grave whose exact location is still unknown. Carrington, however, was important enough to merit a brief death notice and an obituary in the *Richmond Enquirer*. Carrington's death notice first identified her as a daughter and a wife, making her family connections the basic source of her identity and merit: "to have been one of the daughters of Mr. Jacquelin Ambler, a former Treasurer of this Commonwealth, and the widow of Col. Edward Carrington, are circumstances which confer no small distinction on this lady." But the *Enquirer* then praised Carrington for her own virtues: her "cultivated mind; her generous heart; her active and diffusive charity of which the Female Humane Association of Richmond furnishes one enduring memorial; and her practical piety."[38]

Today the Female Humane Association that Carrington helped found still exists as the Memorial Foundation for Children. It no longer has a building or an orphanage, but it does distribute money to organizations that assist children. Carrington's role in the creation of this public institution is worth remembering. Her benevolent work, born of her Revolutionary experiences and nurtured by comforting female friendships, suggests the possibilities and limits of women's public activism in the post-Revolutionary era.

NOTES

1. All letters cited are from the Elizabeth Jacquelin Ambler Papers, 1780–1832, at the Rockefeller Library, Colonial Williamsburg Foundation. All letters are cataloged under the name Elizabeth (or Eliza) Jacquelin Ambler, and my citations retain this usage, regardless of the author's changing surname; most letters are dated with years only. For letters between Betsey Ambler and Mildred Smith during the American Revolution, see Mildred Smith [Dudley] to Eliza Jacquelin Ambler, 1780; Eliza Jacquelin Ambler to Mildred Smith [Dudley], 1780; Eliza Jacquelin Ambler to Mildred Smith [Dudley], Richmond, 1781; and Mildred Smith [Dudley] to Eliza Jacquelin Ambler, 1782. For more on Elizabeth Jacquelin Ambler Brent Carrington, see Catherine Kerrison, "Carrington, Elizabeth Jacquelin Ambler Brent," in *Dictionary of Virginia Biography* (Richmond: Library of Virginia, 1998–), 3:35–37.

2. For more on early American women and infertility, or controlling fertility, see Margaret Marsh and Wanda Ronner, *The Empty Cradle: Infertility in America from Colonial times to the Present* (Baltimore, Md.: Johns Hopkins University Press, 1996); and Susan E. Klepp, *Revolutionary Conceptions: Women, Fertility, and Family Limitation in America, 1760–1820* (Chapel Hill: University of North Carolina Press, 2009).

3. For more on women, the American Revolution, and benevolence, see Linda K. Kerber, *Women of the Republic: Intellect and Ideology in Revolutionary America* (Chapel Hill: University of North Carolina Press, 1980), 111–13, 278; Carol Berkin, *Revolutionary Mothers: Women in the Struggle for America's Independence* (New York: Knopf, 2005), 44–48; Cynthia A. Kierner, *Beyond the Household: Women's Place in the Early South, 1700–1835* (Ithaca, N.Y.: Cornell University Press, 1998), 181, 189–90, 198, 218.

4. See Anne M. Boylan, *Sunday School: The Formation of an American Institution, 1790–1880* (New Haven, Conn.: Yale University Press, 1990). On women, religion, and benevolence, see generally Robert H. Abzug, *Cosmos Crumbling: American Reform and Religious Imagination* (Oxford: Oxford University Press, 2004); Mary P. Ryan, *Cradle of the Middle Class: The Family in Oneida County, New York, 1790–1865* (Cambridge: Cambridge University Press, 1983); Anne M. Boylan,

The Origins of Women's Activism: New York and Boston, 1797–1840 (Chapel Hill: University of North Carolina Press, 2002).

5. For the standard periodization of women's benevolence, see Anne M. Boylan, "Women in Groups: An Analysis of Women's Benevolent Organizations in New York and Boston, 1797–1840," *Journal of American History* 71 (1984): 497–523. Timothy James Lockley has noted that southern women like Carrington typically engaged in benevolence activities in their forties; see *Welfare and Charity in the Antebellum South* (Gainesville: University Press of Florida, 2007), 81. On Carrington's religion, see Catherine Kerrison, *Claiming the Pen: Women and Intellectual Life in the Early American South* (Ithaca, N.Y.: Cornell University Press, 2006), 97.

6. Lockley, *Welfare and Charity*, 143–47. On overseers of the poor, see ibid., 14.

7. On the history of the meaning of the word "friend," see Andrew S. Trees, *The Founding Fathers and the Politics of Character* (Princeton, N.J.: Princeton University Press, 2004), 20–21.

8. Carol F. Karlsen and Laurie Crumpacker, eds., *The Journal of Esther Edwards Burr 1754–1757* (New Haven, Conn.: Yale University Press, 1986), 257; Elise Pinckney, ed., *The Letterbook of Eliza Lucas Pinckney* (Chapel Hill: University of North Carolina Press, 1972), 152.

9. Mildred Smith [Dudley] to Eliza Jacquelin Ambler, 1780; Elizabeth Jacquelin Ambler to Miss [Frances] C[aines], Bristol, 1786; Eliza Jacquelin Ambler to Miss [Frances] C[aines], 1792; Eliza Jacquelin Ambler to Miss [Frances] Caines, Bristol, Richmond, March 1795; Eliza Jacquelin Ambler to Miss [Frances] C[aines], 1802.

10. Anya Jabour, *Scarlett's Sisters: Young Women in the Old South* (Chapel Hill: University of North Carolina Press, 2007), 71, 73. See also Carroll Smith-Rosenberg, "The Female World of Love and Ritual: Relations between Women in Nineteenth-Century America," *Signs* 1 (1975): 1–29; Mildred Smith [Dudley] to Eliza Jacquelin Ambler, York, 1780. On the history of same-sex relationships, see Thomas A. Foster, *Long before Stonewall: Histories of Same-Sex Sexuality in Early America* (New York: New York University Press, 2007); and Richard Godbeer, *The Sexual Revolution in Early America* (Baltimore, Md.: Johns Hopkins University Press, 2004), 11–12, 64–65, 87, 112–15.

11. Mildred Smith [Dudley] to Eliza Jacquelin Ambler, 1780; Mildred Smith [Dudley] to Eliza Jacquelin Ambler, 1782; Eliza Jacquelin Ambler to Mildred Smith [Dudley], 1780.

12. On miasmas and the history of the idea that held that some locations were unhealthy, see Nancy Tomes, *The Gospel of Germs: Men, Women, and the Microbe in American Life* (Cambridge, Mass.: Harvard University Press, 1999), 3, 32–33, 35–36, 51, 95–96; and Sheila Rothman, *Living in the Shadow of Death: Tuberculosis and the Social Experience of Illness in American History* (New York: Basic, 1994), 4, 21–22, 133–37.

13. Eliza Jacquelin Ambler to Mildred Smith [Dudley], 1781.

14. Ibid.

15. Mary Beth Norton, *Liberty's Daughters: The Revolutionary Experience of American Women, 1750–1800* (Boston: Little, Brown, 1980), 55; Catherine Clinton, *The Plantation Mistress: Woman's World in the Old South* (New York: Pantheon, 1982), 113–14; Mildred Smith [Dudley] to Elizabeth Jacquelin Ambler, 1782; Eliza Jacquelin Ambler to Ann [Nancy] Fisher, January 1, 1807; Catherine Kerrison, "By the Book: Eliza Ambler Brent Carrington and Conduct Literature in Late Eighteenth-Century Virginia," *Virginia Magazine of History and Biography* 105 (1997): 39.

16. Mildred Smith [Dudley] to Eliza Jacquelin Ambler, 1782; Eliza Jacquelin Ambler to Mildred Smith [Dudley], Williamsburg, January 10, 1786. On women's responsibility for sexual restraint in the early eighteenth century, see Norton, *Liberty's Daughters*, 53–54.

17. On the ideals of companionate marriage increasing marital unhappiness, see Merrill D. Smith, *Breaking the Bonds: Marital Discord in Pennsylvania, 1730–1830* (New York: New York University

Press, 1993); and Suzanne Lebsock, *The Free Women of Petersburg: Status and Culture in a Southern Town, 1784–1860* (New York: Norton, 1984), chap. 2, esp. 32–35. On divorce in early Virginia, see Thomas E. Buckley, *The Great Catastrophe of My Life: Divorce in the Old Dominion* (Chapel Hill: University of North Carolina Press, 2002). On successful single women, see Karin A. Wulf, *Not All Wives: Women of Colonial Philadelphia* (Philadelphia: University of Pennsylvania Press, 2005). On women's limited legal rights, see generally Marylynn Salmon, *Women and the Law of Property in Early America* (Chapel Hill: University of North Carolina Press, 1986).

18. Mildred Smith [Dudley] to Eliza Jacquelin Ambler, 1782; Kerrison, "By the Book," 37.

19. Eliza Jacquelin Ambler to [Ann] Nancy [Fisher], March 1809; Eliza Jacquelin Ambler to [Ann] Nancy [Fisher], 1810.

20. On novels as advice books, see Cathy N. Davidson, *Revolution and the Word: The Rise of the Novel in America* (New York: Oxford University Press, 2004); and Catherine Kerrison, "The Novel as Teacher: Learning to Be Female in the Eighteenth-Century South," *Journal of Southern History* 69 (2003): 513–48.

21. "Variety; or, The Vicissitudes of Long Life," Elizabeth Jacquelin Ambler Papers, n.d., 3.

22. Essay on family [Eliza Jacquelin Ambler to Ann Ambler Fisher], October 10, 1796, Elizabeth Jacquelin Ambler Papers; Eliza Jacquelin Ambler to Ann Fisher, [1807–9].

23. "An Act Incorporating the Female Humane Association of the City of Richmond: 1810–1811 Va. Acts 52, Jan. 3, 1811," in *Acts Passed at a General Assembly of the Commonwealth of Virginia [beginning 1810]* (Richmond, Va.: Samuel Pleasants Jr., 1811), 86–87; Lockley, *Welfare and Charity*, 67, 74, 76.

24. Samuel Mordecai, *Virginia, Especially Richmond, in By-Gone Days* (Richmond, Va.: West and Johnston, 1860), 255–56; *Memorial Home for Girls, Formerly Female Humane Association, 1805–1938* (Richmond, Va.: n.p., 1938), 12, 13, 15; Bylaws, Memorial Foundation for Children Records, 1827–1965, acc. no. 26532a-w, Library of Virginia.

25. Virginia D. Cox, *Memorial Foundation for Children, formerly Memorial Home for Girls, formerly Female Humane Association* (Richmond, Va.: n.p., 1965), 11, 77.

26. Mary Kelley, *Learning to Stand and Speak: Women, Education, and Public Life in America's Republic* (Chapel Hill: University of North Carolina Press, 2008), 23, 29; Clinton, *Plantation Mistress*, 123–38.

27. Bylaws, Memorial Foundation for Children Records, 8, 1, 7, 10; *Memorial Home for Girls*, 11; Memorial Home for Girls, *Constitution and By-Laws of the Female Humane Association of the City of Richmond, Adopted April 1, 1833* (Richmond, Va.: Shepherd and Colin, 1843), 4.

28. On increasing poverty in nearby Petersburg during this period, see Lebsock, *Free Women of Petersburg*, 203–5. On mortality rates, see Billy G. Smith, *Down and Out in Early America* (University Park: Pennsylvania State University Press, 2004), chaps. 3 and 8 (reference to Charleston on 215); Judith Leavitt and Whitney Walton, "'Going Down to Death's Door': Women's Perceptions of Childbirth in America," in *Women and Health in America: Historical Readings*, ed. Judith Walzer Leavitt (Madison: University of Wisconsin Press, 1984), 155–65. On cholera, see Charles E. Rosenberg, *The Cholera Years: The United States in 1832, 1849, and 1866* (1962; rpt., Chicago: University of Chicago Press, 1987).

29. Matthew A. Crenson, *Building the Invisible Orphanage: A Prehistory of the American Welfare System* (Cambridge, Mass.: Harvard University Press, 2001), 17. See also Timothy A. Hacsi, *Second Home: Orphan Asylums and Poor Families in America* (Cambridge, Mass.: Harvard University Press, 1997), 1; *Memorial Home for Girls*, 5.

30. *Memorial Home for Girls*, 5.

31. Eliza Jacquelin Ambler to Ann [Nancy] Fisher, January 1, 1807.

32. Benjamin B. Weisiger III, comp., *City of Richmond, Virginia Wills 1782–1810* (Richmond, Va.: Benjamin B. Weisiger III, 1983), 70; "Variety; or, The Vicissitudes of Long Life," 4.

33. *Memorial Home for Girls*, 16.

34. Research is needed to explain why women began to write their names as Mrs. Male Name in the 1840s. Suzanne Lebsock notes this shift but does not explain its cause (*Free Women of Petersburg*, 198). For women reducing their other public roles, such as speaking on stage, see Carolyn Eastman, "The Female Cicero: Young Women's Oratory and Gendered Public Participation in the Early American Republic," *Gender and History* 19 (2007): 260–83.

35. *Memorial Home for Girls*, 11, 12.

36. Cox, *Memorial Foundation for Children*, 7, 8.

37. For the obituaries and gravestone inscriptions of Carrington and her two husbands, see *Richmond Virginia Gazette; or, The American Advertiser*, June 25, 1785; Sue Bratt St. Amant, *St. John's Church, Henrico Parish, Richmond, Virginia: A Pictorial History* (Richmond, Va.: St. John's Church Foundation, 1996), 43–44; J. Staunton Moore, ed., *The Annals and History of Henrico Parish, Diocese of Virginia, and St. John's P.E. Church* (Baltimore, Md.: Genealogical Publishing, 1979), 429.

38. Elizabeth Arnold Poe, the mother of Edgar Allan Poe, is also buried in St. John's churchyard, in a grave that went unmarked until 1928, when the Raven Society at the University of Virginia sought to honor Edgar Allan Poe by locating and marking the grave of his mother. Carrington has received no such attention. Her death notice appeared in the *Daily Richmond Whig*, February 16 and 17, 1842; her obituary is in the *Richmond Enquirer*, February 17, 1842.

Dolley Madison

A Case Study in Southern Style

CATHERINE ALLGOR

Though historians tend to avoid ahistorical hypotheses, it is probably safe to say that Dolley Madison would have been very pleased to be included in a volume about Virginia women, though perhaps she would have preferred the term "ladies" or "wives." Dolley was proud of her southern, especially her Virginian, roots. From our perspective, she seems an obvious, even iconic, subject for an entry in this collection. Dolley was the prototypical First Lady and one of the most famous Americans of her time. By her marriage into the Madison clan and her life on a Virginia plantation, she also seems to have been a typical nineteenth-century "southern lady."

According to her own correspondence and the observations of others, Dolley brought a southern style of entertaining to Washington, D.C., forever shaping capital society. Part of that southern style came from Dolley herself: a personality who set the tone for social events, a hostess and a belle, full of that charm, hospitality, and warmth that many people associate with southernness. A closer look at her post-Washington career, however, when Dolley was deep in the heart of the Orange County countryside, presents a different picture, one that complicates our understandings both of Dolley herself and of what it meant to be southern.

With no diary and few self-reflective letters, Dolley did not leave behind much evidence of what she thought about her heritage. Therefore it is interesting to examine what she chose to tell about her origins on the few occasions when someone asked her directly. In 1834, seventeen years after she retired to Montpelier, Dolley's old friend the writer Margaret Bayard Smith contacted her to say that she had been commissioned to write an entry about Dolley for the

DOLLEY MADISON
At the end of her life, Dolley Madison was regarded as an emblem of the republic and as the iconic southern lady. Library of Congress, Prints and Photographs Division.

four-volume *National Portrait Gallery of Distinguished Americans*. Both women were aware of the double honor: Margaret was one of the few women writers invited to contribute, and Dolley was the only female subject in the collection's third volume.

Dolley was both flattered and fearful, openly worrying about accusations of "egotism," but privately fretting that her life would "have so few incidents to make her Biography interesting." She was also of two minds about Margaret as the writer. Though she assured Margaret that her "pen, would be more agreeable to me" over "any other," Dolley not only did not help Margaret gather the necessary materials but actively stonewalled her. At the start of the process, however, before Dolley became evasive, she did answer a set of questions about her early life. To one of Margaret's questions, Dolley replied: "My family are all Virginians except myself, who was born in N. Carolina whilst my Parents were there on a visit of one year, to an Uncle. Their families on both sides were among the most respectable."[1]

This statement stands out and not only because this was one of the few particulars that Dolley shared with Margaret. It is also a subtle untruth: by stating that she was born in North Carolina, Dolley modestly eschewed any claim of being a born and bred Virginian, while unthinkingly inscribing it as a category. But by presenting her North Carolina birth as accidental, and by adding that her parents were widely known as prominent Virginians, Dolley undermined any claim North Carolina had on her. The reality of Dolley's birth was a deeper and darker story. She was born in 1768 after her father, John Payne, converted to the Quaker faith of Dolley's mother, Mary Coles Payne, and moved to the North Carolina frontier to join the New Garden Friends Meeting. Because John Payne sold all his property in Virginia, bought property in North Carolina, and moved his whole family to the frontier, one can assume that the Paynes intended never to return. That after only a short time the Paynes moved back to Virginia at a great financial loss signals that something went terribly wrong in North Carolina. Fragmentary evidence, along with the fact that the Philadelphia Quakers later expelled him from Meeting for sharp business practices, suggests that John Payne might have engaged in shady dealings.[2] Though it is unclear why Dolley presented her birth in the way she did, the sum of her efforts hid any improprieties and created the Virginia childhood that would undergird her claim to a genteel southern heritage.

After James Madison's retirement from politics in 1817, during the 1820s and 1830s he and Dolley were working hard at Montpelier readying his papers, especially those on the Constitutional Convention, for publication. In the days before professional archivists, Dolley gathered and filed letters and papers, editing and transcribing and becoming, literally, a woman who made history. In this atmosphere of historical preservation and dissemination, it is not surprising that Dolley began to think of her own historical legacy. Consequently, in the years after her death in 1849, her niece Mary Estelle Elizabeth Cutts produced a memoir of her famous aunt.

The Cutts Memoir is a troublesome albeit fascinating source. To begin with, it exists as two documents: one bound in two sections that clearly follow one another, the second a loose collection of pages. Their precise order is an editor's guess. But the thorniest issue raised by these fascinating fragments is their status as memoir. Cutts Memoir I begins with Dolley's family tree and her birth and ends in 1814, the year its author, Mary Cutts, was born; Cutts Memoir II also begins before Mary's birth, in 1800, though it continues through the 1830s and beyond, covering the time during which an adult Mary would have known her aunt Dolley and uncle James. Given that Mary was not alive for most of the time covered by her "memoir," it is not a stretch to understand these recollections as the closest form of Dolley's autobiographical voice left to history. That Dolley's memories should exist so filtered makes sense, given her gender and historical context.

Mary, who took pride in her effort as the family historian and worked as a professional writer, was no mere recorder. She approached at least two publishers about her manuscript and would have no doubt seen her "little undertaking," as she called it, in print if not for her untimely death at age forty-one, in 1856, only seven years after Dolley's. (Ultimately, Mary Cutts's own niece Lucia B. Cutts would cobble and bowdlerize the two accounts into one, resulting in the first, and for many years the only, primary source collection about Dolley Madison.)[3] Nowhere does Mary's editorial hand seem more evident than in the treatment of Dolley's early years. From the first pen stroke, it is clear that Mary's (and Dolley's) imperative is to establish Dolley's indisputable Virginia pedigree.

As convention dictated, Mary begins her discussion of Dolley with a family tree, managing to imbue both sides with "First Family of Virginia" status along with the imprimatur of English nobility. For Mary, ancestors that included "an English gentleman of wealth and education," a Scottish earl, and a "Sir Thomas Fleming" showed the superior breeding and blood that produced the subject of the memoir. Family trees can be overwhelming as the branches proliferate, but in this case, Mary makes the most of that multiplicity, embedding Dolley in a welter of southern families—the Coleses, the Winstons, the Dabneys, and the Symes. Just when the weary reader thinks such wanderings have no point, Mary zeros in on Patrick Henry, a famous Virginian and Dolley's "near relative." At first glance, it seems odd that at the beginning of a memoir of Dolley Madison, Mary would spend pages and pages on Patrick Henry. (Lucia B. Cutts apparently agreed, deleting this long discussion from her version.) But Mary connects Dolley and Patrick, asserting that both were "reared under similar auspices in Hanover County, afterwards meeting in Philadelphia." Mary uses Patrick Henry as a mirror, reflecting the great Virginian's historic importance onto his kinswoman. In doing so, she uses a technique to discuss women—especially those from political families—common in both her day and ours: significance by association. Mary also highlights characteristics of Henry's that could apply to Dolley: for instance, being "dazzled by neither, power nor dignity," knowing what it meant to "serve ... in perilous times, when to be highest was only to be exposed foremost to the bolt of the dreaded enemy, or at some conjuncture of civil danger." Given what Mary says later about Dolley's personal influence, she might be speaking of her aunt when she notes Henry's "power of swaying the minds of men." The same could be said when she declares that Henry was not only a noted American but a product of his homeland: "Virginia is proud of that son, who seemed to spring into exist[e]nce as a meteor when most needed by his country."[4]

It is a cliché to say it is not the lie but the cover-up that causes the most trouble. After the digression about Patrick Henry, Mary moves on to Dolley's actual birth and childhood, repeating what Dolley must have told her, stating that her aunt was born "while on a visit to his [John Payne's] relations in North Carolina." While this roughly correlates with what Dolley told Margaret Bayard Smith, note that the lone uncle has expanded to a set of "relations." Unless Dolley had recently discovered a set of kinfolk in North Carolina, she changed her story. Especially coming after the section on Patrick Henry, and in the context of the larger piece, which stresses Dolley's Virginia origins, this statement seems, again, as if Dolley is modestly marking herself as a technical North Carolinian but a bone-deep Virginian. Apparently, this was all too much for the later editor, Lucia, who with a cross-out changed the line to simply "a visit to North Carolina."[5]

Though there is evidence that Dolley's early family life had its difficult moments, the childhood Mary Cutts presents is a southern gentry dream. After the disastrous trip to North Carolina, the family returned to Virginia, and Dolley grew into young womanhood surrounded by her mother's kin, the prominent Coles family. Dolley's maternal side was Virginia royalty. According to Mary, before her marriage Dolley's mother had many admirers, including that Virginian among Virginians, Thomas Jefferson, though there is no evidence that this is true. Putting Dolley's father in the best southern light was a bit more difficult.

Mentions of earls aside, the best Mary can do is to assert that he was a North Carolina planter (a way to account for that mysterious uncle?) and a captain in the Revolutionary War. Neither statement is true.

In Mary's tale, Dolley Payne lives a "tranquil" life in the green, beautiful Hanover County countryside. According to Dolley's memories, the Paynes lived for a while in an enormous plantation house, Scotchtown, with "twenty rooms on a floor, [and] every one had marble hearths and mantels." As Dolley only lived at Scotchtown until the age of three, her specific remembrance of architectural details probably stems from later visits. Not for the only time in the memoir, Mary uses real estate to establish pedigree: Dolley's childhood home not only had been owned by an English nobleman, who dwelt like a feudal lord with his dependents in small attached brick dwellings, but later it would become the property of her kinsman Patrick Henry.[6]

Mary conveys a story of the young Dolley that was undoubtedly chosen to allow readers to marvel at customs both southern and quaint. The ladies of the time, according to Mary, were "so particular ... about the complexion" that little Dolley traveled to school not only with a white sunbonnet on her head but in long white gloves and "sometimes even a white linen mask."[7] Obviously, this practice was peculiar enough to Mary's audience to merit mentioning, and it served Mary's (and Dolley's) purposes well, presenting the image of a child whose white clothes signify an upbringing so refined and pure that she is sheltered even from the sun's rays.

Though neither Mary nor Dolley probably intended it as such, whiteness in complexions and otherwise was a signifier of southernness, as was its opposite, the blackness that symbolized slavery. While the institution of slavery shaped the lives of all white Americans, the issue had special resonance for the Quaker Paynes. Like his Anglican neighbors, John Payne worked his Virginia acres with slaves. Belying the plantation stereotype, the Paynes' was a modest household, with approximately five enslaved black people and nine white members by 1783.[8] Contrast this to the experience of Dolley's future husband, who grew up with a community of over a hundred slaves.

What Dolley's experience with slavery lacked in intensity, however, it made up in intimacy. It was probably natural that a loving child such as Dolley would become attached to the small contingent of enslaved people in her household. And indeed, Mary tells the story of "Mother Amey," Dolley's nurse, who dressed as a Quaker, refused her freedom, and came with the Paynes to Philadelphia. Amy's devotion continued through the unstable Philadelphia years, and she took care of Dolley and her mother during the yellow fever epidemic of 1793. Mary notes that on her death, Amy willed her former charge $500.[9]

Mary's treatment of Dolley Madison and slavery reflects her own position as a woman in the 1850s who had strong ties to both the proslavery South and the increasingly abolitionist North. On one hand, Mary Cutts understood her aunt's pride in her Virginia roots, which she shared. Though Mary's father, Richard Cutts, was a prominent congressman from Massachusetts (later Maine), the young Mary identified more with the southern side of the family, no doubt because of her mother's closeness with Dolley and James Madison and the years she spent with them at Montpelier and in Washington. People who knew Mary as a young woman, such as First Lady Louisa Catherine Johnson Adams, had no trouble referring to her as one of those "southern girls."[10]

On the other hand, Mary came to appreciate her northern family, especially by the 1840s and 1850s, when abolitionism was increasingly seen less as a radical aberration and more as the accepted wisdom of the day. In her depiction of the Payne family's relationship to slavery, then, Mary may have felt that she had two audiences to please. For northern readers, Mary proudly presents John Payne's decision in 1783 to free his slaves and move his family to the seat of American Quakerism, Philadelphia, as an act of Quaker conscience. Without specifying the relatively small number of slaves in question (which does not lessen the moral rectitude of Payne's decision) and by using the word "plantation," Mary imparts the impression of a much greater sacrifice on his part.

Mary's southern audience, however, would have been enchanted by her descriptions of the Paynes' gentry way of life and of the way they treated their slaves (a technique she expands in her later discussions of bucolic Montpelier, with its droves of contented, aged former "servants"). During the first half of the nineteenth century, increasingly under attack by abolitionists who considered slavery immoral, southern apologists defended their "peculiar institution" on a variety of grounds, including that of benevolence. In their paternalistic vision, slave owners ruled their childlike labor force as parents ruled children. Slaves supplied work as part of a system not of violence, but of mutual respect and responsibilities. Slaveholders took material care of slaves, and slaves reciprocated with labor, love, and loyalty.

This vision did not reflect reality, but that did not diminish its rhetorical power, and Mary does not hesitate to invoke "Mother Amey" as evidence of the fantasy of white benevolence and the childlike nature of African Americans. On one hand, Amy's decision to stay with the Paynes illustrates exemplary loyalty. On the other, her shortsightedness in refusing her freedom reinforces the stereotype of the black slave as an immature dependent. Mary does not discuss the issue of slavery or Dolley's attitude toward the institution. Instead, she describes the various warm, reciprocal relationships Dolley had with specific slaves. Such a depiction, which was not the whole truth by any means, could affirm southerners' vision of slavery as benign. At the same time, even the most abolitionist northern readers would be left with the impression of Dolley as a "good mistress" in an evil system.

Moving from the Virginia countryside to the bustling streets of Philadelphia—next to London, the most cosmopolitan city in the English-speaking world—must have been a shock to the teenaged Dolley Payne, who perhaps became newly aware of her southern identity there. Her Philadelphia years were Dolley's first experience of performing southernness for a northern audience. Evidence exists that the tall, shapely brunette with striking blue eyes and pale skin made her mark in the plain Quaker circles of Philadelphia. One of her admirers there, Anthony Morris, who became a lifelong friend and beneficiary of the Madisons' political largesse, characterized Dolley's entrance onto the Philadelphia scene as the "bright dawn of her splendid day." He recalled: "She came upon our comparatively cold hearts in Philad[elphi]a, suddenly & unexpectedly with all the delightful influences of a Summer Sun, from the Sweet South ... with all the warm feelings, & flowing fancies of her Native State." For Morris, Dolley Payne, with "her complexion ... from Scotland, and her soft blue Eyes from Saxony," acted like a southern sun, "rais[ing] the mercury there in the thermometers of the Heart to fever heat."[11]

At the same time, Dolley seemed to be a puzzle to Philadelphia's Quaker community, as were other members of the Payne family. Her delight in frivolities, such as fashion, led to rebukes by female Quaker leaders. For his part, perhaps fired with the zeal of the convert, John Payne had become a man his Virginia neighbors called a "fanatic" because of his Quaker beliefs. When he moved his family to the Quaker capital, he, like his daughter, stood out, but in his case, for his willingness to speak in Meeting.[12] Whether in reaction to their father's religious fervor, or simply because they followed more closely the path of Virginia gentlemen, Dolley's brothers, Walter, William Temple, and Isaac, one by one, were read out of Meeting. Though Walter was expelled for absconding with his creditors' money, the two other brothers were rejected for "worldly" offenses, such as drinking, gambling, and performing military service, all of which were practices that would have seemed de rigueur in their former milieu to the south.

Finally, even Dolley's father was read out of Meeting, not because of debt, as many historians have asserted, but rather because his Quaker brethren suspected him of exploiting the reputation of the Society of Friends for honesty in order to swindle his business associates. According to Mary Cutts, John Payne never got over this shame: he retreated into his room, and he never left or "raised his head" until his death a short time later. Significantly, Mary invokes southernness to explain and excuse Payne's disgrace. Though a leading authority on Dolley Madison, who has edited her papers, has clearly demonstrated that Payne's business practices were the issue, Mary attributes his financial difficulties to his unstintingly generous southern hospitality and his overall inability to adapt to life in a northern city.[13]

Life in Philadelphia clearly did not go well for the Paynes and particularly for Dolley. She lived there for ten years and in that time her father, brothers, and one little sister died. According to Mary's account, though she did not "incline to relinquish her girl hood," Dolley obeyed her father's wishes that she marry a young Quaker, John Todd, which she did in 1790.[14] In 1793 Dolley experienced the trauma of the citywide crisis of yellow fever, during which her husband died, along with their newborn son, William Temple, who had been named for one of Dolley's brothers. In 1794 the young widow Todd, along with her surviving son, John Payne Todd, called "Payne," moved into her mother's boardinghouse.

Philadelphia had been the national capital for four years, and the influx of government officials brought a host of eligible, prominent men from across the nation to Dolley's doorstep. The twenty-five-year-old beauty captured the heart of a forty-three-year-old congressman from Virginia, James Madison. After James's uncharacteristically aggressive courtship, Dolley agreed to be his wife, and they married on September 15, 1794, at Harewood, the Virginia home of Dolley's sister Lucy, who had married into George Washington's family. Looking back, it was clearly a good match. During their decades-long union, James would grow in his appreciation for Dolley, and over time his love would surpass mere sexual attraction. For her part, Dolley would fall deeply and devotedly in love with James, prizing his sterling character and intellect. To the historian's chagrin, they exchanged letters infrequently since they were so devoted to each other that they rarely separated. But all that was later. A close look at how their courtship proceeded provides a significant opportunity to examine the construction of southernness in one person's life.

Though James Madison had a modest romantic track record, it is clear why he fell in love with Dolley. According to Mary Cutts and Madison family lore, he saw the young beauty on the street and was immediately smitten. Why Dolley chose him is less clear. At twenty-five, a gorgeous widow with a nice inheritance, Dolley was hardly withering on the vine. Indeed, her marriage to James Madison would get her read out of the Quaker Meeting not only because James was not of the Society of Friends, but also because of her haste in remarrying only a scant year after her Quaker husband's death. Dolley certainly could have held out for a younger, more sexually charismatic, even richer, suitor. All of the advantages were on her side; even the presence of a young son was not an impediment to remarriage. In an era in which death acted as divorce does now, blended families with stepparents and children were common. Indeed, the existence of Payne could be seen in a positive way, proving that Dolley had a record of fertility.

Surely, Dolley was attracted to James for reasons other than sexual desirability. Not only was James quite a bit older, he was also small, frail, and universally understood to be almost an invalid. Nor did he possess the ineffable erotic charm that seems to transcend physical beauty. It is not at all certain that his massive intellect would have enticed Dolley in the way it might have a more cerebral woman, such as Abigail Adams. Nor could political ambition have played a part in Dolley's calculations. As it happened, James would have a long and successful career in politics, including a two-term presidency, and Dolley Madison would discover and cultivate her own astonishing political potential. But at the moment of decision it had been much more likely that James, who was a leader of the minority Republican Party, would retire from politics, as he then did a few years later, along with his colleague Thomas Jefferson.

The idea of marrying for practicality suggests an answer to the puzzle of why Dolley might have chosen James, who was, as far as the record shows, the first man to ask for her hand after John Todd's death. In the hours before their late afternoon wedding ceremony, Dolley wrote to her friend Eliza Collins Lee of her impending marriage. She did not speak of love, but rather of her son having gained "a generous & tender protector." She also reassured Eliza that she had made proper financial arrangements for her son, forestalling any gossip that her hasty marriage would deprive young John Payne Todd of his late father's estate.[15]

But another advantage that James offered Dolley, besides the romance and security many a beau could offer, was a return to the world of the Virginia gentry. To a young woman who knew only trauma in Philadelphia, whose golden memories of her childhood contrasted sharply with her experience in that northern city, surely the idea of a Virginia homecoming was appealing. She would return to Virginia, moreover, at a higher level than that to which she had been born. The Coleses and Paynes might be "well born," as Mary Cutts asserts in her memoir, but Dolley's natal family had only a farm. By marrying James, Dolley would be the mistress of a plantation grander than any she might have known, aside from the Scotchtown rental.

How much James Madison's Virginia southernness counted for Dolley is only speculation, as is the second issue the Madison marriage raises. If marriage to James meant a return to plantation life, it also meant a return to the world of chattel slavery. It seems beyond imagination that this did not cross Dolley's mind. For an Anglican woman, slavery might not be a consideration when marrying a fellow Virginian, but not so for Quaker Dolley. She certainly heard debates about the issue, whether in her own home or at Meeting. Perhaps, though, Dolley associated antislavery ideas with her family's misfortunes, which began with John Payne's manumissions, and she was only too happy to relax back into a familiar world that included slavery.

After their honeymoon, Dolley and James Madison returned to Philadelphia so that James could finish his term in Congress. Now the wife of a prominent politician and having been read out of Meeting, Dolley indulged her taste for pretty clothes and society. She was finally able to participate in the social life of the capital, over which Martha Washington presided. Like many elite women, the president's wife understood that being American involved more than adopting republican laws or even a new federal Constitution. In her "republican court," Martha instituted ceremonial social events for a new republic. Dressed in simple white, like a "Roman Matron," she welcomed a small number of invited guests to staid receptions at which refreshments were few and modest. Martha truly was an innovator; these formal presentations bore little resemblance to the Virginia society to which she was accustomed.[16] Dolley observed it all.

In 1797 James and Dolley retired from politics, and James brought his bride home to Montpelier. When Dolley alighted from the carriage, with young Payne and her little sister Anna in tow, she saw a beautiful, graceful house. Sitting high on the landscape, Montpelier's every window had dazzling views of fields and orchards, culminating in a stunning vista from the front porch of the Blue Ridge Mountains. Dolley would remain there for three years, and it was under Montpelier's roof that she began her adult education as a southern lady.

Far from retiring, James Madison used those years to build political bases with his neighbor Thomas Jefferson. Their collaboration would result in the success of the Republican Party in the groundbreaking election of 1800, which would bring Jefferson to the presidency and the Madisons to Washington as James became Jefferson's secretary of state. Little correspondence to and from Dolley exists from that period. No doubt she spent her time accustoming Anna and Payne to their new life and establishing her own place at Montpelier. Unlike other brides who came to a husband's home and were immediately expected to take on the duties of a mistress, Dolley joined an already established household that included James's father and mother, along with a slave community of about a hundred people. The senior Madisons were by no means retired, and indeed, though James Sr. would die in 1801, Nelly Conway Madison would continue to manage Montpelier for decades. For a woman of a different temperament, having a mother-in-law firmly in charge could have caused tension, but Dolley seems to have merged into the Madison family easily, ceding what she might have seen as her rightful place with little effort.

Whatever Dolley lost in household power, she gained in freedom. Many a southern belle, raised to be pampered and ornamental, underwent a shock on becoming a wife, when she had to take up the arduous workload and responsibilities of running a plantation household. With Nelly supervising slaves and overseeing myriad household tasks, Dolley had the opportunity to learn on the job without pressure. Some evidence suggests that it was during those years that Dolley truly fell in love with her husband. Given James's premarital ardor, it is not surprising that he addressed her as "my dearest" in one of the few letters from him at this time. More unexpected and delightful is the intimation of playfulness and affection in Dolley's short note to her friend Eliza Collins Lee, thanking her for sending along some hose, though, Dolley added, the stockings were too small for her or even for "my darling little Husband."[17]

During the years at Montpelier, Dolley got to experience genteel southern life. She saw the great houses of the gentry and participated in balls, barbecues, and visits both long and short in those houses. As a new Madison, she socialized with Taylors, Barbours, and Pendletons. She also got to see firsthand how houses and social events functioned in the social, political, and economic life of the region. Echoing gentry customs from the Old World, Virginia elites treated their houses as places of public business, rather than as private havens in a heartless world. In a house such as Montpelier, besides the intimate business of family life, events that moderns would consider public occurred on a daily basis. On any given day, the house might entertain a visiting preacher, a slave trader offering or scouting human chattel, a neighbor with an offer to buy land, or a tourist with letters of introduction. In good traveling weather, a family dinner at a gentry house would host some number of strangers or nonhousehold members. Because business of various kinds was the business of the household, the official and unofficial spheres tended to blur.

These were the ideals and models Dolley took with her when in 1801 she and James traveled to the brand-new capital city of Washington. Though it would be eight years before she could truly fulfill her vision and preside over the nation's society as "Queen Dolley," she began laying her groundwork from the time they took over the house on F Street that would serve as the secretary of state's headquarters. Historians have long asserted that Dolley's role in the widower Jefferson's administration was that of substitute First Lady. This was not so. Jefferson did ask Dolley and her sisters to preside at table when he had female dinner guests if his daughter and official hostess, Martha Jefferson Randolph, was not in town. Claiming this position for Dolley, however, obscures two points. First, Jefferson mostly entertained at small, single-party, all-male dinners, which did not require a female presence. Second, Dolley was involved in her own social and political projects even before her husband succeeded Jefferson as president.

With Jefferson restricting public access to the executive mansion to the Fourth of July and New Year's Day, and presiding over intimate dinner parties of congressmen solely of one party or the other, the Madisons' house on F Street became the social center of Washington. With a succession of parties (large and small), dinners, teas, and other gatherings, Dolley began the work for which she would become justly famous. She brought both Federalists and Republicans together, mixed them with local gentry who had invested in the new capital, and threw in whatever visiting dignitaries or American travelers happened to be in town. Though Dolley could not see into the future, guided by her own instincts she was modeling bipartisanship and facilitating the formation of a ruling class for a two-party democracy. As at the parties she had seen in Virginia, these events in the unofficial sphere of society blurred business (in this case, politics) with pleasure, and furthered them both. John Quincy Adams might be bored to tears at Jefferson's dinner table, surrounded only by his fellow Federalists and with Jefferson dominating the conversation. At the Madisons, John Quincy attended an event with "a company of about seventy persons of both sexes," where he had a chance for a quiet chat, one on one, with James, enjoying "considerable conversation . . . on the subjects now most important to the public."[18]

Ironically, the Madisons' social style was more southern than that of Jefferson, the more famous Virginian president. Dolley and James self-consciously adopted country customs. The wife of the British ambassador, Elizabeth Leathes Merry, might have meant her remark that a Madison dinner resembled a country "harvest home" as an insult, but she may not have been wrong. In fact, Dolley did not disagree, averring that "abundance was preferable to elegance." Like Martha Washington, Dolley understood that everyday decisions, even something as basic as a menu, had larger implications, "that circumstances formed customs, and customs formed taste; and as the profusion, so repugnant to foreign customs, arose from the happy circumstance of the super-abundance and prosperity of our country," Dolley "did not hesitate to sacrifice the delicacy of European taste, for the less elegant, but more liberal fashion of Virginia."[19]

When James Madison was elected to the presidency and Dolley became the head of national society, she brought all the connections and networks that she had made, as well as her style of political socializing, to a larger stage. In the summer of 1809, shortly after the Madison inauguration, Margaret Bayard Smith and her husband, Samuel Harrison Smith, the editor of the *Daily Intelligencer*, left Washington to visit Thomas Jefferson at Monticello and then the Madisons at Montpelier. Margaret used this occasion, which was ostensibly a chance to visit friends in their homes, to subject both homes and families to her kind of political analysis. From her famous account of these trips, it is clear that she saw her mission as bidding ex-president Jefferson farewell and assessing the new national family, the Madisons. Both Thomas Jefferson and Dolley Madison were aware of the evaluative intention of this trip, and accordingly performed the roles of southern host and hostess.[20]

Clearly, one of the lenses through which Margaret viewed her hosts was southernness, specifically as applied to Virginia. As a northern-born woman, her approach was almost anthropological. In her account, one of the primary messages Margaret sent was that Jefferson was safely retired on his mountaintop and would not be meddling in national affairs. To make her case, she presented him in several ways, but certainly as a Virginia planter among the members of his household. Like many writers before her, for all of her adoration of him, Margaret found it hard to really capture Jefferson. She admitted that she could "not converse with him, with ease." Rather than listening to what he said, "my mind is busied in thinking of what he is." When her report turned to the Madisons, however, Margaret was utterly in the moment and her writing reflected that. At the end of the visit, Margaret was confident that the Madisons were indeed the best family to lead the nation.

Margaret had known James almost as long as she had known Jefferson. She apparently had no qualms about him, and accordingly, her description of James at Montpelier—"plain, friendly, communicative, & unceremonious"—was consistently positive. Though Margaret had liked Dolley on their first meeting, she had some concerns about her propriety as she observed the wife of the secretary of state's rise in power. Margaret's final verdict on Dolley, rendered at the end of the visit after speaking to Dolley's enslaved maid Nany—"Truly, in her there is to be found no gaul, but the pure milk of human kindness"—came after pages in which she described Dolley as the consummate Virginia hostess, "uniting to all the elegance & polish of fashion, the unadulterated simplicity, frankness, warmth, & friendliness of her native character & native state." When the Smiths arrived, they had been escorted into the dining room, where the men were drinking wine and smoking "segars." Instantly, Dolley entered the room, embraced Margaret, and took her by the hands, saying, "I will take you out of this smoke to a pleasanter room." Dolley immediately established a more intimate tone, escorting Margaret into her own bedroom where she took her traveling habit and bonnet, and then, to Margaret's delight, "we threw ourselves on her bed." Slaves brought the merry pair "wine, ice, punch & delightful pine-apples." "No restraint, no ceremony," Margaret concluded. Dolley's hospitality was "the presiding genius of this house."

Dolley impressed Margaret with her easy graciousness. When Dolley discovered that Margaret had not wished to impose on her hosts by bringing her daughters along, Dolley laughed and told her that she should have brought them since "we have house room in plenty." Dolley averred that she "should not have known they were here, among all the rest, for at this moment we have only three & twenty in the house." After supper, Margaret ended her evening talking of Washington with Dolley until the "servant" came with candles. Dolley "insisted" on escorting her, helped her undress, and sat talking until Margaret was ready for bed. Margaret marveled: "How unassuming, how kind is this woman. How can any human being be her enemy."

By the time of her last meal with the Madisons, "a most excellent virginian breakfast—tea, coffee, hot wheat bread, light cakes, a pone, or corn loaf—cold ham, nice hashes, chickens, etc.," Margaret was won over. She was sure that the Madisons' "mode of living . . . if it had more elegance than is found among the planters, was characterized by that abundance, that hospitality, & that freedom, we are taught to look for on a virginian plantation," would travel well to the national capital, as would the "presiding genius of th[e] house."[21]

Dolley's career as the president's wife is the most well-known aspect of her life. The accomplishments that ensured her fame and that attract the most attention can be seen as an extension of her southern education. Her redecoration (really, a restructuring) of the executive mansion; her social events that so cemented the mansion into the life of the city and nation that it soon acquired a nickname, the "White House"; the short- and long-term political uses of her famous weekly drawing rooms; her preeminence as a hostess and charismatic figure for the Madison administration—the success of all of these make them seem natural or obvious choices for Dolley to have made. That Dolley Madison's personifying capacity would transcend partisanship and that the burning of the capital city and especially the White House would galvanize the contentious citizenry around the unpopular War of 1812 again may seem unexceptional. The same could be said of the indisputably southern political society that the Madisons left when they departed Washington in 1817, awash in a golden glow of national approbation.

All of these aspects of Dolley's career, however, were consciously chosen, shaped by her Virginia experiences and ideals. She could have made other choices. Dolley could have retained Jefferson's vision for the executive mansion, as a place aloof and isolated from the people. She could have instituted a more conventional social program—as her successor, Elizabeth Kortright Monroe, would do—along European lines, with more formality and restricted access. Or Dolley could have continued Martha Washington's subdued and ceremonial republican court. But she did none of these things.

Her White House was reconstructed in the eighteenth-century Virginia gentry house tradition, with all the money and energy focused on creating large public rooms in which to entertain large and diverse companies of guests. When the renovation was done, Dolley threw open the doors to all, like the southern families she had seen who would invite everyone in the neighborhood to a barbeque. And though Dolley reigned over all in fantastic ensembles of satin and lace, she did so with a charm and down-home friendliness that could only be regarded as southern.

Though Mary Cutts discusses Dolley's years as First Lady, the best way to view them is through the many descriptions of Queen Dolley and her events that pepper correspondence from the early national period. These descriptions are not merely color commentary or celebrity lists; rather, they function as a kind of political analysis. A culture-wide anxiety over the fate of the republic marked the decades after the American Revolution. In a political system lacking a bureaucracy and established institutions, Americans looked to personalities for reassurance, legitimacy, and unity. In the 1780s and 1790s they focused on George Washington, evaluating his mien and movements to assure themselves of his legitimacy as their leader. In the early 1800s public attention shifted to Dolley Madison. People observed and relayed what Dolley wore, how she held herself, and the experience of her drawing room—often in minute detail—because the stakes were so high. From these observations, they drew conclusions about the Madisons' right to govern, the fate of the capital city, and even of the republic itself.[22]

The letters and diaries that discuss Dolley do not use southernness as a category of analysis, but this may be a case of evidential absence speaking loudly. Early nineteenth-century Americans were very aware of regional differences; later in the century, with fears of disunion, they would call these differences "sectionalism." Regionalism, then, was such a pervasive mindset that Dolley's observers did not name it even as they reacted to it. Dolley's southern effect was most noticeable on people from the Northeast like Sophia May, who hailed from Massachusetts and was taken aback when Dolley called her "honey"—which "sound[ed] queer to a Yankee"—but Sophia admitted to Dolley's "sweetness." The many paeans to Dolley's heart—for instance, hailing her as the "Queen of Hearts"—directly address acts of what many people understand to be southern hospitality.[23]

Dolley also enacted southernness when it came to family matters. Family is important in many cultures, but for southerners family connections and descent are an obsession, perhaps stemming from the worry in slaveholding societies about race and race mixing. Dolley took this cultural fixation to a new level. When a young South Carolinian, William Campbell Preston, stood paralyzed with shyness in one of her drawing rooms, Dolley put him at ease by asking, "Are you William Campbell Preston, son of my old friend and most beloved kinswoman, Sally Campbell?" Dolley did not stop there, declaring: "I stand towards [you] in the relation of a parent," and, as William remembered, with all the "easy grace and benignity which no woman in the world could have exceeded," she proceeded to introduce William to important men and reigning belles, urging all to consider him her "protégé."[24] William was *not* clearly related to Dolley by either blood or marriage (his mother was a friend of Dolley's sister Anna), but what was important was that Dolley declared him so. This was part of a larger pattern. Dolley had circles of adopted daughters and sons, all from influential families. Dolley used these fictive family connections, along with her ability to never forget a name, a face, or a family pedigree, as a professional politician would: publicly and to political purpose.

If Dolley Madison as an icon of southern style had ended with her triumphant years in Washington, one could argue that she was the quintessential southern lady—personally warm and charming, a wonderful hostess, and a widely acknowledged representative of her putative native state. However, looking at Dolley in Virginia, to which the Madisons retired in 1817, presents a more ambiguous picture. James was happy to leave the city for his country home. He loved Montpelier and rarely left during his retirement, except to visit Thomas Jefferson while serving as a member of the Board of Visitors for the University of Virginia and to attend a state constitutional convention in Richmond. Dolley loved James and because he did not leave Montpelier, neither did she. At first, work on the papers project provided an excuse for staying close by his side; then, through the 1820s and 1830s, James's failing health was its own reason. Near the end of James's life, Dolley acknowledged that she "never left him half an hour, for the last two years." At one point, she had not left the grounds for eight months, and she did not ride a horse during the last four years of his life. A proposed trip to the courthouse was the occasion for a joke: "It would be quite an event, for me to go there—5 miles from home!"[25]

But Dolley's correspondence shows how much she missed Washington. She enjoyed a lively correspondence with her nieces Mary Cutts and Mary's sister, Dolley's namesake, Dolley Madison Cutts, who were living in the capital. She never ceased advising them on Washington ways, whether it was who to avoid offending or what their reaction should be to the newest dances. During the 1820s she followed the unfolding scandal surrounding Margaret O'Neale Timberlake Eaton—the supposedly adulterous wife of Andrew Jackson's secretary of war—with fascination and horror. And always, whether her correspondent was old or young, family or friend, Dolley pled for news. In 1825 she asked Mary to "get a large paper and place it where you can go and write, as you recollect things.... and if you tell me all the secrets of the nation, they shall be sacred."²⁶

Though she lived at Montpelier for decades in the summers and then full time for over twenty years, Dolley was an uneasy fit for the rural milieu. She may have charmed her Washington neighbors, but the locals did not succumb. She could not even get along with the extended Madison clan. A local historian, W. W. Scott, who knew many members of the Madison family, observed: "the Madison kith and kin did not like 'Dolly.' They heard too much of her 'low neck and short sleeves,' of her 'turban' and her gay life in Washington society."²⁷

They may have felt that way because they saw that Dolley favored her own family over theirs, especially Anna Cutts and her brood and, of course, her own son, Payne Todd. Through the years the local Madisons and their neighbors saw both Dolley and James bail Payne Todd out again and again. A spectacularly dissolute man, Todd accrued debts totaling over $100,000. Dolley and James paid the debts, using what Madison relatives might consider their family's resources. As W. W. Scott concluded, "It was manifest that her indulgence of her spendthrift son, Payne Todd, and her permitting him to waste the estate of her husband, had left a sting in their memories—if they had ever admired her; which is doubtful." After James's death, when Dolley could not cover Payne's debts, she was brought into court. The court's officers, assistant clerk Philip S. Frye and clerk Reynolds Chapman might have been Madison kin, but that did not stop them from pursuing her with zeal.²⁸

Family ties and loyalty are important components in southern culture. Dolley, the darling of diplomats with her famed gifts for reconciliation, boasted a large circle of adopted kin, but she could not win over the Madison family. She could not stop them, for instance, from suing each other or even from suing her, as James's brother William did. One Madison authority presents these family troubles as "a kind of test case of Dolley's ability to—or perhaps desire to—convert enemy to friend through kindness, generosity of spirit, and warmth, or play the role of hostess who brought together opposing factions as she had done in Washington, D.C." She concludes, "All evidence indicates that Dolley failed that test."²⁹

There was one way that Dolley did remain consistent with her southern persona, and sadly that had to do with slavery. It is shocking to hear a woman so famed for her empathy and insight discuss people as commodities, as when she explained to her sister that she "would buy a maid but good ones are rare & as high as 8 & 900$—I should like to know what you gave for yours." Dolley alternately expressed closeness to "her people" and complained about them, a familiar pattern among slaveholders. Like most white women in slaveholding households, when there were problems, Dolley saw the situation more as a personal power struggle than the result of a coercive and unjust institution. She could not understand, as when she complained about her maid Sukey's thefts, why a person whose labor is in effect stolen every day might herself steal from her mistress.[30] Dolley's attitudes regarding slaves not as full people but as childlike and in constant need of supervision lest they shirk their duties may have been typical of her time and place, but they seem doubly discordant in view of her charming and empathetic public persona.

Recently, historians have used the idea of celebrity to understand the public roles of prominent people, especially women, in the early American republic. Unlike fame, which could be garnered through merit or public service, celebrity implies only a public popularity. Dolley Madison was one of the few women of her era who achieved both. While the fame she gained by saving the portrait of George Washington during the British invasion of Washington in 1814 could be seen as national, her celebrity was consciously southern. For her, southernness was a performance, one that was particularly effective outside of traditional southern settings, for regionally mixed or nonsouthern audiences.[31] Performance, however, could take Dolley only so far. In Orange County, Virginia, she failed, unable to adapt her performance to the dense fabric of ordinary southern life, with its focus on agriculture and extensive family obligations.

The one-dimensional ideal of the southern belle hides many facets of southern women's lives. Significantly, Dolley Madison is often linked in the popular mind with the fictional Scarlett O'Hara as the epitome of this ideal.[32] Scarlett's bravery while Atlanta burned seems to echo Dolley's heroism during the burning of Washington. Both women used fashion and personal charm to influence others. That Dolley may have even made a dress out of the famous red velvet curtains that she rescued from the British invaders only reinforces the association. But the character of Scarlett spends most of *Gone with the Wind* fighting the very gender conventions that were supposed to define her; as delineated by author Margaret Mitchell, Scarlett was no lady. In contrast, Dolley was a lady, as her culture understood that term, adapting gender conventions to construct a public persona that brought her celebrity, fame, and political success in Washington.

If Dolley, then, seems more the belle than her fictional southern sister, in the end it may be Dolley who failed the ultimate test of southernness. One could not be part of the southern gentry without the house and land that was both its symbol and the site of production. Scarlett fought to save Tara, even reluctantly relocating to the big city of Atlanta to do so. Though initially the widowed Dolley planned to divide her time between Washington and Orange County, in 1844 she lost Montpelier as a result of debt, a large part of which was (as her

Madison kin feared) owed by her son Payne. So Dolley left Virginia to live full time in the nation's capital, the site of her famous southern performances. She spent her final years being heralded and lauded by Washington audiences as she played the part of the southern lady. By 1846 she was a fixture in the city. The *Boston Cultivator* declared her "one of [Virginia's] monuments." When she died in 1849, Dolley was escorted to her grave not by family or by Orange County neighbors, but by President Zachary Taylor, the Cabinet, members of the House and Senate, the Supreme Court justices, army and navy officers, and crowds of "citizens and strangers" in the largest funeral that Washington had ever seen.[33] For Dolley, home was not the plantation in the Virginia countryside, but the national stage, in the center of the political spotlight, where she made the most of her time by playing the role of a Virginia lady.

NOTES

1. Dolley Payne Todd Madison (hereafter DPTM) to Mary Estelle Elizabeth Cutts (hereafter MEEC), December 2, 1834, March 10, 1835; DPTM to Margaret Bayard Smith (hereafter MBS), August 31, 1834; DPTM to Anna Payne Cutts (hereafter APC), June 6, 1829, all in *Dolley Madison Digital Edition* (hereafter *DMDE*), http://rotunda.upress.virginia.edu/dmde.

2. Catherine Allgor, *A Perfect Union: Dolley Madison and the Creation of the American Nation* (New York: Henry Holt, 2006), 21; Holly C. Shulman, "History, Memory, and Dolley Madison: Notes from a Documentary Editor," in *The Queen of America: Mary Cutts's Life of Dolley Madison*, ed. Catherine Allgor (Charlottesville: University of Virginia Press, 2012), 49–51.

3. Allgor, *Queen of America*, 199. For complete transcripts of both memoirs, as well as framing essays, see ibid.

4. Cutts Memoir I (hereafter CM I), in Allgor, *Queen of America*, 87–88.

5. Ibid., 89.

6. CM I, 89.

7. Ibid., 90.

8. Shulman, "History, Memory, and Dolley Madison," 46.

9. CM I, 90.

10. Louisa Catherine Johnson Adams, [July 1, 1839], "Adventures of a Nobody," Adams Family Papers, Massachusetts Historical Society, Boston.

11. Anthony Morris to Anna Payne, June 26, 1837, cited in *Records of the Columbia Historical Society* 44–45 (1942–43): 217–20.

12. CM I, 90.

13. Shulman, "History, Memory, and Dolley Madison," 47–50; CM I, 91–92.

14. CM I, 92.

15. DPTM to Eliza Collins Lee (hereafter ECL), September 16, [1794], *DMDE*.

16. For more on Martha Washington and the republican court, see Catherine Allgor, *Parlor Politics: In Which the Ladies of Washington Help Build a City and a Government* (Charlottesville: University of Virginia Press, 2000), 18–20; Sandra Moats, *Celebrating the Republic: Presidential Ceremony and Popular Sovereignty, from Washington to Monroe* (DeKalb: Northern Illinois University Press,

2012), chap. 2; David S. Shields and Fredrika J. Teute, "The Republican Court and the Historiography of a Women's Domain in the Public Sphere," paper presented at the Society for Historians of the Early Republic, July 16, 1994, Boston.

17. DPTM to ECL, [October 1794–97], *DMDE*. On the burdens of young southern wives, see Anya Jabour, *Scarlett's Sisters: Young Women in the Old South* (Chapel Hill: University of North Carolina Press, 2007), 194–200; Catherine Clinton, *The Plantation Mistress: Woman's World in the Old South* (New York: Pantheon, 1982), 18–21; Elizabeth Fox-Genovese, *Within the Plantation Household: Black and White Women of the Old South* (Chapel Hill: University of North Carolina Press, 1988), 114–15.

18. John Quincy Adams, Diary, January 11, 1805, and February 13, 1806, Adams Family Papers, Massachusetts Historical Society, Boston.

19. Margaret Bayard Smith, "Mrs. Madison," in *The National Portrait Gallery of Distinguished Americans*, ed. James B. Longacre and James Herring (New York: Hermon Bancroft, 1836), 3:20.

20. Catherine Allgor, "Margaret Bayard Smith's 1809 Journey to Monticello and Montpelier: The Politics of Performance in the Early Republic," *Early American Studies* 10 (2012): 30–68. The original of this account is found in Margaret Bayard Smith, Commonplace Book, box 1, Margaret Bayard Smith Papers, Manuscript Division, Library of Congress. See also "Margaret Bayard Smith's Account of a Visit to Monticello," July 29–August 2, 1809, in Jefferson *The Papers of Thomas Jefferson, Retirement Series*, ed. J. Jefferson Looney (Princeton, N.J.: Princeton University Press, 2004), 1:386–401. This is the only scholarly transcription of MBS's account.

21. MBS, Commonplace Book.

22. Allgor, *Perfect Union*, 241–42.

23. Sophia May, Diary, February 13, 1807, Sophia May Papers, American Antiquarian Society, Worcester, Mass.; Samuel Latham Mitchill to Catharine Akerly Mitchill, January 3, 1802, cited in "Dr. Mitchill's Letters from Washington, 1801–1813," *Harper's New Monthly Magazine* 58 (April 1879): 743.

24. Elizabeth Ellet, *Court Circles of the Republic* (Hartford, Conn.: Hartford Publishing, 1869), 84–87.

25. DPTM to Mary Elizabeth Payne Jackson Allen, February 25, 1834; DPTM to Frances Dandridge Lear, March 1832; DPTM to ECL, July 26, 1836; DPTM to John Payne Todd, July 20, 1832, all in *DMDE*.

26. DPTM to MEEC, March 10, 1833, and March 10, 1835; DPTM to APC, January 25, 1830; DPTM to Dolley Madison Cutts, March 10, 1830; DPTM to MEEC, January 22, 1825, all in *DMDE*. On the so-called Eaton affair, see Allgor, *Parlor Politics*, chap. 5.

27. Qtd. in Shulman, "History, Memory, and Dolley Madison," 57, 56.

28. Ibid.

29. Ibid., 58.

30. DPTM to APC, [c. July 23, 1818], *DMDE*.

31. Charlene M. Boyer Lewis, *Elizabeth Patterson Bonaparte: An American Aristocrat in the Early Republic* (Philadelphia: University of Pennsylvania Press, 2012), 32–34. Andrew S. Jacobs, a scholar of late antiquity, uses celebrity "as a mode of analysis distinct from more familiar terms like *status, authority*, or the nebulous but compelling term *power*," in his examination of the fourth-century bishop and saint Epiphanius of Salamis. See Jacobs, "*Fatuus senex, Pater episcoporum*: Epiphanius of Cyprus and Episcopal Fame," paper presented at the Meeting of the North American Patristics Society, May 25, 2012, Chicago.

32. Jabour, *Scarlett's Sisters*, 1–2, 15.

33. *Boston Cultivator*, April 4, 1846, 8, 14, 104; Allen C. Clark, *Life and Letters of Dolly Madison* (Washington, D.C.: W. F. Roberts, 1914), 450–51.

Harriet Hemings

Daughter of the President's Slave

CATHERINE KERRISON

The weather during the spring of 1822 had been fine as Virginia farmers took to their fields. On his arrival at his Bedford County plantation of Poplar Forest in May, Thomas Jefferson happily reported that "the prepar[atio]ns for a tob[acc]o crop are beyond anything I ever had. 300,000 hills, four fifths of them in ground newly clear, and nearly all planted by the fav[o]r. of the season." With great anticipation, Jefferson looked forward to a splendid tobacco crop. That season was also one of great anticipation for Harriet Hemings, the daughter of Sally Hemings and Thomas Jefferson. She would turn twenty-one that May, a milestone traditionally signifying the end of childhood and the beginning of adulthood. For Harriet, however, it also meant the end of her enslavement at Monticello and the beginning of her freedom. It was a prospect for which she had prepared her whole life, atop Jefferson's "little mountain." Her parents had also been mindful of the coming of this day; each had done what they could to equip her for it. In the end, however, it appears that Harriet followed the trajectory of the plan of education her mother laid out for her, over that of her father. Of the many tales of self-fashioning in the early republic, hers must surely stand apart: a declaration of independence from her origins of such breathtaking scope as to rival that of her father.[1]

The documentary record of Harriet Hemings is sparse, but it lays out the broad chronological outline of her life. She was the second of four surviving children of Sally Hemings; she had three brothers: Beverley, Madison, and Eston; her father's Farm Book shows that she was born in May 1801; and it lists her among the twelve people at work in his textile manufactory on Mulberry Row in 1815. Sometime in 1822, at Jefferson's directive, the overseer Edmund Bacon put Hemings on a stage, paid the fare to Philadelphia, and supplied her with $50. We learn from her brother Madison's account, which appeared in an Ohio newspaper in 1873, that Hemings "married a white man in good standing in Washington City . . . [and] raised a family of children." We also know that Hemings lived until at least 1863, for Madison also observed that he had not heard from her in ten years. But during all those years, he was "not aware that her identity as Harriet Hemings of Monticello ha[d] ever been discovered." So successful was Hemings in obliterating her historical tracks that her trail—even today—remains stone cold. But her invisibility in the written records need not preclude our efforts to try to find her, to reflect on the choices her life presented, and to ruminate on what her decision to leave Monticello says about race and gender in her time and in our own.[2]

The wide-ranging literature that has examined the issue of Thomas Jefferson's connection with Sally Hemings has focused largely on the question from the white Jefferson family's perspective, with but a passing mention of the children of their union.[3] In 2008 Annette Gordon-Reed's award-winning *The Hemingses of Monticello: An American Family* reversed the focus, analyzing the Wayles-Hemings-Jefferson relationships from the Hemings family's perspectives. But Gordon-Reed's story centered largely on the first two generations of Hemingses. This essay explores third-generation Harriet Hemings's life. Pausing as much over the gaps in the records as over the documentary record itself, it is possible to begin to sketch out the contours of a life devoted to the pursuit of happiness—a task eminently befitting a daughter of Thomas Jefferson.

The lives of the Hemings and Jefferson families had been intertwined long before the day that Harriet Hemings left Monticello forever. John Wayles, the father of Jefferson's wife, Martha, had fathered six children with his slave Elizabeth Hemings, one of whom was Sally Hemings. After Wayles's death in 1773, Jefferson inherited the entire Hemings family, including the infant Sally. By 1775 or 1776 the Hemings family had moved to Monticello. In 1782 nine-year-old Sally was present at the death bed of her half-sister Martha Jefferson. In 1787, at fourteen, Sally escorted Jefferson's younger daughter Mary when she joined him in Paris. With the Jeffersons, Sally would return, pregnant, to Virginia in November 1789. Over the course of the next eighteen years at Monticello, Sally Hemings bore seven children, for whose paternity the overwhelming preponderance of the evidence points to Thomas Jefferson.[4]

As a Hemings, Harriet's life was different from that of most slaves at Monticello from the very beginning. Historians have described the Hemings family members as "a caste apart." They experienced a stability of family life uncommon to most slaves, at Monticello or anywhere else; they were employed in

WEAVER'S COTTAGE

Originally built to house the white workers who renovated Monticello, this stone cottage is thought to have later housed Jefferson's textile manufactory. Here, Harriet Hemings learned to operate a twenty-four-spindle spinning jenny, acquiring a skill for self-sufficiency in freedom. Meanwhile, steps away in the great house, her cousins studied history, mathematics, literature, Latin, Spanish, and French. Photo by Catherine Kerrison.

VIEW FROM WEAVER'S COTTAGE

Jefferson's love of classical architecture and his genius in design is clear even from the partial view afforded from Harriet Hemings's vantage point at the bottom of these steps, which today connect Mulberry Row to the main house. From the weaver's cottage where she worked, Harriet could see the graceful curve of the brick exterior of Jefferson's library and the pediment that crowned the four massive pillars at the east entrance of the mansion. Only two dozen steps to the top, but it might have been a world away.

Photo by Catherine Kerrison.

positions of trust (as butlers, valets, chambermaids, and nurses) and skill (as cooks, carpenters, and artisans); and, as products of interracial relationships, they were fairer-skinned than most slaves. Indeed, Harriet Hemings, who was seven-eighths (and therefore, under Virginia law, legally) white, was described by Edmund Bacon as "nearly as white as anybody, and very beautiful."[5]

Harriet Hemings spent her childhood at her mother's side. Deceptively simple, this straightforward fact packs a world of meaning. Harriet was raised by a woman whose experiences as a young girl set her apart from every other slave at Monticello: she had survived the perils of transatlantic travel and had lived in the glittering city of Paris for two years. Sally Hemings had crossed the Atlantic virtually alone: no one provided her with a male protector to shield her from the coarse leers and more of roughened sailors, and she was charged to be nine-year-old Mary Jefferson's travel companion and maid. In Paris, as Annette Gordon-Reed has remarked, Sally Hemings "learned that another type of life was possible." Under the tutelage and guidance of her elder brother James (who had accompanied Jefferson to Paris in 1784), Sally Hemings experienced the sights and sounds of the city, mixed with other people of color to whom James introduced her, learned to speak French, watched the beginnings of a revolution, and knew enough about French law regarding slavery to know that if she chose, she could remain in France as a free woman. She mixed in elite Parisian society as a lady's maid, possibly attending Jefferson's daughters occasionally at their school, but certainly at the balls the elder sister, Martha, attended in her last months in Paris. So integrated was she into the girls' lives that their schoolmates included greetings to "Mademoiselle Sally" in their letters. Sally Hemings was a caste apart, then, before she became Jefferson's "concubine." For the rest of her life, she spoke frequently of those years in Paris. Learning self-reliance at an early age and living in a much wider world than was visible from Monticello, Sally Hemings was a mother of uncommon character and experience in the slave community.[6]

Harriet Hemings would have learned significant lessons at the knee of such a mother. First and foremost, she would have been taught, from her earliest memory, that she was destined for freedom. With her three brothers, she grew up "free from the dread of having to be slaves all our lives long" and, in consequence, "measurably happy." She would have learned that this was the result of her mother's own "treaty" of Paris, an agreement, her brother Madison Hemings recounted, that Sally Hemings had negotiated with Jefferson: if she returned to Monticello with him, their children would be freed at age twenty-one. Harriet would have learned that, in spite of the insidious laws that governed the lives of Virginia slaves (including her mother's), *she* could, with care, craft her own future. And from the mother who had seen that "another type of life was possible," she would have learned how to prepare for a life as a free white woman.⁷

But before that training would begin, Harriet Hemings could first enjoy her childhood. Born at the beginning of Jefferson's presidency, Harriet—like the other house slaves—appreciated the benefits of a slower pace of life during his absences from Monticello. Edmund Bacon, hired in 1806, may have been startled when he was told firmly "to take no control of them [the female house slaves]," but that instruction certainly put him on notice about the status of the Hemings women at Monticello. Lacking the driving presence of master and overseer, and exempt from laboring "in the ground," Sally Hemings had more time than most enslaved women to devote to her small children and her relations at Monticello. The Hemingses were a tightly knit family; their naming patterns are clear and poignant indications of this: for example, Madison Hemings named children after his mother, sister, and both brothers. Thus Harriet grew up in her family's full embrace and under their watchful care, in the relative freedom that Jefferson's absences provided all of them. It is highly likely that Harriet spent time with the Randolphs, the children of Jefferson's elder daughter, Martha Jefferson Randolph. It was not at all unusual for very young children, free and enslaved, to spend their days playing together until they began to learn their respective conditions in life. But unlike any other slaves at Monticello, Harriet and her brothers could look forward to a free adulthood, just as Jefferson's grandchildren did.⁸

Sally Hemings was uniquely positioned to train her daughter for that life. She had seen what lay beyond their little mountain. At balls and at Jefferson's Paris residence, Sally had ample opportunity to observe the manners and tastes of polite society, many of which Jefferson retained back in Virginia. The constant stream of visitors to Monticello after Jefferson's retirement in 1809 kept all the women in the great house from a life of rural isolation. Carefully observant in all these venues, Sally Hemings would have noted the speech, manners, and dress of whites of "good standing" and was ready to prepare her little daughter to take her place among them one day. Their own dress was limited, of course, to that which Jefferson provided, but even so, it set the house servants apart from the rest: not for them the coarse osnaburg, an itchy rough-woven fabric that was the standard uniform of most slaves at Monticello. Rather, Jefferson instructed Bacon to ensure that the Hemingses be dressed in "colored plains," a cloth woven of wool, which was softer next to the skin. Building on the promise of "extraordinary privileges" she had extracted from Jefferson in Paris for her children, Sally Hemings would have taught Harriet from childhood that she was different from any other slave girl on the mountain. She would have taught her to speak, move, and behave so that her manners and conduct accorded with those of white women, so that her upbringing in slavery would never betray her once she attained her freedom.[9]

Sally Hemings would have prepared her daughter for life as a white man's wife in other practical ways as well. Described in the newspaper reports that publicly exposed her life with Jefferson as "an industrious and orderly creature in her behavior," Sally possessed exactly the characteristics Jefferson found so appealing in women. (He had once written to his daughter Martha, "Nothing is so disgusting to our sex as a want of cleanliness and delicacy in yours.") Sally passed to Harriet all the skills she had learned in Paris and at Monticello that would have been expected of a properly raised young white woman: how to sew, care for a range of fabrics and garments, and manage a home. The adoption of these habits of industry and order would recommend Harriet one day as the wife of a respectable white man.[10]

Thomas Jefferson took a somewhat different approach to Harriet's education. Like her brothers, Harriet would be freed in the prime of her life, her adulthood stretching before her. Until then, she required paternal protection and training in a skill by which she could earn her living until she married. The gap in Jefferson's documentary record about Harriet between 1801 and 1815 may be significant for it implies that her childhood deviated from the norm he set down for the rest of his enslaved workforce, in which children under age ten "serve[d] as nurses" (that is, minded younger children); between ten and sixteen "the boys ma[d]e nails, the girls sp[u]n"; and at sixteen they went "into the ground or learn[ed] trades." Not until she was fourteen, however, did Harriet appear in Jefferson's Farm Book as a worker, one of five spinners in his textile factory. Sally Hemings's children enjoyed a longer childhood than most slaves, perhaps in part because of the prospect of permanent separation from their parents when they attained their majority.[11]

There were several possible reasons that Jefferson would have decided to place Harriet in his textile factory. In his own youth, his mother and sisters owned spinning wheels; his sister Martha (who would grow up to marry his best friend, Dabney Carr) received a spinning wheel when she was sixteen. Perhaps Jefferson saw spinning as more a polite hobby and an accomplishment than a productive skill vital to the household economy.[12] In this way, he may have been equipping his daughter for the life of domesticity he expected her to have.

He also had more practical considerations, however, particularly considering how the world had changed from his mother's day to his daughter's, when small textile manufactories were sprouting up all over the country. In his own neighborhood, Jefferson observed in January 1812, "We are all busied in the country with our household manufactures of clothing. I do not believe one fifth of the coarse clothing has been bought this year from the importers which has been heretofore bought." From Philadelphia as early as 1806, James Ronaldson had sent Jefferson "many patterns of a variety of manufactures then carried on" there, auguring the place the city would take in the 1820s as a leading manufacturing center. The thriving textile industry in Philadelphia may explain why Jefferson directed Bacon to pay Harriet's fare to that city. Jefferson believed "household manufacture" to be "really precious; because the same children are employed in them, under the eye & care of their parents, where they are more correctly brought up, and have better opportunities of healthy exercise." It is tempting to sentimentalize Jefferson as thinking of the first year of Harriet's employment in a factory under his "eye & care," but since Madison Hemings complained that Jefferson "was not in the habit of showing partiality or fatherly affection to us children," that is unlikely. Still, Jefferson may well have satisfied himself that he met the obligations of his paternity by the provision he was making for his daughter's future as a housewife in a middling household, virtuously industrious, with her children about her.[13]

Working in the textile factory was not altogether unpleasant for Harriet. The workers were young (eight of the twelve were teenagers), and the factory seemed to lack strict oversight. Supervision of the factory's output apparently fell to Martha Jefferson Randolph, in whose presence the "work used to be weighed out . . . and partly with her own hands." But if she attempted to impose a rigid order on the textile workers, she was unsuccessful. Fifty years after Jefferson's death, one of his former spinners at Monticello chuckled that "we were so bad, so troublesome, I wonder how mistress had the patience to bear with us as she did." The work of spinners and weavers was not so engrossing as to preclude sharing stories, jokes, gossip, riotous laughter, and other behaviors that Randolph found "troublesome." That four teenage boys were among the factory crew would only have added to the boisterousness. Clearly, Harriet did not spend her working days under a strict regime enforced by the lash. Instead, she worked in the company of other young people in a somewhat relaxed but productive environment.[14]

Harriet's work was less onerous and physically taxing than most slave labor on the plantation, even in the textile factory. She worked with wool, which is much easier to handle than flax or hemp. It is the easiest of all fibers to spin, and wool's natural lanolin would have been softer on her hands than the stiffness of flax. And since Jefferson gave wool for stockings to those slaves "who will have it spun and knit for themselves," Harriet was in an occasional position to put her skills to work for her family's interests. The overseer Edmund Bacon recalled that Harriet "never did any hard work," although whether he referred to her performance in the textile factory, or was comparing the ease of factory versus field labor, is unclear.[15]

Nor was Harriet Hemings ever far from her family as she worked. The original stone house thought to have been the textile manufactory still stands at Monticello, at the bottom of the slope near the house where her mother worked. Its very location could well have been an important reason for Harriet's assignment there. Working in close proximity to her parents by day, surrounded by a regular staff of co-workers, Harriet would have been protected from the sexual advances typically suffered by young enslaved women. That would help account for the fact that she remained childless until after her departure at age twenty-one; most enslaved women experienced their first pregnancy by age eighteen.[16] Such an arrangement would comport completely with Jefferson's preference to deal quietly rather than publicly with his obligations to his daughter, affording her remarkable protection without raising unwanted notice.

It is unlikely, however, that these skills would have given Harriet Hemings the social cachet necessary for success in the marriage market. Jefferson was training his daughter in skills that provided her with earning power but kept her in a class below his white granddaughters. He thought spinning the labor best suited to Indian women, for example, and early in his presidency he envisioned Native men settling down to "cultivate their lands; and their women to spin and weave for their families." Even in the northern states, where such work was not consigned to slaves, spinning was falling out of favor as a badge of good housewifery. By the 1820s most northern women were buying rather than making cloth; spinning and, later, mechanized weaving were moving out of homes to factories, large and small. So it is unlikely that laboring as a spinner in one of the many small manufactories in Philadelphia would have positioned Harriet to raise her status by marrying up.[17]

On southern plantations, spinning and weaving were typically the work of slaves, supervised by white mistresses. Jefferson's interest in manufacturing coarse cloth for his enslaved workforce was widely shared in the region. But there was little probability that Harriet would remain there: in 1806 Virginia had decreed that freed slaves must vacate the state within twelve months of manumission, unless their owner sought a legislative waiver. This, Jefferson would never do, since it would place his private life before the scrutiny of the state legislators. Moreover, not two years earlier, Jefferson had calculated that "a [slave] woman who brings a child every two years [is] more profitable than the best man of the farm." To act in a way so counter to his own acute financial interests would require explanations he was not prepared to give.[18] Thus only his quiet release of her, hidden by his public notation in his Farm Book, "run," would suit his—and his white descendants'—purposes. Legally, then, Harriet would forever remain a fugitive slave, her freedom predicated on her removal from the state. So she would no more have envisioned a future as a slaveholding mistress than one as a slave.

At first glance, Harriet's transfer from the great house to the textile factory at age fourteen was not as dramatic as that of her mother, at the same age, from Virginia to Paris. Harriet's journey was literally a matter of steps, not thousands of miles. Yet even if it did not offer a blueprint for her future, Jefferson's plan for Harriet was deeply significant. Sally Hemings returned to Virginia as she had left it, a personal maid. But—whether of his own volition or persuaded by Sally—Jefferson did not make a maid of his daughter.[19] He placed her, as he had his Hemings sons, among people who could teach her a skill, which he intended to lead to self-sufficiency. It is quite possible—even likely—that Harriet preferred the education she received from her mother, calculating that it was more likely to ensure her passage into free white society and a better opportunity to marry well, than that offered by her father. But in any event, it was clear that in her adult life Harriet Hemings would not be anyone's servant.

Where she was headed the day she left Monticello, we do not know for sure. Jefferson's Farm Book merely notes "Sally's [daughter]. run. [18]22."[20] Bacon recalled that he put her on a stage to Philadelphia, but Madison Hemings tells us that she married and raised her family in Washington. These accounts are not mutually exclusive, of course, but whatever Harriet's choice, we know it was the right one, for her ability to remake her life was absolute: she obliterated her slave past and re-created herself as a free-born white woman.

For several reasons, she could have decided that Philadelphia was the ideal place to begin her new life. Her father had paid the full fare; it was far enough away from Monticello and Charlottesville that the Hemings name (if indeed she kept it) might not betray her origins; and it would be easier to disappear into anonymity in Philadelphia (with its population of 63,802) than in the considerably smaller city of Washington. After the Revolution, Philadelphia attracted many newly freed men and women from Delaware, Maryland, Virginia, and the Pennsylvania hinterlands. The city's reputation for abolitionism and tolerance appears to have been confirmed by the 1820 Census, which for the first time entered a zero under the category of "Slave." In her desire to expunge her slave past, Hemings would have stayed far away from the free black community; but for a fugitive, as Harriet was without freedom papers, Philadelphians' lack of interest in upholding the institution of slavery may have reassured her of the city's comparative safety.[21]

Jefferson would not have sent her to Philadelphia without making careful arrangements for her initial placement and care. He had known the city well in his days in the Continental Congress and later as secretary of state, and he still had close and trusted friends there. Whether or not Jefferson entrusted his secret to anyone in Philadelphia, the city would only have been a possible destination for Harriet Hemings if her father made it so. One intriguing record, still available on the genealogical website of the Church of Latter-day Saints, places Harriet in Philadelphia and lists the names of her husband and six children. The pursuit of this lead provides a classic cautionary tale for genealogists. After weeks of fruitless searches in Philadelphia archives, the information on the website was revealed to be fictional. An LDS member had read a novel about Harriet and, persuaded that all its characters were actual historical figures, entered their names on the website and even arranged for their posthumous baptism.[22]

Even if Philadelphia was a viable option in Jefferson's view, it does not necessarily follow that Harriet Hemings or her mother agreed. They may have thought of her textile skills as a kind of safety net if all else failed, but they probably had very different ideas about creating her life as a free woman. The stage Harriet boarded in Charlottesville was the Lynchburg line that terminated in Washington; following Jefferson's plan for her to go to Philadelphia would have required her to transfer to another line.[23] But Madison Hemings's account suggests that Harriet chose to alight from the stage in Washington instead. If she did, it was because the Hemingses had made other plans that did not include Harriet supporting herself by spinning. A new and growing city, Washington offered a wide array of employment possibilities—with the notable exception of textile manufacturing.

It is curious that Beverley Hemings, Sally's eldest child, who had turned twenty-one on April 1, 1819, did not immediately leave Monticello, according to the terms his mother had negotiated with his father. Instead, he waited, in slavery, until his sister's arrival at that benchmark age. Beverley's exact departure date is unknown: Jefferson's Farm Book shows that he received his last woolen and shirting allowance in 1819–20 and that he "ran away" in 1822.[24] That Beverley waited so long suggests a Hemings family plan, rather than a Jeffersonian one. There were several good reasons for the siblings to choose to go to Washington, and it would make sense for the elder brother, trained in carpentry, to go ahead to scout out living quarters and work prospects to establish himself shortly before his sister joined him.

Washington was a capital still very much in the making in 1822, a mix of affluent planters from the outlying areas and Alexandria and Georgetown merchants, joined by an array of government clerks and officeholders. When

Harriet and Beverley arrived in Washington, its population was only thirteen thousand, but growing. In the next decade, it would increase almost 50 percent to nineteen thousand, with an influx of government workers to staff a growing bureaucracy and of newly manumitted men and women. The city was a jumble of distinct neighborhoods: brick townhouses after the London style dominated the residential areas of merchants and the middle class, while Chesapeake-style frame homes dominated less affluent areas.[25] Opportunities for work for skilled carpenters were ubiquitous, making Washington City a perfect place for Beverley Hemings to begin his new life.

Under the protective wing of her brother, Harriet could also make a life for herself. Few government employees who boarded in the city brought their families with them in these early years, so working women supplied the needs ordinarily tended to at home by wives and daughters. The directory to the city published the year that Beverley and Harriet arrived shows that women ran boardinghouses, schools, grocery stores, and "fancy" stores; they were milliners, seamstresses, and in a couple of cases "tailoresses," who undoubtedly catered to a male clientele. Harriet could have begun a tailoring business (her mother was a talented seamstress and passed that skill to her daughter) or, if she was literate, she may have applied to teach in one of several small schools headed by women. The infant city was ripe for talented, hard-working people looking to make their way in the world.[26]

Washington's relatively smaller population might not have posed an obstacle to attaining anonymity since, in a city of transients, new faces were not suspect. Nor were the Hemingses' former owners interested in tracking them down. Years later Jefferson's granddaughter Ellen Wayles Randolph Coolidge would assert that the whereabouts of "three young men and one girl, who walked away and staid away . . . were perfectly known but they were left to themselves." It was Jefferson's "principle," she explained, "to allow such of his slaves as were sufficiently white to pass for white men, to withdraw quietly from the plantation; it was called running away, but they were never reclaimed."[27] And if the path of Harriet Hemings ever crossed those of Martha Jefferson Randolph and her children (who resided for a time in the city after Jefferson's death), the family records are silent on the matter.

Although there were many opportunities for well-trained ambitious white men and women, life was harder for freed blacks. Since the District of Columbia did not impose restrictions on newly manumitted men and women, the free black population expanded rapidly, to the growing alarm of whites. Initial regulations governing free black workers had resembled those of northern cities. The 1820 Washington city charter required only that they post a bond to ensure they would not become a public charge. By 1827, however, the city fathers attempted to slow the numbers of free blacks entering the city by requiring residency permits and to control any attempts at resistance by placing limits on their ability to assemble in groups. A dozen years after their arrival, Beverley and Harriet might have witnessed riots in Washington in 1835, "which targeted successful black property owners, [and] caused the city to exclude blacks from a number of occupations." From that point, one historian observes, "the overwhelming majority [of free black people] cooked meals, cleaned houses, dug foundations, and shifted piles of goods and building materials as servants and laborers." Very quickly, then, anywhere they turned in their adopted city, Beverley and Harriet could see the fate they had escaped when they decided to pass.[28]

Unmarked by their enslaved past, brother and sister evaded the notice of white Washingtonians. Official records likewise failed to notice them. Marriage records between 1811 (when the District of Columbia first required all marriages to be registered) and 1830 yield no clues. Although the District's marriage record lists the names of the bride and groom and their wedding date, Harriet and Beverley apparently dropped their last name; there is not a single Hemings listed in the entire book. Church records are sparser still. Only two of the original churches remaining in the city today possess records dating to this period: the short list of marriages at First Presbyterian Church does not contain any bride named Harriet. Nor do the records of St. John's Episcopal Church reveal any information about Harriet Hemings. Searches in each church's baptismal records for children with any of the distinctive Hemings family first names also turn up nothing.[29]

Harriet Hemings may have slipped through church and city marriage records; she may have refused to provide information for the directories. (S. A. Elliot, the editor of the 1827 directory, regretted that "many, at first, through a misconception of the intention of the publisher, refused to give their names altogether.") But surely the Census would have found her, at age forty-nine, established and the mother of several children. The 1850 federal Census was the first to list the name, sex, age, and occupation of every member of the household. A city of forty thousand residents by 1850, Washington's population had tripled since Harriet's arrival. One building at a time, in each of the city's six wards, Census takers knocked at the doors of businesses, private homes, and boardinghouses, and carefully inscribed the required information in their own hand. Rather than exposing her past, the Census would have confirmed her life as she now lived it, blending seamlessly with other white families of Washington. But whether she greeted the Census taker with fear, apprehension, or confidence, she was successful in claiming the ultimate privilege of whiteness: invisibility. Nothing gave her away, then or now.[30]

But at what cost did Harriet Hemings purchase this life? Telling his family's story almost fifty years after his father's death, Madison Hemings chose his words carefully as he recounted his sister's choice. "She thought it to her interest, on going to Washington, to assume the role of a white woman," he said evenly, "and by her dress and conduct as such I am not aware that her identity as Harriet Hemings of Monticello has ever been discovered."[31] Madison was the only child of Sally Hemings to live his life as "black," with all the freight that category has carried in the American experience. The record is silent about why. Perhaps his skin, hair, or features would not have permitted passing, or perhaps he preferred to identify himself with the community of his origins, or to forever retain his mother's name. Whatever the case, his words "she thought it to her interest" are pregnant with a sense of the moral tensions of Harriet's decision to pass as a free-born white person.

Harriet's departure from Monticello in the year of her twenty-first birthday suggests that she always knew she would leave the mountain and planned accordingly. Freedom and invisibility were incomparable prizes in antebellum America, but she must have pondered the costs of passing: giving up the precious Hemings name (too many people in Washington had visited Monticello and would recognize it, if not her; and there had been a lot of talk among the neighbors in Charlottesville on her departure); permanent separation from her mother and her younger brothers, a state of living death they would all have to endure; eternal vigilance that she never betray her enslaved origins and fugitive status; and the loneliness that such a secret would forever inscribe on all her relationships, particularly if she kept it from the family she would create in Washington. Only with Beverley would she be able to be most truly herself, but even he was not as accessible to her as he had been in the early days of their freedom: with his marriage, he may have left the city to live in Maryland.[32]

But if she wanted a life different from her mother's, Harriet Hemings had to leave Charlottesville; and if she wanted a better life in antebellum America, she had to pass. Her options were different from those of her brothers, who were trained in carpentry and music, both crafts that enabled them to marry and support families. Female self-sufficiency in this period was synonymous with poverty, so a good marriage was Harriet's best route to financial security and respectability. Perhaps Sally Hemings hoped that Harriet would remain in Charlottesville and marry a white man there, as had Sally's sister Mary Hemings Bell. But lacking a legislative waiver allowing her to remain in Virginia, Harriet's freedom in Charlottesville would have relied entirely on a community consensus, which may or may not have been stable.[33] How much better her prospects as a beautiful, young, white woman to marry up, to a man in "good standing," in a growing city where no one knew her enslaved origins.[34] Less than ten years later, her younger brothers would marry free women of mixed racial parentage in their old neighborhood, continuing the process of freeing the succeeding generation. But ever since 1662, Virginia law had mandated that children take on the condition of the mother. The only way Harriet could ensure freedom for her children was to leave Charlottesville and her origins forever.

Successful passing requires that no record be left behind, and neither Harriet nor Beverley left a trace. In a sense, their passing was aided by a Virginia law of 1785, which changed the racial dividing line from one-eighth to one-quarter African blood. An attempt to codify the implications of racial mixing in the new nation's legal system, the law was silent on the status of those with less than one-eighth African ancestry. Rather than clarifying matters, it made identifying a person's race more complex and subjective, even a matter for local juries. A case in Virginia in 1809, for example, had specified, "where white persons are claimed as slaves, the *onus pro bandi* lies upon the claimant." For this reason, Virginians rarely bought light or white slaves on the auction block, fearing how easily they could escape and blend into white society, and the difficulties of proving their legal condition.[35] One-eighth African, the children of Sally Hemings were thus legally white; and, white in aspect as she was, Harriet Hemings could play on all the presumptions of freedom accorded to whites in a white supremacist society.

Stories of passing from the antebellum period give us an idea of how Harriet accomplished her deception. One escaped slave, "being well dressed, and of genteel deportment," boarded a steamboat in New Orleans in 1852, "sat at the first table, in the cabin, near the ladies," and made it as far as Memphis before he aroused any suspicion. With the "appearance of an unassuming gentleman," he had traveled almost eight hundred miles, "freely mingling with society," before he was discovered. In another case, a "Monsieur Dukay" arrived in Memphis in 1838 with a manufactured history: in his affected French accent, Dukay told his new friends that he sought to escape the malarial climate of the South. Charming the ladies, "who smiled delightedly in his presence," and talking "eloquently of finance" and of his two sugar plantations, "no party or fashionable assemblage [that summer] was complete" without him. Fleeing his newly made "dear old friends," Dukay left town with a new horse, a saddle, a bridle, and even a diamond ring for "his only sister." In what was probably a much more common scenario, a young seamstress passed for white in the home of the mother of a young tradesman, who became enamored of her and married her in 1849 "in the full belief that she was free and a white woman." The subsequent discovery that she was "a negress and a slave" voided the marriage, but her story shows how it was possible to cross the color line even without the flamboyant performing skills of "Monsieur Dukay."[36] From Madison's comment on Harriet's "dress and conduct," it is likely that, amply supplied by her mother's superior sewing skills, Harriet Hemings made her appearance in Washington "well dressed." And, with her mother's training, she had acquired the "genteel deportment" that won her a husband of "good standing." Unlike the fugitive on the steamboat, however, she was never discovered.

But neither did she completely disappear. It is clear that Harriet Hemings kept in contact with her brother Madison for forty years after she bid him good-bye, even though no letters remain. He knew where she was; he could name her husband "but w[ould] not for prudential reasons"; he knew she raised "a family of children," that in all those years no one ever guessed her secret, and that she was still living as late as 1863. So, despite passing, she had not cut off all ties to her birth family. How she remained in contact with Madison is unknown. She may have possessed at least rudimentary literacy: several Hemings family members could read and write, including Madison, and Harriet had been able to secure a husband who was in "good standing," a less likely feat for an uneducated illiterate.[37] But what risks might she have taken in writing and receiving letters? Had Beverley been their conduit for news of each other? Possessing greater mobility and a presumption of privacy for business papers and affairs, a nineteenth-century man could keep up a surreptitious correspondence more easily than could a woman, especially a wife. But Beverley was apparently still alive in 1873—Madison did not report his death—and yet Madison had not heard from his sister in ten years. It seems likely, then, that Harriet and Madison corresponded directly. It is possible that the moment finally arrived when the risk of communication was too great and Harriet had to make the agonizing choice between protecting her white children's racial identity and maintaining a connection with her brother.

Such decisions would be replicated time and again among the descendants of Sally Hemings. Interviews with the succeeding generations of Madison Hemings's family revealed that some followed him in retaining their black identity; others abandoned their family connections to cross the color line forever; others crossed and returned, tired and broken from the high costs such strategies demanded in a society whose racism continued unabated after the Civil War. Unwilling to continue suffering the penalties his African ancestry elicited from his white neighbors, Eston Hemings moved his wife and three children to Wisconsin in 1852, hid the Hemings name behind an innocuous middle initial, took the surname Jefferson, and passed as white. While this move saved his descendants from the wrenching separations that Madison's family suffered, it is possible that the high rates of early death among Eston's male descendants constituted a different kind of cost.[38] Harriet Hemings's choice may have shielded her descendants from both fates, since they were oblivious to their slave origins, unlike Eston's children, who were teenagers when they moved from Ohio and would have known their family story. Nor, apparently, did an infant of questionable skin color ever give her away.

Even today, passing remains fraught with pain, judgment, recriminations, and loss. As one cultural studies critic has concluded, "the moral in each version of the story [of passing] is the same. Passing, if not altogether bad, is at least a really bad idea, and society, or life itself, will punish the 'passer' for breaking the rules." Passing is a "bad idea" because—depending on one's perspective—it requires the deliberate rejection of one's identity, family, and origins; it involves deceit; it upends notions of a strict racial order and a natural hierarchy; or, conversely, by failing to challenge those notions, it is complicit in the very oppressive regime that it strives to escape. More recent commentaries have attempted to counter this view by arguing that passing is an expression of American individualism: since individualism is about one's *consent* mattering more than one's *descent*, what you make of yourself is more important than where you came from. "The widely shared public bias against hereditary privilege ... has strongly favored *achieved* rather than *ascribed* identity," one literary critic explains, "and supported 'self-determination' and 'independence' from ancestral, parental, and external definitions."[39]

Passing remains problematic in our own day. The 1990 death of Anatole Broyard, a literary critic for the *New York Times* who had passed as white, prompted the reflection that "in a system where whiteness is the default, racelessness is never a possibility. You cannot opt out." The generations between Hemings's time and Broyard's have not eliminated the racial divide that continues to separate families like the Broyards: in the twentieth century, a black family member carefully tended Broyard graves in the black section of a New Orleans cemetery, but felt constrained from attending to family members' graves in the white section by "the unspoken code that kept the white and black branches of the family from mixing." Long after Harriet Hemings's time and decades after the civil rights movement, mixed-race ancestry continues to be associated with slavery and shame, to have real social and economic reverberations, and to separate family members from each other in a vortex of denial, anger, silence, and resignation.[40]

Passing can also be about "the creation and establishment of an alternative set of narratives." With her brother, Harriet Hemings would have had to create a new story of their origins for their life in Washington. This would not necessarily have been a new experience for her, but rather a continuation of her project of self-creation. If it is true that "every subject's history is a work in progress—a set of stories we tell ourselves in order to make sense or coherence out of a frequently confusing and complicated past"—Harriet had been working on that history long before she left Monticello. To do so, she needed to sort out the contradictions between what she knew to be true about her humanity and her parentage, and what the Virginia laws of property and the Jefferson-Randolph family alleged to be true. One of the "yellow children" to whom Ellen Randolph Coolidge referred, Harriet was disconnected from the rarefied world of the Jefferson-Randolph family even as she lived among them.[41] Yet, having seen herself with courage and clarity, she would be ready to leave for the world beyond the mountain.

And that may have been what Madison Hemings found distressing. Watching his elder sister learn to conduct herself as a white woman, preparing for the day of her departure, Madison must have anticipated her decision with a combination of puzzlement, hurt, foresight, understanding, and bitterness. It is a curious feature of his account that while "colored" blood "coursed" in the veins of Beverley's daughter and Eston's wife, Harriet was not suspected of the "taint" of "African" blood. Perhaps he sensed an emotional drawing away as she prepared herself for separation; anthropologists have observed that those most likely to pass were those who did not have strong ties to the black community.[42] Perhaps Harriet summarily cut off communications with her brother in 1863; ten years later his sarcastic use of the pejorative "taint" suggests that he continued to harbor resentment against her. But if he doubted her attachment to her brothers after her departure, Madison nonetheless gave eloquent proof of his love for her and of the importance of family ties when he named his second daughter after her.

Passing precipitates pain; Madison Hemings knew that. So did his sister. But ultimately Harriet's decision to pass was not a rejection of him, or of her mother, or even of the decision her mother made all those years before in Paris. As Harriet was growing up, Virginia and the other southern states had begun to articulate a regional identity built around a racial order, calcified as a natural creation and underscored by reference to scripture. Even as Harriet entered adulthood, Jefferson was building a university to provide an alternative for the sons of Virginia to those "northern seminaries" where they were "imbibing opinions and principles in discord with those of their own country."[43] Thirty-five years earlier, her mother, living in revolutionary France, could be forgiven if she anticipated an upward trajectory for her life that European and American trends toward manumission and abolition seemed to forecast. No such hope existed in Harriet's day; the Missouri Compromise in 1820 had signaled a trend toward a national accommodation of slavery, rather than its abolition. If her decision inflicted pain, it was because no decision within such a system—stay or go—could fail to do so.

Ultimately, Harriet's decision was about bringing order to her world, passing as human, and claiming for herself the human rights to life, liberty, and the pursuit of happiness. It has been observed that "passing never feels natural. It is a second skin that never adheres."[44] Maybe. But for Harriet Hemings, it was the artificiality of the legal codes that rendered her black and it was being enslaved that did not feel natural; passing, she could do.

NOTES

1. Thomas Jefferson (hereafter TJ) to Bernard Peyton, May 25, 1822, in Edwin Morris Betts, ed., *Thomas Jefferson's Farm Book* (Charlottesville: Thomas Jefferson Memorial Foundation, 1999), 307 (hereafter *TJ's Farm Book*).

2. Facsimile of Thomas Jefferson's Farm Book (hereafter FB), 128, 152; *TJ's Farm Book*; Hamilton Wilcox Pierson, ed., *Jefferson at Monticello: The Private Life of Thomas Jefferson from Entirely New Materials* (New York: Charles Scribner, 1862), 110; Madison Hemings, "Life among the Lowly, No. 1," *Pike County* (Ohio) *Republican*, March 13, 1873, reprinted in Annette Gordon-Reed, *Thomas Jefferson and Sally Hemings: An American Controversy* (Charlottesville: University of Virginia Press, 1997), 246.

3. Historians who have denied the connection include Merrill Peterson, *The Jefferson Image in the American Mind* (New York: Oxford University Press, 1960); Dumas Malone, *Jefferson the President: First Term* (Boston: Little, Brown, 1970), 212–16, 494–98; John Chester Miller, *The Wolf by the Ears: Thomas Jefferson and Slavery* (New York: Free Press, 1977). Winthrop Jordan contextualizes the question of the Hemings connection in a larger story of race and slavery in *White over Black: American Attitudes toward the Negro, 1550–1812* (Chapel Hill: University of North Carolina Press, 1968). Fawn M. Brodie's *Thomas Jefferson: An Intimate History* (New York: Norton, 1974) was the first to investigate seriously the claims of the Hemings family. See also Gordon-Reed, *Thomas Jefferson and Sally Hemings*; and Jan Ellen Lewis and Peter S. Onuf, eds., *Sally Hemings and Thomas Jefferson: History, Memory, and Civic Culture* (Charlottesville: University of Virginia Press, 1999).

4. The best summary and analysis of the evidence is in Gordon-Reed, *Thomas Jefferson and Sally Hemings*.

5. Lucia Stanton, *Free Some Day: The African-American Families of Monticello* (Charlottesville, Va.: Thomas Jefferson Foundation, 2000), 105; Annette Gordon-Reed, *The Hemingses of Monticello: An American Family* (New York: Norton, 2008), 27–28; Pierson, *Jefferson at Monticello*, 107.

6. Gordon-Reed, *Hemingses of Monticello*, 193, chaps. 8–12; Marie de Botidoux to Martha Jefferson, November 1789–January 1790, Marie Jacinthe de Botidoux, Letters, 1788–1847, to Martha Jefferson Randolph, acc. no, 5385-aa, Small Special Collections Library, University of Virginia, Charlottesville; Pierson, *Jefferson at Monticello*, 108. The eighteenth-century meaning of the term "concubine" was a woman who lived with a man without being married to him. Virginia law prohibited the marriage of enslaved women to white men, so Sally Hemings could never have been Jefferson's legal

wife. Nor would the term "mistress," defined as a woman having sexual relations with a married man, be applicable to her situation (Gordon-Reed, *Hemingses of Monticello*, 107).

7. Hemings, "Life among the Lowly," in Gordon-Reed, *Thomas Jefferson and Sally Hemings*, 248.

8. Stanton, *Free Some Day*, 105; Pierson, *Jefferson at Monticello*, 107. For the eighteenth century, see Hunter Farish, ed., *Journal and Letters of Philip Vickers Fithian: A Plantation Tutor in the Old Dominion, 1773–1774* (Williamsburg, Va.: Colonial Williamsburg Foundation, 1943); and Mechal Sobel, *The World They Made Together: Black and White Values in Eighteenth-Century Virginia* (Princeton, N.J.: Princeton University Press, 1987); for the nineteenth century, see David Blight, ed., *The Narrative of the Life of Frederick Douglass* (Boston: Bedford, 2003).

9. Hemings, "Life among the Lowly," in Gordon-Reed, *Thomas Jefferson and Sally Hemings*, 246; TJ memorandums to Edmund Bacon (1805–6), in *TJ's Farm Book*, 25. Martha Jefferson Randolph attended to the clothing worn by the most prominent house servants, that is, "Peter Hemings, Burwell, Edwin, Critta, and Sally" (TJ to Bacon, 1805–6). Melvin Ely has shown that speech patterns among blacks and whites in the antebellum South may have been similar, unlike the stereotypes of black speech that became common with segregation under Jim Crow. See Ely, *Israel on the Appomattox: A Southern Experiment in Black Freedom from the 1790s through the Civil War* (New York: Knopf, 2004), 290–95.

10. *Frederick-Town Herald*, reprinted in *Richmond Recorder*, December 8, 1802; TJ to Martha Jefferson, December 22, 1783, in Edwin Morris Betts and James Adam Bear Jr., eds., *The Family Letters of Thomas Jefferson* (1966; rpt., Charlottesville: University of Virginia Press, 1986), 22.

11. Gordon-Reed, *Thomas Jefferson and Sally Hemings*, 52; FB, 77, 152. TJ's notations on the latter page are undated, but they are found in pages between those dated 1814 and 1816. See Hemings, "Life among the Lowly," in Gordon-Reed, *Thomas Jefferson and Sally Hemings*, 248.

12. Susan Kern, "The Material World of the Jeffersons at Shadwell," *William and Mary Quarterly*, 3rd ser., 62 (2005): 24.

13. TJ to William Thornton, January 14, 1812, in *TJ's Farm Book*, 469; TJ to James Ronaldson, October 13, 1808, ibid., 466; Philip Scranton, *Proprietary Capitalism: The Textile Manufacture at Philadelphia, 1800–1885* (Cambridge: Cambridge University Press, 1983), 75–134; TJ to Charles Willson Peale, May 8, 1816, in *TJ's Farm Book*, 490; Hemings, "Life among the Lowly," in Gordon-Reed, *Thomas Jefferson and Sally Hemings*, 247.

14. Sarah Nicholas Randolph to [H. S. Randall], quoting Ellen Wayles Randolph Coolidge, February 30 [*sic*], 1876, Papers of the Randolph Family of Edgehill, box 11, acc. no. 1397, Small Special Collections Library, University of Virginia, Charlottesville; Stanton, *Free Some Day*, 93.

15. Author's interview of Linda Eaton, head curator of textiles, Winterthur Museum, April 6, 2009; Pierson, *Jefferson at Monticello*, 48, 110.

16. Alan Kulikoff, *Tobacco and Slaves: The Development of Southern Cultures in the Chesapeake* (Chapel Hill: University of North Carolina Press, 1988), 72; Richard Follet, *The Sugar Masters: Planters and Slaves in Louisiana's Cane World, 1820–1860* (Baton Rouge: Louisiana State University Press, 2005), 57.

17. TJ to Handsome Lake, November 3, 1802, Thomas Jefferson Papers, Library of Congress; Jeanne Boydston, *Home and Work: Housework, Wages, and the Ideology of Labor in the Early Republic* (New York: Oxford University Press, 1990), 125; Jane C. Nylander, *Our Own Snug Fireside: Images of the New England Home 1760–1860* (New York: Knopf, 1994), 182.

18. TJ to John Wayles Eppes, June 30, 1820, in *TJ's Farm Book*, 45–46; Gordon-Reed, *Thomas Jefferson and Sally Hemings*, 29–30.

19. Gordon-Reed, *Hemingses of Monticello*, 598.

20. FB, 130.

21. 1820 Census, http://www.census.gov/history/www/fast_facts/012344.html (accessed April 14, 2009); Gary Nash, *Forging Freedom: The Foundation of Philadelphia's Black Community* (Cambridge, Mass.: Harvard University Press, 1988), 137. White Philadelphians responded to the growing black population with laws and practices that increasingly restricted their rights, including barring black men from the franchise by 1838. See Gary Nash and Jean Soderlund, *Freedom by Degrees: Emancipation in Pennsylvania and Its Aftermath* (New York: Oxford University Press, 1991).

22. I am grateful to Beverly Gray, the oral historian at Monticello's Getting Word project, for sharing with me her theory that Harriet Hemings may have begun her free life in Philadelphia (phone interview, April 3, 2009). Harriet's uncle James, who lived in Philadelphia after his manumission, had died in 1801 and so could not have eased her transition into the city, as Dumas Malone has speculated (*Jefferson the President*, 496). The erroneous information is still available on www.family search.org. I am grateful to Lucia Stanton and Henry Weincek for alerting me to the provenance of the information, which is Barbara Chase-Riboud's novel *The President's Daughter* (1994).

23. John Melish, *The Traveller's Directory through the United States* (Philadelphia: printed for the author, 1815), 3–4, 15–16; Samuel Augustus Mitchell, *Mitchell's Travel Guide through the United States* (Philadelphia: Mitchell and Hinman, 1836), 43.

24. "Roll of the negroes according to their ages. Albemarle," FB, 130.

25. Carl Abbott, *Political Terrain: Washington, D.C., from Tidewater Town to Global Metropolis* (Chapel Hill: University of North Carolina Press, 1999), 28–38, 47–48.

26. Judah Delano, ed., *Washington Directory: Showing the Name, Occupation, and Residence of Each Head of a Family and Person in Business* (Washington, D.C.: William Duncan, 1822), 33. There is no evidence to prove that either Sally Hemings or her daughter were literate, although there are many reasons to suspect that they were. Several Hemings men were literate, and at least a rudimentary education would have been imperative in order for Harriet to pass as white. See Gordon-Reed, *Hemingses of Monticello*, 403–6.

27. Ellen Wayles Randolph Coolidge to Joseph Coolidge, October 24, 1858, Ellen Wayles Randolph Coolidge Letterbook, Coolidge Collection, acc. no. 9090, Small Special Collections Library, University of Virginia, Charlottesville.

28. Kathleen M. Lesko, *Black Georgetown Remembered: A History of Its Black Community from the Founding of "the Town of George" in 1751 to the Present Day* (Washington, D.C.: Georgetown University Press, 1991), 12; Abbott, *Political Terrain*, 49.

29. Session Records, vol. 1, 1812–1840, First Presbyterian Church, Washington, D.C. I am grateful to J. Theodore Anderson for his assistance. See also Marriage and Baptism Record Book, St. John's Episcopal Church, Lafayette Square, Washington, D.C. I am grateful to Hayden Bryan, who provided access to this record.

30. S. A. Elliot, comp., *The Washington Directory, Showing the Names, Occupation, and Residence, of Each Head of a Family and Persons in Business Together with Other Useful Information* (Washington, D.C.: S. A. Elliot, 1827), iii; Hemings, "Life among the Lowly," in Gordon-Reed, *Thomas Jefferson and Sally Hemings*, 246. Nor did a search of the 1860 Census reveal her. I am grateful to my graduate assistant, Claire Bohall, for her work on the 1860 Census.

31. Hemings, "Life among the Lowly," in Gordon-Reed, *Thomas Jefferson and Sally Hemings*, 246. The following discussion will be limited to race passing from "black" to "white."

32. Ibid.

33. One scholar has suggested that free blacks and mixed-race couples lived undisturbed in Albe-

marle County, however. See Kirt Von Daacke, *Freedom Has a Face: Race, Identity, and Community in Jefferson's Virginia* (Charlottesville: University of Virginia Press, 2012).

34. Ibid.

35. James Hugo Johnston, *Race Relations in Virginia and Miscegenation in the South 1776-1860* (Amherst: University of Massachusetts Press, 1970), 191-94, 213.

36. Ibid., 207-10.

37. Items such as letters, recipes, and inventories attest to the reading and writing literacy of John Hemmings, James Hemings, and Robert Hemings. Madison Hemings noted, with some bitterness, that his father did not teach him to write, but he learned from the Randolph children instead. See Gordon-Reed, *Thomas Jefferson and Sally Hemings*, 246, 149, 247.

38. Lucia Stanton and Dianne Swann-Wright, "Bonds of Memory: Identity and the Hemings Family," in Lewis and Onuf, *Sally Hemings and Thomas Jefferson*, 163-69.

39. Brooke Kroeger, *Passing: When People Can't Be Who They Are* (New York: Public Affairs, 2003), 2; Werner Sellors qtd. in Kathleen Pfeiffer, *Race Passing and American Individualism* (Amherst: University of Massachusetts Press, 2003), 5.

40. Qtd. in Kroeger, *Passing*, 25; see also Bliss Broyard, *One Drop: My Father's Hidden Life: A Story of Race and Family Secrets* (New York: Little, Brown, 2007), 250.

41. Linda Schlossberg, "Rites of Passing," in *Passing: Identity and Interpretation in Sexuality, Race, and Religion*, ed. Maria Carla Sánchez and Linda Schlossberg (New York: New York University Press, 2001), 4. The different stories invented by the Randolph grandchildren to explain the "yellow" children at Monticello show that they, too, needed to make sense of their complicated past. See Ellen Wayles Randolph Coolidge to Joseph Coolidge, October 24, 1858, *Jefferson Quotes and Family Letters*, http:www.monticello.org/familyletters; Thomas Jefferson Randolph to TJ, n.d., acc. no. 8937, box 3, Small Special Collections Library, University of Virginia, Charlottesville.

42. St. Clair Drake and Horace R. Clayton, *Black Metropolis: A Study of Negro Life in a Northern City* (1962; rpt., Chicago: University of Chicago Press, 1993).

43. TJ to James Breckinridge, February, 15, 1821, Thomas Jefferson Papers, Library of Congress.

44. Kroeger, *Passing*, 8.

Edy Turner

The Nottoway Indians' "Female Chief"

HELEN C. ROUNTREE

Only one Nottoway Indian ever generated enough records of any sort to make even a sketchy biography possible, and that individual is an even rarer bird in the Virginia records because she was female. Edy (Edith) Turner was born around 1754, but she did not become prominent until she was in her mid-fifties. As so often happened with nonliterate Native Americans, she gained that prominence in the eyes of the record makers by irritating powerful whites. By the early 1800s she was one of only two elders left in the tribe, the other being a blind man three years her junior. Her other contemporaries had either died or moved away to escape a tribe that was in serious decline while local whites waited impatiently for its final demise. The tribe's age-old language and mixed hunting and farming culture were dying for lack of practitioners and the loss of the land base needed to support them.

In 1806 a series of events occurred that conclusively demonstrated the Nottoway tribe's fatal apathy even toward its own children, and in its wake, Turner apparently snapped. Her plan seems to have been to try to salvage something of the old ways while adapting to the intensive farming the whites insisted on. Ironically, it was her long experience as an Indian woman, in a world where farming was women's business, which enabled her to work out a plan for adaptation while the unemployed male hunters sat around and drank rather than considering change. But the Nottoways' decline was too far advanced for her scheme to do any more than to slow down the process of dissolution. Ultimately, Edy Turner threw in the towel, helped behind the scenes to get it over with, and made the best of a bad situation.

The Nottoways had never been an easy people for the English in Virginia to deal with.[1] Because of their location well south of the James River, near the Carolina border, unlike the Powhatans they inhabited lands that were for decades relatively peripheral to the Virginia colony. As a result, the Nottoways remained a fairly strong nation even into the eighteenth century. That fact made the colonists in Virginia wary of them, in spite of their signing peace treaties with England in 1677 and 1714.[2] Proof of that wariness is shown by the English insistence on the latter treaty, even though they had successfully kept the Nottoways from joining their fellow Iroquoian-speakers, the Tuscaroras, in the Tuscarora War. It is true that some Nottoways chose to leave their land and move north with the Tuscaroras, who joined the Five Nations Iroquois and made them the Six Nations after that war was over. But it was the spread of English settlers, eager for land, that would spell disaster for the Nottoways who remained in Virginia.

Any Indian people who wanted to retain their age-old way of life had to live by a combination of farming and hunting; the latter required enormous tracts of land compared to what the Europeans' domesticated animals took up in pasturage. Thus when the Nottoways parted with tracts of hunting land, they made themselves poorer because Nottoway men, who considered themselves professional hunters and fishermen, refused to learn what they considered the women's work of farming. Like most Native people, the Nottoways were also uninterested in animal husbandry, in part because hunting wild animals kept the men prepared to go to war to defend their land and families. The weapons and techniques they used for fighting enemies and hunting animals were the same and also militarily essential, because raiding went back and forth until the Nottoways' last significant wars with other Indians ended in the 1730s. Men had traditionally conducted the contacts—hostile or peaceful—with outsiders, and henceforward those outsiders would be whites. The loss of Nottoway land led to poverty, which some sought to escape through drinking—which, in turn, cost them both whatever they gave to Europeans in exchange for the alcohol and also their clearheadedness, which then often led to the loss of yet more land. It was a vicious cycle.[3]

Problems with whites selling liquor to the Nottoways surfaced in 1703, and since Indians' drinking made them sitting ducks for predators who wanted to get them into debt for both liquor and trade goods and then take their land in payment, no amount of legislation thereafter could stem the tide. The Nottoway population decreased rapidly, from an estimated ninety able-bodied men in 1669 to about thirty in 1730, as a result of alcoholism (best documented for the early nineteenth century), disease, war with other tribes like the Saponis,

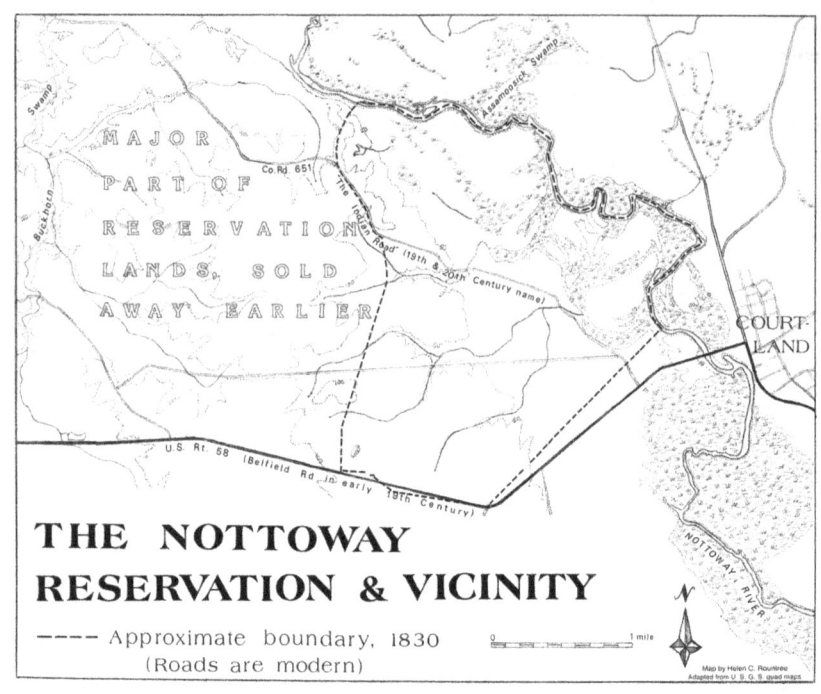

OLD NOTTOWAY RESERVATION
Map by Helen C. Rountree.

EDY TURNER'S SIGNATURE ON THE 1821 PETITION
Library of Virginia.

and the departure of people, either to join the Iroquois or to assimilate into English society. Virginia authorities assigned the Nottoways two large tracts of land in what are now the counties of Surry and Southampton, but the tribe began selling off pieces of it as early as 1734. The sales were conducted, after permission was given by the colonial legislature as required by the treaties, by Anglo-Virginian trustees who were locally important landowners. Regrettably, most of the trustees' records for that period, other than the deeds themselves, have been lost.[4]

Edy Turner was born around 1754—her age in 1808 was given as fifty-four—when the land sales were already well under way. Nothing was recorded about her birth, childhood, or young womanhood, but she probably lived on the square tract south of the Nottoway River, which the tribe held under a ruling of 1705 and the treaty of 1714. This reservation began a mile or so upstream from what came to be Southampton County's seat, now called Courtland. The Nottoway population had been bolstered in the 1740s with the addition of remnants of the Weyanocks and a group of Nansemonds, formerly part of the Algonquian-speaking Powhatans. Other Indians under pressure from white settlers, as well as some non-Indians, also may have joined what had become a fairly strong refugee community, where a reasonably traditional way of life could still be practiced. Edy Turner's ancestry may therefore not have been entirely Nottoway, but since she was born in the 1750s, there was still a good chance that she was a full-blooded Native American. She certainly grew up speaking the Nottoway language, which was the primary language of the people around her. She spoke fluent English in her old age, but she never learned to read or write, like most of her contemporaries (including many white men and most white women). She signed documents with her mark, which changed from one document to another, indicating that she was not trying to imitate any particular letter or sign.[5]

Edy Turner (whose personal Nottoway name was Wané Roonseraw) probably grew up within the traditional kinship system of the Nottoways. Judging from later records, that system seems to have been matrilineal—meaning that descent and inheritance were traced through the mother's line—but nothing else was ever recorded about it. We do not know if people lived in matrilineal extended families that included grandparents, unmarried children, married daughters, and their husbands and children, nor do we know if the Nottoways had even larger kinship groups or clans.

However, by the end of the eighteenth century poverty and alcoholism would have undermined any traditional structures that had survived in Nottoway society. According to the accounts of the tribe's trustees, the Nottoway people neither adopted English customs nor worked together in a more traditional way to help themselves: hence their continuing need to raise cash by selling land. Matrilineal rule also began working against the survival of the tribe because its population had become so small that people had to marry outside the tribe if they were to avoid committing incest. Native people with plenty of land could afford to take in nontribal husbands and confer full rights on those husbands and their children. But once the Nottoways' land base was greatly reduced, tribal rights became more precious, and Natives and their white trustees became more restrictive in offering access to land, essentially saying that only the children of female Nottoways would be deemed "Indian."[6] As one Nottoway man observed in 1823, male Nottoways who married outside the tribe could not pass tribal membership on to their children. As a result, they had little reason to exert themselves for the good of the community, or even to remain for long in it.[7]

By contrast, Nottoway women could marry outside their tribe without losing status, and Edy Turner apparently did. The Nottoways kept no marriage records, but one source indicates that Turner had a husband when she was in her fifties, and he was apparently not Native (because he is mentioned only in passing and not as a member of her "Indian" family). Nothing is known about whether she had a previous husband or any children. Her role as a wife is relatively easy to reconstruct, for it very probably was similar to that of women in more thoroughly documented eastern woodland Indian societies. Except for occasional trading, women left negotiations with whites to the men. They bore and then reared children, especially the girls. They made the family's clothing and household utensils, which included going some distance from home to collect the materials for the latter. Women and their children were the procurers of the firewood their families used for fuel. Finally, and most relevant to Edy Turner's story, they were the farmers of the family. Turner was brought up to be a farmer, so it should be no surprise that in her later years she was a good one, winning the approval of white observers. In the matter of occupation as in inheritance, it was the men in Edy's world who were at a disadvantage later on. They were brought up to the manly profession of hunting animals and people, but the guerrilla warfare had ended, and the tribe's hunting territory continually shrank. It was the women who had it better in the last years of the Nottoway reservation.[8]

Indeed, Edy Turner first appears in the historical record as a result of a land-related transaction. The surviving records do not mention chiefs (called *terheers*) among the Nottoways after the early eighteenth century, nor is there any indication of how an individual attained this position while it existed. Matrilineal inheritance may have played a part, but we cannot be certain. By the middle of the eighteenth century, Nottoway documents were being signed by all the adult men, who perhaps wielded some collective authority because of the overall smallness of the tribe's population. Their signing of documents, without official reference to the women, was certainly within traditional custom. But that tradition changed a few decades later. By 1780 Thomas Jefferson believed that there were few Native Americans left in his entire state and that the Nottoways in particular had been reduced to only "a few women." He was slightly off the mark: in 1792 the seven remaining Nottoway men signed a petition addressed to the state legislature in Richmond concerning the sale of yet more land, and then all the surviving adult Nottoways—seven men and three women—signed the resulting deeds. These deeds are Turner's first appearance in the historical record. When the next Nottoway petition went to Richmond in 1803, all nine surviving adult Nottoways signed it.[9]

Edy Turner would begin her rise to prominence soon thereafter, mainly by default on the part of her male contemporaries. The crisis began in 1806, when the last Nansemond living on the Nottoway reservation died, leaving behind three young people (relationship not recorded): Fanny and Solomon Bartlett, and Alexander Rogers. These youngsters had no relatives among the Nottoways and, according to the tribe's white trustees, at that time "not one of the Nottoways came to take care of them, or to inquire what was to be done with them." Rather than let them starve, the trustees took them into their own households. About the same time, young Billy Woodson's Nottoway mother died, and his white father, Micajah Bozeman, took him in. All four children were living within three miles of the reservation, but not actually on it. Their living away because nobody wanted to care for them constituted another drain on the Nottoway population, and Edy Turner became increasingly angry about it. Perhaps she asked the trustees to let her have the children, though there is no record of such a request. Or maybe she knew not to ask because the fact that she was related to none of the children might have made the trustees reluctant to consign them to her, though she is known to have taken other youngsters into her home by 1808.[10]

Edy's anger reached the ears of Governor William H. Cabell, probably through the trustees (no document survives), in the form of a charge that the four children were being detained by white people as servants without the permission of the tribe. That, if true, was illegal, so on June 5, 1808, the governor asked the trustees for a census of the Natives and a detailed report on the tribe's condition. The trustees obliged and, luckily for us, that document *does* survive. The July 1808 census is a time capsule that gives many details about the Nottoways, their families, and the trustees' attitude toward them all.[11]

In 1808, according to the census, there were only seventeen "real" Nottoways left, none of them with Indian spouses. Hints in the trustees' wording indicate a number of sequential unions, in and out of wedlock—county registers show no Nottoway marriages in this period—and blended or matrifocal families. The census takers reported that most of the reservation land was not being "used"—meaning that the Nottoways were not engaged in animal husbandry or farming—and that drunkenness was a major problem. They concluded that the Nottoway people were living in poverty that they had brought on themselves. Edy Turner, age fifty-four, had a husband, who had hired two "negroes" to cultivate the land she was using at the time. The trustees believed that she worked at "knitting, sewing, and what is usual in common housewifery"—in other words, the sorts of work thought to be appropriate for Anglo-Virginian (though not Indian) women. Edy's husband, about whom nothing further is known, did not count as an Indian in the trustees' eyes. "Her family consists of herself, Polly Woodson, and John Woodson," they reported. The Woodsons, who were aged fourteen and twelve, respectively, were possibly relatives.[12]

As for the four children living off-reservation, they were not being treated as servants. As it turned out, Billy Woodson—who later went by the name of William G. Bozeman—was being treated by his father as a son. The other three, the trustees reported, were also doing well. None of the Nottoways except Edy Turner was taking an interest in them, and the trustees had become very frustrated with what they apparently considered to be her nagging. In what may have been a sexual slur, they wrote to the governor that "we doubt much whether it would be possible for her to be satisfied long with the united attentions of every man in Virginia." At the very least, the staunchly patriarchal trustees were finding it hard to comprehend why this Indian woman believed she deserved serious attention, much less eventual satisfaction, from prominent white men such as themselves. It does not seem to have occurred to them that Edy may have lost patience with her fellow Nottoways' apathy over the dissolution of their tribe, and that she might have hoped to save them by training them in Anglo-style farming. She had probably surmised that taking a seemingly maternal interest in these motherless children was one approach that could secure sympathy and help from the trustees. Her efforts failed, at least initially, because the trustees' letter resulted in the children being left where they were.

Apparently, however, Edy kept on complaining to the trustees and others, including the governor, and she was aided by the fact that the Nottoways had some genuine legal problems. Some of the non-Indians leasing Nottoway land were not paying as they should, while other non-Indians were moving onto Native land as squatters. On December 14, 1808, Cabell's successor, Governor John Tyler, wrote a letter to the trustees in which he stated that the bylaws for the tribe were "incomplete" because they did not prevent such abuses. But the governor also went on to order that all four of the children who were living off-reservation were to be "immediately restored to the tribe," after which, paradoxically, they were to be "put to school, or bound [as] apprentices" with the permission of the Nottoways. Either one of those educational avenues would have meant removing them from the reservation again, but at least this time it would be done with the approval of the adult Nottoways.[13] So Billy Woodson would be taken away from his own father, thanks to Edy Turner's determination to try to keep young people in her Indian community. But he had stayed with his father long enough to learn to read and write, making him the only literate Nottoway of his time.

The trustees duly had all the children returned to the reservation, though they never mentioned with whom the youngsters lived once they got there. The likely candidate was Edy Turner, who with her own successful adaptation could teach them how usefully to blend Indian and white ways and become intensive farmers. Jedidiah Morse, a New Englander who toured the United States in 1820 "under a commission from the president . . . for the purpose of ascertaining . . . the actual state of the Indian tribes in our country," described Turner as the "reigning Queen" of the Nottoways and as one who had "good sense [i.e., she showed evidence of thinking as he did], easy and fluent in [English] conversation." His report added that she "manages her farming and other business with discretion and profit."[14]

The trustees, however, were not interested in Natives staying on the reservation as farmers. They wanted to see Indian youngsters become craftsmen, but they would have to live off-reservation in order to practice their crafts. Thus the trustees had little success getting the Nottoways' permission to enroll the children in the desired schools or apprenticeships. If the tribal members thought further ahead at all, they probably thought that Edy's plan made more sense than apprenticeships, because farming not only kept young people close to home but it was also a viable occupation for whites and Indians alike. Indeed, some of Virginia's Powhatan tribes had already adapted to their own dire circumstances by becoming Anglo-style farmers, though the Nottoways may not have been aware of that development.[15]

Hence the frustrated trustees informed the governor on February 17, 1809:

> We have already used every argument in our power to induce them to use the habits of sobriety, industry, frugality, &c., but without effect. If your Excellency would have the goodness to direct us how we are to manage, or what kind of rules will be proper for a people destitute of those habits, we shall acknowledge it as a

particular favour, and pursue the direction willingly. Schooling the children belonging to the Tribe has been mentioned to the grown Indians [in accordance with the 1714 treaty], and the propriety of it made as plain to them as we could make it. They sometimes seem willing to send them to [boarding] school, but that is as far as they have progressed, and we fear as they ever will without compulsion, which we have no authority to use. . . . Since the receipt of your letter the subject of binding the children [as] apprentices [to white neighbors] has been mentioned to the Tribe, to which they answered that an Indian was never known as [an] apprentice. There is, therefore, no prospect of an artisan from among them.

Not only that, but the Nottoways no longer wanted any more land leased out to bring in cash, even though they were near to starving. "Their objections are that the white people are already as near them as they wish them to be, and that if they are to have nearer neighbors they desire to have the choosing [of] them."[16]

Lack of Native literacy, in the trustees' view, compounded the problems they faced in dealing with the generally untrustworthy Nottoways. In 1809, when Governor Tyler inquired about tribal finances (in a letter that has not survived), the trustees replied that it was very hard to be certain about the state of the Nottoways' affairs, much less to keep records of them. "Application may be made for a little money; it is furnished; the articles are charged, but where are the vouchers in support of such charges to be obtained from?" they complained, adding, "The Indians don't write, and if they did their receipts in such cases would avail but little without a witness." In June 1809 Virginia's attorney general nevertheless gave the trustees directions about how to defend the tribe's land better from nonpaying lessees and illegal squatters. And there matters rested, as far as the historical record is concerned: no further correspondence survives for a time.[17]

The Nottoways apparently went on living precariously, and the four children finished growing up on the reservation. Edy Turner's prominence grew during that time and apparently became legitimated somehow. In an 1818 petition to the Virginia General Assembly, she had the person writing on her behalf call her the "female chief" of the Nottoways, while the trustees and other white observers occasionally called her the Nottoway "queen." During these years she was one of only three people on the reservation who could still speak the Nottoway language, the other two being a blind man and a male invalid. Her own health seems to have been good. Apparently thinking that her farming-education program would work with the younger people, her policy as chief was to try to sell off more land. Later, her objective would be to divide the remaining lands among individual Indians, each of whom would enjoy the right of private possession and ownership.

In the 1818 petition to the general assembly, endorsed with a note from the trustees, Edy Turner—along with Anny and Polly Woodson, Fanny Bartlett, Henry Turner, and Alex Rogers—asked for the trustees' permission to sell all the remaining reservation land and invest the proceeds in "some profitable stock."[18] Though the six of them constituted only part of the Nottoway tribe, the petitioners asked for the authority to dispose of all of the Nottoways' land. The legislators were only partially cooperative, allowing the trustees to sell about one-third of the land, which they did.[19] In 1821 Edy Turner and her supporters tried a new tactic, this time petitioning for permission to have the remaining land divided among them, to be owned by the individuals in fee simple (in other words, absolutely).[20]

Farming on individual plots might have been workable for Edy's faction, but for most of the Nottoways the situation was sufficiently difficult that the trustees endorsed the 1821 petition only with reservations. They informed the legislators that the tribe had increased to about thirty people—up from twenty-six in 1818—most of whom were "women with large families of children," adding that "Edy Turner their Queen is nearly 70 years of age" and that the "principal male of their tribe" was older than she and completely blind. Not only that, but one young man, Alex Rogers, had incurred legal bills after he was tried twice for murder in the Southampton County Superior Court.[21]

This situation was enough to set off an alarm in the legislators' minds, so on December 27, a member of the House of Delegates asked the trustees for further information. The reply, four days later, from trustee Jeremiah Cobb was positively scathing. Most of the Indians were drunkards, he averred:

> Altho their lands are capable of producing any & every crop common for this section of the country, & blessed with the finest Cattle & Hog range, yet they dont make a support [of themselves] by one half; owing entirely to their indolence and fondness for spirituous liquors; there is no property they would not sacrifice for this article.... I have no hesitation in saying that they are destitute of both economy, prudence, or industry, and were their lands to be divided among them at discretion, they would scarcely have a hut to shelter themselves in five years....
> I am therefore of opinion that should the legislature pass a law agreeably to the prayer of their petition, that in a few years this county will be faced with them on the parish [i.e., on public relief].

Understandably, the legislature balked at granting the petition.[22]

The unsuccessful 1821 petition has a special interest for anthropologists and historians because in it, for the one and only time, Edy Turner and some of her young followers gave their Nottoway names as well as their English ones. The exception was "T. M." (probably William) Bozeman—the former Billy Woodson—who had no Nottoway name and who also signed for himself, proving he was literate at least to the extent that he could sign his name. The likely explanation of why Edy Turner, Polly Woodson, and Solomon Rogers (who may be the same person as Solomon Bartlett) wanted their names on the document in both languages is that some of their neighbors had recently been taking an interest in them *as Indians*. The March 17, 1820, issue of a Petersburg newspaper included an anonymous four-paragraph report on the Nottoways, mainly focusing on an interview with Edy Turner. Jedidiah Morse later republished the piece as part of his larger report on American Indians that had been commissioned by the federal government.[23]

As we have seen, Morse's brief but positive assessment of Edy Turner was the complete opposite of Jeremiah Cobb's unflattering description of the Nottoway people. Also significant was the visitor's report that Edy and two other tribal elders were the only remaining people who knew how to speak the Nottoway language. That observation stirred the interest of students of linguistics, with the result that two word lists (but regrettably, no full sentences in Nottoway) were recorded and published in the next few decades. The source of the word lists, gathered independently by neighbors J. Wood and James Trezvant, was Edy Turner.[24]

Unfortunately, it was too late for Edy's efforts to perpetuate her people's language to take hold. Keeping a language alive requires a large community of speakers, most of whom have most of their dealings with each other in their own language, rather than with outsiders in the language of those outsiders. That kind of regular immersion was impossible, because the tiny Nottoway community in 1820 was very far from being that self-sufficient. The Nottoways were surrounded by, and to a great extent dependent on, English-speaking Virginians.

Turner finally got her way, however, in terms of the allotment and disposal of the reservation lands. In this effort, the support of Billy Woodson/William G. Bozeman was instrumental. In 1823, probably with her encouragement, Bozeman presented a very persuasive petition, in which he presented himself as just the sort of serious, ambitious, and hardworking man that the legislators were apt to take seriously. A promising young man who, because of the matrilineal system of tribal membership, would never see any of his children become tribal members, Bozeman declared that he wanted to leave the moribund tribe and make his own way, but he needed his share of the tribe's land and money to do it. The trustees wrote him a glowing endorsement, without mentioning any desire they may have had to see all the troublesome Nottoways vanish into the distance. The general assembly granted Bozeman's wish—and also, probably, Edy's wish—not only because it allowed Bozeman to get his share, but also because the special law it passed for him in 1824 also provided that more Indians in the future could apply for and get land through their county court. That provision effectively let the legislature turn the dissolution of the reservation over to Southampton County authorities.[25]

The first Nottoways to claim their allotments were Edy Turner and William Bozeman, but they waited until May 1830 to do so. We cannot be sure why they waited, but it is easy to conjecture about their reasons for doing it when they did. Nat Turner's 1831 insurrection—a major slave revolt that took place in Southampton County, a few miles away from the Nottoway reservation—was fifteen months in the future, and no Nottoways would be involved in it. But it would have been common knowledge early in 1830 that public pressure from whites was making the Virginia legislature move toward passing laws that would discriminate severely against free people of color—meaning all nonwhites—which in fact happened in the 1831–32 session, in the aftermath of the insurrection.[26]

By 1830 it was already illegal in Virginia for free people of color to marry whites, hold office, testify in court except against slaves, vote, live and work without keeping a certificate of free birth ready to show questioners, or use a gun without a county license. Since 1806 it had been illegal to teach nonwhite children, if they were orphans bound out by the county overseer of the poor, how to read. Less than a year after Edy Turner and William Bozeman sold their land, a new statute made it illegal to teach *any* nonwhites in the state to read, which drastically reduced their ability to communicate among themselves (and with white abolitionists). During the spring after the insurrection, a raft of new laws went into effect: any assemblies were forbidden to all nonwhites, except for church services conducted by white clergy; no guns were allowed them under any circumstances (even for hunting for food); and any free nonwhite accused of a felony was to be tried in a Court of Oyer and Terminer, rather than getting a trial by jury. Virginia was becoming a very difficult place for free people of color, which is what most Natives who cut ties with their reservation would legally become.[27]

In March 1830 Turner and Bozeman asked for and got their land, and two months later they sold all of it except for two acres, on which Edy would presumably continue to live. Interestingly, the land they received as a result of their petition was the least valuable part of the reservation, according to the surveyors. The original county court decree and the report of the surveyors have been lost, but copies remain archived in the folder with Bozeman's 1823 petition. After the sale, there were 3,109 acres left of the reservation and twenty-six people entitled to share in them. The least valuable land would have been near the Nottoway River, on its marshy floodplain. The river did not form the boundary of any subsequent allotments. Given the short time they owned the land, Turner and Bozeman may have selected it deliberately, knowing they would shortly sell it and wishing to leave the remaining tribal members with the better farmland.[28]

Bozeman disappears thereafter from the Virginia records, presumably leaving the state, as did many young Virginians in the early nineteenth century. A troubled economy, coupled with the various punitive statutes enacted to control nonwhites in the aftermath of Nat Turner's insurrection, made the early 1830s an excellent time for Bozeman or any young Nottoway to think about leaving.[29] Edy Turner was too old to leave, being by then in her late seventies. She may also have rejected the idea of leaving her homeland and the last of her people, who were as yet making no move to sell out. Indeed, some of them would hold out beyond the 1850s.

Edy Turner died in 1838. The fact that she left a will—which, after all, was an Anglo-Virginian legal device—made her unique among the Nottoways. Turner's will, which was made on February 26 and proved on March 19, was brief, and it mentioned no children or any other relatives. Edy directed that her estate pay any debts she owed, and she left the remainder, including her personal property (a mare, a cart and wheels, a yearling bull, a sow, farming utensils, kitchen furniture, plus four "house pigs") to "Edwin Turner, one of the Indian tribe." One last time, Edy Turner was helping a protégé. Although his relationship to her is impossible to reconstruct, the 1870 Census listed him as living in Southampton County with his wife and eleven children, the youngest of whom was named Edie. Edwin Turner proved to be the most entrepreneurial Nottoway of his generation: by 1870 he owned land worth five thousand dollars and personal property worth one thousand dollars. When he died, some time during the 1870s, he bequeathed some land to his children, though there is evidence that his fortunes had declined somewhat during Reconstruction.[30]

The Nottoways' only recorded "female chief" appeared late in the tribe's history—too late to save it. It was late in her own lifetime too, indicating that she may not have taken action willingly, at least initially. Edy Turner was in her fifties (which counted as old in those days), her people had traveled far down the road to dissolution, and the white trustees appointed to protect them had reached the end of their patience with Natives who wanted to remain traditional, unrealistic as that desire was by the early nineteenth century. It is ironic that the economic course Turner advocated—intensive agriculture and land use—coincided with the ideas and customs of many white men of her era, which for the Nottoways were doomed to failure. Neither selling off the rest of the reservation land nor allotting it to individuals would make the Indians, especially most of the men, into Anglo-style farmers who could hold their community together. Long after the tribe had been reduced to less than two dozen people, Edy Turner tried to keep the Nottoways intact, an effort that proved to be fruitless. She did, however, cooperate with some local whites who recorded some of the Nottoway language's words, and for that scholars remain everlastingly grateful to her.

NOTES

1. For a history of the tribe, see Lewis R. Binford, "An Ethnohistory of the Nottoway, Meherrin and Weanock Indians of Southeastern Virginia," *Ethnohistory* 14 (1967): 103–218; and Helen C. Rountree, "The Termination and Dispersal of the Nottoway Indians of Virginia," *Virginia Magazine of History and Biography* 95 (1987): 193–214.

2. Treaty between Virginia and the Indians, 1677, in "Virginia Colonial Records," *Virginia Magazine of History and Biography* 14 (1906–7): 289–96; Treaty, 1714, in *Early American Indian Documents: Treaties and Laws 1607–1789*, ed. W. Stitt Robinson (Frederick, Md.: University Publications of America, 1983), 4:216–20.

3. H. R. McIlwaine et al., eds., *Executive Journals of the Council of Colonial Virginia*, 6 vols. (Richmond: Virginia State Library, 1925–66), 4:303. On Indians' antipathy toward domesticated livestock, especially cattle, see Virginia DeJohn Anderson, *Creatures of Empire: How Domestic Animals Transformed Early America* (New York: Oxford University Press, 2004), esp. chap. 7.

4. On the Nottoway population over time, see McIlwaine et al., *Executive Journals*, 2:315–16; William Noel Sainsbury et al., eds., *Calendar of State Papers, Colonial Series*, 60 vols. (London: HMSO, 1860–1912), 21:376–77, 37:217–18; William Waller Hening, comp., *The Statutes at Large: Being a Collection of All the Laws of Virginia*, 13 vols. (Richmond, Va.: Samuel Pleasants Jr., 1810–23), 2:274. On land sales, see Hening, *Statutes at Large*, 4:459–61; H. L. McIlwaine et al., eds., *Legislative Journals of the Council of Colonial Virginia*, 3 vols. (Richmond: Virginia State Library, 1918); and Deed Books of Isle of Wight and Southampton Counties, cited in Rountree, "Termination and Dispersal."

5. Rountree, "Termination and Dispersal," 193–99; H. R. McIlwaine et al., eds., *Journal of the House of Burgesses*, 13 vols. (Richmond: Virginia State Library, 1915) 4:98; Robinson, *Early American Indian Documents*, 4:216–20. The reservation originated in a treaty between the Nottoways and Great Britain. In 1776 the newly independent Commonwealth of Virginia (not yet officially part of a larger confederation) assumed the responsibilities for the reservation that the treaty had assigned to the British monarch.

6. The trustees' 1808 census plainly shows this narrowing definition of who officially counted as Indians. In this census, the children of male Natives—all of whom had non-Indian wives—are not listed, but the children of Native women are recorded by name on the census list.

7. Petition of William Bozeman, December 13, 1823, Legislative Petitions, Southampton County, Library of Virginia.

8. Peace with the Saponis came in 1733; the last threat from the Catawbas was in 1735. See McIlwaine et al., *Executive Journals*, 4:303, 356. On Edy Turner's husband, see Commonwealth of Virginia, Executive Papers, July 18, 1808, Library of Virginia.

9. Petitions of the Nottoway Indians, December 11, 1792, and December 9, 1803, Legislative Peti-

tions, Southampton County; and Southampton County Deeds 8:97 and following, all in Library of Virginia. See also Thomas Jefferson, *Notes on the State of Virginia*, in *The Portable Thomas Jefferson*, ed. Merrill D. Peterson (New York: Penguin, 1975), 134–38.

10. Commonwealth of Virginia, Executive Papers, July 18, 1808.

11. Ibid.

12. Ibid.

13. Ibid., December 14, 1808. The attorney general's advice to the governor, which prompted this letter, is filed along with the letter.

14. Jedidiah Morse, *A Report . . . on Indian Affairs* (New Haven, Conn.: S. Converse, 1822), 31.

15. Helen C. Rountree, *Pocahontas's People: The Powhatan Indians of Virginia through Four Centuries* (Norman: University of Oklahoma Press, 1990), chaps. 7–8.

16. William P. Palmer et al., eds., *Calendar of Virginia State Papers*, 11 vols. (Richmond, Va.: H. W. Flournoy, 1875–93), 10:46–47; Petition of William Bozeman, December 13, 1823, Legislative Petitions, Southampton County.

17. Palmer et al., *Calendar of Virginia State Papers*, 10:52–53, 63–69.

18. Petition of Edy Turner et al., December 16, 1818, Legislative Petitions, Southampton County.

19. Southampton County Deeds 17:97–104, 21:287.

20. Petition of Edy Turner et al., December 11, 1821, Legislative Petitions, Southampton County.

21. Petition of Nottoway Indians, December 10, 1821, ibid.; Southampton County Common Law Order Books of Superior Court, 1:416, 419, 440, 444; 2:1.

22. Jeremiah Cobb letter, December 31, 1821, in Legislative Petitions, Southampton County.

23. The newspaper article is reprinted in Morse, *Report . . . on Indian Affairs*, 31.

24. Albert Gallatin, "Appendix: Vocabularies," in "A Synopsis of the Indian Tribes of North America," *Archaeologia Americana: Transactions and Collections of the American Antiquarian Society* 2 (1836): 307–67; Gallatin, "Hale's Indians of North-west America, and Vocabularies of North America, with an Introduction," *Transactions of the American Ethnological Society* 2 (1847): 115.

25. Petition of William Bozeman, December 13, 1823, Legislative Petitions, Southampton County.

26. For a concise account of the Nat Turner insurrection and its aftermath, see Lacy K. Ford, *Deliver Us from Evil: The Slavery Question in the Old South* (New York: Oxford University Press, 2009), 338–57.

27. Hening, *Statutes at Large*, 3:87, 251, 298; 4:122; Samuel Shepherd, ed., *The Statutes at Large of Virginia . . . Being a Continuation of Hening*, 3 vols. (Richmond, Va.: Samuel Shepherd, 1835), 1:238, 2:417–18, 3:274.

28. Southampton County Deeds, 21:381.

29. See, for instance, Philip J. Schwarz, *Migrants against Slavery: Virginians and the Nation* (Charlottesville: University of Virginia Press, 2001).

30. Southampton County Deeds, 28:699; Southampton County Wills 12:106, Library of Virginia; 1870 Census, Southampton County, Boykins Depot Township, 21.

Ann R. Page and Mary L. Custis

From Annfield and Arlington to Africa, with Love

DEBORAH A. LEE

First, she emancipated herself. In 1810 Ann Randolph Meade Page—the daughter of slaveholders and, with her husband, Matthew Page, one of the largest slaveholders in Frederick County, Virginia—could no longer uphold the status quo. By her own account, an old, blind black woman rescued her from a deep depression, a quagmire of guilt and self-condemnation, and helped her to see the world with fresh eyes, infused with the joy and power of evangelical religion. She realized that slaveholding could not be reconciled with the spirit of Christianity. She acted on her new spiritual convictions and found solidarity with her cousin Mary Lee Fitzhugh Custis—known as Molly—the wife of George Washington Parke Custis of Arlington. Together they labored to end slavery and prepare those in bondage for freedom.

At first frustrated by their inability to work beyond their households, the women found agency through the American Colonization Society (ACS), which was founded in Washington, D.C., in December 1816 to colonize free people of color on the west coast of Africa. The women hoped that this organization would encourage manumissions and gradually end slavery. They worked tirelessly for the organization, advocating, collecting donations, recruiting, mentoring male leaders in the cause, and preparing and emancipating emigrants. They developed social networks that crossed the Atlantic Ocean and religious, gender, and racial boundaries. Their activism shows how certain white slaveholding women, influenced by their close relationships with enslaved people and acting on an expanded social consciousness and sense of responsibility, exercised leadership in transforming the nation and the world. The people they emancipated helped establish and develop the colony of Liberia, which became the first independent republic in Africa in 1847. While their legacy is profoundly mixed, their intentions, activism, and effects should be acknowledged and understood.[1]

Although (and because) they were affluent slaveholders, few antislavery activists, northern or southern, were as committed and influential as Ann R. Page and Mary L. Custis. They embraced colonization, a movement that began and had its greatest support in the Upper South, because it relied on moral suasion, offered African Americans a refuge from the prejudice and legal inequality they suffered in the United States, and helped to defuse whites' fears about the growing number of free blacks. They believed their efforts would benefit Africa by helping to end the illegal slave trade, spread Christianity, and boost commerce. Colonization was also the limit of what was possible for southern antislavery activists, especially elites, at that time. Unlike many white southerners who opposed slavery, however, Page and Custis wanted to end slavery for the benefit of black people as well as white. In the 1830s, as moral suasion yielded little progress, northerners increasingly supported abolitionist demands for immediate, unconditional emancipation. While colonization and abolition had markedly different philosophies, strategies, and tactics, they shared the humanitarian goals of ending slavery and uplifting African Americans.[2]

Ann Randolph Meade Page and Mary Lee Fitzhugh Custis's transformation into antislavery crusaders began with their mothers, who were close kin. Ann's mother, Mary Fitzhugh Grymes Meade, was a niece of Molly's parents, Ann Bolling Randolph and William Fitzhugh of Chatham in Fredericksburg. Ann Meade was born at Chatham in 1781. Ann Fitzhugh's first child, Mary Lee, followed in 1788. The two girls were thus first cousins, one generation removed. Their mothers worked to instill values of Christian piety and republican simplicity, along with that sense of order, entitlement, and responsibility that came with being at the top of a hierarchical society. Mary Meade recognized enslaved people's humanity, taught them to read, and saw that they were cared for. She warned her children, "Your guests see your well-spread table, but God sees in the negro's cabin," and in her will she allowed the enslaved people to choose their new owners from among her heirs. At the same time, Meade cautioned her children not to mix with their slaves socially lest they lose their respect. Ann Fitzhugh seemed similarly inclined. Ann Meade copied extracts from Fitzhugh's writings, such as "Narrow is that man's soul, which the good of himself, or his own immediate family, engrosseth. But he who with benevolence, warm as the heat of the sun, and diffusive as its light, takes in, all mankind, and is sincerely interested for the welfare of the whole, enjoys all the good that is

ANN RANDOLPH MEADE PAGE

Soon after marrying a wealthy slaveholder in 1799, Ann Page experienced a spiritual crisis and renewal. Slavery, she then understood, was irreconcilable with the teachings of Christ. Wielding power from her religion and social position, she enacted reforms and manumissions in her household, promoted emancipation and the education of black people, and campaigned to end slavery through the American Colonization Society.

Frontispiece of C. W. Andrews, *Memoir of Mrs. Ann R. Page* (New York: Protestant Episcopal Society for the Promotion of Evangelical Knowledge, 1856).

MARY LEE FITZHUGH CUSTIS

From her home at what is now known as Arlington House, the Robert E. Lee Memorial, Mary L. Custis was a leader in the movement for the gradual end of slavery. A key figure in a network of uneasy slaveholders and progressive clergy in the Upper South, Custis worked closely with managers of the American Colonization Society. Her daughter Mary married R. E. Lee, who, like many others, admired Custis for her intelligence and character.
Virginia Historical Society.

done in the world." Such socialization prepared the girls for benevolent work in the future.³

Their world had its dark side, however, which was exposed in a violent incident in 1805. On January 2, after the enslaved people at Chatham had enjoyed their customary six-day Christmas holiday, the overseer ordered them back to work. Six men refused. When the overseer became more forceful, the Fitzhugh slaves tied him up and whipped him, then allowed him to escape. The overseer returned with four "gentlemen," but "these were also secured by the negroes, and underwent a severe corporal punishment." The white men were released, but returned with warrants and an armed posse. They shot and killed one enslaved man and severely wounded another as they attempted to escape; a third drowned in the river. Three men apprehended were tried for "conspiracy and insurrection" and condemned to death, though two were instead transported out of the country. One white man later died of the injuries sustained in the beating. Whether they were present or not, surely this violent conflict made a considerable impression on the young women, and probably reminded them of Gabriel's thwarted slave insurrection in Richmond five years earlier.⁴

While such events might frighten one into questioning slavery, there were also religious reasons to do so. On March 23, 1799, Ann Randolph Meade had married Matthew Page, a wealthy planter, who owned roughly one hundred slaves and a large plantation in Frederick County near Berryville. Page renamed his estate "Annfield" in honor of his new wife. As Ann adjusted to life as a plantation mistress, she began to question slavery and sank into a deep depression. Her spiritual conversion was facilitated by an elderly, blind black woman, who came into her bedchamber when no other white person was near. On that occasion, Ann later recalled, "We began a conversation in which she used expressions respecting entire confidence in Christ, which made an indelible impression upon my mind." After this exchange, Ann often visited this spiritual counselor—who lived nearby but not on the Page plantation—in her cottage. Ann believed that this woman was "a living example of Christ formed in the soul," and admitted, "I think I owe her, under God, much of my religious joy in after-years."⁵ In other words, the meeting changed her life.

Ann's cousin Mary Lee Fitzhugh Custis of Arlington became her close confidante and ally in family matters and in the antislavery cause. Molly married George Washington Parke Custis, a grandson of Martha Washington, in July 1804 and moved into a partially completed house at Arlington. The columned home with its large collection of Washington family artifacts, situated high on the banks of the Potomac overlooking the capital city, signified its residents' high status. Nevertheless, the ensuing years were challenging for Molly, who lost her parents, gave birth to four children, and buried three. There is evidence that her husband also fathered children with enslaved women.[6] In 1807 Molly Custis was at Annfield when she gave birth to a daughter, Mary Anna Randolph Custis. This future wife of Robert E. Lee, the hero of the Confederacy, came to share her mother's evangelical religious views and antislavery sentiments.[7]

After Ann Randolph Page's conversion experience, she found slavery unconscionable and devoted herself to improving conditions for the people who suffered as a result of it. She excluded herself from Sunday "dining about" and spent more time and money to elevate the lives of those in bondage at Annfield. She conducted classes for children and others "not employed on the plantations," teaching them to read and giving them Bibles. To replace the old dormitory-style slave dwellings, she designed duplex quarters with corner cupboards, fenced yards for the safety of young children, and bedrooms for the girls to support nuclear family life and values. In one case, she protected an orphaned girl from the predations of their overseer. She conducted religious services for those who would attend. She wrote, "I earnestly desire to fix on a plan for the most speedy and advantageous delivery of these slaves from bondage, not only temporal but spiritual." She talked with white visitors to Annfield about religion and the immorality of slavery, and kept a supply of tracts and pamphlets to distribute among them. Meanwhile, Molly Custis undertook similar efforts at Arlington.[8]

While a number of enslaved people at Annfield and Arlington learned to read and write, and some eventually professed Christianity, they often resisted their mistresses' efforts to further shape their lives. Ann Page poured out her frustrations in pages of written prayers, lamenting the "murmuring and rebellious language toward me," while reminding herself of her own shortcomings and need for a proper spirit and self-control. After visiting both Annfield and the home of Ann's brother William Meade, Ann C. Robinson remarked, "I could not help being a little comforted . . . by finding that the servants of William and Mrs Page are not more Godly than my own; I was comforted not by finding sin abounded in the families of my friends, but because I hoped all the evil which I see at home, is not caused by my unfaithful teaching." At Arlington, the situation was even less controlled; the estate was notorious for the unruliness of its enslaved workers and the haplessness of the Custis and Lee families in governing them. Since many of these individuals proved accomplished both in slavery and in freedom, their behavior probably reflected their natural resistance to slavery itself. Selina Gray, for example, managed the household and the Washington artifacts admirably when Mary C. Lee left Arlington during the Civil War, and afterward operated a fifteen-acre produce farm and business with her husband.[9]

Both Page and Custis cultivated emotionally intimate relationships with their enslaved people, especially the women, most demonstrably when they were sick or dying. When Page's son-in-law the Reverend Charles W. Andrews overheard her speaking to an enslaved woman "in the most sweet and heavenly manner," it moved him to tears. Not all slaves appreciated this sort of intervention, however: Anna, an enslaved woman at Annfield, died suddenly of an abscess without professing faith in God. Nonetheless a bond had existed between Ann and Anna. "She was so much in my affection from different circumstances of friendship and attention and feeling, she had often shewn me when I have been in trouble," Page lamented. "I know I will miss her so much. . . . I did not know how much I loved her till now." The distraught mistress decided to "take hope even against hope" that "*some* must possess the requisite gifts of the new covenant without knowing it—while others who possess knowledge have not the true spirit."[10]

One who deeply appreciated such ministrations was Lilly, whom Molly Custis had attended during a prolonged and serious illness. Unable to reciprocate when Molly herself became ill, Lilly wrote her a long letter in which she credited her own survival to Molly's visiting in "all weathers to read & encourage me to persevere," adding, "you are the person I love next to God & it must be a gift from God or I could not love you as I do." Now it was Lilly's turn to minister. "'Jesus whispered to my heart & told me I was his,'" she wrote. "*I not only felt glory in my heart* but the whole house seemed enlightened[.] *I felt that my heart could not be the same* that it had been. I felt in an entirely new frame. I hope you have felt the same." These women—free and enslaved—shared some of their deepest and most meaningful life experiences through the language of Christian love. These relationships were not true friendships because the inherent violence of slavery made trust across the color line problematic. But the black women demonstrated a strength of character and a generosity of spirit that reinforced the white women's religious antislavery convictions. Lilly lived in New York City by 1845 and remained in touch with the Custises who, without formally emancipating her, likely allowed her to live as free.[11]

Many of Ann Page's peers criticized her activities as "endangering the peace of the community." Others called her a slave to her slaves. As son-in-law Andrews explained, "The troubles of those who undertake to labor for the slaves in the Southern States can not well be conceived, if the laborer's standard of duty rises much above that of the community. He has to do with a subject on which people quickly become violent, and on which too many Christians are soon angry. This state of things tries the fidelity of ministers, and strongly tempts them to keep back things which can not be kept back consistently with a good conscience." Ann Page attested that "the fear of God enabled me to overcome the fear of man." She had the tacit support of her husband, who allowed her to conduct the school and religious services and agreed not to sell his slaves—and thereby separate slave families—though he forbade manumissions.[12]

The women saw the opportunity to expand their efforts beyond their households when, in 1815, they read about the antislavery ideas of the Congregationalist minister Samuel John Mills and the Presbyterian minister Robert F. Finley, who advocated forming an organization to establish a colony for free blacks on the west coast of Africa. The clergymen hoped that colonization would encourage manumissions, which had become more difficult in Virginia after 1806, when a new law required any former slave to leave the state within a year of receiving freedom. Mills and Finley, both northerners, had many allies in the mid-Atlantic region, including the northern Virginia congressman Charles Fenton Mercer and Maryland's Francis Scott Key. To Ann Page, the plan appeared as a distant candle in the darkness. Surely she and Molly Custis encouraged participation in the American Colonization Society's organizing meeting in Washington in December 1816. Ralph Gurley, the longtime secretary of the ACS, later recognized their early antislavery activism. He remarked that even "long before the formation of the Colonization Society, . . . a few devout ladies in Virginia" devoted themselves "to teach, comfort and save" the "afflicted Africans," and through their "zeal and charity . . . inspired ministers and statesmen . . . in their cause." For the rest of their lives, their support and commitment never wavered.[13]

Ann Page and Molly Custis mentored men in the colonization movement, beginning with their younger brothers, William Meade and William Henry Fitzhugh. Their mothers had chosen the College of New Jersey at Princeton for their sons because of its evangelical orientation. The cousins tied for first honors. William Meade delivered the valedictory address on the importance of education for women; a copy of the oration is written in his sister Ann's hand. He felt called to enter the ministry, but Ann and Molly believed that he was not ready, and Molly arranged for him to continue his studies under Walter Addison, an evangelically inclined Episcopal minister in Georgetown. Under Addison's tutelage, the earnest young man experienced the requisite spiritual conversion and recognized the immorality of slavery. He was ordained in 1811, helped revive the Episcopal Church in Virginia, and was ordained the bishop of Virginia in 1829. Throughout his career, Meade considered African Americans an important part of his ministry.[14]

Meade also became a founder of the American Colonization Society and an early agent for it. He traveled the east coast, speaking and establishing auxiliary societies. His local ACS group, the Frederick County Auxiliary, was the first one formed and contributed more money than any other in the commonwealth. Its published 1820 annual report was a bracing antislavery document that recognized the merits and potential of people of color and maintained that their exclusion from full political participation was a danger to the republic: "Who would submit to a negro president or a negro chief justice? The very idea inspires indignation and contempt. Thus degraded in the scale of existence, the emancipated negro must be habitually prone to infamy and rebellion." Conceding that white elites considered race prejudice nearly immutable, the report maintained that African colonization would reduce racial tensions in the United States and would offer black Americans a place where they could live and work free of such prejudice. While Africa would benefit from Western-style civilization, commerce, and Christianity, white Americans would have an opportunity to atone for the sin of slavery.[15]

William Meade was circumspect about criticizing slavery in public, but he made his feelings clear in private. In 1823 he confessed to his cousin Molly Custis that he regarded the issue "as the first in importance to our unhappy and I must say guilty land." He lamented, "We make the sins of our Fathers our own, we clasp our chains, entail misery & vice upon our children by not adopting the most effectual means of removing an evil which grows with our growth and strengthens with our strength, and will soon outgrow us & bear us to the ground." Meade emancipated his own slaves—he held eleven in 1830—and honored their wishes by helping them to settle in Pennsylvania. After his sister Ann died in 1838, however, he became less involved in the colonization movement and, like most white male Virginians in the 1830s, he backed away from antislavery. Later in his life, another clergyman wishing to emancipate his slaves sought Meade's counsel. According to his memoirist, Meade advised that "if he could not retain his servants himself, he should provide them with good masters."[16]

Ann Page and Molly Custis similarly worked with Molly's younger brother William Henry Fitzhugh. He and his wife, Anna Maria, lived at Ravensworth, the largest farm in Fairfax County. Their home served as a place of gathering and retreat for a large network of extended family and friends. The women urged William to build single-family slave quarters at Ravensworth rather than the dormitory style. Fitzhugh became the ACS's vice president in 1820 and eloquently defended the colonization cause against both proslavery and antislavery critics in the 1820s. He developed an emancipation plan and a promising pilot program for his slaves at Ravensworth, by which they rented his farmland and received credit for the goods they produced, with the surplus going toward the purchase of their freedom. Fitzhugh served in the state legislature and as a delegate to the Virginia Constitutional Convention of 1829–30, where he supported democratic reforms. He died tragically in 1830. In his will, he directed that his slaves be freed in 1850 and provided funds for their resettlement outside of Virginia, as the law required, plus a $50 incentive if they chose to go to Liberia. The delay provided financial support for his widow and time for Liberia to develop, but these freed people chose to remain in the United States. Molly Custis and Mary Lee forewent cash bequests of $1,000 to enable the executor, Anna Maria Fitzhugh, to better manage the estate and carry out the desired emancipations.[17]

Ann Page also mentored the Vermont Congregationalist Charles Wesley Andrews, who came to Virginia and worked as a tutor for her brother Richard Meade. Andrews was ordained in the Episcopal Church in 1832 and married Page's eldest daughter, Sarah, the following year. The couple lived at Annfield while he worked as Bishop William Meade's assistant and as general agent for the Virginia Colonization Society. In 1836 Andrews traveled throughout the state and heard many people remark that "they had never felt any particular interest in the condition of slaves, or had their conscience awakened respecting them, until they heard of the efforts of Mrs. Page." A colleague observed that Andrews "was very much impressed by the earnestness and devotion of her Christian life," and "her influence upon himself he gratefully recognized, especially as deepening and enlarging his views of Christian and ministerial obligation." After her death in 1838 he wrote a memoir of his mother-in-law, the first of his many publications.[18]

Ann Page and Molly Custis cultivated other young men outside their families for the colonization cause. The Scottish immigrant Robert Munro spent time in Frederick County, likely at Annfield, where he found "much joy and comfort" with the "Christian females" who "eagerly watched for opportunities to strengthen his pious resolutions," and soon he had a spiritual conversion. He joined the Presbyterian Church in Georgetown, adopted the colonization cause, and organized Sunday schools in Washington for white and black students. He reported to Page that there were a total of 360 students and 50 teachers in these two schools in 1818. Page and Custis mentioned Munro frequently in letters. Ann believed that "God sent him at this critical period of our course to lend us heavenly assistance," but his death in 1821 ended his promising career. When Ann sent Molly another young man burning with enthusiasm for the ministry, she advised her to "speak with him fully & freely on the sorrows of heart respecting slavery—on the sad burden of conscience—on your desire that your child never marry without the preliminary of holding continual power to liberate, as fast as the colony preparing, will receive them."[19]

Of all the men who worked closely with women in the colonization movement, none was more kind, effective, and enduring than Ralph R. Gurley. He and Molly Custis made a truly remarkable team. The Yale-educated son of a Connecticut Congregationalist minister and his wife, Gurley moved to Washington in 1818. A good writer and orator, he was licensed to preach in the Presbyterian Church and served three terms as chaplain to the U.S. Congress. In 1822 the ACS hired him as an agent. Two years later he traveled to Liberia and negotiated a settlement between the settlers and governing agent Jehudi Ashmun, which included settlers in the colony's governance. Gurley was a man of integrity whose promotion to executive secretary in 1825 signaled a turn toward more benevolence and voluntarism for the ACS. The Washington socialite and writer Margaret Bayard Smith called him "a most interesting man; in his looks, a hero of romance; in his temper and life, one of the most perfect Christians I ever saw." Gurley hated slavery and devoted his life to "the elevation of the negro race" in the way he thought most promising. "The measures of the Society," he believed, "tend to elevate most surely and rapidly a community of men of colour, who may exhibit to the whole world the capabilities of the colored race for high moral and social improvement, and self-government."[20]

How Gurley's personal and professional relationship with Molly Custis developed is unclear, but a letter he wrote her from New England in 1826 revealed their intimacy. Addressing her as "My Dearest Sister and Friend," he informed her of his intent to marry his cousin Eliza McClellan, whom he hoped Custis would embrace "with delight" as a sister. Gurley also reported on various aspects of ACS business. He concluded, "You perceive that I have not only *valued* but *taken* your advice, I hope you will be encouraged to give it freely at all times for you stand finest & unequalled on my list of friends."[21] Ralph and Eliza Gurley indeed were accepted as virtual members of the Custis family. He seemed much more invested than most male colonizationists in the emigrants and their well-being. After Molly Custis's death, Gurley remained close to her daughter Mary Lee. He also corresponded with the black emigrants who eventually left Arlington to settle in Liberia.[22]

Such close personal and working relationships between activist women and men were important for effective social action. As the abolitionist Lydia Maria Child observed, one sex trying to work alone would "be like half a pair of scissors."[23] Colonization enabled these elite women to participate in the public sphere while conducting their private lives; indeed, their letters show that it is difficult to separate the two. They not only influenced men; they also *led* (morally and intellectually), and they recruited, trained, and continuously collaborated.[24]

While relationships with men were important, women also valued their relationships with one another for emotional and physical support, personal and spiritual growth, and social and political action. Their antislavery views complicated their lives and made their jobs as household managers more difficult. They complained often to one another, questioned their motivations and methods, and found comfort and encouragement in the colonization movement. Ann C. Robinson was particularly candid in her letters to Molly Custis. "Send me all the information you can collect about the colonization society," she wrote. "I grow more and more anxious to be relieved from the burden of slavery, and am in constant trouble for fear what I am doing should not be in the right spirit, sometimes." She and others frequently consulted Molly Custis for advice. "Do you think it would be right to compel men and women to learn to read against their will?" Robinson asked, adding, "I should not like to be forced to do anything for my own good against my inclination, and there is no authority that I can find in scripture which seems to authorise making people do things for their own good against their will. Sometimes I am afraid my arguing in this way is dictated by a love of ease, for it would be much more pleasant to spend my evenings reading than teaching those who are compelled to learn." One historian of colonization observed that these women viewed "slave emancipation as their own emancipation" and envisioned a "domestic utopia" without bonded labor.[25]

Mary Lee Fitzhugh Custis seemed unique among her circle of correspondents, as she rarely complained and seemed to possess a calm cheerfulness that usually escaped the others. That quality coupled with her compassion, intelligence, and knowledge made her a valuable counselor. Elizabeth Carter Turner wrote, "You always seemed to me, my dear Molly to be one of the happiest Christians I ever knew; and I have always thought I would give worlds to resemble you." Rosalie Stier Calvert concurred, observing, "she is a woman in a thousand."[26]

In their correspondence and conversations with one another and with men, these women explored and discussed the theological and philosophical underpinnings of their faith and social action. They often shared books. Ann Page read William Wilberforce, the British evangelical antislavery politician, at Custis's recommendation. National and international politics related to slavery concerned them as well: "I live in too constant a knowledge of the sin & sorrow of Slavery to have any hope of comfort but in its extinction—Mr Brougham in the British Parliament, is of the right mind" in introducing a bill to make slave trading a felony.[27]

The women also became emancipators, although only some of the people they freed were willing to go to Africa. In 1823 Ann and William's younger sisters Susan and Lucy Meade died of fevers on the same day; their wills emancipated their slaves for Liberia, but even Ann Page could not convince them to go. Some settled near Arlington, probably in Washington, D.C., and occasionally contacted Molly Custis for assistance.[28]

The opportunity for Ann Page to act on the emancipatory imperatives of her heart came with the death of her husband, Matthew, in 1826. In widowhood, Page grieved and prayed for protection for their "helpless female band." Because she would not sell slaves, their population grew to about two hundred—many of them children. Matthew's estate was mired in debt, however, and his executors had to sell personal property to settle the estate. Slaves counted as personal property; both Page and her enslaved people feared that traders would purchase them for sale in the Deep South, separating families, a fate that befell many enslaved Virginians as planters increasingly divested themselves of slave property to pay their mounting debts. Page's fifteen-year-old daughter Sarah consoled her by saying that now she need "wait ... *only only* upon God," and, legally helpless, Ann and others prayed mightily. The executors held two large sales at Annfield, and approximately one hundred people were sold, but surviving records indicate that community members purchased them with the intention of keeping families together. Some remained with Ann and others went to her daughters. Sarah signed her slaves back to her mother "so that she may have it in her power to liberate & send them to Africa or elsewhere whenever she desires to do so."[29]

In 1830 Christian Blackburn of Jefferson County, whose sisters married into the Washington family there, became the first in this kinship network to emancipate emigrants to Liberia: the Greens and the Hatters. Andrew and Priscilla Green named their first son George Washington and the youngest Lott Cary, after the already renowned black missionary in Liberia. Blackburn's brother-in-law Bushrod Corbin Washington emancipated Priscilla Green's mother so she could accompany them. Blackburn had carefully groomed Elizabeth Hatter to become a teacher in the colony and sent with her "a pretty good library... and a dozen spelling books." She purchased and freed her husband, Reuben Hatter, so the couple could remain together. After the ship arrived in Liberia, Blackburn was frantic for news. Her sister Judith wrote to Ralph Gurley, asking for "any minute tidings of the dear people who left us," adding that Christian "suffers much anxiety of mind about Elizabeth Hatter, a young woman she reared with great tenderness." At first taken aback by the rough conditions, and likely, too, the tropical diseases that especially afflicted newcomers, the Hatters later sent back favorable reports. "I never was better satisfied in my life, if I only had my dear relations and friends with me," Elizabeth wrote. "We enjoy the same liberty that our masters and mistresses do in America."[30]

Ann Page continued to educate and prepare the remaining enslaved people at Annfield for freedom. She stepped up classes and religious services and assembled stores of goods they would need to live for a year and practice their trades. Even though she was candid about the hardships and dangers they could expect to face, a considerable number were willing to go. Between 1832 and 1836, thirty-two interrelated people, almost all with the Page surname, sailed for Liberia in four groups.[31]

In a long letter to Ralph Gurley after the first group embarked, Ann Page reported that she told the departing black Virginians that, while she expected them to prosper in Liberia, she had sent them there to "live an upright life before God" and "be as a light set on a hill." She related that "I yearn to have you in a situation where your children cannot be sold from you, *that* bitter woe to my view—your children will receive *education* there." She explained, "I cannot set you free here. . . . You cannot expect that as white people have taken the trouble to settle this country they will give it up to you, so as that you could have sufficient advantages here to become an independent people—that will not be—to continue together must be to continue in bondage, and of course liable to be sold at the will and for the debt of white people. I cannot die in peace without using all the means in my power to place you safe from that dire anguish, giving up your children for sale."[32]

Historians have debated southern slaveholding women's sincerity and motivations in wanting to end slavery. The prayers of Ann Page are unequivocal: "'O my father Thou seest I would never have chosen it—Thou seest how Thy grace has taught me to desire above all earthly things, the abolition of Slavery." It is clear, too, that women like Ann Page considered ending slavery to be important for both races, and that they empathized considerably with people of color. These women's expenditures in time, energy, and money furthering antislavery and preparing African Americans for freedom bear out their words. Their faith both empowered and constrained them, as they strove to be virtuous and exemplary wives, mothers, citizens, teachers, and managers in a slaveholding society. They had a utopian vision in which Africa redeemed them and the American nation for the sin of slaveholding. But they were practical, too, in wanting people of color to enjoy real freedom in the present, to keep their families intact, and to educate their children in a way that was impossible in the United States, or at least in Virginia.[33]

The colonizationists' strategy proved inadequate, however, and their vision of the separation of the races too conservative. Most people of color did not want to leave the country they had helped build and where they had deep roots, nor could the ACS afford to send even the small number who wanted to emigrate to Africa. Liberia struggled, and mortality rates due to tropical diseases there were high. Northern antislavery activists increasingly supported the movement for immediate, unconditional emancipation. Abolitionists' bold and insistent rhetoric fed the fears of Virginia's colonizationists. Many colonization women shifted their energy into mission schools, and members of the Page-Custis network were likewise committed to that cause.[34]

Indeed, Ann Page and Molly Custis's legacy passed to their family members, colleagues, emigrants, and descendants. Page died in 1838, but the Pages in Liberia corresponded for decades with her son-in-law and daughter Charles Wesley and Sarah Andrews. In 1839 the emigrant Robert M. Page reported from Liberia, "Africa is a new country with some inconveniences, yet we enjoy many blessed privileges. We have to work hard, but we get a toler[a]ble comfortable support." Peggue Potter testified in 1847 that "any man can live heare that will Work and if a man is got money he can live[.] all the Fault I find in this Place the things is so deare that I has to work to get something for me and my children to Eat and as fast as I can get a little money I have to take it all the Buey [buy] some Cloths for my Children to ware." Around 1850 Sarah Page Andrews replied to letters from John, Peter, and Solomon Page, who had been young children when they left Annfield. She rejoiced to hear they were well, obtaining good educations, and that Peter had "become pious," declaring, "I loved you & your Parents before you." She recalled each of them clearly along with the "delight I used to take in your little ways and words when you were little children." In 1855 John M. Page wrote to Charles Wesley Andrews about coming to visit and bringing African goods with him, referring to Andrews's offer to reimburse him for the cost of his passage. All of the letters are filled with family news, including the latest, from Peter Mead Page to Ralph Gurley in 1858, twenty-six years after the first emigrants sailed.[35]

The Arlington emigrants left for Liberia after Molly Custis died suddenly in the spring of 1853. In her grief, Mary C. Lee reflected on her mother's life, perused her papers, and concluded that "the great desire of her soul was that all our slaves should be enabled to emigrate to Africa—For years this has been the subject of her hopes & prayers not only for their own benefit but that they ... might aid in the mighty work of carrying light & Christianity to that Dark heathen country." She then addressed her family: "May you all feel it as a sacred duty to unite in its accomplishment." And if her mother's wishes were not enough, she added, "If you were only to consult your own comfort & happiness you would rid yourself of them & I am sure you would never wish to do it in any other way than by liberation. Let it be done gradually & surely. William & his family who I hope will go to Africa this fall will act as pioneers." She also pledged to make good on a promise made to Eliza years ago that she would free her, and penciled a note in 1860 to say she had done so, apparently unofficially.[36]

William Burke and his wife, Rosabella, the enslaved servants to whom Mary C. Lee referred, were grieved to hear of Molly Custis's death, but seemed to welcome the opportunity to gain their freedom and sail to Liberia. The family was living in Baltimore, and William responded to Mary Lee's letter to Rosabella with some of his own reflections. "Although I might not have done all that I might or ought to have done for her comfort when I was with her," he admitted, "yet her kindness & instruction to me in my youth is what I can never forget." He imagined that, as she crossed over, a heavenly voice told her, "Well done. Enter into the joys of thy Lord." The Burkes' reason for being in Baltimore is unclear. William may have been hired out or he may have hired himself out, as he wrote, "If you want me to do any thing for you I can Leave my work at any time."[37]

The Burkes were emancipated, according to ACS records, by Colonel Robert E. Lee. They sailed from Baltimore in November 1853 on the *Banshee* with their children, Cornelia, seven years old; Grandison, six; Alexander, three; and William, four months. The overcrowded ship landed safely in Monrovia, Liberia's capital; from there the Burkes headed upland on the St. Paul River and settled in the new town of Clay-Ashland. William expressed satisfaction with the place and the ACS provisions for new settlers, and asked for books and papers so he could begin teaching. By August he had managed to clear land and build a cabin, twenty-two by thirteen feet—quite an accomplishment given that many settlers as well as Native people lived in thatch huts. He was recovering from the acclimating fever and worked during the heat of the day as a shoemaker when he could get leather. Rosabella Burke reported to Mary C. Lee that they had met with President Joseph Jenkins Roberts in Monrovia, but she was uncomfortable among the society people there. She liked Clay-Ashland and their new home. It seemed a modest version of Arlington: "We have a lot and house upon a beautiful hill in the township, which we have named Mount Rest. It is about 200 yards from the river, overlooking the town." William was ordained a Baptist minister in 1858.[38]

The Burkes loved Liberia and were among their nation's biggest boosters. William Burke and Ralph Gurley were frequent correspondents. The letters are warm, affectionate, respectful, and full of news about family members and friends along with concern and hope for Liberia and its agriculture. Some were published in the ACS's quarterly, *African Repository*. Five years after their arrival, William Burke reported having experienced the sort of hardships and the difficulties "common to the first settlement in any new country," but he was not "disappointed or discouraged . . . and so far from being dissatisfied with the country, I bless the Lord that ever my lot was cast in this part of the earth . . . for which I feel that I can never be sufficiently thankful." Still, he cautioned that because many who were persuaded to go to Africa were unhappy and returned to the United States, only those who were prepared to "take everything just as they find it, and be satisfied" should emigrate. Rosabella Burke's letter to Mary C. Lee followed her husband's. She reported on the children, their health and schooling, and said that she often thought of the Lee family, asking particularly to "give my love to Mary Ann, and tell her for me that she must try and behave herself, that it will do her good in the end"; she added, "I have thought and dreamt much about you lately." Rosabella asked her correspondent to tell aunt Elleanor "that I love Africa, and would not change it for America," and requested that Mary write about Rosabella's father as "he never will write to me." While the letter could have been written between white friends, she closed it, "Yours humbly."[39]

Perhaps because of the changing times and the lack of substantial progress in the colonization movement, Sarah Page Andrews and Mary C. Lee did not carry on the work of their mothers. Nor were they particularly active in another cause. They held quiet Unionist sentiments until after Virginia seceded in April 1861. They did, however, continue to hold the emigrants in their hearts. In 1867 Mary C. Lee sent a photograph of her husband, General Lee, to the Burkes. William Burke thanked her and said that their four-year-old son born in Liberia, Robert Edward, "is quite proud of it, and calls it his Gen. Lee, and is very anxious to share it, when any one comes in—he is a remarkable fine child."[40] The affection was returned and passed along.

Ann Page and Molly Custis's legacy also continued through the men they mentored and influenced and through the Liberians they trained and emancipated. In 1857 George Washington Parke Custis died and by will decreed that his slaves should go free within five years. Robert E. Lee reluctantly executed the manumission of his father-in-law's slaves during the Civil War but, perhaps because these black Virginians sensed the imminent attainment of freedom at home; none wanted to go to Liberia. After the Civil War, Charles Wesley Andrews helped black residents establish an African Methodist Episcopal Church and a school, and gave Bibles to students who learned to read. A Freedmen's Bureau teacher remarked, "He has always been a friend to the colored people." Ralph Gurley carried on the colonization work, including two additional trips to Liberia, until the late 1860s. William Burke studied Greek and Latin for a deeper understanding of the Bible, and in 1859 he was the preacher at nearby Millsburg, where the pious Peter Mead Page, formerly of Annfield, was the teacher. Burke also expressed respect for and community with Liberia's indigenous people—qualities that were often lacking in other Westerners—and concern for the poor. He and Rosabella took in refugees from a captured slave ship who had been released in Liberia.[41]

Although women have received relatively little attention in histories of Liberia, in part because primary sources are scarce, they played important roles in its development. Americo-Liberian women tended to share the sense of superiority of their former owners and of Westerners generally. Indigenous women conducted formal "sende" schools for older girls to teach skills they needed for adulthood in their own cultures, but Americo-Liberians dismissed them as "bush" schools. They instead encouraged girls and boys alike to attend mission schools where they would learn English, reading, writing, and Christianity. Officials there gave them English names and encouraged them to wear Western dress. Girls and boys alike worked as servants, sometimes indentured, in the homes of Americo-Liberians, including that of the Burke family, often in exchange for education. Inevitably, the cultures mixed, especially noticeably in architecture and foodways, and indigenous women eventually began organizing mutual aid societies within their own religions.[42]

Sometimes, indigenous people embraced Western culture and intermarried with Americo-Liberian families. The Page family provides an interesting example. Mary Louise Page, born in 1883 to Thomas Page and Angie Tucker of Little Bassa, was likely a granddaughter of Annfield emigrants. Because few documents have survived, many American descendants cannot definitively document their lineage, but naming patterns provide considerable evidence. Mary, her father, and her uncles Peter and Sol all shared given and surnames with Annfield emigrants. In 1904 Mary married Albert Komoyah Peabody, an indigenous man of the Bassa tribe who had been educated at the Presbyterian mission—where he was given his Western name—and at Lincoln University in Pennsylvania and Storer College in Harpers Ferry, not far from Annfield. The couple taught school in Liberia, had three children, and adopted a nephew. Ann Page would have been pleased to read this line in Mary Louise's obituary: "In her earlier days, one of her greatest concern[s] was how she could have all of her children trained, educated and christianized to be of benefit to her, themselves and the Church and State." Her goals were accomplished, and her legacy has continued through the lives of grandchildren such as Stanton Peabody, an acclaimed Liberian journalist, and Christian Peabody, a dentist in the United States who has been researching their family history. He visited Annfield and was deeply moved by the tangible connection to his American ancestors.[43]

After decades of social and political turmoil and civil war stemming from tensions between Americo-Liberians and indigenous people, Liberia is now recovering, with women playing notable roles. Leymah Gbowee led a women's movement credited with ending the second civil war in 2003 and electing Ellen Johnson Sirleaf as president in 2006. Sirleaf was the first female head of state in Africa, and a Nobel Peace Prize recipient with Gbowee and a woman from Yemen. Sirleaf wrote a memoir with a brief history of Liberia in which she mentioned William and Rosabella Burke and their ties to Robert E. Lee. "Liberia," she surmised, "is a wonderful, beautiful, mixed-up country struggling mightily to find itself."[44] Since the civil wars, Liberians with American ancestry have felt pressure to keep it hidden, even if they personally value it. Despite conflicted feelings about their nation's African American heritage, Liberians generally feel a kinship to the United States. They have many American influences in their culture, and some American institutions, such as the Library of Congress, recognize those connections.[45]

In 2010 National Park Service (NPS) staff members associated with Arlington House, the Robert E. Lee Memorial—Kendell Thompson, Emily Weisner, and Mary Troy—obtained a travel grant and researched the Burke family in Liberia. Despite wartime-like security measures, they enjoyed warm hospitality everywhere they went. They interviewed a Burke descendant, Robert Lee "Ray" Burke, whose father was Edward Lee Burke. His family has retained the naming patterns and an oral history of association with Robert E. Lee and his family. Ray Burke said that his line's births and deaths were recorded in the old family Bible, but when they attempted to escape the violence, carrying it and the General Lee photograph, militants snatched and burned the items. The NPS team also visited the Reverend Dr. Olu Menjay, the principal of Ricks Institute, a Baptist-affiliated school in Clay-Ashland named for the benefactor Moses Ricks, another successful Virginia emigrant. Menjay showed them the ruins of the Baptist church where William Burke served as pastor, the overgrown cemetery where he is likely buried, and Burke Hill, where the family lived. Reflecting on their visit, Kendell Thompson, then the site manager of Arlington, recalled the warm smiles of the Liberian people despite the pervasive devastation and decay, coupled with their deep sense of abandonment by the American people.[46]

Americans, by and large, know little about the complex and fascinating history the two nations share, and still less about women's roles in Virginia's antislavery movement and the fruit it bore in Africa. The vision of the NPS staff is to incorporate research on William and Rosabella Burke—and on Mary Lee Fitzhugh Custis's antislavery activities—into their interpretation of the Lee family property at Arlington. Telling these transatlantic colonization stories complicates the history of America's grand manor houses and their inhabitants, slavery and the opposition to slavery, the ideals and realities of white southern womanhood, and the history of Liberia. These stories explore the nature of loving relationships that were unequal and constrained, but that found expression in religion and the flawed but important work of colonization. They reveal nineteenth-century elite white women using their strength in service of a vision, exercising leadership, and changing the world.

NOTES

1. For colonization, including women's roles, see Marie Tyler-McGraw, *An African Republic: Black and White Virginians in the Making of Liberia* (Chapel Hill: University of North Carolina Press, 2007).

2. Elizabeth R. Varon, *We Mean to Be Counted: White Women and Politics in Antebellum Virginia* (Chapel Hill: University of North Carolina Press, 1998), chap. 2.

3. C. W. Andrews, *Memoir of Mrs. Ann R. Page* (New York: Protestant Episcopal Society for the Promotion of Evangelical Knowledge, 1856), 8, 27; John Johns, *Memoir of . . . William Meade* (Baltimore, Md.: Innes, 1867), 110; Mary Meade, will proved September 7, 1813, Will Book 9:251, Frederick County Courthouse, Winchester, Va.; Page, "Valuable extracts; selected by my dear aunt Fitzhugh" (n.d.), Annfield Collection, Clarke County Historical Association, Berryville, Va. (hereafter CCHA).

4. *Virginia Herald*, January 4, 1805; and Ronald W. Johnson, *Preliminary Historic Resource Study: Chatham, Fredericksburg, and Spotsylvania County Battlefields Memorial National Military Park, Virginia* (Denver, Colo.: U.S. Dept. of the Interior, 1982), 50–52. On Gabriel's Rebellion, see generally, Douglas R. Egerton, *Gabriel's Rebellion: The Virginia Slave Conspiracies of 1800 and 1802* (Chapel Hill: University of North Carolina Press, 1993), 50–118.

5. Andrews, *Memoir of Mrs. Ann R. Page*, 10, 18–19.

6. Elizabeth Brown Pryor, *Reading the Man: A Portrait of Robert E. Lee through His Private Letters* (New York: Penguin, 2008), 138–39.

7. National Park Service, *Arlington House: The Robert E. Lee Memorial* (Washington, D.C.: Division of Publications, National Park Service, Department of the Interior, 1985), 12–14.

8. Andrews, *Memoir of Mrs. Ann R. Page*, 18–19, 27, 30–32.

9. Ibid., 47; Robinson to Custis, September 14, 1818, Mary Custis Lee Papers, 1694–1917, Virginia Historical Society (hereafter VHS); Pryor, *Reading the Man*, 128–31; the Black Heritage Museum of Arlington, Virginia, Virtual Exhibits, "The Gray Family" and "The Syphax Family," http://www.arlingtonblackheritage.org/exhibits.html (accessed May 1, 2013); Karen Byrne, "The Remarkable Legacy of Selina Gray," *Cultural Resources Management* 4 (1998): 20–22.

10. Andrews, *Memoir of Mrs. Ann R. Page*, 31; Page to Susan and Lucy Meade, [1823], Charles Wesley Andrews Papers, David M. Rubenstein Rare Book & Manuscript Library, Duke University, Durham, N.C.

11. Lilly to Custis, [n.d.], VHS; Mary A. R. [Custis] Lee to Mary Lee [Fitzhugh] Custis, June 18, [c. 1844–45], Custis-Lee-Mason Family Papers, 1756–1863, Library of Virginia.

12. Andrews, *Memoir of Mrs. Ann R. Page*, 18, 21, 33–35; Frederick D. Goodwin, "The Diary of Rev. Frederick D. Goodwin," *Proceedings of the Clarke County Historical Association* 4 (1944): 38–39; Page to Mary L. Custis, May 12, 1817, Mary Custis Lee Papers, VHS.

13. Andrews, *Memoir of Mrs. Ann R. Page*, 37–39; Tyler-McGraw, *African Republic*, 20, 26–35; Ralph Randolph Gurley, *Life of Jehudi Ashmun, Late Colonial Agent in Liberia* (Washington, D.C.: printed by J. C. Dunn, 1835), qtd. in C. W. Andrews, "Obituary [for Ann R. Page]," *African Repository and Colonial Journal* 14, no. 4 (April 1838): 123–27.

14. William Meade, Oration, [n.d.], William Meade Correspondence, St. Mark's Library, Union Theological Seminary, New York; Mary Meade to Mary Lee (Fitzhugh) Custis, July 12, 1808, Mary Lee Custis Papers, VHS; William Meade to Custis, August 1 and 9, 1808, ibid. See also David Lynn Holmes, "Wlliam Meade and the Church of Virginia, 1789–1829" (PhD diss., Princeton University, 1971), and Arthur Dicken Thomas, "The Second Great Awakening in Virginia and Slavery Reform, 1785–1837" (PhD diss., Union Theological Seminary, 1981).

15. *The Annual Report of the Auxiliary Society of Frederick County, Va., for Colonizing the Free People of Color of the United States* (Winchester, Va.: Auxiliary Society, 1820), 14; Deborah A. Lee, "The Frederick County Auxiliary of the American Colonization Society, Est. 1817," *Winchester-Frederick County Historical Society Journal* 9 (1996): 17–40.

16. Meade to Custis, April 9, 1823, Mary Custis Lee Papers, VHS; Johns, *Memoir of . . . William Meade*, 77; Varon, *We Mean to Be Counted*, 59–62, 65.

17. Page to Susan Meade, [c. 1815], Charles Wesley Andrews Papers, Duke University, Durham, N.C.; "William H. Fitzhugh, Esq.," *African Repository* 3, no. 6 (August 1827): 185; "Obituary Memoir," *African Repository* 6, no. 3 (May 1830): 91–96; William H. Fitzhugh Will, August 16, 1830, Fairfax County, Va., Will Book Q-1, 57–59; Will of Mrs. A. M. Fitzhugh, August 23, 1870, VHS.

18. Andrews, *Memoir of Mrs. Ann R. Page*, 52; Cornelius Walker, *Memoir of Rev. C. W. Andrews, D.D.* (New York: Thomas Whittaker, 1877), 49–50; Marie Tyler-McGraw, "Charles Wesley Andrews," in *Dictionary of Virginia Biography* (Richmond: Library of Virginia, 1998–), 1:163–64.

19. "B.," "Sketch of the Life and Character of Robert Munro," *Christian Herald* (July 21, 1821): 132; Munro to Page, April 15, 1818, Annfield Collection, CCHA; Page to Custis, [n.d.], Mary Custis Lee Papers, VHS; Page to Custis, May 12, 1817, ibid.

20. P. J. Staudenraus, *The African Colonization Movement, 1816–1865* (New York: Columbia University Press, 1961), 15, 78, 99; R. R. Gurley, "Remarks on the Principles of the Colonization Society," *African Repository* 10, no. 3 (May 1834): 68.

21. Gurley to Custis, November 16, 1826, Mary Custis Lee Papers, VHS.

22. See, for example, Gurley to Lee, October 6, 1858, ibid.

23. Lydia Maria Child to Lucretia Mott, March 5, 1839, qtd. in Dorothy Sterling, *Ahead of Her Time: Abby Kelley and the Politics of Antislavery* (New York: Norton, 1994), 80.

24. See, generally, Varon, *We Mean to Be Counted*, chap. 2.

25. Robinson to Custis, March 16, [1810s], and others also from the 1810s, in Mary Custis Lee Papers, VHS. See also Tyler-McGraw, *African Republic*, 87–88.

26. Turner to Custis, May 26, 1833, George Bolling Lee Papers, 1872–1948, VHS; Calvert to Isabelle van Havre, July 15, 1811, in *Mistress of Riversdale: The Plantation Letters of Rosalie Stier Calvert*, ed. Margaret Law Callcott (Baltimore, Md.: Johns Hopkins University Press, 1991), 240, both cited in Pryor, *Reading the Man*, 228–29.

27. Page to Custis, December 6, 1810, and October 17, [1820s], Mary Lee Custis Papers, VHS.

28. Susan Meade Will, dated July 3, 1820, proved June 8, 1827; and Lucy F. Meade Will, August 1, 1820, Frederick County Will Book, 15:5–7; William Meade to Mary Lee Custis, April 18, 1836, Mary Lee Custis Papers, VHS.

29. Andrews, *Memoir of Mrs. Ann R. Page*, 45; Matthew Page estate accounts, December 28, 1826,

and August 17, 1827, Frederick County Will Book 15:75–77; Ann R. Page, prayer, n.d., Annfield Collection, CCHA; Sarah W. Page to Ann R. Page, February 28, 1833, Charles Wesley Andrews Papers, Duke University.

30. Jane Ailes and Marie Tyler-McGraw, "Leaving Virginia for Liberia: Western Virginia Emigrants and Emancipators," *West Virginia History* 6 (2012): 1–34 (quotations on 11–12).

31. For more on the Page emigrants, see *Virginia Emigrants to Liberia*, http://www.vcdh.virginia.edu/liberia (accessed December 31, 2013).

32. Ann R. Page to Ralph R. Gurley, April 4, 1831, American Colonization Society Records, Library of Congress (hereafter ACS Records).

33. Two overviews of the vast literature on slaveholding women are Tyler-McGraw, *African Republic*, 203–4n6; and Varon, *We Mean to Be Counted*, 179n1. See also Page, prayer, November 1823, Annfield Collection, CCHA.

34. Varon, *We Mean to Be Counted*, 59–60; Ann R. Page, African Missionary Registry from 1820, Charles Wesley Andrews Papers, Duke University; Ann R. Page to Mary Lee [Fitzhugh] Custis, August 30, [1823], Mary Lee Custis Papers, VHS.

35. Page to C. W. Andrews, May 6, 1839, Charles Wesley Andrews Papers, Duke University; Potter to C. W. Andrews, December 29, 1847; and Sarah W. Andrews to John, Peter, and Solomon Page, [c. 1850], both in Mary F. Goodwin, "From the Society's Collections: I. A Liberian Packet," *Virginia Magazine of History and Biography* 59 (1951): 86–87; Page to C. W. Andrews, April 1, 1855, ibid., 85; Page to Gurley, January 31, 1858, Incoming Correspondence, ACS Records.

36. Mary A. R. Custis Lee, Diary, 1852–58, Lee Family Papers, VHS.

37. Burke to Robert Mary A. R. Custis Lee, May 8, 1853, Robert E. Lee Papers, David M. Rubenstein Rare Book & Manuscript Library, Duke University, Durham, N.C.

38. "List of Emigrants," *African Repository* 30, no. 1 (January 1854): 19–20; William C. Burke to Ralph R. Gurley, January 4, 1854; Burke to William McLain, January 16, 1854; and Rosabella Burke to Lee, August 21, 1854, all in John Blassingame, ed., *Slave Testimony: Two Centuries of Letters, Speeches, Interviews, and Autobiographies* (Baton Rouge: Louisiana State University Press, 1977), 98–102; Gurley to Burke, April 23, 1858, Outgoing Correspondence, ACS Records.

39. Burke to Lee, February 20, 1859, in *African Repository* 35, no. 7 (July 1859): 213–16.

40. Sarah Andrews to Nanny Andrews, May 31, [1853], C. W. Andrews Papers, Duke University; Pryor, *Reading the Man*, 566n77; Burke to Lee, August 16, 1867, Mary Custis Lee Papers, VHS.

41. Pryor, *Reading the Man*, 261–75; Anna Wright, "Freedmen's Mission," *Dover* (N.H.) *Morning Star*, February 28, 1866, qtd. in *Sarah Jane Foster: Teacher of the Freedmen: A Diary and Letters*, ed. Wayne E. Reilly (Charlottesville: University of Virginia Press, 1990), 141n39, see also 116 and 147n88; Bell I. Wiley, *Slaves No More: Letters from Liberia, 1833–1869* (Lexington: University Press of Kentucky, 1980), 188–214; "Southern Baptist Missions," *African Repository* 35, no. 9 (September 1859): 262–63.

42. Joanna Tenneh Diggs Hoff, "The Role of Women in National Development in Liberia, 1800–1900" (PhD diss., University of Illinois, 1989), 78.

43. George B. Peabody, *Bahr-Fofoe: A Bassa Boy* (Lancaster, Pa.: New Era, 1891); Albert K. Peabody obituary, (Liberian) *Weekly Mirror* (c. September 22, 1938); Mary Louise Peabody obituary, February 1956 (in possession of author); Stanton Peabody obituary, *All Voices Global News*, May 17, 2011; telephone interview with Christian Peabody, April 13, 2010.

44. Ellen Johnson Sirleaf, *This Child Will Be Great: Memoir of a Remarkable Life by Africa's First Woman President* (New York: Harper, 2009), 1, 14.

45. See, for instance, "The African American Mosaic: Liberia," http://www.loc.gov/exhibits/african/afam003.html (accessed December 31, 2013).

46. Katrina Lashley, Deborah Lee, Emily Weisner Thompson, Kendell Thompson, and Mary Troy, "Interpreting Historic Sites Transnationally: A Case Study Stretching from Virginia to Liberia," panel presentation at the Annual Meeting of the Organization of American Historians and the National Council on Public History, Milwaukee, Wis., April 2012.

Ellen Wayles Randolph Coolidge

Thomas Jefferson's Granddaughter in New England and Beyond

LISA A. FRANCAVILLA

On a spring day in May 1825, in the parlor at Monticello, Thomas Jefferson's granddaughter Ellen Wayles Randolph married Joseph Coolidge, the son of a Boston merchant. After a brief few weeks, Ellen left the home and family she loved in Virginia and traveled north to start her life in New England. Ellen's education, her elite upbringing on a large slaveholding plantation, and indeed every aspect of her life up to the point of her marriage made her assimilation into New England society difficult. For several years after her marriage she struggled to adapt to a world that was vastly different from her Virginia home. Plagued by feelings of isolation and worried about how others perceived her, she contemplated how she should define herself. Was she a southerner or a Yankee, a Virginian or a Bostonian, the granddaughter of a former president or the wife of a prosperous merchant? Could she be these things simultaneously, to herself or to others? When Joseph's business interests took him overseas, Ellen accompanied him. Her experiences abroad brought new and more expansive contemplations of self-identity.

Ellen Coolidge's many letters and diaries record her impressions of wherever she lived, but they also reveal a woman who was curious, and even sometimes confused and uncertain, about her own place in the world. Virginia was never far from her thoughts, continually influencing her perceptions of herself, how she interacted with others, and her observations of the world around her. Despite decades living away from Virginia, across distances great and small, through economic hardships, wars overseas, and a civil war at home, the constant in

ELLEN WAYLES RANDOLPH COOLIDGE

Portrait by Francis Alexander, 1836. With appreciation to Ellen Eddy Thorndike.
Thomas Jefferson Foundation, Inc., at Monticello.

PRAYA GRANDE, MACAO BAY

Engraving by George Philip Reinagle from the original by George Chinnery, c. 1818–35. Ellen Coolidge resided here for eighteen months beginning in November 1839.

©The Trustees of the British Museum. All rights reserved.

Ellen's life was her connection to her grandfather Thomas Jefferson and her lost Virginia home.[1]

Born at Monticello in 1796, Ellen was the fourth of twelve children of Jefferson's daughter Martha and Thomas Mann Randolph. When Jefferson retired from the presidency in 1809, the Randolph family joined him at Monticello, and until the time of her marriage the "little mountain" was her home and her grandfather her most treasured companion. Outside, there were flower gardens, groves, a vineyard, a fishpond, and a terraced kitchen garden. Inside the home there were thousands of books to read on hundreds of topics, artifacts from the Lewis and Clark expedition to the West, an assortment of maps, fossilized mammoth and mastodon bones, and a model of the pyramid of Cheops, all exhibited alongside fine paintings and sculptures.[2]

This was truly a unique environment in which to live, and Ellen thrived in it. Her conversations with the statesmen, diplomats, scholars, scientists, artists, and authors who visited not only expanded her knowledge greatly but gave her confidence and the ability to adapt to almost any social setting. It was in her studies, however, that Ellen found her greatest satisfaction. She relished the occasional trips with her grandfather to Poplar Forest, Jefferson's Bedford County retreat, because there, away from the bustle of Monticello, she could spend several uninterrupted hours a day with her books. By the time she had grown to womanhood she could read French, Italian, and Latin; discuss history, philosophy, art, and literature; and was familiar with many of the political, social, and economic issues of her time. She was lively and intelligent, possessed a dry wit, and was an astute—albeit occasionally critical—observer of society and human nature. Jefferson was especially fond of Ellen and praised her as possessing "a good heart, good temper, a sound head, and great range of information."[3]

But Monticello and Poplar Forest were part of the larger slave society that was antebellum Virginia, and life among slaves had a profound effect on Ellen. As historians of elite southern women have argued, though slaves and their mistresses were often close, both physically and emotionally, their relationship was fundamentally antagonistic. Most white slaveholding women were elitist and racist, and Ellen was no exception. Life among slaves at Monticello had a lasting influence not only on her expectations for domestic ease but also on her perceptions of self and her understandings of race and class.[4]

Ellen entered formal society at the age of nineteen, enjoying the privileges that her connections bestowed on her as a member of two of the oldest and most distinguished families in Virginia, as the favored granddaughter of Jefferson, and as a resident of the most uniquely beautiful (though not very prosperous) plantation in the state. Young women typically regarded this portion of their lives with either pleasure or apprehension, recognizing the enormous significance of the social customs and ceremonies that marked their new status and identity as marriageable young ladies. Ellen delighted in the cycle of balls, dinners, and other excursions, evaluated other young ladies in attendance, and fancied one potential beau after another. Her debut challenged her to adapt to social milieus with unfamiliar rules and expectations—including Washington, D.C., and the state capital of Richmond—but gradually she became accustomed to participating in "frivolous and insipid conversations" and dancing with young men who, though wealthy and attractive, she deemed intellectually stunted. Her initial aloofness and "feelings of loathing and disgust" were soon replaced by an "anxiety to please" and to "excite admiration."[5]

There is no evidence to suggest that Ellen intentionally tried to avoid entanglements in order to extend her time in society, as some young women did. Rather, it seems that although her elegance and intelligence enthralled many potential suitors, her lack of fortune ultimately failed to attract a proposal that suited her. Ellen's father and grandfather were both struggling financially. Economic depression, compounded by disappointing crop yields, falling land prices, and ever-increasing debts meant that both men had to scrimp and borrow to supply Ellen with the necessary funds for her debut. The family hoped that Ellen could make an advantageous marriage for her sake, but she undoubtedly felt pressure to do so for theirs as well. By December 1818, at the advanced age of twenty-two, the strain and disappointment were beginning to wear on her, and after playfully relaying the latest gossip to her mother, Ellen closed her letter with "for Heaven's sake my dear Mama, laugh at this nonsense if you can, but do not let it go farther, for I am beginning to experience serious mortifications on this ridiculous subject—& I have been already held to the world as a fortune-hunter in petticoats."[6]

The height of Ellen's popularity seems to have occurred during the Washington season that stretched from December 1821 until well into the spring of 1822, when she attracted the attentions of not one, but several, middle-aged statesmen. Chief among her rumored conquests was the forty-year-old New York senator Martin Van Buren. Ellen cared less about the geographical origins of a potential match than whether he was intelligent and from a high-ranking family. She reported to her mother that Van Buren was "a very well bred and agreeable man, & exceedingly influential in his own State.... these advantages combined with a large fortune would make him what is called a speculation, were he not a widower encumbered with five children, & of decidedly plebian birth." Though rumors of romance between Ellen and Van Buren persisted for several months, nothing ever came of them. Whether it was his children or his "plebian birth" that prevented her from accepting an offer, or whether he never formally made one, is unknown.[7]

In 1824, when she was past the age when most Virginia belles married, Ellen met Joseph Coolidge. One of seven children born to Joseph and Elizabeth Bulfinch Coolidge, young Joseph was part of a prosperous and prominent Boston family, had graduated from Harvard, and was traveling through the middle Atlantic states after having spent nearly four years touring Europe. George Washington's step-granddaughter Eleanor Parke Custis Lewis was taken with him when he visited her in May, just before appearing at Monticello. "I think him the finest young man I have ever known," she wrote. "He is highly improved by Books & travel—his conversation is the most agreeable possible, free from affectation, parade or pedantry. He is modest, frank, unassuming . . . very genteel in his appearance, elegant in his manners, a very sweet voice & smile. In short I have not, in these degenerate days seen any one to compare with him."[8]

A letter of introduction from the Harvard scholar George Ticknor presented Joseph Coolidge to Thomas Jefferson, and his two-week stay and subsequent correspondence with Ellen and Jefferson garnered an invitation from the latter for a return visit in the fall of that year. Jefferson had observed Ellen and Joseph together during the course of Joseph's first visit and had learned of their attachment "with pleasure." Although it would mean Ellen's removal from Virginia, Jefferson and Ellen's mother, Martha, were very pleased with the engagement. In a ceremony conducted by the Reverend Frederick W. Hatch, Ellen and Joseph were married at Monticello on May 27, 1825.[9]

Three weeks later, as the newly wedded Coolidges made their long and roundabout journey from Monticello to Boston, Ellen became painfully aware not only of all she was leaving behind but also of the vast differences between her birthplace and the region that would now become her home. She struggled with her feelings, fought off regrets and tears, and was grateful for her husband's patience and understanding. While they visited the towns and toured the countryside, Ellen confided her impressions of what she saw to her mother and her grandfather. In letters to both, she described the landscape and the "respectable appearance" of the villages and their inhabitants. To Martha she expressed her apprehensions about the climate of New England, where, she explained, "the principle [sic] growth . . . is of miserable, pinched & poverty-stricken pines, so ragged & wretched that it makes your heart ache to look at them. . . . in the houses you are alarmed at the sight of stove-pipes running in every direction, & when you go out, great piles of wood already cut & prepared for winter's use, speak volumes of the horrors of a climate where such precautions are necessary."

Her "southern eye" was shocked to find that sleighs were always readily available, and she was horrified to learn from a servant girl that there were five to six feet of snow every year.[10]

But the journey also prompted comparisons of a different sort, which she shared with Jefferson. Ellen declared that the tour had "given me an idea of prosperity & improvement, such as I fear our Southern States cannot hope for, whilst the canker of slavery eats into their hearts, & diseases the whole body. . . . when I consider the immense advantages of soil & climate which we possess over these people, it grieves me to think that such great gifts of Nature should have failed to produce any thing like the wealth and improvement which the New-Englanders have wrung from the hard bosom of a stubborn & ungrateful land. . . . I should judge from appearances that they are at least a century in advance of us in all the arts & embellishments of life."[11]

Ellen's tour of New England led her to ponder the effects of slavery on white southerners and white southern society, but never on the slaves themselves. She wrote as a Virginian and a newly self-conscious southerner who was distressed only by the stark contrasts in economic and intellectual development between the regions, and she found in black slavery an explanation for the sad disadvantages of white southerners. Perhaps conversations with her New England husband prompted these reflections, but Jefferson had been writing for decades about slavery, often in similar terms, and it was likely that Ellen was aware of her grandfather's opinions on the subject. Like her grandfather, Ellen neither challenged the existence of slavery nor advocated its abolition. Indeed, it is likely that she never imagined living without it.

At Monticello, her life had been inextricably linked with the lives of slaves. Some of these relationships were complex, as in the case of the Hemings family. John Hemmings, a half-brother of Sally Hemings, was one of Jefferson's most valued slaves and a favorite among his grandchildren, who gave Hemmings books and relayed messages on his behalf in their own letters home to Monticello. "Daddy Hemmings," whom Ellen described as "an excellent creature," was a literate and highly skilled craftsman. He made Ellen's first writing desk, according to her grandfather's design, and its loss with most of her personal belongings in a shipwreck shortly after her marriage upset him deeply. John's half-sister Sally Hemings—also the half-sister of Ellen's grandmother (and therefore Ellen's great-aunt)—and her children were also members of the Monticello household. Most historians today believe that Jefferson fathered Sally Hemings's children, including her sons Madison and Eston, who frequently worked with their uncle John and accompanied him to Poplar Forest. These trips sometimes overlapped with Jefferson's own visits in the company of Ellen and her sisters.

Sally and her children, though enslaved, were related to Ellen by blood. Yet John Hemmings is the only family member whose name appears in any of the available Jefferson family correspondence. That the names of other household slaves often appear in letters makes these Hemings family members conspicuous by their absence and suggests the tension that arose from the ambiguous status of the enslaved Hemingses in Ellen's childhood home.[12]

As a young, southern, slaveholding woman learning how to manage a household, Ellen worked closely with the family's enslaved domestics. In a plan designed by their mother to prepare them for plantation housekeeping, Ellen and her sisters took turns "carrying the keys" for a month at a time, supervising the work of the household slaves, overseeing the preparation of meals, managing the stores, settling household disputes, and acting as hostess to Monticello's visitors and guests. Although the keys served as a symbol of their power and control over the household, each Randolph daughter "reluctantly" assumed the duty of "housekeeping," complained of the time they would have to spend away from other pursuits, and eagerly planned for when they could turn the keys over to an equally reluctant sister.[13]

Managing household slaves was part of Ellen's duties before she was married, and learning how to train and supervise a personal servant was another. Ellen first experienced personal control over an enslaved worker when, though only a girl herself, she received ten-year-old Sally Cottrell as her personal maid. Ellen kept a keen eye on Sally and ensured that she was always kept busy, even when Ellen was away from Monticello. She owned Sally until her marriage, when ownership transferred to her husband, Joseph, under the common law of coverture. Ellen's brother Thomas Jefferson Randolph then sold Sally on Joseph's behalf, but not before Ellen stipulated that Sally be allowed to set the terms of her disposition, whether she be sold or hired out, and to whom. Yet giving Sally her freedom was not among the options Ellen considered. Letters from Ellen's sisters relayed Sally's messages of "love to her mistress" and assured Ellen that Sally seemed happy in her new home, suggesting that they believed Ellen would want this information. But Ellen rarely mentioned Sally and when she did it was not as a person whose company she missed but rather as a valuable and reliable servant and source of income. It was Sally's subsequent owner who ultimately freed her.[14]

Ellen's experience with and acceptance of chattel slavery was not the only difference between her and her Boston in-laws. Joseph had not chosen a home for his new wife before their marriage, so they lodged temporarily with his family in their Beacon Hill house, where she learned that even elite northerners did not enjoy the ease of her former Virginia home. Ellen was unaccustomed to rising and dressing as early as the Coolidges did, particularly without Sally's help, so she was often late to breakfast, appearing in her wrapper "because it is the only dress I can put on in haste & without assistance." She learned that the maid-of-all-work would appear in the morning to make the bed and tidy up the room, but that she would not return to take care of any of the clothes Ellen discarded throughout the day or to help with her toilette. Ellen found Boston fare inedible, being too heavy with meats and puddings, and grumbled that there was no literature in the house, for "books are never spoken of, & reading," she suspected, was "considered a waste of time." She also learned that manners were different in Boston and worried endlessly that she would do something to offend her in-laws or embarrass her husband. She wrote her mother that she moved like "one who is fettered in every limb" and lived in "perpetual fear of violating some established rule, of sinning against the laws of propriety as they are understood here.... I weigh every word before I utter it, curb every sally of imagination, regulate my very countenance, & try to look, speak[,] walk, & sit just as I ought to do."[15]

Ellen had never resided in a city for any length of time, and Boston, with the bustle of its commerce and people, was vastly different from any place she had visited before. Joseph was certain that she would be happy in Boston society and equally certain that if her impressions were unfavorable at first, they would change with time. He also believed she would discover that the "reports of inconvenient independance in our domestics are very much exaggerated!" As Ellen and Joseph debated the merits of Virginia versus New England, his letters to her family indicate that she was very deliberately thinking and speaking of herself as a Virginian. In a letter to his mother-in-law, Joseph wrote that Ellen was beginning to discover for herself that "our claims to the character of a rational hospitality are not, as she supposed, wholly unfounded; and, if not quite satisfied with the politics '*of these parts*' is, at least, not disappointed in the views of religion which she finds to exist among us—; indeed, I do not despair altogether of making her something of a Yankee, yet." Still, he reassured Martha that Ellen would not love Virginia less just because she might come to love Boston as well. "Her affections," he knew, were "too strongly given to the South to be soon eradicated." To Ellen's brother-in-law Nicholas Trist, Joseph admitted, "I do not mean to make her to forget Virginia—this would be impossible, but I hope to make her satisfied with New England."[16]

Boston friends and family treated Ellen kindly, but she suffered from loneliness and feelings of isolation nonetheless. In Virginia she was accustomed to having her large family about her, as well as many close friends with whom she visited, sometimes at their homes and often at Monticello. Though she defended

New Englanders—whose politics, she believed, caused them to be "misunderstood at the South"—she also lamented that even after many months, she was "not *intimate* with a single person." She was mystified by New England perceptions of feminine beauty, which to her completely lacked the "romance," "brightness," or "holy calm" of many of the young women she had known back home. She admired the Boston women as housekeepers and managers, but was perplexed by their reserve and regretted that there was "not one drop of the essence of poetry in their whole composition." The young men, too, lacked "that witchery of genius & imagination which so often fascinates in our southern scape-graces." The intellectually stunted men she had known as a belle were, by comparison, more appealing. If nothing else, they knew how to enjoy themselves and be entertaining company.[17]

Joseph urged his in-laws to visit Ellen often to ease her loneliness. Ellen's mother and her sisters Mary and Cornelia took turns staying with her, but there were months when no one from Virginia could be in Boston. Over the next six years Ellen gave birth to six children, including one set of twins, and the assistance of a sister during these times was essential to her. But the Coolidge household was often in turmoil. Neighbors could hear children fussing and crying, and although they said nothing to Ellen, servants carried their comments and criticisms back to her.[18]

Those servants were frequently the cause of Ellen's troubles, despite her husband's optimism. Unlike slaves, northern wage-earning servants were generally white, could come and go as they pleased, and would leave employment without notice. They often played employers against one another to improve their salaries and work schedules. High demand meant that they were difficult to replace and, of course, troublesome, since free servants could not be disciplined or punished like slaves. Ellen had, at best, a cook, a nurse, a maid, and a manservant, but she seldom managed to have all of them at once. She knew that they were "Yankee" servants and must be managed in "Yankee" fashion, but she resented their freedom and presumption of social equality, and believed they were unreliable, insolent, duplicitous, lazy, and even occasionally thieves. Unaccustomed as she was to white servants, Ellen deemed them preferable to the "*northern* blacks" who, she declared, were "a detestable race," presumably because they were not sufficiently subservient. Attempts to obtain free blacks from Virginia proved fruitless. Ellen's struggles made her long for the "trusted" slaves of Monticello, especially when Joseph's business took him to Canton, China, in 1832 and kept him away, with only a brief visit home, for nearly five years.[19]

During her first decade away from Virginia, Ellen's health deteriorated, due in part to her frequent pregnancies, but more from the strain of having to cope with so much on her own. Diphtheria, measles, scarlet fever, cholera, and various other diseases plagued Boston, and the often-precarious health of Ellen's children kept her moving in and out of the city to protect them. The management of household finances, negotiation of contracts, wrangling with Boston tradespeople, and ongoing struggles to find reliable servants all took their toll on her. This was not the life she had been prepared for at Monticello, where there were slaves to manage the children, tend the sick, mend clothing, and perform other daily household tasks. Over the course of this same ten years, Ellen lost several members of her Virginia family, including her beloved grandfather. The family also lost Monticello, and most of Jefferson's belongings, including his slaves, were sold at auction. Family letters kept Ellen informed of events, but the news arrived days or even weeks later. The death of Ellen's mother in October 1836 was a dreadful blow and, as with other losses, she learned of it long after it occurred and grieved alone.

Joseph returned to Boston in late 1837, and by March 1838 he had determined to take Ellen with him when he returned to China, believing it essential to her physical and mental health. Ellen would join him in London and after a few weeks of rest and sightseeing, the two of them would make their way to China. In June, with the children dispersed to relatives in New York and Virginia and to Boston boarding schools, Ellen departed from New York aboard the *Wellington*, joining the swell of Americans who were traveling overseas in increasing numbers. Although extended travel was still primarily reserved for the wealthy, this exclusivity was beginning to change. Incomes were rising; transatlantic transportation was faster, more comfortable, and affordable; and there were new guidebooks to help travelers plan their voyages and excursions. Ellen journeyed in order to join Joseph, who was in London on business, but like most of her fellow travelers, she was going as a tourist. This voyage marked the beginning of a new phase in her life: for most of the next ten years, she lived outside of the United States.[20]

When Ellen arrived in London in early July 1838, she was delighted to find that Joseph had provided her with a lady's maid, a luxury she had not had since parting from her slave Sally Cottrell many years earlier. "When I was a girl, living in Virginia," she wrote in her diary, "I had an excellent lady's maid who did every thing for me. When I married and went to New England where every lady is her own maid, and waits upon herself, and dresses her own hair, I felt as if I should never be able to perform such Herculean tasks. Thirteen years of persevering effort, however, made these things so easy to me that I fancied I should never desire to be waited on again. . . . But it was a mistaken thought. In five minutes I had relapsed into old habits—allowed my maid to undress and put me to bed the night of my arrival, and now cannot stick a pin or smooth a hair without her."[21]

In between Joseph's business activities, the Coolidges visited museums, toured the Tower of London and the tunnel under the Thames, and attended the theater and the opera. With the critical eye of one who had lived most of her life among black slaves, Ellen watched as Thomas Rice performed his wildly popular character "Jim Crow" at London's Adelphi Theater. She observed later that Rice "does the negro pretty well. He has the laugh, the loud 'gaffaw' to perfection, and so the movement in dancing, as far as the straight limbs and small feet of the Caucasian race can imitate a motion peculiar to the crooked shin and broad flat foot. . . . The negroes dance in perfect time to the music, and in this respect, Jem Crow is a good representative of his black brethren." Those in the audience around her enthusiastically applauded Rice's songs and dances, but Ellen sought authenticity in the portrayal of the slaves she knew in Virginia. She watched and judged whether the white actor could accurately represent the motions, voice, and mannerisms of what she considered a familiar but inferior race.[22]

On extended trips to the countryside and excursions in the city, the softly rolling green hills, the biscuits eaten at a restaurant, and the smell of tobacco in a London warehouse all reminded Ellen of Virginia, prompting reminiscences of her girlhood, her grandfather, and her mother. But as the weeks passed, Ellen grew tired of sightseeing. When Sarah Coles Stevenson, the wife of Andrew Stevenson, the American ambassador in London, learned of her presence, Ellen's social engagements multiplied. Stevenson was a native Virginian, a first cousin of Dolley Madison and a sister of Jefferson's former secretary and friend Isaac Coles. She was also a girlhood acquaintance of Ellen and was pleased to have "the advantage of introducing her to these *fastidious* people as the granddaughter of our immortal Jefferson." Stevenson took particular pride in Ellen's success in London society, and Ellen reveled in it as well. In a letter to her niece, Stevenson reported, "Ellen has rather taken here. The desire to see Mr. *Jefferson's* Granddaughter extends to all classes—tory & radicals—& I whisper around, very *like him*—educated by him. . . . She goes to many of the places *without Mr Coolidge* & seems much at her ease, she has the repose of manner which is so English & great self possession—with an air of modesty & sweetness."[23]

Circulating in London society reinvigorated Ellen intellectually as well as physically, even as it refreshed her sense of social superiority. The Coolidges attended balls and dinner parties with members of the aristocracy; mingled with radical politicians and reformers; breakfasted with noteworthy authors, poets, and artists; gained entrée to private residences and art studios; and had the rare privilege of attending Queen Victoria's opening of Parliament in February 1839. Ellen was observant of hierarchy, attentive to manners and rituals, and noted approvingly the presence of deferential servants. Now that she was in England, she began to think more expansively about her identity. Comparing Boston with Virginia, she had always considered herself a Virginian, even when playfully encouraging her Virginia family not to forget about their "Yankee" relatives to the north. In England, however, she saw herself as an American and, while certain places and things reminded her of Virginia or brought her grandfather and mother to mind, it was to America and Americans that she compared London and the British.

Still, Ellen was an American with claims to an illustrious heritage—a notable who mingled with other notables—and unlike many American travelers, who gravitated toward each other when abroad, she made no deliberate attempts to seek out other Americans in London. Instead she criticized her compatriots for failing to behave properly in British society, observing in a letter to her sister Virginia Trist that "many of them behave very ill" with "a union of swaggering and servility, of self conceit & the spirit of *Toadyism*," which she found "inexpressibly disgusting and disgraceful." Even Sarah Coles Stevenson, despite her Virginia roots and her connections to the Madisons, was a source of potential embarrassment to Ellen. When Ellen learned that the Stevensons were to visit Queen Victoria at Windsor, she fretted to her sister Virginia: "I wish they were better calculated to do honour to the intelligence and refinement of their country. But they are 'old Virginny' to the very uncouthest vulgarisms of pronunciation & manners. . . . Oh that they may not say 'charmber' & 'yarnder' & 'mighty good,' but they will, they surely will!" At the same time, Ellen was not completely enamored of the British. She criticized English women especially for "their ignorance of all that relates to America & Americans."[24]

The Coolidges returned to the United States in June 1839, visited briefly with family, made long-term arrangements for their children, and departed a month later for China, carrying with them Ellen's French maid (Josephine), a cow, and two canary birds. The forty-three-year-old Ellen now perceived herself as middle-aged, and the lengthy voyage gave her ample free time for contemplation. Monticello and Virginia once again occupied her thoughts, taking on the wistful, rosy hues of nostalgia. "For three months past I have had little more to do than think over my bygone days," she wrote to her sister Virginia, who was also living abroad, in Saint-Servan, France. "The years and friends of my youth, as well as later ties and affections. Monticello, my early home and history, my grandfather, mother, sisters, brothers, friends, these were the images always before my eyes, and my memory."[25]

One scholar has observed that travel and travel writing, "whatever else it might be, was an American exercise in 'othering' for purposes of self-definition," involving the reduction of peoples to a list of physical characteristics, thereby documenting their inferiority to the traveler. Ellen did this while watching Rice perform in England, and when she arrived at Batavia, now Jakarta, in October 1839, she made othering assessments of the "natives" there as well. To Virginia she wrote condescendingly that she "envied the natives, men women and children, whom I saw making their toilettes in the water; often plunging head and all beneath, and often clothed in their single garment, a piece of cotton cloth reaching from the waist to the knee.... The women had their coal black hair hanging on their shoulders, or were just twisting it, still wet, in a knot on the back of the head. These females have ugly flat faces, but fine busts & clean looking skins." Unlike their supposed counterparts in her native Virginia, Ellen was pleased to declare that these "dark picturesque figures" and "blackies" were "not slaves."[26]

When the Coolidges arrived in Macao in late November, Ellen was not impressed with her new home. The island was barren and bleak with "a cold, hollow wind blowing that shrivels me like a frost bitten tobacco plant, I feel as if I were blackening & withering and my leaves drooping as I have so often seen it the case with my national Virginian emblem, in the first cold of autumn." Taking up residence in a house "immediately on the great street of the Praya Grande," where "the sea rolls just under my windows," she was disappointed to find that there was little in the way of society. Most of the British had been forced to leave due to escalating tensions between London and China, so aside from a few other American merchants, the only person whose company Ellen enjoyed was the British artist George Chinnery. Housekeeping was different than she had experienced in Boston, but had some reassuring similarity to life on a slaveholding plantation. Male servants performed all domestic service, and Ellen had only to give her directions to an overseer, or "comprador," who in turn hired the servants, supervised their performance, paid their wages, provisioned the house, and finally balanced all accounts with his mistress. Ellen found little reason to complain of her servants in Macao. "No Chinese servant thinks of opposing his will to yours or of uttering a murmur at your behests," she explained to her sister, conceding that "you are cheated of course, by these men, but it is by rule and measure.... It is hopeless to try to get along without them."[27]

In Macao, Ellen missed her children and missed her husband, and as it turned out, the tropical climate that she had hoped would be similar to that of a Virginia summer instead plagued her with repeated fevers that sapped her strength and turned her hair to gray. She remained in Macao for eighteen months, during which Joseph's business in Canton was so demanding that he was only able to visit twice. Chinese regulations prohibited the presence of foreign women in Canton, so it was impossible for her to go to him. By late 1840 Ellen was on her way back to America to collect her daughter, then departed again to join her boys in Geneva, Switzerland, where they were attending school.[28]

In Geneva, Ellen came face to face with one of the flaws of her Monticello education. Although she had learned to read French, she had not learned to speak it and was unaccustomed to hearing it spoken, so she was unable to communicate with anyone who did not speak English. Frustrated and suspicious, she grumbled at "the shameful manner" in which she was "plucked & pigeoned in this far worse than Yankee town," and decided that "the Yankees are guileless as babes compared with the Genevese." This time, unlike in London, she preferred to socialize with the few Americans in residence; she also wrote to her English friends and devoted herself to the care of her children, supervising their educations while she waited for Joseph to join them. In the summer of 1842, still reminiscing about her youth, her grandfather, and her mother, she took her daughter Ellen to Paris but was "disappointed, disgusted, dismayed" when she could find no one to help her locate the houses where Jefferson and his daughter had resided in the 1780s. Ellen especially wanted to see the convent where her mother had attended school when she lived in Paris with her father, but she discovered that "the Abbaye Royale de Panthemont was an unknown name" and was unable to "receive a single intelligible answer" to any of her inquiries.[29]

Ellen and her family lived for extended periods in various villages and towns in England, France, Germany, Switzerland, and Italy, and in her letters she often characterized herself as a wanderer or vagabond, and her family as homeless. She did not circulate as much among Europeans as she had done during her first visit to England, but rather spent more time with other Americans living abroad. By 1843 Ellen clearly longed to return to the home of her youth. "How I wish I could pass this summer in Virginia," she sighed to her sister-in-law Jane, who lived with her large family near Monticello. "I long to re-visit *home*, to see my native mountains, to breathe the fragrance of the yellow jessamine, hear the cry of the Whip-poor-will, and find myself once more in the midst of friends."[30]

Ellen remained in Europe, however, for several years more. The timing of her family's travels, as it turned out, was fortunate. She had left Macao just before the outbreak of the Opium War and so was not there when her husband was temporarily imprisoned and violence reigned in Canton. In 1846 she was in Geneva "through a revolution, [and] some days of civil war," and was "for one day at least a prisoner" in her residence, with "all the streets guarded by armed men" and the sound of a cannonade ringing in her ears. Leaving their sons Joseph Randolph, Algernon, and Sidney at military school in Dresden, Joseph accompanied Ellen and their two remaining children to Boston from Paris in the fall of 1847, just as tensions were increasing in the French capital. He returned immediately to Paris to meet nineteen-year-old Joseph Randolph there, just in time for the two of them to witness the early stage of the revolution that ultimately overthrew the Orléans monarchy.[31]

Back in Boston in 1848, Joseph turned his attention primarily to investments in real estate, utilities, and railroads, and made occasional business trips abroad, while Ellen sought the company and comfort of her family. Her unmarried sisters Mary and Cornelia took turns visiting again and her sister-in-law Jane resumed sending pippin apples, preserves, and Virginia hams and sausages as she had done during the first years of Ellen's marriage. Ellen made short trips to visit family in Philadelphia, New York, and Virginia, often with her companion Fanny Pecchi, whom Ellen had taken on while the Coolidges lived in Italy. One 1850 trip to Virginia was especially upsetting. While staying at Edgehill, the home of her brother Thomas Jefferson Randolph and his wife, Jane, Ellen visited Monticello. Her grandfather's home was now desolate, gloomy, filthy, and falling to ruin, and Ellen came away sick at heart.[32]

So, too, was Boston changing in ways that made it even more antipathetic to Ellen's Virginia sensibilities and values. Men and women "just emancipated from the nursery" led society now, and though these included members of her own family and she and Joseph were still invited to parties and dinners, they felt increasingly "like owls in a company of singing birds." Ellen also observed with apprehension the "iniquitous coalition" developing between the "blacks & their white abettors the black hearted abolitionists." When Harriet Beecher Stowe's *Uncle Tom's Cabin* appeared in 1852 and created "an immense sensation," Ellen's concern turned to fear, anger, and frustration. To her the book, like other "incendiary works" appearing at the time, fomented "hatred against the slaveholder & enthusiasm for the slaves in a way to make moderate people fear for the consequences." Ellen protested that though the "comic scenes & characters are very well done, with a true knowledge of negro manners & dialect" and while "no one can have a greater horror of slavery as a system than I have ... to say that its workings are uniformly what this Beecher fanatic makes them, is to put forward the rare exception as the rule."[33]

Growing sectional tensions prompted Ellen again to ponder her allegiance and identity, both of which were still firmly Virginian. At the outset of the Civil War, she declared herself a "true Southern woman," her affection for the South unshaken despite decades living elsewhere. Ellen understood and agreed with the southern doctrine of states' rights, but she believed that secession should have been a last resort and held South Carolina responsible for acting hastily and prompting other slave states to follow. She believed that the unity of the country was of the utmost importance and trembled for the future of her geographically, and now also politically, divided family. She commiserated with her sister Cornelia, who was living with the Trists in Philadelphia. "Your last letter was after my own heart," she wrote. "I find that we sympathize in our feelings & opinions—disapprobation of the doings of the South, & yet fond recollections of our Southern homes & affections. I lie awake at night & think of Monticello— of early days & early friends[,] of all that was when 'life was young & promised to be happy.' The beautiful scenery, the charming climate, the balmy air. . . . I am & I must ever be a true daughter of the South."[34]

Ellen's Virginia identity and family connections placed her on uncomfortable ground in Boston, and her connection to Jefferson made the details of her divided family fodder for the newspapers. Several of Ellen's nephews were fighting for the Confederacy, and her youngest brother, George Wythe Randolph, who had been educated in Boston before joining the navy, served briefly as Jefferson Davis's secretary of war. Learning anything about their whereabouts or how conditions were in Virginia was nearly impossible. Ellen sent frequent letters southward but rarely received any in return. She gathered what information she could, talking with Union soldiers who were home on furlough and reading the newspapers for the locations of battles and skirmishes. She and Joseph watched for familiar names among those taken prisoner, in case they could provide clothing, money, or anything else that could bring comfort. She had to be cautious in her inquiries, however, because, as one historian has argued, families "with opposing political loyalties raised questions about that family's character, reputation, and, most significantly in this time of war, potential for disloyalty or even treason." Ellen was aware of this danger, remarking bitterly, in a letter that was censored to protect her identity and that of her intended recipient, that "there is in Boston, a fierce, fanatical hatred of the South which restrains every expression of interest, sympathy, or natural affection."[35]

By April 1862 Ellen's son Algernon, a surgeon, was tending the Union wounded at Fortress Monroe in Hampton, Virginia, and his twin brother, Sidney, was a major in the Sixteenth U.S. Infantry. Ellen wrote worriedly to Cornelia, "my heart is sick at the thought of my son being in arms as it were against my brothers. *He* has deep regrets but no doubts as to the justice of the cause. With all his kind feelings for my relations he considers that the South has put herself so completely in the wrong that no northern man can hesitate as to what is to be done." As Sidney oversaw recruitment and training in Illinois and Ohio, Ellen was torn between the calm of knowing that he was safe and the disappointment she knew he would suffer if he was never called to the field. That call finally came in early

1863, and while serving as part of the Army of the Cumberland under General William Rosecrans, Major Philip Sidney Coolidge was lost during the Battle of Chickamauga in September of that year. Newspaper reports disagreed: some said Sidney was wounded and taken prisoner; others declared he was missing; and still others that he had been killed. For months the Coolidges could learn nothing definite. Algernon, from his post in Virginia and through his contacts both north and south, tried unsuccessfully to learn what had become of his brother. By January 1864 the family was losing hope. Ellen took to her bed, not leaving her room for days and alternating between calm and hysterics, unable even to attend a church service held for Sidney and other lost soldiers. Later that year, the Union general Benjamin Franklin Butler returned Sidney's sword to his youngest brother, Thomas Jefferson Coolidge. The engraving on it traced the sword's movements back and forth across battle lines.[36]

Several months before, at Gettysburg, Ellen's nephew Bennett Taylor, a captain in the Nineteenth Virginia Infantry, was wounded "slightly" and taken prisoner following his participation in the disastrous action later known as Pickett's Charge. While they grieved for the loss of their own son, Ellen and Joseph worked tirelessly to negotiate Taylor's exchange in December 1864 and the early months of 1865. She wrote frequent letters to him at the Union prison camp on Johnson's Island, and in every one reminded him that she loved him and would not forget about him. Perhaps as Ellen wrote to her nephew, she clung to a faint hope that her son would also turn up in a prisoners' camp. Two years later the Coolidges were still trying to learn what had become of Sidney.[37]

By then, Ellen and Joseph had returned to Europe. Ellen thought she would be happier if she could escape the turmoil and sadness in her own country. The Coolidges remained there, traveling in France, Italy, Spain, and Switzerland, often in the company of one or another of their children's families, until September 1870. Ellen returned home to her native Virginia for the last time just a few months before she died in April 1876. She was buried at Mount Auburn Cemetery in Cambridge, Massachusetts.[38]

Ellen Coolidge wrote prolifically throughout the course of her life, and in her letters and diaries we can trace the evolution of her identity. She saw herself initially as an elite Virginian in Boston, then as an American in foreign lands, and later as a "true Southern woman" in perilous times. Throughout her long and peripatetic life, however, she was always a Virginia lady. As a woman whose place of residence was determined by men—first her father and grandfather, and later her husband—she spent a long and eventful life in a remarkable array of exotic and interesting locales, but Monticello was her only true home.

Indeed she was most at ease when she could write about her life there with her grandfather and the rest of her family. In whatever other ways she ultimately defined herself, regardless of where she was living, in her mind and heart, Ellen was always a Virginian and the granddaughter of Thomas Jefferson.

NOTES

1. Much of the material in this chapter was first presented to the Society for Historians of the Early American Republic in July 2007, and later to the Southern Association for Women Historians in June 2009. All manuscript collections are in the Albert and Shirley Small Special Collections Library at the University of Virginia, unless otherwise specified. All quoted material retains the original spellings, punctuation, and emphases.

2. For more on Monticello, see Peter Hatch, "*A Rich Spot of Earth*": *Thomas Jefferson's Revolutionary Garden at Monticello* (New Haven, Conn.: Yale University and Thomas Jefferson Foundation, 2012); Susan Stein, *The Worlds of Thomas Jefferson at Monticello* (New York: Abrams, 1993).

3. Thomas Jefferson to William Short, May 5, 1816, Thomas Jefferson Papers, College of William and Mary.

4. See, for instance, Elizabeth Fox-Genovese, *Within the Plantation Household: Black and White Women of the Old South* (Chapel Hill: University of North Carolina, 1988), 35, and esp. chap. 7.

5. Ellen W. Randolph Coolidge (hereafter EWRC) to Martha Jefferson Randolph (hereafter MJR), February 7–17, 1816, January 28, [c. December 29], 1818, and May 18, 1820, all in Ellen Wayles Randolph Coolidge Correspondence, University of Virginia (hereafter UV: Coolidge), in *Jefferson Quotes and Family Letters*, http://www.monticello.org/familyletters (hereafter *JFL*); Anya Jabour, *Scarlett's Sisters: Young Women in the Old South* (Chapel Hill: University of North Carolina, 2007), 117; Catherine Clinton, *The Plantation Mistress: Woman's World in the Old South* (New York: Pantheon, 1982), 58–63.

6. EWRC to MJR, [c. March 26, 1816], January 28 and December 29, 1818, April 9, [1819], January 13, 1822; and EWRC to Thomas Mann Randolph, March 26, 1816, all in UV: Coolidge, *JFL*; Jabour, *Scarlett's Sisters*, 129.

7. EWRC to MJR, December 30–31, 1821, and January 13, 1822, UV: Coolidge; MJR to Nicholas P. Trist, March 21, 1822, Nicholas P. Trist Papers, Southern Historical Collection, University of North Carolina, Chapel Hill, all in *JFL*.

8. *Proceedings of the Massachusetts Historical Society, 1835–1855* 2 (1880): 209–10; *Genealogy of Some of the Descendants of John Coollidge of Watertown, Mass, 1630* (Boston: privately printed, 1903), 23, 26–30; Henry Wilder Foote, *Annals of King's Chapel*, 2 vols. (Boston: Little, Brown, 1896), 2:370, 475–76, 608; Eleanor Parke Custis Lewis to Elizabeth Bordley Gibson, May 2, 1824, in *George Washington's Beautiful Nelly: The Letters of Eleanor Parke Custis Lewis to Elizabeth Bordley Gibson, 1794–1851*, ed. Patricia Brady (Columbia: University of South Carolina Press, 1991), 148–49.

9. Joseph Coolidge to Thomas Jefferson, October 13, 1824, Coolidge Collection of Thomas Jefferson Papers, Massachusetts Historical Society (hereafter MHS: Coolidge); Thomas Jefferson to Joseph Coolidge, October 24, 1824, in private collection; Thomas Jefferson to Dabney C. Terrell, June 23, 1825, Thomas Jefferson Papers, Library of Congress; *Richmond Enquirer*, June 24, 1825.

10. EWRC to Thomas Jefferson, August 1, 1825, MHS: Coolidge; EWRC and Joseph Coolidge to MJR, July 7–8, 1825, and EWRC to MJR, July 26, 1825, both in UV: Coolidge.

11. EWRC to Thomas Jefferson, August 1, 1825, MHS: Coolidge.

12. EWRC to MJR, July 28, 1819, UV: Coolidge, *JFL*; Thomas Jefferson to EWRC, November 14, 1825, Thomas Jefferson Papers, College of William and Mary. John Hemmings's name appears as he spelled it. Sally Hemings was the daughter of John Wayles and Elizabeth Hemings, his slave. Wayles was also the father of Jefferson's wife, Martha Wayles Skelton Jefferson. On the Thomas Jefferson–Sally Hemings relationship, see Annette Gordon-Reed, *Thomas Jefferson and Sally Hemings: An American Controversy* (Charlottesville: University of Virginia Press, 1997); Gordon-Reed, *The Hemingses of Monticello: An American Family* (New York: Norton, 2008); Jan E. Lewis and Peter S. Onuf, eds., *Sally Hemings and Thomas Jefferson: History, Memory, and Civic Culture* (Charlottesville: University of Virginia Press, 1999); Helen F. M. Leary, "Sally Hemings's Children: A Genealogical Analysis of the Evidence," *National Genealogical Society Quarterly* 89 (2001): 165–207. On Harriet Hemings, see also the chapter by Catherine Kerrison in this volume.

13. See, for example, EWRC to MJR, September 27–30, 1816; Mary J. Randolph and Virginia J. Randolph Trist to EWRC, September 11–13, 1825; Cornelia J. Randolph to Coolidge, November 24, 1825, and September 11, 1826, all in UV: Coolidge, *JFL*; Wilma King, "The Mistress and Her Maids: White and Black Women in a Louisiana Household, 1858–1868," in *Discovering the Women in Slavery: Emancipating Perspectives on the American Past*, ed. Patricia Morton (Athens: University of Georgia Press, 1996), 90–91; Clinton, *Plantation Mistress*, 19–20, 110.

14. EWRC to MJR, [after August 29, 1817], c. 1819–21, June 26–27, 1825, and May 6, 1828, and to Virginia J. Randolph Trist, May 9–10, 1826; Cornelia J. Randolph to EWRC, July 13, 1825; Virginia J. Randolph Trist to EWRC, December 4, 1825; and Mary J. Randolph to Coolidge, April 16, 1826, and July 29, 1827, all in UV: Coolidge, *JFL*; Documents in Negotiation with Thomas H. Key, July 21, 1827, Nicholas Philip Trist Papers, Library of Congress. Sally's age at the time she was given to Ellen is approximate. For more on the slaves of Monticello, see Lucia C. Stanton, *Free Some Day: The African-American Families of Monticello* (Charlottesville, Va.: Thomas Jefferson Foundation, 2000).

15. EWRC to MJR, [August 1825], UV: Coolidge, *JFL*.

16. Joseph Coolidge and EWRC to MJR, [August 10, 1825], and Joseph Coolidge to MJR, November 11, 1825, both in UV: Coolidge; Joseph Coolidge to Nicholas P. Trist, October 5, 1825, Trist Papers; all in *JFL*.

17. EWRC to MJR, January 2, February 27, and March 23, 1826, all in UV: Coolidge, *JFL*.

18. Ellen's children were Ellen (b. 1826), Joseph Randolph (b. 1828), twins Algernon Sidney and Philip Sidney (b. 1830), and Thomas Jefferson (b. 1831). The Coolidges lost their daughter Elizabeth (b. 1827) to scarlet fever in 1832.

19. EWRC to Virginia J. Randolph Trist, March 20, 1827, March 13, 1829, October 15, 1830, and September 6, 1836; EWRC to MJR, May 28–29, 1828; EWRC, personal note, July 13, 1828, all in UV: Coolidge, *JFL*; Virginia J. Randolph Trist to Nicholas P. Trist, May 5, 1835; and Joseph Coolidge to Mary J. Randolph, May 17, 1835, both in Trist Papers.

20. Joseph Coolidge to Nicholas P. Trist, March 6, 1838, Trist Papers, *JFL*; Daniel Kilbride, *Being American in Europe, 1750–1860* (Baltimore, Md.: Johns Hopkins University Press, 2013), 2–5, 80. See also William W. Stowe, *Going Abroad: European Travel in Nineteenth-Century American Culture* (Princeton, N.J.: Princeton University Press, 1994).

21. Ann Lucas Birle and Lisa A. Francavilla, eds., *Thomas Jefferson's Granddaughter in Queen Victoria's England: The Travel Diary of Ellen Wayles Coolidge, 1838–1839* (Charlottesville: University of Virginia Press, 2011), 20.

22. Ibid., 183–84.

23. Sarah Coles Stevenson to Miss [Emily] Coles, January 12, 1839; and Stevenson to Sarah Rutherford, February 23, 1839, both in Sarah Coles Stevenson Papers, Duke University, Durham, N.C.

24. EWRC to Virginia J. Randolph Trist, December 8–11, 1838, in Trist Papers; Birle and Francavilla, *Thomas Jefferson's Granddaughter*, 105, 212–19, 314–15; Kilbride, *Being American in Europe*, 76.

25. EWRC to Augustine Heard, October 5, [1839], Heard Family Papers, Harvard University; EWRC to Virginia J. Randolph Trist, October 11, 1839, Trist Papers.

26. EWRC to Augustine Heard, October 5, [1839], Heard Papers; EWRC to Virginia J. Randolph Trist, October 11, 1839, Trist Papers; Mary Suzanne Schriber, *Writing Home: American Women Abroad, 1830–1920* (Charlottesville: University of Virginia Press, 1997), 77.

27. EWRC to Augustine Heard, November 29, 1839, Heard Papers; EWRC to Virginia J. Randolph Trist, January 29, 1840, Trist Papers.

28. EWRC to Virginia J. Randolph Trist, September 28, 1840, Trist Papers. For more on trade in Canton, see Jacques M. Downs, *Golden Ghetto: The American Commercial Community at Canton and the Shaping of American China Policy, 1784–1844* (Bethlehem, Pa.: Lehigh University Press, 1997).

29. EWRC to Virginia J. Randolph Trist, January 19, May 25, and July 22, 1842, May 16, 1843, Trist Papers.

30. EWRC to Jane H. Nicholas Randolph, May 17, 1843, UV: Coolidge.

31. EWRC to Virginia J. Randolph Trist, October 27, 1846, and March 26, 1848; and EWRC to Nicholas P. Trist, July 22, 1848, all in Trist Papers; Tim Sturgis, *Rivalry in Canton: The Control of Russell & Co. 1838–1840 and the Founding of Augustine Heard & Co. 1840* (London: Warren Press, 2006). Following early childhood, the family referred to Philip Sidney by his middle name.

32. Mary J. Randolph to Martha J. Trist, May 7, 1850, Trist Papers. For how Monticello fared under a succession of owners after Jefferson's death, see Marc Leepson, *Saving Monticello: The Levy Family's Epic Quest to Save the House That Jefferson Built* (Charlottesville: University of Virginia Press, 2003), chaps. 1–2.

33. EWRC to Martha J. Trist, January 20 and February 20, 1851; and EWRC to Nicholas P. Trist, May 6, 1852, all in Trist Papers.

34. Transcript of EWRC to Benjamin F. Randolph, February 6, 1861, in the hand of Martha J. Trist Burke, JFL; EWRC to Cornelia J. Randolph, January 19, 1862, Trist Papers.

35. Amy Murrell Taylor, *The Divided Family in Civil War America* (Chapel Hill: University of North Carolina Press, 2005), 7, 32–34; EWRC to Elizabeth(?), July 13, [1862], Trist Papers. See *Cleveland Daily Herald*, November 16, 1863; and *Philadelphia Inquirer*, December 7, 1863, for an extract from a letter written by Jefferson's biographer Henry S. Randall, lamenting the divisions among Jefferson's descendants (JFL).

36. EWRC to Cornelia J. Randolph, July 11, 1861, and March 2, 1863; Mary J. Randolph to Cornelia J. Randolph, January 5, 1864, all in Trist Papers; *Philadelphia Inquirer*, September 24, 1863; *Boston Daily Advertiser*, September 29 and October 12, 1863, January 2, 1864; and Thomas Jefferson Coolidge, *Autobiography of T. Jefferson Coolidge, 1831–1920* (Boston: Houghton Mifflin, 1923), 39–43, all in JFL. In his autobiography, Sidney's youngest brother noted that he had the sword engraved "Major Sidney Coolidge, 16. Infantry U.S.A., From T. J. C., Sept. 5. 1862," but beneath that now appeared "Captured at the battle of Chickamauga by Col. D. D. Gowan, 2. Arks. Reg., Sept. 19. 1863," followed by "Recaptured from Brig. Gen. Gowan at the battle of Jonesboro Sept. 1864."

37. Bennett Taylor to John C. R. Taylor, July 9, 1863; Joseph Coolidge to Bennett Taylor, with postscript by EWRC, December 17, [1864]; EWRC to Bennett Taylor, January 10 and 27, February 17 and 21, 1865 (photocopies in Bennett Taylor Papers), all in JFL.

38. EWRC to Bennett Taylor, January 10, 1865, Taylor Papers, *JFL*; EWRC to Cornelia J. Randolph, August 8 and November 28, 1865, March 10, 1866; and EWRC to Martha J. Trist Burke, September 24, 1870, all in Trist Papers; EWRC to Carolina Ramsay Randolph, August 17, 1866, Randolph Family Papers, UV; EWRC to Sarah N. Randolph, January 6, 1876, Edgehill-Randolph Papers, UV; Thomas Jefferson Coolidge, *Autobiography*, 82; gravestone inscription, Mount Auburn Cemetery, Cambridge, Mass.

Elizabeth Van Lew

Southern Lady, Union Spy

ELIZABETH R. VARON

Born in 1818, Elizabeth Van Lew lived a long and dramatic life; since her death in 1900, she has had a bizarre and fascinating afterlife that sheds light on America's remembrance of the Civil War era. Van Lew, despite the richness of her story, is in many ways a problematic subject for the biographer. The vast majority of Americans have never heard of her; for most of the reading public she is an utterly obscure figure. At the same time, for the sizable community of Civil War buffs, she is a mythical figure, the subject of all sorts of twice-told tales. Finally, for people in Richmond, the native city with which she had an intense love-hate relationship, Van Lew is a household name and a very polarizing figure: she is regarded as a heroine in some quarters and, to this very day, as a pariah in others. This chapter sketches the Van Lew myth, then offers a corrective to that myth, and closes with a few words about the scholarly significance for southern history and women's history of Van Lew's remarkable story.[1]

The principal features of the Van Lew legend are as follows: Van Lew was a rare elite white southern abolitionist, whose antislavery sentiments can be traced to her northern parentage and her education in Philadelphia. Motivated by her opposition to slavery, Van Lew headed up a Union spy ring in the Confederate capital that aided Federal prisoners there and gathered intelligence for the U.S. army; its greatest achievements were the breakout of 109 Union inmates from Libby Prison and the clandestine reburial of the slain Union colonel Ulric Dahlgren, both in the spring of 1864. (The underground disinterred Dahlgren's body from a Confederate cemetery and reburied it on the farm of a Virginia Unionist.) The fact that Van Lew, both during and after the war, destroyed most of her dispatches means that we cannot know much about the inner workings

ELIZABETH VAN LEW, A SYMBOL OF VIRGINIA UNIONISM
"It was my sad privilege," she wrote, "to differ in many things from the perceived opinions in my locality."
Virginia Historical Society.

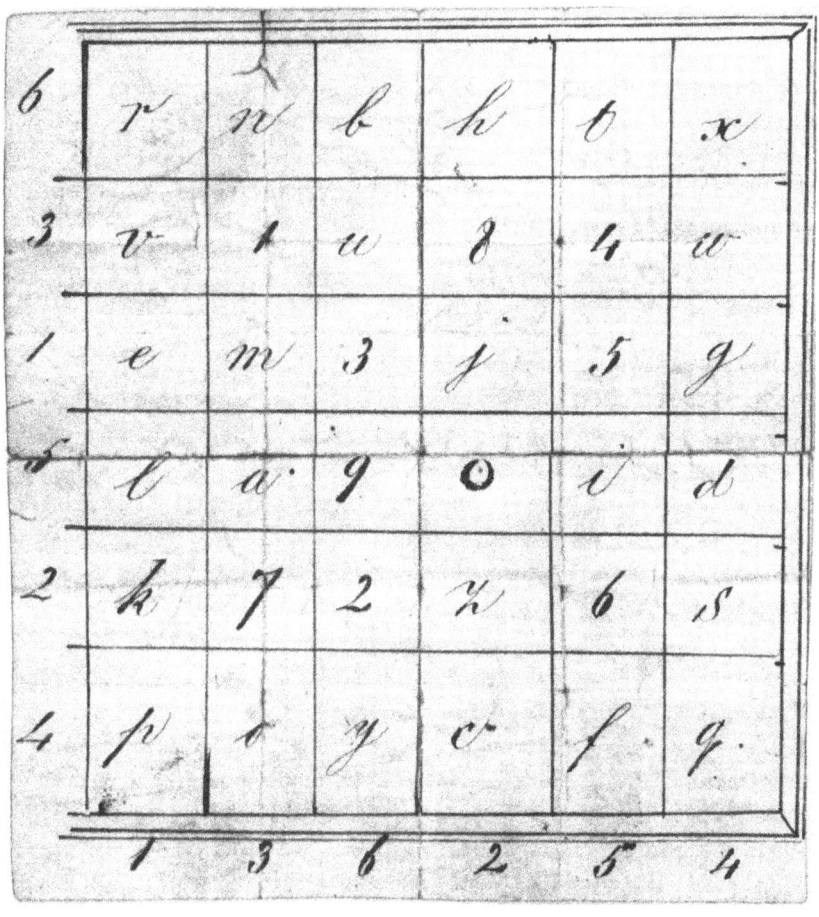

CIPHER

Van Lew's crude but effective spycraft relied on devices such as this cipher for coding and decoding messages. Elizabeth Van Lew Papers, Manuscripts and Archives Division, The New York Public Library, Astor, Lenox, and Tilden Foundations.

of her intelligence operation. Although her Union sympathies were well known to many Confederate Richmonders, Van Lew avoided detection and incarceration during the war by crafting a reputation as an imbalanced and therefore essentially harmless eccentric old spinster; hence her contemporaries knew her and she has been remembered as "Crazy Bet." Many a treatment of Van Lew has suggested that the role of Crazy Bet came easily to her because she was in fact an odd and eccentric woman.[2]

This mythologized view has proven resilient and difficult to dispel in part because of the nature of the sources available to us. Van Lew left behind a tattered, disorganized, and largely illegible set of personal papers: part diary, part reminiscence, part collected correspondence, and part news clippings. During the war, she kept these papers hidden, buried in an undisclosed location, so Confederate authorities would not seize them should they search her house. But by plumbing the murky depths of these papers and putting them in their historical context, and by recovering other voices and perspectives on Van Lew, we can discern that the true story of Van Lew and her fabled Unionist underground is far more compelling and significant than the mythological version that has been passed down over the generations since the war. Four themes are especially salient: Van Lew's views on slavery; the significance of her spy network; the issue of why she never got caught by the Confederates; and the origins of and problems with the Crazy Bet persona.

According to the Van Lew myth, she was an abolitionist, someone who, from the time that she was a child, knew slavery was wrong and committed herself to emancipation. The word abolitionism of course was and is a loaded term. For Van Lew's detractors, those sympathetic to the Confederacy, calling her an abolitionist was a way to brand her as an outsider, as someone who, thanks to both her northern parentage and her heretical views, was never a real Virginian.[3] For Van Lew's defenders, calling her an abolitionist has been a way to paint her as a moral paragon, as someone who saw the true evil of slavery when her fellow southern whites could not.

But a close reading of the sources reveals that Van Lew was not an abolitionist in the sense that William Lloyd Garrison and Frederick Douglass were. Instead of rejecting slavery and the company of slaveholders, Van Lew and her family carefully staked out a position on the tenuous middle ground between abolitionism and the proslavery creed. The Van Lews, who lived in a mansion in Richmond's most elegant neighborhood, made every effort to fully assimilate into southern society, and during the antebellum period they owned dozens of slaves. At the same time that her family held blacks in bondage, Van Lew and her mother, Eliza, lamented the evils of slavery, hoping all the while that through individual acts of kindness, charity, and manumission they could erode slavery gradually, from the inside. Indeed Van Lew and her family supported African colonization, the controversial movement to deport—or repatriate, as some euphemistically put it—American black people to Africa. Elizabeth Van Lew sent her family's most valued slave, Mary Richards, to Liberia as a teenager, only to ask that Mary be returned to her, and to slavery, in Richmond a few years later. While there is evidence that Van Lew secretly freed some of her slaves, her family had de jure ownership of at least a half dozen bondspeople, Mary Richards among them, well into the Civil War.[4]

Van Lew's stubborn belief in gradual, voluntary emancipation was no northern heresy; rather, as far as Elizabeth was concerned, it was a distinctly Virginian outlook. The key to understanding Van Lew's life and her spy career is to recognize that she did not see herself as someone who repudiated and betrayed the South; rather, she believed that secessionists and Confederates were the traitors to the South. It was they who, in the wake of Abraham Lincoln's 1860 election, abandoned Virginia's heritage of political moderation; it was they who rejected reform and compromise and became blinded by their virulent proslavery creed. Secession represented for Van Lew, in other words, both a catastrophe and an epiphany. Van Lew did eventually elaborate a sophisticated critique of slavery, but it was forged in the firestorm of secession. Slavery, she came to conclude by the eve of the war, had made southern whites antidemocratic, coercive, intellectually backward, and dangerously self-righteous and arrogant; slavery was the root cause of the madness of secession. Van Lew's estrangement from proslavery whites in Richmond deepened her empathy for and even identification with the city's blacks. "Looking upon slavery as it really is," Van Lew in the wake of secession explicitly repudiated the southern position that abolitionists had exaggerated slavery's evils. "What is more absurd than the idea that 'Uncle Tom's Cabin' could be an exaggeration!" she wrote. "No pen, no book, no time can do justice to slavery's wrongs, its horrors."[5]

Tantalizing evidence suggests that Van Lew may have been influenced by the black people working in her household to view slavery in a framework of sin and redemption. Not long after secession, Van Lew remembered, one of the family's servants predicted the downfall of the Confederacy, telling her, "You will see.... They shall fall down slain. That is the fulfillment of prophecy." Van Lew recorded the words in her journal, followed by a brief and empathetic postscript: "So said with clear eye and bright hope, the intelligent colored man, William Roane, that called us owners." Van Lew shared this "bright hope" and looked to the Union army to fulfill Roane's prophecy. During the war she would take measures to promote emancipation and to help black people, including her own servants, flee the South.[6]

Thus, it was only after secession closed off the middle ground, dashing her hope that the white South might reform itself, that Elizabeth Van Lew embraced abolition. She chose to stay in Richmond during the war and after, although she could have easily decamped to the North, where she had relatives, because she felt she had an "awful responsibility," as she put it, to her fellow Virginians, particularly the black people in her orbit. In short, Van Lew was not born and raised an abolitionist but evolved into one. She would bring to her war work and postwar crusades the special zeal—born of guilt and regret—of a latecomer to the truth.

But how was she to fulfill that awful responsibility? It has long been established that Van Lew rallied to the assistance of Union prisoners of war, helping them to survive and to escape, in the first two years of the Civil War; in the second half of the war, she headed an intelligence operation that gathered vital information for General Ulysses S. Grant's Army of the Potomac. But this aspect of her story has been cloaked in myth. According to the Crazy Bet legend, Van Lew was regarded as so harmless that she was allowed to wander Confederate prisons at will, hatching plans with the prisoners and gathering data to send to Union forces. Van Lew did, during the first year of the war, have access to Confederate prisons in Richmond, and she did befriend and assist inmates, but she secured that access by manipulating her image as a southern lady. She publicly justified her ministrations to Union soldiers as acts of charity to the supposedly unworthy, in keeping with the female imperative to be benevolent. The main weapons in Van Lew's Unionist arsenal at this stage were her family's wealth, which she spent liberally to bribe Confederate prison guards and officials, and her family's social standing, which she parlayed into numerous favors from influential Confederates, such as Provost Marshal John Winder. For example, she flattered and cajoled the vain Winder into reinstating her permission to visit Federal soldiers in prison hospitals after an irate Confederate surgeon had turned her away. But after President Jefferson Davis imposed martial law in Richmond on March 1, 1862—a measure that was followed by the arrests of dozens of suspected Unionists—Van Lew no longer could visit with Union prisoners; indeed, she was never allowed to enter the notorious Libby Prison.[7]

The Union underground that coalesced under Van Lew's leadership in the wake of the March 1862 arrests managed, in spite of the new atmosphere of scrutiny of civilian dissenters, to provide relief and means of escape for Union soldiers imprisoned in Richmond, and helped white and black civilian Unionists to flee the Confederacy and find refuge in the North. Richmond Unionists worked with Van Lew to provide escapees with safe houses, with passes and disguises, and with guides and contacts to take them to the Union lines. Van Lew frequently resorted to play-acting to get her way, and her favored role continued to be that of the loyal, respectable Confederate lady. When in the presence of Confederate officialdom, she and her mother, Eliza, did their best to "talk Southern Confederacy," as Elizabeth put it, and they took in Confederate boarders and opened their home to the rebel wounded. But perhaps the most important asset for the Union underground was the cooperation of African American Unionists. According to the memoirs of Colonel David B. Parker, who was stationed at General Grant's headquarters at City Point, Virginia, during the last year of the war: "Miss Van Lew kept two or three bright, sharp colored men on the watch near Libby prison who were always ready to conduct an escaped prisoner to a place of safety." Thanks to Elizabeth's discretion and that of her servants, her family mansion proved a safe way station for fugitives on the perilous journey beyond the Confederate lines.[8]

The most fabled—and most elusive—of Van Lew's African American co-workers was the mysterious Mary Elizabeth Bowser. Rumors began circulating after Van Lew's death that during the war she had planted an African American servant as a spy in the inner sanctum of the Confederate White House. An article published in the *Richmond Evening Leader* in July 1900, as Van Lew lay dying, told the story of how one of Van Lew's "maids, of more than usual intelligence, was sent by her mistress to Philadelphia to receive a superior education and then given her liberty and sent to Liberia." Then, Van Lew, "feeling that a trusted, educated employee would be convenient to have around," sent for this charge, who came back to Richmond and was arrested for being at large without a pass and brought before a judge. In her defense, the woman "declared that she had never been given her freedom but had only been permitted to go away on a visit." The court remanded her into the custody of her former mistress, Eliza Van Lew. This same mysterious slave—whom the newspaper did not name—was planted, the article revealed, by Elizabeth Van Lew in the Confederate White House, where in her guise as a domestic servant she gathered intelligence for the Union spy network.[9]

This story took on new life when Van Lew's executor, John Reynolds Jr., purportedly ascertained the identity of the White House spy. In 1910, at the request of William Gilmore Beymer, who was preparing an article on Van Lew for *Harper's Monthly*, Reynolds interviewed Van Lew's niece Annie Randolph Van Lew Hall, and asked if she remembered the name of the servant who had worked for Jefferson Davis. Hall confidently identified the African American spy as "Mary Elizabeth Bowser." When asked if she had knowledge of anything that Bowser had reported from the Davis White House, Hall replied, "No, I don't know of anything. Of course I was just ten when the war was all over, and they wouldn't let the children know what was going on." Reynolds passed the name Bowser on to Beymer, who made the information public in a 1911 article on Van Lew for *Harper's Monthly*.[10]

But evidence has come to light establishing that the woman remembered as Mary Elizabeth Bowser was actually Mary Jane Richards. The records of the American Colonization Society and the Freedman's Bureau, along with other sources, demonstrate that she was the slave girl named Mary Richards, whom the Van Lews sent north to be educated, then sent on to Liberia, and then eventually summoned back to Richmond on the eve of the war. Richards stayed one step ahead of the authorities by using a series of aliases, including Mary Henly and Mary Jones. During Reconstruction, Richards revealed in letters to the Freedman's Bureau that she served as a Federal agent during the war. In other words, the details of Mary Richards's life lend credence to the irresistible legend of Mary Bowser: those details allow us to confirm that the Van Lews did educate an African American servant in the North who eventually returned to Virginia and worked for the Union underground during the war. The most striking single piece of evidence concerning Richards's wartime exploits is a newspaper article covering a speech she gave in September 1865 at New York's Abyssinian Baptist Church. Published in the black-owned newspaper the *Anglo-African* under the title "Richmonia Richards," the article credits Richards with having "gone into President Davis's house while he was absent, seeking for washing," and making her way into a "private office" where she "opened the drawers of a cabinet and scrutinized the papers." It also quotes her telling her audience, "Young ladies and young gentlemen, turn your attention to the education and adornment of your minds"—for education was the "great lever" of African Americans' "elevation as a people." Van Lew would have surely endorsed this message.[11]

Beginning in the winter of 1863, Van Lew's double life became considerably more risky, as she and her fellow Unionists were formally enlisted into the Federal secret service by Union general Benjamin F. Butler. From that point on, the Van Lew mansion was the nerve center of the Richmond underground. Van Lew's role is best described as that of spymaster, since she oversaw and deployed a devoted group of Unionist operatives who were willing to take her orders without question. The very existence of this network undercuts the Crazy Bet theory; it is hard to believe that men and women would have trusted their lives to Van Lew if she made a practice of acting erratically in public. Van Lew's network reached far beyond the city itself and into the neighboring counties. Her operatives practiced a primitive but effective spy tradecraft, using code names and invisible ink and carrying messages hidden in their shoes and clothing. Their work had profound tactical, strategic, and symbolic significance for the Union war effort.

Van Lew's spy network conveyed to Federal authorities some intelligence that had immediate tactical applications—information, in other words, that they could use in planning battles. In the last year of the war, as Grant struck blows at General Robert E. Lee's trench line that reached from Petersburg to Richmond, the Richmond underground furnished Grant with key insights about the movements of men and materiel in the vicinity of Richmond, and about the strength of the picket posts and fortified lines that girded the rebel capital. Thus the underground helped prepare the Federals for launching offensives, such as the successful Federal assault at Chaffin's Farm, which resulted in the capture of the Confederate Fort Harrison.[12]

More important than contributions to specific engagements were the underground's strategic insights. At a time when Grant was having to fight simultaneously on two fronts in Virginia—along the Richmond-Petersburg corridor and in the Shenandoah Valley—Van Lew's operatives provided key information on the movements of Confederate reinforcements back and forth between Lee's army in the east and General Jubal Early's army in the west. When the underground was able to report that troops were leaving the Richmond perimeter and being transferred to the valley (an insight agents gleaned from keeping an eye on the railroad depots), Grant struck blows at the Richmond defenses. In the fall of 1864, when Union intelligence revealed that a crucial division of Early's troops had been sent east to Lee, the Federal cavalry under Major General Philip H. Sheridan struck with a series of attacks in the valley that left Early reeling. Sheridan's and Grant's victories can be attributed in no small part to the efforts of agents in Richmond, who kept the high command apprised of Confederate strategic maneuvers.[13]

Van Lew and her fellow Unionists knew that Grant relied on them not only for military intelligence but also for assessments of the political atmosphere and living conditions in the besieged capital. Taken together, the Unionists' reports from the last year of the war provide a picture of increasing desolation in the Confederate capital: business suspended; rampant inflation; old men and boys being herded into the army; public bitterness at the fall of Atlanta to General William Tecumseh Sherman and at Lincoln's reelection; and constant rumors that Richmond was to be evacuated. This kind of information had a vital strategic importance, since it confirmed for Grant, during a time in which he was under a lot of public criticism, that his grand strategy of attrition was working and that his siege was draining Confederate resources and sapping rebel morale. Just how much the Federal high command valued insight into Richmonders' morale was revealed by staff officers Horace Porter and Adam Badeau, who later recalled that the Union commander was so eager for news from Richmond that he sometimes met in person with scouts who had come through the lines to City Point, and that one of the favorite topics of conversation around the campfires at night for the officers at Union headquarters were the latest reports from the Richmond underground.[14]

Moreover, the work of the Richmond underground influenced public opinion in both the North and the South. The testimony of the scores of escapees and refugees from Richmond who were aided by Van Lew and her band provided the northern press with evidence to support its case that the Confederate regime was repressive and thereby stoked the fires of Yankee patriotism. Escaped prisoners often attested that they had been aided in their escape by southern black people, and this positive image of African American courage helped to foster sympathy for slaves and support for emancipation in the North. Finally, the underground's efforts undermined Confederate morale. The two most dramatic feats of Richmond's Unionists were the escape of 109 Union officers from Libby Prison and the reburial on Unionist soil of the slain Union colonel Ulric Dahlgren, who had been killed leading an abortive raid on Richmond. The Confederate press called these incidents the "Great Escape" and the "Great Resurrection" (because when they tried to dig up Dahlgren's body to return it to Federal authorities, at the request of Dahlgren's father, they found it was missing!). Taken together, the two episodes seemed to suggest that the Richmond underground was capable of working miracles, and this understandably was unnerving to Confederates.[15]

It is fitting that the most cogent summary of Van Lew's significance to the Union war effort comes from the pen of George Sharpe, the Union chief of military intelligence for the Army of the Potomac. He wrote in a postwar letter that "for a long, long time, she represented all that was left of the power of the U.S. government in the city of Richmond." This is a remarkable statement for a nineteenth-century man to make about a nineteenth-century woman.[16]

Why then, given the riskiness and impact of Van Lew's espionage work, was she not caught? The Crazy Bet myth suggests that Van Lew's mantle of madness gave her a kind of impunity, but that is just not so. With Elizabeth's agents traveling to and from her house with dispatches, orders, and missions, the Van Lew family was vulnerable to exposure by false friends or suspicious neighbors. The moment of reckoning came in September 1864 when, evidently acting on a tip, Confederate authorities launched a formal investigation of the Van Lews. The Confederate state police sought to build a case against the Van Lew women by getting inside their social circle. They interrogated the Van Lews' friends, but those friends did nothing to betray the family. Ironically, the authorities found their star witness among Van Lew's kinfolk, in the person of Mary C. Van Lew, the estranged wife of Elizabeth's brother John Newton Van Lew. In September 1864 Mary Van Lew swore in a deposition that she had "often heard [Elizabeth and her mother] express ardent desire for the success of Federal arms and the failure of the Confederate States to establish its independence—that they are strong abolitionist[s]—that they sent a negro woman North to be educated—that [Elizabeth's brother] John N. Van Lew has gone North on account of his preference for that Government."[17]

Soon after this deposition was taken, Provost Marshal Isaac Carrington sent a copy of it to the adjutant and inspector general's office, asking, "shall other evidence be taken with a view to the removal of these parties from [the Confederacy]?" and noting that "they are people of wealth and position." The reply Carrington received to his query about the Van Lews sheds more light than any other extant document on how Elizabeth Van Lew got away with her espionage activities. Charles Blackford of the adjutant general's office, having gleaned over the course of the investigation that Elizabeth and not her mother was the proper target of the Confederate probe, stipulated that "Miss El. Van Lew of this city is very unfriendly in her sentiments towards the Govt." But, he went on, "it does not appear that she has ever done anything to infirm the cause—Like most of her sex she seems to have talked freely ... in the presence of female friends, who have informed on her. The question is whether she shall be sent beyond the lines because of her opinion?" Blackford's superiors were evidently persuaded by the argument that Elizabeth had not actually "done anything" disloyal: the ultimate finding in her case was "no action to be taken."[18]

The salient qualities imputed to Van Lew by those judging her were the "wealth and position" of her family and her bad habit—a conventionally feminine one, they asserted—of talking too much. Confederate prejudices served to insulate Van Lew. The sexism of the men whose job it was to root out disloyalty disinclined them to believe that a frail spinster "lady" was capable of politically significant acts of disloyalty. Van Lew did not, as the myth of Crazy Bet suggests, recklessly broadcast her Unionism in public, but only shared her feelings with those she considered part of her inner circle. It was only when the authorities infiltrated Van Lew's family that they were able to gather evidence of her disloyal sentiments, and even then, they could not find hard proof of disloyal actions. Van Lew was acute enough to overestimate her enemies, even as they foolishly underestimated her.

When Richmond finally fell to Union forces in April 1865, Van Lew felt it a personal vindication. "Oh, army of my country, how glorious was your welcome!" she confided to her journal. But at that historic moment she also confronted the truth that so many white Americans could not bring themselves to face: although the war was ending, the work of reckoning with racism had only just begun. It would be a long time yet before America would confront the grim truth of what whites had done to blacks: "when eternity shall unknot the records of time," Van Lew wrote in her journal, "you will see written for them [black people] by the Almighty their unpenned stories, then to be read before a listening universe."[19]

Van Lew's private journal speaks to us in tones both solemn and poignant, revealing that she hoped history would prize her for her honesty and vision. It is for her rationality that Van Lew wanted to be remembered; for that reason more than any other, the Crazy Bet story does her an injustice. A central theme running through Van Lew's journal is her conviction that she, during the war and its aftermath, was a pillar of sanity in a world gone mad. The tragedy of Van Lew's life is that again and again the world has rejected her vision of herself, rebuffed her attempts to project an image of competence, and instead saw her through the prism of sexism. The story of Van Lew's wartime exploits first became widely known when she was appointed to be the postmaster of Richmond by President Ulysses S. Grant in 1869. While white Richmonders railed against the appointment of a female spy to the postmastership, no one charged Van Lew with craziness—yet. In her eight years in office, Van Lew, by her own account, tried to project a public image of fairness and efficiency. She refused to ally herself fully with any one political faction, "being friendly," as she put it, to the "good men" across the political spectrum. At the same time she adopted the mantle of truth teller on the subject of race relations, writing letters to the northern press on the repressive treatment of black people in Richmond, trying to convey the "facts as they really are."[20]

Neither the white Republicans whom she sought to represent nor the white Democrats whose policies she opposed were willing to concede Van Lew's competence and rationality. Only the city's African Americans were willing to honor her, and she made the unprecedented move of hiring black people to work in the post office and used her office as a bully pulpit for the cause of civil rights. In 1877, as she battled in vain to retain her office, a committee of African American men headed up by William C. Roane, a kinsman of a former Van Lew slave, passed a resolution in her support, declaring that "if any other person is appointed postmaster the colored people will have no chance whatever of getting employment in the office." White men across the political spectrum responded with the allegation that Van Lew was "erratic" and "hysterical." It was this backlash against her officeholding, more than her wartime comportment, that inclined some white Richmonders to regard Van Lew in her old age as "crazy." In her waning years, Van Lew was so estranged from white Richmond that it was all too easy to mistake her alienation for a kind of madness.[21]

Curiously, the myth of her craziness took on a new life after her death. The first time that the success of her spy ring was attributed to her tactic of feigning madness was in 1900, when Van Lew's executor, John Reynolds Jr., published a series of notices in newspapers around the country describing how "Crazy Van Lew" fooled the Confederacy into letting her enter Libby Prison to aid Union soldiers there. (Reynolds was the nephew of the late Colonel Paul Revere, a Union soldier whom Van Lew had aided during the war. He also represented a group of influential Bostonians who felt indebted to Van Lew for her service to Massachusetts soldiers and who helped to sustain her financially in her old age.) Although Reynolds's claim was directly contravened by Van Lew herself, who stated plainly in her journal that she was "never permitted" to enter Libby Prison, the claim became a staple of Van Lew lore, thanks in large part to the influence Reynolds was able to exert over William Gilmore Beymer, who produced the first extensive biographical piece on Van Lew in 1911.[22]

Beymer's personal papers contain his revealing correspondence with Reynolds. Beymer first wrote to Reynolds in 1908, hoping that he could serve as a source for the *Harper's* article and that the executor would give Beymer access to the Van Lew manuscripts in his possession. Reynolds initially demurred, responding that he was no expert on Van Lew. While he had met with her on a few occasions in her waning years, he explained, she had only talked about the past with him in a "meagre way" and had "always [been] reticent" about her accomplishments. Reynolds went on to offer his opinion about the personal papers Van Lew had willed to him: he declared them "perfectly valueless for purposes of publication, as [they] contain long chapters on her views on slavery, women's rights, and all sorts of other uninteresting things."[23]

To make a long story short, Beymer eventually cajoled Reynolds into taking a proprietary interest in the article he was writing. Indeed, by 1910 Reynolds had repositioned himself as the authority on Van Lew's life and was trying to dictate to Beymer how he should tell her story. When Beymer sent Reynolds an initial draft of the *Harper's* piece, Reynolds took him to task for not putting enough emphasis on Van Lew's reputation for eccentricity. Reynolds even scribbled in the margins of his letter to Beymer that Van Lew was known as "Old Crazy Bet." He succeeded in influencing Beymer, whose *Harper's* article features the theme of Crazy Bet prominently. The article became the single most-frequently quoted secondary source on Van Lew.[24]

If wartime and Reconstruction sources do not support the theory that Civil War Richmonders regarded Van Lew as crazy, then why did Reynolds and subsequent chroniclers seize on the notion? Reynolds made Van Lew's acquaintance after Reconstruction, when she was in her late sixties. Her political troubles and family tensions had taken a toll both on her nerves and on her public reputation. Reynolds did not see the Van Lew who had cannily manipulated the Confederate authorities nor the one who had inspired the devotion of Unionists; he did not see the Van Lew whose professionalism in the post office had won the grudging praise even of Richmond's most conservative newspapers. Rather, he saw a frightened, paranoid old woman who was shunned by the "good" people of her city and obsessed with the theme of her own persecution. Like so many others did, Reynolds projected what he knew of the elderly Van Lew back into the past. The image of the bedraggled, nervous, poverty-stricken crone—of Crazy Bet—effaced the image of the articulate, razor-sharp, and efficient spymaster and politician.

But thanks to modern scholarship on gender and the Civil War, Van Lew's life and legacy have at last come into clear focus. Recent scholarship has trained our attention on the contributions of women to the war efforts of both the Union and the Confederacy and on the political divisions within the South and how they contributed to the demise of the Confederacy. These themes in turn underscore the complex interrelatedness of the homefront and the battlefront, and the need for scholars to focus on both at once. Van Lew's life dramatically connects the themes of women's war work and southern Unionism.

For a long time, the standard narrative of women and the Civil War, inscribed in scholarship and popular culture, was the story of women's unflagging devotion to the cause—the Union or especially the Confederate one. While male civic duty in wartime was synonymous with the exercise of courage on the battlefield, women's duty was synonymous with sacrifice and benevolence, and especially with the willingness to send their men off to war and to channel their domestic skills into helping the troops. This patriotic division of labor reflected the predominant gender ideals of the Victorian era, particularly the idea that women's proper place was in the domestic sphere. Through the 1960s the vast majority of historical writing on women and the war told us how women fulfilled those duties.[25]

Since the advent of women's history as a field in the 1970s, a more fascinating story has come to light: we now see aspects of the Civil War as a conflict over gender roles and relations. Scholars have found provocative examples of women who felt that the prevailing ideal of sacrifice and benevolence asked too much of them—women who resisted the demands of patriotism in draft riots in the North and in bread riots in the South, and who in countless letters begged their men to desert the army or asked the government to exempt them from the draft. Much of this discontent and disillusionment flowed from the perception, strongest in the South, that the Civil War was a "rich man's war but a poor man's fight" and the more general belief that common people had been made to bear the brunt of wartime sacrifice.[26]

Scholars have also found provocative examples of women who felt that the prevailing ideal asked too little of them. A common lament in women's wartime letters and diaries was "I wish I was a man." In a society that valorized male courage as the highest virtue, these women wanted to give the full measure of devotion. In that spirit, countless women transgressed the boundary of women's prescribed sphere, the line between the homefront and the battlefront. These included thousands of female hospital workers, whose ranks were made up of orderlies, nurses, hospital managers, and even a few physicians. Even more surprising has been historians' discovery and documentation of 250 cases of women who disguised themselves as men and fought as soldiers in the Union and Confederate ranks. Van Lew was one of the countless women who were determined to do more than fulfill the prescribed gender conventions of their time, which relegated women to often passive supporting roles.[27]

Elizabeth Van Lew also was part of a larger—but often overlooked—tradition of southern dissent. It is commonplace for us, all of us, to equate the Confederacy and the South: for instance, we say that the South lost the Civil War. But as a number of recent studies show, that shorthand glosses over crucial divisions within the South and obscures the strong presence of southern Unionists who opposed the Confederacy. The South was divided by a number of regional fault lines, most notably the line dividing the mountainous upcountry "white belts" from the lowcountry "black belts" where plantation slavery predominated, and the line dividing what we might call the Border South or the Upper South—states like Virginia—from the Deep South. Upper South states had close cultural and economic ties to the North and stronger cohorts of Unionists than Deep South states did. There were, in a sense, many Souths—and many Virginias.

We can translate these divisions into striking numbers. Some 450,000 men from slave states fought in Union blue: 150,000 of these were African Americans; 200,000 were whites in the four slave states (Missouri, Kentucky, Delaware, and Maryland) that did not secede; and 100,000 were whites from Confederate states like Virginia. These 450,000 were half as many men as the entire Confederate army. These statistics give us a new perspective on an old debate: did the Confederacy lose because of the overwhelming numbers and resources of the North, or did the Confederacy die of internal causes, because of its own failure of will? If we confront the presence of Unionists in the South, we can fuse these two explanations and see that internal divisions in the South contributed to the North's advantages. The Confederacy could not and did not command the loyalty of the entire South. Among the legions of unconditional Unionists in the South, Van Lew was among the most prominent and significant.[28]

She is also a key transitional figure in an indigenous reform tradition in the South, a tradition represented by colonizationists, scalawags, readjusters/

fusionists, populists, and progressives.[29] Her story reminds us that such reformers have so often been doomed to failure not only because reactionaries were willing to use violence and fraud but because conservatives have suppressed the memory of these reform efforts. Not content with merely driving Van Lew and other native-born Republicans from office, former Confederates and their like-minded descendants also sought to write them out of existence. The myth that Van Lew was a crazy, lonely, old spinster—a "lone vixen," as one Richmond paper put it—was far less dangerous ideologically than the image of her as head of a brave, efficacious, and far-flung interracial network of reform-minded Virginians.

Finally, Van Lew's life sheds light on a foundational debate in southern women's history: was the Civil War a watershed, a turning point, for women?[30] Van Lew's postwar trials suggest that yes, the war was a turning point for women, though not in the simple sense that the war was good for them or advanced their quest for rights. What the war did was lend credence to the doctrine of female accountability—the notion that women are not innocents in wartime, but rather that they are agents who could be punished or rewarded for political acts. The central theme of Van Lew's embattled postmastership, and of her Reconstruction officeholding, was accountability: she was accountable for her work and rewarded for her services to the state. Ex-Confederates, though they had been blind to Van Lew's political agency during the war, held her accountable afterward for her wartime sins, and they accordingly refused to accept her attempts to cast herself as a nonpartisan civil servant. They instead cast her as traitor, whose punishment for her disloyalty should be a lifetime of derision and ostracism.

Interestingly, at the same time that the press was circulating stories of "Crazy Van Lew," Elizabeth's oldest friend, a fellow Unionist, longtime neighbor, and coworker in the post office, Eliza Griffin Carrington Nowland, was trying in vain to publish her own account of Elizabeth's life. "In a few brief pages I propose to portray the patriotic and philanthropic characteristics of Elizabeth Van Lew," Eliza began her manuscript, which was rejected by a Boston publisher. "Possessed of a logical mind," Nowland continued, Van Lew "believed slavery to be a blot on the nation. . . . When Patrick Henry stood in historic old St. John's Church and shouted 'Give me liberty or give me death,' the walls of the Old Van Lew mansion . . . echoed . . . and Elizabeth Van Lew's heart caught up the refrain and cried 'Give *them* liberty or give me death.' . . . Love for her family sustained her in her trials through her life. . . . I have never known as noble a woman."[31]

We owe it to this noble woman to put the myth of Crazy Bet in its proper place and context, and to recover a sense of the real Elizabeth Van Lew, a woman whom we should remember not only for her intelligence gathering but for her intelligence, not only for her ability to conceal the truth but for her ability to tell it.

NOTES

1. For an extensive treatment of Van Lew's life and documentation of the relevant sources, see Elizabeth R. Varon, *Southern Lady, Yankee Spy: The True Story of Elizabeth Van Lew, a Union Agent in the Heart of the Confederacy* (New York: Oxford University Press, 2003).

2. For the Van Lew myth, see, for example, David D. Ryan, ed., *A Yankee Spy in Richmond: The Civil War Diary of "Crazy Bet" Van Lew* (Mechanicsburg, Pa.: Stackpole, 1996), 59; Elizabeth D. Leonard, *All the Daring of the Soldier: Women of the Civil War Armies* (New York: Norton, 1999), 55; William Gilmore Beymer, "Miss Van Lew," *Harper's Monthly* (June 1911): 89–91.

3. The influential newspaper the *Richmond Enquirer* led the Reconstruction-era campaign to brand Van Lew as an outsider and a political heretic. See, for example, *Richmond Enquirer*, March 18, April 11 and 29, May 3 and 6, 1877.

4. Varon, *Southern Lady, Yankee Spy*, 20–32; on Richards, see, for example, Elizabeth Van Lew (hereafter EVL) to William McLain, April 20, September 29, and October 2, 1854, April 24, 1857, December 2, 1858, April 21, 1859, American Colonization Society Papers, Library of Congress.

5. Varon, *Southern Lady, Yankee Spy*, 45–51; Elizabeth Van Lew Papers, microfilm edition, Library of Virginia (hereafter EVLP), frames 41–42, 113. (Because many pages in Van Lew's papers are not clearly numbered, I have assigned a number to each microfilm frame; when clear page numbers are available, I list them first, followed by the frame numbers.) Van Lew's notion of Virginians as politically moderate on slavery and other issues is supported by the historical record. See, for instance, Lacy K. Ford, *Deliver Us from Evil: The Slavery Question in the Old South* (New York: Oxford University Press, 2009), esp. chap. 12.

6. EVL, "Notes on Her Ancestry," EVLP, frame 244.

7. Varon, *Southern Lady, Yankee Spy*, 56–57, 68; EVL, "Personal Narrative," EVLP, 17–18, frames 94–96.

8. Qtd. in Varon, *Southern Lady, Yankee Spy*, 88–93; *Richmond Dispatch*, July 17, 1883.

9. *Richmond Evening Leader*, July 27, 1900.

10. Beymer, "Miss Van Lew"; interview with Mrs. Annie R. [Van Lew] Hall, December 9, 1910, William Gilmore Beymer Papers, Center for American History, University of Texas, Austin.

11. Varon, *Southern Lady, Yankee Spy*, 209–12; *Anglo-African* (New York), October 7, 1865.

12. Varon, *Southern Lady, Yankee Spy*, 168–75; *Richmond Dispatch*, March 18, 1869, and July 17, 1883; *Richmond News Leader*, September 25, 1900.

13. Varon, *Southern Lady, Yankee Spy*, 168–75.

14. Horace Porter, *Campaigning with Grant* (1897; rpt., New York: Konecky and Konecky, 1991), 392; Adam Badeau, *Military History of General Ulysses S. Grant, from April, 1861 to April, 1865* (New York: Appleton, 1881), 2:243.

15. On the Libby Prison breakout, see Varon, *Southern Lady, Yankee Spy*, 118–33; on the Dahlgren reburial, see ibid., 135–43.

16. George Henry Sharpe to Cyrus Constock, January 1867, EVLP, frames 129–35.

17. Varon, *Southern Lady, Yankee Spy*, 178–82; Testimony of Mary C. Van Lew, Letters Received by the Confederate Adjutant and Inspector General, 1861–65, October 15, 1864, RG 109, National Archives.

18. Order of Charles Blackford, October 18, 1864, Letters Received by the Confederate Adjutant and Inspector General, 1861–65, RG 109, National Archives.

19. EVL, "Personal Narrative," April 2 and 3, 1865, EVLP, 730–33, frames 54–55.

20. Varon, *Southern Lady, Yankee Spy*, 220–31; EVL, "Article in Response to 'Men and Monopolists,'" EVLP, frames 216–18.

21. *Richmond Whig*, April 14, 1877; *Richmond Enquirer*, April 29, 1877.

22. *Boston Evening Transcript*, September 26, 1900; Ryan, *A Yankee Spy in Richmond*, 41.

23. Reynolds to Beymer, December 14, 1908, April 22 and 29, December 6, 1910, Beymer Papers.

24. Reynolds to Beymer, December 14, 1908, April 22 and 29, December 6, 1910, Beymer Papers.

25. See, for example, Mary Elizabeth Massey, *Bonnet Brigades: American Women and the Civil War* (New York: Knopf, 1966).

26. See, for example, Stephanie McCurry, *Confederate Reckoning: Power and Politics in the Civil War South* (Cambridge, Mass.: Harvard University Press, 2010); Drew Faust, *Mothers of Invention: Women of the Slaveholding South in the American Civil War* (Chapel Hill: University of North Carolina Press, 1996); George Rable, *Civil Wars: Women and the Crisis of Southern Nationalism* (Champaign: University of Illinois Press, 1991).

27. See, for example, Leonard, *All the Daring of the Soldier*; Nina Silber, *Gender and the Sectional Conflict* (Chapel Hill: University of North Carolina Press, 2009); DeAnne Blanton and Lauren M. Cook, *They Fought like Demons: Women Soldiers in the Civil War* (Baton Rouge: Louisiana State University Press, 2002).

28. William W. Freehling, *The South vs. the South: How Anti-Confederate Southerners Shaped the Course of the Civil War* (New York: Oxford University Press, 2002).

29. Carl Degler, *The Other South: Southern Dissenters in the Nineteenth Century* (New York: Harper & Row, 1974).

30. On this debate, see Anne Firor Scott, *The Southern Lady: From Pedestal to Politics, 1830–1930* (Chicago: University of Chicago Press, 1970); Faust, *Mothers of Invention*; Rable, *Civil Wars*; Silber, *Gender and the Sectional Conflict*.

31. Eliza Griffin [Carrington Nowland], "Reminiscences of Elizabeth Van Lew," EVLP, frames 180–87.

Antonia Ford Willard

Southern Belle, Yankee Wife

MICHELLE A. KROWL

Sometimes a single event can change the course of a person's life. For Antonia Ford of Fairfax Court House, Virginia, the capture of Union general Edwin H. Stoughton by Confederate lieutenant John S. Mosby on March 9, 1863, proved to be just such an event. Federal authorities suspected Antonia of complicity in Mosby's Fairfax raid. Her arrest and subsequent imprisonment garnered national attention, made her a heroine in the Confederacy, and eventually secured her a place in history with other female spies of the Civil War. More important for Antonia, however, her imprisonment attracted the attention of a major in the Union army, with whom she would fall in love and marry—a wartime act requiring more bravery than any espionage she might have committed. At the same time, the months she spent in prison may have adversely affected her health, which childbirth did nothing to improve, leading to her death at the age of thirty-two. Thus, Mosby's capture of Stoughton in 1863 brought Antonia Ford Willard love, loss, and a legacy.

Antonia's residence in the northernmost county in the Confederacy, adjacent to the enemy capital in Washington, constantly exposed her to soldiers, officials, and civilian adherents on both sides. The real Antonia Ford Willard may or may not have been a Confederate spy, but the historical record reveals her to have been intelligent, mischievous, courageous, entertaining, attractive, devoted to the people she loved, and willing to cross the boundaries of proper southern womanhood when she felt the cause to be a worthy one. During the war, two seemingly contradictory causes—support for the Confederacy and love for a Union officer—tested her resolve. She passed both tests. Her remarkable story shows how gender could be a source of both constraint and flexibility for women in such perilous times.

ANTONIA FORD WILLARD

The year of this photograph and the name of the photographer are unknown.
Library of Congress, Manuscript Division.

ANTONIA FORD LETTER

Antonia wrote frequently to her "dearest Major" in the days leading up to their wedding, assuring him of her eternal devotion. Here, she insists that she will cling to him even if his divorce causes a scandal.

Her closing, "Your own Antonia," is at the upper right.

Library of Congress, Manuscript Division.

Born on July 23, 1838, Antonia J. Ford was the eldest child of the prosperous Fairfax Court House merchant Edward R. Ford and his wife, Julia F. Ford. Antonia first attended school at nearby Coombe Cottage before moving on to more advanced studies in 1855 at Virginia's first women's college, the Buckingham Female Collegiate Institute in Buckingham County. Like many young students living away from home for the first time, Antonia initially succumbed to homesickness, but soon wrote to friends about her "dear school" and "her darling schoolmates" and her hopes to remain at Buckingham as a French teacher after graduation.[1]

Despite her upbringing as an educated young Virginia lady, contemporary accounts also reveal a mischievous side to Antonia's personality. At the Buckingham Institute she "tried one of [her] tricks to scare" her new schoolmates, but was disappointed when "they screamed so loud a teacher scolded me for the sin of a practical joke!" Others remembered her as "fond of mischief," "spirited, and fearless." As she grew older, she became known for her good looks, for being "a wit and gifted conversationalist," and for "tact and repartee." She also had some familiarity with northerners, as many had moved to northern Virginia for economic opportunities in the antebellum years. In fact, Antonia at first expressed "disappointment" with the southern girls she met at Buckingham Institute, considering them "as chilling as icebergs, nothing like the Northern girls I am accustomed to." Thus, Antonia Ford on the eve of the Civil War was a young woman who could be described as a "lady of great delicacy and refinement" and "very much admired & courted," comfortable interacting with northerners, while also willing to step beyond conventional boundaries for a bit of adventure.[2]

Courtship and eventual marriage were the presumed destiny of all southern belles. Antonia must have become very adept at being "admired & courted" by the end of 1861, since several men had succumbed to her charms. The unidentified "A. J.," for example, wrote Antonia in November 1861 claiming that despite a brief acquaintance, he had "long regarded [her] with much favor" after the first time he "beheld [her] beautiful countenance and through it received a glimpse of the noble [soul] that animates it." Since then his heart had alternated between "delightful hope and dispairing fear" of her feelings toward him. Since A. J. does not appear again in Antonia's correspondence, she most likely made him a "most *miserable* of mortals" by not encouraging his romantic pursuit.[3]

For Antonia to have been serious about a suitor early in the war, he would have had to sympathize with the Confederacy, since her most intimate associates were "rebels." Some historians have referred to Antonia's father as "a dedicated secessionist" and "strongly Southern." E. R. Ford's loyalty to the Confederacy led General J. E. B. Stuart to provide him with a pass to travel the Little River Turnpike freely in order to "procure supplies for the families at Fairfax Court House." Antonia's beloved brother Charles, a cadet at the Virginia Military Institute, attached himself to the Second South Carolina Infantry during the First Battle of Manassas in July 1861, and then enlisted as a second lieutenant in Stuart's Light Horse Artillery.[4]

To what extent Antonia's identification with the Confederate cause rested on her own political opinions or on the influence of her family is unclear. Her surviving correspondence fails to record her thoughts on secession, slavery, or the Union, nor did she articulate an understanding of the principles underlying the Confederate nation. Some scholarship suggests that unlike Unionist ideology during the Civil War, which emphasized duty to the nation before one's family or personal affiliations, Confederate nationalism drew to a far greater extent on loyalty to home and family. Consequently, for many Confederate women who might not have formulated independent political opinions (as well as for many who did), devotion to their families and deference to the political allegiances of the family patriarch contributed to their identity with and support for the new Confederate nation.[5] Regardless of whether her Confederate identity was based on political, philosophical, or emotional grounds, Antonia Ford allied herself with the Confederacy throughout the war.

The military buildup in Fairfax County brought additional admirers into Antonia's orbit. A politically divided northern county in the contested border state of Virginia, Fairfax County saw encampments of both Union and Confederate troops. Although Union military authorities often occupied Fairfax Court House itself, the Confederates maintained a presence in nearby Centreville and elsewhere in Fairfax County early in the war. These fluid boundaries allowed Antonia to socialize with nearby Confederates. The Confederate officer Thomas Lafayette Rosser developed a fondness for her, and General Stuart referred to Rosser specifically as "Miss Antonia's friend." Antonia's friend Laura Ratcliffe of Frying Pan (near Chantilly) drew her further into association with Stuart. The married general flirted with Ratcliffe, and some of his invitations to dinner and sleigh rides included Antonia as well. It was during these jolly days that Stuart made Antonia Ford an honorary member of his staff. On October 7, 1861, he wrote out a commission that read in part: "That reposing special confidence in the patriotism, fidelity, and ability of Miss [Ford], I, James E. B. Stuart . . . do hereby appoint and commission her my honorary aid-de-camp, to rank as such from this date. She will be obeyed, respected, and admired by all the lovers of a noble nature." While Stuart no doubt appreciated Antonia's loyalty to the Confederacy, he likely gave her the commission as a lark, without any expectation of actual service. Antonia, however, kept the commission as a treasured document.[6]

Barred from expressing their loyalty through military service or traditional political acts, some Confederate women in contested areas overcame their feelings of "uselessness" through espionage, among other activities on behalf of the cause, and Antonia's residence in Fairfax put her in a perfect location for gathering intelligence. Its proximity to both Confederate lines and Washington, D.C., as well as to major transportation routes in northern Virginia, made Fairfax an early target for Union occupation. The large and centrally located Ford house made it an early target for Union occupation as well. Union officers frequently lodged or entertained at the Ford home, even though much of the family was still in residence. Despite their known Confederate sympathies, the Fords seem to have maintained relatively pleasant relations with the Federal officers, and Antonia especially employed her charming personality to befriend the Yankees in the neighborhood. "Mr. Ford's house was a centre of attraction," remembered an acquaintance. "Officers of high and low degree gathered there and were entertained, drawn no doubt, by the fact that it was Antonia's home." Antonia's beauty and intelligent conversation lowered the guard of her new acquaintances, who likely shared more information about military matters than was wise. One contemporary described Antonia's gentle probing as being done "in an apparently very careless and no-interest-to-me-I-assure-you manner, which quite deceived the men." As one historian of southern women has noted, "long expert in managing men, Confederate women in wartime simply turned these skills to new purposes."[7]

Antonia's historical fame as an alleged spy, however, rests on one military operation in particular. Union authorities in occupied Fairfax were perfectly aware of the threat posed by Confederate rangers under John S. Mosby and by the hostile civilians still residing in northern Virginia. On March 1, 1863, Union general Edwin H. Stoughton wrote two dispatches warning of a breach in the Union picket lines near Fairfax and of spies in his vicinity. He urged that "women and other irresponsible persons in this neighborhood" be forced to take a loyalty oath or be expelled from his lines since these "rampant secessionists" were in the habit of keeping "their friends in the rebel service" well informed on Union military movements. If Stoughton felt that Fairfax women were so subversive as to be classified with "other irresponsible persons," it is unclear why forcing them to take an oath of allegiance to the United States would stop them from conveying information to Confederate friends, since an oath of allegiance is only as effective as the sincerity with which it is taken.[8]

One historian cites Stoughton's suggestion of forced oaths as indicative of a new willingness on the part of Union authorities to think of women as political actors. If southern women were capable of political allegiance and agency, they should be held "more accountable for their anti-Union sentiments." Had disloyal women in Fairfax County actually been compelled to swear allegiance to the United States in March 1863, the action might be interpreted as evidence of shifting views on the impact of women's actions on the homefront, and perhaps as a precursor to harsher tactics toward Confederate women, such as Union general Philip Sheridan's banishment of the Confederate Mary Greenhow Lee from Winchester, Virginia, in 1865.[9] As it was, Stoughton's warnings went unheeded, and the women remained both oathless and behind Union lines in Fairfax as of March 9.

Mosby's target on his nighttime raid was Colonel Percy Wyndham, who had insulted Mosby by referring to him as a horse thief. When Mosby's forces arrived in Fairfax at about 2:00 a.m. on March 9, they discovered that Wyndham had gone to Washington. While Mosby's men fanned out to capture horses and Federal prisoners, Mosby went to the Gunnell house, where General Stoughton slept. By posing as members of the Fifth New York Cavalry delivering a message to the general, Mosby's men gained access to the house and announced to the general that he had been captured. The raiders then reassembled in the courthouse square and fled back through Union lines with their haul of Union prisoners and even more valuable horses.[10]

In the aftermath of Stoughton's capture, Union authorities launched an investigation of the embarrassing incident. Not surprisingly, attention immediately focused on civilians in Fairfax who might have provided information to Mosby about weaknesses in the Union lines and the locations of officers in Fairfax. Antonia Ford's name especially came under scrutiny due to an article printed in the *New York Times* on March 14 in which a Vermont man claimed to have received a letter dated March 5, 1863, from a source in Fairfax. The letter noted that Stoughton made his headquarters several miles away from his brigade, leaving him vulnerable in case of attack. Furthermore, Antonia Ford, who held a commission from J. E. B. Stuart, was allowed to reside in Fairfax. "Why our people do not send her beyond the lines is another question," the author of the letter wondered. "I understand that she and Stoughton are very intimate," and the source predicted, "*If he gets picked up some night he may thank her for it.*" With such an accusation leveled at Antonia in a major national newspaper, which found the story credible enough to publish, she inevitably became a prime suspect.[11]

With attention now centered on Antonia's possible contribution to the raid, Union provost marshal Lafayette C. Baker assigned Frankie Abel, one of his female detectives, to visit Fairfax in the guise of a southern woman trying to reach friends behind Confederate lines. The Fords welcomed Abel into their home, and she shared a bedroom with Antonia, who apparently believed Abel's cover story. If Antonia was truly an accomplished spy, she displayed an exceptional lack of judgment in bragging about her exploits to Abel, and showing off the commission given to her by General Stuart in 1861. Abel's report triggered a search of Antonia's room, in which Union authorities found the commission and documents from Confederate officers. Backed by the authority of the secretary of war, Baker ordered Antonia's arrest and confinement at Old Capitol Prison in Washington, D.C.[12]

Antonia's commission garnered national attention and was widely reprinted in both northern and southern newspapers. The *Boston Herald* published the text of the commission and called Antonia "the Virginia Delilah who betrayed Brig. Gen. Stoughton." *Harper's Weekly* ran a cartoon of "General Stuart's New Aid," depicting Antonia on horseback, a drum and her skirts flying behind her as she briskly rides through a camp of cheering soldiers. Southern papers also reprinted Antonia's commission, but focused on the absence of chivalry among the Yankees, who persecuted women. This followed a pattern in Confederate press coverage of celebrating women's transgressions on behalf of the southern cause while also casting them as victims of northern aggression. The *Charleston Mercury* referred to Federal authorities as "the valiant warriors upon women" and called Lafayette Baker "a cowardly brute." Confederate John Esten Cooke claimed to have been present when Stuart presented Antonia with the commission. "Who could have ever imagined that the gay jest of the moment—that paper which was written by a brave soldier and presented with mock formality to the fair young lady . . . would in these days become the ground of a grave accusation against the maiden," he wrote. He then accused the Union of making war on Confederate women: "So they go—these people. They cannot catch our partisans, but they arrest our young [ladies]." In reporting on Antonia's case, the political war between the states became a gender conflict as well.[13]

The tantalizing question remains: was she guilty? If Antonia did provide Mosby with intelligence about Stoughton and the military situation in Fairfax, she was certainly not his only source of information. A leading authority on Mosby's Rangers states that Antonia played no role in the raid itself, even if she had passed along "unguarded remarks" made in her presence by Union soldiers. Mosby planned his raid based on a combination of reconnaissance, civilian intelligence, and information provided by Union prisoners and deserters. Mosby told a correspondent in 1914 that "Antonia was as innocent as Abraham Lincoln" in terms of participating in the Fairfax raid. Perhaps the authors of *Mosby's Confederacy* have provided the most accurate assessment of her complicity: "Whether Antonia Ford provided Mosby with information that helped make his raid a success has been, and probably always will be, a matter of controversy."[14]

Unlike other Confederate women accused of spying, such as Rose Greenhow and Belle Boyd, Antonia never wrote a memoir or spoke publicly about her wartime adventures, so her actions remain open to speculation, interpretation, and embellishment. However, many Civil War women in contested areas used their femininity to their advantage, knowing that male assumptions about female incapability often placed them above suspicion. To think that Antonia Ford actively spied for the Confederacy, and perhaps on more than one occasion, is certainly reasonable. The story of Antonia racing to Confederate lines with vital intelligence prior to the Second Battle of Manassas in 1862 is mirrored in a similar tale told of Belle Boyd flirting her way through Union lines in the Shenandoah Valley to deliver timely information to Confederate general Stonewall Jackson. Mosby credited Laura Ratcliffe with defying Union expectations by being able to reach Mosby in time to warn him of a trap. "This was not the only time during the war," Mosby recalled in his memoirs, "when I owed my escape from danger to the tact of a Southern woman." In Richmond, Elizabeth Van Lew relied on her status as a southern lady to deflect suspicion from her continued devotion to the United States and her far more dangerous and ongoing work in a successful Union espionage ring, despite living in the Confederate capital.[15]

Regardless of Antonia's guilt or innocence in connection with the Mosby raid, the discovery of Stuart's commission and other Confederate-related documents provided enough evidence of her disloyalty to the United States to justify her incarceration. Antonia, her father, and several other male civilians from Fairfax were all arrested as "rebel sympathizers" in March 1863 and sent to the Old Capitol Prison complex on Capitol Hill in Washington. Arrested as a "rebel spy" on March 16, Antonia appears to have been incarcerated in Carroll Prison, which was located next to Old Capitol and served as an annex.[16]

Officials allowed Antonia to write her mother with assurances that she and her father were both "comfortably fixed and very well," though she urged her mother to "make a clean sweep in gathering up my things," suggesting that perhaps incriminating articles still lurked among her possessions. The prison superintendent, William Wood, permitted Antonia to receive unsealed letters from home and to send for a trunk filled with items she thought necessary for prison life. Antonia requested an impressively long list of practical items, as well as the novel *Les Misérables* and sheet music for "The Bonnie Blue Flag" and "Dixie," which seemed to push the limits of what a Confederate inmate in a Union prison ought to possess. Antonia's prison poetry also reflected her continued Confederate allegiance: "On some auspicious day / We'll meet, I'll be with 'the advance,' / By gallant Stuart led; / With Rosser, Charlie by my side / Waving—'Red white and red.'"[17]

On May 11, 1863, Antonia was transferred from prison and sent across the lines for exchange at City Point, near Petersburg, Virginia. Her father was likewise sent to City Point the next month. Neither Ford had taken an oath of allegiance to the United States, which meant they could both be rearrested should they return to Union-occupied Fairfax. Antonia and her father separately moved north from City Point, and both were again arrested shortly after arriving in Fairfax, Antonia on September 12, 1863. The Unionist *Alexandria News* expressed the hope that Antonia's recapture would force her to "reflect upon the evil of her ways." In fact, within days of returning to Old Capitol both Fords took the oath of allegiance, and Antonia received a military pass on September 18 allowing her to return safely to Fairfax Court House. For E. R. Ford, taking the oath of allegiance may have been a matter of practicality, but Antonia's willingness to renounce her Confederate allegiance in deed, if perhaps not in thought, may have been prompted by love. The heart of the "rebel spy" had been captured by Union major Joseph C. Willard.[18]

Born in Vermont in 1820, Joseph Clapp Willard co-owned the prosperous Willard Hotel in Washington, D.C., with his brother Henry. At the outbreak of the war, the Willard brothers relinquished active management of the hotel to a leasing company, and Joseph enlisted in the Union army on March 4, 1862, ultimately achieving the rank of major. He first served under General Irvin McDowell, and by 1863 had joined the staff of General Samuel P. Heintzelman, who oversaw the defenses of Washington. Willard remained in the Washington area for much of his service with McDowell and Heintzelman, and his duties took him to the Union outpost of Fairfax Court House, where he first met the Fords in April 1862. After dining at the Ford home with General John Pope and his wife, Willard received orders from Pope to place a protective guard at the house. The Fords expressed their appreciation, and Willard noted in his diary that "Miss Ford says if I am taken prisoner I must come to her house." By September 1862 Antonia and Joseph had made a noticeable impression on one another.[19]

Interaction between Union officers and southern civilians occurred frequently in what one historian has termed "garrison towns," urban areas securely occupied by Union forces. While the proximity of Confederate troops near Fairfax Court House in the first years of the war and the lingering threat of partisan raids thereafter qualified it as more of a "no man's land" between Washington, D.C., and the Confederate lines than as a typical garrison town, the early arrival and prolonged stay of Union authorities meant that Antonia Ford's hometown settled into a pattern of Union occupation at a time during which relations between the two sides were relatively friendly. During this period Union authorities tolerated a certain amount of Confederate sympathies among the populace, especially the women. In garrison towns, the interaction between Confederates and Yankees often developed into relationships that humanized the enemy and allowed for socializing, and sometimes the development of romantic relationships. Furthermore, Fairfax's history of antebellum settlement by northerners and local Unionist presence during the war may have led to less fraught relations between Union military authorities and residents in occupied Fairfax than in other areas of Virginia—where embittered Confederates resented the unfamiliar and increasingly draconian Yankee conquerors—further easing the association between Major Willard and the Fords.[20]

Whatever the nature of the relationship between Antonia and Joseph before March 1863, it blossomed into romance after Antonia's arrest. Given her lenient treatment at Carroll Prison, it is possible that Willard's military connections in Washington and high standing in the community as the owner of the Willard Hotel allowed him to secure Antonia the privileges afforded her. Benjamin O. Tayloe wrote to Willard on March 23 expressing hope that the Major's "chivalry ought to be rewarded by your being permitted to see the lady in whom of course you feel a lively interest," and he offered to help Willard to provide Antonia with whatever items she needed for her "comfort & convenience." By the time of Antonia's final release from prison in September 1863, she and Major Willard clearly had fallen in love. Telegrams and military passes document his continued interest in Antonia's welfare, and his multiple trips across the lines to and from Fairfax certainly included visits to the Ford home. If any doubt remained as to the depth of their feelings for one another, despite the problems presented by their romance, their love letters from then on provide passionate and indisputable evidence of their devotion.[21]

By December 1863 Joseph's ardor for Antonia was so strong that he proposed they enter into "a private marriage" in which they would enjoy the emotional bonds of matrimony, but not the legal or religious sanction of an official marriage. Antonia responded on New Year's Eve with an extraordinary letter assuring him of her devotion, but rejecting his unusual proposal. "You *know* I love you, but Major I can *never* consent to a private marriage," she explained. "My parents and relatives would be mortified and distressed to death; acquaintances would disown me; it would be illegal, and above all it would be *wrong*." Could she make him "the happiest man in the world" without compromising her principles, she would. "You ask for my 'heart and hand,'" she continued. "The heart is yours already. When *your* hand is free and you can claim mine before the world, *then that also is yours.* Surely you are now satisfied. I've promised in 'black and white[']' to marry you when you are at *liberty* to *marry*. . . . Remember Major, the obstacle is with you, not me." Antonia then explained that she thought "fate has a good deal to do with us any how. . . . I was literally thrown in your way by a power above us, call it *Destiny* I think that a prettier word than *fate*. Now, Major, let's be hopeful, and expect Destiny, (as she has taken *our fate* in her hands) to work out something joyful for us."[22]

Historians have often mistakenly argued that the obstacle preventing Antonia from marrying Willard was his blue Federal uniform. Despite her oath of allegiance to the United States, her brother Charles still served under J. E. B. Stuart and the Confederacy still claimed her sympathies. As long as Willard remained in the Union army, this interpretation seems plausible: Antonia perhaps felt herself unable to wed a man who was actively engaged in defeating the Confederacy and those who stood for it. The truth, however, was more complicated. In 1863 Willard's hand was not free to claim any woman's because legally it still belonged to his wife. Major Willard was a married man.

Joseph Willard had married Caroline Moore in New York in 1849, but the fact that Willard did not inform his wife of his brief move to California in 1851 suggests the marriage quickly ran into trouble.[23] When Joseph returned to the east coast to join his brother in the hotel business, he collected Caroline and they both moved to Washington. Although they lived together, the marriage broke down irretrievably and they took the unusual step of obtaining a formal legal separation in March 1862. While they "lived separately, and apart . . . and wholly estranged, the one from the other," and Joseph had provided Caroline with a comfortable financial settlement, they remained married in the eyes of the law.[24] When Antonia reminded Joseph in December 1863 that "the obstacle is with you," she correctly noted that it would be illegal for them to wed, and she was not willing to live in sin as only his de facto wife.

In mid-February 1864 Caroline Willard filed for divorce on the grounds of Joseph's adultery, but not on the basis of his affection for Antonia. In her petition Caroline claimed that Joseph had had sexual relationships with "women of damaged reputations, and yielding virtue" at the Willard Hotel and that he had installed his mistress, Caroline Rosekrans, in the family home in the winter of 1859, a claim to which two former Willard slaves, Mary Cecilia Ratcliffe and John Thomas, testified. In his reply, Willard denied any association with "women of damaged reputations," but admitted having committed adultery after his loveless marriage had "wrecked" his "domestic happiness." The court agreed that the Willard marriage "should be severed" and granted a divorce decree on March 2, 1864.[25] Destiny had made Joseph Willard a free man, but at the cost of a failed marriage, a public divorce, and court documents recording allegations of adultery—none of which diminished Antonia's love.

With "the Major," as he was known in the Ford family, now in possession of Antonia's heart and a pledge for her hand once his divorce proceedings were completed, the two forged ahead with plans to marry, but kept their engagement secret. Antonia knew her marriage would be met with scorn locally, since Joseph was still a married (until March 2), much-older New England–born Yankee officer, whom many in the community would consider an unsuitable match for a twenty-five-year-old Virginia girl with southern sympathies and a brother in the Confederate military. Thus, Antonia prepared to cast off any disapproving acquaintances in Fairfax and find all the companionship she needed in the bosom of her immediate family. Confederate sympathizers in Fairfax would forgive as a passing act of patriotism Antonia's public transgression of prevailing gender conventions when she allegedly spied for the Confederate cause. Marrying a Yankee, however, was quite a different thing, and in doing so she would demonstrate even more courage to be with the man she loved. "Who cares what they all say," she proclaimed to Joseph, "as long as we are satisfied and happy!" Truthfully she *did* care what her neighbors said, but she willingly chose a life with the Major over the approval of her community.[26]

Although both Antonia and Joseph were determined to wed someone whose political allegiances were contrary to their own, gender shaped how others perceived their choices. Perhaps because many contemporaries believed that women's political allegiance was at worst inconceivable and at best informed by emotion and personal connections, Joseph was unlikely to be censured for marrying a southern woman. Antonia's choice was more transgressive: the Unionist loyalties of her fiancé were both unquestionable and deeply entrenched, and his military commission signified that he was able to inflict real harm on Confederate communities. Perhaps Antonia hoped that the widespread belief that women privileged romance over politics would help people in her community to accept the Major as her intended spouse.

As the wedding approached, Antonia wrote to her fiancé nearly every day, revealing both the challenges they faced to be united and the deep devotion that would see them through each ensuing crisis. Willard submitted his resignation from the army, which went into effect on March 1, 1864, the day prior to his divorce from Caroline. Antonia feared that both events would be traumatic for him. She hoped he did not regret his resignation, or the possible rejection of his

Union sympathies that his resignation might imply. "*No one has ever* accused you of being anything but the *most decided* unionist," she assured him. "I know you are true to the government, but I *love you none the less* for it." While she could not join him in endorsing *the* Union, she pledged her faith in *their* union. She congratulated him on his divorce, but worried that the associated scandal had depressed his spirits. "You had just passed through a great trouble; one undertaken solely on my account," she wrote, sympathetically. "What if they do talk! We dont care," she reassured him. "Darling dont allow it to sadden you, the more dearly I will love you and more closely cling to you."[27]

The couple also struggled to make practical arrangements for their wedding, which the war further complicated. Without any recognized authority in northern Virginia who could issue marriage licenses, they decided to marry in Washington, D.C. With Confederate raiders still patrolling the roads to Fairfax, they negotiated the safest travel arrangements they could: the Major would come for Antonia on the morning of their wedding and return to Washington with her and her father, hopefully without anyone being captured along the way.[28]

Despite these obstacles, the couple was sustained by the blessings of many close friends and family members. Benjamin Tayloe assured Willard he would "'not think less' of you for marrying a poor but intelligent and more than, all a *respectable Virginian*," and wished the couple much happiness. Antonia assured Joseph that none of her immediate family members objected to their marriage, not even her brother Charlie, who still fought for the Confederacy. Major Willard had also made a favorable personal impression on a number of Fairfax residents, who dropped hints to Antonia about his virtues, little knowing she already had pledged to be his wife. That Willard served as an officer in the Union army and owned a successful hotel may have ameliorated some objections to the Major, since he at least belonged to an equivalent social class as that of the Fords, and may have been viewed as a possible patron for the family and community. The status of being an officer, as opposed to an enlisted man, smoothed relations between combatants in more than one occupied town during the war, whereas Antonia's "respectability" as a lady counted in her favor with Willard's northern friends.[29]

When March 10, 1864, finally arrived, Antonia and Joseph were married at the Metropolitan Hotel by Pastor P. D. Gurley of the New York Avenue Presbyterian Church. The *Evening Star* reported on the nuptials, commenting that Antonia "visits the city this time under more agreeable auspices" than her previous trips to prison. The newlyweds then boarded a train for Philadelphia, where they spent their honeymoon. Despite displaying confidence during her previous adventures, like many new brides Antonia suffered from wedding night jitters.

Her more experienced husband soon put her at ease, and she confessed to her mother that he "succeeded much better than I supposed could be the case."[30]

On returning from Philadelphia, the Willards set up housekeeping in Washington. Just before their marriage Antonia had written Joseph that "they say a married life is *not all* sunshine, but I must confess I cant *conceive* of shade while with you." But shade did indeed fall over the early months of the Willard marriage as they negotiated the realities of living as a divided family on the North-South border. Living away from home, Antonia missed her mother terribly. "Many a night I can't sleep or even lie still for thinking of the separation from you," she wrote. Out of the military and without an active occupation, Joseph initially felt restless and irritable and, to Antonia's horror, contemplated returning to the army. Antonia endured his crossness when directed at her, but she felt isolated and friendless in the city. Having given up so much of her previous life to marry the Major, she keenly realized her complete dependence on him when he was physically or emotionally absent.[31]

News from Fairfax in those early days depressed her further. She experienced pangs of guilt in enjoying such bounty in Washington, knowing that her family in nearby war-ravaged northern Virginia went without. "I have no pleasure in eating when I think of you all being deprived of what I have," she wrote to her mother. Her mood was not improved by the knowledge that some in Fairfax still gossiped maliciously about her marriage, which the Major greatly resented after having tried to show the community every kindness. Then, crushing news reached Antonia just a couple of months into her married life: her beloved brother Charlie had been killed in May 1864 during the fighting in Virginia, and had been buried in Hollywood Cemetery in Richmond. It must have been difficult for her to mourn a Confederate death while living in the U.S. capital. While other southern women wrestled with the prospect of continuing to sacrifice loved ones and physical comforts for Confederate men and for the Confederate cause that increasingly failed to ensure their "care and protection," Antonia instead wrestled with having her needs met by marrying a Yankee, while her family still suffered for the cause she still supported. All in all, Antonia wondered if her sister should marry a Virginian to avoid such cross-sectional difficulties.[32]

Eventually, the sun began to shine on the Willards once more. After the slightly rough start to their marriage, they established comfortable patterns of life. The Major agreed to let Antonia's teenaged sister, Pattie, live with them while she attended school in Washington, which also gave Antonia a trusted confidante. Then, just as the war ended, the Willard household celebrated the birth of Joseph Edward Willard in May 1865. Jodie, as he was commonly known, became the center of his parents' lives, especially Antonia's. Soon Antonia found that she could even joke about her mixed marriage, commenting to Joseph that unlike a childless couple she knew, the Willards represented "the prolific combination of Secesh & Yankee." A friend later recalled that when asked why she had married a Union man, Antonia mischievously replied, "I know I could not revenge myself on the nation but was fully capable of tormenting one Yankee to death so took the Major."[33]

Early in her married life Antonia established a precedent of returning to her family home in Fairfax during the summer. The heat was less intense in the countryside than in the city, and her devoted family helped her care for Jodie. As neither Antonia's nor Jodie's health was always robust, Antonia credited the time in Fairfax as "the baby's salvation," as well as her own.[34] Reminiscent of their courting days, Antonia and Joseph maintained their relationship primarily through letter writing during their months apart, which were punctuated by the Major's brief visits to Fairfax. Like most domestic correspondence, in these letters the everyday business of living predominated. Jodie's variable health and his childhood antics inspired frequent commentary by Antonia. She also described her days, confided her despair of truly becoming a good Christian, and thanked her husband for the supplies he sent to Fairfax, which was still recovering from wartime shortages. Many of Antonia's letters resemble those of her flirtatious courtship days in assuring the Major of her continuing love and devotion to him. "Wont it be funny if our letters are opened and read?" she teased. "Unless they knew they would suppose we were just married. Four years is a right long *honey*-moon, is it not?"[35]

Tragically, the honeymoon was not to last. Ill health had plagued Antonia for several years, which some observers blamed on her brief stay in prison, but which was likely more attributable to her multiple pregnancies and miscarriages. Whatever its origin, Antonia's frailty frustrated her, and she felt like a burden to her family. "I feel so keenly my utter helplessness to you," she told her husband. "You require a *strong robust hopeful* wife [and] I'm just the reverse—a bill of expense and no use under heaven." In March 1868, convinced that she was near death, Antonia wrote her mother two goodbye letters, saying how hard it was for her to leave those she loved. She also wondered if someone had poisoned her "for marrying the Major," which not only demonstrated the agony of her medical condition but also suggested that there was lingering resentment about her marriage, or perhaps some sort of subconscious guilt as she faced judgment day. After Jodie's birth Antonia became pregnant at least three additional times, giving birth to two sons, Charlie and Archie, who both died in infancy. As was the case for many women in the nineteenth century, the pregnancies further weakened Antonia's already fragile constitution, and the birth of Archie on February 9, 1871, likely led to Antonia's death five days later.[36]

Crushed by the loss of his beloved wife, Joseph Willard remained a widower until his death in 1897. While many in Washington viewed him as unsociable and reclusive in his later years, what society did not see were the brief but sentimental entries in his financial journals that noted the important anniversaries in his short life with Antonia, and how happy they had been with one another. Willard also grieved for the loss of his close friend and father-in-law, E. R. Ford, who died in November 1871, nine months after Antonia. Antonia's dying wish had been for her son to be raised in Fairfax by her sister, Pattie, who had been devoted to Jodie since his birth. Joseph acquiesced to Antonia's wish, and Pattie raised Jodie as her own, while also ensuring the Major's presence in his son's life. Willard, in turn, made sure that Jodie and the Ford family wanted for nothing, and assumed a fatherly role during his young brother-in-law Frank's adolescent years.[37]

In death Antonia Ford Willard crossed the boundary between life and legend. Each generation seems to return to and perpetuate her story, whether to celebrate her contribution to the Confederate cause, discuss her supposed espionage as part of a general survey of female spies of the Civil War, cite her relationship with Major Willard as an example of North-South courtship during the war, or present it as a love story with a Romeo-and-Juliet quality. By far the most popular threads of Antonia's story for journalists, novelists, and amateur and professional historians alike have always been her spying for the Confederates and her romance with Major Willard. Both feature characteristics that are eternally appealing for historical and human interest stories: adventure, espionage, danger, forbidden love, and tragedy. Together, they also demonstrate how women could negotiate personal and political challenges in a uniquely volatile era. The seemingly contradictory choices she made about political allegiances and personal relationships brought her love and loss and an enduring historical legacy.

NOTES

1. Marker F-54, "Female Collegiate Institute," in *A Guidebook to Virginia's Historical Markers*, rev. ed., comp. John S. Salmon (Charlottesville: University of Virginia Press, 1996), 40; Antonia Ford (hereafter AF) to Frances Carper, 1855, in Cordelia Grantham Sansone, *Journey to Bloomfield: Lives and Letters of 19th Century Virginia Families* (Fairfax, Va.: AlphaGraphics Printshops of the Future, 2004), 55, 76; AF to Frances Carper, June 1856, ibid., 83; AF to Julia F. Ford (hereafter JFF), October 10,

1864, container I: 167; and diploma, container I: OV-1, Willard Family Papers, Manuscript Division, Library of Congress.

2. AF to Frances Carper, spring 1855, in Sansone, *Journey to Bloomfield*, 55–56; Sallie Ford to Holly, July 8, 1924, and Kate F. Willcoxon to Belle W. Willard, n.d., container I: 173, Willard Papers; Ben H. Miller, "Antonia Ford, Confederate Spy," *The Sun* (Baltimore), January 3, 1932; typed transcript of John Eston Cooke article in *Southern Illustrated News*, August 15, 1863, container I: 173, Willard Papers.

3. "A. J." to AF, November 27, 1861, container I: 167, Willard Papers. See, generally, Anya Jabour, *Scarlett's Sisters: Young Women in the Old South* (Chapel Hill: University of North Carolina Press, 2007), esp. chap. 4.

4. "Antonia Ford Willard," National Park Service, www.nps.gov/resources/person.htm?id=134 (accessed August 25, 2012); Ernest B. Furgurson, "The Spy Who Loved Him," *Washington Post Magazine* (October 31, 2004), 13; military pass dated November 25, 1861, container I: 172, Willard Papers; entry for "Charles Edward Ford (Confederate)," in the American Civil War Research Database, http://asp6new.alexanderstreet.com/cwdb; C. E. Ford to JFF, March 5, 1862, container I: 167, Willard Papers.

5. Nina Silber, *Gender and the Sectional Conflict* (Chapel Hill: University of North Carolina Press, 2009), 19, 40–41; George C. Rable, *Civil Wars: Women and the Crisis of Southern Nationalism* (Urbana: University of Illinois Press, 1991), 63, 145.

6. T. Lafayette Rosser to AF, September 11, 1861, container I: 167, Willard Papers; photostatic copy of J. E. B. Stuart to Laura Ratcliffe, January 6, 1862, and Stuart to Laura Ratcliffe and AF, January 30, 1862, both in Jeb Stuart Correspondence, 1861–62, Manuscript Division, Library of Congress; commission qtd. in L. C. Baker, *History of the United States Secret Service* (1867; rpt., Bowie, Md.: Heritage Books, 1992), 172. The location of the original commission given to Antonia Ford by Stuart is unknown. Baker claimed to have it in his possession in his March 1863 report to Secretary of War Stanton. As of 1950, the commission could not be found in the Baker-Turner Papers at the National Archives. See Wayne C. Grover to Mrs. Kermit Roosevelt, July 28, 1950, container I: 172, Willard Papers.

7. Drew Gilpin Faust, "Altars of Sacrifice: Confederate Women and the Narratives of War," *Journal of American History* 76 (1990): 1206; George W. Shreve to Belle W. Willard, December 1934, container I: 173, Willard Papers; Harnett T. Kane, *Spies for the Blue and Gray* (Garden City, N.Y.: Hanover House, 1954), 170; Drew Gilpin Faust, *Mothers of Invention: Women of the Slaveholding South in the American Civil War* (Chapel Hill: University of North Carolina Press, 1996), 218, 198.

8. E. H. Stoughton to C. H. Potter, March 1, 1863, in *The War of the Rebellion: A Compilation of the Official Records of the Union and Confederate Armies* (hereafter *OR*), ser. 1, vol. 25, pt. II (Washington, D.C.: Government Printing Office, 1880–1901), 114–15.

9. Silber, *Gender and the Sectional Conflict*, 61; Sheila R. Phipps, *Genteel Rebel: The Life of Mary Greenhow Lee* (Baton Rouge: Louisiana State University Press, 2004), 199–201.

10. Jeffry D. Wert, *Mosby's Rangers* (New York: Simon & Schuster, 1990), 18–22; John S. Mosby to J. E. B. Stuart, March 11, 1863, *OR*, ser. 1, vol. 25, pt. I, 1121–22.

11. Thomas J. Evans and James M. Moyer, *Mosby's Confederacy: A Guide to the Roads and Sites of Colonel John Singleton Mosby* (Shippensburg, Pa.: White Mane, 1991), 1; *New York Times*, March 14 and 16, 1863.

12. Baker, *History of the United States Secret Service*, 171–73.

13. *Boston Herald*, March 20, 1863; *Harper's Weekly*, April 4, 1863, 211; Elizabeth R. Varon, *South-*

ern Lady, Yankee Spy: The True Story of Elizabeth Van Lew, a Union Agent in the Heart of the Confederacy (New York: Oxford University Press, 2003), 62; *Charleston Mercury*, March 25, 1863; typed transcript of John Esten Cooke article in *Southern Illustrated News*, August 15, 1863, container I: 173, Willard Papers.

14. Wert, *Mosby's Rangers*, 48 (quote), 18, 43; copy of John S. Mosby to Mrs. Merchant, December 9, 1914, container I: 172, Willard Papers; Evans and Moyer, *Mosby's Confederacy*, 5.

15. Ernest B. Furgurson, *Freedom Rising: Washington in the Civil War* (New York: Knopf, 2004), 262; *The Sun* (Baltimore), January 3, 1932; Kane, *Spies for the Blue and Gray*, 171; Faust, *Mothers of Invention*, 215–17; Elizabeth D. Leonard, *All the Daring of the Soldier: Women of the Civil War Armies* (New York: Norton, 1999), 28–29; Charles V. Mauro, *A Southern Spy in Northern Virginia: The Civil War Album of Laura Ratcliffe* (Charleston, S.C.: History Press, 2009), 98; John S. Mosby, *Mosby's War Reminiscences, Stuart's Cavalry Campaigns* (1887; rpt., New York: Dodd, Mead, 1898), 66; Varon, *Southern Lady, Yankee Spy*, 52–193. On Van Lew, see also the chapter in this volume.

16. For the imprisonment records of Antonia and E. R. Ford, see primarily Book Records (Prisoner Registers & Statements), vols. B, E, and F, entry 179B, Baker-Turner Papers, 1862–65, RG 94, Records of the Adjutant General's Office, 1780s–1917, National Archives and Records Administration (hereafter NARA); Register of Prisoners Compiled by the Office of the Commissary General of Prisoners, vol. 349, Old Capitol Prison, Washington, D.C., Selected Records of the War Department Relating to Confederate Prisoners of War (National Archives Microfilm Publication M-598), reel 110, frames 79–80; Curtis Carroll Davis, "The 'Old Capitol' and Its Keeper: How William P. Wood Ran a Civil War Prison," *Records of the Columbia Historical Society* 52 (1989): 214. Depending on the register consulted, the arrest, exchange, and release dates for the Fords can vary by several days.

17. AF to JFF, n.d., container I: 170, Willard Papers; list of items requested from prison by AF, n.d., container I: 173, ibid.; poem by AF, n.d., ibid.

18. *Evening Star* (Washington, D.C.), May 14, 1863; see also the imprisonment records referenced above. Dabney Ball to AF, June 18, 1863, container I: 167, Willard Papers; E. R. Ford to AF, June 29, 1863, ibid.; *Alexandria News*, September 15, 1863, reprinted in *Evening Star* (Washington, D.C.), September 16, 1863; vols. B and E, entry 179B, Baker-Turner Papers, RG 94, NARA. E. R. Ford was arrested on September 15, 1863, and released on September 21. Military pass, September 18, 1863, pt. II, container 1, Willard Papers.

19. Garnett Laidlaw Eskew, *Willard's of Washington: The Epic of a Capital Caravansary* (New York: Coward-McCann, 1954), 17–18; Richard Wallace Carr and Marie Pinak Carr, *The Willard Hotel: An Illustrated History* (Washington: Dicmar Publishing, 1986, 2005), 15–17; Henry Kellogg Willard, "Henry Augustus Willard: His Life and Times," *Records of the Columbia Historical Society* 20 (1917): 246; "Joseph Clapp Willard," U.S. Civil War Soldier Records and Profiles, www.ancestry.com (accessed August 23, 2012); testimony by Joseph C. Willard (hereafter JCW), December 31, 1862, OR, ser. 1, vol. 12, pt. I, 161; endorsement by Irvin McDowell, draft of JCW to Edwin M. Stanton, February 28, 1863, container I: 9, Willard Papers; JCW to Susan D. Willard, May 13, 1863, container I: 167, ibid.; JCW diary transcription, April 9, 1862, and JCW diary, April 9, 1884, and September 1–2, 1862, all in container I: 1, ibid.

20. Stephen V. Ash, *When the Yankees Came: Conflict and Chaos in the Occupied South, 1861–1865* (Chapel Hill: University of North Carolina Press, 1995), esp. 42–43, 218–20; Amy Murrell Taylor, *The Divided Family in Civil War America* (Chapel Hill: University of North Carolina Press, 2005), 51; Nan Netherton et al., *Fairfax County, Virginia: A History* (Fairfax, Va.: Fairfax County Board of Supervisors, 1978), 352.

21. Taylor, *Divided Family*, 52–53; *Evening Star* (Washington, D.C.), May 14, 1863; Benjamin Ogle Tayloe to JCW, March 23, 1863, container I: 9, Willard Papers; AF to JCW, February 26, 1864, container I: 167, ibid. For telegrams and military passes, see container I: 9, ibid.

22. AF to JCW, December 31, 1863, container I: 167, Willard Papers.

23. Divorce proceedings between Caroline M. Willard and Joseph C. Willard, case 163, Equity Case Files, 1863–1938, entry 69, Records of the District Courts of the United States, RG 21, NARA (hereafter Willard Divorce Proceedings); Henry A. Willard to JCW, June 8, 1851, container I: 3, Willard Papers; Henry A. Willard to JCW, February 22 and June 22, 1852; JCW to Susan D. Willard, March 15, 1862; and Henry A. Willard to JCW, October 10, 1852, all in container I: 167, ibid.

24. Willard Divorce Proceedings; P. W. Tayloe to Mrs. Moore, March 6, 1862, container I: 9, Willard Papers.

25. Willard Divorce Proceedings; *Evening Star* (Washington, D.C.), March 2, 1864; H. Donald Winkler, *Stealing Secrets: How a Few Daring Women Deceived Generals, Impacted Battles, and Altered the Course of the Civil War* (Naperville, Ill.: Cumberland House, 2010), 190–91.

26. AF to JCW, March 1, [1864], container I: 167, Willard Papers; Silber, *Gender and the Sectional Conflict*, xiii. For another example of a southern community's response to the marriage of a Union officer and a Confederate woman, see Suzy Barile, *Undaunted Heart: The True Story of a Southern Belle and a Yankee General* (Hillsborough, N.C.: Eno Publishers, 2009).

27. James A. Hardee to JCW, February 11, 1864, container I: 9; extract copy of Special Orders no. 70, Adjutant General's Office, February 12, 1864; AF to JCW, February 28, 1864; AF to JCW, February 29, 1864; AF to JCW, March 5, [1864], all in container I: 167, Willard Papers.

28. AF to JCW, February 22, 1864; AF to JCW, February 29, 1864, and March 5, [1864], all in container I: 167, Willard Papers.

29. Benjamin Ogle Tayloe to JCW, March 6, 1864; AF to JCW, March 1, [1864]; AF to JCW, February 22 and 24, 1864, all in container I: 167, Willard Papers; Margaret Creighton, "Gettysburg Out of Bounds: Women and Soldiers in the Embattled Borough, 1863," in *Occupied Women: Gender and Military Occupation and the American Civil War*, ed. LeeAnn Whites and Alecia P. Long (Baton Rouge: Louisiana State University Press, 2009), 74; Cita Cook, "The Practical Ladies of Occupied Natchez," ibid., 133–34.

30. Marriage license, issued on March 8 and endorsed on March 10, 1864, container I: 172, Willard Papers; *Evening Star* (Washington, D.C.), March 15, 1864; AF to JFF, March 19, 1864, container I: 167, Willard Papers.

31. AF to JCW, March 3, [1864]; and AF to JFF, c. 1864, both in container I: 167; AF to JFF, undated letters; and AF to JCW, July 23, [no year], all in container I: 170, all in Willard Papers; Taylor, *Divided Family*, 3.

32. AF to JFF, undated fragment; AF to JFF, undated fragment, c. 1864, both in container I: 170; G. W. B. to [the Fords?], October 1864, container I: 171; AF to JFF, n.d., container I: 170, all in Willard Papers; Faust, "Altars of Sacrifice," 1220 (quote); Faust, *Mothers of Invention*, 234–47.

33. AF to JFF, October 10, 1864, container I: 167; AF to JCW, September 2, 1870, container I: 169; Sallie Ford to Holly, July 8, 1924, container I: 173, all in Willard Papers.

34. AF to JCW, July 11, 1865, container I: 168, ibid.

35. AF to JCW, June 20, 1866; and AF to JCW, June 12, [1868], both ibid.

36. AF to JCW, August 14, 1866; and AF to JFF, March 9 and 10, 1868, all ibid.; JCW diary entry of February 14, 1871, container I: 1, ibid.; *Evening Star* (Washington, D.C.), February 14, 1871. The birthdate of Archie Willard is listed in the burial record associated with lot 689 at Oak Hill Cemetery in Georgetown, Washington, D.C. See www.oakhillcemeterydc.org/burialrecords.html (accessed

August 31, 2012). On family size and maternal mortality generally, see V. Lynn Kennedy, *Born Southern: Childbirth, Motherhood, and Social Networks in the Old South* (Baltimore, Md.: Johns Hopkins University Press, 2009), esp. 42–45, 70–73.

37. *The Sun* (Baltimore), January 18, 1897; *Washington Post*, January 18, 1897; JCW diaries, container I: 1, Willard Papers; Kate F. Willcoxon to Belle W. Willard, n.d., container I: 173, ibid.; biographical sketch of Joseph E. Willard, February 6, 1929, container I: 157, ibid.; correspondence from JFF and Pattie Ford to JCW, container II: 2; and Frank R. Ford to JCW, container II: 1, ibid.

Sally Louisa Tompkins

Confederate Healer

E. SUSAN BARBER

On April 27, 1966, the Women of the Confederacy Memorial Committee met at the home of Mary Reynolds to consider designs for a statue intended to memorialize Sally Louisa Tompkins, a Richmond woman who operated a highly successful hospital for sick and wounded Confederate soldiers during the Civil War. The statue was to be installed on the city's famed Monument Avenue, where it would take its place beside massive likenesses of Confederate heroes Robert E. Lee, Stonewall Jackson, and J. E. B. Stuart. Coming as it did in the mid-1960s, the idea of adding a female figure to the Monument Avenue display may have been the planners' nod to the emergent women's rights movement and the call to include women in the American historical narrative. Among the artists who submitted designs for the proposed statue was the noted surrealist Salvador Dalí. The artist did not attend the meeting, but he sent an envoy, Captain Peter J. Moore, who had arrived in the Virginia capital earlier in the month to scout the monument site, accompanied by the artist's pet ocelot. Dalí's design, as sketched for the committee by a local artist, Bill Wynne, depicted Tompkins as a barefooted, feminized version of St. George, clad in a Grecian gown and slaying the dragon of disease and infection with a huge sword. The pedestal supporting the statue was a twenty-foot reproduction of Dalí's little finger.[1]

News of the meeting made the front page of the *Richmond News-Leader* and later reverberated in a series of letters to the newspaper's editor. Most Richmonders who took their Civil War history seriously were not inspired by Dalí's design. "Though I have no desire to bring up the subject of the aesthetic value of Salvador Dalí's art," Roy Tyler wrote, "I would like to take this opportunity to comment upon the proposed work of art Dalí might be contracted to do for Monument Avenue.... To put this statue on Monument Avenue with the statues already there would be like putting a Gothic cathedral such as Notre Dame in the middle of Dulles International Airport.... I cannot see how this hideous monstrosity would have any connection with its surroundings." Tyler, a student at Washington and Lee University, was joined in his objections by H. M. Cowardin, a self-described senior citizen who had grown up hearing tales of Civil War heroism from Confederate veterans. With his tongue firmly lodged in his cheek, Cowardin opined that "the idea of the monument being supported on a tiny little twenty-foot model of Dalí's little finger seems wholly inadequate. I feel sure that if other aluminum companies were solicited they would be glad to add to the thousand pounds already donated. This would suffice for a higher pedestal, a model of the genius himself, supporting Captain Sally on his head." A third writer reflected on the impact the Dalí statue would make on Richmond's reputation as a repository of Lost Cause iconography. "From time to time," Thomas Temple wrote, "I enjoy showing out-of-town visitors the many beautiful areas of Richmond, including Monument Avenue. If anything resembling the propose[d] Dalí statue is erected, I shall drive as far out of the way as necessary to avoid showing it to anyone." Writing from his home in Overland Park, Kansas, G. Christian Guvernator III dismissed the statue with a single word: "Nauseating!"[2]

The final word on the controversy was perhaps voiced by "J. P. L." in a piece titled "Monuments Are for the Living Generation." "Captain Sally already has a monument," the author wrote, "and it's on Franklin Street a block or two before it turns into Monument [Avenue].... The memorial, as many Richmonders already know, is a stained-glass window in St. James's Episcopal Church, where Sally appears serene in the full-skirted nurse's dress of the 1860's. In her arm, she holds the Bible; and behind her rises the Angel of Mercy. In a vignette at the top is sketched her white clapboard house at Fourth and Main that was her hospital during the war.... Here is no militant harridan of the suffragette movement, whacking away at a reluctant dragon.... Sally dispensed not drugs but Christian charity to the dying men in Grey.... There is no evidence that Sally aspired to any other sort of memory than that allotted to the just soul—which may be why the window at St. James's seems to present her in just the right aspect."[3]

By the time this last article appeared in print, the members of the Women of the Confederacy Memorial Committee had beaten a hasty retreat from Dalí and announced plans to turn the project into a competition among local artists. Eventually the idea was utterly abandoned, and no other controversy arose to disturb the tranquility of Civil War memories along Monument Avenue until the statue of tennis star Arthur Ashe was installed there in the mid-1990s.[4]

One wonders what Sally Tompkins herself would have thought of a plan to

PROPOSED STATUE OF SALLY LOUISA TOMPKINS

The design was by Salvador Dalí; the sketch is by the Richmond artist Bill Wynne.
Virginia Historical Society.

SALLY LOUISA TOMPKINS
Hand-retouched photographic print, c. 1860s.
Virginia Historical Society.

chisel her wartime likeness into stately marble or even to freeze her image into stained glass at her beloved St. James Church. She was certainly no "militant harridan," yet no woman—except perhaps the notorious Elizabeth Van Lew—ever rose to a higher level of prominence in the Confederate capital's history than Sally Louisa Tompkins. Between 1861 and 1865 Tompkins operated a highly successful hospital that treated more than thirteen hundred sick and wounded soldiers with only seventy-three fatalities. Indeed her success rate exceeded all other private and military hospitals in the city, even Chimborazo, the crown jewel of the Confederate military hospital system. This was quite a remarkable feat for a single woman in her late twenties whose primary exposure to illness and death, up to this point, had been the personal losses she experienced through the deaths of her beloved father and siblings. Tompkins's legendary status as a Civil War icon was further secured by the fact that she was the only woman ever commissioned as a captain in the Confederate army. Yet she seldom sought the limelight and all but disappeared from public view after the war ended, living quietly for more than forty years, with only occasional appearances at Civil War celebrations until she entered the Richmond Home for Confederate Women in 1905. And despite Tompkins's wartime popularity, no Civil War historian has undertaken a serious book-length biography of her life and work.[5]

This chapter attempts to move beyond the mythical Captain Sally of Civil War fame to examine Tompkins's life in the context of the social roles and expectations regarding elite white southern women during the late nineteenth and early twentieth centuries. From that perspective, Sally Tompkins's life reveals a woman of contrasts. On the one hand, she was a bold, innovative administrator whose extraordinary record of wartime nursing challenged gender expectations and helped to expand roles for women in hospital management; on the other, she remained a dutiful southern daughter enmeshed in the more traditional gender expectations regarding a woman's obligations to friends and family, which gave structure and meaning to her life.

Information about Sally Louisa Tompkins's early life is sketchy. Born on November 9, 1833, at Poplar Grove in Mathews County, Virginia, Tompkins was the youngest child of Christopher Tompkins, a Tidewater planter and former militia commander, and his second wife, Maria Booth Patterson. Maria Tompkins's family was affluent, and young Sally spent her early life in apparent comfort surrounded by her brothers and sisters whose needs were ministered to by an array of household slaves. Even Christopher Tompkins's death in 1838, when Sally was just five years of age, did little to disturb the lifestyle that the Tompkins family enjoyed since most of her parents' wealth—including the three-hundred-acre Poplar Grove plantation, its mansion, and its slaves—was derived from Sally's mother's side of the family. The 1840 Census for Mathews County shows the widowed Maria Tompkins as the head of a household composed of ten white dependents, mostly females between the ages of five and fifty, and eighty-six slaves.[6] Two years later, however, the sudden deaths of three of Sally's older siblings—Martha Tabb, Elizabeth, and Harriet Tompkins—during a yellow fever epidemic that swept through the South in 1842 shook the family to its core. It also orphaned Martha Tabb's three young daughters—Lucy, Sally, and Mary—who came to live in the Tompkins household. Five years later in 1847, Sally's brother Benjamin succumbed to consumption, leaving Sally, her sister Maria, and her stepbrother Christopher as the only survivors of her father's eight children.[7]

Since the medical profession was still in its infancy in the mid-nineteenth century, women and girls frequently functioned as the first line of defense, nursing sick and injured relatives. This was no doubt the case with the Tompkins family in the 1840s. A recipe book published in 1863 provides ample evidence of the centrality of women's role in this regard with its inclusion of remedies for many common ailments, including diphtheria, whooping cough, scarlet fever, asthma, camp itch, boils, and warts.[8] When their ministrations failed to effect a cure, it was the women and girls in the family who washed and dressed the bodies of their deceased kin and laid them out for mourning. Tompkins's hagiographers have suggested that Sally's interest in working as a Civil War healer was piqued by caring for sick slaves and wounded birds and animals on the Poplar Grove estate.[9] No evidence has survived that supports this point of view. Rather, a more likely explanation for her later hospital work is that Sally was thrust into a caretaking role in the early 1840s when she assisted her mother in caring for her dying siblings.

With a household now composed largely of young girls in need of an education, Maria Tompkins in 1847 hired a governess for $300 to tutor the Poplar Grove children.[10] But the deaths of the Tompkins siblings must have been a devastating blow that taxed Maria's physical, if not her financial, resources. By 1849 she had left Poplar Grove and moved with her two daughters and eight of the family's slaves to Norfolk, where Sally studied English for a year at the Norfolk Female Institute. This may have been the end of Tompkins's formal education since no further mention of it appears in any of the existing records.[11]

Southern girlhood has been described as a series of rites of passage through which elite females progressed on their way to adulthood. In particular, their roles as sociable students in female academies and their debuts as marriageable young women represented significant developmental milestones. Neither seems to have been part of the experience of Sally Louisa Tompkins or her older sister, Maria, who both remained single throughout their lives. Sally's year at the Norfolk Female Institute provided her with little opportunity to cultivate the lifelong friendships that historians have described as an essential component in the development of adolescent southern girls. And except for a brief flirtation with a young man named Edmund at the Cherry Hill home of her cousin Mary Ann Taylor, Tompkins may have experienced no youthful romantic involvement.[12]

These departures from the anticipated developmental expectations for genteel girls like Sally and her sister were most likely due less to the early death of her father than to the series of sibling deaths the family encountered between 1842 and 1847. Coming as they did when Sally and Maria were entering puberty, the deaths must have diverted Maria Tompkins's attention away from preparing her two surviving daughters for a proper entry into Virginia society. By March 1854 Sally's mother, Maria Tompkins, had also died (from pleurisy at the age of fifty-nine), orphaning Sally and her sister and leaving them as heirs to the Poplar Grove estate. Rather than settling permanently at Poplar Grove, however, Sally and Maria moved to Richmond where by 1860 they had taken up residence at Arlington House, a large boardinghouse on the corner of Sixth and Main. As the secession crisis deepened in the spring of 1861, the two young women therefore had a front row seat to the spectacle of civil war. Maria eventually retreated to Port Royal in northwestern Virginia, but Sally remained in Richmond, where she became a close witness to the war's destruction through her service to sick and wounded Confederate soldiers.[13]

Scholars who write about the American Civil War emphasize its horrific carnage and the ways in which neither side was prepared to meet its duty to care for the sick and wounded who streamed from the battlefields. More than 618,000 boys and men between the ages of thirteen and forty-three on both sides of the conflict were wartime casualties, a figure that exceeded the sum of American military deaths in all other wars, including World Wars I and II, until sometime in the middle of the war in Vietnam. The overall demographic impact of these losses varied significantly by region, however, because the North's population was so much larger than the South's. Although more Union than Confederate soldiers perished in the war, the North's dead accounted for only 6 percent of its white male population; in the South, 18 percent of the region's white men—or one of every four men of military age—died in the Civil War. Thousands more were injured but survived, often with permanent disabilities due to amputations, the effects of exposure, or what we now understand today as post-traumatic stress disorder.[14]

As the capital of the Confederate States of America, Richmond was the seat of a national government. But since the city also served as the capital of the state of Virginia, most of its available government buildings were quickly overextended. More significant, the city became a major training and staging area for the war's eastern theater, which resulted in not only a tripling of the city's population between 1860 and 1865 but also a heavy demand for hospitals to care for wartime casualties. Thus every available Richmond building—including tobacco warehouses, church basements, and the Richmond Female Institute—was pressed into service.

The number of hospitalized soldiers was astounding both to civilian Richmonders and to contemporary scholars. Chimborazo Hospital, opened in 1861 on the city's eastern boundary, was the largest hospital in the world. It divided its sick and wounded soldiers into divisions according to the state they served and had a capacity of more than 5,000 beds, with cone-shaped Sibley tents strategically placed around the grounds to handle the overflow from the Virginia battlefields. Chimborazo also boasted a brewery, a bakery, blacksmith and carpenter shops, a soap factory, and a herd of cows and goats. A few hospitals of middling size appear to have functioned as triage units. For example, General Hospital No. 9, which had beds for 900 patients, took in a total of 3,752 men during the four days of fighting at Chancellorsville in 1863, usually dismissing the sick and wounded to other smaller hospitals at the end of each day. Other Richmond hospitals were quite small by comparison, having beds for only 30 or 40 men. An 1862 report on sick and wounded soldiers published in the *Richmond Enquirer* listed forty-two military and private hospitals, which had treated more than 99,500 soldiers overall since their inception. All of these hospitals were frequently inundated with wounded men after major battles.[15]

Richmond newspapers routinely carried these hospital reports as well as pleas for volunteers, aimed primarily at the city's women, to go to the hospitals to help care for and comfort the wounded. One oft-repeated appeal, titled "Ladies! To the Hospital!" took the form of a lengthy poem that instructed women to put away their "bright tinted dresses" and to braid back their hair "in a serious way" and to come to the hospitals "with their souls on their faces / To meet the stern wants of the hour!" The poem's ensuing verses completed the picture with vivid descriptions of heads with gunshot wounds, shattered hands, and dying men raving for the comforts of home, a cautionary primer for any woman considering hospital nursing as a calling.[16] All manner of Richmond women responded, including elite women from the upper echelons of society, several orders of Catholic nuns, and a portion of the city's female slaves, who were contracted by their owners for hospital work. Only a few women, like

Sally Tompkins and Maria Clopton, the wife of a Richmond judge, founded and directed hospitals on their own.[17]

Tompkins opened Robertson Hospital—located in the former home of John Robertson, a Richmond judge—in July 1861, shortly after the First Battle of Manassas (Bull Run), the first engagement of the Civil War. Situated on the corner of Third Street and Main, the three-story wooden building had a forty-bed capacity—quite modest when compared to others in the area—and was surrounded by a generous lawn and a few outbuildings. It was staffed by five Tompkins slaves, including the Poplar Grove cook, Phoebe, who cared for patients under the supervision of Tompkins and Dr. A. Y. P. Garnett, a contract surgeon originally from Washington, D.C., who also treated patients at General Hospital No. 3, one of the military hospitals in the Confederate capital. A few disabled soldiers worked at the hospital as well, maintaining the buildings and grounds.

Women's Civil War hospital work encompassed a wide variety of functions, including reading the scriptures to soldiers, writing letters to their family members, and feeding the men "delicacies," or foodstuffs that reminded them of home, which the medical staff hoped would help restore them to full health. These good offices were often the purview of the city's elite, such as Mary Boykin Chesnut, the wife of James Chesnut Jr., a wealthy South Carolina planter who served as an aide to Confederate president Jefferson Davis during the early years of the war. She and other elite Richmonders volunteered their time at Robertson Hospital, offering comfort to convalescent soldiers. Other women took on the more difficult and grueling paid labor of hospital nursing, which involved bathing the injured, dressing wounds, preparing the dead for burial, and assisting in the countless amputations, which were the most common treatment for a damaged limb. This type of wartime nursing proved too much for some women. "As I passed by the rows of occupied cots," wrote Sarah Rice Pryor, "I saw a nurse kneeling beside one of them, holding a pan for a surgeon. The red stump of an amputated arm was held over it. The next thing I knew I was myself lying on a cot and a spray of cold water was falling over my face. I had fainted." Pryor was sent home as "unfit" for hospital work.[18]

Women entering Civil War hospitals in either the North or the South confronted a world that was both strange and familiar. While women's nineteenth-century domestic duties encompassed caring for sick family members of both sexes, nursing in military hospitals raised questions of propriety. Wartime nursing represented a significant departure from women's traditional role as caregivers in that it exposed women to the mangled, naked bodies of men who were both strangers and often from a lower social class. In the South, this kind of work might have been acceptable for working-class white women or female slaves, but some worried that it was beneath the dignity of elite women like Tompkins and that such indelicate work might sully their reputations. Others worried that hospital nursing would become a haven for prostitutes, who might view military hospitals as convenient pools of prospective clients. Sally Tompkins chose to address these concerns at Robertson Hospital by dressing in simple dark clothing, with her auburn hair pulled back and sometimes encased in a kepi—a cap worn by Confederate soldiers—with an attached veil, perhaps a nod to the veils worn by the Sisters of Charity, who operated another private hospital in the city. She also was often described as walking through the hospital with a medical case attached to her belt and a Bible in her hand, an image captured in an early photograph. By conflating women's hospital work with both religious and patriotic callings, Tompkins effectively silenced critics who might have objected to a young single woman being engaged in such a pioneering enterprise.

As many as twenty thousand women may have performed some kind of hospital work during the American Civil War, but a regional comparison of military hospitals reveals some stark contrasts that directly affected women workers. In the North, nurses were trained hospital workers who served under the direction of Dorothea Dix, the superintendent of nursing for the Union armies. In this position, Dix carefully screened female applicants, only hiring plain women over thirty who dressed simply in brown or black with no bows or frills.[19] She also established specific protocols for military nurses and advocated for them to receive postwar pensions. In the South, no such system existed. There was no female director of nursing with supervisory authority. Instead, Tompkins's Robertson Hospital at the beginning of the war was part of a two-tiered Confederate hospital system composed of a small number of private hospitals operated independently by women and a larger number of military hospitals, all under the direction of Confederate surgeon general Samuel P. Moore. In Confederate military hospitals, white women usually worked as matrons, supervisors whose primary responsibilities were to see that the wards were kept clean, that linens were properly laundered, and that special diets for convalescent soldiers were correctly prepared. Most of this actual work was accomplished by poor white women and slaves. The less prestigious title of "nurse" was reserved for white men—often convalescent or disabled soldiers—and slaves of both sexes. Nurses were responsible for bathing patients and assisting with their treatment. In truth, none of these specific titles mattered much when ambulances arrived from the battlefields carrying soldiers with life-threatening injuries. Everyone stepped in to lend a hand, thrusting fingers into spurting arteries or helping to bind a shattered limb.[20]

By the fall of 1862, however, the Medical Department of the Confederate military reorganized its hospital system, closing some private hospitals that it deemed inefficient and bringing the remainder into the military hospital system where they would be under the scrutiny of the medical director and the surgeon general. In effect, this move put all female hospital employees under the supervision of male military officers, who often resented the women's presence as an intrusion and responded to them with a combination of condescension, derision, and outright hostility, especially when the women seemed to challenge their authority. Phoebe Yates Pember, for example, a matron of Ward 2 at Chimborazo Hospital, labored under the disdainful gaze of hospital surgeons while she made a concerted effort to protect the hospital's liquor supply, which was rationed daily to the patients, from the predations of the surgeons and other male hospital staff.[21]

There are several possible reasons for this hospital reorganization effort. One explanation was that these changes would make the Confederate hospital system more efficient by avoiding duplication of effort. Concern about the propriety of private hospitals operated by women also may have contributed to this decision, which was to be enforced under a regulation that stipulated that no soldier could be treated in a hospital where the director held a rank lower than captain, a measure that effectively closed all of the hospitals operated by women. Finally, this effort might have been an attempt to address vocal dissatisfaction with the South's military hospital system. For months, the Richmond press had been publishing articles that were highly critical of public military hospitals, prompting those men who could afford it to seek treatment in the private ones. Whatever the reason, Tompkins's Robertson Hospital, along with a handful of others, was slated for closure.[22]

What happened next is the stuff from which legend is often formed. Most accounts maintain that Tompkins immediately asked for an audience with Jefferson Davis, where she presented evidence of her hospital's success, including its remarkable death rate of only 5.5 percent—this at a time when the death rate for military hospitals was averaging around 10 percent. Davis's response was to commission the twenty-nine-year-old woman as an unassigned captain in the Confederate army, thereby enabling her to continue to direct a hospital under the new regulations. Tompkins was the only woman to be so recognized in either the North or the South, with the exception of some of the more than four hundred cross-dressing women who served as Civil War soldiers.[23]

While many descriptions of this event have overlaid it with a patina of southern gallantry—one source even suggests that the dashing cavalry officer J. E. B. Stuart championed Tompkins's cause—Davis may have had a more pragmatic reason for his unusual gesture. Tompkins's commission provided additional benefits to her hospital by allowing her to draw rations and medicines for the men under her care. At the very least, it enabled her to keep her hospital open until several weeks after the city was occupied by Union troops in April 1865. At some point after the war, Tompkins appended this note on the bottom of her commission: "I accepted the above commission as Captain in the C.S.A. when it was issued. But I would not allow my name to be placed upon the pay roll of the army." This note suggests that, rather than seeking the limelight as the first woman to hold a military rank, Tompkins viewed her commission as a means of keeping her hospital running effectively, an activity inspired by her overwhelming loyalty to the Confederacy and her sense of her caretaking as a patriotic calling.[24]

Although Tompkins's commission as captain successfully negated the attempt to close Robertson Hospital, her single-minded commitment to her work was continuously surrounded by controversy, which sometimes caused tension between her and medical director William A. Carrington and chief surgeon A. Y. P. Garnett. One particularly revealing example is chronicled in a series of letters written in early June 1864. It began on June 6 with a letter from Carrington, which was apparently prompted by a hospital morning report indicating that Robertson Hospital was caring for forty-four patients. The letter was addressed to Garnett and ignored Tompkins's role completely. "Sir," Carrington wrote, "you are directed to transfer 25 of the patients in Robertson without delay . . . and not receive into the Hos[pital] in future more than 19—the number you were ordered by the Surgeon Genl. to receive. If such resolution of orders and disregard for the safety of the sick and wounded occurs again the Hospital will necessarily be closed as a nuisance." Garnett replied the next day, saying that he would reduce the number of patients to twenty-two immediately, indicating that the hospital's patients included a number of men who lived in nearby quarters but were "subsisted by the hospital," an "arrangement . . . adopted by the lady in charge without consultation with me." On June 8 Carrington sent a similar letter to J. J. Gravatt, a surgeon at General Hospital No. 9, directing him to send no more patients to Robertson.[25]

Tompkins responded directly to Carrington on June 9 in a letter that dripped with righteous indignation toward Carrington and a sense of betrayal by Garnett. "Dr. Garnett's endorsement on the morning report," Tompkins wrote, "was written under a misapprehension of fact. The number allowed (by measurement) was 22, but in consideration of the number of chambers, it was extended to 25." She continued:

> Dr. Garnett found on *examination* that there were occupying beds in the hospital *at that time* but 22 patients. The remainder—entirely with his approbation, sleeping in private quarters, but fed and tended in this Hospital. Had Dr. Garnett but *suggested*

that he considered the sick & wounded too much crowded, I certainly would have had them transferred to other hospitals.... Dr. Garnett's numerous engagements have prevented his giving much of his time & attention to his patients of late—notwithstanding I think the register of this Hospital will show as great success in its management of the sick and wounded as any other.

Carrington revoked his order for the hospital's closure on June 15 in a caustic letter to Garnett, admonishing him that the ladies at the hospital should "confine themselves to duties assigned ... to matrons of hospitals and be under your authority as such," and that "if anything in the orders relating to reports, therapeutic or hygienic arrangements, are not executed, you alone will be considered responsible." Despite Carrington's determination to ignore Tompkins's role as the hospital manager, she continued to remain in charge of a growing staff, which now included eight additional surgeons.[26]

Clearly, Tompkins was not a woman who could easily be dismissed, even by men who were twenty years her senior. A letter to Sally Tompkins from her sister, Maria, then residing in Port Royal, draws a sharp contrast between the sisters' personalities and underscores Sally's extraordinary wartime service. "I have written for so many things that were necessary to my comfort & which you have not noticed," Maria peevishly wrote to her sister in March 1863, "that my heart fails me to write again, but I must make one more effort.... My clothes are in a horrid condition—my chemises & stockings are literally falling off me ... & I cannot imagine why I am so ignored. I asked you to send me a cake of soap & am now actually without any, & you may know what a trial it is to me, whose happiness is easily disturbed by *soiled* fingers and nails." In the two months before Maria wrote this letter, Sally's hospital had taken in a total of fifty-three soldiers suffering from a variety of ailments such as pneumonia, persistent fevers, dysentery, bronchitis and hepatitis, in addition to a myriad of war-related injuries. Further, Garnett, the hospital's primary surgeon, was embroiled in writing a series of contentious letters to the Confederate president, Jefferson Davis, and the secretary of war, Judah P. Benjamin, to refute accusations that the surgeon had somehow disrespected First Lady Varina Davis at a social gathering.[27] Tompkins was also busy fending off another attempt by William Carrington to shut down Robertson Hospital.[28]

When the last patient was discharged in June 1865, Tompkins closed Robertson Hospital and this chapter of her life. She did not seek to continue her career as a hospital administrator by opening a private hospital in postwar Richmond, although her example may have inspired other women to do so. Instead, with the hospital's closure Tompkins slipped into a period of relative obscurity during which she nearly disappeared from the public stage; the records of her activities during the late 1860s and 1870s are fragmentary at best. Instead, in the war's immediate aftermath she turned her attention to a pressing family matter. Sally's sister, Maria, had died in July 1864 in Norfolk, but she had not been buried in the family plot at Poplar Grove, perhaps because the plantation had been partially decimated by Union troops. In 1866 Sally arranged for Maria's remains to be relocated next to those of their mother and for her brother, Christopher, to purchase suitable tombstones for the women's graves.[29] By this time, Poplar Grove had been sold to Judge Griffin Taylor Garnett, but the Tompkins family continued to maintain a burial plot there until well into the twentieth century.[30]

During the latter part of the 1860s and through much of the 1870s, Tompkins lived and worked in Richmond, teaching Sunday school classes at St. James Church and actively participating in annual reunions of Civil War veterans. By the 1880s, however, she resumed her work as a healer, moving back and forth between Richmond, Norfolk, and Port Royal to care for an extended network of family and friends. The caregiving she performed in this postwar period was more like the traditional sorts of nursing southern women provided for close family and friends than her pathbreaking work as a hospital director during the Civil War.

Tompkins's correspondence with her cousin Lucy Parke Chamberlayne Bagby, the wife of George W. Bagby, editor of the *Southern Literary Messenger*, reveals the extent to which these caretaking activities dominated her life. In 1881, for example, she spent part of the summer caring for a young Richmond woman who was ill with typhoid fever, and she devoted part of the fall to attending to a sick mother and son. Between 1886 and 1888 she spent much of her time at Riverview, a Greek revival home on the Rappahannock River in Port Royal, nursing members of the John B. Lightfoot family through a series of protracted illnesses.[31]

In October 1886 Tompkins was called to the bedside of Dr. John James Gravatt, the surgeon who had worked at Robertson Hospital during the Civil War, to nurse him through his final illness. At this juncture, it becomes evident that her reputation as a healer might have been comparable to those of male medical professionals in the area, although there is no evidence that she ever garnered either hostility or acclaim from them. "Our dear good doctor was ill nearly five weeks," she wrote on October 7, 1886. "I staid with him every day from 6 a.m. till 11 or 12 p.m. towards the last I came home earlier at night.... There is no physician near here now [in Port Royal] that we have any confidence in. Since Dr. G. died I have staid with Mrs. G. She is quite sick & thinks I can prescribe for her. . . . I stay with her every night and most of the day. There is a great deal of sickness here—not any that can be attributed to the climate—but old chronic cases & old people & they think I can help them so I am obliged to go and of course I am not only willing but truly thankful to be of use—but my time is *occupied*."[32]

Although Tompkins's work as a healer placed a high premium on her time, she maintained her practice until the early years of the twentieth century. "I have hardly ever been more constantly occupied than this Fall and Winter," she began a Christmas Eve letter to her cousin Parke in 1888. "Just now I am occupied with a poor old friend here who is the most destitute person you ever saw—she is almost, if not quite, 90 years old, lives entirely alone. . . . now the poor old thing has typhoid fever. . . . I go to see her five and six times a day . . . & my last visit is about ten p.m." A letter to Parke in February 1899 indicates the toll that years of this work was taking on Tompkins's health. "Ever since I left dear Richmond Nov. 1st I have wanted to write to you, & especially at Christmas," she wrote, "but writing is not as easy to one at sixty-five as it was—and where there is sickness I am usually in that room."[33]

In January 1904, in a letter to Walter Herron, a lifelong friend and financial advisor, Tompkins revealed a new worry that was weighing on her mind. "Have you heard what to me is a real distress," she wrote. "Our dear little church—Christ Church, Kingston Parish, Mathews County—is *burned* to the ground except the brick walls—all in ashes! . . . This is the church my sister Lizzie built in 1839 with the assistance of your father and other friends in Norfolk." Tompkins had been an Episcopalian from birth and her faith played a significant role in her life. For many southern women, the church represented not only a house of worship but also the institutional source of women's social and political activism. When in Richmond, Tompkins regularly attended St. James Church, which was presided over by the Reverend Joshua Peterkin. When Peterkin died in 1892, Tompkins poured out her grief to her cousin Parke. "I cannot express the deep sorrow I feel," she wrote, "in the loss of our dear Pastor. . . . Since I was nineteen years old and I lost my mother . . . [I] have looked to him more than any other human being for counsel and comfort." Having just received the last payment from the sale of the Riverview estate—which Tompkins had purchased from the Lightfoots in 1886—she now instructed Herron to devote a portion of those funds to rebuilding Christ Church, closing her letter by saying, "fix it so if I die before it is used, the church will get it."[34]

As Christ Church rose from the ashes in Mathews County, Tompkins's own health was beginning to decline. During her life, she had expended a great deal of energy in service to others. Now in her seventies and with her eyesight failing, there was no one to take care of her. By then, too, her finances were strained. Tompkins had apparently retained enough of her inheritance to support herself until the beginning of the twentieth century, living alone in Richmond for several postwar decades as the city's economy struggled to recover. During this time she indulged in an occasional riverboat trip to visit friends, rented suites of rooms to entertain her former patients at Confederate veterans' reunions, and visited Richmond in 1890 for the unveiling of the Lee statue on Monument Avenue. In 1886 she had even purchased the palatial Riverview house on the Rappahannock. By 1905, however, with her fortune almost depleted, Tompkins accepted an invitation to become a resident of the Richmond Home for Needy Confederate Women, where she lived until her death on July 25, 1916, at the age of eighty-two. She was buried at Christ Church Cemetery in Mathews County, in a coffin draped with a Confederate flag, as was the custom for all Confederate veterans, following a funeral with full military honors.[35]

In a pioneering study of Petersburg's free women, white and black, a leading historian concluded that women and men disposed of their estates differently and that this striking contrast was, in turn, indicative of their fundamentally different personal values. Men tended to divide their estates equally between their legal heirs, but women wrote wills to distribute their wealth according to the ideals of "personalism," allocating their assets on the basis of personal need, especially in the case of female relatives. Women testators also frequently remembered individual women with special pieces of clothing, jewelry, or other personal items.[36]

Sally Tompkins's will, written in 1907, indicates that, much like the women of Petersburg, she may have been guided by personalism in the disposal of her estate. Of the twelve heirs mentioned in Tompkins's will, ten were women. Although most received $150, Tompkins's niece Clementine received a lifetime income from investments in real estate loans and other securities. In addition to cash settlements, Tompkins also bequeathed almost all of her personal property to women, leaving her cousin Ellen Tabb her black silk skirt; her cousin Kate Robertson her astrakhan cape; and a niece, Ellen Wise, a silver sugar dish and cream pot.[37]

Tompkins used her will to assert her personal authority, but she did so in ways that comported with the ideals of white southern womanhood. In so doing, she maintained the careful balance between self-actualization and conformity that she had honed during the crisis years of the Civil War. Had Tompkins been privy to the discussion surrounding her immortalization on Monument Avenue in the 1960s, she would probably have agreed with "J. P. L.," who noted that the stained-glass window at St. James Church, where she was surrounded by images of faith, home, and family, was all the recognition she would have desired. Although Tompkins stepped briefly beyond the conventional confines of nineteenth-century southern womanhood to provide extraordinary service to the Confederacy through her pioneering work as the director of a highly successful Civil War hospital, she remained, through much of her life, a woman steeped in and shaped by the customs and mores of nineteenth-century southern culture.

NOTES

1. For a detailed account of Dalí's interest in the Sally Tompkins statue, see Kevin Colcannon, "Dalí in Virginia," *SECAC Review* 1 (1967): 598–607.

2. *Richmond News Leader*, April 27, May 2, and May 7, 1966.

3. Ibid., May 14, 1966.

4. *New York Times*, June 18, 1995.

5. Two brief book-length studies of Tompkins's life are Shirley E. Gillespie, *The Lady with the Milk White Hands: A Biography of Sally Louisa Tompkins* (Chandler, Ariz.: Two Dogs, 2005); and Keppel Hagerman, *Dearest of Captains: A Biography of Sally Louisa Tompkins* (White Stone, Va.: Brandylane, 1996). The latter is a biographical poem. In addition, several biographical essays have appeared in the *UDC Magazine*, a publication of the United Daughters of the Confederacy. See, for example, Tommie Phillips LaCavera, "Captain Sally Tompkins: Angel of Mercy," *UDC Magazine* 55 (March 1992): 8–10; Deanna Riley Bryant, "Captain Sally Tompkins," *UDC Magazine* 74 (March 2011): 10–11; and Jonathan Hicks, "Sally Louisa Tompkins: Personal Sacrifice and Spiritual Commitment," *UDC Magazine* 65, no. 8 (September 2002): 33–34. Most of these and other writings about Tompkins's life take the form of hagiography. For example, see Elizabeth Dabney Coleman, "The Captain Was a Lady," *Virginia Cavalcade* 6 (1956–57): 35–41.

6. 1840 Census, Mathews County, Virginia, roll 565, p. 356, National Archives and Records Administration (hereafter NARA).

7. Martha Tabb Tompkins (1807–42) and Harriet Pauline Tompkins (1809–42) were daughters from Christopher Tompkins's first marriage to Elizabeth Cary Smith, who died in 1814. The couple's third child, Henry, died in infancy (Gillespie, *Lady with the Milk White Hands*, ix). The only surviving son from that first union, Christopher Quarles Tompkins (1813–77), a mining engineer, enjoyed a brief military career during the Civil War. Martha Tabb Tompkins, the eldest daughter, married her cousin Henry Wythe Tabb in 1828 and had given birth to five children by the time of her death in 1842.

8. West and Johnston, Publishers, comps., *Confederate Receipt Book: A Compilation of Over One Hundred Receipts Adapted to the Times*, rev. ed. (1863; rpt., Athens: University of Georgia Press, 1960), 21–23.

9. See, for example, Hagerman, *Dearest of Captains*, 5–12.

10. Adam Foster to his daughter Cynthia, January 7, 1847, qtd. in Gillespie, *Lady with the Milk White Hands*, 13.

11. Gillespie, *Lady with the Milk White Hands*, 2; 1850 U.S. Census, Slave Schedule, NARA.

12. Gillespie, *Lady with the Milk White Hands*, 15. On southern girlhood and adolescence gener-

ally, see Anya Jabour, *Scarlett's Sisters: Young Women in the Old South* (Chapel Hill: University of North Carolina Press, 2007), esp. chaps. 1, 2, and 4; Giselle Roberts, *The Confederate Belle* (Columbia: University of Missouri Press, 2003), 15–35.

13. Gillespie, *Lady with the Milk White Hands*, 2–25.

14. An excellent starting point for considering the war's demographic impact is Maris Vinovskis, "Have Social Historians Lost the Civil War?" *Journal of American History* 76 (1989): 34–58. For the cultural impact of the quantity and quality of wartime casualties, see Drew Gilpin Faust, *This Republic of Suffering: Death and the American Civil War* (New York: Knopf, 2008).

15. *Richmond Enquirer*, September 29, 1862; Francis B. Simkins and James W. Patton, "The Work of Southern Women among the Sick and Wounded of the Confederate Armies," *Journal of Southern History* 1 (1935): 475.

16. "Ladies! To the Hospital!" *Southern Churchman*, September 26, 1862.

17. Founded in October 1862, Maria Clopton's hospital, located on Franklin Avenue, was only in operation for six months. See E. Susan Barber, "'Sisters of the Capital': White Women in Richmond Virginia, 1860–1880" (PhD diss., University of Maryland, 1997), 91–96.

18. Sarah Rice [Mrs. Roger] Pryor, "The Hospital Was Filled to Overflowing," in *Reminiscences of Peace and War*, reprinted in *Ladies of Richmond*, ed. Katherine Jones (Indianapolis, Ind.: Bobbs-Merrill, 1962), 127–28. An excellent examination of Civil War nursing is Jane E. Schultz, "The Inhospitable Hospital: Gender and Professionalism in Civil War Medicine," *Signs* 17 (1992): 363–92. See also Louise Oates, "Civil War Nurses," *American Journal of Nursing* 28 (1928): 207–12; and Simkins and Patton, "Work of Southern Women," 475–96.

19. Schultz, "The Inhospitable Hospital," 366–67; Oates, "Civil War Nurses," 207.

20. Barber, "Sisters of the Capital," 79–119.

21. Report of William A. Carrington, Surgeon and Inspector of Hospitals, October 24, 1862, M331, RG 109, Records of the Confederate Government, 1861–65, NARA; Phoebe Yates Pember, *A Southern Woman's Story: Life in Confederate Richmond*, ed. Bell I. Wiley (St. Simons, Ga.: Mockingbird Books, 1974).

22. Confederate States of America, Congress, Senate Select Committee to Examine into the Condition of Hospitals, 1862, reprinted in *Richmond Enquirer*, September 29, 1862. For a discussion of hospitals run by women, see, for example, *Richmond Enquirer*, September 3, 1861, June 11, 1862; *Richmond Examiner*, October 3, 1861; *Religious Herald*, October 2, 1862; *Southern Churchman*, December 20, 1861, September 11, 1862; and *Southern Illustrated News*, November 22, 1862.

23. On cross dressing female soldiers, see Lauren Burgess and James McPherson, eds., *An Uncommon Soldier: The Civil War Letters of Sarah Rosetta Wakeman, alias Pvt. Lyons Wakeman, 153rd Regiment, New York State Volunteers, 1862–1864* (New York: Oxford University Press, 1996); DeAnne Blanton and Lauren M. Cook, *They Fought like Demons: Women Soldiers in the Civil War* (New York: Vintage, 2003). For hospital death rates, see *Religious Herald*, October 2, 1862.

24. Commission of Sally Louisa Tompkins, C.S.A., Eleanor S. Brockenbrough Library, Museum of the Confederacy, Richmond, Va. The date of Tompkins's emendation is unknown.

25. William A. Carrington to A. Y. P. Garnett, June 6, 1864, Letters Sent and Received, Medical Director's Office, 1864–65, ch. 6, vol. 364, RG 109, General Records of the Confederate Government, 1861–65, NARA; Alexander Y. P. Garnett to William A. Carrington, June 7, 1864, ibid.; William A. Carrington to J. J. Gravatt, June 8, 1864, Letters Received and Sent, General Hospital No. 9, ibid.

26. Sally Louisa Tompkins to William A. Carrington, June 9, 1864, Letters Sent and Received, Medical Director's Office, 1864–65, ch. 6, vol. 364 (emphasis in original); William A. Carrington to A. Y. P. Garnett, June 15, 1864, ibid.; Robertson Hospital Register, Sally Louisa Tompkins–

Robertson Hospital Collection, Eleanor S. Brockenbrough Library, Museum of the Confederacy, Richmond, Va.

27. A. Y. P. Garnett to Judah P. Benjamin and Jefferson Davis, January 28–November 11, 1863, B16, sec. 8, Garnett Family Papers, Virginia Historical Society, Richmond. After the war, Garnett continued his highly successful medical practice and was elected president of the American Medical Association in 1886. See "Memorial of Dr. A. Y. P. Garnett," *Transactions of the American Clinical and Climatological Association* 7 (1890): 324.

28. Maria Mason Tompkins to Sally Louisa Tompkins, March 7, 1863, Sally Louisa Tompkins–Robertson Hospital Collection (emphasis in original); "Statistical Report of Hospitals, Richmond, Virginia, 1862–1864", vol. 51, ch. 6, p. 51, RG 109, General Records of the Confederate Government, 1861–65, NARA; William A. Carrington, Inspector of Hospitals, to Sally L. Tompkins, January 28, 1863, M331, ibid.

29. Sally Tompkins to Christopher Quarles Tompkins, December 7, 1866, Sally Louisa Tompkins Papers, Library of Virginia.

30. In another twist of historical fate, in the late 1960s, Poplar Grove was acquired by John Lennon and Yoko Ono, who later deeded the property to the New Beginning Boys Home. See Frances Christian and Susan Archer, eds., *Homes and Gardens in Old Virginia* (Richmond, Va.: Garrett and Massie, 1962), 187; Nomination Form for Poplar Grove and Mill House, 1969, National Register of Historic Places, U.S. Department of the Interior, National Park Service, Washington, D.C.

31. Sally Tompkins to Parke Bagby, August 9 and November 19, 1881, November 13, 1886, Bagby Family Papers, Virginia Historical Society. Harriet Field Lightfoot was Sally Tompkins's cousin.

32. Sally Tompkins to Parke Bagby, October 7, 1886, ibid.

33. Sally Tompkins to Parke Bagby, December 24, 1888, ibid.; Sally Louisa Tompkins to Parke Bagby, February 7, 1899, ibid.

34. Sally Louisa Tompkins to Walter Herron Taylor, January 28, 1904, Walter Herron Taylor Papers, Library of Virginia (emphasis in original); Sally Tompkins to Parke Bagby, June 7, 1892, Bagby Family Papers, Virginia Historical Society. On the connection between religion and southern women's activism, see, for instance, Anne Firor Scott, *Natural Allies: Women's Associations in American History* (Chicago: University of Illinois Press, 1992), esp. chaps. 1 and 4; Timothy James Lockley, *Welfare and Charity in the Antebellum South* (Gainesville: University of Florida Press, 2007), chap. 2; Elizabeth R. Varon, *We Mean to Be Counted: White Women and Politics in Antebellum Virginia* (Chapel Hill: University of North Carolina Press, 1998), esp. chaps. 1 and 2.

35. Sally Louisa Tompkins to Lucy Parke Chamberlayne Bagby, May 16, 1890, Bagby Family Papers; Sally Louisa Tompkins obituary, *Richmond Times-Dispatch*, July 26, 1916.

36. Suzanne Lebsock, *The Free Women of Petersburg: Status and Culture in a Southern Town, 1784–1860* (New York: Norton, 1984), esp. chap. 5.

37. Last will and testament, Sally Louisa Tompkins, April 16, 1907, Sally Tompkins Papers, Eleanor S. Brockenbrough Library, Museum of the Confederacy.

Contributors

CATHERINE ALLGOR is the Nadine and Robert Skotheim Director of Education at the Huntington Library, Art Collections, and Botanical Gardens, and a professor of history and UC Presidential Chair at the University of California, Riverside. Her books include *Parlor Politics: In Which the Ladies of Washington Help Build a City and a Government* (2000), *A Perfect Union: Dolley Madison and the Creation of the American Nation* (2006), *Dolley Madison: The Problem of National Unity* (2012), and *The Queen of America: Mary Cutts's Life of Dolley Madison* (2012). President Barack Obama has appointed Allgor to the James Madison Memorial Fellowship Foundation.

E. SUSAN BARBER is associate professor of history at Notre Dame of Maryland University. Her published essays include "Cartridge Makers and Myrmidon Viragos," in *Negotiating the Boundaries of Southern Womanhood*, edited by Janet Coryell et al. (2000), "Lewd and Abandoned Women," in *Neither Slave nor Lady*, edited by Susanna Delfino and Michele Gillespie (2002), and, coauthored with Charles F. Ritter, "'Unlawfully and against Her Consent': Sexual Violence and the Military during the American Civil War," in *Sexual Violence in Conflict Zones*, edited by Elizabeth D. Heineman (2011).

MARY C. FERRARI is professor of history at Radford University. A specialist in colonial and Revolutionary Virginia and South Carolina history, her two most recent articles are "Charity, Folly and Politics: Charles Town's Social Clubs on the Eve of the Revolution" and "'Obliged to Earn Subsistence for Themselves': Women Artisans in Charleston, South Carolina, 1763–1808," both published in *South Carolina Historical Magazine*. She is the recipient of the Radford University College of Arts and Sciences Distinguished Teaching Award.

LISA A. FRANCAVILLA is managing editor of the *Papers of Thomas Jefferson: Retirement Series*, and coeditor, with Ann Lucas Birle, of *Thomas Jefferson's Granddaughter in Queen Victoria's England: The Travel Diary of Ellen Wayles Coolidge, 1838–1839* (2011). A doctoral candidate in history at George Mason University, her research focuses on gender, family, society, and material culture in nineteenth-century America.

CATHERINE KERRISON is associate professor of history at Villanova University. She specializes in gender, intellectual, and southern history in the colonial and early national periods. She is the author of several articles and *Claiming the Pen: Women and Intellectual Life in the Early American South* (2006), which won the Outstanding Book Award for 2007 from the History of Education Society. She is the recipient of numerous awards, including fellowships from the Virginia Foundation of the Humanities and the Association of American University Women. She is currently at work on her next book, *Jefferson's Daughters*.

CYNTHIA A. KIERNER is professor of history at George Mason University. A specialist in early America, women and gender, and early southern history, she is the author or editor of seven books, including *Scandal at Bizarre: Rumor and Reputation in Jefferson's America* (2004) and the award-winning *Martha Jefferson Randolph, Daughter of Monticello: Her Life and Times* (2012). She is also the coauthor, with Megan Taylor Shockley and Jennifer R. Loux, of *Changing History: Virginia Women through Four Centuries* (2013), and is a past president of the Southern Association for Women Historians.

MARTHA J. KING is associate editor of the *Papers of Thomas Jefferson*. A historian of early America, she is the author of "'What Providence Has Brought Them to Be': Widows, Work, and the Print Culture of Colonial Charleston," in *Women and Freedom in Early America*, edited by Larry D. Eldridge (1997). She is working on a book manuscript about other women printers of the Revolutionary era.

MICHELLE A. KROWL is the Civil War and Reconstruction specialist in the Manuscript Division at the Library of Congress. She was previously assistant professor at Northern Virginia Community College, and a research assistant for the historian Doris Kearns Goodwin. She is the author of *Women of the Civil War* (2006), *The World War II Memorial: Honoring the Price of Freedom* (2007), and coauthor, with Bradley E. Gernand, of *Quantico: Semper Progredi, Always Forward* (2004).

JON KUKLA is currently writing a biography of Patrick Henry. His books include *Mr. Jefferson's Women* (2007) and *A Wilderness So Immense: The Louisiana Purchase and the Destiny of America* (2003). Kukla directed the publications program of the Library of Virginia in the 1970s and 1980s, the Historic New Orleans Collection in the 1990s, and the Patrick Henry Memorial Foundation from 2000 to 2007.

DEBORAH A. LEE is an independent scholar and consulting historian who holds a doctorate in cultural studies from George Mason University. She is the author of *Honoring Their Paths: African American Contributions along the Journey through Hallowed Ground* (2009) and the codeveloper, with Marie Tyler-McGraw, of the website *Virginia Emigrants to Liberia*. She has received fellowships at the Virginia Foundation for the Humanities and the Virginia Historical Society and research grants at Duke University's Special Collections Library.

SARAH HAND MEACHAM is associate professor of history at Virginia Commonwealth University. She specializes in the social, scientific, and cultural history of eighteenth-century America. She is the author of *Every Home a Distillery: Alcohol, Gender, and Technology in the Early Chesapeake* (2009), "Pets, Status, and Slavery in the Late-Eighteenth-Century Chesapeake," *Journal of Southern History* (2011), and "Mark Catesby's World in Virginia," in *Mark Catesby: An Eighteenth-Century Naturalist and Artist Explores the New World* (2014). She is working on a book about the history of emotions in early America.

HELEN C. ROUNTREE is professor emerita of anthropology at Old Dominion University. An ethnohistorian specializing in the Indians of the mid-Atlantic region, she is the author of many books, including *Pocahontas's People: The Powhatan Indians of Virginia through Four Centuries* (1990) and *Pocahontas, Powhatan, Opechancanough: Three Indian Lives Changed by Jamestown* (2005). She is also the coauthor, with Thomas E. Davidson, of *Eastern Shore Indians of Virginia and Maryland* (1997); with E. Randolph Turner III, of *Before and after Jamestown: Virginia's Powhatans and Their Predecessors* (2002); and with Wayne E. Clark, Kent Mountford, and Robert A. Carter, of *John Smith's Chesapeake Voyages, 1607–1609* (2007). She is also the editor of *Powhatan Foreign Relations, 1500–1722* (1993). A past president of the American Society for Ethnohistory, she is also the 1995 winner of an Outstanding Faculty Award from the State Council on Higher Education in Virginia for teaching and research.

KRISTALYN M. SHEFVELAND, a specialist in colonial and Native American history, is assistant professor of history at the University of Southern Indiana. She is the author of "'Willingly complyed and removed to the Fort': The Secret History of Anglo-Indian Visions of Virginia's Southwest," in *Beyond Two Worlds: Thinking with Place, Space, and Landscape in Native North American History*, edited by C. Joseph Genetin-Pilawa and James Buss (2014). Her current project is a book manuscript based on her dissertation, "'Wholly Subjected'?: Anglo-Indian Interaction in Colonial Virginia 1646–1718."

TERRI L. SNYDER is professor of history at California State University, Fullerton. Her research focuses on the intersections of gender, race, and the law in early modern North America. She is the author of two books, *Brabbling Women: Disorderly Speech and the Law in Early Virginia* (2003) and *The Power to Die: Slavery and Suicide in North America, 1619–1830* (2014). Her articles have been published in *Journal of American History*, *William and Mary Quarterly*, and *Law and History Review*.

LINDA L. STURTZ is the Corlis Professor of History at Beloit College in Wisconsin. She is the author of *Within Her Power: Propertied Women in Colonial Virginia* (2002) and "Mary Johnson Rose, 'White' African Jamaican Woman?: Race and Gender in Eighteenth-Century Jamaica," in *Gendering the African Diaspora: Women, Culture, and Historical Change in the Caribbean and Nigerian Hinterland*, edited by Judith A. Byfield,

LaRay Denzer, and Anthea Morrison (2010). She is currently writing on African Jamaican women's festive culture during the eighteenth and early nineteenth centuries.

GAIL S. TERRY is the author of *Documenting Women's Lives: A User's Guide to Manuscripts at the Virginia Historical Society* and essays on family and migration in early America, including the prize-winning "Sustaining Bonds of Kinship in a Trans-Appalachian Migration, 1790–1811: The Cabell-Breckinridge Slaves Move West," *Virginia Magazine of History and Biography* (1994). She served as interim director of the D'Arcy McNickle Center for American Indian and Indigenous Studies at the Newberry Library in Chicago and currently teaches history at DePaul University.

SANDRA GIOIA TREADWAY is director of the Library of Virginia in Richmond. She is the author of *Women of Mark: A History of the Woman's Club of Richmond, Virginia, 1894–1994* (1995), and the coeditor, with Janet Lee Coryell, Thomas H. Appleton Jr., and Anastatia Sims, of *Negotiating Boundaries of Southern Womanhood: Dealing with the Powers That Be* (2000); with Janet Lee Coryell, Martha H. Swain, and Elizabeth Turner, of *Beyond Image and Convention: Explorations in Southern Women's History* (1998); and with Sara B. Bearss, John T. Kneebone, J. Jefferson Looney, and Brent Tarter, of the first three volumes of the *Dictionary of Virginia Biography* (1998–2006). She served as president of the Southern Association for Women Historians in 2002.

ELIZABETH R. VARON is Langbourne M. Williams Professor of American History at the University of Virginia. A specialist in the Civil War era and the nineteenth-century South, she is the author of *We Mean to Be Counted: White Women and Politics in Antebellum Virginia* (1998); *Southern Lady, Yankee Spy: The True Story of Elizabeth Van Lew, a Union Agent in the Heart of the Confederacy* (2003), which won the Lillian Smith Prize of the Southern Regional Council; *Disunion!: The Coming of the American Civil War, 1789–1859* (2008); and *Appomattox: Victory, Defeat, and Freedom at the End of the Civil War* (2013).

Index

Italicized page numbers refer to illustrations.

Abel, Frankie, 329–30
abolitionist movement, 191, 207, 261, 274, 298, 305, 308. *See also* slavery
Act of Union (1707), 99
Adams, James, 75
Adams, John Quincy, 213
Adams, Louisa Catherine Johnson, 207
Addison, Walter, 267
Africa, 9, 260–61, 267–68, 270–79, 309, 312. *See also* slavery
African Americans: colonization movement, 9, 260–79, 309, 312; employment, 316; exclusion from white charities, 195; free people of color, 55–70, 70n6, 233–34, 236, 242n33, 256, 261, 359; passing as white, 233–40; religion, 172, 276; stereotypes, 207, 241n9; struggle for equality, 4; Union army activism for, 311–12, 314, 316, 319; use of legal system, 9, 60–61, 66–68, 195; and women's political agency, 3–4, 55, 59–70. *See also* race and racial identity; slavery
African Methodist Episcopal Church, 276
African Repository, 275
Aicheson, Rebecca, 107
Alexander, Francis, 284
Alexandria News, 332
Ambler, Jacquelin, 180, 187, 197
Ambler, Rebecca Burwell, 180, 187
American Colonization Society, 9, 260, 262, 263, 267–71, 312
American Revolution: commerce and political allegiance in, 95, 98–110; historical sources on, 7–8, 134; impact on women's political agency, 4, 102, 180–81, 184, 197; and Indians, 124; political propaganda, 88–89; and slavery, 103; Virginia frontier support for, 110–12, 116–17, 122, 124–25, 150–51, 164–65

Anderson, H. P., 154
Andrews, Charles Wesley, 266–67, 269, 274, 276
Andrews, Sarah Page, 274, 276
Anglican religion, 17, 83, 160, 161, 163. *See also* religion
Anglo-African (Richmond), 312
Anglo-Powhatan war, 39–40
Anna (enslaved woman), 266
antislavery movement. *See* slavery
Appeal (D. Walker), 71n8
Appeal to Matter of Fact and Common Sense, An (Fletcher), 167
Arnold, Benedict, 108–9
Asbury, Francis, 167–68, 172, 173
Ashe, Arthur, 345
Ashmun, Jehudi, 270

Bacon, Edmund, 222, 226, 227, 229–30
Bacon, Nathaniel, 42, 54n41. *See also* Bacon's Rebellion
Bacon's Rebellion (1676), 1, 3, 17, 33–37, 40–51, 54n41
Badeau, Adam, 313
Bagby, George W., 357
Bagby, Lucy Parke Chamberlayne, 357, 358
Baker, Lafayette C., 329–30
Baptist Church, 167. *See also* religion
Barnes, Anthony, 19–21, 24
Barnes, Elizabeth, 19–21, 23–24
Bartlett, Fanny, 250, 254–55
Bartlett, Solomon, 250
Battle of Bloody Run, 34, 40, 44
Baum, L. Frank, 27–28
Behn, Aphra, 37–38, 50, 54n41
Bell, Mrs. John, 196
Bell, Mary Hemings, 235

Benjamin, Judah P., 356
Berkeley, Frances, 1, 14, 37, 43
Berkeley, William, 33, 37, 42–43, 45, 46–47
Beymer, William Gilmore, 311–12, 317
bipartisanship, 213
birth control and abortion, 181, 197n2
Blackburn, Christian, 272
Blackford, Charles, 315
blacks. *See* African Americans; race and racial identity; slavery
Blackstone, William, 166
Blair, John, 81
Bland, Richard, 89
Bobbitt, Lorena, 2
"Bonnie Blue Flag, The" (song), 331
Boston, 88, 181, 291, 293, 298–99
Boston Cultivator, 220
Boston Herald, 330
Boston Tea Party, 88, 122
Bowser, Mary Elizabeth, 311–12
Boyd, Belle, 331
Boyle, Sarah Patton, 3
Bozeman, Micajah, 250
Bozeman, William G. (Billy Woodson; "T. M."), 250–52, 255–56
Braine, Edward, 49–50
Bray, Plomer, 18, 22
Brent, William, 181
Britain: colonial allegiance to, 95, 98, 99, 107, 111; colonial policies, 88, 95, 98–99, 104–12, 125, 150, 165, 180–81; Indian relations, 39–42, 138–46, 142–43, 151–52, 258n5; War of 1812, 215
Brocke, William, 19
Broyard, Anatole, 238
Bullitt, Alexander Scott, 128–29, 130–31, 133
burial customs, 78, 133, 183, 196, 200n38, 220, 357
Burke, Alexander, 275
Burke, Cornelia, 275
Burke, Edward Lee, 278
Burke, Grandison, 275
Burke, Robert Lee "Ray," 278
Burke, Rosabella, 275
Burke, William, 275–77
Burr, Esther, 185
Butler, Benjamin Franklin, 300, 312
Byrd, Anne, 17
Byrd, John, 17, 20
Byrd, Lucy Parke, 14
Byrd, Mary Willing, 99, 108–10, 111

Byrd, Thomas, 108
Byrd, William, 33, 34, 37, 40–42, 46, 49
Byrd, William, III, 108

Cabell, William H., 250
Cable, Thomas, 67
Caines, Frances, 186
Calvert, Rosalie Stier, 271
Campbell, Arthur, 166
Campbell, Charles Henry, 164
Campbell, Margaret Buchanan, 164
Campbell, Sally, 217
Campbell, Sarah Buchanan, 164, 166
Campbell, William, 160, 164–65, 173
Capps, Richard, 19, 20, 21, 24, 25
Capps, William, Jr., 19
Carrington, Edward, 181, *183*
Carrington, Elizabeth Jacquelin Ambler Brent, 7, 9, 180–97
Carrington, Isaac, 315
Carrington, William A., 355–56
Cartwright, Alice, 17
census records, 231, 234, 250–51, 257, 258n6, 349. *See also* historical sources
Cesar (enslaved man), 68, 73n36
Chapman, Reynolds, 218
charitable organizations, 184–85, 191
Charles II (king), 37, 48
Charleston Mercury, 330
Charlton, Jane, 86
Chase-Riboud, Barbara, 242n22
Cherokee Indians, 124–25, 164–65. *See also* Indians
Chesnut, James, Jr., 352
Chesnut, Mary Boykin, 352
Chickahominy Indians, 40, 49. *See also* Indians
Child, Lydia Maria, 270
children: enslavement of, 41, 60–69; indentured servitude, 72n20; in mixed-status marriages, 60–61; property rights of, 108
Chimborazo Hospital, 348, 351, 354
China, 295–97
Chinnery, George, 285, 296
Christian, Anne Henry, 8, 116–34, *118*, *119*, 164
Christian, Elizabeth, 127, 129, 132
Christian, Israel, 129, 130
Christian, Prissy, 120, 128
Christian, Sarah Henry, 121
Christian, William, 116–17, 120–29, 164

Index

Christianity, 260, 261, 265–67, 268, 277. *See also* religion
Civil War: African American and southern white Union support, 311–12, 314, 316, 319; class divisions, 318; female soldiers and commissions, 319, 327–28, 330, 348, 354; female spies, 305–21, *307*, 323, 327–33, 339; gender roles in, 3–5, 318, 319; loyalty oaths, 328–29, 332; medical care and nursing, 348–56, 361nn17–18; mortality and casualty rates, 37, 193, 350–51, 361n14; opposing family loyalties in, 299; and southern identity, 298–99
Clayton, John, 43
Cline, Patsy, 3
Clinton, Henry, 103
Clopton, Maria, 352, 361n17
cloth and clothing production, 144, 148–49, 181, 224–25, 227–30, 249, 296
Cobb, Jeremiah, 254, 255
Cockacoeske (Pamunkey Indian leader), 6, 33, 35, 36–51, 54n33
Cocke, Christopher, 25
Coercive Acts (1774), 88, 122
Coles, Isaac, 294
College of William and Mary, 100
Collins, Isaac, 75
Colonial Williamsburg Foundation, 93n36
colonization movement, 9, 260–79, 309, 312. *See also* slavery
concubine, 226, 240n6
Confederate army: commission of women in, 327–28, 330, 348; medical care and nursing, 348–56; political divisions within, 319; role of female spies, 323, 327–33, 339. *See also* Civil War
Constitutional Convention (1787), 203–4
Cooke, John Esten, 330
Coolidge, Algernon Sidney, 297, 299–300, 302n18
Coolidge, Elizabeth, 302n18
Coolidge, Elizabeth Bulfinch, 288
Coolidge, Ellen (daughter), 302n18
Coolidge, Ellen Wayles Randolph, 6, 8, 233, 239, 243n41, 283–301, *284*
Coolidge, Joseph, 243n41, 283, 287–88, 297–98
Coolidge, Joseph (father), 288
Coolidge, Joseph Randolph, 297, 302n18
Coolidge, Philip Sidney, 297, 299–300, 302n18
Coolidge, Thomas Jefferson, 300, 302n18

Cooper (enslaved man), 103
Cottrell, Sally, 290
Countrey Justice (Dalton), 14, 23
coverture: and legal liability, 46, 50; and mixed-status marriages, 61–62; and property rights, 4, 78, 98, 110, 166, 189, 290. *See also* marriage
Cowardin, H. M., 345
Culpeper, Thomas, 48
Cunningham, Robert G., 13
Cushing, Jonathan P., 27
Custis, George Washington Parke, 260, 264, 276
Custis, Mary Anna Randolph, 263, 265
Custis, Mary Lee Fitzhugh, 9, 260–79, *263*
Cutts, Anna, 218
Cutts, Dolley Madison, 217
Cutts, Lucia B., 204–5
Cutts, Mary Estelle Elizabeth, 204–7, 209, 210, 216
Cutts, Richard, 207

Dahlgren, Ulric, 305, 314
Dalí, Salvador, 344–45, 346
Dalton, Michael, 14, 23
Daughters of Liberty, 181
Davenport, Peachy, 91n9
Davies, Samuel, 163
Davis, Jefferson, 310, 311, 352, 354, 356
Davis, Varina, 356
Dawson, William, 161
defamation suits, 16–21, 19, 30n20, 38, 65–66
Delaware Indians, 143
De Veaux, James, 162
Dick (enslaved man), 75, 88
Dickinson, Elizabeth, 86
Dinwiddie, Robert, 142, 145–46
Discovery of Witches, The (Hopkins), 24
disorderly speech, 65–66. *See also* defamation suits
divorce, 189
Dix, Dorothea, 353
"Dixie" (song), 332
Dixon, John, 74, 75, 78, 84, 86
domestic service, 192–94, 292, 296
Douglass, Frederick, 308
dower rights, 22, 78–79, 108, 171. *See also* inheritance; widows
Dragging Canoe (Cherokee Indian leader), 124
Draper, Betty, 143, 152

Draper, Eleanor, 139, 142, 143, 149
Draper, George, 139, 142
Draper, Lyman C., 152
Driggus, Thomas, 62–63
Dudley, Mildred Smith, 185, 186, 187
Duggless, James, 150
Dunmore, Earl of (John Murray), 88, 103, 108, 121–23
Dunmore, Lady (Charlotte Stewart Murray), 87

Early, Jubal, 313
eastern shore, 59–60
Eastman, Carolyn, 200n34
Eaton, Margaret O'Neale Timberlake, 217
Edinburgh (enslaved man), 132
education, 5, 105–7, 190, 192–93, 256, 269, 273
Ellegood, Mary, 107
Ely, Melvin, 241n9
emancipation, 261–62, 268–69, 271, 274, 308–9, 314. *See also* slavery
Emory, John, 173
Emory and Henry College, 173
employment, 85–86, 232–33, 316. *See also* women's work
English Civil War, 37
English domestic ideals, 36
Episcopalian Church, 168–69. *See also* religion
Equal Rights Amendment, 2, 5, 10n7
Escape from Indian Captivity (J. Ingles), 139, 152, 157n13
Ester (enslaved woman), 147
evangelical movement: and antislavery sentiment, 265, 271; Great Awakening, 160–74, 181, 183–84; growth of, 9, 160–61, 163, 166–70, 174; revival meetings, 167–68, 171–72; women's role in, 181, 184. *See also* religion
Evans, Thomas J., 331

Fairfax County (Va.), 327–28, 332–33
Falls Plantation, *34*, 40, 41
farming methods, 244–45, 251–54, 257
Faust, Drew Gilpin, 361n14
Female Cicero, The (Eastman), 200n34
female friendship, 185–87
Female Humane Association, 9, 181, 182, 191–95, 197
Female Society for the Relief of the Distressed, 191

female stereotypes: deference to men, 47, 79, 84, 93n29, 105, 108, 109; and women's political agency, 47, 98, 105, 315, 331
feme covert and feme sole, 62, 70, 78, 80, 83. *See also* coverture
feminism, 5, 8, 27–28, 109, 155
Fincastle Resolves, 150
Finley, Robert F., 267
Fisher, Nancy Ambler, 190
Fitzhugh, Anna Maria, 268–69
Fitzhugh, William (father), 261
Fitzhugh, William Henry (son), 267–69
Fleming, Anne, 117, 121, 130
Fleming, Lenny, 120–21
Fleming, Thomas, 204
Fleming, William, 117, 120, 121, 126
Fletcher, John William, 167
Flournoy, Matthew, 130–31
Floyd, Benjamin Rush, 152, 156
Floyd, Letitia Preston, 152–53
Follow the River (Thom), 155
Ford, Antonia, 8
Ford, Charles, 327, 334, 337
Ford, Edward R., 326, 327, 331, 332, 339, 341n16
Ford, Julia F., 326
Ford, Pattie, 337, 339
Fort Vause, 146
Franklin, John Hope, 71n8
Frederick County Auxiliary, 268
Free and Accepted Masons, 74, 84
"Free Black Experience in Antebellum Wilmington, North Carolina, The" (Rohrs), 71n8
Freedmen's Bureau, 312
Free Negro in North Carolina (Franklin), 71n8
Free Women of Petersburg (Lebsock), 200n34
French and Indian War, 100, 121–22, 143
frontier exchange economy, 51
Frye, Philip S., 218

Gage, Matilda Joslyn, 27
Garnett, Alexander Y. P., 352, 355–56, 362n27
Garnett, Griffin Taylor, 357
Garrison, William Lloyd, 308
garrison towns, 332–33
gender and gender roles and conventions: English domestic ideals of, 36; Indians, 38–39, 47–49, 249–51; and motherhood, 139; patriarchy, 4–5, 78, 84, 163, 172, 251, 327; property rights and inheritance, 105–6,

359; and punishment, 16, 46; scholarship on, 2–3, 58, 318; in slavery, 7, 227–31; use as protection in legal case, 50; and use of women's married names, 196; widows, 37–38, 78, 82–83, 109, 133; witchcraft accusations, 21–22; and women's political allegiance, 335. *See also* female stereotypes; sexual attitudes and conventions
George III (king), 89, 95
Getting Word project, 242n22
Gisbourne, Jane, 19–21, 24, 25
Gisbourne, John, 19–21, 24, 25
Glasgow, Ellen, 3, 7
Gone with the Wind (Mitchell), 219
Goodrich, Margaret, 107
Gordon-Reed, Annette, 226; *Hemingses of Monticello*, 223, 242n26; *Thomas Jefferson and Sally Hemings*, 243n37
Gower, Abel, 49
Grant, Ulysses S., 310, 313, 316
Gravatt, John James, 355, 357
Gray, Beverly, 242n22
Gray, Selina, 265
Great Awakening movements, 160–74, 181, 183–84. *See also* evangelical movement; religion
Green, Abigail, 92n20
Green, Andrew, 272
Green, Anne Catharine Hoof, 81–82
Green, George Washington, 272
Green, Jonas, 74, 81, 92n20
Green, Lott Cary, 272
Green, Priscilla, 272
Green children, 82
Greenhow, Rose, 331
Grendon, Sarah Harris Stegge, 6, 33–34, 36–43, 46–47, 49–51
Grendon, Thomas, 36, 37, 41–42, 47, 49
Gunderson, Joan, 177n33
Gurley, P. D., 336
Gurley, Ralph, 267, 270, 272, 274–76
Guvernator, G. Christian, III, 345

Hale, John P., 156; *Trans-Allegheny Pioneers*, 153
Hall, Annie Randolph Van Lew, 311
Hamilton, Henry, 149–50
Hancock, George, 25
Hannah (enslaved woman), 103
Harmanson, George, 65
Harmon, Adam, 142, 145

Harper's Weekly, 330
Harris, George, 37
Harrison, Benjamin, 89
Hatter, Elizabeth, 272
Hatter, Reuben, 272
"Have Social Historians Lost the Civil War?" (Vinovskis), 361n14
Haviland, Anthony, 37
Haviland, Mrs., 43, 46
Heintzelman, Samuel P., 332
Hemings, Beverley, 222, 232–33, 235
Hemings, Elizabeth, 223, 302n12
Hemings, Eston, 222, 237, 289
Hemings, Harriet, 3, 7, 222–40
Hemings, James, 226, 242n22, 243n37
Hemings, Madison, 222–23, 226, 235, 237, 239, 243n37, 289
Hemings, Robert, 243n37
Hemings, Sally: family of, 231–32, 235, 289, 302n12; historical research on, 58, 69; racial identity of, 7, 236–37; relationship with Thomas Jefferson, 222–23, 226–28, 240n6
Hemingses of Monticello (Gordon-Reed), 223, 242n26
Hemmings, John, 243n37, 289, 302n12
Henry, John, 117, 160, 161, 163
Henry, Patrick: family of, 8, 116, 117, 160, 161, 204–5; military and political career, 89, 121, 122, 124, 131, 164, 173
Henry, Sarah Shelton, 163
Herring, James, 203, 221n19
Herron, Walter, 358
Hicks, Joseph, 147
Hill, Edward, 40
Hill, Luke and Elizabeth, 22–23, 24–25
historical research, 3–4, 10, 21, 58, 219, 221n31
historical sources: accuracy of genealogical, 232; archaeological and ethnographic, 39; census records, 231, 234, 250–51, 257, 258n6, 349; Farm Book of Thomas Jefferson, 222, 228, 231, 232; legal records, 28n3, 55–58, 70, 254–55; obstacles in documenting women's experiences, 3–4, 6–7, 36, 149, 195–96, 308, 317–18; *Virginia Gazette*, 89; women's letters as, 8, 116–20, 133–34
Holt, William, 101, 102–3
Hopkins, Francis, 165
Hopkins, Matthew, 24
Horsmanden, Warham, 49
Hunter, Margaret, 86

Hunter, William, 75
hunting, 121, 244–45, 249, 256

indentured servitude, 58–61, 65, 72n20
Indians. *See* Native Americans
Ingles, George, 142, 145
Ingles, John, 143, 145, 148, 152–53, 156; *Escape from Indian Captivity*, 139, 152, 157n13
Ingles, Mary, 146, 148
Ingles, Mary Draper, 6, 138–56, *140–41*, 157n11, 157n13
Ingles, Rhoda, 146
Ingles, Susanna, 146
Ingles, Thomas, 142, 145, 148, 151
Ingles, William, 138, 139, 146–47, 150, 151
inheritance: law of escheat, 22, 26, 104–5; matrilineal, 38, 50, 248–49; protection of children's, 16, 131, 133, 166; rights of widows, 41, 76, 78, 84–85, 101–2, 108, 148, 165–66; of slaves as property, 148, 178n41, 195, 223; use of wills, 101–2, 106, 129, 132, 148, 257, 359
"Inhospitable Hospital, The" (Schultz), 361n18
Iroquois Indians, 121, 245, 248. *See also* Indians
itinerant ministers, 167–72. *See also* religion

Jackson, Thomas, 18
Jackson, Thomas "Stonewall," 331, 344
Jacobs, Andrew S., 221n31
James (enslaved man), 147
James I (king), 24
Jamestown, 1, 2
Jefferies, John, 141
Jefferson, Martha, 223, 286
Jefferson, Martha Wayles Skelton, 302n12
Jefferson, Mary, 223, 226
Jefferson, Thomas: family of, 3, 7, 228–29, 231, 283, 288; historical research on, 58; political career, 88–89, 109, 211, 212; relationship with Sally Hemings, 222–23, 226–28, 240n6; *A Summary View of the Rights of British America*, 77, 88–89; and *Virginia Gazette*, 85, 91n4
Jefferson the President (Malone), 242n22
Jeffreys, Herbert, 48
Jenking, Joan, 17
Jerdone, Francis, 95, 99–102
Jerdone, Francis, Jr., 103–4, 111
Jerdone, Isabella, 110
Jerdone, John, 104
Jerdone, Sarah Macon, 8, 95–112, *96*

Jerdone Castle, 95, *96*, 100, 111
Jessup, Georgia Mills, 35
Jim Crow, 5, 241n9, 294. *See also* race and racial identity

Kaine, Timothy M., 11
Keckley, Elizabeth, 1
Kent (enslaved man), 103
Key, Francis Scott, 267
King, Sarah, 62–63
Kobler, John, 169

Lafayette, Marquis de (Gilbert du Motier), 165
land ownership, 26, 126–27, 147–48, 157–58n17, 245, 248, 253–54
land speculation, 126, 142–43
language: and gender roles, 47, 79, 84, 93, 105; preservation of Nottoway Indian, 253, 255, 258
law of coverture. *See* coverture
law of escheat, 22, 26, 104–5. *See also* inheritance
Lawson, Cecil C., 157n13
Lebsock, Suzanne, 200n34
Lee, Arthur, 109
Lee, Eliza Collins, 210, 212
Lee, Hannah Ludwell, 86
Lee, Mary C., 276
Lee, Mary Greenhow, 239
Lee, Richard Henry, 89, 124
Lee, Robert E., 5, 263, 265, 275, 276, 344
Left (enslaved man), 55, 61, 63–64, 65, 69
Left, Jane, 3, 6, 9, 55–70, *56*, 73n30
legal system, 4, 9, 60–61, 63, 66–69, 195
Lennon, John, 362n30
Lerner, Gerda, 10n2
lesbian mothers, 3
Les Misérables (Hugo), 331
Lewis, Andrew, 145–46
Lewis, Eleanor Parke Custis, 288
Libby Prison (Richmond), 310, 311, 314
Liberia, 9, 261, 270–79. *See also* slavery
Lightfoot, John B., 357
Lilly (enslaved woman), 266
Lincoln, Abraham, 309, 313
Lincoln, Mary Todd, 1
literacy, 6–7, 237, 242n26, 243n37, 248, 253, 256. *See also* education; print culture
London, 293–95
Longacre, James B., 203, 221n19

Long Way Home, The (E. H. Smith), 154–56
Lower Norfolk County, 16–17
Ludwell, Thomas, 49

Macao, 296–97
Macaulay, Alexander, 102, 113n12
Macaulay, Elizabeth Jerdone, 110, 113n12
Madison, Anna, 211
Madison, Dolley, 3, 6, 8, 201–20, *202*, 294
Madison, James, 172–73, 203, 209–11, 217
Madison, James, Sr., 211
Madison, Nelly Conway, 211
Madison, William, 218
Malone, Dumas, 242n22
Manley, Gabriel, 66
manumission: by antislavery activists, 276, 308; British offer to volunteers, 103, 108, 123; colonization movement strategy, 260, 262; methods and terms of, 60, 65, 71n13, 230. *See also* slavery
marriage: interracial, 60, 71n8, 240n6, 242n33, 256; legal status of women, 46, 50, 166; of mixed-status couples, 58–64, 71n8; property rights in, 4, 78, 98, 110, 166, 189, 290; social and economic benefit for women, 189, 235. *See also* inheritance; widows
Marshall, John, 196
Maryland Gazette, 81–82
matrilineal descent and inheritance, 33, 36, 38–39, 50, 248–49. *See also* inheritance
May, Sophia, 216
McAnally, David Rice, 175n15
McClellan, Eliza, 270
McCleskey, Turk, 157n17
McDowell, Irvin, 332
Mead, Stith, 169–70, 172
Meade, Lucy, 271
Meade, Mary Fitzhugh Grymes, 261
Meade, Richard, 269
Meade, Susan, 271
Meade, William, 265, 267–68
medical care and hospitals. *See* Civil War; women's work
Memorial Foundation for Children, 197
Memorial Home for Girls (Richmond), *182*, 192, 196
Mercer, Charles Fenton, 267
Meredith, Samuel, 175n15
Merry, Elizabeth Leathes, 213
Methodist Church, 167–74. *See also* religion

Mills, Samuel John, 267
Minor, Jane, 1
Missouri Compromise, 240
Mitchell, Margaret, 219
Monroe, Elizabeth Kortright, 215
Monticello, 224, 225, 286, 287. *See also* plantation economy
Moore, Peter J., 344
Moore, Samuel P., 353
Morris, Anthony, 208
Morse, Jedidiah, 252, 255
Mosby, John S., 323, 328–31
Mosby's Confederacy (Evans and Moyer), 331
Mother Amey (enslaved woman), 206, 207
motherhood, 4, 109, 139, 186, 187, 189–90, 236
Motier, Gilbert du (Marquis de Lafayette), 165
Moyer, James M., 331
Mulligan, Margery, 19
Munro, Robert, 269
Murray, Charlotte Stewart (Lady Dunmore), 87
Murray, John (Earl of Dunmore), 88, 103, 108, 121–23

names and naming conventions, 69, 196, 200n34, 227, 254–55, 277–78
Nansemond Indians, 48, 248, 250. *See also* Indians
Nany (enslaved woman), 214
Nanzatico Indians, 46. *See also* Indians
National Portrait Gallery of Distinguished Americans (Longacre and Herring), 203
Native Americans: abduction of Mary Draper Ingles, 138–39, 142–46, 151–56; alcohol and alcoholism, 245, 248, 254; and American Revolution, 124–25; Bacon's Rebellion, 1, 3, 6, 17, 33, 36–50; captivity narratives, 152–56; children of, 252–53, 258n6; Cockacoeske, 6, 33, *35*, 36–51, 54n33; as free people of color, 256; French and Indian War, 100, 121–22, 143–44, 146; hunting and farming methods, 121, 244–45, 251–54, 256, 257; land ownership, 244–45, *246*, 248–50, 255–57, 258n5; language, 253, 255, 258; matrilineal inheritance and descent, 33, 36, 38–39, 50, 248–49; organization of society, 38–39; slave trade of, 33, 37, 40–41, 51; tribal membership, 258n6; tributary agreements, 39–40, 43; Turner, Edith "Edy," 6, 244–58, *247*; westward migration, 39, 43, 127; women's roles, 36, 38–39, 44, 47–49, 249, 251, 389

Nat Turner's Rebellion (1831), 256
Necotowance (Powhatan Indian chief), 39, 40
Nelson, Thomas, 109
"New and Accurate Map of Virginia, A" (J. Henry), 161
New River Valley, 138, 142–47, 150, 154
Nicholas, Mrs. Philip Norborne, 195, 196
Nineteenth Amendment, 5; women's suffrage, 2, 5, 8
Nordlinger, Zelda Kingoff, 1
Nottoway Indians, 48, 244–58, *246–47*, 258nn5–6. *See also* Indians
Nowland, Eliza Griffin Carrington, 320
nursing, 349–56, 361n18

Occoneechee Indians, 37. *See also* Indians
Ohio Indians, 142–43. *See also* Indians
Ono, Yoko, 362n30
Opechancanough (Powhatan Indian chief), 39, 49
Opitchapam (Powhatan Indian chief), 38
Opium War (1839–42), 298
orphans and orphanages, 189, 191–95

Page, Ann Randolph Meade, 9, 260–79, *262*
Page, John, 274
Page, Mary Louise, 277
Page, Matthew, 260, 264, 272
Page, Peter Mead, 274, 276
Page, Robert M., 274
Page, Solomon, 274
Page, Thomas, 277
Pamunkey Indians, 33, 36, 38–39, 40, 54n33. *See also* Indians
Paris, 223, 226–28, 297–98
Parker, David B., 311
Parker, Margaret, 107
Parks, William, 75
Parrish, Anne, 191
patriarchy, 4–5, 78, 84, 163, 172, 251, 327. *See also* gender and gender roles and conventions
Patterson, Maria Booth, 348–49
Patton, James, 142, 143–44, 152
Payne, Isaac, 208
Payne, John, 203
Payne, Lucy, 209
Payne, Mary Coles, 203
Payne, Walter, 208
Payne, William Temple, 208

Peabody, Albert Komoyah, 277
Peabody, Christian, 277
Peabody, Stanton, 277
Pecchi, Fanny, 298
Pelham, Peter, 74
Pember, Phoebe Yates, 354
Pendleton, Edmund, 89
Peterkin, Joshua, 358
Philadelphia, 208, 229, 231–32, 305
Philipsburg Proclamation, 103
Phoebe (enslaved woman), 352
Pickett's Charge, 300
Pinckney, Eliza Lucas, 185
Pinkney, John, 75, 80, 82, 83–84, 90
"Placing Women in History" (Lerner), 10n2
plantation economy, 33, 36, 51, 100, 224–25, 228–30, 286–87, 290
Pocahontas, 1–2, 11, 14
Poe, Edgar Allan, 200n38
Poe, Elizabeth Arnold, 200n38
Pope, Alexander, 97, 100
Pope, John, 332
Porter, Horace, 313
Potter, Peggue, 274
Powell, Mark, 22
Powhatan, Rose, 35
Powhatan Indians, 1, 38–41, 248, 252. *See also* Indians
Praya Grande, 285
Prentis, Robert, 80
Presbyterian Church, 163, 167. *See also* religion
President's Daughter, The (Chase-Riboud), 242n22
Preston, Francis, 171, 173
Preston, Sarah Campbell, 171
Preston, Thomas L., 173
Preston, William, 150, 152
Preston, William Campbell, 216–17
print culture, 7, 85–86, 89, 90, 190
Proclamation Line of 1763, 121, 126
property rights, 98–101, 104–8, 107–8. *See also* inheritance; marriage; slavery; widows
prostitution, 7, 193, 194–95, 353
Protestants, 17, 142, 160, 170. *See also* religion
Providence Forge, 100, 101, 102–3
Pryor, Sarah Rice, 352
Purdie, Alexander, 75, 78, 84, 86, 91n9
Purdie, Mary, 91n9
Puritans, 17, 20. *See also* religion

Quaker religion, 17, 191, 203, 207–9, 210. *See also* religion
Quebec Act (1774), 122, 126
Queen of America, The (M. E. E. Cutts), 204–7, 209, 210, 216
Queen ye Queen, Betty, 50

race and racial identity: and gender, 7; interracial marriage, 60, 71n8, 240n6, 242n33, 256; and legal system, 5, 59, 65, 69, 238, 241n9, 294; passing as white, 233–40; post–Civil War discrimination, 4–5, 316; race mixing and southern descent, 216, 238; and women's history, 3, 5, 58, 68, 70, 139. *See also* African Americans; slavery
Randolph, Ann Bolling, 261
Randolph, Cornelia, 292, 298, 299
Randolph, George Wythe, 299
Randolph, Martha Jefferson, 58, 69, 212, 227, 229, 292
Randolph, Mary, 1, 292, 298
Randolph, Peyton, 89
Randolph, Thomas Jefferson, 290, 292, 298
Randolph, Thomas Mann, 286
Rappahannock Indians, 49. *See also* Indians
Ratcliffe, Laura, 327, 331
Ratcliffe, Mary Cecilia, 334
Rathell, Catherine, 1, 86
Reconstruction, 3, 312, 317, 320
regionalism, 216, 239, 289
Reinagle, George Philip, 285
religion: and accusations of witchcraft, 17, 20–21; church organization and ideals, 177n33, 208–9; evangelical and Great Awakening movements, 9, 160–74, 181, 183–84; itinerant ministers, 167–72; and slavery, 207, 260–67, 2/1; and social class, 167–68; state-sponsored churches, 174; and widows, 83; and women's benevolence movement, 181, 184, 191; and women's political agency, 358
Republican Party, 211
Revere, Paul, 317
Reynolds, John, Jr., 311–12, 317
Reynolds, Mary, 344
Rice, Thomas, 294
Richards, Mary, 309
Richards, Mary Jane (Bowser, Mary Elizabeth), 312
Richmond: Civil War hospitals, 350–56; Civil War monuments, 344–45, *346*; Union spies and political activists in, 310–14, 316, 331; women's benevolence work in, 181–82, 191–93
Richmond Enquirer, 196–97, 321n3
"Richmonia Richards" *(Anglo-African)*, 312
Rind, Alexander, 92n20
Rind, Clementina, 7, 74–90, *76*, 91n3, 92n20
Rind, William, 74–75, 92n20
Rind children, 75, 84, 91n6
Roan, John, 163
Roane, Spencer, 173
Roane, William, 309
Roane, William C., 316
Roberts, Humphrey, 107
Roberts, Joseph Jenkins, 275
Robertson, John, 352
Robertson, Kate, 359
Robertson Hospital (Richmond), 352–56
Robinson, Ann C., 265, 271
Rochambeau, Viscount, 188–89
Rogers, Alexander, 250, 254
Rogers, Solomon, 255
Rohrs, Richard C., 71n8
Rolfe, John, 11
Ronaldson, James, 229
Roonseraw, Wané, 6, 244–58, *247*
Rosecrans, William, 300
Rosekrans, Caroline, 334
Rosser, Thomas Lafayette, 327
Royle, Joseph, 75
Russell, Elizabeth Henry Campbell, 9, 116, 160–74, *162*, 175n15
Russell, William, 160, 165–68, 173

Salem, Mass., 20–21, 27
salt production, 126–27, 129–32, 166
Savage, Esther, 67, 71n11
Savage, Thomas, 55, 61, 63, 65–67, 69
Savage, Thomas, III, 73n38
Schultz, Jane E., 361n18
Scott, W. W., 218
Scottish settlers, 99, 143, 161
secession, 298, 309, 327. *See also* Civil War
Second Continental Congress, 123
Seneca Falls Convention (1848), 8. *See also* women's rights movement
sewing, 148–49, 185, 233, 237, 251
sexual attitudes and conventions, 16, 19, 188–90, 195, 230, 265
sexual orientation, 3, 186

Sharpe, George, 314
Shawnee Indians, 121, 127, 138, 143–44, 146, 151. *See also* Indians
Shepard, Lee, 30n20
Sheridan, Philip H., 313
Sherman, William Tecumseh, 313
Sherwood, Grace, 6, 11–28, 13, 31n33
Sherwood, James, 17–22, 26
Sherwood, Richard, 26
Shingas (Delaware Indian war captain), 145
Six Nations, 245. *See also* Indians
slavery: abolitionist movement, 191, 207, 261, 274, 298, 305, 308; colonization movement, 260–76; emancipation, 261–62, 268–69, 271, 274, 308–9, 314; family life in, 132, 223, 226, 227, 235–38; and free blacks, 57, 65, 68–69; of Indians, 33, 37, 40–41, 51; Missouri Compromise, 240; mixed-race children, 243n41; mixed-status marriage, 58–64, 71n8; Nat Turner's Rebellion, 256; and plantation economy, 33, 100, 161, 228–30; relationships with white women owners, 206–7, 210–11, 218–19, 286, 289–90, 308; and religion, 171, 207, 260–67, 271; slave owners, 132, 147, 207–8, 218–19, 230–31, 265–67, 273; southern opposition to, 5, 9, 305; and stereotypes, 241n9; taxation of, as property, 147. *See also* manumission
Smith, Earl Hobson, 154–56
Smith, Elizabeth Cary, 360n7
Smith, George, 50
Smith, John, 11
Smith, Margaret Bayard, 201, 205, 213–15, 270
Smith, Mildred, 180, 189
Smith, Samuel Harrison, 213
social class: and antislavery sentiment, 286, 305; and Civil War, 318; political activism of elite women, 270–71, 348, 352–53, 359–60; and religion, 167–68; and women's rights, 5
Society for the Relief of Poor Widows, 191
Society of Friends, 17, 191, 203, 207–9, 210. *See also* religion
Sons of Liberty, 181
southern identity, 102, 209, 213–17, 298–301
southern reform tradition, 319–20
Stanton, Lucia, 242n22
states' rights, 298. *See also* Civil War
Stegge, Thomas, 33, 36, 37, 40–41
Steuben, F. W. von, 109
Stevenson, Andrew, 294

Stevenson, Sarah Coles, 294, 295
St. James Episcopal Church, 345, 348, 357, 360
Stoughton, Edwin H., 323, 328–31
Stowe, Harriet Beecher, 298, 309
Stuart, James E. B., 327–30, 332, 334, 344, 354
Sukey (enslaved woman), 219
Summary View of the Rights of British America, A (T. Jefferson), 77, 88–89
Susquehannock Indians, 42, 44. *See also* Indians
Sutton, Mary, 12
Syme, John, Jr., 160
Syme, John, Sr., 161
Syme, Sarah Winston, 117, 160

Tabb, Ellen, 359
Tabb, Henry Wythe, 360n7
Tabb, Lucy, 349
Tabb, Mary, 349
Tabb, Sally, 349
taverns, 147, 148
taxation: of free black women, 60, 65, 71n9; of livestock, 151; without representation, 88, 93n43, 122, 181; of slaves as property, 147
Tayloe, Benjamin O., 333, 336
Taylor, Bennett, 300
Taylor, Beverly, 154–55
Taylor, Mary Ann, 350
temperance, 191
Temple, Thomas, 345
terheers, 249
Terrell, Anne Dabney, 1
textile industry. *See* cloth and clothing production
This Republic of Suffering (Faust), 361n14
Thom, James Alexander, 155
Thomas, John, 334
Thomas Jefferson and Sally Hemings (Gordon-Reed), 243n37
Thompson, Jane Russell, 171
Thompson, Kendell, 278
Thorndike, Ellen Eddy, 284
Thornton, Charlotte, 98–99, 110, 111
Thornton, Presley, 1–7
Ticknor, George, 288
Tillson, Albert, 157n17
"Title Book" (W. Byrd), 34, 40
tobacco, 16, 25, 46, 89, 99, 160–61, 222
Todd, John, 209
Todd, John Payne, 209, 210, 218, 220

Todd, William Temple, 209
Tompkins, Benjamin, 349
Tompkins, Christopher, 348–49
Tompkins, Christopher Quarles, 357, 360n7
Tompkins, Clementine, 359
Tompkins, Elizabeth, 349
Tompkins, Harriet Pauline, 349, 360n7
Tompkins, Henry, 360n7
Tompkins, Maria, 350, 357
Tompkins, Martha Tabb, 349, 360n7
Tompkins, Sally Louisa, 9, 344–60, *346–47*, 362
Totopotomoy (Pamunkey Indian leader), 40, 44
Trans-Allegheny Pioneers (Hale), 153
transatlantic economy, 99, 101, 106
travel and travel writing, 293, 295–96
treason, 6, 46–47, 107, 109, 150, 299
Treaty of Middle Plantation (1677), 47–50
Trezvant, James, 255
Trist, Nicholas, 291
Troy, Mary, 278
Tucker, Angie, 277
Tunnell, John, 167
Turner, Edith "Edy," 6, 244–58, *247*
Turner, Edwin, 257
Turner, Elizabeth Carter, 271
Turner, Henry, 254
Tuscarora War, 245
Tyler, John, 251–52, 253
Tyler, Roy, 344–45

Uncle Tom's Cabin (Stowe), 298, 309
Union army: role of African Americans and southern whites, 311, 312, 319; role of female spies, 305–21, *307*. See also Civil War
unruly speech, 38. See also defamation suits
unwed mothers, 188–90. See also sexual attitudes and conventions

Valentine, Lila Meade, 1
Van Buren, Martin, 287–88
Van Lew, Elizabeth, 3, 9, 305–21, *306*, 321n3, 348
Van Lew, John Newton, 315
Van Lew, Mary C., 314–15
Vause, Ephraim, 146
Vinovskis, Maris, 361n14
Virginia Colonization Society, 269. See also colonization movement

Virginia Constitutional Convention (1829–30), 269
Virginia Convention (1775), 123
Virginia frontier settlements, 138–48, 150, 157n17
Virginia Gazette (1766–74), 7, 26, 74–90, *76*, 91n4
Virginia General Court, 15–16, 17, 23–25, 131
Vobe, Jane, 85

Wahunsonacock (Powhatan Indian chief), 38
Walker, David, 71n8
Walker, Thomas, 145
Wallace, Caleb, 128
Wallace, Rosanna, 128
Ware, Thomas, 167
War for Independence. See American Revolution
War of 1812, 215
Warrenton, Camille, 188
Warrenton, Lewis, 188
Warrenton, Rachel, 180–81, 185, 187, 188–89
Washington, Bushrod Corbin, 272
Washington, D.C., 213, 217–18, 219, 232–34
Washington, George, 85, 89, 95, 109, 196, 216
Washington, Martha, 109, 211, 215, 264
Wayles, John, 223, 302n12
Webb, Daniel, 59
Webb, Dinah, 66, 70
Webb, Elisha, 57, 66–68, 70, 73n36
Webb, Jane, 3, 6, 9, 55–70, *56*, 73n30
Weincek, Henry, 242n22
Weisner, Emily, 278
Wentworth, Daniel, 57
weronsquas and *weroances*, 38–39, 44
Wesley, John, 163, 167, 171–72
Wesley, Samuel, 163, 171
Wesleyan movement, 167–72, 174. See also religion
West, John, 44, 48, 50
Westo Indians, 40–41. See also Indians
westward migration, 4, 116–17, 126–27, 138–52
Weyanock Indians, 48, 248. See also Indians
White, John, 17–18
Whitefield, George, 163, 171
White House, 215–16, 311–12
white supremacy, 4–5. See also race and racial identity
Widdow Ranter, The (Behn), 37–38, 50–51, 54n41

widows: community and family resources, 83–84, 90, 168, 184–85; economic independence, 80–82, 130; historical views of, 3–4, 79; legal and property rights, 22, 74–79, 82–83, 98, 101–2, 108, 128, 171; one-third share, 22, 78–79, 108; social and political position, 37–38, 78, 82–83, 109, 133. *See also* inheritance; marriage

Wilberforce, William, 271

Wilderness Road, 127

Willard, Antonia Ford, 323–39, *324–25*, 341n16

Willard, Archie, 338

Willard, Caroline Moore, 334–35

Willard, Charles, 338

Willard, Henry, 332

Willard, Joseph Clapp, 332–39

Willard, Joseph Edward, *337*, 339

Williams, Ann, 59

Williams, Elizabeth and Thomas, 21

Williams, Jane, 3, 6, 9, 55–70, *56*, 73n30

Williamsburg, 83, 86, 90, 93n36

Winder, John, 310

Winston, Isaac, 163

Wise, Ellen, 359

Witchcraft Act (1736), 26

witches, 3, 6, 11–28, 31n27, 31n30

Women of the Confederacy Memorial Committee, 344, 345

women's benevolence movement, 9, 181–85, 191–97

women's history: Civil War, 318–19, 320, 344; diversity of experience, 1–2, 4–5; race and status, 57–58, 69–70; research on, 2–3, 57–58; and stereotypes, 10; and westward migration, 153–56

women's letter writing: and family connections, 237, 283, 286, 288–89, 338; and female friendship, 185–86; as historical source, 8, 116–20, 133–34; and identity, 300

women soldiers, 319, 354. *See also* Civil War

women's political agency: African Americans, 3–4, 55, 59–70; antislavery activism, 260–79; Bacon's Rebellion, 33; benevolence movement, 181, 183–85, 191–95; Civil War, 305–21, 323, 327–33, 339, 359–60; collaboration between men and women, 270–71; colonial Virginia politics and society, 50–51; and female stereotypes, 310–11, 315–16; and gender conventions, 4, 107, 335; of Indians, 6, 36–51, 244–58, 389; political allegiance, 102, 327, 339; in public sphere, 89–90, 105, 111–12, 196, 200n34; restrictions on free speech, 38; role of churches, 358

women's rights movement, 5, 8, 27–28, 191, 317, 344

women's suffrage, 2, 5, 8

women's work: caregiver roles, 349, 352–53, 357–58; colonial commerce, 79, 85–86; domestic service, 192–94, 233, 292–94; family businesses, 75, 78–82, 101, 128–32, 138; farms and plantations, 148–49, 244, 258, 290; free women of color, 233–34; hospital management and nursing, 348–56; and indentured servitude, 60; Indians, 144, 249, 251, 296; and slavery, 228–31; textile and clothing production, 148–49, 185, 227–28, 230, 233, 237, 251; widowed printers, 74–90; women shopkeepers, 86

Wonderful Wizard of Oz, The (Baum), 27–28

Wood, J., 255

Wood, Jean Moncure, 195–96

Wood, William, 331

Woodson, Anny, 254

Woodson, Billy (William G. Bozeman; "T.M"), 250–52, 255–56

Woodson, Polly, 254–55

Wormeley, John, 106–7

Wormeley, Ralph, 106–7

Wyndham, Percy, 239

Wynne, Bill, 344, 346

Wythe, George, 196

www.ingramcontent.com/pod-product-compliance
Lightning Source LLC
LaVergne TN
LVHW040731250326
834688LV00031B/245